WILLIAM BARTRAM

WILLIAM BARTRAM

TRAVELS AND OTHER WRITINGS

*Travels Through
North and South Carolina, Georgia,
East and West Florida*

*Travels in Georgia and Florida, 1773–74:
A Report to Dr. John Fothergill*

Miscellaneous Writings

THE LIBRARY OF AMERICA

Distributed to the trade in the United States
by Penguin Books USA Inc
and in Canada by Penguin Books Canada Ltd.

Library of Congress Catalog Number: 95–23727
For cataloging information, see end of Index.
ISBN: 1–883011–11–6

First Printing
The Library of America—84

Manufactured in the United States of America

THOMAS P. SLAUGHTER

SELECTED THE CONTENTS AND WROTE THE NOTES
FOR THIS VOLUME

The Library of America wishes to acknowledge the work of the late Francis Harper, Research Associate, the John Bartram Association, Philadelphia, whose scholarship greatly aided the preparation of this volume.

Contents

Illustrations

PLATES

APS: Courtesy American Philosophical Society, B. S. Delafield Collection.
MA: Courtesy Sterling Morton Library. The Morton Arboretum. Lisle, Illinois.
NHML: Courtesy Natural History Museum, London. PC: Private Collection/
Ron White, photographer.

TRAVELS

TRAVELS

THROUGH

NORTH AND SOUTH CAROLINA,

GEORGIA,

EAST AND WEST FLORIDA,

THE CHEROKEE COUNTRY,

THE EXTENSIVE TERRITORIES OF THE MUSCOGULGES

OR CREEK CONFEDERACY,

AND THE COUNTRY OF THE CHACTAWS.

CONTAINING

AN ACCOUNT OF THE SOIL AND NATURAL
PRODUCTIONS OF THOSE REGIONS;

TOGETHER WITH

OBSERVATIONS ON THE MANNERS OF THE INDIANS.

Mico Chlucco the Long Warrior,
or King of the Siminoles.

CONTENTS.

PART I.

INTRODUCTION.

CHAP. VII.

CHAP. VI.

CHAP. VII.

CHAP. VIII.

PART IV.

CHAP. I.

CHAP. II.

and maintains great influence in their constitution and councils of
state—these Indians not idolaters—they adore the Great Spirit, the
giver and taker away of the breath of life, with the most profound
homage and purity—anecdote   394

CHAP. III.

Dress, feasts, and divertisements—youth of both sexes are fond of
decorations with respect to dress—their ears lacerated—diadem
plumes, &c.—paint their skin—dress of the females different from
that of the men—great horned owl skin stuffed and born about by
the priests—insignia of wisdom and divination—fond of music, dancing, and routs—different classes of songs—variety of steps in their
dances—sensible and powerful effects—ball play—festival of the
Busk   399

CHAP. IV.

Concerning property, agriculture, arts, and manufactures—private
property—produce of their agricultural labours—common plantation—king's crib—public treasury—women the most ingenious and
vigilant in mechanic arts and manufactures   406

CHAP. V.

Marriages and funeral rites—polygamy—take wives whilst they are
yet young children—adultery—Muscogulges bury their dead in a sitting posture—strange customs of the Chactaws relative to duties to
the deceased—bone-house—dirges—feast to the dead—methods
which the nurses pursue to flatten the infant's skull and retain its
form   408

CHAP. VI.

Language and monuments—Muscogulge language spoken
throughout the confederacy—agreeable to the ear—Cherokee language loud—pyramidal artificial hills or mounts, terraces, obelisks—
high ways and artifical lakes—chunk yards—slave posts   412

Introduction

T HE ATTENTION of a traveller should be particularly turned, in the first place, to the various works of Nature, to mark the distinctions of the climates he may explore, and to offer such useful observations on the different productions as may occur. Men and manners undoubtedly hold the first rank—whatever may contribute to our existence is also of equal importance, whether it be found in the animal or vegetable kingdom; neither are the various articles, which tend to promote the happiness and convenience of mankind, to be disregarded. How far the writer of the following sheets has succeeded in furnishing information on these subjects, the reader will be capable of determining. From the advantages the journalist enjoyed under his father JOHN BARTRAM, botanist to the king of Great Britain, and fellow of the Royal Society, it is hoped that his labours will present new as well as useful information to the botanist and zoologist.

This world, as a glorious apartment of the boundless palace of the sovereign Creator, is furnished with an infinite variety of animated scenes, inexpressibly beautiful and pleasing, equally free to the inspection and enjoyment of all his creatures.

Perhaps there is not any part of creation, within the reach of our observations, which exhibits a more glorious display of the Almighty hand, than the vegetable world; such a variety of pleasing scenes, ever changing throughout the seasons, arising from various causes, and assigned each to the purpose and use determined.

It is difficult to pronounce which division of the earth, between the polar circles, produces the greatest variety. The tropical division certainly affords those which principally contribute to the more luxurious scenes of splendour, as Myrtus communis, Myrt. caryophyllata, Myrt. pimenta, Caryophyllus aromaticus, Laurus cinnam. Laurus camphor. Laurus Persica, Nux mosch. Illicium, Camellia, Punica, Cactus melo-cactus, Cactus grandiflora, Gloriosa superba, Theobroma, Adansonia digitata, Nyctanthes, Psidium, Musa paradisica, Musa sapientum, Garcinia mangostana, Cocos nucifera, Citrus, Citrus aurantium, Cucurbita citrullus, Hyacinthus, Amaryllis, Narcissus, Poinciana pulcherrima, Crinum, Cactus cochinellifer.

But the temperate zone (including by far the greater portion of the earth, and a climate the most favourable to the increase and support of animal life, as well as for the exercise and activity of the human faculties) exhibits scenes of infinitely greater variety, magnificence, and consequence, with respect to human economy, in regard to the various uses of vegetables.

For instance; Triticum Cereale, which affords us bread, and is termed, by way of eminence, the staff of life, the most pleasant and nourishing food to all terrestrial animals. Vitis vinifera, whose exhilarating juice is said to cheer the hearts of gods and men. Oryza, Zea, Pyrus, Pyrus malus, Prunus, Pr. cerasus, Ficus, Nectarin, Apricot, Cydonia. Next follow the illustrious families of forest-trees, as the Magnolia grandiflora and Quercus sempervirens, which form the venerated groves and solemn shades, on the Mississippi, Alatamaha and Florida; the magnificent Cupressus disticha of Carolina and Florida; the beautiful Water Oak*, whose vast hemispheric head presents the likeness of a distant grove in the fields and savannas of Carolina; the gigantic Black Oak[†], Platanus occidentalis, Liquidambar styraciflua, Liriodendron tulipifera, Fagus castania, Fagus sylvatica, Juglans nigra, Juglans cinerea, Jug. pecan, Ulmus, Acer saccharinum, of Virginia and Pennsylvania; Pinus phœnix, Pinus tæda, Magnolia acuminata, Nyssa aquatica, Populus heterophylla, and the floriferous Gordonia lasianthus, of Carolina and Florida; the exalted Pinus strobus, Pin. balsamica, Pin. abies, Pin. Canadensis, Pin. larix, Fraxinus excelsior, Robinia pseudacacia, Guilandina dioica, Æsculus Virginica, Magnolia acuminata, of Virginia, Maryland, Pennsylvania, New Jersey, New York, New England, Ohio, and the regions of Erie and the Illinois; and the aromatic and floriferous shrubs, as Azalea coccinia, Azalea rosea, Rosa, Rhododendron, Kalmia, Syringa, Gardenia, Calycanthus, Daphne, Franklinia, Styrax and others equally celebrated.

In every order of nature we perceive a variety of qualities distributed amongst individuals, designed for different pur-

---

*Quercus Hemispherica.
[†]Quercus tinctoria.

poses and uses; yet it appears evident, that the great Author has impartially distributed his favours to his creatures, so that the attributes of each one seem to be of sufficient importance to manifest the divine and inimitable workmanship. The pompous Palms of Florida, and glorious Magnolia, strike us with the sense of dignity and magnificence; the expansive umbrageous Live Oak* with awful veneration, the Carica papaya seems supercilious with all the harmony of beauty and gracefulness; the Lilium superbum represents pride and vanity; Kalmia latifolia and Azalea coccinea, exhibit a perfect show of mirth and gaiety; the Illicium Floridanum, Crinum Floridanum, Convallaria majalis of the Cherokees, and Calycanthus floridus, charm with their beauty and fragrance. Yet they are not to be compared for usefulness with the nutritious Triticum, Zea, Oryza, Solanum tuberosum, Musa, Convolvulus Batata, Rapa, Orchis, Vitis vinifera, Pyrus, Olea; for clothing with Linum Cannabis, Gossypium, Morus; for medicinal virtues with Hyssopus, Thymus, Anthemis nobilis, Papaver somniferum, Quinquina, Rheum rhabarbarum, Pisum, &c. Though none of these most useful tribes are conspicuous for stateliness, figure, or splendour, yet their valuable qualities and virtues excite love, gratitude, and adoration to the great Creator, who was pleased to endow them with such eminent qualities, and reveal them to us for our sustenance, amusement, and delight.

But there remain of the vegetable world several tribes that are distinguished by very remarkable properties, which excite our admiration, some for the elegance, singularity, and splendour of their vestment, as the Tulipa, Fritillaria, Colchicum, Primula, Lilium superbum, Kalmia, &c.: others astonish us by their figure and disposal of their vesture, as if designed only to embellish and please the observer, as the Nepenthes distillatoria, Ophrys insectoria, Cypripedium calceolus, Hydrangia quercifolia, Bartramia bracteata, Viburnum Canadense, Bartsia, &c.

Observe these green meadows how they are decorated; they seem enamelled with the beds of flowers. The blushing Chironia and Rhexia, the spiral Ophrys with immaculate white

*Quercus sempervirens.

flowers, the Limodorum, Arethusa pulcherrima, Sarracenia purpurea, Sarracenia galeata, Sarracenia lacunosa, Sarracenia flava. Shall we analyze these beautiful plants, since they seem cheerfully to invite us? How greatly the flowers of the yellow Sarracenia represent a silken canopy? the yellow pendant petals are the curtains, and the hollow leaves are not unlike the cornucopia or Amalthea's horn; what a quantity of water a leaf is capable of containing, about a pint! taste of it—how cool and animating—limpid as the morning dew: nature seems to have furnished them with this cordated appendage or lid, which turns over, to prevent a too sudden and copious supply of water from heavy showers of rain, which would bend down the leaves, never to rise again; because their straight parallel nerves, which extend and support them, are so rigid and fragile, the leaf would inevitably break when bent down to a right angle; therefore I suppose the waters which contribute to their supply, are the rebounding drops or horizontal streams wafted by the winds, which adventitiously find their way into them, when a blast of wind shifts the lid: see these short stiff hairs, they all point downwards, which direct the condensed vapours down into the funiculum; these stiff hairs also prevent the varieties of insects, which are caught from returning, being invited down to sip the mellifluous exudation, from the interior surface of the tube, where they inevitably perish; what quantities there are of them! These latent waters undoubtedly contribute to the support and refreshment of the plant: perhaps designed as a reservoir in case of long continued droughts, or other casualties, since these plants naturally dwell in low savannas liable to overflows, from rain water: for although I am not of the opinion that vegetables receive their nourishment only through the ascending part of the plant, as the stem, branches, leaves, &c.; and that their descending parts, as the root and fibres, only serve to hold and retain them in their places; yet I believe they imbibe rain and dews through their leaves, stems, and branches, by extremely minute pores, which open on both surfaces of the leaves and on the branches, which may communicate to little auxiliary ducts or vessels; or, perhaps the cool dews and showers, by constricting these pores, and thereby preventing a too free perspiration, may recover and again invigorate the languid nerves of those which seem to suffer for want of water, in great heats and droughts; but whether the insects caught in their leaves, and which dissolve and mix with the fluid, serve for aliment or support to these kind of plants, is doubtful. All the Sarracenias are insect catchers, and so is the Drosera rotundifolia.

But admirable are the properties of the extraordinary Dionea muscipula! A great extent on each side of that serpentine rivulet is occupied by those sportive vegetables—let us advance to the spot in which nature has seated them. Astonishing production! see the incarnate lobes expanding, how gay and sportive they appear! ready on the spring to intrap incautious deluded insects! what artifice! there behold one of the leaves just closed upon a struggling fly; another has gotten a worm; its hold is sure, its prey can never escape—carnivorous vegetable! Can we after viewing this object, hesitate a moment to confess, that vegetable beings are endued with some sensible faculties or attributes, similar to those that dignify animal nature; they are organical, living, and self-moving bodies, for we see here, in this plant, motion and volition.

What power or faculty is it, that directs the cirri of the Cucurbita, Momordica, Vitis, and other climbers, towards the twigs of shrubs, trees, and other friendly support? we see them invariably leaning, extending, and like the fingers of the human hand, reaching to catch hold of what is nearest, just as if they had eyes to see with; and when their hold is fixed, to coil the tendril in a spiral form, by which artifice it becomes more elastic and effectual, than if it had remained in a direct line, for every revolution of the coil adds a portion of strength; and thus collected, they are enabled to dilate and contract as occasion or necessity requires, and thus by yielding to, and humouring the motion of the limbs and twigs, or other support on which they depend, are not so liable to be torn off by sudden blasts of wind or other assaults: is it sense or instinct that influences their actions? it must be some impulse; or does the hand of the Almighty act and perform this work in our sight?

The vital principle or efficient cause of motion and action, in the animal and vegetable* system, perhaps, may be more

*Vid. Sponsalia plantarum, Amœn. Acad l. n. 12. Linn.

similar than we generally apprehend. Where is the essential difference between the seed of peas, peaches, and other tribes of plants and trees, and the eggs of oviparous animals, as of birds, snakes, or butterflies, spawn of fish, &c.? Let us begin at the source of terrestrial existence. Are not the seeds of vegetables, and the eggs of oviparous animals fecundated, or influenced with the vivific principle of life, through the approximation and intimacy of the sexes? and immediately after the eggs and seeds are hatched, does not the young larva and infant plant, by heat and moisture, rise into existence, increase, and in due time arrive to a state of perfect maturity? The physiologists agree in opinion, that the work of generation in viviparous animals, is exactly similar, only more secret and enveloped. The mode of operation that nature pursues in the production of vegetables, and oviparous animals, is infinitely more uniform and manifest, than that which is or can be discovered to take place in viviparous animals.

The most apparent difference between animals and vegetables is, that animals have the powers of sound, and are locomotive, whereas vegetables are not able to shift themselves from the places where nature has planted them: yet vegetables have the power of moving and exercising their members, and have the means of transplanting or colonising their tribes almost over the surface of the whole earth; some seeds, for instance, grapes, nuts, smilax, peas, and others, whose pulp or kernel is food for animals, will remain several days without being injured in stomachs of pigeons and other birds of passage; by this means such sorts are distributed from place to place, even across seas; indeed some seeds require this preparation by the digestive heat of the stomach of animals, to dissolve and detach the oily, viscid pulp, or to soften the hard shells. Small seeds are sometimes furnished with rays of hair or down; and others with thin light membranes attached to them, which serve the purpose of wings, on which they mount upward, leaving the earth, float in the air, and are carried away by the swift winds to very remote regions before they settle on the earth; some are furnished with hooks, which catch hold of the wool and hair of animals passing by them, and are by that means spread abroad; other seeds ripen in pericarpes, which open with elastic force, and shoot their seed to a very great distance round about; some other seeds, as of the Mosses and Fungi, are so very minute as to be invisible, light as atoms, and these mixing with the air, are wafted all over the world.

The animal creation also excites our admiration, and equally manifests the almighty power, wisdom, and beneficence of the Supreme Creator and Sovereign Lord of the universe; some in their vast size and strength, as the mammoth, the elephant, the whale, the lion, and alligator; others in agility; others in their beauty and elegance of colour, plumage, and rapidity of flight, having the faculty of moving and living in the air; others for their immediate and indispensable use and convenience to man, in furnishing means for our clothing and sustenance, and administering to our help in the toils and labours of life: how wonderful is the mechanism of these finely formed self-moving beings, how complicated their system, yet what unerring uniformity prevails through every tribe and particular species! the effect we see and contemplate, the cause is invisible, incomprehensible; how can it be otherwise? when we cannot see the end or origin of a nerve or vein, while the divisibility of matter or fluid, is infinite. We admire the mechanism of a watch, and the fabric of a piece of brocade, as being the production of art; these merit our admiration, and must excite our esteem for the ingenious artist or modifier; but nature is the work of God omnipotent; and an elephant, nay even this world, is comparatively but a very minute part of his works. If then the visible, the mechanical part of the animal creation, the mere material part, is so admirably beautiful, harmonious, and incomprehensible, what must be the intellectual system? that inexpressibly more essential principle, which secretly operates within? that which animates the inimitable machines, which gives them motion, impowers them to act, speak, and perform, this must be divine and immortal?

I am sensible that the general opinion of philosophers, has distinguished the moral system of the brute creature from that of mankind, by an epithet which implies a mere mechanical impulse, which leads and impels them to necessary actions, without any premeditated design or contrivance; this we term instinct, which faculty we suppose to be inferior to reason in man.

The parental and filial affections seem to be as ardent, their sensibility and attachment as active and faithful, as those observed in human nature.

When travelling on the east coast of the isthmus of Florida, ascending the south Musquito river, in a canoe, we observed numbers of deer and bears, near the banks, and on the islands of the river; the bears were feeding on the fruit of the dwarf creeping Chamærops; (this fruit is of the form and size of dates, and is delicious and nourishing food:) we saw eleven bears in the course of the day, they seemed no way surprised or affrighted at the sight of us. In the evening, my hunter, who was an excellent marksman, said that he would shoot one of them, for the sake of the skin and oil, for we had plenty and variety of provisions in our bark. We accordingly, on sight of two of them, planned our approaches as artfully as possible, by crossing over to the opposite shore, in order to get under cover of a small island; this we cautiously coasted round, to a point, which we apprehended would take us within shot of the bears; but here finding ourselves at too great a distance from them, and discovering that we must openly show ourselves, we had no other alternative to effect our purpose, but making oblique approaches. We gained gradually on our prey by this artifice, without their noticing us: finding ourselves near enough, the hunter fired, and laid the largest dead on the spot where she stood; when presently the other, not seeming the least moved at the report of our piece, approached the dead body, smelled, and pawed it, and appearing in agony, fell to weeping and looking upwards, then towards us, and cried out like a child. Whilst our boat approached very near, the hunter was loading his rifle in order to shoot the survivor, which was a young cub, and the slain supposed to be the dam. The continual cries of this afflicted child, bereft of its parent, affected me very sensibly; I was moved with compassion, and charging myself as if accessary to what now appeared to be a cruel murder, endeavoured to prevail on the hunter to save its life, but to no effect! for by habit he had become insensible to compassion towards the brute creation: being now within a few yards of the harmless devoted victim, he fired, and laid it dead upon the body of the dam.

If we bestow but very little attention to the economy of the animal creation, we shall find manifest examples of premeditation, perseverance, resolution, and consummate artifice, in order to effect their purposes. The next morning, after the slaughter of the bears, whilst my companions were striking our tent and preparing to re-embark, I resolved to make a little botanical excursion alone: crossing over a narrow isthmus of sand hills which separated the river from the ocean, I passed over a pretty high hill, its summit crested with a few palm trees, surrounded with an Orange grove: this hill, whose base was washed on one side by the floods of the Musquitoe river, and on the other side by the billows of the ocean, was about one hundred yards diameter, and seemed to be an entire heap of sea shells. I continued along the beach a quarter of a mile, and came up to a forest of the Agave vivipara (though composed of herbaceous plants, I term it a forest, because their scapes or flower-stems arose erect near 30 feet high): their tops regularly branching in the form of a pyramidal tree, and these plants growing near to each other, occupied a space of ground of several acres: when their seeds are ripe they vegetate, and grow on the branches, until the scape dries, when the young plants fall to the ground, take root, and fix themselves in the sand: the plant grows to a prodigious size before the scape shoots up from its centre. Having contemplated this admirable grove, I proceeded towards the shrubberies on the banks of the river, and though it was now late in December, the aromatic groves appeared in full bloom. The broad-leaved sweet Myrtus, Erythrina corallodendrum, Cactus cochinellifer, Cacalia suffruticosa, and particularly, Rhizophora conjugata, which stood close to and in the salt water of the river, were in full bloom, with beautiful white sweet scented flowers, which attracted to them two or three species of very beautiful butterflies, one of which was black, the upper pair of its wings very long and narrow, marked with transverse stripes of pale yellow, with some spots of a crimson colour near the body. Another species remarkable for splendour, was of a larger size; the wings were undulated and obtusely crenated round their ends, the nether pair terminating near the body, with a long narrow forked tail; the ground light yellow, striped oblique-transversely, with stripes of pale celestial blue, the ends of them adorned with little eyes encircled with the finest blue and crimson, which represented a very brilliant rosary. But those which were the most numerous were as white as snow, their wings large, their ends lightly crenated and ciliated, forming a fringed border, faintly marked with little black crescents, their points downward, with a cluster of little brilliant orbs of blue and crimson, on the nether wings near the body; the numbers were incredible, and there seemed to be scarcely a flower for each fly, multitudinous as they were, besides clouds of them hovering over the mellifluous groves. Besides these papiles, a variety of other insects come in for a share, particularly several species of bees.

As I was gathering specimens of flowers from the shrubs, I was greatly surprised at the sudden appearance of a remarkably large spider on a leaf, of the genus Araneus saliens: at sight of me he boldly faced about, and raised himself up, as if ready to spring upon me; his body was about the size of a pigeon's egg, of a buff colour, which, with his legs, were covered with short silky hair; on the top of the abdomen was a round red spot or ocelle encircled with black. After I had recovered from the surprise, observing that the wary hunter had retired under cover, I drew near again, and presently discovered that I had surprised him on predatory attempts against the insect tribes. I was therefore determined to watch his proceedings. I soon noticed that the object of his wishes was a large fat bomble bee (apis bombylicus), that was visiting the flowers, and piercing their nectariferous tubes: this cunning intrepid hunter conducted his subtil approaches with the circumspection and perseverance of a Siminole when hunting a deer, advancing with slow steps obliquely, or under cover of dense foliage, and behind the limbs, and when the bee was engaged in probing a flower, he would leap nearer, and then instantly retire out of sight, under a leaf or behind a branch, at the same time keeping a sharp eye upon me. When he had now gotten within two feet of his prey, and the bee was intent on sipping the delicious nectar from a flower, with his back next the spider, he instantly sprang upon him, and grasped him over the back and shoulder, when for some moments they both disappeared. I expected the bee had carried off his enemy, but to my surprise, they both together rebounded back again, suspended at the extremity of a strong elastic thread or web, which the spider had artfully let fall, or fixed on the twig, the instant he leaped from it: the rapidity of the bee's wings, endeavouring to extricate himself, made them both together appear as a moving vapour, until the bee became fatigued by whirling round, first one way and then back again: at length, in about a quarter of an hour, the bee quite exhausted by his struggles, and the repeated wounds of the butcher, became motionless, and quickly expired in the arms of the devouring spider, who, ascending the rope with his game, retired to feast on it under cover of the leaves; and perhaps before night, became himself the delicious evening repast of a bird or lizard.

Birds are in general social and benevolent creatures; intelligent, ingenious, volatile, active beings; and this order of animal creation consists of various nations, bands, or tribes, as may be observed from their different structure, manners, and languages, or voice; each nation, though subdivided into many different tribes, retaining its general form or structure, a similarity of customs, and a sort of dialect or language, particular to that nation or genus from which those tribes seem to have descended or separated. What I mean by a language in birds, is the common notes or speech, that they use when employed in feeding themselves and their young, calling on one another, as well as their menaces against their enemy; for their songs seem to be musical compositions, performed only by the males, about the time of incubation, in part to divert and amuse the female, entertaining her with melody, &c. This harmony, with the tender solicitude of the male, alleviates the toils, cares, and distresses of the female, consoles her in solitary retirement whilst sitting, and animates her with affection and attachment to himself in preference to any other. The volatility of their species, and operation of their passions and affections, are particularly conspicuous in the different tribes of the thrush, famous for song. On a sweet May morning we see the red thrushes (turdus rufus) perched on an elevated sprig of the snowy Hawthorn, sweet flowering Crab, or other hedge shrub, exerting their accomplishments in song, striving by varying and elevating their voices to excel each other; we observe a very agreeable variation, not only in tone but in modulation; the voice of one is shrill, of another lively and elevated, of others sonorous and quivering. The mock-bird (turdus polyglottos) who excels, distinguishes himself in a variety of action as well as air; from a turret he bounds aloft with the celerity of an arrow, as it were to recover or recal his very soul, expired in the last elevated strain. The high forests are filled with the symphony of the song or wood thrush (turdus minor).

Both sexes of some tribes of birds sing equally finely; and it is remarkable, that these reciprocally assist in their domestic cares, as building their nests and sitting on their eggs, feeding and defending their young brood, &c. The oriolus (icterus, Cat.) is an instance of this case; and the female of the icterus minor is a bird of more splendid and gay dress than the male bird. Some tribes of birds will relieve and rear up the young and helpless, of their own and other tribes, when abandoned. Animal substance seems to be the first food of all birds, even the granivorous tribes.

Having passed through some remarks, which appeared of sufficient consequence to be offered to the public, and which were most suitable to have a place in the introduction, I shall now offer such observations as must necessarily occur, from a careful attention to, and investigation of, the manners of the Indian nations; being induced, while traveling among them, to associate with them, that I might judge for myself, whether they were deserving of the severe censure which prevailed against them among the white people, that they were incapable of civilization.

In the consideration of this important subject it will be necessary to inquire, whether they were inclined to adopt the European modes of civil society? Whether such a reformation could be obtained, without using coercive or violent means? And lastly, whether such a revolution would be productive of real benefit to them, and consequently beneficial to the public? I was satisfied in discovering that they were desirous of becoming united with us, in civil and religious society.

It may, therefore, not be foreign to the subject, to point out the propriety of sending men of ability and virtue, under the authority of government, as friendly visitors, into their towns: let these men he instructed to learn perfectly their languages, and by a liberal and friendly intimacy become acquainted with their customs and usages, religious and civil; their system of legislation and police, as well as their most ancient and present traditions and history. These men thus enlightened and instructed would be qualified to judge equitably, and when returned to us, to make true and just reports, which might assist the legislature of the United States to form, and offer to them, a judicious plan for their civilization and union with us.

But I presume not to dictate in these high concerns of government, and I am fully convinced that such important matters are far above my ability; the duty and respect we owe to religion and rectitude, the most acceptable incense we offer to the Almighty, as an atonement for our negligence in the care of the present and future wellbeing of our Indian brethren, induce me to mention this matter, though perhaps of greater concernment than we generally are aware.

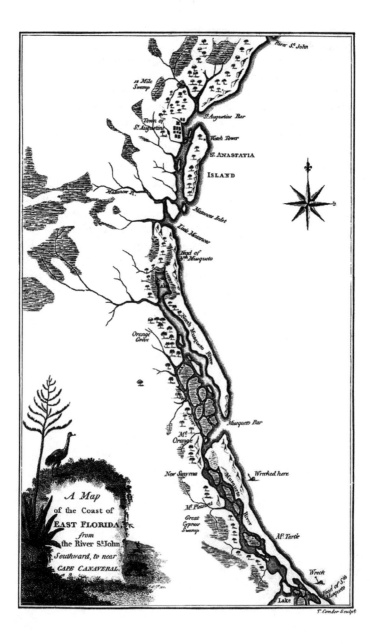

Rivar St. John

11 Mile Swamp

S. Augustine Bar

Town of St. Augustine

Watch Tower

St. ANASTATIA

ISLAND

Matanca R.

Matanca Inlet

Tide Matanca

Head of Nth Musqueto

North Musqueto River

Orange Grove

Musqueto Bar

Mt. Orange

New Smyrna

Wrecked here

Mt. Plaistick

Musqueto River

Great Cypress Swamp

Mt. Turtle

Wreck

A Map
of the Coast of
EAST FLORIDA
from
the River St. John
Southward, to near
CAPE CANAVERAL.

Lake

Head of Sth. Musqueto

T. Conder Sculpt.

CHAP. I.

THE AUTHOR SETS SAIL FROM PHILADELPHIA, AND ARRIVES AT CHARLESTON, FROM WHENCE HE BEGINS HIS TRAVELS.

At the request of Dr. Fothergill, of London, to search the Floridas, and the western parts of Carolina and Georgia, for the discovery of rare and useful productions of nature, chiefly in the vegetable kingdom; in April, 1773, I embarked for Charleston, South Carolina, on board the brigantine Charleston packet, captain Wright, the brig ——, captain Mason, being in company with us, and bound to the same port. We had a pleasant run down the Delaware, 150 miles to cape Henlopen, the two vessels entering the Atlantic together. For the first twenty-four hours we had a prosperous gale, and were cheerful and happy in the prospect of a quick and pleasant voyage; but, alas! how vain and uncertain are human expectations! how quickly is the flattering scene changed! The powerful winds, now rushing forth from their secret abodes, suddenly spread terror and devastation; and the wide ocean, which, a few moments past, was gentle and placid, is now thrown into disorder, and heaped into mountains, whose white curling crests seem to sweep the skies!

This furious gale continued near two days and nights, and not a little damaged our sails, cabin furniture, and state-rooms, besides retarding our passage. The storm having abated, a lively gale from N. W. continued four or five days, when shifting to N. and lastly to N. E. on the tenth of our departure from cape Henlopen, early in the morning, we descried a sail astern, and in a short time discovered it to be capt. Mason, who soon came up with us. We hailed each other, being joyful to meet again, after so many dangers. He suffered greatly by the gale, but providentially made a good harbour within cape Hatteras. As he ran by us, he threw on board ten or a dozen bass, a large and delicious fish, having caught a great number of them whilst he was detained in harbour. He got into Charleston that evening, and we the next morning, about eleven o'clock.

There are few objects out at sea to attract the notice of the traveller, but what are sublime, awful, and majestic: the seas themselves, in a tempest, exhibit a tremendous scene, where the winds assert their power, and, in furious conflict, seem to set the ocean on fire. On the other hand, nothing can be more sublime than the view of the encircling horizon, after the turbulent winds have taken their flight, and the lately agitated bosom of the deep has again become calm and pacific; the gentle moon rising in dignity from the east, attended by thousands of glittering orbs; the luminous appearance of the seas at night, when all the waters seem transmuted into liquid silver; the prodigious bands of porpoises foreboding tempest, that appear to cover the ocean; the mighty whale, sovereign of the watery realms, who cleaves the seas in his course; the sudden appearance of land from the sea, the strand stretching each way, beyond the utmost reach of sight; the alternate appearance and recess of the coast, whilst the far distant blue hills slowly retreat and disappear; or, as we approach the coast, the capes and promontories first strike our sight, emerging from the watery expanse, and, like mighty giants, elevating their crests towards the skies; the water suddenly alive with its scaly inhabitants; squadrons of sea-fowl sweeping through the air, impregnated with the breath of fragrant aromatic trees and flowers; the amplitude and magnificence of these scenes are great indeed, and may present to the imagination, an idea of the first appearance of the earth to man at the creation.

On my arrival at Charleston, I waited on doctor Chalmer, a gentleman of eminence in his profession and public employments, to whom I was recommended by my worthy patron, and to whom I was to apply for counsel and assistance, for carrying into effect my intended travels. The doctor received me with perfect politeness, and, on every occasion, treated me with friendship; and by means of the countenance which he gave me, and the marks of esteem with which he honoured me, I became acquainted with many of the worthy families, not only of Carolina and Georgia, but also in the distant countries of Florida.

CHAP. II.

ARRIVING in Carolina very early in the spring, vegetation was not sufficiently advanced to invite me into the western parts of this state; from which circumstance, I concluded to make an excursion into Georgia; accordingly, I embarked on board a coasting vessel, and in twenty-four hours arrived in Savanna, the capital, where, acquainting the governor, Sir J. Wright, with my business, his excellency received me with great politeness, shewed me every mark of esteem and regard, and furnished me with letters to the principal inhabitants of the state, which were of great service to me. Another circumstance very opportunely occurred on my arrival: the assembly was then sitting in Savanna, and several members lodging in the same house where I took up my quarters, I became acquainted with several worthy characters, who invited me to call at their seats occasionally, as I passed through the country; particularly the hon. B. Andrews, esq. a distinguished, patriotic, and liberal character. This gentleman's seat, and well cultivated plantations, are situated near the south high road, which I often travelled; and I seldom passed his house without calling to see him, for it was the seat of virtue, where hospitality, piety, and philosophy, formed the happy family; where the weary traveller and stranger found a hearty welcome, and from whence it must be his own fault if he departed without being greatly benefited.

After resting, and a little recreation for a few days in Savanna, and having in the mean time purchased a good horse, and equipped myself for a journey southward, I sat off early in the morning for Sunbury, a sea-port town, beautifully situated on the main, between Medway and Newport rivers, about fifteen miles south of great Ogeeche river. The town and harbour are defended from the fury of the seas by the north and south points of St. Helena and South Catharine's islands; between which is the bar and entrance into the sound: the harbour is capacious and safe, and has water enough for ships of great burthen. I arrived here in the evening, in company with a gentleman, one of the inhabitants, who politely

29

introduced me to one of the principal families, where I supped
and spent the evening in a circle of genteel and polite ladies
and gentlemen. Next day, being desirous of visiting the islands, I forded a narrow shoal, part of the sound, and landed
on one of them, which employed me the whole day to explore. The surface and vegetable mould here is generally a
loose sand, not very fertile, except some spots bordering on
the sound and inlets, where are found heaps or mounds of
sea-shell, either formerly brought there by the Indians, who
inhabited the island, or which were perhaps thrown up in
ridges, by the beating surface of the sea: possibly both these
circumstances may have contributed to their formation. These
sea shells, through length of time, and the subtle penetrating
effects of the air, which dissolve them to earth, render these
ridges very fertile; and, when clear of their trees, and cultivated, they become profusely productive of almost every kind
of vegetable. Here are also large plantations of indigo, corn,
and potatoes*, with many other sorts of esculent plants. I
observed, amongst the shells of the conical mounds, fragments of earthen vessels, and of other utensils, the manufacture of the ancients: about the centre of one of them, the rim
of an earthen pot appeared amongst the shells and earth,
which I carefully removed, and drew it out, almost whole: this
pot was curiously wrought all over the outside, representing
basket work, and was undoubtedly esteemed a very ingenious
performance, by the people, at the age of its construction. The
natural produce of these testaceous ridges, besides many of
less note, are, the great Laurel Tree, (Magnolia grandiflora)
Pinus tæda, Laurus Borbonia, Quercus sempervirens, or Live
Oak, Prunus Lauro-cerasus, Ilex aquifolium, Corypha palma,
Juniperus Americana. The general surface of the island being
low, and generally level, produces a very great variety of trees,
shrubs, and herbaceous plants; particularly the great long-
leaved Pitch-Pine, or Broom-Pine, Pinus palustris, Pinus
squarosa, Pinus lutea, Gordonia Lasianthus, Liquid ambar
(Styraciflua) Acer rubrum, Fraxinus excelcior, Fraxinus aquatica, Quercus aquatica, Quercus phillos, Quercus dentata,
Quercus pumila varietas, Vaccinium varietas, Andromeda

*Convolvulus batata.

varietas, Prinos varietas, Ilex varietas, Viburnum prunifolium, V. dentatum, Cornus florida, C. alba, C. sanguinea, Carpinus betula, C. ostrya, Itea Clethra alnifolia, Halesia tetraptera, H. diptera, Iva, Rhamnus frangula, Callicarpa, Morus rubra, Sapindus, Cassine, and of such as grow near watercourses, round about ponds and savannas, Fothergilla gardini, Myrica cerifera, Olea Americana, Cyrilla racemiflora, Magnolia glauca, Magnolia pyramidata, Cercis, Kalmia angustifolia, Kalmia ciliata, Chionanthus, Cephalanthos, Æsculus pavia; and the intermediate spaces, surrounding and lying between the ridges and savannas, are intersected with plains of the dwarf prickly fan-leaved Palmetto, and lawns of grass variegated with stately trees of the great Broom-Pine, and the spreading ever-green Water-Oak, either disposed in clumps, or scatteringly planted by nature. The upper surface, or vegetative soil of the island, lies on a foundation, or stratum, of tenacious cinereous-coloured clay, which perhaps is the principal support of the vast growth of timber that arises from the surface, which is little more than a mixture of fine white sand and dissolved vegetables, serving as a nursery bed to hatch or bring into existence the infant plant, and to supply it with aliment and food, suitable to its delicacy and tender frame, until the roots, acquiring sufficient extent and solidity to lay hold of the clay, soon attain a magnitude and stability sufficient to maintain its station. Probably if this clay were dug out, and cast upon the surface, after being meliorated by the saline or nitrous qualities of the air, it would kindly incorporate with the loose sand, and become a productive and lasting manure.

The roebuck, or deer, are numerous on this island; the tyger, wolf, and bear, hold yet some possession; as also raccoons, foxes, hares, squirrels, rats, and mice, but I think no moles. There is a large ground rat, more than twice the size of the common Norway rat. In the night time it throws out the earth, forming little mounds, or hillocks. Opossums are here in abundance, as also pole-cats, wild-cats, rattle-snakes, glass-snake, coach-whip snake, and a variety of other serpents.

Here are also a great variety of birds, throughout the seasons, inhabiting both sea and land. First I shall name the eagle, of which there are three species. The great grey eagle is the largest, of great strength and high flight; he chiefly preys on fawns and other young quadrupeds.

The bald eagle is likewise a large, strong, and very active bird, but an execrable tyrant: he supports his assumed dignity and grandeur by rapine and violence, extorting unreasonable tribute and subsidy from all the feathered nations.

The last of this race I shall mention is the falco piscatorius, or fishing-hawk: this is a large bird, of high and rapid flight; his wings are very long and pointed, and he spreads a vast sail, in proportion to the volume of his body. This princely bird subsists entirely on fish which he takes himself, scorning to live and grow fat on the dear earned labours of another; he also contributes liberally to the support of the bald eagle.

Water-fowl, and the various species of land-birds, also abound, most of which are mentioned by Catesby, in his Hist. of Carolina, particularly his painted finch (Emberiza Ciris Linn.) exceeded by none of the feathered tribes, either in variety and splendour of dress, or melody of song.

Catesby's ground doves are also here in abundance: they are remarkably beautiful, about the size of a sparrow, and their soft and plaintive cooing perfectly enchanting.

> How chaste the dove! "never known to violate the
>   conjugal contract."
> She flees the seats of envy and strife, and seeks the
>   retired paths of peace.

The sight of this delightful and productive island, placed in front of the rising city of Sunbury, quickly induced me to explore it; which I apprehended, from former visits to this coast, would exhibit a comprehensive epitome of the history of all the sea-coast islands of Carolina and Georgia, as likewise in general of the coast of the main. And though I considered this excursion along the coast of Georgia and northern border of Florida, a deviation from the high road of my intended travels, yet I performed it in order to employ to the most advantage the time on my hands, before the treaty of Augusta came on, where I was to attend, about May or June, by desire of the Superintendant, J. Stewart, esq. who, when I was in Charleston, proposed, in order to facilitate my travels in the

Indian territories, that, if I would be present at the Congress, he would introduce my business to the chiefs of the Cherokees, Creeks, and other nations, and recommend me to their friendship and protection; which promise he fully performed, and it proved of great service to me.

Obedient to the admonitions of my attendant spirit, curiosity, as well as to gratify the expectations of my worthy patron, I again sat off on my southern excursion, and left Sunbury, in company with several of its polite inhabitants, who were going to Medway meeting, a very large and well constructed place of worship, in St. John's parish, where I associated with them in religious exercise, and heard a very excellent sermon, delivered by their pious and truly venerable pastor, the Rev. —— Osgood. This respectable congregation is independent, and consist chiefly of families, and proselytes to a flock, which this pious man led about forty years ago, from South Carolina, and settled in this fruitful district. It is about nine miles from Sunbury to Medway meeting-house, which stands on the high road opposite the Sunbury road. As soon as the congregation broke up, I re-assumed my travels, proceeding down the high road towards Fort Barrington, on the Alatamaha, passing through a level country, well watered by large streams, branches of Medway and Newport rivers, coursing from extensive swamps and marshes, their sources: these swamps are daily clearing and improving into large fruitful rice plantations, aggrandizing the well inhabited and rich district of St. John's parish. The road is straight, spacious, and kept in excellent repair by the industrious inhabitants; and is generally bordered on each side with a light grove, consisting of the following trees and shrubs: Myrica Cerifera, Calycanthus, Halesia tetraptera, Itea stewartia, Andromeda nitida, Cyrella racemiflora, entwined with bands and garlands of Bignonia sempervirens, B. crucigera, Lonicera sempervirens and Glycene frutescens; these were overshadowed by tall and spreading trees, as the Magnolia grandiflora, Liquid ambar, Liriodendron, Catalpa, Quercus sempervirens, Quercus dentata, Q. Phillos; and on the verges of the canals, where the road was causwayed, stood the Cupressus disticha, Gordonia Lacianthus, and Magnolia glauca, all planted by nature, and left standing, by the virtuous inhabitants, to shade the road, and perfume the sultry air. The extensive plantations of rice and corn, now in early verdure, decorated here and there with groves of floriferous and fragrant trees and shrubs, under the cover and protection of pyramidal laurels and plumed palms, which now and then break through upon the sight from both sides of the way as we pass along; the eye at intervals stealing a view at the humble, but elegant and neat habitation, of the happy proprietor, amidst arbours and groves, all day, and moon-light nights, filled with the melody of the cheerful mockbird, warbling nonpareil, and plaintive turtle-dove, altogether present a view of magnificence and joy, inexpressibly charming and animating.

In the evening I arrived at the seat of the Hon. B. Andrews, esq. who received and entertained me in every respect, as a worthy gentleman could a stranger, that is, with hearty welcome, plain but plentiful board, free conversation and liberality of sentiment. I spent the evening very agreeably, and the day following (for I was not permitted to depart sooner): I viewed with pleasure this gentleman's exemplary improvements in agriculture; particularly in the growth of rice, and in his machines for shelling that valuable grain, which stands in the water almost from the time it is sown, until within a few days before it is reaped, when they draw off the water by sluices, which ripens it all at once, and when the heads or panicles are dry ripe, it is reaped and left standing in the field, in small ricks, until the straw is quite dry, when it is hauled, and stacked in the barn yard. The machines for cleaning the rice are worked by the force of water. They stand on the great reservoir which contains the waters that flood the rice fields below.

Towards the evening we made a little party at fishing. We chose a shaded retreat, in a beautiful grove of magnolias, myrtles, and sweet bay trees, which were left standing on the bank of a fine creek, that, from this place, took a slow serpentine course through the plantation. We presently took some fish, one kind of which is very beautiful; they call it the red-belly. It is as large as a man's hand, nearly oval and thin, being compressed on each side; the tail is beautifully formed; the top of the head and back of an olive green, besprinkled with russet specks; the sides of a sea green, inclining to azure, insensibly blended with the olive above, and beneath lightens to a silvery white, or pearl colour, elegantly powdered with specks of the finest green, russet and gold; the belly is of a bright scarlet red, or vermilion, darting up rays or fiery streaks into the pearl on each side; the ultimate angle of the branchiostega extends backwards with a long spatula, ending with a round or oval particoloured spot, representing the eye in the long feathers of a peacock's train, verged round with a thin flame-coloured membrane, and appears like a brilliant ruby fixed on the side of the fish; the eyes are large, encircled with a fiery iris; they are a voracious fish, and are easily caught with a suitable bait.

The next morning I took leave of this worthy family, and sat off for the settlements on the Alatamaha, still pursuing the high road for Fort Barrington, till towards noon, when I turned off to the left, following the road to Darian, a settlement on the river twenty miles lower down, and near the coast. The fore part of this day's journey was pleasant, the plantations frequent, and the roads in tolerable good repair; but the country being now less cultivated, the roads became bad. I pursued my journey almost continually through swamps and creeks, waters of Newport and Sapello, till night, when I lost my way; but coming up to a fence, I saw a glimmering light, which conducted me to a house, where I stayed all night, and met with very civil entertainment. Early next morning I sat off again, in company with the overseer of the farm, who piloted me through a large and difficult swamp, when we parted; he in chase of deer, and I towards Darian. I rode several miles through a high forest of pines, thinly growing on a level plain, which admitted an ample view, and a free circulation of air, to another swamp; and crossing a considerable branch of Sapello river, I then came to a small plantation by the side of another swamp: the people were remarkably civil and hospitable. The man's name was M'Intosh, a family of the first colony established in Georgia, under the conduct of general Oglethorpe. Was there ever such a scene of primitive simplicity, as was here exhibited, since the days of the good king Tammany! The venerable grey headed Caledonian smilingly meets me coming up to his house. "Welcome, stranger; come in, and rest; the air is now very sultry;

it is a very hot day." I was there treated with some excellent venison, and here found friendly and secure shelter from a tremendous thunder storm, which came up from the N. W. and soon after my arrival began to discharge its fury all around. Stepping to the door to observe the progress and direction of the tempest, the fulgour and rapidity of the streams of lightning, passing from cloud to cloud, and from the clouds to the earth, exhibited a very awful scene; when instantly the lightning, as it were, opening a fiery chasm in the black cloud, darted with inconceivable rapidity on the trunk of a large pine tree, that stood thirty or forty yards from me, and set it in a blaze. The flame instantly ascended upwards of ten or twelve feet, and continued flaming about fifteen minutes, when it was gradually extinguished by the deluges of rain that fell upon it.

I saw here a remarkably large turkey of the native wild breed: his head was above three feet from the ground when he stood erect; he was a stately beautiful bird, of a very dark dusky brown colour, the tips of the feathers of his neck, breast, back, and shoulders, edged with a copper colour, which in a certain exposure looked like burnished gold, and he seemed not insensible of the splendid appearance he made. He was reared from an egg, found in the forest, and hatched by a hen of the common domestic fowl.

Our turkey of America is a very different species from the meleagris of Asia and Europe; they are nearly thrice their size and weight. I have seen several that have weighed between twenty and thirty pounds, and some have been killed that weighed near forty. They are taller, and have a much longer neck proportionally, and likewise longer legs, and stand more erect; they are also very different in colour. Ours are all, male and female, of a dark brown colour, not having a black feather on them; but the male exceedingly splendid, with changeable colours. In other particulars they differ not.

The tempest being over, I waited till the floods of rain had run off the ground, then took leave of my friends, and departed. The air was now cool and salubrious, and riding seven or eight miles, through a pine forest, I came to Sapello bridge, to which the salt tide flows. I here stopped, at Mr. Bailey's, to deliver a letter from the governor. This gentleman received me very civilly, inviting me to stay with him; but upon my urging the necessity of my accelerating my journey, he permitted me to proceed to Mr. L. M'Intosh's, near the river, to whose friendship I was recommended by Mr. B. Andrews.

Perhaps, to a grateful mind, there is no intellectual enjoyment, which regards human concerns, of a more excellent nature, than the remembrance of real acts of friendship. The heart expands at the pleasing recollection. When I came up to his door, the friendly man, smiling, and with a grace and dignity peculiar to himself, took me by the hand, and accosted me thus: "Friend Bartram, come under my roof, and I desire you to make my house your home, as long as convenient to yourself; remember, from this moment, that you are a part of my family, and, on my part, I shall endeavour to make it agreeable," which was verified during my continuance in, and about, the southern territories of Georgia and Florida; for I found here sincerity in union with all the virtues, under the influence of religion. I shall yet mention a remarkable instance of Mr. M'Intosh's friendship and respect for me; which was, recommending his eldest son, Mr. John M'Intosh, as a companion in my travels. He was a sensible virtuous youth, and a very agreeable companion through a long and toilsome journey of near a thousand miles.

Having been greatly refreshed, by continuing a few days with this kind and agreeable family, I prepared to prosecute my journey southerly.

CHAP. III.

I SAT off early in the morning for the Indian trading-house, in the river St. Mary, and took the road up the N. E. side of the Alatamaha to Fort-Barrington. I passed through a well inhabited district, mostly rice plantations, on the waters of Cathead creek, a branch of the Alatamaha. On drawing near the fort, I was greatly delighted at the appearance of two new beautiful shrubs, in all their blooming graces. One of them appeared to be a species of Gordonia*, but the flowers are larger, and more fragrant than those of the Gordonia Lascanthus, and are sessile; the seed vessel is also very different. The other was equally distinguished for beauty and singularity; it grows twelve or fifteen feet high, the branches ascendant and opposite, and terminate with large panicles of pale blue tubular flowers, specked on the inside with crimson; but, what is singular, these panicles are ornamented with a number of ovate large bracteæ, as white, and like fine paper, their tops and verges stained with a rose red, which, at a little distance, has the appearance of clusters of roses, at the extremities of the limbs: the flowers are of the Cl. Pentandria monogynia; the leaves are nearly ovate, pointed and petioled, standing opposite to one another on the branches.

After fifteen miles riding, I arrived at the ferry, which is near the site of the fort. Here is a considerable height and bluff on the river, and evident vestiges of an ancient Indian town may be seen, such as old extensive fields, and conical mounds, or artificial heaps of earth. I here crossed the river, which is about five hundred yards over, in a good large boat, rowed by a Creek Indian, who was married to a white woman; he seemed an active, civil, and sensible man. I saw large, tall trees of the Nyssa coccinea, si. Ogeeche, growing on the banks of the river. They grow in the water, near the shore. There is no tree that exhibits a more desirable appearance than this, in the autumn, when the fruit is ripe, and the tree divested of its leaves; for then they look as red as scarlet, with their fruit, which is of that colour also. It is of the shape, but larger than

*Franklinia Alatahama.

38

the olive, containing an agreeable acid juice. The leaves are oblong lanceolate and entire, somewhat hoary underneath; their upper surface of a full green, and shining; the petioles short, pedunculis multifloris. The most northern settlement of this tree, yet known, is on Great Ogeeche, where they are called Ogeeche limes, from their acid fruit being about the size of limes, and their being sometimes used in their stead.

Being safely landed on the opposite bank, I mounted my horse, and followed the high road to the ferry on St. Ille, about sixty miles south of the Alatamaha, passing through an uninhabited wilderness. The sudden transition from rich cultivated settlements, to high pine forests, dark and grassy savannas, forms in my opinion no disagreeable contrasts; and the new objects of observation in the works of nature soon reconcile the surprised imagination to the change. As soon as I had lost sight of the river, ascending some sand-hills, I observed a new and most beautiful species of Annona, having clusters of large white fragrant flowers; and a diminutive but elegant Kalmia. The stems are very small, feeble, and for the most part undivided, furnished with little ovate pointed leaves, and terminate with a simple racemi, or spike of flowers, salver formed, and of a deep rose red. The whole plant is ciliated. It grows in abundance all over the moist savannas, but more especially near ponds and bay-swamps. In similar situations, and commonly a near neighbour to this new Kalmia, is seen a very curious species of Annona. It is very dwarf, the stems seldom extending from the earth more than a foot or eighteen inches, and are weak and almost decumbent. The leaves are long, extremely narrow, almost linear. However, small as they are, they retain the figure common to the species, that is, lanceolate, broadest at the upper end, and attenuating down to the petiole, which is very short; their leaves stand alternately, nearly erect, forming two series, or wings, on the arcuated stems. The flowers, both in size and colour, resemble those of the Annona triloba, and are single from the axillæ of the leaves on incurved pedunculi, nodding downwards. I never saw the fruit. The dens, or caverns, dug in the sand-hills, by the great land-tortoise, called here Gopher*, present

*Testudo Polyphemus.

a very singular appearance: these vast caves are their castles and diurnal retreats, from whence they issue forth in the night, in search of prey. The little mounds, or hillocks of fresh earth, thrown up in great numbers in the night, have also a curious appearance.

In the evening I arrived at a cow-pen, where there was a habitation, and the people received me very civilly. I staid here all night, and had for supper plenty of milk, butter, and very good cheese of their own make, which is a novelty in the maritime parts of Carolina and Georgia; the inhabitants being chiefly supplied with it from Europe and the northern states. The next day's progress, in general, presented scenes similar to the preceding, though the land is lower, more level and humid, and the produce more varied: high open forests of stately pines, flowery plains, and extensive green savannas, chequered with the incarnate Chironia pulcherrima, and Asclepias fragrans, perfumed the air whilst they pleased the eye. I met with some troublesome cane swamps, saw herds of horned cattle, horses and deer, and took notice of a procumbent species of Hibiscus, the leaves palmated, the flowers large and expanded, pale yellow and white, having a deep crimson eye; the whole plant, except the corolla, armed with stiff hair. I also saw a beautiful species of Lupin, having pale green villous lingulate* leaves; the flowers are disposed in long erect spikes; some plants produce flowers of the finest celestial blue, others incarnate, and some milk white, and though they all three seem to be varieties of one species, yet they associate in separate communities, sometimes approaching near each other's border, or in sight at a distance. Their districts are situated on dry sandy heights, in open pine forests, which are naturally thin of undergrowth, and appear to great advantage; generally, where they are found, they occupy many acres of surface. The vegetative mould is composed of fine white sand, mixed, and coloured, with dissolved and calcined vegetable substances; but this stratum is not very deep, and covers one of a tenacious cinereous coloured clay, as we may observe by the earth adhering to the roots of trees, torn up by storms, &c. and by the little chimnies, or air holes of cray-fish, which perforate

---

*Lupinus biennis, foliis integerimis oblongis villosis.

Annona Pygmea.

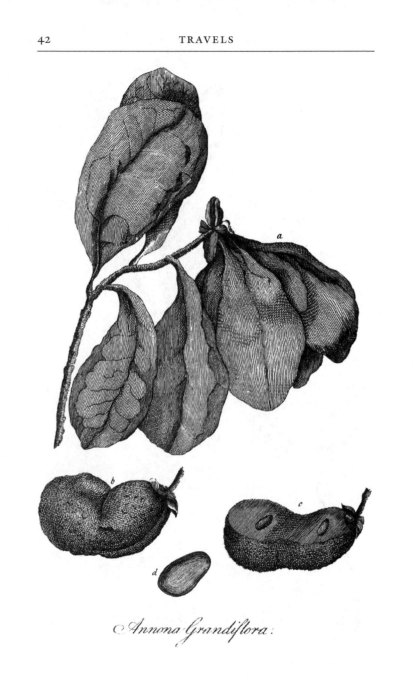

Annona Grandiflora.

the savannas. Turkeys, quails, and small birds, are here to be seen; but birds are not numerous in desert forests; they draw near to the habitations of men, as I have constantly observed in all my travels.

I arrived at St. Ille's in the evening, where I lodged; and next morning, having crossed over in a ferry boat, sat forward for St. Mary's. The situation of the territory, its soil and productions, between these two last rivers, are nearly similar to those which I had passed over, except that the savannas are more frequent and extensive.

It may be proper to observe, that I had now passed the utmost frontier of the white settlements on that border. It was drawing on towards the close of day, the skies serene and calm, the air temperately cool, and gentle zephyrs breathing through the fragrant pines; the prospect around enchantingly varied and beautiful; endless green savannas, chequered with coppices of fragrant shrubs, filled the air with the richest perfume. The gaily attired plants which enamelled the green had begun to imbibe the pearly dew of evening; nature seemed silent, and nothing appeared to ruffle the happy moments of evening contemplation; when, on a sudden, an Indian appeared crossing the path, at a considerable distance before me. On perceiving that he was armed with a rifle, the first sight of him startled me, and I endeavoured to elude his sight, by stopping my pace, and keeping large trees between us; but he espied me, and turning short about, sat spurs to his horse, and came up on full gallop. I never before this was afraid at the sight of an Indian, but at this time, I must own that my spirits were very much agitated: I saw at once, that being unarmed, I was in his power; and having now but a few moments to prepare, I resigned myself entirely to the will of the Almighty, trusting to his mercies for my preservation: my mind then became tranquil, and I resolved to meet the dreaded foe with resolution and chearful confidence. The intrepid Siminole stopped suddenly, three or four yards before me, and silently viewed me, his countenance angry and fierce, shifting his rifle from shoulder to shoulder, and looking about instantly on all sides. I advanced towards him, and with an air of confidence offered him my hand, hailing him, brother; at this he hastily jerked back his arm, with a look of malice, rage, and disdain, seeming every way discontented; when again looking at me more attentively, he instantly spurred up to me, and with dignity in his look and action, gave me his hand. Possibly the silent language of his soul, during the moment of suspense (for I believe his design was to kill me when he first came up) was after this manner: "White man, thou art my enemy, and thou and thy brethren may have killed mine; yet it may not be so, and even were that the case, thou art now alone, and in my power. Live; the Great Spirit forbids me to touch thy life; go to thy brethren, tell them thou sawest an Indian in the forests, who knew how to be humane and compassionate." In fine, we shook hands, and parted in a friendly manner, in the midst of a dreary wilderness; and he informed me of the course and distance to the trading-house, where I found he had been extremely ill-treated the day before.

I now sat forward again, and after eight or ten miles riding, arrived at the banks of St. Mary's, opposite the stores, and got safe over before dark. The river is here about one hundred yards across, has ten feet water, and, following its course, about sixty miles to the sea, though but about twenty miles by land. The trading company here received and treated me with great civility. On relating my adventures on the road, particularly the last with the Indian, the chief replied, with a countenance that at once bespoke surprise and pleasure, "My friend, consider yourself a fortunate man: that fellow," said he, "is one of the greatest villains on earth, a noted murderer, and outlawed by his countrymen. Last evening he was here, we took his gun from him, broke it in pieces, and gave him a severe drubbing: he, however, made his escape, carrying off a new rifle gun, with which, he said, going off, he would kill the first white man he met."

On seriously contemplating the behaviour of this Indian towards me, so soon after his ill treatment, the following train of sentiments insensibly crowded in upon my mind.

Can it be denied, but that the moral principle, which directs the savages to virtuous and praiseworthy actions, is natural or innate? It is certain they have not the assistance of letters, or those means of education in the schools of philosophy, where the virtuous sentiments and actions of the most illustrious characters are recorded, and carefully laid before the youth of civilized nations: therefore this moral principle must be innate, or they must be under the immediate influence and guidance of a more divine and powerful preceptor, who, on these occasions, instantly inspires them, and as with a ray of divine light, points out to them at once the dignity, propriety, and beauty of virtue.

The land on, and adjacent to, this river, notwithstanding its arenaceous surface, appears naturally fertile. The peach trees are large, healthy, and fruitful; and Indian corn, rice, cotton, and indigo, thrive exceedingly. This sandy surface, one would suppose, from its loose texture, would possess a percolating quality, and suffer the rainwaters quickly to drain off; but it is quite the contrary, at least in these low maritime sandy countries of Carolina and Florida, beneath the mountains; for in the sands, even the heights, where the arenaceous stratum is perhaps five, eight, and ten feet above the clay, the earth, even in the longest droughts, is moist an inch or two under the surface; whereas, in the rich tenacious low lands, at such times, the ground is dry, and, as it were, baked many inches, and sometimes some feet deep, and the crops, as well as almost all vegetation, suffer in such soils and situations. The reason of this may be, that this kind of earth admits more freely of a transpiration of vapours, arising from intestine watery canals to the surface; and probably these vapours are impregnated with saline or nitrous principles, friendly and nutritive to vegetables; however, of these causes and secret operations of nature I am ignorant, and resume again my proper employment, that of discovering and collecting data for the exercise of more able physiologists.

The savannas about St. Mary's, at this season, display a very charming appearance of flowers and verdure; their more elevated borders are varied with beds of violets, lupins, Amaryllis atamasco, and plants of a new and very beautiful species of Mimosa sensitiva, which I think as admirable and more charming than the celebrated Humble plant, equally chaste and fearful of the hastly touch of the surprised admirer. The flower is larger, of a bright damask rose colour, and exceedingly fragrant: the whole plant is destitute of prickles, but hairy: it is procumbent, reclining itself upon the green turf, and from these trailing branches proceeds an upright peduncle, six or eight inches high, supporting an oblong head of flowerets, which altogether, at a small distance, have the appearance of an exuberant field of clover; and, what is singular, and richly varies the scene, there are interspersed patches of the same species of plants, having flowers of the finest golden yellow, and others snow white; but the incarnate is most prevalent. Magnolia glauca, Itea Clethra, Chionanthus, Gordonia lasianthus, Ilex angustifolium, Olea Americana, Hopea tinctoria, &c. are seated in detached groves or clumps, round about the ponds or little lakes, at the lower end of the savannas. I observed, growing on the banks of this sequestered river, the following trees and shrubs: Quercus sempervirens, Q. aquatica, Q. Phillos, Q. dentata, Nyssa aquatica, N. sylvatica, N. Ogeeche, si. coccinea, Cupressus disticha, Fraxinus aquatica, Rhamnus frangula, Prunus laurocerasa, Cyrilla racemiflora, Myrica cerifera, Andromeda ferruginia, Andr. nitida, and the great evergreen Andromeda of Florida, called Pipe-stem Wood, to which I gave the name of Andromeda formosissima, as it far exceeds in beauty every one of this family.

The river St. Mary has its source from a vast lake, or marsh, called Ouaquaphenogaw, which lies between Flint and Oakmulge rivers, and occupies a space of near three hundred miles in circuit. This vast accumulation of waters, in the wet season, appears as a lake, and contains some large islands or knolls, of rich high land; one of which the present generation of the Creeks represent to be a most blissful spot of the earth: they say it is inhabited by a peculiar race of Indians, whose women are incomparably beautiful; they also tell you that this terrestrial paradise has been seen by some of their enterprising hunters, when in pursuit of game, who being lost in inextricable swamps and bogs, and on the point of perishing, were unexpectedly relieved by a company of beautiful women, whom they call daughters of the sun, who kindly gave them such provisions as they had with them, which were chiefly fruit, oranges, dates, &c. and some corn cakes, and then enjoined them to fly for safety to their own country; for that their husbands were fierce men, and cruel to strangers: they further say, that these hunters had a view of their settlements, situated on the elevated banks of an island, or promontory, in a beautiful lake; but that in their endeavours to approach it, they were involved in perpetual labyrinths, and, like enchanted land, still as they imagined they had just gained it, it seemed to fly before them, alternately appearing and disappearing. They resolved, at length, to leave the delusive pursuit, and to return; which, after a number of inexpressible difficulties, they effected. When they reported their adventures to their countrymen, their young warriors were enflamed with an irresistible desire to invade, and make a conquest of, so charming a country; but all their attempts hitherto have proved abortive, never having been able again to find that enchanting spot, nor even any road or pathway to it; yet they say that they frequently meet with certain signs of its being inhabited, as the building of canoes, footsteps of men, &c. They tell another story concerning the inhabitants of this sequestered country, which seems probable enough, which is, that they are the posterity of a fugitive remnant of the ancient Yamases, who escaped massacre after a bloody and decisive conflict between them and the Creek nation (who, it is certain, conquered, and nearly exterminated, that once powerful people), and here found an asylum, remote and secure from the fury of their proud conquerors. It is, however, certain that there is a vast lake, or drowned swamp, well known, and often visited both by white and Indian hunters, and on its environs the most valuable hunting grounds in Florida, well worth contending for, by those powers whose territories border upon it. From this great source of rivers*, St. Mary arises, and meanders through a vast plain and pine forest, near an hundred and fifty miles to the ocean, with which it communicates, between the points of Amelia and Talbert islands; the waters flow deep and gently down from its source to the sea.

Having made my observations on the vegetable productions of this part of the country, and obtained specimens and seeds of some curious trees and shrubs (which were the principal objects of this excursion) I returned by the same road to the Alatamaha, and arrived safe again at the seat of my good

---

*Source of rivers. It is said, that St. Ille, St. Mary, and the beautiful river Little St. Juan, which discharges its waters into the bay of Apalachi, at St. Mark's, take their rise from this swamp.

friend, L. M'Intosh, Esq. where I tarried a few days to rest and refresh myself, and to wait for my young companion and fellow pilgrim, Mr. John M'Intosh, who, being fond of the enterprise, had been so active during my absence, in the necessary preparations, that we had nothing to wait for now but Mrs. M'Intosh's final consent to give up her son to the perils and hardships of so long a journey; which difficult point being settled, we set off with the prayers and benevolent wishes of my companion's worthy parents.

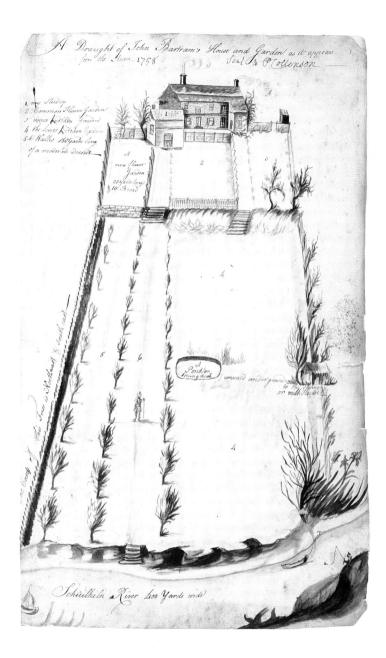

A Draught of John Bartram's House and Garden as it appears from the River 1758 Sent to P. Collinson

1 my Study
2 Common Flower Garden
3 upper Kitchen Garden
4 the Lower Kitchen Garden
5.6 Walks 150 yards long
of a moderate descent

A new Flower Garden 25 yards long & 10 broad

A Pond or Spring head conveyd underground to My Spring or milk House

the Course A the Fence to Northeast & South east

Schuilkiln River 200 Yards wide

PLATE I

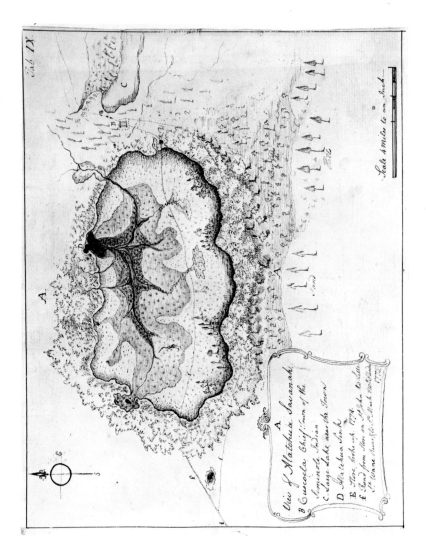

Tab. IX.

A
View of Alachua Savanah
B Cuscowilla Chief Town of the
Seminole Indian
C Large Lake near the Town
D Alachua Sink
E Here broke up A. 1774
F Sand from Stone on St. John to Lake
St Wars River West Mark 140 Chains
1774

Scale 4 miles to an Inch

PLATE 2

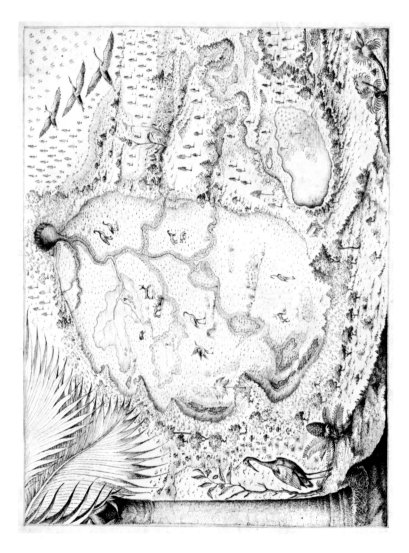

Plate 3

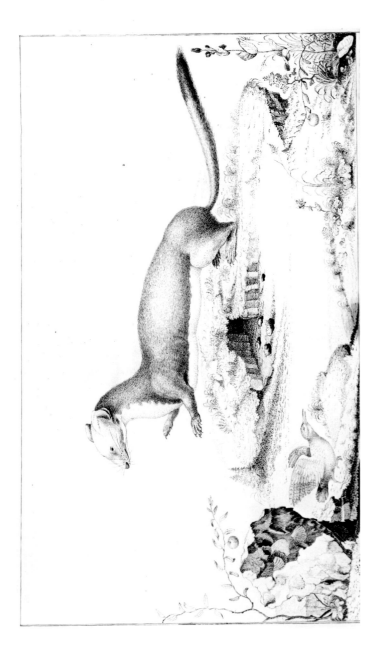

PLATE 4

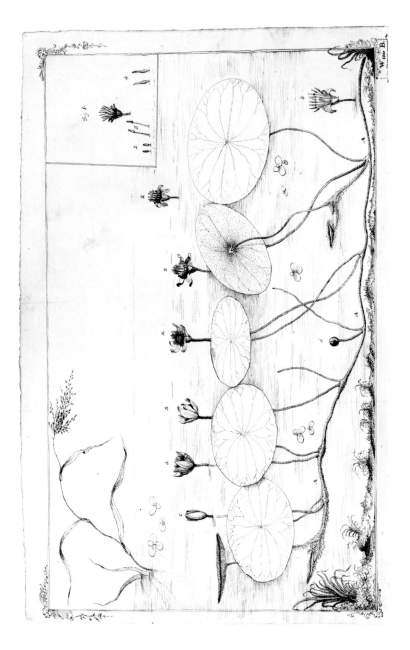

PLATE 5

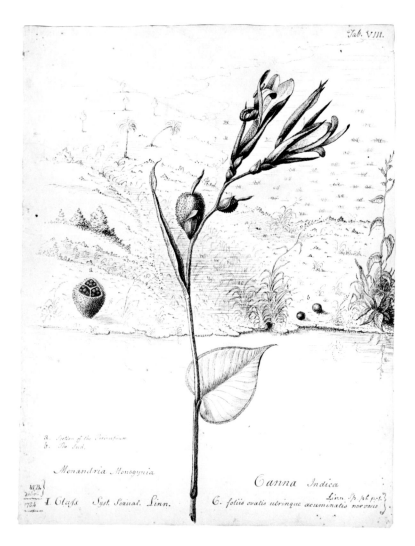

Tab. VIII.

a. Section of the Pericarpium
b. The Seed.

Monandria Monogynia

Canna Indica

W.B.
delin.
1784 I. Class   Syst. Sexual. Linn.

Linn. Sp. pl. p. 1.
C. foliis ovatis utrinque acuminatis nervosis

PLATE 6

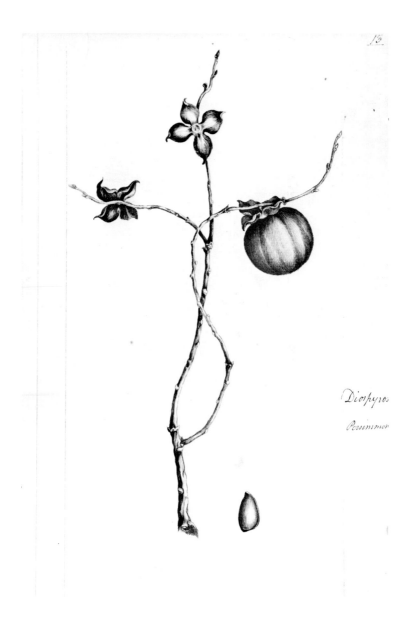

13.

Diospyros

Persimmon

PLATE 7

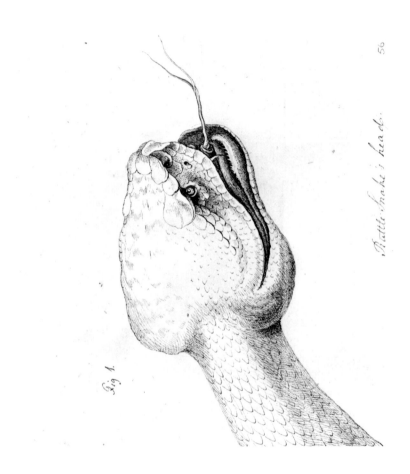

Rattle Snake's head.

Fig. 1.

PLATE 8

The Apgalargo of John.

PLATE 9

Fig. 1.

Fig. 1. Arethusa divaricata. Radice subrotunda scapi folio foliisque spathaceis lanceolatis, petal. is exterioribus adscendentibus. Gron. virg. 139.

Helleborine lilii folio caulem ambiente, flore uno hexapetalo tribus petalis longis angustis obscure purpurascis, caloris brevioribus rosaceis. Catesb. car. 1. p. 58. ta. 58.

2. Arethusa scapo tenui, &c. the 3 or 6 ovate-lanced vais deep, may be termed such, which, according to Linnaeus are the Spatha. This species of Arethusa seems not to be described or mentioned. It is a native of Pennsylvania and N. Jersey and is the 4th species native to N. America.

Co. B. Esq.

PLATE 10

Plate I.

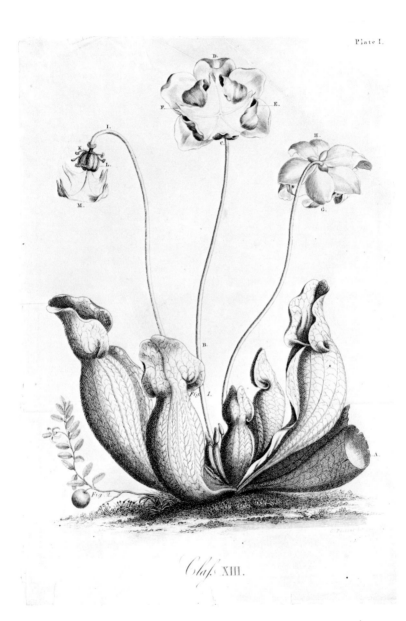

Claſs XIII.

PLATE II

Podophyllum peltatum.

PLATE 12

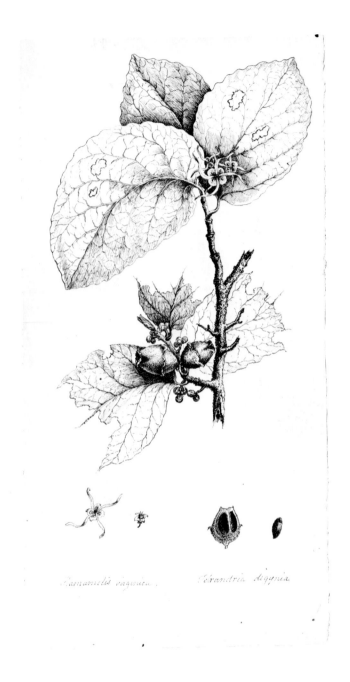

Hamamelis virginica   *Tetrandria digynia*

PLATE 13

PLATE 14

PLATE 15

PLATE 16

CHAP. IV.

EARLY in the morning, we mounted our horses, and in two days arrived in Savanna; here we learned that the superintendant of Indian affairs had left the capital, and was on his way to Augusta. I remained but one day in Savanna, which was employed in making up and forwarding the collections for Charleston.

The day following we set off for Augusta, which is on Savanna river, at least an hundred and fifty miles by land from the capital, and about three hundred by water. We followed the course of the river, and arrived there after having had a prosperous journey, though a little incommoded by the heats of the season.

As nothing very material occurred on the road, I shall proceed to give a summary account of the observations I made concerning the soil, situation, and natural productions of the country.

In our progress from the sea coast, we rise gradually, by several steps or ascents, in the following manner: First, from the sea-coast, fifty miles back, is a level plain, generally of a loose sandy soil, producing spacious high forests, of Pinus tæda, P. lutea, P. squarrosa, P. echinata, 1. Quercus sempervirens, 2. Quercus aquatica, 3. Q. phillos, 4. Q. tinctoria, 5. Q. dentata, 6. Q. prinos, 7. Q. alba, 8. Q. sinuata, 9. Q. rubra, Liriodendron tulipifera, Liquidambar styraciflua, Morus rubra, Cercis tilia, Populus heterophylla, Platanus occidentalis, Laurus sassafras, Laurus Borbonia, Hopea tinctoria, Fraxinus excelsior, Nyssa, Ulmus, Juglans exaltata, Halesa, Stewartia. Nearly one third of this vast plain is what the inhabitants call swamps, which are the sources of numerous small rivers and their branches: these they call salt rivers, because the tides flow near to their sources, and generally carry a good depth and breadth of water for small craft, twenty or thirty miles upwards from the sea, when they branch and spread abroad like an

1. Live Oak. 2. Delta-leaved Water Oak. 3. Willow-leaved Oak. 4. Great Black Oak. 5. Narrow leaved Wintergreen Oak. 6. Swamp White Oak. 7. White Oak. 8. Spanish Oak. 9. Red Oak.

open hand, interlocking with each other, and forming a chain of swamps across the Carolinas and Georgia, several hundred miles parallel with the sea coast. These swamps are fed and replenished constantly by an infinite number of rivulets and rills, which spring out of the first bank or ascent: their native trees and shrubs are, besides most of those already enumerated above, as follow: Acer rubrum, Nyssa aquatica, Chionanthus, Celtis, Fagus sylvatica, Sambucus; and the higher knolls afford beautiful clumps of Azalea nuda and Azalea viscosa, Corypha palma, Corypha pumila, and Magnolia grandiflora; besides, the whole surface of the ground between the trees and shrubs appear to be occupied with canes (Arundo gigantea) entangled with festoons of the floriferous Glycine frutescens, Bignonia sempervirens, Glycine apios, Smilax, various species, Bignonia crucigera, Bign. radicans, Lonicera sempervirens, and a multitude of other trees, shrubs, and plants less conspicuous; and, in very wet places, Cupressus disticha. The upper soil of these swamps is a perfectly black, soapy, rich earth, or stiff mud, two or three feet deep, on a foundation or stratum of calcareous fossil, which the inhabitants call white marle; and this is the heart or strength of these swamps: they never wear out or become poor, but, on the contrary, are more fertile by tillage; for when they turn up this white marle, the air and winter frosts causing it to fall like quicklime, it manures the surface: but it has one disadvantage, that is, in great droughts, when they cannot have water sufficient in their reservoirs to lay the surface of the ground under water, it binds, and becomes so tough as to burn and kill the crops, especially the old cleared lands; as, while it was fresh and new, the great quantity of rotten wood, roots, leaves, &c. kept the surface loose and open. Severe droughts seldom happen near the sea coast.

We now rise a bank of considerable height, which runs nearly parallel to the coast, through Carolina and Georgia: the ascent is gradual by several flights or steps, for eight or ten miles, the perpendicular height whereof, above the level of the ocean, may be two or three hundred feet (and these are called the sand-hills), when we find ourselves on the entrance of a vast plain, generally level, which extends west sixty or seventy miles, rising gently as the former, but more perceptibly.

This plain is mostly a forest of the great long-leaved pine (P. palustris Linn.) the earth covered with grass, interspersed with an infinite variety of herbaceous plants, and embellished with extensive savannas, always green, sparkling with ponds of water, and ornamented with clumps of evergreen, and other trees and shrubs, as Magnolia grandiflora, Magnolia glauca, Gordonia, Illex aquifolium, Quercus, various species, Laurus Borbonia, Chionanthus, Hopea tinctoria, Cyrilla, Kalmia angustifolia, Andromeda, varieties, Viburnum, Azalea, Rhus vernix, Prinos, varieties, Fothergilla, and a new shrub of great beauty and singularity: it grows erect, seven or eight feet high; a multitude of erect stems arise from its root; these divide themselves into ascendant branches, which are garnished with abundance of narrow lanceolate obtuse pointed leaves, of a light green, smooth and shining. These branches, with their many subdivisions, terminate in simple racemes of pale incarnate flowers, which make a fine appearance among the leaves; the flowers are succeeded by desiccated triquetrous pericarpi, each containing a single kernel.

The lowest sides of these savannas are generally joined by a great cane swamp, varied with coppices and hommocks of the various trees and shrubs already mentioned. In these swamps several rivulets take their rise, which drain them and the adjoining savannas, and thence meandering to the rivers through the forests, with their banks decorated with shrubs and trees. The earth under this level plain may be described after the following manner: the upper surface, or vegetative mould, is a light sandy loam, generally nine inches or a foot deep, on a stratum of cinereous coloured clay, except the sand-hills, where the loose sandy surface is much deeper upon the clay; stone of any fort, or gravel, is seldom seen.

The next ascent, or flight, is of much greater and more abrupt elevation, and continues rising by broken ridges and narrow levels, or vales, for ten or fifteen miles, when we rest again on another extensive nearly level plain of pine forests, mixed with various other forest trees, which continues west forty or fifty miles farther, and exhibits much the same appearance with the great forest last mentioned; its vegetable productions nearly the same, excepting that the broken ridges by which we ascend to the plain are of a better soil; the vegetative mould is mixed with particles of clay and small gravel, and the soil of a dusky brown colour, lying on a stratum of reddish brown tough clay. The trees and shrubs are, Pinus tæda, great black Oak, Quercus tinctoria, Q. rubra, Laurus, Sassafras, Magnolia grandiflora, Cornus Florida, Cercis, Halesia, Juglans acuminata, Juglans exaltata, Andromeda arborea: and, by the sides of rivulets (which wind about and between these hills and swamps, in the vales) Styrax latifolia, Ptelea trifoliata, Stewartia, Calycanthus, Chionanthus, Magnolia tripetala, Azalea, and others.

Thus have I endeavoured to give the reader a short and natural description of the vast plain lying between the region of Augusta and the sea coast; for from Augusta the mountainous country begins (when compared to the level sandy plain already passed), although it is at least an hundred and fifty miles west, thence to the Cherokee or Apalachean mountains; and this space may with propriety be called the hilly country, every where fertile and delightful, continually replenished by innumerable rivulets, either coursing about the fragrant hills, or springing from the rocky precipices, and forming many cascades; the coolness and purity of which waters invigorate the air of this otherwise hot and sultry climate.

The village of Augusta is situated on a rich and fertile plain, on the Savanna river; the buildings are near its banks, and extend nearly two miles up to the cataracts, or falls, which are formed by the first chain of rocky hills, through which this famous river forces itself, as if impatient to repose on the extensive plain before it invades the ocean. When the river is low, which is during the summer months, the cataracts are four or five feet in height across the river, and the waters continue rapid and broken, rushing over rocks five miles higher up: this river is near five hundred yards broad at Augusta.

A few days after our arrival at Augusta, the chiefs and warriors of the Creeks and Cherokees being arrived, the Congress and the business of the treaty came on, and the negociations continued undetermined many days; the merchants of Georgia demanding at least two millions of acres of land from the Indians, as a discharge of their debts, due, and of long standing: the Creeks, on the other hand, being a powerful and proud spirited people, their young warriors were unwilling to

submit to so large a demand, and their conduct evidently be-
trayed a disposition to dispute the ground by force of arms,
and they could not at first be brought to listen to reason and
amicable terms; however, at length, the cool and deliberate
counsels of the ancient venerable chiefs, enforced by liberal
presents of suitable goods, were too powerful inducements for
them any longer to resist, and finally prevailed. The treaty
concluded in unanimity, peace, and good order; and the honourable superintendant, not forgetting his promise to me, at
the conclusion, mentioned my business, and recommended
me to the protection of the Indian chiefs and warriors. The
presents being distributed amongst the Indians, they departed, returning home to their towns. A company of surveyors were appointed, by the governor and council, to
ascertain the boundaries of the new purchase; they were to
be attended by chiefs of the Indians, selected and delegated
by their countrymen, to assist, and be witnesses that the
articles of the treaty were fulfilled, as agreed to by both parties
in Congress.

Col. Barnet, who was chosen to conduct this business on
the part of the Georgians, a gentleman every way qualified for
that important trust, in a very friendly and obliging manner,
gave me an invitation to accompany him on this tour.

It was now about the middle of the month of May; vegetation, in perfection, appeared with all her attractive charms,
breathing fragrance every where; the atmosphere was now animated with the efficient principle of vegetative life; the ar-
bustive hills, gay lawns, and green meadows, which on every
side invest the villa of Augusta, had already received my frequent visits; and although here much delighted with the new
beauties in the vegetable kingdom, and many eminent ones
have their sequestered residence near this place, yet, as I was
never long satisfied with present possession, however endowed
with every possible charm to attract the sight, or intrinsic
value to engage and fix the esteem, I was restless to be searching for more, my curiosity being insatiable.

Thus it is with regard to our affections and attachments, in
the more important and interesting concerns of human life.

Upon the rich rocky hills at the cataracts of Augusta, I first
observed the perfumed rhododendron ferrugineum, white-

robed philadelphus inodorus, and cerulean malva; but nothing in vegetable nature was more pleasing than the odoriferous pancratium fluitans, which almost alone possesses the little rocky islets which just appear above the water.

The preparatory business of the surveyors being now accomplished, Mr. J. M'Intosh, yet anxious for travelling, and desirous to accompany me on this tour, joined with me the caravan, consisting of surveyors, astronomers, artisans, chain-carriers, markers, guides, and hunters, besides a very respectable number of gentlemen, who joined us, in order to speculate in the lands, together with ten or twelve Indians, altogether to the number of eighty or ninety men, all or most of us well mounted on horseback, besides twenty or thirty pack-horses, loaded with provisions, tents, and camp equipage.

The summer season now rapidly advancing, the air at midday, about this region, was insufferably hot and sultry. We sat off from Augusta, early in the morning, for the Great Buffalo Lick, on the Great Ridge, which separates the waters of the Savanna and Alatamaha, about eighty miles distant from Augusta. At this Lick the surveyors were to separate themselves, and form three companies, to proceed on different routes. On the evening of the second day's journey, we arrived at a small village on Little River, a branch of the Savanna: this village, called Wrightsborough, was founded by Jos. Mattock, esq., of the sect called quakers. This public spirited man having obtained for himself and his followers a district, comprehending upwards of forty thousand acres of land, gave the new town this name, in honour of sir James Wright, then governor of Georgia, who greatly promoted the establishment of the settlement. Mr. Mattock, who is now about seventy years of age, healthy and active, and presides as chief magistrate of the settlement, received us with great hospitality. The distance from Augusta to this place is about thirty miles; the face of the country is chiefly a plain of high forests, savannas, and cane swamps, until we approach Little River, when the landscape varies, presenting to view high hills and rich vales. The soil is a deep, rich, dark mould, on a deep stratum of reddish brown tenacious clay, and that on a foundation of rocks which often break through both strata, lifting their backs above the surface. The forest trees are chiefly of the deciduous order, as, quercus tinctoria, q. laciniata, q. alba, q. rubra, q. prinus, with many other species; celtis, fagus sylvatica, and, on the rocky hills, fagus castanea, fag. pumila, quercus castanea; in the rich vales, juglans nigra, jug. cinerea, gleditsia triacanthos, magnolia acuminata, liriodendron, platanus, fraxinus excelsior, cercis, juglans exaltata, carpinus, morus rubra, calycanthus, halesia, æsculus pavia, æsc. arborea.

Leaving the pleasant town of Wrightsborough we continued eight or nine miles through a fertile plain and high forest, to the north branch of Little River, being the largest of the two, crossing which, we entered an extensive fertile plain, bordering on the river, and shaded by trees of vast growth, which at once spoke its fertility. Continuing some time through these shady groves, the scene opens, and discloses to view the most magnificent forest I had ever seen. We rose gradually a sloping bank of twenty or thirty feet elevation, and immediately entered this sublime forest. The ground is perfectly a level green plain, thinly planted by nature with the most stately forest trees, such as the gigantic black* oak (q. tinctoria), liriodendron, juglans nigra, platanus, juglans exaltata, fagus sylvatica, ulmus sylvatica, liquidambar styraciflua, whose mighty trunks, seemingly of an equal height, appeared like superb columns. To keep within the bounds of truth and reality, in describing the magnitude and grandeur of these trees, would, I fear, fail of credibility; yet, I think I can assert, that many of the black oaks measured eight, nine, ten, and eleven feet diameter five feet above the ground, as we measured several that were above thirty feet girt, and from hence they ascend perfectly straight, with a gradual taper, forty or fifty feet to the limbs; but, below five or six feet, these trunks would measure a third more in circumference, on account of the projecting jambs, or supports, which are more or less, according to the number of horizontal roots that they arise from: the tulip tree, liquidambar, and beech, were equally stately.

Not far distant from the terrace, or eminence, overlooking the low grounds of the river, many very magnificent monuments of the power and industry of the ancient inhabitants of

---

*Gigantic black oak. Querc, tinctoria; the bark of this species of oak is found to afford a valuable yellow dye. This tree is known by the name of black oak in Pennsylvania, New-Jersey, New-York, and New-England.

these lands are visible. I observed a stupendous conical pyramid, or artificial mount of earth, vast tetragon terraces, and a
large sunken area, of a cubical form, encompassed with banks
of earth; and certain traces of a larger Indian town, the work
of a powerful nation, whose period of grandeur perhaps long
preceded the discovery of this continent.

After about seven miles progress through this forest of
gigantic black oaks, we enter on territories which exhibit more
varied scenes: the land rises almost insensibly by gentle ascents, exhibiting desart plains, high forests, gravelly and stony
ridges, ever in sight of rapid rivulets; the soil, as already described. We then passed over large rich savannas, or natural
meadows, wide spreading cane swamps, and frequently old
Indian settlements, now deserted and overgrown with forests.
These are always on or near the banks of rivers, or great
swamps, the artificial mounts and terraces elevating them
above the surrounding groves. I observed, in the ancient cultivated fields, 1. diospyros, 2. gleditsia triacanthos, 3. prunus
chicasaw, 4. callicarpa, 5. morus rubra, 6. juglans exaltata,
7. juglans nigra, which inform us, that these trees were cultivated by the ancients, on account of their fruit, as being
wholesome and nourishing food. Though these are natives of
the forest*, yet they thrive better, and are more fruitful, in
cultivated plantations, and the fruit is in great estimation with
the present generation of Indians, particularly juglans exaltata,
commonly called shell-barked hiccory. The Creeks store up
the last in their towns. I have seen above an hundred bushels
of these nuts belonging to one family. They pound them to
pieces, and then cast them into boiling water, which, after
passing through fine strainers, preserves the most oily part of
the liquid: this they call by a name which signifies hiccory
milk; it is as sweet and rich as fresh cream, and is an ingredient
in most of their cookery, especially homony and corn cakes.

After four days moderate and pleasant travelling, we arrived
in the evening at the Buffalo Lick. This extraordinary place
occupies several acres of ground, at the foot of the S. E. prom-

---

*The Chicasaw plumb I think must be excepted, for though certainly a
native of America, yet I never saw it wild in the forests, but always in old
deserted Indian plantations: I suppose it to have been brought from the
S. W. beyond the Missisippi, by the Chicasaws.

ontory of the Great Ridge, which, as before observed, divides the rivers Savanna and Alatamaha. A large cane swamp and meadows, forming an immense plain, lie S. E. from it; in this swamp I believe the head branches of the great Ogeeche river take their rise. The place called the Lick contains three or four acres, is nearly level, and lies between the head of the cane swamp and the ascent of the Ridge. The earth, from the superficies to an unknown depth, is an almost white or cinereous coloured tenacious fattish clay, which all kinds of cattle lick into great caves, pursuing the delicious vein. It is the common opinion of the inhabitants, that this clay is impregnated with saline vapours, arising from fossile salts deep in the earth; but I could discover nothing saline in its taste, but I imagined an insipid sweetness. Horned cattle, horses, and deer, are immoderately fond of it, insomuch, that their excrement, which almost totally covers the earth to some distance round this place, appears to be perfect clay; which, when dried by the sun and air, is almost as hard as brick.

We were detained at this place one day, in adjusting and planning the several branches of the survey. A circumstance occurred during this time, which was a remarkable instance of Indian sagacity, and had nearly disconcerted all our plans, and put an end to the business. The surveyor having fixed his compass on the staff, and being about to ascertain the course from our place of departure, which was to strike Savanna river at the confluence of a certain river, about seventy miles distance from us; just as he had determined upon the point, the Indian chief came up, and observing the course he had fixed upon, spoke, and said it was not right; but that the course to the place was so and so, holding up his hand, and pointing. The surveyor replied, that he himself was certainly right, adding, that that little instrument (pointing to the compass) told him so, which, he said, could not err. The Indian answered, he knew better, and that the little wicked instrument was a liar; and he would not acquiesce in its decisions, since it would wrong the Indians out of their land. This mistake (the surveyor proving to be in the wrong) displeased the Indians; the dispute arose to that height, that the chief and his party had determined to break up the business, and return the shortest way home, and forbad the surveyors to proceed any farther:

however, after some delay, the complaisance and prudent conduct of the colonel made them change their resolution; the
chief became reconciled, upon condition that the compass
should be discarded, and rendered incapable of serving on this
business; that the chief himself should lead the survey; and,
moreover, receive an order for a very considerable quantity of
goods.

Matters being now amicably settled, under this new regulation, the colonel having detached two companies on separate
routes, Mr. M'Intosh and myself attaching ourselves to the
colonel's party, whose excursion was likely to be the most
extensive and varied, we sat off from the Buffalo Lick, and
the Indian chief, heading the party, conducted us on a straight
line, as appeared by collateral observation, to the desired
place. We pursued nearly a north course up the Great Ridge,
until we came near the branches of Broad River, when we
turned off to the right hand, and encamped on a considerable
branch of it. At this place we continued almost a whole day,
constituting surveyors and astronomers, who were to take the
course, distance, and observations on Broad River, and from
thence down to its confluence with the Savanna.

The Great Ridge consists of a continued high forest; the
soil fertile, and broken into moderately elevated hills, by the
many rivulets which have their sources in it. The heights and
precipices abound in rock and stone. The forest trees and
other vegetable productions are the same as already mentioned about Little River: I observed halesia, styrax, æsculus
pavia, æsc. sylvatica, robinia hispida, magnolia acuminata,
mag. tripetala, and some very curious new shrubs and plants,
particularly the physic-nut, or Indian olive. The stems arise
many from a root, two or three feet high; the leaves sit opposite, on very short petioles; they are broad, lanceolate, entire, and undulated, having smooth surfaces of a deep green
colour. From the bosom of each leaf is produced a single oval
drupe, standing erect, on long slender stems; it has a large
kernel, and thin pulp. The fruit is yellow when ripe, and about
the size of an olive. The Indians, when they go in pursuit of
deer, carry this fruit with them, supposing that it has the
power of charming or drawing that creature to them; from
whence, with the traders, it has obtained the name of the

physic-nut, which means, with them, charming, conjuring, or fascinating. Malva scandens, filix scandens, perhaps a species of trichomanes; the leaves are palmated, or radiated; it climbs and roves about, on shrubs, in moist ground. A very singular and elegant plant, of an unknown family, called Indian lettuce, made its first appearance in these rich vales; it is a biennial; the primary or radical leaves are somewhat spatuled, or broad, lanceolate, and obtuse pointed, of a pale yellowish green, smooth surface, and of a delicate frame, or texture; these leaves spread equally on every side, almost reclining on the ground; from their centre arises a straight upright stem, five, six, or seven feet high, smooth and polished; the ground of a dark purple colour, which is elegantly powdered with greenish yellow specks; the stems, three-fourths of its length, is embellished with narrow leaves, nearly of the same form with the radical ones, placed at regular distances, in verticilate order. The superior one-fourth division of this stem is formed into a pyramidal spike of flowers, rather diffuse; these flowers are of the hexandria, large, and expanded; of a dark purple colour, delicately powdered with green, yellow, and red, and divided into six parts, or petals; these are succeeded by triquetrous dry pericarpi, when ripe.

This great ridge is a vast extended projection of the Cherokee or Alegany mountains, gradually increasing in height and extent, from its extremity at the Lick, to its union with the high ridge of mountains anciently called the Apalachian mountains; it every where approaches much nearer the waters of the Alatamaha than those of the Savanna. At one particular place, where we encamped, on the Great Ridge, during our repose there part of a day, our hunters going out, understanding that their route was to the low lands on the Ocone, I accompanied them: we had not rode above three miles before we came to the banks of that beautiful river. The cane swamps, of immense extent, and the oak forests, on the level lands, are incredibly fertile; which appears from the tall reeds of the one, and the heavy timber of the other.

Before we left the waters of Broad River, having encamped in the evening on one of its considerable branches, and left my companions, to retire, as usual, on botanical researches, on ascending a steep rocky hill, I accidentally discovered a new species of caryophyllata (geum odoratissimum); on reaching to a shrub my foot slipped, and, in recovering myself, I tore up some of the plants, whose roots filled the air with animating scents of cloves and spicy perfumes.

On my return towards camp, I met my philosophic companion, Mr. M'Intosh, who was seated on the bank of a rivulet, and whom I found highly entertained by a very novel and curious natural exhibition, in which I participated with high relish. The waters at this place were still and shoal, and flowed over a bed of gravel just beneath a rocky rapid: in this eddy shoal were a number of little gravelly pyramidal hills, whose summits rose almost to the surface of the water, very artfully constructed by a species of small cray-fish (cancer macrourus) which inhabited them: here seemed to be their citadel, or place of retreat for their young against the attacks and ravages of their enemy, the gold-fish: these, in numerous bands, continually infested them, except at short intervals, when small detachments of veteran cray-fish sallied out upon them, from their cells within the gravelly pyramids, at which time a brilliant sight presented: the little gold fish instantly fled from every side, darting through the transparent waters like streams of lightning; some even sprang above the surface, into the air, but all quickly returned to the charge, surrounding the pyramids as before, on the retreat of the cray-fish; in this manner the war seemed to be continual.

The gold-fish is about the size of the anchovy, nearly four inches long, of a neat slender form; the head is covered with a salade of an ultramarine blue, the back of a reddish brown, the sides and belly of a flame, or of the colour of a fine red lead; a narrow dusky line runs along each side, from the gills to the tail; the eyes are large, with the iris like burnished gold. This branch of Broad River is about twelve yards wide, and has two, three, and four feet depth of water, and winds through a fertile vale, almost overshadowed on one side by a ridge of high hills, well timbered with oak, hiccory, liriodendron, magnolia acuminata, pavia sylvatica, and on their rocky summits, fagus castanea rhododendron ferrugineum, kalmia latifolia, cornus Florida, &c.

One of our Indian young men, this evening, caught a very large salmon trout, weighing about fifteen pounds, which he presented to the colonel, who ordered it to be served up for supper. The Indian struck this fish, with a reed harpoon, pointed very sharp, barbed, and hardened by the fire. The fish lay close under the steep bank, which the Indian discovered and struck with his reed; instantly the fish darted off with it, whilst the Indian pursued, without extracting the harpoon, and with repeated thrusts drowned it, and then dragged it to shore.

After leaving Broad River, the land rises very sensibly, and the country being mountainous, our progress became daily more difficult and slow; yet the varied scenes of pyramidal hills, high forests, rich vales, serpentine rivers, and cataracts, fully compensated for our difficulties and delays. I observed the great aconitum napellus, delphinium peregrinum, the carminative angelica lucida*, and cerulean malva.

We at length happily accomplished our line, arriving at the little river, where our hunters bringing in plenty of venison and turkeys, we had a plentiful feast at supper. Next morning we marked the corner tree, at the confluence of Little River and the Savanna; and, soon after, the Indians amicably took leave of us, returning home to their towns.

The rocks and fossils, which constitute the hills of this middle region, are of various species, as, quartsum, ferrum, cos, silex, glarea, arena, ochra, stalactites, saxum, mica, &c. I saw no signs of marble, plaster, or lime-stone; yet there are, near Augusta, in the forests, great piles of a porous friable white rock, in large and nearly horizontal masses, which seems to be an heterogeneous concrete, consisting of pulverized sea shells, with a small proportion of sand; it is soft, and easily wrought into any form, yet of sufficient consistence for constructing any building.

As for the animal productions, they are the same which originally inhabited this part of North America, except such as have been affrighted away since the invasion of the Europeans. The buffalo (urus) once so very numerous, is not at this day to be seen in this part of the country; there are but few elks, and those only in the Apalachian mountains. The dreaded and formidable rattle-snake is yet too common, and

*Called nondo in Virginia: by the Creek and Cherokee traders, white root.

a variety of other serpents abound, particularly that admirable creature the glass-snake: I saw a very large and beautiful one, a little distance from our camp. The alligator, a species of crocodile, abounds in the rivers and swamps, near the sea coast, but is not to be seen above Augusta. Bears, tygers*, wolves, and wild cats (felis cauda truncata) are numerous enough: and there is a very great variety of papilio and phalena, many of which are admirably beautiful, as well as other insects of infinite variety.

The surveyors having completed their observations, we sat off next day on our return to Augusta, taking our route generally through the low lands on the banks of the Savanna. We crossed Broad River, at a newly settled plantation, near its confluence with the Savanna. On my arrival at Augusta, finding myself a little fatigued, I staid there a day or two, and then sat off again for Savanna, the capital, where we arrived in good health.

Having, in this journey, met with extraordinary success, not only in the enjoyment of an uninterrupted state of good health, and escaping ill accidents, incident to such excursions, through uninhabited wildernesses, and an Indian frontier, but also in making a very extensive collection of new discoveries of natural productions; on the recollection of so many and great favours and blessings, I now, with a high sense of gratitude, presume to offer up my sincere thanks to the Almighty, the Creator and Preserver.

*This creature is called, in Pennsylvania and the northern States, panther; but in Carolina and the southern States, is called tyger; it is very strong, much larger than any dog, of a yellowish brown, or clay colour, having a very long tail: it is a mischievous animal, and preys on calves, young colts, &c.

CHAP. V.

HAVING completed my Hortus Siccus, and made up my collections of seeds and growing roots, the fruits of my late western tour, and sent them to Charleston, to be forwarded to Europe, I spent the remaining part of this season in botanical excursions to the low countries, between Carolina and East Florida, and collected seeds, roots, and specimens, making drawings of such curious subjects as could not be preserved in their native state of excellence.

During this recess from the high road of my travels, having obtained the use of a neat light cypress canoe, at Broughton Island, a plantation, the property of the Hon. Henry Laurens, Esq. I stored myself with necessaries for the voyage, and resolved upon a trip up the Alatamaha.

I ascended this beautiful river, on whose fruitful banks the generous and true sons of liberty securely dwell, fifty miles above the white settlements.

How gently flow thy peaceful floods, O Alatamaha! How sublimely rise to view, on thy elevated shores, yon magnolian groves, from whose tops the surrounding expanse is perfumed, by clouds of incense, blended with the exhaling balm of the liquidambar, and odours continually arising from circumambient aromatic groves of illicium, myrica, laurus, and bignonia.

When wearied with working my canoe against the impetuous current (which becomes stronger by reason of the mighty floods of the river, with collected force, pressing through the first hilly ascents, where the shores on each side present to view rocky cliffs rising above the surface of the water, in nearly flat horizontal masses, washed smooth by the descending floods, and which appear to be a composition, or concrete, of sandy lime-stone) I resigned my bark to the friendly current, reserving to myself the controul of the helm. My progress was rendered delightful by the sylvan elegance of the groves, cheerful meadows, and high distant forests, which in grand order presented themselves to view. The winding banks of the river, and the high projecting promontories, unfolded fresh scenes of grandeur and sublimity. The deep forests and distant hills re-echoed the cheering social lowings of domestic herds. The air was filled with the loud and shrill whooping of the wary sharp-sighted crane. Behold, on yon decayed, defoliated cypress tree, the solitary wood-pelican, dejectedly perched upon its utmost elevated spire; he there, like an ancient venerable sage, sets himself up as a mark of derision, for the safety of his kindred tribes. The crying-bird, another faithful guardian, screaming in the gloomy thickets, warns the feathered tribes of approaching peril; and the plumage of the swift failing squadrons of Spanish curlews (white as the immaculate robe of innocence) gleams in the cerulean skies.

Thus secure and tranquil, and meditating on the marvellous scenes of primitive nature, as yet unmodified by the hand of man, I gently descended the peaceful stream, on whose polished surface were depicted the mutable shadows from its pensile banks; whilst myriads of finny inhabitants sported in its pellucid floods.

The glorious sovereign of day, clothed in light refulgent, rolling on his gilded chariot, hastened to revisit the western realms. Grey pensive eve now admonished us of gloomy night's hasty approach: I was roused by care to seek a place of secure repose, ere darkness came on.

Drawing near the high shores, I ascended the steep banks, where stood a venerable oak. An ancient Indian field, verdured over with succulent grass, and chequered with coppices of fragrant shrubs, offered to my view the Myrica cerifera, Magnolia glauca, Laurus benzoin, Laur. Borbonia, Rhamnus frangula, Prunus Chicasaw, Prun. laurocerasus, and others. It was nearly encircled with an open forest of stately pines (Pinus palustris) through which appeared the extensive savanna, the secure range of the swift roebuck. In front of my landing, and due east, I had a fine prospect of the river and low lands on each side, which gradually widened to the sea coast, and gave me an unconfined prospect, whilst the far distant sea-coast islands, like a coronet, limited the hoary horizon.

My barque being securely moored, and having reconnoitred the surrounding groves, and collected fire-wood, I spread my skins and blanket by my cheerful fire, under the protecting shade of the hospitable Live-oak, and reclined my head on my hard but healthy couch. I listened, undisturbed, to the divine hymns of the feathered songsters of the groves, whilst the softly whispering breezes faintly died away.

The sun now below the western horizon, the moon majestically rising in the east; again the tuneful birds became inspired: how melodious is the social mock-bird! the groves resound the unceasing cries of the whip-poor-will; the moon about an hour above the horizon; lo! a dark eclipse* of her glorious brightness came slowly on; at length, a silver thread alone encircled her temples: at this boding change, an universal silence prevailed.

Nature now weary, I resigned myself to rest; the night passed over; the cool dews of the morning awoke me; my fire burnt low; the blue smoke scarce rose above the moistened embers; all was gloomy: the late starry skies, now overcast by thick clouds, warned me to rise and be going. The livid purple clouds thickened on the frowning brows of the morning; the tumultuous winds from the east now exerted their power. O peaceful Alatamaha! gentle by nature! how thou wert ruffled! thy wavy surface disfigured every object, presenting them obscurely to the sight, and they at length totally disappeared, whilst the furious winds and sweeping rains bent the lofty groves, and prostrated the quaking grass, driving the affrighted creatures to their dens and caverns.

The tempest now relaxed, its impetus being spent, and a calm serenity gradually took place; by noon the clouds broke away, the blue sky appeared, the fulgid sun-beams spread abroad their animating light, and the steady western wind resumed his peaceful reign. The waters were purified, the waves subsided, and the beautiful river regained its native calmness. So it is with the varied and mutable scenes of human events on the stream of life. The higher powers and affections of the soul are so blended and connected with the inferior passions, that the most painful feelings are excited in the mind when the latter are crossed: thus in the moral system, which we have planned for our conduct, as a ladder whereby to mount to the summit of terrestrial glory and happiness, and from

---

*The air at this time being serene, and not a cloud to be seen, I saw this annual almost total autumnal eclipse in its highest degree of perfection.

whence we perhaps meditated our flight to heaven itself, at the very moment when we vainly imagine ourselves to have attained its point, some unforeseen accident intervenes, and surprises us; the chain is violently shaken, we quit our hold and fall: the well contrived system at once becomes a chaos; every idea of happiness recedes; the splendour of glory darkens, and at length totally disappears; every pleasing object is defaced, all is deranged, and the flattering scene passes quite away; a gloomy cloud pervades the understanding, and when we see our progress retarded, and our best intentions frustrated, we are apt to deviate from the admonitions and convictions of virtue, to shut our eyes upon our guide and protector, doubt of his power, and despair of his assistance. But let us wait and rely on our God, who in due time will shine forth in brightness, dissipate the envious cloud, and reveal to us how finite and circumscribed is human power, when assuming to itself independent wisdom.

But, before I leave the river Alatamaha, we will proceed to give a further and more particular account of it. It has its source in the Cherokee mountains, near the head of Tugilo, the great west branch of Savanna, and, before it leaves them, is joined and augmented by innumerable rivulets; thence it descends through the hilly country, with all its collateral branches, and winds rapidly amongst the hills two hundred and fifty miles, and then enters the flat plain country, by the name of the Oakmulge; thence meandering an hundred and fifty miles, it is joined on the east side by the Ocone, which likewise heads in the lower ridges of the mountains. After this confluence, having now gained a vast acquisition of waters, it assumes the name of Alatamaha, when it becomes a large majestic river, flowing with gentle windings through a vast plain forest, near an hundred miles, and enters the Atlantic by several mouths. The north channel, or entrance, glides by the heights of Darien, on the east bank, about ten miles above the bar, and running from thence with several turnings, enters the ocean between Sapello and Wolf islands. The south channel, which is esteemed the largest and deepest, after its separation from the north, descends gently, winding by M'Intosh's and Broughton islands; and lastly, by the west coast of St. Simon's island, enters the ocean, through St. Simon's sound, between the south end of the island of that name and the north end of Jekyl island. On the west banks of the south channel, ten or twelve miles above its mouth, and nearly opposite Darien, are to be seen the remains of an ancient fort, or fortification; it is now a regular tetragon terrace, about four feet high, with bastions at each angle; the area may contain about an acre of ground, but the fosse which surrounded it is nearly filled up. There are large Live Oak, Pines, and other trees, growing upon it, and in the old fields adjoining. It is supposed to have been the work of the French or Spaniards. A large swamp lies betwixt it and the river, and a considerable creek runs close by the works, and enters the river through the swamp, a small distance above Broughton island. About seventy or eighty miles above the confluence of the Oakmulge and Ocone, the trading path, from Augusta to the Creek nation, crosses these fine rivers, which are there forty miles apart. On the east banks of the Oakmulge, this trading road runs nearly two miles through ancient Indian fields, which are called the Oakmulge fields: they are the rich low lands of the river. On the heights of these low grounds are yet visible monuments, or traces, of an ancient town, such as artificial mounts or terraces, squares and banks, encircling considerable areas. Their old fields and planting land extend up and down the river, fifteen or twenty miles from this site.

If we are to give credit to the account the Creeks give of themselves, this place is remarkable for being the first town or settlement, when they sat down (as they term it) or established themselves, after their emigration from the west, beyond the Missisippi, their original native country. On this long journey they suffered great and innumerable difficulties, encountering and vanquishing numerous and valiant tribes of Indians, who opposed and retarded their march. Having crossed the river, still pushing eastward, they were obliged to make a stand, and fortify themselves in this place, as their only remaining hope, being to the last degree persecuted and weakened by their surrounding foes. Having formed for themselves this retreat, and driven off the inhabitants by degrees, they recovered their spirits, and again faced their enemies, when they came off victorious in a memorable and decisive battle. They afterwards gradually subdued their surrounding enemies, strengthening themselves by taking into confederacy the vanquished tribes.

And they say, also, that about this period the English were establishing the colony of Carolina; and the Creeks, understanding that they were a powerful, warlike people, sent deputies to Charleston, their capital, offering them their friendship and alliance, which was accepted, and, in consequence thereof, a treaty took place between them, which has remained inviolable to this day. They never ceased war against the numerous and potent bands of Indians, who then surrounded and cramped the English plantations, as the Savannas, Ogeeches, Wapoos, Santees, Yamasees, Utinas, Icosans, Paticas, and others, until they had extirpated them. The Yamasees and their adherents sheltering themselves under the power and protection of the Spaniards of East Florida, they pursued them to the very gates of St. Augustine; and the Spaniards refusing to deliver them up, these faithful intrepid allies had the courage to declare war against them, and incessantly persecuted them, until they entirely broke up and ruined their settlements, driving them before them, till at length they were obliged to retire within the walls of St. Augustine and a few inferior fortified posts on the sea coast.

After a few days I returned to Broughton island. The Cherokees and their confederates being yet discontented, and on bad terms with the white people, it was unsafe to pursue my travels in the north western regions of Carolina. And recollecting many subjects of natural history, which I had observed in the south of the isthmus of Florida, when on a journey some years ago with my father, John Bartram, that were interesting, and not taken notice of by any traveller; and as it was then in the autumn and winter, having reason to think that very many curious subjects had escaped our researches; I now formed the resolution of travelling into East Florida; accordingly, I immediately wrote to doctor Fothergill, in order that he might know where to direct to me.

PART II

CHAP. I.

W E ARE, all of us, subject to crosses and disappointments, but more especially the traveller; and when they surprise us, we frequently become restless and impatient under them: but let us rely on Providence, and by studying and contemplating the works and power of the Creator, learn wisdom and understanding in the economy of nature, and be seriously attentive to the divine monitor within. Let us be obedient to the ruling powers in such things as regard human affairs, our duties to each other, and all creatures and concerns that are submitted to our care and controul.

In the month of March, 1774, I sat off from Savanna, for Florida, proceeding by land to the Alatamaha, where I diverted my time agreeably in short excursions, picking up curiosities, until the arrival of a small vessel at Frederica, from Savanna, which was destined to an Indian trading house high up St. John's, in East Florida. Upon information of this vessel's arrival, I immediately took boat and descended the Alatamaha, calling by the way of Broughton island, where I was kindly received by Mr. James Bailey, Mr. Laurens's agent. Leaving Broughton island in the evening, I continued descending the south channel nine or ten miles, when, after crossing the sound, I arrived at Frederica, on the island of St. Simon, where I was well received and entertained by James Spalding, esq. This gentleman carrying on a very considerable trade, and having extensive connections with the Indian tribes of East Florida, gave me letters to his agents residing at his trading houses, ordering them to furnish me with horses, guides, and every other convenient assistance.

Before the vessel was ready to sail again for St. John's, I had time to explore the island. In the cool of the morning early, I rode out of the town, directing my course to the south end of the island. After penetrating a thick grove of oaks, which almost surrounded the town on the land-side, suddenly a very extensive and beautiful green savanna opened to view, in length nearly two miles, and in breadth near a mile, well stocked with horned cattle, horses, sheep, and deer. Following an old highway, now out of repair, across the Savanna, I ascended the sloping green bank, and entered a noble forest of lofty pines, and then a venerable grove of Live Oaks, under whose shady spreading boughs opened a spacious avenue, leading to the former seat of general Oglethorpe, but now the property of capt. Raimond Demere. After leaving this town, I was led into a high pine forest; the trees were tall, and generally of the species called Broom-pine (P. palustris Linn.) the surface of the ground covered with grass, herbage, and some shrubbery: I continued through this forest nearly in a direct line towards the sea coast, five or six miles, when the land became uneven, with ridges of sand-hills, mixed with sea shells, and covered by almost impenetrable thickets, consisting of Live Oaks, Sweet-bay (L. Borbonia), Myrica, Ilex aquifolium, Rhamnus frangula, Cassine, Sideroxylon, Ptelea, Halesia, Callicarpa, Carpinus, entangled with Smilax pseudochina, and other species, Bignonia sempervirens, B. crucigera, Rhamnus volubilis, &c. This dark labyrinth is succeeded by a great extent of salt plains, beyond which the boundless ocean is seen. Betwixt the dark forest and the salt plains, I crossed a rivulet of fresh water, where I sat down a while to rest myself, under the shadow of sweet Bays and Oaks; the lively breezes were perfumed by the fragrant breath of the superb Crinum, called by the inhabitants, White Lily. This admirable beauty of the sea-coast-islands dwells in the humid shady groves, where the soil is made fertile and mellow by the admixture of sea shells. The delicate structure of its spadix, its green broad leaves, and the texture and whiteness of its flowers, at once charmed me. The Euphorbia picta, Salvia coccinea, and Ipomea erecta, were also seated in front of my resting place, as well as the Lycium salsum (perhaps L. Afrum Linn.) a very beautiful ever-green shrub, its cerulean flowers, and coral red berries, always on its branches, forming not the least of its beauties.

Time now admonishing me to rise and be going, I, with reluctance, broke away from this assembly of maritime beauties.

Continuing on, southward, the salt plains on my left hand insensibly became narrower, and I at length reached the strand, which was level, firm, and paved with shells, and afforded me a grand view of the boundless ocean.

O thou Creator supreme, almighty! how infinite and incomprehensible thy works! most perfect, and every way astonishing!

I continued nearly a mile along this firm sandy beach, the waves of the sea sometimes washing my horse's feet. I observed a great variety of shell-fish, as Echinitis, Corallinus, Patella, Medusa, Buccina, Concha venerea, Auris marina, Cancer, Squilla, &c. some alive, and others dead, having been cast upon the beach by the seas, in times of tempest, where they became a prey to sea fowl, and other maritime animals, or perished by the heat of the sun and burning sands. At length I doubled the utmost south point of St. Simon's, which forms the north cape of the south channel of the great river Alatamaha. The sound, just within this cape, forms an excellent bay, or cove, on the south end of the island, on the opposite side of which I beheld a house and farm, where I soon arrived. This delightful habitation was situated in the midst of a spacious grove of Live Oaks and Palms, near the strand of the bay, commanding a view of the inlet. A cool area surrounded the low but convenient buildings, from whence, through the groves, was a spacious avenue into the island, terminated by a large savanna; each side of the avenue was lined with bee-hives, to the number of fifty or sixty; they seemed to be well peopled, and exhibited a lively image of a colony that has attained to a state of power and affluence, by the practice of virtue and industry.

When I approached the house, the good man, who was reclining on a bear-skin, spread under the shade of a Live Oak, smoking his pipe, rose and saluted me: "Welcome, stranger, I am indulging the rational dictates of nature, taking a little rest, having just come in from the chace and fishing." After some conversation and rest, his servant brought a bowl of honey and water, a very refreshing and agreeable liquor, of which I drank. On rising to take my departure, he objected, and requested me to stay and dine with him; and on my pleading, for excuse, the necessity of my being at Frederica, "Yet, I pray you, stay a little, I will soon have some refreshment for you." Presently was laid before us a plentiful repast of venison,

&c.; our drink being honey and water, strengthened by the addition of brandy. Our rural table was spread under the shadow of Oaks, Palms, and Sweet Bays, fanned by the lively salubrious breezes wafted from the spicy groves. Our music was the responsive love-lays of the painted nonpareil, and the alert and gay mockbird; whilst the brilliant humming-bird darted through the flowery groves, suspended in air, and drank nectar from the flowers of the yellow Jasmine, Lonicera, Andromeda, and sweet Azalea.

But yet, how awfully great and sublime is the majestic scene eastward! the solemn sound of the beating surf strikes our ears; the dashing of yon liquid mountains, like mighty giants, in vain assail the skies; they are beaten back, and fall prostrate upon the shores of the trembling island.

Taking leave of my sylvan friend, I sat off on my return to the town, where I arrived before night, having observed, on the way, many curious vegetable productions, particularly Corypha Palma (or great Cabbage Palm) Corypha pumila, Corypha repens, frondibus expansis, flabelliformibus, plicatis, stipit. spinosis (Dwarf Saw Palmetto) Corypha obliqua, caudice arboreo adscendente, frondibus expansis, flabelliformibus, plicatis, stipit. serratis, Cyrilla, Tillandsia monostachya, Till. lingulata, or Wild Pine; both these curious vegetables are parasites, living on the substance of others, particularly on the limbs of the Live Oak; the latter species is a very large flourishing plant, greatly resembling, at some distance, a well grown plant of the Bromelia Ananas: the large deep green leaves are placed in an imbricated order, and ascendant; but their extremities are reflex, their bases gibbous and hollowed, like a ladle, and capable of containing near a pint of water: heavy tempests of wind and rain tear these plants from the trees; yet they live and flourish on the earth, under the shadow of these great Live Oaks. A very large part of this island had formerly been cleared and planted by the English, as appeared evidently to me, by vestiges of plantations, ruins of costly buildings, highways, &c. but it is now overgrown with forests. Frederica was the first town built by the English in Georgia, and was founded by general Oglethorpe, who began and established the colony. The fortress was regular and beautiful, constructed chiefly with brick, and was the largest, most regular, and perhaps most costly, of any in North America, of British construction: it is now in ruins, yet occupied by a small garrison; the ruins also of the town only remain; peach trees, figs, pomegranates, and other shrubs, grow out of the ruinous walls of former spacious and expensive buildings, not only in the town, but at a distance in various parts of the island; yet there are a few neat houses in good repair, and inhabited: it seems now recovering again, owing to the public and liberal spirit and exertions of J. Spalding, esq. who is president of the island, and engaged in very extensive mercantile concerns.

CHAP. II.

THE VESSEL in which I was to embark for East Florida, being now ready to pursue her voyage, we sat sail with a fair wind and tide. Our course was south, through the sound, betwixt a chain of sea-coast-islands, and the main. In the evening we came to, at the south end of St. Simon's, having been hindered by the flood tide making against us. The captain and myself, with one of our crew, went on shore, with a view of getting some venison and sea fowl. We had not the good fortune to see any deer, yet we were not altogether unsuccessful, having taken three young racoons (Ursus cauda elongata) which are excellent meat: we had them for supper, served up in a pillo. Next morning early, we again got under way, running by Jekyl and Cumberland Islands, large, beautiful, and fertile, yet thinly inhabited, and consequently excellent haunts for deer, bears, and other game.

As we ran by Cumberland Isle, keeping the channel through the sound, we saw a sail a head coming up towards us. Our captain knew it to be the trading schooner from the stores on St. John's, and immediately predicted bad news, as she was not to sail until our arrival there. As she approached us, his apprensions were more and more confirmed, from the appearance of a number of passengers on deck. We laid to, until she came up, when we hailed her, "What news?" "Bad; the Indians have plundered the upper store, and the traders have escaped, only with their lives." Upon this both vessels came to anchor very near each other, when, learning the particulars, it appeared, that a large party of Indians had surprised and plundered two trading houses, in the isthmus, beyond the river St. John's; and a third being timely apprised of their hostile intentions, by a faithful runner, had time to carry off part of the effects, which they secreted in a swamp at some distance from it, covering them with skins. The upper store had saved their goods in like manner; and the lower store, to which we were bound, had removed the chief of theirs, and deposited them on a small island, in the river, about five miles below the store. With these effects was my chest, which I had forwarded in this vessel, from Savanna, not being at that time determined whether to make this journey by land, or water. The captain of our vessel, resolved to put about and return to Frederica, for fresh instructions how to proceed; but for my part, I was determined to proceed for the island up St. John's, where my chest was lodged, there being some valuable books and papers in it, which I could not do well without. I accordingly desired our captain to put me on shore, on Little St. Simon's, which was not far distant, intending to walk a few miles to a fort, at the south end of that island, where some fishermen resided, who, as I expected, would set me over on Amelia Island, where was a large plantation, the property of Lord Egmont, a British nobleman, whose agent, while I was at Frederica, gave me an invitation to call on him, as I passed toward East Florida; and here I had expectations of getting a boat to carry me to St. John's. Agreeably to my desire, the captain put me on shore, with a young man, a passenger, for East Florida, who promised to continue with me, and share my adventures. We landed safely; the captain wishing us a prosperous journey, returned on board his vessel, and we proceeded for the fort, encountering some harsh treatment from thorny thickets, and prickly vines. However we reached the fort in the evening. The commander was out in the forest, hunting. My companion being tired, or indolent, betook himself to rest, while I made a tour round the south point of the island, walking the shelly paved sea beach, and picking up novelties. I had not gone above a mile, before I came up to a roebuck, lying slain on the sands; and hearing the report of a gun, not far off, and supposing it to be from the captain of the fort, whom I expected soon to return to take up his game, I retired to a little distance, mounted the sand hills, and sat down, enjoying a fine prospect of the rolling billows and foaming breakers, beating on the bar, and north promontory of Amelia Isle, opposite to me. The captain of the fort soon came up, with a slain buck on his shoulders. We hailed each other, and returned together to the fort, where we were well treated, and next morning, at my request, the captain obligingly sat us over, landing us safely on Amelia. After walking through a spacious forest of Live Oaks and Palms, and crossing a creek that ran through a narrow salt marsh, I and my fellow traveller arrived safe at the plantation, where the agent, Mr. Egan, received us very politely and hospitably. This gentleman is a very intelligent and able planter, having already greatly improved the estate, particularly in the cultivation of indigo. Great part of this island consists of excellent hommocky land, which is the soil this plant delights in, as well as cotton, corn, batatas, and almost every other esculent vegetable. Mr. Egan politely rode with me over great part of the island. On Egmont estate are several very large Indian tumuli, which are called Ogeeche mounts, so named from that nation of Indians, who took shelter here, after being driven from their native settlements on the main near Ogeeche river. Here they were constantly harassed by the Carolinians and Creeks, and at length slain by their conquerors, and their bones entombed in these heaps of earth and shells. I observed here the ravages of the common grey caterpillar (Phalena periodica), so destructive to forest and fruit trees, in Pennsylvania, and through the northern states, by stripping them of their leaves, in the spring, while young and tender.

Mr. Egan having business of importance to transact in St. Augustine, pressed me to continue with him a few days, when he would accompany me to that place, and, if I chose, I should have a passage, as far as the Cow-ford, on St. John's, where he would procure me a boat to prosecute my voyage.

It may be a subject worthy of some inquiry, why those fine islands, on the coast of Georgia, are so thinly inhabited; though perhaps Amelia may in some degree plead an exemption, as it is a very fertile island, on the north border of East Florida, and at the Capes of St. Mary, the finest harbour in this new colony. If I should give my opinion, the following seem to be the most probable reasons: the greatest part of these are as yet the property of a few wealthy planters, who having their residence on the continent, where lands on the large rivers, as Savanna, Ogeeche, Alatamaha, St. Ille, and others, are of a nature and quality adapted to the growth of rice, which the planters chiefly rely upon for obtaining ready cash, and purchasing family articles; they settle a few poor families on their insular estates, who rear stocks of horned cattle, horses, swine, and poultry, and protect the game for their proprietors. The inhabitants of these islands also lie open to the invasion and ravages of pirates, and in case of a war, to incursions from their enemies armed vessels; in which case they must either remove with their families and effects to the main, or be stripped of all their moveables, and their houses laid in ruins.

The soil of these islands appears to be particularly favourable to the culture of indigo and cotton, and there are on them some few large plantations for the cultivation and manufacture of those valuable articles. The cotton is planted only by the poorer class of people, just enough for their family consumption: they plant two species of it, the annual and West Indian; the former is low, and planted every year; the balls of this are very large, and the phlox long, strong, and perfectly white; the West Indian is a tall perennial plant, the stalk somewhat shrubby, several of which rise up from the root for several years successively, the stems of the former year being killed by the winter frosts. The balls of this latter species are not quite so large as those of the herbaceous cotton; but the phlox, or wool, is long, extremely fine, silky, and white. A plantation of this kind will last several years, with moderate labour and care, whereas the annual sort is planted every year.

The coasts, sounds, and inlets, environing these islands, abound with a variety of excellent fish, particularly Rock, Bass, Drum, Mullet, Sheepshead, Whiting, Grooper, Flounder, Sea Trout, [this last seems to be a species of Cod] Skate, Skipjack, Stingray. The Shark, and great Black Stingray, are insatiable cannibals, and very troublesome to the fishermen. The bays and lagoons are stored with oysters, and varieties of other shell-fish, crabs, shrimp, &c. The clams, in particular, are large, their meat white, tender, and delicate.

There is a large space betwixt this chain of sea-coast-islands and the main land, perhaps generally near three leagues in breadth; but all this space is not covered with water: I estimate nearly two-thirds of it to consist of low salt plains, which produce Barilla, Sedge, Rushes, &c. and which border on the main land, and the western coasts of the islands. The east sides of these islands are, for the most part, clean, hard, sandy beaches, exposed to the wash of the ocean. Between these islands are the mouths or entrances of some rivers, which run down from the continent, winding about through these low salt marshes, and delivering their waters into the sounds, which are very extensive capacious harbours, from three to five and six to eight miles over, and communicate with each other by parallel salt rivers, or passes, that flow into the sound: they afford an extensive and secure inland navigation for most craft, such as large schooners, sloops, pettiaugers, boats, and canoes; and this inland communication of waters extends along the sea coast with but few and short interruptions, from the bay of Chesapeak, in Virginia, to the Missisippi, and how much farther I know not, perhaps as far as Vera Cruz. Whether this chain of sea-coast-islands is a step, or advance, which this part of our continent is now making on the Atlantic ocean, we must leave to future ages to determine. But it seems evident, even to demonstration, that those salt marshes adjoining the coast of the main, and the reedy and grassy islands and marshes in the rivers, which are now overflowed at every tide, were formerly high swamps of firm land, affording forests of Cypress, Tupilo, Magnolia grandiflora, Oak, Ash, Sweet Bay, and other timber trees, the same as are now growing on the river swamps, whose surface is two feet or more above the spring tides that flow at this day; and it is plainly to be seen by every planter along the coast of Carolina, Georgia, and Florida, to the Missisippi, when they bank in these grassy tide marshes for cultivation, that they cannot sink their drains above three or four feet below the surface, before they come to strata of Cypress stumps and other trees, as close together as they now grow in the swamps.

CHAP. III.

BEING NOW in readiness to prosecute our voyage to St. John's, we sat sail in a handsome pleasure-boat, manned with four stout negro slaves, to row in case of necessity. After passing Amelia Narrows, we had a pleasant run across fort George's sound, where, observing the pelicans fishing, Mr. Egan shot one of them, which he took into the boat. I was greatly surprised on observing the pouch or sack, which hangs under the bill: it is capable of being expanded to a prodigious size. One of the people on board, said, that he had seen more than half a bushel of bran crammed into one of their pouches. The body is larger than that of a tame goose, the legs extremely short, the feet webbed, the bill of a great length, bent inwards like a scythe, the wings extend near seven feet from tip to tip, the tail is very short, the head, neck, and breast, nearly white, the body of a light bluish gray, except the quill feathers of the wings, which are black. They seem to be of the gull kind, both in form and structure, as well as manner of fishing. The evening following, we landed on the main. It was a promontory of high land, covered with orange-trees, and projecting into the sound, forming a convenient port. We pitched our tent under the shelter of a forest of Live Oaks, Palms, and Sweet Bays; and having in the course of the day, procured plenty of sea fowl, such as curlews, willets, snipes, sand birds, and others; we had them dressed for supper, and seasoned with excellent oysters, which lay in heaps in the water, close to our landing-place. The shrub Capsicum growing here in abundance, afforded us a very good pepper: we drank of a well of fresh water just at hand, amidst a grove of Myrtles (Myrica cerifera.) Our repose however was incomplete, from the stings of musquetoes, the roaring of crocodiles, and the continual noise and restlessness of the sea fowl, thousands of them having their roosting-places very near us, particularly loons of various species, herons, pelicans, Spanish curlews, &c. all promiscuously lodging together, and in such incredible numbers, that the trees were entirely covered. They roost in inaccessible islets in the salt marshes, surrounded by

lagoons, and shallow water. Just without the trees, betwixt
them, the water and marshes, is a barricade of Palmetto royal
(Yucca gloriosa) or Adam's needle, which grows so thick together, that a rat or bird can scarcely pass through them; and
the stiff leaves of this sword plant, standing nearly horizontally, are as impenetrable to man, or any other animal, as if
they were a regiment of grenadiers with their bayonets
pointed at you. The Palmetto royal is, however, a very singular
and beautiful production. It may be termed a tree, from its
durability and magnitude, as likewise from the ligneous quality of its stem, or trunk, when old; yet from its form and
texture, I should be inclined to rank it amongst the herbaceous plants, for even the glorious Palm, although it rises to
the altitude of a tree, and even transcends most of them, yet
it bears the characters of the herbaceous ones: and this, like
the Palm tree, rises with a straight, erect stem, about ten or
twelve feet high, crowned with a beautiful chaplet of sword
or dagger-like leaves, of a perfect green colour, each terminated with a stiff, sharp spur, and their edges finely crenated.
This thorny crown is crested with a pyramid of silver white
flowers, each resembling a tulip or lily. These flowers are succeeded by a large fruit, nearly of the form and size of a slender
cucumber, which when ripe, is of a deep purple colour, the
skin smooth and shining, its pulp soft, very juicy, and of an
agreeable aromatic flavour, but rather bitter to the taste; it is,
however, frequently eaten, but if eaten to excess, proves violently purgative. The seeds are numerous, flat, and lunated.

The plant, or tree, when grown old, sometimes divides into
two or three stems, which seem of equal height and thickness,
and indeed nearly of the same thickness with the main stem;
but generally, when they arrive to this age and magnitude,
their own weight brings them to the ground, where they soon
decay, the heart or pith first, leaving a hollow fibrous reticu-
lated trunk or sleeve, which likewise soon after decays, and in
fine, all is again reduced to its original earth, and replaces the
vegetative mould. But the deceased are soon replaced by others, as there are younger ones of all ages and stature, ready to
succeed their predecessors, and flourish for a time, with the
same regal pomp and splendor. These plants are so multitudinous, where-ever they get a footing, that the earth is com-

pletely occupied by them, and scarcely any other vegetable is to be seen, where they are; yet they are sometimes scattered amongst other trees and vegetables.

In three days after leaving Amelia, we arrived at the Cowford, a public ferry, over St. John's, about thirty miles above the bar or capes, the river here being above a mile wide.

Mr. Egan, after procuring a neat little sail-boat for me, at a large indigo plantation near the ferry, and for which I paid three guineas, departed for St. Augustine, which is on the seacoast, about forty-five miles over land.

It was now about the middle of April. Vegetation appearing every where in high progress, I was anxious to be advancing southerly; and having at this plantation stored myself with necessaries for my voyage, I sailed in the morning, with a fair wind. I was now again alone, for the young man, my fellow traveller, though stouter and heartier than myself, having repented of his promise to accompany me to the Indian trading houses, I suppose not relishing the hardships and dangers, which might perhaps befal us, chose rather to stay behind, amongst the settlements. His leaving me, however, I did not greatly regret, as I could not consider it a disappointment much to my disadvantage at the moment. Our views were probably totally opposite; he, a young mechanic on his adventures, seemed to be actuated by no other motives, than either to establish himself in some well inhabited part of the country, where, by following his occupation, he might be enabled to procure, without much toil and danger, the necessaries and conveniencies of life; or by industry and frugality, perhaps establish his fortune. Whilst I, continually impelled by a restless spirit of curiosity, in pursuit of new productions of nature, my chief happiness consisted in tracing and admiring the infinite power, majesty, and perfection of the great Almighty Creator, and in the contemplation, that through divine aid and permission, I might be instrumental in discovering, and introducing into my native country, some original productions of nature, which might become useful to society. Each of our pursuits was perhaps equally laudable; and upon this supposition, I was quite willing to part with him upon amicable terms.

My little vessel being furnished with a good sail, and having fishing tackle, a neat light fusee, powder and ball, I found myself well equipped for my voyage, about one hundred miles to the trading house.

I crossed the river to a high promontory of wood-land, on the west shore, and being struck with the magnificence of a venerable grove of Live Oak, Palms, and Laurel (Magnolia grandiflora) I stepped on shore to take a view of the place. Orange trees were in full bloom, and filled the air with fragrance.

It was now past noon, and this place being about eight miles above the Cow-ford, and the river near three miles in breadth, I wanted to reach a plantation in sight, on the opposite shore, in order to get some repairs, my vessel having sustained some damage from the violence of the wind, in crossing over. I arrived late in the evening, and finding a convenient landing-place and harbour, I concluded to remain here till morning, and then coast it close along shore to the plantation.

It beginning to thunder, I was sufficiently warned to prepare against a wet night; and observing a very large Oak tree, which had been thrown down by a hurricane, and offered me a convenient shelter, as its enormous limbs bore up the trunk a sufficient height from the earth to admit me to sit or lie down under it, I spread my sail, slanting from the trunk of the tree to the ground, on the windward side; and having collected a quantity of wood, sufficient to keep up a fire during the night, I struck one up in front, and spreading skins on the ground, and upon these placing a blanket, one half I lay down upon, turning the other over me for a covering.

The storm came up, with a furious wind and tremendous thunder and lightning, from the opposite N. W. coast, but luckily for me, little rain fell, and I rested very well. But as the wind next morning blew very fresh, right in upon the shore, there was no possibility of moving, with safety, from my present situation. I however arose to reconnoitre the ground round about my habitation, being roused by the report of a musket not far off. I had not left sight of my encampment, following a winding path through a grove of Live Oak, Laurel (Magn. grandiflora) and Sapindus, before an Indian stepped out of a thicket, and crossed the path just before me, having a large turkey cock flung across his shoulders: he saw me, and stepping up and smiling, spoke to me in English, bidding me good morning. I saluted him with "It's well, brother," led him to my camp, and treated him with a dram. This friendly Indian informed me that he lived at the next plantation, employed as a hunter. I asked him how far it was to the house; he answered about half a mile by land, and invited me to go there, telling me that his master was a very good, kind man, and would be glad to see me. I replied, that I would, if my boat and effects in the mean time could be safe. He said that he would immediately return to the house, and acquaint his master with it, who would send trusty negroes to bring my vessel round the point, to the landing. I thanked him for his civility, and not willing to be troublesome, I told him I would leave my boat, and follow after him; so taking my fusee on my shoulder, after dragging my bark as high up on shore as I could, I followed the Indian, and soon reached the house.

The gentleman received me in the most polite manner; and, after hearing my situation, he requested me to make my abode with him a few days, to rest and refresh myself. I thanked him, and told him I would stay a day. He immediately sent slaves who brought my boat round; and having carpenters at work on a new building, he sat them about repairing my vessel, which by night was completely refitted.

I spent the day in the most agreeable manner, in the society of this man of singular worth. He led me over his extensive improvements, and we returned in company with several of his neighbours. In the afternoon, the most sultry time of the day, we retired to the fragrant shades of an orange grove. The house was situated on an eminence, about one hundred and fifty yards from the river. On the right hand was the orangery, consisting of many hundred trees, natives of the place, and left standing, when the ground about it was cleared. These trees were large, flourishing, and in perfect bloom, and loaded with their ripe golden fruit. On the other side was a spacious garden, occupying a regular slope of ground, down to the water; and a pleasant lawn lay between. Here were large plantations of the Indigo plant, which appeared in a very thriving condition: it was then about five or six inches high, growing in strait parallel rows, about eighteen inches apart. The Corn

(Zea) and Potatoes (Convolv. Batata) were greatly advanced
in growth, and promised a plentiful crop. The Indigo made
in East Florida is esteemed almost equal to the best Spanish,
especially that sort, which they call Flora. Mr. Marshall presented me with a specimen of his own manufacture, at this
plantation: it was very little, if any, inferior to the best Prussian
blue.

In the morning following, intimating my intentions of proceeding on my voyage, Mr. Marshall again importuned me to
stay; but I obtained his consent to depart, on my promising
to visit him at my return to Georgia. After breakfast I therefore took my leave, attended to the shore by several slaves,
loaded with ammunition and provisions, which my friend had
provided for me. On my expressing some difficulty in receiving so large a share of his bounty, he civilly replied, that it was
too little to mention, and that, if I had continued with him a
day or two longer, he should have had time to have served
me in a much better manner.

Taking my leave of Mr. Marshall, I again embarked alone
on board my little vessel, and blessed with a favourable steady
gale, I set sail. The day was extremely pleasant; the late thunder storm had purified the air, by disuniting and dissipating
the noxious vapours. The falling of heavy showers, with thunder and brisk winds, from the cool regions of the N. W. contributes greatly towards restoring the salubrity of the air, and
purity of the waters, by precipitating the putrescent scum, that
rises from the bottom, and floats upon the surface, near the
shores of the rivers, in these southern climates, during the hot
seasons. The shores of this great river St. Juan are very level
and shoal, extending, in some places, a mile or two into the
river, betwixt the high land and the clear waters of the river,
which is so level, as to be covered not above a foot or two
deep with water, and at a little distance appears as a green
meadow, having water-grass and other amphibious vegetables
growing in the oozy bottom, and floating upon the water.

Having a lively leading breeze, I kept as near the East shore
as possible, often surprised by the plunging of alligators, and
greatly delighted with the pleasing prospect of cultivation, and
the increase of human industry, which frequently struck my
view from the elevated, distant shores.

At night I ran in shore, at a convenient harbour, where I was received and welcomed by the gentleman, who was agent for the plantation, and at whose pleasant habitation, near the harbour, I took up my quarters for the night.

This very civil man happened to be a person with whom I had formerly been acquainted in St. Augustine; and as he lived about twenty miles distant from it, I had good reason to expect that he would be a proper person to obtain intelligence from, concerning the disturbances which were thought still to subsist, between the Lower Creeks and the white inhabitants of East Florida. Upon inquiry, and conversation with him, I found my conjectures on that head to have been well founded. My friend informed me, that there had, but a few days since, been a council held at St. Augustine, between the governor of East Florida and the chiefs of the Lower Creeks. They had been delegated by their towns, to make inquiry concerning the late alarm and depredations committed by the Indians upon the traders; which the nation being apprised of, recommended these deputies to be chosen and sent, as soon as possible, in order to make reasonable concessions, before the flame, already kindled, should spread into a general war. The parties accordingly met in St. Augustine, and the affair was amicably adjusted, to the satisfaction of both parties. The chiefs of the delinquent bands, whose young warriors had committed the mischief, promised to indemnify the traders for the loss of their goods, and requested that they might return to their store-houses, with goods as usual, and that they should be safe in their persons and property. The traders at this time were actually preparing to return. It appeared, upon a strict investigation of facts, that the affair had taken its rise from the licentious conduct of a few vagrant young hunters of the Siminole nation, who, imagining themselves to have been ill treated in their dealings with the traders (which by the bye was likely enough to be true) took this violent method of doing themselves justice. The culprits however endeavoured to exculpate themselves, by asserting, that they had no design or intention of robbing the traders of their effects, but meant it only as a threat; and that the traders, from a consciousness of their dishonesty, had been terrified and fled, leaving their stores, which they took possession of, to prevent their being totally lost. This troublesome affair being adjusted, was very agreeable news to me, as I could now, without apprehensions, ascend this grand river, and visit its delightful shores, where and when I pleased.

Bidding adieu to my obliging friend, I spread my sail to the favourable breeze, and by noon came to a-breast of fort Picolata; where, being desirous of gaining yet farther intelligence, I landed; but, to my disappointment, found the fort dismantled and deserted. This fortress is very ancient, and was built by the Spaniards. It is a square tower, thirty feet high, invested with a high wall, without bastions, about breast high, pierced with loop holes and surrounded with a deep ditch. The upper story is open on each side, with battlements, supporting a cupola or roof: these battlements were formerly mounted with eight four pounders, two on each side.

The works are constructed with hewn stone, cemented with lime. The stone was cut out of quarries on St. Anastatius Island, opposite St. Augustine: it is of a pale reddish brick colour, and a testaceous composition, consisting of small fragments of sea-shells and fine sand. It is well adapted to the constructing of fortifications. It lies in horizontal masses in the quarry, and constitutes the foundation of that island. The castle at St. Augustine, and most of the buildings of the town, are of this stone.

Leaving Picolata, I continued to ascend the river. I observed this day, during my progress up the river, incredible numbers of small flying insects, of the genus termed by naturalists Ephemera, continually emerging from the shallow water near shore, some of them immediately taking their flight to the land, whilst myriads crept up the grass and herbage, where remaining for a short time, as they acquired sufficient strength, they took their flight also, following their kindred to the main land. This resurrection from the deep, if I may so express it, commences early in the morning, and ceases after the sun is up. At evening they are seen in clouds of innumerable millions, swarming and wantoning in the still air, gradually drawing near the river. They descend upon its surface, and there quickly end their day, after committing their eggs to the deep; which being for a little while tossed about, enveloped in a viscid scum, are hatched, and the little Larva descend into their secure and dark habitation, in the oozy bed beneath, where they remain, gradually increasing in size, until the returning spring: they then change to a Nymph, when the genial heat brings them, as it were, into existence, and they again arise into the world. This fly seems to be delicious food for birds, frogs, and fish. In the morning, when they arise, and in the evening, when they return, the tumult is great indeed, and the surface of the water along shore broken into bubbles, or spirted into the air, by the contending aquatic tribes; and such is the avidity of the fish and frogs, that they spring into the air after this delicious prey.

Early in the evening, after a pleasant day's voyage, I made a convenient and safe harbour, in a little lagoon, under an elevated bank, on the West shore of the river; where I shall entreat the reader's patience, whilst we behold the closing scene of the short-lived Ephemera, and communicate to each other the reflections which so singular an exhibition might rationally suggest to an inquisitive mind. Our place of observation is happily situated under the protecting shade of majestic Live Oaks, glorious Magnolias, and the fragrant Orange, open to the view of the great river and still waters of the lagoon just before us.

At the cool eve's approach, the sweet enchanting melody of the feathered songsters gradually ceases, and they betake themselves to their leafy coverts for security and repose.

Solemnly and slowly move onward, to the river's shore, the rustling clouds of the Ephemera. How awful the procession! innumerable millions of winged beings, voluntarily verging on to destruction, to the brink of the grave, where they behold bands of their enemies with wide open jaws, ready to receive them. But as if insensible of their danger, gay and tranquil each meets his beloved mate in the still air, inimitably bedecked in their new nuptial robes. What eye can trace them, in their varied wanton amorous chaces, bounding and fluttering on the odoriferous air! With what peace, love, and joy, do they end the last moments of their existence?

I think we may assert, without any fear of exaggeration, that there are annually of these beautiful winged beings, which rise into existence, and for a few moments take a transient view of the glory of the Creator's works, a number greater than the whole race of mankind that have ever existed since the creation; and that, only from the shores of this river. How many then must have been produced since the creation, when we consider the number of large rivers in America, in comparison with which, this river is but a brook or rivulet.

The importance of the existence of these beautiful and delicately formed little creatures, whose frame and organization are equally wonderful, more delicate, and perhaps as complicated as those of the most perfect human being, is well worth a few moments contemplation; I mean particularly when they appear in the fly state. And if we consider the very short period of that stage of existence, which we may reasonably suppose to be the only space of their life that admits of pleasure and enjoyment, what a lesson doth it not afford us of the vanity of our own pursuits!

Their whole existence in this world is but one complete year: and at least three hundred and sixty days of that time they are in the form of an ugly grub, buried in mud, eighteen inches under water, and in this condition scarcely locomotive, as each Larva or grub has but its own narrow solitary cell, from which it never travels or moves, but in a perpendicular progression of a few inches, up and down, from the bottom to the surface of the mud, in order to intercept the passing atoms for its food, and get a momentary respiration of fresh air; and even here it must be perpetually on its guard, in order to escape the troops of fish and shrimps watching to catch it, and from whom it has no escape, but by instantly retreating back into its cell. One would be apt almost to imagine them created merely for the food of fish and other animals.

Having rested very well during the night, I was awakened in the morning early, by the cheering converse of the wild turkey-cocks (Meleagris occidentalis) saluting each other, from the sun-brightened tops of the lofty Cupressus disticha and Magnolia grandiflora. They begin at early dawn, and continue till sun rise, from March to the last of April. The high forests ring with the noise, like the crowing of the domestic cock, of these social centinels; the watch-word being caught and repeated, from one to another, for hundreds of miles around; insomuch that the whole country is for an hour or more in an universal shout. A little after sun-rise, their crowing gradually ceases, they quit their high lodging places, and alight on the earth, where, expanding their silver bordered train, they strut and dance round about the coy female, while the deep forests seem to tremble with their shrill noise.

This morning the winds on the great river were high and against me; I was therefore obliged to keep in port a great part of the day, which I employed in little excursions round about my encampment. The Live Oaks are of an astonishing magnitude, and one tree contains a prodigious quantity of timber; yet, comparatively, they are not tall, even in these forests, where growing on strong land, in company with others of great altitude (such as Fagus sylvatica, Liquidambar, Magnolia grandiflora, and the high Palm tree) they strive while young to be upon an equality with their neighbours, and to enjoy the influence of the sun-beams, and of the pure animating air. But the others at last prevail, and their proud heads are seen at a great distance, towering far above the rest of the forest, which consists chiefly of this species of oak, Fraxinus, Ulmus, Acer rubrum, Laurus Borbonia, Quercus dentata, Ilex aquifolium, Olea Americana, Morus, Gleditsia triacanthus, and, I believe, a species of Sapindus. But the latter spreads abroad his brawny arms, to a great distance. The trunk of the Live Oak is generally from twelve to eighteen feet in girt, and rises ten or twelve feet erect from the earth, some I have seen eighteen or twenty; then divides itself into three, four, or five great limbs, which continue to grow in nearly an horizontal direction, each limb forming a gentle curve, or arch, from its base to its extremity. I have stepped above fifty paces, on a strait line, from the trunk of one of these trees, to the extremity of the limbs. It is evergreen, and the wood almost incorruptible, even in the open air. It bears a prodigious quantity of fruit; the acorn is small, but sweet and agreeable to the taste when roasted, and is food for almost all animals. The Indians obtain from it a sweet oil, which they use in the cooking of hommony, rice, &c.; and they also roast it in hot embers, eating it as we do chestnuts.

The wind being fair in the evening, I sat sail again, and crossing the river, made a good harbour on the East shore, where I pitched my tent for the night. The bank of the river was about twelve or fifteen feet perpendicular from its surface, but the ascent gentle. Although I arrived here early in the evening, I found sufficient attractions to choose it for my lodging-place, and an ample field for botanical employment. It was a high, airy situation, and commanded an extensive and varied prospect of the river and its shores, up and down.

Behold yon promontory, projecting far into the great river, beyond the still lagoon, half a mile distant from me: what a magnificent grove arises on its banks! how glorious the Palm! how majestically stands the Laurel, its head forming a perfect cone! its dark green foliage seems silvered over with milk-white flowers. They are so large, as to be distinctly visible at the distance of a mile or more. The Laurel Magnolias, which grow on this river, are the most beautiful and tall that I have any where seen, unless we except those, which stand on the banks of the Missisippi; yet even these must yield to those of St. Juan, in neatness of form, beauty of foliage, and, I think, in largeness and fragrance of flower. Their usual height is about one hundred feet, and some greatly exceed that. The trunk is perfectly erect, rising in the form of a beautiful column, and supporting a head like an obtuse cone. The flowers are on the extremities of the subdivisions of the branches, in the center of a coronet of dark green, shining, ovate pointed entire leaves: they are large, perfectly white, and expanded like a full blown Rose. They are polypetalous, consisting of fifteen, twenty, or twenty-five petals: these are of a thick coriaceous texture, and deeply concave, their edges being somewhat reflex, when mature. In the center stands the young cone; which is large, of a flesh colour, and elegantly studded with a gold coloured stigma, that by the end of summer is greatly enlarged, and in the autumn ripens to a large crimson cone or strobile, disclosing multitudes of large coral red berries, which for a time hang down from them, suspended by a fine, white, silky thread, four, six, or even nine inches in length. The flowers of this tree are the largest and most complete of any yet known: when fully expanded, they are of six, eight, and nine inches diameter. The pericarpium and berries possess an agreeable spicy scent, and an aromatic bitter taste. The wood when seasoned is of a straw colour, compact, and harder and firmer than that of the poplar.

It is really astonishing to behold the Grape-Vines in this place. From their bulk and strength, one would imagine, they were combined to pull down these mighty trees to the earth; when, in fact, amongst other good purposes, they serve to uphold them. They are frequently nine, ten, and twelve inches in diameter, and twine round the trunks of the trees, climb to their very tops, and then spread along their limbs, from tree to tree, throughout the forest: the fruit is but small and ill tasted. The Grape vines, with the Rhamnus volubilis, Bignonia radicans, Bignonia crucigera, and another rambling shrubby vine, which seems allied to the Rhamnus, perhaps Zizyphus scandens, seem to tie the trees together with garlands and festoons, and form enchanting shades. The long moss, so called, (Tillandsea usneaoides), is a singular and surprising vegetable production: it grows from the limbs and twigs of all trees in these southern regions, from N. lat. 35 down as far as 28, and I believe every where within the tropics. Wherever it fixes itself, on a limb, or branch, it spreads into short and intricate divarications; these in time collect dust, wafted by the wind, which, probably by the moisture it absorbs, softens the bark and sappy part of the tree, about the roots of the plant, and renders it more fit for it to establish itself; and from this small beginning, it increases, by sending downwards and obliquely, on all sides, long pendant branches, which divide and subdivide themselves ad infinitum. It is common to find the spaces betwixt the limbs of large trees, almost occupied by this plant: it also hangs waving in the wind, like streamers, from the lower limbs, to the length of fifteen or twenty feet, and of bulk and weight, more than several men together could carry; and in some places, cart loads of it are lying on the ground, torn off by the violence of the wind. Any part of the living plant, torn off and caught in the limbs of a tree, will presently take root, grow, and increase, in the same degree of perfection, as if it had sprung up from the seed. When fresh, cattle and deer will eat it in the winter season. It seems particularly adapted to the purpose of stuffing mattresses, chairs, saddles, collars, &c.; and for these purposes, nothing yet known equals it. The Spaniards in South America and the West-Indies, work it into cables, that are said to be very strong and durable; but, in order to render it useful, it ought to be thrown into shallow ponds of water, and exposed to the sun, where it soon rots, and the outside furry substance is dissolved. It is then taken out of the water, and spread to dry; when, after a little beating and shaking, it is sufficiently clean, nothing remaining but the interior, hard, black, elastic filament, entangled together, and greatly resembling horse-hair.

The Zanthoxylum clava Herculis also grows here. It is a beautiful spreading tree, and much like a well grown apple tree. Its aromatic berry is delicious food for the little turtle dove; and epicures say, that it gives their flesh a fine flavour.

Having finished my observations, I betook myself to rest; and when the plunging and roaring of the crocodiles, and the croaking of the frogs, had ceased, I slept very well during the remainder of the night; as a breeze from the river had scattered the clouds of musquitoes that at first infested me.

It being a fine cool morning, and fair wind, I sat sail early, and saw, this day, vast quantities of the Pistia stratiotes, a very singular aquatic plant. It associates in large communities, or floating islands, some of them a quarter of a mile in extent, which are impelled to and fro, as the wind and current may direct. They are first produced on, or close to the shore, in eddy water, where they gradually spread themselves into the river, forming most delightful green plains, several miles in length, and in some places a quarter of a mile in breadth. These plants are nourished and kept in their proper horizontal situation, by means of long fibrous roots, which descend from the nether center, downwards, towards the muddy bottom. Each plant, when full grown, bears a general resemblance to a well grown plant of garden lettuce, though the leaves are more nervous, of a firmer contexture, and of a full green colour, inclining to yellow. It vegetates on the surface of the still stagnant water; and in its natural situation, is propagated from seed only. In great storms of wind and rain, when the river is suddenly raised, large masses of these floating plains are broken loose, and driven from the shores, into the wide water, where they have the appearance of islets, and float about, until broken to pieces by the winds and waves; or driven again to shore, on some distant coast of the river, where they again find footing, and there, forming new colonies, spread and extend themselves again, until again broken up and dispersed as before. These floating islands present a very entertaining prospect; for although we behold an assemblage of the primary productions of nature only, yet the imagination seems to remain in suspense and doubt; as in order to enliven the delusion, and form a most picturesque appearance, we see not only flowery plants, clumps of shrubs, old weather-beaten trees, hoary and barbed, with the long moss waving from their snags, but we also see them completely inhabited, and alive, with crocodiles, serpents, frogs, otters, crows, herons, curlews, jackdaws, &c. There seems, in short, nothing wanted but the appearance of a wigwam and a canoe to complete the scene.

Keeping along the West or Indian shore, I saw basking, on the sedgy banks, numbers of alligators*, some of them of an enormous size.

The high forests on this coast now wore a grand and sublime appearance; the earth rising gradually from the river westward, by easy swelling ridges, behind one another, lifting the distant groves up into the skies. The trees are of the lofty kind, as the grand laurel magnolia, palma elata, liquidambar styraciflua, fagus sylvatica, querci, juglans hiccory, fraxinus, and others.

On my doubling a long point of land, the river appeared surprisingly widened, forming a large bay, of an oval form, and several miles in extent. On the West side it was bordered round with low marshes, and invested with a swamp of Cypress, the trees so lofty, as to preclude the sight of the highland forests beyond them; and these trees, having flat tops, and all of equal height, seemed to be a green plain, lifted up and supported upon columns in the air, round the West side of the bay.

The cupressus disticha stands in the first order of North American trees. Its majestic stature is surprising; and on approaching it, we are struck with a kind of awe, at beholding the stateliness of the trunk, lifting its cumbrous top towards the skies, and casting a wide shade upon the ground, as a dark intervening cloud, which, for a time, excludes the rays of the

---

*I have made use of the terms alligator and crocodile indiscriminately for this animal, alligator being the country name.

sun. The delicacy of its colour and texture of its leaves, exceed
every thing in vegetation. It generally grows in the water, or
in low flat lands, near the banks of great rivers and lakes, that
are covered, great part of the year, with two or three feet
depth of water; and that part of the trunk which is subject to
be under water, and four or five feet higher up, is greatly
enlarged by prodigious buttresses, or pilasters, which, in full
grown trees, project out on every side, to such a distance, that
several men might easily hide themselves in the hollows between. Each pilaster terminates under ground, in a very large,
strong, serpentine root, which strikes off, and branches every
way, just under the surface of the earth: and from these roots
grow woody cones, called cypress knees, four, five, and six
feet high, and from six to eighteen inches and two feet in
diameter at their bases. The large ones are hollow, and serve
very well for bee-hives; a small space of the tree itself is hollow,
nearly as high as the buttresses already mentioned. From this
place, the tree, as it were, takes another beginning, forming a
grand straight column eighty or ninety feet high, when it divides every way around into an extensive flat horizontal top,
like an umbrella, where eagles have their secure nests, and
cranes and storks their temporary resting places; and what
adds to the magnificence of their appearance is the streamers
of long moss that hang from the lofty limbs and float in the
winds. This is their majestic appearance when standing alone,
in large rice plantations, or thinly planted on the banks of
great rivers.

Parroquets are commonly seen hovering and fluttering on
their tops: they delight to shell the balls, its seed being their
favourite food. The trunks of these trees, when hallowed out,
make large and durable pettiaugers and canoes, and afford
excellent shingles, boards, and other timber, adapted to every
purpose in frame buildings. When the planters fell these
mighty trees, they raise a stage round them, as high as to reach
above the buttresses; on this stage, eight or ten negroes ascend with their axes, and fall to work round its trunk. I have
seen trunks of these trees that would measure eight, ten, and
twelve feet in diameter, for forty and fifty feet straight shaft.

As I continued coasting the Indian shore of this bay, on
doubling a promontory, I suddenly saw before me an Indian

settlement, or village. It was a fine situation, the bank rising gradually from the water. There were eight or ten habitations, in a row, or street, fronting the water, and about fifty yards distance from it. Some of the youth were naked, up to their hips in the water, fishing with rods and lines; whilst others, younger, were diverting themselves in shooting frogs with bows and arrows. On my near approach, the little children took to their heels, and ran to some women who were hoeing corn; but the stouter youth stood their ground, and, smiling, called to me. As I passed along, I observed some elderly people reclined on skins spread on the ground, under the cool shade of spreading Oaks and Palms, that were ranged in front of their houses: they arose, and eyed me as I passed, but perceiving that I kept on without stopping, they resumed their former position. They were civil, and appeared happy in their situation.

There was a large Orange grove at the upper end of their village; the trees were large, carefully pruned, and the ground under them clean, open, and airy. There seemed to be several hundred acres of cleared land about the village; a considerable portion of which was planted, chiefly with corn (Zea), Batatas, Beans, Pompions, Squashes (Cucurbita verrucosa), Melons (Cucurbita citrullus), Tobacco (Nicotiana), &c. abundantly sufficient for the inhabitants of the village.

After leaving this village, and coasting a considerable cove of the lake, I perceived the river before me much contracted within its late bounds, but still retaining the appearance of a wide and deep river, both coasts bordered for several miles with rich deep swamps, well timbered with Cypress, Ash, Elm, Oak, Hiccory, Scarlet Maple, Nyssa aquatica, Nyssa tupilo, Gordonia lasianthus, Corypha palma, Corypha pumila, Laurus Borbonia, &c. The river gradually narrowing, I came in sight of Charlotia, where it is not above half a mile wide, but deep; and as there was a considerable current against me, I came here to an anchor. This town was founded by Den. Rolle, esq. and is situated on a high bluff, on the east coast, fifteen or twenty feet perpendicular from the river, and is in length half a mile, or more, upon its banks. The upper stratum of the earth consists entirely of several species of fresh water Cochleæ, as Coch. helix, Coch. labyrinthus, and Coch. voluta;

the second, of marine shells, as Concha mytulus, Conc. ostrea, Conc. peeton, Haliotis auris marina, Hal. patella, &c. mixed with sea sand; and the third, or lower stratum, which was a little above the common level of the river, of horizontal masses of a pretty hard rock, composed almost entirely of the above shell, generally whole, and lying in every direction, petrified or cemented together, with fine white sand; and these rocks were bedded in a stratum of clay. I saw many fragments of the earthen ware of the ancient inhabitants, and bones of animals, amongst the shells, and mixed with the earth, to a great depth. This high shelly bank continues, by gentle parallel ridges, near a quarter of a mile back from the river, gradually diminishing to the level of the sandy plains, which widen before and on each side eastward, to a seemingly unlimited distance, and appear green and delightful, being covered with grass and the Corypha repens, and thinly planted with trees of the long leaved, or Broom Pine, and decorated with clumps, or coppices, of floriferous, evergreen, and aromatic shrubs, and enamelled with patches of the beautiful little Kalmea ciliata. These shelly ridges have a vegetable surface of loose black mould, very fertile, which naturally produces Orange groves, Live Oak, Laurus Borbonia, Palma elata, Carica papaya, Sapindus, Liquidambar, Fraxinus exelsior, Morus rubra, Ulmus, Tilia, Sambucus, Ptelea, Tallow-nut or Wild Lime, and many others.

Mr. Rolle obtained from the crown a grant of forty thousand acres of land, in any part of East Florida, where the land was unlocated. It seems, his views were to take up his grant near St. Mark's, in the bay of Apalatchi; and he sat sail from England, with about one hundred families, for that place; but by contrary winds, and stress of weather, he missed his aim; and being obliged to put into St. Juan's, he, with some of the principal of his adherents, ascended the river in a boat, and being struck with its majesty, the grand situations of its banks, and fertility of its lands, and at the same time, considering the extensive navigation of the river, and its near vicinity to St. Augustine, the capital and seat of government, he altered his views on St. Mark's, and suddenly determined on this place, where he landed his first little colony. But it seems, from an ill concerted plan in its infant establishment, negligence, or extreme parsimony in sending proper recruits and other necessaries, together with a bad choice of citizens, the settlement by degrees grew weaker, and at length totally fell to the ground. Those of them who escaped the constant contagious fevers, fled the dreaded place, betaking themselves for subsistence to the more fruitful and populous regions of Georgia and Carolina.

The remaining old habitations are mouldering to earth, except the mansion house, which is a large frame building, of cypress wood, yet in tolerable repair, and inhabited by an overseer and his family. There is also a blacksmith with his shop and family, at a small distance from it. The most valuable district belonging to Mr. Rolle's grant, lies on Dun's lake, and on a little river, which runs from it into St. Juan. This district consists of a vast body of rich swamp land, fit for the growth of rice, and some very excellent high land surrounding it. Large swamps of excellent rice land are also situated on the west shore of the river, opposite to Charlotia.

The aborigines of America had a very great town in this place, as appears from the great tumuli, and conical mounts of earth and shells, and other traces of a settlement which yet remain. There grew in the old fields on these heights, great quantities of callicarpa, and of the beautiful shrub annona: the flowers of the latter are large, white, and sweet scented.

Having obtained from the people here directions for discovering the little remote island where the traders and their goods were secreted, which was about seven miles higher up, I sat sail again, with a fair wind, and in about one hour and an half arrived at the desired place, having fortunately taken the right channel of the river, amongst a multitude of others, occasioned by a number of low swampy islands. But I should have run by the landing, if the centinels had not by chance seen me drawing near them; who perceiving that I was a white man, ventured to hail me; upon which I immediately struck sail, and came to. Upon my landing they conducted me to their encampment, forty or fifty yards from the river, in an almost impenetrable thicket. Upon my inquiry, they confirmed the accounts of the amicable treaty at St. Augustine, and in consequence thereof, they had already removed great part of the goods to the trading-house, which was a few miles higher up, on the Indian shore. They showed me my chest, which had been carefully preserved, and upon inspection I found every thing in good order. Having learned from them, that all the effects would, in a few days time, be removed to the store-house, I bid adieu to them, and in a little time arrived at the trading-house, where I was received with great politeness, and treated, during a residence of several months, with the utmost civility and friendship, by Mr. C. M'Latche, Messrs. Spalding and Kelsall's agent.

The river almost from Charlotia, and for near twelve miles higher up, is divided into many channels by a great number of islands.

CHAP. IV.

Having rested myself a few days, and by ranging about the neighbouring plains and groves, surrounding this pleasant place, pretty well recovered my strength and spirits, I began to think of planning my future excursions, at a distance round about this centre. I found, from frequent conferences with Mr. M'Latche, that I might with safety extend my journeys every way, and with prudence, even into the towns and settlements of the Indians, as they were perfectly reconciled to us, and sincerely wished for the renewal of our trade.

There were three trading-houses to be established this summer, each of which had its supplies from the store on St. Juan, where I now had my residence, and in which the produce or returns were to centre annually, in order to be shipped for Savanna or Sunbury, and from thence to Europe.

One of these trading-houses was to be fixed about sixty miles higher up the river, from this place, by the name of Spalding's upper store; a second at Alachua, about fifty miles west from the river St. Juan; and a third at Talahasochte, a considerable town of the Siminoles, on the river Little St. Juan, near the bay of Apalachi, about one hundred and twenty miles distance. Each of these places I designed to visit, before the return of the vessel to Frederica in the autumn, that I might avail myself of an opportunity so favourable for transporting my collections so far on their way towards Charleston.

The company for Alachua were to set off in about a month; that to Little St. Juan, in July, which suited me exceedingly well, as I might make my tour to the upper store directly, that part of the country being at this season enrobed in its richest and gayest apparel.

About the middle of May, every thing being in readiness to proceed up the river, we sat sail. The traders with their goods in a large boat went a-head, and myself in my little vessel followed them; and as their boat was large, and deeply laden, I found that I could easily keep up with them, and, if I chose, out-sail them; but I preferred keeping them company, as well for the sake of collecting what I could from conversation, as on account of my safety in crossing the great lake, expecting to return alone, and descend the river at my own leisure.

We had a pleasant day, the wind fair and moderate, and ran by Mount Hope, so named by my father John Bartram, when he ascended this river, about fifteen years ago. It is a very high shelly bluff, upon the little lake. It was at that time a fine Orange grove, but now cleared and converted into a large indigo plantation, the property of an English gentleman, under the care of an agent. In the evening we arrived at Mount Royal, where we came to, and stayed all night: we were treated with great civility, by a gentleman whose name was —— Kean, and who had been an Indian trader.

From this place we enjoyed a most enchanting prospect of the great Lake George, through a grand avenue, if I may so term this narrow reach of the river, which widens gradually for about two miles, towards its entrance into the lake, so as to elude the exact rules of perspective, and appears of an equal width.

At about fifty yards distance from the landing place, stands a magnificent Indian mount. About fifteen years ago I visited this place, at which time there were no settlements of white people, but all appeared wild and savage; yet in that uncultivated state it possessed an almost inexpressible air of grandeur, which was now entirely changed. At that time there was a very considerable extent of old fields round about the mount; there was also a large orange grove, together with palms and live oaks, extending from near the mount, along the banks, downwards, all of which has since been cleared away to make room for planting ground. But what greatly contributed towards completing the magnificence of the scene, was a noble Indian highway, which led from the great mount, on a straight line, three quarters of a mile, first through a point or wing of the orange grove, and continuing thence through an awful forest of live oaks, it was terminated by palms and laurel magnolias, on the verge of an oblong artificial lake, which was on the edge of an extensive green level savanna. This grand highway was about fifty yards wide, sunk a little below the common level, and the earth thrown up on each side, making a bank of about two feet high. Neither nature nor art could any where present a more striking contrast, as you approached this savanna. The glittering water pond played on the sight, through the dark grove, like a brilliant diamond, on the bosom of the illumined savanna, bordered with various flowery shrubs and plants; and as we advanced into the plain, the sight was agreeably relieved by a distant view of the forests, which partly environed the green expanse on the left hand, whilst the imagination was still flattered and entertained by the far distant misty points of the surrounding forests, which projected into the plain, alternately appearing and disappearing, making a grand sweep round on the right, to the distant banks of the great lake. But that venerable grove is now no more. All has been cleared away and planted with indigo, corn, and cotton, but since deserted: there was now scarcely five acres of ground under fence. It appeared like a desart to a great extent, and terminated, on the land side, by frightful thickets, and open pine forests.

It appears, however, that the late proprietor had some taste, as he has preserved the mount and this little adjoining grove inviolate. The prospect from this station is so happily situated by nature, as to comprise at one view the whole of the sublime and pleasing.

At the reanimating appearance of the rising sun, nature again revives; and I obey the cheerful summons of the gentle monitors of the meads and groves.

Ye vigilant and faithful servants of the Most High! ye who worship the Creator morning, noon, and eve, in simplicity of heart! I haste to join the universal anthem. My heart and voice unite with yours, in sincere homage to the great Creator, the universal sovereign.

O may I be permitted to approach the throne of mercy! May these my humble and penitent supplications, amidst the universal shouts of homage from thy creatures, meet with thy acceptance!

And although I am sensible, that my service cannot increase or diminish thy glory, yet it is pleasing to thy servant to be permitted to sound thy praise; for, O sovereign Lord! we know that thou alone art perfect, and worthy to be worshipped. O universal Father! look down upon us, we beseech thee, with an eye of pity and compassion, and grant that universal peace and love may prevail in the earth, even that divine harmony which fills the heavens, thy glorious habitation!

And, O sovereign Lord! since it has pleased thee to endue man with power and pre-eminence here on earth, and establish his dominion over all creatures, may we look up to thee, that our understanding may be so illuminated with wisdom, and our hearts warmed and animated with a due sense of charity, that we may be enabled to do thy will, and perform our duty towards those submitted to our service and protection, and be merciful to them, even as we hope for mercy.

Thus may we be worthy of the dignity and superiority of the high and distinguished station in which thou hast placed us here on earth.

The morning being fair, and having a gentle favourable gale, we left our pleasant harbour, in pursuit of our desired port.

Now as we approach the capes, behold the little ocean of Lake George, the distant circular coast gradually rising to view, from his misty fringed horizon. I cannot entirely suppress my apprehensions of danger. My vessel at once diminished to a nut-shell on the swelling seas, and at the distance of a few miles, must appear to the surprised observer as some aquatic animal, at intervals emerging from its surface. This lake is a large and beautiful piece of water; it is a dilatation of the river St. Juan, and is about fifteen miles wide, and generally about fifteen or twenty feet deep, excepting at the entrance of the river, where lies a bar, which carries eight or nine feet water. The lake is beautified with two or three fertile islands. The first lies in the bay, as we ascend into the lake, near the west coast, about S. W. from Mount Royal, from whence it appears to form part of the west shore of the bay. The second island seems to ride on the lake before us as we enter, about a mile within it. This island is about two miles in breadth, and three quarters of a mile where broadest, mostly high land, well timbered and fertile. The third and last lies at the south end of the lake, and near the entrance of the river; it is nearly circular, and contains but a few acres of land, the earth high and fertile, and almost an entire orange grove, with grand magnolias and palms.

Soon after entering the lake, the wind blew so briskly from the west, with thunder-clouds gathering upon the horizon, that we were obliged to seek a shelter from the approaching tempest, on the large beautiful island before mentioned; where, having gained the south promontory, we met with an excellent harbour, in which we continued the remaining part of the day and the night. This circumstance gave me an opportunity to explore the greatest part of it.

This island appears, from obvious vestiges, to have been once the chosen residence of an Indian prince, there being to this day evident remains of a large town of the Aborigines. It was situated on an eminence, near the banks of the lake, and commanded a comprehensive and charming prospect of the waters, islands, east and west shores of the lake, the capes, the bay, and Mount Royal; and to the south the view is in a manner infinite, where the skies and waters seem to unite. On the site of this ancient town, stands a very pompous Indian mount, or conical pyramid of earth, from which runs in a strait line a grand avenue or Indian highway, through a magnificent grove of magnolias, live oaks, palms, and orange trees, terminating at the verge of a large green level savanna. This island appears to have been well inhabited, as is very evident, from the quantities of fragments of Indian earthenware, bones of animals and other remains, particularly in the shelly heights and ridges all over the island. There are no habitations at present on the island, but a great number of deer, turkeys, bears, wolves, wild cats, squirrels, racoons, and opossums. The bears are invited here to partake of the fruit of the orange tree, which they are immoderately fond of; and both they and turkeys are made extremely fat and delicious, from their feeding on the sweet acorns of the live oak.

There grow on this island many curious shrubs, particularly a beautiful species of lantana (perhaps lant. camerara, Lin. Syst. Veget. p. 473). It grows in coppices in old fields, about five or six feet high, the branches adorned with rough serrated leaves, which sit opposite, and the twigs terminated with umbelliferous tufts of orange coloured blossoms, which are succeeded by a cluster of small blue berries: the flowers are of various colours, on the same plant, and even in the same cluster, as crimson, scarlet, orange and golden yellow: the whole plant is of a most agreeable scent. The orange-flowered shrub Hibiscus is also conspicuously beautiful (perhaps Hibisc. spinifex of Linn.) It grows five or six feet high, and subramous. The branches are divergent, and furnished with cordated leaves, which are crenated. The flowers are of a moderate size, and of a deep splendid yellow. The pericarpii are spiny. I also saw a new and beautiful palmated leaved convolvulus*. This vine rambles over the shrubs, and strolls about on the ground; its leaves are elegantly sinuated, of a deep grass green, and sit on long petioles. The flowers are very large, infundibuliform, of a pale incarnate colour, having a deep crimson eye.

There are some rich swamps on the shores of the island, and these are verged on the outside with large marshes, covered entirely with tall grass, rushes, and herbaceous plants; amongst these are several species of Hibiscus, particularly the hibiscus coccineus. This most stately of all herbaceous plants grows ten or twelve feet high, branching regularly, so as to form a sharp cone. These branches also divide again, and are embellished with large expanded crimson flowers. I have seen this plant of the size and figure of a beautiful little tree, having at once several hundred of these splendid flowers, which may be then seen at a great distance. They continue to flower in succession all summer and autumn, when the stems wither and decay; but the perennial root sends forth new stems the next spring, and so on for many years. Its leaves are large, deeply and elegantly sinuated, having six or seven very narrow dentated segments; the surface of the leaves, and of the whole plant, is smooth and polished. Another species of hibiscus, worthy of particular notice, is likewise a tall flourishing plant; several strong stems arise from a root, five, six, and seven feet high, embellished with ovate lanciolate leaves, covered with a fine down on their nether surfaces: the flowers are very large, and of a deep incarnate colour.

The last we shall now mention seems nearly allied to the alcea; the flowers are a size less than the hibiscus, and of a fine damask rose colour, and are produced in great profusion on the tall pyramidal stems.

*Convol. dissectus.

The lobelia cardinalis grows in great plenty here, and has a most splendid appearance amidst extensive meadows of the golden corymbous jacobea (senecio jabobea) and odorous pancratium.

Having finished my tour on this princely island, I prepared for repose. A calm evening had succeeded the stormy day. The late tumultuous winds had now ceased, the face of the lake had become placid, and the skies serene; the balmy winds breathed the animating odours of the groves around me; and as I reclined on the elevated banks of the lake, at the foot of a live oak, I enjoyed the prospect of its wide waters, its fringed coasts, and the distant horizon.

The squadrons of aquatic fowls, emerging out of the water, and hastening to their leafy coverts on shore, closed the varied scenes of the past day. I was lulled asleep by the mixed sounds of the wearied surf, lapsing on the hard beaten shore, and the tender warblings of the painted nonpareil and other winged inhabitants of the grove.

At the approach of day the dreaded voice of the alligators shook the isle, and resounded along the neighbouring coasts, proclaiming the appearance of the glorious sun. I arose, and prepared to accomplish my daily task. A gentle favourable gale led us out of the harbour: we sailed across the lake, and towards evening entered the river on the opposite south coast, where we made a pleasant and safe harbour, at a shelly promontory, the east cape of the river on that side of the lake. It is a most desirable situation, commanding a full view of the lake. The cape opposite to us was a vast cypress swamp, environed by a border of grassy marshes, which were projected farther into the lake by floating fields of the bright green pistia stratiotes, which rose and fell alternately with the waters. Just to leeward of this point, and about half a mile in the lake is the little round island already mentioned. But let us take notice of our harbour and its environs: it is a beautiful little cove, just within the sandy point, which defends it from the beating surf of the lake. From a shelly bank, ten or twelve feet perpendicular from the water, we entered a grove of live oaks, palm, magnolia, and orange trees, which grow amongst shelly hills, and low ridges, occupying about three acres of ground, comprehending the isthmus, and a part of the peninsula, which joins it to the grassy plains. This enchanting little forest is partly encircled by a deep creek, a branch of the river, that has its source in the high forests of the main, south east from us; and winds through the extensive grassy plains which surround this peninsula, to an almost infinite distance, and then unites its waters with those of the river, in this little bay which formed our harbour. This bay, about the mouth of the creek, is almost covered with the leaves of the nymphæa nelumbo: its large sweet-scented yellow flowers are lifted up two or three feet above the surface of the water, each upon a green standard, representing the cap of liberty.

The evening drawing on, and there being no convenient landing place for several miles higher up the river, we concluded to remain here all night. Whilst my fellow travellers were employing themselves in collecting fire-wood, and fixing our camp, I improved the opportunity, in reconnoitering our ground; and taking my fusee with me, I penetrated the grove, and afterwards entered some almost unlimited savannas and plains, which were absolutely enchanting; they had been lately burnt by the Indian hunters, and had just now recovered their vernal verdure and gaiety.

How happily situated is this retired spot of earth! What an elysium it is! where the wandering Siminole, the naked red warrior, roams at large, and after the vigorous chase retires from the scorching heat of the meridian sun. Here he reclines, and reposes under the odoriferous shades of Zanthoxylon, his verdant couch guarded by the Deity; Liberty, and the Muses, inspiring him with wisdom and valour, whilst the balmy zephyrs fan him to sleep.

Seduced by these sublime enchanting scenes of primitive nature, and these visions of terrestrial happiness, I had roved far away from Cedar Point, but awakening to my cares, I turned about, and in the evening regained our camp.

On my return, I found some of my companions fishing for trout, round about the edges of the floating nymphæa, and not unsuccessfully, having then caught more than sufficient for us all. As the method of taking these fish is curious and singular, I shall just mention it.

They are taken with a hook and line, but without any bait. Two people are in a little canoe, one sitting in the stern to steer, and the other near the bow, having a rod ten or twelve feet in length, to one end of which is tied a strong line, about twenty inches in length, to which are fastened three large hooks, back to back. These are fixed very securely, and covered with the white hair of a deer's tail, shreds of a red garter, and some particoloured feathers, all which form a tuft, or tassel, nearly as large as one's fist, and entirely cover and conceal the hooks: this is called a bob. The steersman paddles softly, and proceeds slowly along shore, keeping the boat parallel to it, at a distance just sufficient to admit the fisherman to reach the edge of the floating weeds along shore; he now ingeniously swings the bob backwards and forwards, just above the surface, and sometimes tips the water with it; when the unfortunate cheated trout instantly springs from under the weeds, and seizes the supposed prey. Thus he is caught without a possibility of escape, unless he break the hooks, line, or rod, which he, however, sometimes does by dint of strength; but, to prevent this, the fisherman used to the sport is careful not to raise the reed suddenly up, but jerks it instantly backwards, then steadily drags the sturdy reluctant fish to the side of the canoe, and with a sudden upright jerk brings him into it.

The head of this fish makes about one third of his length, and consequently the mouth is very large: birds, fish, frogs, and even serpents, are frequently found in its stomach.

The trout is of a lead colour, inclining to a deep blue, and marked with transverse waved lists, of a deep slate colour, and when fully grown, has a cast of red or brick colour. The fins, with the tail, which is large and beautifully formed, are of a light reddish purple, or flesh colour; the whole body is covered with large scales. But what is most singular, this fish is remarkably ravenous; nothing living that he can seize upon escapes his jaws; and the opening and extending of the branchiostega, at the moment he rises to the surface to seize his prey, discovering his bright red gills through the transparent waters, give him a very terrible appearance. Indeed it may be observed, that all fish of prey have this opening and covering of the gills very large, in order to discharge the great quantity of water which they take in at their mouth, when they strike at their prey. This fish is nearly cuneiform, the body tapering gradually from the breast to the tail, and lightly compressed on each side. They frequently weigh fifteen, twenty, and thirty pounds, and are delicious food.

My companion, the trader, being desirous of crossing the river to the opposite shore, in hopes of getting a turkey, I chose to accompany him, as it offered a good opportunity to observe the natural productions of those rich swamps and islands of the river. Having crossed the river, which is here five or six hundred yards wide, we entered a narrow channel, which, after a serpentine course for some miles, rejoins the main river again, above; forming a large fertile island, of rich low land. We landed on this island, and soon saw a fine roe-buck* at some distance from us, who appeared leader of a company of deer that were feeding near him on the verge of a green meadow. My companion parted from me in pursuit of the deer, one way; and I, observing a flock of turkeys at some distance, on the other, directed my steps towards them, and with great caution got near them; when, singling out a large cock, and being just on the point of firing, I observed that several young cocks were affrighted, and in their language warned the rest to be on their guard against an enemy, whom I plainly perceived was industriously making his subtile approaches towards them, behind the fallen trunk of a tree, about twenty yards from me. This cunning fellow-hunter was a large fat wild cat (lynx): he saw me, and at times seemed to watch my motions, as if determined to seize the delicious prey before me. Upon which I changed my object, and levelled my piece at him. At that instant, my companion, at a distance, also discharged his piece at the deer, the report of which alarmed the flock of turkeys; and my fellow-hunter, the cat, sprang over the log and trotted off. The trader also missed his deer: thus we foiled each other. By this time it being near night, we returned to camp, where having a delicious meal ready prepared for our hungry stomachs, we sat down in a circle round our wholesome repast.

How supremely blessed were our hours at this time! plenty of delicious and healthful food, our stomachs keen, with contented minds; under no controul, but what reason and

*Cervus sylvaticus. The American deer.

ordinate passions dictated, far removed from the seats of strife.

Our situation was like that of the primitive state of man, peaceable, contented, and sociable. The simple and necessary calls of nature being satisfied, we were altogether as brethren of one family, strangers to envy, malice, and rapine.

The night being over we arose, and pursued our course up the river; and in the evening reached the trading-house, Spalding's upper store, where I took up my quarters for several weeks.

On our arrival at the upper store, we found it occupied by a white trader, who had for a companion a very handsome Siminole young woman. Her father, who was a prince, by the name of the White Captain, was an old chief of the Siminoles, and with part of his family, to the number of ten or twelve, was encamped in an orange grove near the stores, having lately come in from a hunt.

This white trader, soon after our arrival, delivered up the goods and store-houses to my companion, and joined his father-in-law's camp, and soon after went away into the forests on hunting and trading amongst the flying camps of Siminoles.

He is at this time unhappy in his connexions with his beautiful savage. It is but a few years since he came here, I think from North Carolina, a stout genteel well-bred man, active, and of a heroic and amiable disposition; and by his industry, honesty, and engaging manners, had gained the affections of the Indians, and soon made a little fortune by traffic with the Siminoles: when unfortunately meeting with this little charmer, they were married in the Indian manner. He loves her sincerely, as she possesses every perfection in her person to render a man happy. Her features are beautiful, and manners engaging. Innocence, modesty, and love, appear to a stranger in every action and movement; and these powerful graces she has so artfully played upon her beguiled and vanquished lover, and unhappy slave, as to have already drained him of all his possessions, which she dishonestly distributes amongst her savage relations. He is now poor, emaciated, and half distracted, often threatening to shoot her, and afterwards put an end to his own life; yet he has not resolution even to leave her; but now endeavours to drown and forget his sorrows in deep draughts of brandy. Her father condemns her dishonest and cruel conduct.

These particulars were related to me by my old friend the trader, directly after a long conference which he had with the White Captain on the subject, his son-in-law being present. The scene was affecting; they both shed tears plentifully. My reasons for mentioning this affair, so foreign to my business, was to exhibit an instance of the power of beauty in a savage, and her art and finesse in improving it to her private ends. It is, however, but doing justice to the virtue and moral conduct of the Siminoles, and American aborigines in general, to observe, that the character of this woman is condemned and detested by her own people of both sexes; and if her husband should turn her away, according to the customs and usages of these people, she would not get a husband again, as a divorce seldom takes place but in consequence of a deliberate impartial trial, and public condemnation, and then she would be looked upon as a harlot.

Such is the virtue of these untutored savages: but I am afraid this is a common phrase epithet, having no meaning, or at least improperly applied; for these people are both well tutored and civil; and it is apparent to an impartial observer, who resides but a little time amongst them, that it is from the most delicate sense of the honour and reputation of their tribes and families, that their laws and customs receive their force and energy. This is the divine principle which influences their moral conduct, and solely preserves their constitution and civil government in that purity in which they are found to prevail amongst them.

CHAP. V.

BEING DESIROUS of continuing my travels and observations higher up the river, and having an invitation from a gentleman who was agent for, and resident at, a large plantation, the property of an English gentleman, about sixty miles higher up, I resolved to pursue my researches to that place; and having engaged in my service a young Indian, nephew to the White Captain, he agreed to assist me in working my vessel up as high as a certain bluff, where I was, by agreement, to land him, on the West or Indian shore, whence he designed to go in quest of the camp of the White Trader, his relation.

Provisions and all necessaries being procured, and the morning pleasant, we went on board and stood up the river. We passed for several miles on the left, by islands of high swamp land, exceedingly fertile, their banks for a good distance from the water, much higher than the interior part, and sufficiently so to build upon, and be out of the reach of inundations. They consist of a loose black mould, with a mixture of sand, shells, and dissolved vegetables. The opposite Indian coast is a perpendicular bluff, ten or twelve feet high, consisting of a black sandy earth, mixed with a large proportion of shells, chiefly various species of fresh water cochleæ and mytuli. Near the river, on this high shore, grew corypha palma, magnolia grandiflora, live oak, callicarpa, myrica cerifera, hybiscus spinifex, and the beautiful evergreen shrub called wild lime or tallow nut. This last shrub grows six or eight feet high, many erect stems spring from a root; the leaves are lanceolate and entire, two or three inches in length and one in breadth, of a deep green colour, and polished; at the foot of each leaf grows a stiff sharp thorn; the flowers are small and in clusters, of a greenish yellow colour, and sweet scented; they are succeeded by a large oval fruit, of the shape and size of an ordinary plumb, of a fine yellow colour when ripe; a soft sweet pulp covers a nut which has a thin shell, enclosing a white kernel somewhat of the consistence and taste of the sweet almond, but more oily and very much like hard tallow, which induced my father when he first observed it, to call it the tallow-nut.

At the upper end of this bluff is a fine orange grove. Here my Indian companion requested me to set him on shore, being already tired of rowing under a fervid sun, and having for some time intimated a dislike to his situation. I readily complied with his desire, knowing the impossibility of compelling an Indian against his own inclinations, or even prevailing upon him by reasonable arguments, when labour is in the question. Before my vessel reached the shore, he sprang out of her and landed, when uttering a shrill and terrible whoop, he bounded off like a roebuck, and I lost sight of him. I at first apprehended, that as he took his gun with him, he intended to hunt for some game and return to me in the evening. The day being excessively hot and sultry, I concluded to take up my quarters here until next morning.

The Indian not returning this morning, I sat sail alone. The coasts on each side had much the same appearance as already described. The palm trees here seem to be of a different species from the cabbage tree; their straight trunks are sixty, eighty, or ninety feet high, with a beautiful taper, of a bright ash colour, until within six or seven feet of the top, where it is a fine green colour, crowned with an orb of rich green plumed leaves: I have measured the stem of these plumes fifteen feet in length, besides the plume, which is nearly of the same length.

The little lake, which is an expansion of the river, now appeared in view; on the east side are extensive marshes, and on the other, high forests and orange groves, and then a bay, lined with vast cypress swamps, both coasts gradually approaching each other, to the opening of the river again, which is in this place about three hundred yards wide. Evening now drawing on, I was anxious to reach some high bank of the river, where I intended to lodge; and agreeably to my wishes, I soon after discovered on the west shore a little promontory, at the turning of the river, contracting it here to about one hundred and fifty yards in width. This promontory is a peninsula, containing about three acres of high ground, and is one entire orange grove, with a few live oaks, magnolias and palms. Upon doubling the point, I arrived at the landing, which is a circular harbour, at the foot of the bluff, the top of which is about twelve feet high; the back of it is a large cypress swamp, that spreads each way, the right wing forming the west coast of the little lake, and the left stretching up the river many miles, and encompassing a vast space of low grassy marshes. From this promontory, looking eastward across the river, I beheld a landscape of low country, unparalleled as I think; on the left is the east coast of the little lake, which I had just passed; and from the orange bluff at the lower end, the high forests begin, and increase in breadth from the shore of the lake, making a circular sweep to the right, and contain many hundred thousand acres of meadow; and this grand sweep of high forests encircles, as I apprehend, at least twenty miles of these green fields, interspersed with hommocks or islets of evergreen trees, where the sovereign magnolia and lordly palm stand conspicuous. The islets are high shelly knolls, on the sides of creeks or branches of the river, which wind about and drain off the super-abundant waters that cover these meadows during the winter season.

The evening was temperately cool and calm. The crocodiles began to roar and appear in uncommon numbers along the shores and in the river. I fixed my camp in an open plain, near the utmost projection of the promontory, under the shelter of a large live oak, which stood on the highest part of the ground, and but a few yards from my boat. From this open, high situation, I had a free prospect of the river, which was a matter of no trivial consideration to me, having good reason to dread the subtle attacks of the alligators, who were crowding about my harbour. Having collected a good quantity of wood for the purpose of keeping up a light and smoke during the night, I began to think of preparing my supper, when, upon examining my stores, I found but a scanty provision. I thereupon determined, as the most expeditious way of supplying my necessities, to take my bob and try for some trout. About one hundred yards above my harbour began a cove or bay of the river, out of which opened a large lagoon. The mouth or entrance from the river to it was narrow, but the waters soon after spread and formed a little lake, extending into the marshes: its entrance and shores within I observed to be verged with floating lawns of the pistia and nymphea and other aquatic plants; these I knew were excellent haunts for trout.

The verges and islets of the lagoon were elegantly embellished with flowering plants and shrubs; the laughing coots with wings half spread were tripping over the little coves and hiding themselves in the tufts of grass; young broods of the painted summer teal, skimming the still surface of the waters, and following the watchful parent unconscious of danger, were frequently surprised by the voracious trout; and he, in turn, as often by the subtle greedy alligator. Behold him rushing forth from the flags and reeds. His enormous body swells. His plaited tail brandished high, floats upon the lake. The waters like a cataract descend from his opening jaws. Clouds of smoke issue from his dilated nostrils. The earth trembles with his thunder. When immediately from the opposite coast of the lagoon, emerges from the deep his rival champion. They suddenly dart upon each other. The boiling surface of the lake marks their rapid course, and a terrific conflict commences. They now sink to the bottom folded together in horrid wreaths. The water becomes thick and discoloured. Again they rise, their jaws clap together, re-echoing through the deep surrounding forests. Again they sink, when the contest ends at the muddy bottom of the lake, and the vanquished makes a hazardous escape, hiding himself in the muddy turbulent waters and sedge on a distant shore. The proud victor exulting returns to the place of action. The shores and forests resound his dreadful roar, together with the triumphing shouts of the plaited tribes around, witnesses of the horrid combat.

My apprehensions were highly alarmed after being a spectator of so dreadful a battle. It was obvious that every delay would but tend to encrease my dangers and difficulties, as the sun was near setting, and the alligators gathered around my harbour from all quarters. From these considerations I concluded to be expeditious in my trip to the lagoon, in order to take some fish. Not thinking it prudent to take my fusee with me, lest I might lose it overboard in case of a battle, which I had every reason to dread before my return, I therefore furnished myself with a club for my defence, went on board, and penetrating the first line of those which surrounded my harbour, they gave way; but being pursued by several very large ones, I kept strictly on the watch, and paddled with all my might towards the entrance of the lagoon, hoping to be sheltered there from the multitude of my assailants; but ere I had half-way reached the place, I was attacked on all sides, several endeavouring to overset the canoe. My situation now became precarious to the last degree: two very large ones attacked me closely, at the same instant, rushing up with their heads and part of their bodies above the water, roaring terribly and belching floods of water over me. They struck their jaws together so close to my ears, as almost to stun me, and I expected every moment to be dragged out of the boat and instantly devoured. But I applied my weapons so effectually about me, though at random, that I was so successful as to beat them off a little; when, finding that they designed to renew the battle, I made for the shore, as the only means left me for my preservation; for, by keeping close to it, I should have my enemies on one side of me only, whereas I was before surrounded by them; and there was a probability, if pushed to the last extremity, of saving myself, by jumping out of the canoe on shore, as it is easy to outwalk them on land, although comparatively as swift as lightning in the water. I found this last expedient alone could fully answer my expectations, for as soon as I gained the shore, they drew off and kept aloof. This was a happy relief, as my confidence was, in some degree, recovered by it. On recollecting myself, I discovered that I had almost reached the entrance of the lagoon, and determined to venture in, if possible, to take a few fish, and then return to my harbour, while day-light continued; for I could now, with caution and resolution, make my way with safety along shore; and indeed there was no other way to regain my camp, without leaving my boat and making my retreat through the marshes and reeds, which, if I could even effect, would have been in a manner throwing myself away, for then there would have been no hopes of ever recovering my bark, and returning in safety to any settlements of men. I accordingly proceeded, and made good my entrance into the lagoon, though not without opposition from the alligators, who formed a line across the entrance, but did not pursue me into it, nor was I molested by any there, though there were

some very large ones in a cove at the upper end. I soon caught
more trout than I had present occasion for, and the air was
too hot and sultry to admit of their being kept for many
hours, even though salted or barbecued. I now prepared for
my return to camp, which I succeeded in with but little trouble, by keeping close to the shore; yet I was opposed upon
re-entering the river out of the lagoon, and pursued near to
my landing (though not closely attacked), particularly by an
old daring one, about twelve feet in length, who kept close
after me; and when I stepped on shore and turned about, in
order to draw up my canoe, he rushed up near my feet, and
lay there for some time, looking me in the face, his head and
shoulders out of water. I resolved he should pay for his te-
merity, and having a heavy load in my fusee, I ran to my camp,
and returning with my piece, found him with his foot on the
gunwale of the boat, in search of fish. On my coming up he
withdrew sullenly and slowly into the water, but soon returned and placed himself in his former position, looking at
me, and seeming neither fearful nor any way disturbed. I soon
dispatched him by lodging the contents of my gun in his head,
and then proceeded to cleanse and prepare my fish for supper;
and accordingly took them out of the boat, laid them down
on the sand close to the water, and began to scale them; when,
raising my head, I saw before me, through the clear water,
the head and shoulders of a very large alligator, moving slowly
towards me. I instantly stepped back, when, with a sweep of
his tail, he brushed off several of my fish. It was certainly most
providential that I looked up at that instant, as the monster
would probably, in less than a minute, have seized and
dragged me into the river. This incredible boldness of the
animal disturbed me greatly, supposing there could now be
no reasonable safety for me during the night, but by keeping
continually on the watch: I therefore, as soon as I had prepared the fish, proceeded to secure myself and effects in the
best manner I could. In the first place, I hauled my bark upon
the shore, almost clear out of the water, to prevent their over-
setting or sinking her; after this, every moveable was taken
out and carried to my camp, which was but a few yards off;
then ranging some dry wood in such order as was the most
convenient, I cleared the ground round about it, that there

might be no impediment in my way, in case of an attack in the night, either from the water or the land; for I discovered by this time, that this small isthmus, from its remote situation and fruitfulness, was resorted to by bears and wolves. Having prepared myself in the best manner I could, I charged my gun and proceeded to reconnoitre my camp and the adjacent grounds; when I discovered that the peninsula and grove, at the distance of about two hundred yards from my encampment, on the land side, were invested by a cypress swamp, covered with water, which below was joined to the shore of the little lake, and above to the marshes surrounding the lagoon; so that I was confined to an islet exceedingly circumscribed, and I found there was no other retreat for me, in case of an attack, but by either ascending one of the large oaks, or pushing off with my boat.

It was by this time dusk, and the alligators had nearly ceased their roar, when I was again alarmed by a tumultuous noise that seemed to be in my harbour, and therefore engaged my immediate attention. Returning to my camp, I found it undisturbed, and then continued on to the extreme point of the promontory, where I saw a scene, new and surprising, which at first threw my senses into such a tumult, that it was some time before I could comprehend what was the matter; however, I soon accounted for the prodigious assemblage of crocodiles at this place, which exceeded every thing of the kind I had ever heard of.

How shall I express myself so as to convey an adequate idea of it to the reader, and at the same time avoid raising suspicions of my veracity. Should I say, that the river (in this place) from shore to shore, and perhaps near half a mile above and below me, appeared to be one solid bank of fish, of various kinds, pushing through this narrow pass of St. Juan's into the little lake, on their return down the river, and that the alligators were in such incredible numbers, and so close together from shore to shore, that it would have been easy to have walked across on their heads, had the animals been harmless? What expressions can sufficiently declare the shocking scene that for some minutes continued, whilst this mighty army of fish were forcing the pass? During this attempt, thousands, I may say hundreds of thousands, of them were caught and swallowed by the devouring alligators. I have seen an alligator take up out of the water several great fish at a time, and just squeeze them betwixt his jaws, while the tails of the great trout flapped about his eyes and lips, ere he had swallowed them. The horrid noise of their closing jaws, their plunging amidst the broken banks of fish, and rising with their prey some feet upright above the water, the floods of water and blood rushing out of their mouths, and the clouds of vapour issuing from their wide nostrils, were truly frightful. This scene continued at intervals during the night, as the fish came to the pass. After this sight, shocking and tremendous as it was, I found myself somewhat easier and more reconciled to my situation; being convinced that their extraordinary assemblage here was owing to this annual feast of fish; and that they were so well employed in their own element, that I had little occasion to fear their paying me a visit.

It being now almost night, I returned to my camp, where I had left my fish broiling, and my kettle of rice stewing; and having with me oil, pepper, and salt, and excellent oranges hanging in abundance over my head (a valuable substitute for vinegar) I sat down and regaled myself cheerfully. Having finished my repast, I rekindled my fire for light, and whilst I was revising the notes of my past day's journey, I was suddenly roused with a noise behind me toward the main land. I sprang up on my feet, and listening, I distinctly heard some creature wading in the water of the isthmus. I seized my gun and went cautiously from my camp, directing my steps towards the noise: when I had advanced about thirty yards, I halted behind a coppice of orange trees, and soon perceived two very large bears, which had made their way through the water, and had landed in the grove, about one hundred yards distance from me, and were advancing towards me. I waited until they were within thirty yards of me: they there began to snuff and look towards my camp: I snapped my piece, but it flashed, on which they both turned about and galloped off, plunging through the water and swamp, never halting, as I suppose, until they reached fast land, as I could hear them leaping and plunging a long time. They did not presume to return again, nor was I molested by any other creature, except being occasionally awakened by the whooping of owls, screaming of bitterns, or the wood-rats running amongst the leaves.

The wood-rat is a very curious animal. It is not half the size of the domestic rat; of a dark brown or black colour; its tail slender and shorter in proportion, and covered thinly with short hair. It is singular with respect to its ingenuity and great labour in the construction of its habitation, which is a conical pyramid about three or four feet high, constructed with dry branches, which it collects with great labour and perseverance, and piles up without any apparent order; yet they are so interwoven with one another, that it would take a bear or wild-cat some time to pull one of these castles to pieces, and allow the animals sufficient time to secure a retreat with their young.

The noise of the crocodiles kept me awake the greater part of the night; but when I arose in the morning, contrary to my expectations, there was perfect peace; very few of them to be seen, and those were asleep on the shore. Yet I was not able to suppress my fears and apprehensions of being attacked by them in future; and indeed yesterday's combat with them, notwithstanding I came off in a manner victorious, or at least made a safe retreat, had left sufficient impression on my mind to damp my courage; and it seemed too much for one of my strength, being alone in a very small boat, to encounter such collected danger. To pursue my voyage up the river, and be obliged every evening to pass such dangerous defiles, appeared to me as perilous as running the gauntlet betwixt two rows of Indians armed with knives and firebrands. I however resolved to continue my voyage one day longer, if I possibly could with safety, and then return down the river, should I find the like difficulties to oppose. Accordingly I got every thing on board, charged my gun, and set sail cautiously, along shore. As I passed by Battle lagoon, I began to tremble and keep a good look out; when suddenly a huge alligator rushed out of the reeds, and with a tremendous roar came up, and darted as swift as an arrow under my boat, emerging upright on my lee quarter, with open jaws, and belching water and smoke that fell upon me like rain in a hurricane. I laid soundly about his head with my club and beat him off; and after plunging and darting about my boat, he went off on a straight line through the water, seemingly with the rapidity of lightning, and entered the cape of the lagoon. I now employed my time to the very best advantage in paddling close along shore, but could not forbear looking now and then behind me, and presently perceived one of them coming up again. The water of the river hereabouts was shoal and very clear; the monster came up with the usual roar and menaces, and passed close by the side of my boat, when I could distinctly see a young brood of alligators, to the number of one hundred or more, following after her in a long train. They kept close together in a column without straggling off to the one side or the other; the young appeared to be of an equal size, about fifteen inches in length, almost black, with pale yellow transverse waved clouds or blotches, much like rattlesnakes in colour. I now lost sight of my enemy again.

Still keeping close along shore, on turning a point or projection of the river bank, at once I beheld a great number of hillocks or small pyramids, resembling hay-cocks, ranged like an encampment along the banks. They stood fifteen or twenty yards distant from the water, on a high marsh, about four feet perpendicular above the water. I knew them to be the nests of the crocodile, having had a description of them before; and now expected a furious and general attack, as I saw several large crocodiles swimming abreast of these buildings. These nests being so great a curiosity to me, I was determined at all events immediately to land and examine them. Accordingly, I ran my bark on shore at one of their landing-places, which was a sort of nick or little dock, from which ascended a sloping path or road up to the edge of the meadow, where their nests were; most of them were deserted, and the great thick whitish egg-shells lay broken and scattered upon the ground round about them.

The nests or hillocks are of the form of an obtuse cone, four feet high and four or five feet in diameter at their bases; they are constructed with mud, grass, and herbage. At first they lay a floor of this kind of tempered mortar on the ground, upon which they deposit a layer of eggs, and upon this a stratum of mortar seven or eight inches in thickness, and then another layer of eggs, and in this manner one stratum upon another, nearly to the top. I believe they commonly lay from one to two hundred eggs in a nest: these are hatched,

I suppose, by the heat of the sun; and perhaps the vegetable substances mixed with the earth, being acted upon by the sun, may cause a small degree of fermentation, and so increase the heat in those hillocks. The ground for several acres about these nests shewed evident marks of a continual resort of alligators; the grass was every where beaten down, hardly a blade or straw was left standing; whereas, all about, at a distance, it was five or six feet high, and as thick as it could grow together. The female, as I imagine, carefully watches her own nest of eggs until they are all hatched; or perhaps while she is attending her own brood, she takes under her care and protection as many as she can get at one time, either from her own particular nest or others: but certain it is, that the young are not left to shift for themselves; for I have had frequent opportunities of seeing the female alligator leading about the shores her train of young ones, just as a hen does her brood of chickens; and she is equally assiduous and courageous in defending the young, which are under her care, and providing for their subsistence; and when she is basking upon the warm banks, with her brood around her, you may hear the young ones continually whining and barking, like young puppies. I believe but few of a brood live to the years of full growth and magnitude, as the old feed on the young as long as they can make prey of them.

The alligator when full grown is a very large and terrible creature, and of prodigious strength, activity, and swiftness in the water. I have seen them twenty feet in length, and some are supposed to be twenty-two or twenty-three feet. Their body is as large as that of a horse; their shape exactly resembles that of a lizard, except their tail, which is flat or cuneiform, being compressed on each side, and gradually diminishing from the abdomen to the extremity, which, with the whole body is covered with horny plates or squammæ, impenetrable when on the body of the live animal, even to a rifle ball, except about their head and just behind their fore-legs or arms, where it is said they are only vulnerable. The head of a full grown one is about three feet, and the mouth opens nearly the same length; their eyes are small in proportion and seem sunk deep in the head, by means of the prominency of the brows; the nostrils are large, inflated and prominent on the top, so that the head in the water resembles, at a distance, a great chunk of wood floating about. Only the upper jaw moves, which they raise almost perpendicular, so as to form a right angle with the lower one. In the fore-part of the upper jaw, on each side, just under the nostrils, are two very large, thick, strong teeth or tusks, not very sharp, but rather the shape of a cone: these are as white as the finest polished ivory, and are not covered by any skin or lips, and always in sight, which gives the creature a frightful appearance: in the lower jaw are holes opposite to these teeth, to receive them: when they clap their jaws together it causes a surprising noise, like that which is made by forcing a heavy plank with violence upon the ground, and may be heard at a great distance.

But what is yet more surprising to a stranger, is the incredible loud and terrifying roar, which they are capable of making, especially in the spring season, their breeding time. It most resembles very heavy distant thunder, not only shaking the air and waters, but causing the earth to tremble; and when hundreds and thousands are roaring at the same time, you can scarcely be persuaded, but that the whole globe is violently and dangerously agitated.

An old champion, who is perhaps absolute sovereign of a little lake or lagoon (when fifty less than himself are obliged to content themselves with swelling and roaring in little coves round about) darts forth from the reedy coverts all at once, on the surface of the waters, in a right line; at first seemingly as rapid as lightning, but gradually more slowly until he arrives at the center of the lake, when he stops. He now swells himself by drawing in wind and water through his mouth, which causes a loud sonorous rattling in the throat for near a minute, but it is immediately forced out again through his mouth and nostrils, with a loud noise, brandishing his tail in the air, and the vapour ascending from his nostrils like smoke. At other times, when swollen to an extent ready to burst, his head and tail lifted up, he spins or twirls round on the surface of the water. He acts his part like an Indian chief when rehearsing his feats of war; and then retiring, the exhibition is continued by others who dare to step forth, and strive to excel each other, to gain the attention of the favourite female.

Having gratified my curiosity at this general breeding-place and nursery of crocodiles, I continued my voyage up the river without being greatly disturbed by them. In my way I observed islets or floating fields of the bright green Pistia, decorated with other amphibious plants, as Senecio Jacobea, Persicaria amphibia, Coreopsis bidens, Hydrocotyle fluitans, and many others of less note.

The swamps on the banks and islands of the river are generally three or four feet above the surface of the water, and very level; the timber large and growing thinly, more so than what is observed to be in the swamps below lake George; the black rich earth is covered with moderately tall, and very succulent tender grass, which when chewed is sweet and agreeable to the taste, somewhat like young sugar-cane: it is a jointed decumbent grass, sending out radiculæ at the joints into the earth, and so spreads itself, by creeping over its surface.

The large timber trees, which possess the low lands, are Acer rubrum, Ac. negundo, Ac. glaucum, Ulmus sylvatica, Fraxinus excelsior, Frax. aquatica, Ulmus suberifer, Gleditsia monosperma, Gledit. triacanthus, Diospyros Virginica, Nyssa aquatica, Nyssa sylvatica, Juglans cinerea, Quercus dentata, Quercus phillos, Hopea tinctoria, Corypha palma, Morus rubra, and many more. The palm grows on the edges of the banks, where they are raised higher than the adjacent level ground, by the accumulation of sand, river-shells, &c. I passed along several miles by those rich swamps: the channels of the river which encircle the several fertile islands I had passed, now uniting, formed one deep channel near three hundred yards over. The banks of the river on each side, began to rise and present shelly bluffs, adorned by beautiful Orange groves, Laurels and Live Oaks. And now appeared in sight, a tree that claimed my whole attention: it was the Carica papaya, both male and female, which were in flower; and the latter both in flower and fruit, some of which were ripe, as large, and of the form of a pear, and of a most charming appearance.

This admirable tree is certainly the most beautiful of any vegetable production I know of; the towering Laurel Magnolia, and exalted Palm, indeed exceed it in grandeur and magnificence, but not in elegance, delicacy, and gracefulness. It rises erect to the height of fifteen or twenty feet, with a

perfectly straight tapering stem, which is smooth and polished, of a bright ash colour, resembling leaf silver, curiously
inscribed with the footsteps of the fallen leaves; and these vestiges are placed in a very regular uniform imbricated order,
which has a fine effect, as if the little column were elegantly
carved all over. Its perfectly spherical top is formed of very
large lobe-sinuate leaves, supported on very long footstalks;
the lower leaves are the largest as well as their petioles the
longest, and make a graceful sweep or flourish, like the long
s or the branches of a sconce candlestick. The ripe and green
fruit are placed round about the stem or trunk, from the low-
ermost leaves, where the ripe fruit are, and upwards almost to
the top; the heart or inmost pithy part of the trunk is in a
manner hollow, or at best consists of very thin porous medullæ
or membranes. The tree very seldom branches or divides into
limbs, I believe never unless the top is by accident broke off
when very young: I saw one which had two tops or heads,
the stem of which divided near the earth. It is always green,
ornamented at the same time with flowers and fruit, which
like figs come out singly from the trunk or stem.

After resting and refreshing myself in these delightful
shades, I left them with reluctance. Embarking again after the
fervid heats of the meridian sun was abated, for some time I
passed by broken ridges of shelly high land, covered with
groves of Live Oak, Palm, Olea Americana, and Orange trees;
frequently observing floating islets and green fields of the
Pistia near the shores of the river and lagoons.

Here is in this river and in the waters all over Florida, a very
curious and handsome species of birds; the people call them
Snake Birds; I think I have seen paintings of them on the
Chinese screens and other India pictures: they seem to be a
species of cormorant or loon (Colymbus cauda elongata), but
far more beautiful and delicately formed than any other species that I have ever seen. The head and neck of this bird are
extremely small and slender, the latter very long indeed, almost out of all proportion; the bill long, straight, and slender,
tapering from its ball to a sharp point; all the upper side, the
abdomen and thighs, are as black and glossy as a raven's, covered with feathers so firm and elastic, that they in some degree
resemble fish-scales; the breast and upper part of the belly are

covered with feathers of a cream colour; the tail is very long, of a deep black, and tipped with a silvery white, and when spread, represents an unfurled fan. They delight to sit in little peaceable communities, on the dry limbs of trees, hanging over the still waters, with their wings and tails expanded, I suppose to cool and air themselves, when at the same time they behold their images in the watery mirrour. At such times, when we approach them, they drop off the limbs into the water as if dead, and for a minute or two are not to be seen; when on a sudden, at a vast distance, their long slender head and neck only appear, and have very much the appearance of a snake, and no other part of them is to be seen when swimming in the water, except sometimes the tip end of their tail. In the heat of the day they are seen in great numbers, sailing very high in the air, over lakes and rivers.

I doubt not but if this bird had been an inhabitant of the Tiber in Ovid's days, it would have furnished him with a subject for some beautiful and entertaining metamorphoses. I believe it feeds intirely on fish, for its flesh smells and tastes intolerably strong of it; it is scarcely to be eaten unless constrained by insufferable hunger.

I had now swamps and marshes on both sides of me; and evening coming on apace, I began to look out for high land to encamp on; but the extensive marshes seemed to have no bounds, and it was almost dark when I found a tolerably suitable place, and at last was constrained to take up with a narrow strip of high shelly bank, on the west side. Great numbers of crocodiles were in sight on both shores. I ran my bark on shore at a perpendicular bank four or five feet above the water, just by the roots and under the spreading limbs of a great Live Oak: this appeared to have been an ancient camping place by Indians and strolling adventurers, from ash heaps and old rotten fire brands and chunks, scattered about on the surface of the ground; but was now evidently the harbour and landing place of some sovereign alligator: there led up from it a deep beaten path or road, which was a convenient ascent.

I did not approve of my intended habitation from these circumstances; and no sooner had I landed and moored my canoe to the roots of the tree, than I saw a huge crocodile

rising up from the bottom close by me, who, when he perceived that I saw him, plunged down again under my vessel.
This determined me to be on my guard, and in time to provide against a troublesome night. I took out of my boat every
moveable, which I carried upon the bank; then chose my
lodging close to my canoe, under the spreading Oak, as hereabouts only, the ground was open and clear of high grass and
bushes, and consequently I had some room to stir and look
round about. I then proceeded to collect firewood, which I
found difficult to procure. Here were standing a few Orange
trees. As for provisions, I had saved one or two barbecued
trout, the remains of my last evening's collection, in tolerable
good order, though the sultry heats of the day had injured
them; yet by stewing them up afresh with the lively juice of
Oranges, they served well enough for my supper, as I had by
this time but little relish or appetite for my victuals; for constant watching at night against the attacks of alligators, stinging of musquitoes and sultry heats of the day; together with
the fatigues of working my bark, had almost deprived me of
every desire but that of ending my troubles as speedily as possible. I had the good fortune to collect together a sufficiency
of dry sticks to keep up a light and smoke, which I laid by
me, and then spread my skins and blankets upon the ground,
kindled up a little fire, and supped before it was quite dark.
The evening was however extremely pleasant; a brisk cool
breeze sprang up, and the skies were perfectly serene, the stars
twinkling with uncommon brilliancy. I stretched myself along
before my fire; having the river, my little harbour, and the
stern of my vessel in view; and now through fatigue and weari-
ness I fell asleep. But this happy temporary release from cares
and troubles I enjoyed but a few moments, when I was awakened and greatly surprised, by the terrifying screams of Owls
in the deep swamps around me; and what increased my extreme misery was the difficulty of getting quite awake, and
yet hearing at the same time such screaming and shouting,
which increased and spread every way for miles around, in
dreadful peals vibrating through the dark extensive forests,
meadows, and lakes. I could not after this surprise recover my
former peaceable state and tranquillity of mind and repose,
during the long night; and I believe it was happy for me that

I was awakened, for at that moment the crocodile was dashing my canoe against the roots of the tree, endeavouring to get into her for the fish, which I however prevented. Another time in the night I believe I narrowly escaped being dragged into the river by him; for when again through excessive fatigue I had fallen asleep, but was again awakened by the screaming owl, I found the monster on the top of the bank, his head towards me not above two yards distant; when starting up and seizing my fusee well loaded, which I always kept under my head in the night time, he drew back and plunged into the water. After this, I roused up my fire, and kept a light during the remaining part of the night, being determined not to be caught napping so again: indeed the musquitoes alone would have been abundantly sufficient to keep any creature awake that possessed their perfect senses; but I was overcome and stupified with incessant watching and labour. As soon as I discovered the first signs of day-light, I arose, got all my effects and implements on board, and set sail, proceeding upwards, hoping to give the musquitoes the slip, who were now, by the cool morning dews and breezes, driven to their shelter and hiding places. I was mistaken however in these conjectures, for great numbers of them, which had concealed themselves in my boat, as soon as the sun arose, began to revive, and sting me on my legs, which obliged me to land in order to get bushes to beat them out of their quarters.

It is very pleasing to observe the banks of the river ornamented with hanging garlands, composed of varieties of climbing vegetables, both shrubs and plants, forming perpendicular green walls, with projecting jambs, pilasters, and deep apartments, twenty or thirty feet high, and completely covered with Glycine frutescens, Glyc. apios, Vitis labrusca, Vitis vulpina, Rajana, Hedera quinquifolia, Hedera arborea, Eupatorium scandens, Bignonia crucigera, and various species of Convolvulus, particularly an amazing tall climber of this genus, or perhaps an Ipomea. This has a very large white flower, as big as a small funnel; its tube is five or six inches in length, and not thicker than a pipe stem; the leaves are also very large, oblong, and cordated, sometimes dentated or angled, near the insertion of the foot-stalk; they are of a thin texture, and of a deep green colour. It is exceedingly curious to behold the

Wild Squash* climbing over the lofty limbs of the trees; its yellow fruit, somewhat of the size and figure of a large orange, pendant from the extremities of the limbs over the water.

Towards noon, the sultry heats being intolerable, I put into shore, at a middling high bank, five or six feet above the surface of the river. This low sandy testaceous ridge along the river side was but narrow; the surface light, black, and exceedingly fertile, producing very large venerable Live Oaks, Palms, and grand Magnolias, scatteringly planted by nature. There being no underwood to prevent the play of the breezes from the river, it afforded a desirable retreat from the sun's heat. Immediately at the back of this narrow ridge, were deep wet swamps, where stood some astonishingly tall and spreading Cypress trees. And now being weary and drowsy, I was induced to indulge and listen to the dictates of reason and invitations to repose; which consenting to, after securing my boat and reconnoitering the ground, I spread my blanket under the Oaks near my boat, on which I extended myself, where, falling to sleep, I instantaneously passed away the sultry hours of noon. What a blissful tranquil repose! Undisturbed I awoke, refreshed and strengthened; I cheerfully stepped on board again and continued to ascend the river. The afternoon being cool and pleasant, and the trees very lofty on the higher western banks of the river, by keeping near that shore I passed under agreeable shades the remaining part of the day. During almost all this day's voyage, the banks of the river on both shores were middling high, perpendicular, and washed by the brisk current: the shores were not lined with the green lawns of floating aquatics, and consequently not very commodious resorts or harbours for crocodiles; I therefore was not disturbed by them, and saw but few, but those were very large. I however did not like to lodge on those narrow ridges, invested by such dreary swamps; and evening approaching, I began to be anxious for high land for a camping place. It was quite dark before I came up to a bluff, which I had in view a long time, over a very extensive point of meadows. I landed however at last, in the best manner I could, at a magnificent forest of Orange groves, Oaks, and Palms. I

*Cucurbita peregrina.

here, with little labour or difficulty, soon collected a sufficient quantity of dry wood: there was a pleasant vista of grass betwixt the grove and the edge of the river bank, which afforded a very convenient, open, airy encamping place, under the protection of some spreading Oaks.

This was a high perpendicular bluff, fronting more than one hundred yards on the river, the earth black, loose, and fertile: it is a composition of river-shells, sand, &c. At the back of it from the river, were open Pine forests and savannas. I met with a circumstance here, that, with some, may be reckoned worthy of mentioning, since it regards the monuments of the ancients. As I have already observed, when I landed it was quite dark; and in collecting wood for my fire, strolling in the dark about the groves, I found the surface of the ground very uneven, by means of little mounts and ridges. In the morning I found I had taken up my lodging on the border of an ancient burying ground, containing sepulchres or tumuli of the Yamasees, who were here slain by the Creeks in the last decisive battle, the Creeks having driven them into this point, between the doubling of the river, where few of them escaped the fury of the conquerors. These graves occupied the whole grove, consisting of two or three acres of ground: there were near thirty of these cemeteries of the dead, nearly of an equal size and form, being oblong, twenty feet in length, ten or twelve feet in width, and three or four feet high, now overgrown with orange trees, live oaks, laurel magnolias, red bays and other trees and shrubs, composing dark and solemn shades.

I here, for the first time since I left the trading house, enjoyed a night of peaceful repose. I arose, greatly refreshed and in good spirits, stepped on board my bark, and continued my voyage. After doubling the point, I passed by swamps and meadows on each side of me. The river here is something more contracted within perpendicular banks; the land of an excellent quality, fertile, and producing prodigiously large timber and luxuriant herbage.

The air continued sultry, and scarcely enough wind to flutter the leaves on the trees. The Eastern coast of the river now opens, and presents to view ample plains, consisting of grassy marshes and green meadows, and affords a prospect almost unlimited and extremely pleasing. The opposite shore exhibits a sublime contrast; a high bluff bearing magnificent forests of grand magnolia, glorious palms, fruitful orange groves, live oaks, bays and other trees. This grand elevation continues four or five hundred yards, describing a gentle curve on the river, ornamented by a sublime grove of palms, consisting of many hundreds of trees together; they entirely shade the ground under them. Above and below the bluff, the grounds gradually descend to the common level swamps on the river: at the back of this eminence open to view expansive green meadows or savannas, in which are to be seen glittering ponds of water, surrounded at a great distance by high open pine forests and hommocks, and islets of oaks and bays projecting into the savannas. After ranging about these solitary groves and peaceful shades, I re-embarked and continued some miles up the river, between elevated banks of the swamps or low lands; when on the East shore, in a capacious cove or winding of the river, were pleasing floating fields of pistia; and in the bottom of this cove opened to view a large creek or branch of the river, which I knew to be the entrance to a beautiful lake, on the banks of which was the farm I was going to visit, and which I designed should be the last extent of my voyage up the river.

About noon the weather became extremely sultry, not a breath of wind stirring, hazy or cloudy, with very heavy distant thunder, which was answered by the crocodiles, sure presage of a storm!

Soon after ascending this branch of the river, on the right hand presents itself to view a delightful little bluff, consisting chiefly of shells, and covered with a dark grove of red cedar, Zanthoxylon and myrtle. I could not resist the temptation to stop here, although the tremendous thunder all around the hemisphere alarmed me greatly, having a large lake to cross. From this grove appears to view an expansive and pleasing prospect. The beauteous long lake in front, about North East from me, its most distant East shores adorned with dark, high forests of stately trees; North and South almost endless green plains and meadows, embellished with islets and projecting promontories of high, dark forests, where the pyramidal magnolia grandiflora, palma elata, and shady oak, conspicuously tower.

Being heretofore so closely invested by high forests and deep swamps of the great river, I was prevented from seeing the progress and increase of the approaching tempest, the terrific appearance of which now at once confounded me. How purple and fiery appeared the tumultuous clouds, swiftly ascending or darting from the horizon upwards! they seemed to oppose and dash against each other; the skies appeared streaked with blood or purple flame overhead, the flaming lightning streaming and darting about in every direction around, seemed to fill the world with fire; whilst the heavy thunder kept the earth in a constant tremor. I had yet some hopes of crossing the lake to the plantation in sight. On the opposite shore of the creek before me, and on the cape as we enter the lake, stood a large islet or grove of oaks and palms. Here I intended to seek shelter and abide till the fury of the hurricane was overpast, if I found it too violent to permit me to cross the lake. In consequence of this precipitate determination, I stepped into my boat and pushed off. What a dreadful rushing and roaring there was every where around me! and to my utter confusion and astonishment, I could not find from what particular quarter its strongest current or direction came, whereby I might have a proper chance of taking measures for securing a harbour or running from it. The high forests behind me bent to the blast; and the sturdy limbs of the trees cracked. I had by this time got up abreast of the grove or hommock: the hurricane close by, pursuing me, I found it dangerous and imprudent in the highest degree to put in here, as the groves were already torn up, and the spreading limbs of the ancient live oaks were flying over my head, and carried about in the air as leaves and stubble. I ran by and boldly entered the lake (being hurried in by a strong current, which seemed a prodigy, the violent wind driving the stream of the creek back again into the lake), and as soon as possible took shelter under the high reedy bank of the lake, and made fast my bark to the boughs of a low shrubby Hickory, that leaned over the water. Such was the violence of the wind, that it raised the waters on the opposite shores of the lake several feet perpendicular, and there was a rapid flow of water from the creek into it, which was contrary to its natural course. Such floods of rain fell during the space of half or three quarters of an hour, that my boat was filled, and I expected every moment when I should see her sink to the bottom of the lake; and the violence of the wind kept the cable so constantly extended, that it was beyond my ability to get to her. My box which contained my books of specimens and other collections, was floating about in her; and for a great part of the time the rain came down with such rapidity and fell in such quantities, that every object was totally obscured, excepting the continual streams or rivers of lightning, pouring from the clouds. All seemed a frightful chaos. When the wind and rain abated, I was overjoyed to see the face of nature again appear.

It took me an hour or more to clear the water out of my bark. I then crossed the lake before a brisk and favourable breeze (it was about a mile over), and landed safely at the plantation.

When I arrived, my friend was affrighted to see me, and immediately inquired of me in what manner I came there; supposing it impossible (until I had showed him my boat) that I could have arrived by water, through so tremendous a hurricane.

Indeed I saw plainly that they were greatly terrified, having suffered almost irreparable damages from the violence of the storm. All the buildings on the plantation, except his own dwelling-house, were laid almost flat to the ground, or the logs and roof rent asunder and twisted about; the mansion-house shook and reeled over their heads. He had nearly one hundred acres of the Indigo plant almost ripe for the first cutting, which were nearly ruined; and several acres of very promising sugar-cane, totally spoiled for the season. The great live oaks which had been left standing about the fields, were torn to pieces, their limbs lying scattered over the ground: and one very large one which stood near his house torn down, which could not have been done by the united strength of a thousand men. But what is incredible, in the midst of this devastation and ruin, providentially no lives were lost; although there were about sixty Negro slaves on the plantation, and most of them in their huts when the storm came on, yet they escaped with their lives, though several were badly wounded.

I continued here three days: indeed it took most of the time of my abode with him, to dry my books and specimens of plants. But with attention and care I saved the greatest number of them; though some were naturally so delicate and fragile, that it was impossible to recover them. Here is a vast body of land belonging to this estate; of high ridges fit for the culture of corn, indigo, cotton, batatas, &c. and of low swamps and marshes, which when properly drained and tilled, would be suitable for rice. These rich low grounds, when drained and ridged, are as productive as the natural high land, and vastly more durable, especially for sugar-cane, corn, and even indigo; but this branch of agriculture being more expensive, these rich lands are neglected, and the upland only is under culture. The farm is situated on the East shore of the beautiful Long Lake, which is above two miles long, and near a mile broad. This lake communicates with the St. Juan, by the little river that I ascended, which is about one mile and an half in length, and thirty or forty yards wide. The river, as well as the lake, abounds with fish and wild fowl of various kinds, and incredible numbers, especially during the winter season, when the geese and ducks arrive here from the north.

New Smyrna*, a pretty thriving town, is a colony of Greeks and Minorquines, established by Mr. Turnbull, on the Musquito river, and very near its mouth; it is about thirty miles over land from this farm.

My friend rode with me, about four miles distance from the house, to show me a vast fountain of warm, or rather hot mineral water, which issued from a high ridge or bank on the

---

*New Smyrna is built on a high shelly bluff, on the West bank of the South branch of Musquito river, about ten miles above the capes of that river, which is about thirty miles North of Cape Canaveral, Lat. 28. I was there about ten years ago, when the surveyor run the lines or precincts of the colony, where there was neither habitation nor cleared field. It was then a famous orange grove, the upper or South promontory of a ridge, nearly half a mile wide, and stretching North about forty miles, to the head of the North branch of the Musquito, to where the Tomoko river unites with it, nearly parallel to the sea coast, and not above two miles across to the sea beach. All this ridge was then one entire orange grove, with live oaks, magnolias, palms, red bays, and others: I observed then, near where New Smyrna now stands, a spacious Indian mount and avenue, which stood near the banks of the river: the avenue ran on a strait line back, through the groves, across the ridge, and terminated at the verge of natural savannas and ponds.

river, in a great cove or bay, a few miles above the mouth of the creek which I ascended to the lake; it boils up with great force, forming immediately a vast circular bason, capacious enough for several shallops to ride in, and runs with rapidity into the river three or four hundred yards distance. This creek, which is formed instantly by this admirable fountain, is wide and deep enough for a sloop to sail up into the bason. The water is perfectly diaphanous, and here are continually a prodigious number and variety of fish; they appear as plain as though lying on a table before your eyes, although many feet deep in the water. This tepid water has a most disagreeable taste, brassy and vitriolic, and very offensive to the smell, much like bilge water or the washings of a gun-barrel, and is smelt at a great distance. A pale bluish or pearl coloured coagulum covers every inanimate substance that lies in the water, as logs, limbs of trees, &c. Alligators and gar were numerous in the bason, even at the apertures where the ebullition emerges through the rocks; as also many other tribes of fish. In the winter season several kinds of fish and aquatic animals migrate to these warm fountains. The forbidding taste and smell of these waters seems to be owing to vitriolic and sulphureous fumes or vapours; and these being condensed, form this coagulum, which represents flakes of pearly clouds in the clear cerulean waters in the bason. A charming orange grove, with magnolias, oaks, and palms, half surrounded this vast fountain. A delightful stream of cool salubrious water issues from the ridge, meandering along and entering the creek just below the bason. I returned in the evening, and next day sat off again down the river.

My hospitable friend, after supplying me with necessaries, prevailed on me to accept of the company and assistance of his purveyor, one day's voyage down the river, whom I was to set on shore at a certain bluff, upwards of twenty miles below, but not above one third that distance by land; he was to be out in the forests one day, on a hunt for turkeys.

The current of the river being here confined within its perpendicular banks, ran briskly down: we cheerfully descended the grand river St. Juan, enjoying enchanting prospects.

Before night we reached the destined port, at a spacious orange grove. Next morning we separated, and I proceeded down the river. The prospects on either hand are now pleasing, and I view them at leisure, and without toil or dread.

Induced by the beautiful appearance of the green meadows, which open to the Eastward, I determined not to pass this Elysium without a visit. Behold the loud, sonorous, watchful savanna cranes (grus pratensis) with musical clangor, in detached squadrons. They spread their light elastic sail: at first they move from the earth heavy and slow; they labour and beat the dense air; they form the line with wide extended wings, tip to tip; they all rise and fall together as one bird; now they mount aloft, gradually wheeling about; each squadron performs its evolution, encircling the expansive plains, observing each one its own orbit; then lowering sail, descend on the verge of some glittering lake; whilst other squadrons, ascending aloft in spiral circles, bound on interesting discoveries, wheel round and double the promontory, in the silver regions of the clouded skies, where, far from the scope of eye, they carefully observe the verdant meadows on the borders of the East Lake; then contract their plumes and descend to the earth, where, after resting a while on some verdant eminence, near the flowery border of the lake, they, with dignified, yet slow, respectful steps, approach the kindred band, confer, and treat for habitation; the bounds and precincts being settled, they confederate and take possession.

There is inhabiting the low shores and swamps of this river and the lakes of Florida, as well as Georgia, a very curious bird*, called by an Indian name (Ephouskyca) which signifies in our language the crying bird. I cannot determine what genus of European birds to join it with. It is about the size of a large domestic hen: all the body, above and beneath, is of a dark lead colour, every feather edged or tipped with white, which makes the bird appear speckled on a near view; the eye is large and placed high on the head, which is very prominent; the bill or beak is five or six inches in length, arched or bent gradually downwards, in that respect to be compared to one half of a bent bow; it is large or thick near the base, compressed on each side, and flatted at top and beneath, which makes it appear four square for more than an inch, where the

*Tantalus pictus.

nostrils are placed, from whence, to their tips, both mandibles are round, gradually lessening or tapering to their extremities, which are thicker for about half an inch than immediately above, by which the mandibles never fit quite close their whole length; the upper mandible is a small matter longer than the under; the bill is of a dusky green colour, more bright and yellowish about the base and angles of the mouth; the tail is very short, and the middle feather the longest; the others on each side shorten gradually, and are of the colour of the rest of the bird, only somewhat darker; the two shortest or outermost feathers are perfectly white, which the bird has a faculty of flirting out on either side, as quick as a flash of lightning, especially when he hears or sees any thing that disturbs him, uttering at the same instant an extreme harsh and loud shriek; his neck is long and slender; and his legs are also long and bare of feathers above the knee, like those of the bittern, and are black or of a dark lead colour.

There are two other species of this genus, which agree in almost every particular with the above description, except in size and colour. The first[*] of these I shall mention is a perfect white, except the prime quill feathers, which are as black as those of a crow; the bill and legs of a beautiful clear red, as also a space clear of feathers about the eyes. The other species[†] is black on the upper side, the breast and belly white, and the legs and beak as white as snow. Both these species are about half the size of the crying bird. They fly in large flocks or squadrons, evening and morning, to and from their feeding place or roosts; both species are called Spanish curlews: these and the crying bird feed chiefly on cray fish, whose cells they probe, and with their strong pinching bills drag them out: all the three species are esteemed excellent food.

It is a pleasing sight at times of high winds and heavy thunderstorms, to observe the numerous squadrons of these Spanish curlews driving to and fro, turning and tacking about, high up in the air, when by their various evolutions in the different and opposite currents of the wind high in the clouds,

[*]Tantalus albus. Numinus albus. Cat.
[†]Tantalus versicolor. Numinus fuscus. Cat.

their silvery white plumage gleams and sparkles like the brightest crystal, reflecting the sun-beams that dart upon them between the dark clouds.

Since I have turned my observations upon the birds of this country I shall notice another very singular one, though already most curiously and exactly figured by Catesby, which seems to be nearly allied to those before mentioned; I mean the bird which he calls the wood pelican*. This is a large bird, perhaps near three feet high when standing erect. The bill is very long and strong, bending with a moderate curve from the base to the tip; the upper mandible is the largest, and receives the edges of the nether one into it its whole length; the edges are very sharp and firm; the whole of a dark ash or horn colour; the forehead round the base of the beak and sides of the head is bare of feathers, and of a dark greenish colour, in which space is placed the eyes, which are very large; the remainder of the head and neck is of a nut brown colour; the back of a light bluish grey; upper part of the wings, breast, and belly, almost white, with some slight dashes of grey; the quill-feathers and tail, which are very short, are of a dark slate colour, almost black; the legs, which are very long, and bare of feathers a great length above the knees, are of a dark dull greenish colour: it has a small bag or pouch under its throat: it feeds on serpents, young alligators, frogs, and other reptiles.

This solitary bird does not associate in flocks, but is generally seen alone; commonly near the banks of great rivers, in vast marshes or meadows, especially such as are caused by inundations; and also in the vast deserted rice plantations: he stands alone on the topmost limb of tall dead cypress trees, his neck contracted or drawn in upon his shoulders, and beak resting like a long scythe upon his breast: in this pensive posture and solitary situation, it looks extremely grave, sorrowful, and melancholy, as if in the deepest thought. They are never seen on the salt sea coast, and yet are never found at a great distance from it. I take this bird to be of a different genus from the tantalus, and perhaps it approaches the nearest to the Egyptian ibis of any other bird yet known.

*Tantalus loculator. Linn.

There are two species of vultures* in these regions, I think
not mentioned in history: the first we shall describe is a beautiful bird, near the size of a turkey buzzard[†], but his wings
are much shorter, and consequently he falls greatly below that
admirable bird in sail. I shall call this bird the painted vulture.
The bill is long and straight almost to the point, when it is
hooked or bent suddenly down and sharp; the head and neck
bare of feathers nearly down to the stomach, when the feathers begin to cover the skin, and soon become long and of a
soft texture, forming a ruff or tippet, in which the bird by
contracting his neck can hide that as well as his head; the bare
skin on the neck appears loose and wrinkled, and is of a deep
bright yellow colour, intermixed with coral red; the hinder
part of the neck is nearly covered with short, stiff hair; and
the skin of this part of the neck is of a dun-purple colour,
gradually becoming red as it approaches the yellow of the sides
and fore part. The crown of the head is red; there are lobed
lappets of a reddish orange colour, which lie on the base of
the upper mandible. But what is singular, a large portion of
the stomach hangs down on the breast of the bird, in the
likeness of a sack or half wallet, and seems to be a duplicature
of the craw, which is naked and of a reddish flesh colour; this
is partly concealed by the feathers of the breast, unless when
it is loaded with food (which is commonly, I believe, roasted
reptiles), and then it appears prominent. The plumage of the
bird is generally white or cream colour, except the quill-feathers of the wings and two or three rows of the coverts, which
are of a beautiful dark brown; the tail, which is large and
white, is tipped with this dark brown or black; the legs and
feet of a clear white; the eye is encircled with a gold coloured
iris; the pupil black.

The Creeks or Muscogulges construct their royal standard
of the tail feather of this bird, which is called by a name signifying the eagle's tail: this they carry with them when they
go to battle, but then it is painted with a zone of red within
the brown tips; and in peaceable negociations it is displayed
new, clean, and white: this standard is held most sacred by

*Vultur sacra.
[†]Vultur aurea.

them on all occasions, and is constructed and ornamented with great ingenuity. These birds seldom appear but when the deserts are set on fire (which happens almost every day throughout the year, in some part or other, by the Indians, for the purpose of rousing the game, as also by the light-ning:) when they are seen at a distance soaring on the wing, gathering from every quarter, and gradually approaching the burnt plains, where they alight upon the ground yet smoking with hot embers: they gather up the roasted serpents, frogs, and lizards, filling their sacks with them: at this time a person may shoot them at pleasure, they not being willing to quit the feast, and indeed seeming to brave all danger.

The other species may very properly be called the coped vulture, and is by the inhabitants called the carrion crow. As to bulk or weight, he is nearly equal to either of the others before mentioned. His wings are not long and sharp pointed, but broad and round at their extremities, having a clumsy appearance; the tail is remarkably short, which he spreads like a little fan, when on the wing. They have a heavy laborious flight, flapping their wings, then sail a little and then flap their wings again, and so on as if recovering them-selves when falling. The beak is very long and straight, until it makes a sudden hook at the point, in the manner of the other vultures. The whole bird is of a sable or mourning colour; the head and neck down to the breast is bare of feathers, and the skin wrinkled; this unfeathered skin is of a deep livid purple, appearing black and thinly set with short black hair. He has a ruff or tippet of long soft feathers, like a collar, bearing on his breast, in which he can conceal his neck and head at pleasure.

Having agreeably diverted away the intolerable heats of sultry noon in fruitful fragrant groves, with renewed vigour I again resume my sylvan pilgrimage. The afternoon and evening moderately warm, and exceeding pleasant views from the river and its varied shores. I passed by Battle la-goon and the bluff, without much opposition; but the croc-odiles were already assembling in the pass. Before night I came to, at a charming orange grove bluff, on the East side of the little lake; and after fixing my camp on a high open situation, and collecting a plenty of dry wood for fuel, I had

time to get some fine trout for supper, and joyfully return to
my camp.

What a most beautiful creature is this fish before me! gliding to and fro, and figuring in the still clear waters, with his
orient attendants and associates: the yellow bream* or sun
fish. It is about eight inches in length, nearly of the shape of
the trout, but rather larger in proportion over the shoulders
and breast; the mouth large, and the branchiostega opens
wide; the whole fish is of a pale gold (or burnished brass)
colour, darker on the back and upper sides; the scales are of
a proportionable size, regularly placed, and every where vari-
ably powdered with red, russet, silver, blue, and green specks,
so laid on the scales as to appear like real dust or opaque
bodies, each apparent particle being so projected by light and
shade, and the various attitudes of the fish, as to deceive the
sight; for in reality nothing can be of a more plain and polished surface than the scales and whole body of the fish. The
fins are of an orange colour; and, like all the species of the
bream, the ultimate angle of the branchiostega terminates by
a little spatula, the extreme end of which represents a crescent
of the finest ultramarine blue, encircled with silver and velvet
black, like the eye in the feathers of a peacock's train. He is a
fish of prodigious strength and activity in the water; a warrior
in a gilded coat of mail; and gives no rest or quarter to small
fish, which he preys upon. They are delicious food and in great
abundance.

The orange grove is but narrow, betwixt the river banks and
ancient Indian fields, where there are evident traces of the
habitations of the ancients, surrounded with groves of live oak,
laurel magnolia, zanthoxylon, liquidambar, and others.

How harmonious and soothing is this native sylvan music
now at still evening! inexpressibly tender are the responsive
cooings of the innocent dove, in the fragrant zanthoxylon
groves, and the variable and tuneful warblings of the nonpareil, with the more sprightly and elevated strains of the blue
linnet and golden icterus: this is indeed harmony, even amidst
the incessant croaking of the frogs: the shades of silent night

*Cyprinus coronarius.

are made more cheerful, with the shrill voice of the whip-poor-will* and active mock-bird.

My situation high and airy: a brisk and cool breeze steadily and incessantly passing over the clear waters of the lake, and fluttering over me through the surrounding groves, wings its way to the moon-light savannas, while I repose on my sweet and healthy couch of the soft tillandsia usnea-adscites, and the latter gloomy and still hours of night pass rapidly away as it were in a moment. I arose, strengthened and cheerful, in the morning. Having some repairs to make in the tackle of my vessel, I paid my first attention to them; which being accomplished, my curiosity prompted me to penetrate the grove and view the illumined plains.

What a beautiful display of vegetation is here before me! seemingly unlimited in extent and variety: how the dew-drops twinkle and play upon the sight, trembling on the tips of the lucid, green savanna, sparkling as the gem that flames on the turban of the eastern prince. See the pearly tears rolling off the buds of the expanding Granadilla†; behold the azure fields of cerulean Ixea! what can equal the rich golden flowers of the Canna lutea, which ornament the banks of yon serpentine rivulet, meandering over the meadows; the almost endless varieties of the gay Phlox, that enamel the swelling green banks, associated with the purple Verbena corymbosa, Viola, pearly Gnaphalium, and silvery Perdicium? How fantastical looks the libertine Clitoria, mantling the shrubs, on the vistas skirting the groves! My morning excursion finished, I returned to my camp, breakfasted, then went on board my boat, gently descended the noble river, and passed by several openings of extensive plains and meadows, environing the east lake, charming beyond compare. At evening I came to at a good harbour, under the high banks of the river, and rested during the night amidst the fragrant groves, exposed to the constant breezes from the river: here I made ample collections of specimens and growing roots of curious vegetables, which kept

---

*Caprimulgus rufus, called chuck-will's-widow, from a fancied resemblance of his notes to these words: it inhabits the maritime parts of Carolina and Florida, and is more than twice the size of the night hawk or whip-poor-will.

†Passiflora incarnata, called May-Apple.

me fully employed the greatest part of the day; and in the evening arrived at a charming spot on the east bank, which I had marked on my ascent up the river, where I made some addition to my collections; and the next day I employed myself in the same manner, putting into shore frequently, at convenient places, which I had noticed; and in the evening arrived again at the upper store, where I had the pleasure of finding my old friend, the trader, in good health and cheerful, and his affairs in a prosperous way. There were also a small party of Indians here, who had lately arrived with their hunts to purchase goods. I continued a few days at this post, searching its environs for curious vegetable productions, collecting seeds and planting growing roots in boxes, to be transported to the lower trading house.

Now, having procured necessaries to accommodate me on my voyage down to the lower store, I bid adieu to my old friend and benefactor, Mr. Job Wiggens, embarked alone on board my little fortunate vessel, and set sail. I chose to follow the easternmost channel of the river to the Great Lake, because it ran by high banks and bluffs of the eastern main the greatest part of the distance, which afforded me an opportunity of observing a far greater variety of natural subjects, than if I had taken the western or middle channel, which flowed through swamps and marshes.

At evening I arrived at Cedar Point, my former safe and pleasant harbour, at the east cape of the Great Lake, where I had noticed some curious shrubs and plants; here I rested, and on the smooth and gentle current launch again into the little ocean of Lake George, meaning now, on my return, to coast his western shores in search of new beauties in the bounteous kingdom of Flora.

I was however induced to deviate a little from my intended course, and touch at the inchanting little Isle of Palms. This delightful spot, planted by nature, is almost an entire grove of Palms, with a few pyramidal Magnolias, Live Oaks, golden Orange, and the animating Zanthoxylon. What a beautiful retreat is here! blessed unviolated spot of earth, rising from the limpid waters of the lake: its fragrant groves and blooming lawns invested and protected by encircling ranks of the Yucca gloriosa. A fascinating atmosphere surrounds this blissful

Ixia Cælestina.

Rad . *bulbosa subrotunda .*
Caulis. *teret. vaginatis .*
Foliis . *Lineari lanceolatis .*
Floribus. *expansis magnis cæruleis .*

Vide Tournefort.

garden; the balmy Lantana, ambrosial Citra, perfumed Crinum, perspiring their mingled odours, wasted through Zanthoxylon groves. I at last broke away from the enchanting
spot, and stepped on board my boat, hoisted sail, and soon
approached the coast of the main, at the cool eve of day: then
traversing a capacious semicircular cove of the lake, verged by
low, extensive grassy meadows, I at length by dusk made a
safe harbour, in a little lagoon, on the sea shore or strand of
a bold sandy point, which descended from the surf of the lake.
This was a clean sandy beach, hard and firm by the beating
surf, when the wind sets from the east coast. I drew up my
light vessel on the sloping shore, that she might be safe from
the beating waves in case of a sudden storm of wind in the
night. A few yards back the land was a little elevated, and
overgrown with thickets of shrubs and low trees, consisting
chiefly of Zanthoxylon, Olea Americana, Rhamnus frangula,
Sideroxylon, Morus, Ptelea, Halesia, Querci, Myrica cerifera,
and others. These groves were but low, yet sufficiently high
to shelter me from the chilling dews; and being but a few
yards distance from my vessel, here I fixed my encampment.
A brisk wind arising from the lake, drove away the clouds of
musquitoes into the thickets. I now, with difficulty and industry, collected a sufficiency of dry wood to keep up a light
during the night, and to roast some trout which I had caught
when descending the river: their heads I stewed in the juice
of Oranges, which, with boiled rice, afforded me a wholesome
and delicious supper: I hung the remainder of my broiled fish
on the snags of some shrubs over my head. I at last, after
reconnoitring my habitation, returned, spread abroad my
skins and blanket upon the clean sands by my fire side, and
betook myself to repose.

How glorious the powerful sun, minister of the Most High
in the rule and government of this earth, leaves our hemisphere, retiring from our sight beyond the western forests! I
behold with gratitude his departing smiles, tinging the fleecy
roseate clouds, now riding far away on the eastern horizon;
behold they vanish from sight in the azure skies!

All now silent and peaceable, I suddenly fell asleep. At midnight I awake; when, raising my head erect, I find myself alone
in the wilderness of Florida, on the shores of Lake George.

Alone indeed, but under the care of the Almighty, and protected by the invisible hand of my guardian angel.

When quite awake, I started at the heavy tread of some animal; the dry limbs of trees upon the ground crack under his feet; the close shrubby thickets part and bend under him as he rushes off.

I rekindle my sleepy fire; lay in contact the exfoliated smoking brands damp with the dew of heaven.

The bright flame ascends and illuminates the ground and groves around me.

When looking up, I found my fish carried off, though I had thought them safe on the shrubs, just over my head; but their scent, carried to a great distance by the damp nocturnal breezes, I suppose were too powerful attractions to resist.

Perhaps it may not be time lost, to rest a while here, and reflect on the unexpected and unaccountable incident, which however pointed out to me an extraordinary deliverance or protection of my life, from the rapacious wolf that stole my fish from over my head.

How much easier and more eligible might it have been for him to have leaped upon my breast in the dead of sleep, and torn my throat, which would have instantly deprived me of life, and then glutted his stomach for the present with my warm blood, and dragged off my body, which would have made a feast afterwards for him and his howling associates! I say, would not this have been a wiser step, than to have made protracted and circular approaches, and then after, by chance, espying the fish over my head, with the greatest caution and silence rear up, and take them off the snags one by one, then make off with them, and that so cunningly as not to awaken me until he had fairly accomplished his purpose?

The morning being clear, I sat sail with a favourable breeze, coasting along the shores; when on a sudden the waters became transparent, and discovered the sandy bottom, and the several nations of fish, passing and repassing each other. Following this course I was led to the cape of the little river, descending from Six Mile Springs, and meandering six miles from its source through green meadows. I entered this pellucid stream, sailing over the heads of innumerable squadrons of fish, which, although many feet deep in the water, were distinctly to be seen. I passed by charming islets of flourishing trees, as Palm, Red Bay, Ash, Maple, Nyssa, and others. As I approached the distant high forest on the main, the river widened, floating fields of the green Pistia surrounded me, the rapid stream winding through them. What an alluring scene was now before me! A vast bason or little lake of crystal waters, half encircled by swelling hills, clad with Orange and odoriferous Illicium groves, the towering Magnolia, itself a grove, and the exalted Palm, as if conscious of their transcendent glories, tossed about their lofty heads, painting, with mutable shades, the green floating fields beneath. The social prattling coot enrobed in blue, and the squeeling water-hen, with wings half expanded, tripped after each other, over the watery mirrour.

I put in at an ancient landing place, which is a sloping ascent to a level grassy plain, an old Indian field. As I intended to make my most considerable collections at this place, I proceeded immediately to fix my encampment but a few yards from my safe harbour, where I securely fastened my boat to a Live Oak which overshadowed my port.

After collecting a good quantity of fire-wood, as it was about the middle of the afternoon, I resolved to reconnoitre the ground about my encampment. Having penetrated the groves next to me, I came to the open forests, consisting of exceedingly tall straight Pines (Pinus Palustris) that stood at a considerable distance from each other, through which appeared at N. W. an almost unlimited plain of grassy savannas, embellished with a chain of shallow ponds, as far as the sight could reach. Here is a species of Magnolia that associates with the Gordonia lasianthus; it is a tall tree, sixty or eighty feet in heighth; the trunk straight; its head terminating in the form of a sharp cone; the leaves are oblong, lanceolate, of a fine deep green, and glaucous beneath; the flowers are large, perfectly white and extremely fragrant; with respect to its flowers and leaves, it differs very little from the Magnolia glauca. The silvery whiteness of the leaves of this tree had a striking and pleasing effect on the sight, as it stood amidst the dark green of the Quercus dentata, Nyssa sylvatica, Nys. aquatica, Gordonia lasianthus, and many others of the same hue. The tall aspiring Gordonia lasianthus, which now stood in my view in all its splendour, is every way deserving of our admiration. Its thick foliage, of a dark green colour, is flowered over with large milk-white fragrant blossoms, on long slender elastic peduncles, at the extremities of its numerous branches, from the bosom of the leaves, and renewed every morning; and that in such incredible profusion, that the tree appears silvered over with them, and the ground beneath covered with the fallen flowers. It at the same time continually pushes forth new twigs, with young buds on them; and in the winter and spring, the third year's leaves, now partly concealed by the new and perfect ones, are gradually changing colour, from green to golden yellow, from that to a scarlet, from scarlet to crimson; and lastly to a brownish purple, and then fall to the ground. So that the Gordonia lasianthus may be said to change and renew its garments every morning throughout the year; and every day appears with unfading lustre. And moreover, after the general flowering is past, there is a thin succession of scattering blossoms to be seen, on some parts of the tree, almost every day throughout the remaining months, until the floral season returns again. Its natural situation, when growing, is on the edges of shallow ponds, or low wet grounds on rivers, in a sandy soil, the nearest to the water of any other tree, so that in droughty seasons its long serpentine roots which run near or upon the surface of the earth, may reach into the water. When the tree has arrived to the period of perfect magnitude, it is sixty, eighty, or an hundred feet high, forming a pyramidal head. The wood of old trees when sawn into plank is deservedly admired in cabinet-work or furniture; it has a cinnamon coloured ground, marbled and veined with many colours: the inner bark is used for dying a reddish or sorrel colour; it imparts this colour to wool, cotton, linen, and dressed deer skins, and is highly esteemed by tanners.

The Zamia pumila, the Erythryna corallodendrum, and the Cactus opuntia, grow here in great abundance and perfection. The first grows in the open pine forests, in tufts or clumps, a large conical strobile disclosing its large coral red fruit, which appears singularly beautiful amidst the deep green fern-like pinnated leaves.

The Erythryna corallodendrum is six or eight feet high; its prickly limbs stride and wreathe about with singular freedom, and its spikes of crimson flowers have a fine effect amidst the delicate foliage.

The Cactus opuntia is very tall, erect, and large, and strong enough to bear the weight of a man: some are seven or eight feet high: the whole plant or tree seems to be formed of great oval compressed leaves or articulations; those near the earth continually increase, magnify and indurate as the tree advances in years, and at length lose the bright green colour and glossy surface of their youth, acquiring a ligneous quality, with a whitish scabrous cortex. Every part of the plant is nearly destitute of aculea, or those fascicles of barbed bristles which are in such plenty on the common dwarf Indian Fig. The cochineal insects were feeding on the leaves. The female of this insect is very large and fleshy, covered with a fine white silk or cottony web, which feels always moist or dewy, and seems designed by nature to protect them from the violent heat of the sun. The males are very small in comparison to the females, and but very few in number: they each have two oblong pellucid wings. The large polypetalous flowers are produced on the edges of the last year's leaves, are of a fine splendid yellow, and are succeeded by very large pear-shaped fruit, of a dark livid purple when ripe: its pulp is charged with a juice of a fine transparent crimson colour, and has a cool pleasant taste, somewhat like that of a pomegranate. Soon after eating this fruit the urine becomes of the same crimson colour, which very much surprises and affrights a stranger, but is attended with no other ill consequence; on the contrary, it is esteemed wholesome, though powerfully diuretic.

On the left hand of those open forests and savannas, as we turn our eyes southward, south-west and west, we behold an endless wild desert, the upper stratum of the earth of which is a fine white sand, with small pebbles, and at some distance appears entirely covered with low trees and shrubs of various kinds, and of equal heighth, as dwarf Sweet Bay, (Laurus Borbonia) Olea Americana, Morus rubra, Myrica cerifera, Ptelea, Æsculus pavia, Quercus Ilex, Q. glandifer, Q. maritima, foliis cuneiformibus obsolete trilobis minoribus, Q. pumila, Rhamnus frangula, Halesia diptera, & tetraptera, Cassine, Ilex aquifolium, Callicarpa Johnsonia, Erythryna corallodendrum, Hibiscus spinifex, Zanthoxylon, Hopea tinctoria, Sideroxylum, with a multitude of other shrubs, many of which were new to me, and some of them admirably beautiful and singular. One of them particularly engaged my notice, which, from its fructification, I took to be a species of Cacalia. It is an evergreen shrub, about six or eight feet high; the leaves are generally somewhat cuneiform, fleshy, and of a pale whitish green, both surfaces being covered with a hoary pubescence and vesiculæ, that when pressed feels clammy, and emits an agreeable scent; the ascendent branches terminate with large tufts or corymbes of rose coloured flowers, of the same agreeable scent; these clusters of flowers, at a distance, look like a large Carnation or fringed Poppy flower (Syngenesia Polyg. Æqul. Linn.), Cacalia heterophylla, foliis cuneiformibus, carnosis, papil. viscidis.

Here is also another species of the same genus, but it does not grow quite so large; the leaves are smaller, of a yet duller green colour, and the flowers are of a pale rose; they are both valuable evergreens.

The trees and shrubs which cover these extensive wilds, are about five or six feet high, and seem to be kept down by the annual firing of the deserts, rather than the barrenness of the soil, as I saw a few large Live Oaks, Mulberry trees and Hiccories, which evidently have withstood the devouring flames. These adjoining wild plains, forests, and savannas, are situated lower than the hilly groves on the banks of the lake and river; but what should be the natural cause of it I cannot even pretend to conjecture, unless one may suppose that those high hills, which we call bluffs, on the banks of this great river and its lakes, and which support those magnificent groves and high forests, and are generally composed of shells and sand, were thrown up to their present heighth by the winds and waves, when the bed of the river was nearer the level of the present surface of the earth; but then, to rest upon such a supposition, would be admitting that the waters were heretofore in greater quantities than at this time, or that their present channels and receptacles are worn deeper into the earth.

I now directed my steps towards my encampment, in a different direction. I seated myself upon a swelling green knoll, at the head of the crystal bason. Near me, on the left, was a point or projection of an entire grove of the aromatic Illicium

Floridanum; on my right and all around behind me, was a fruitful Orange grove, with Palms and Magnolias interspersed; in front, just under my feet, was the inchanting and amazing crystal fountain, which incessantly threw up, from dark, rocky caverns below, tons of water every minute, forming a bason, capacious enough for large shallops to ride in, and a creek of four or five feet depth of water, and near twenty yards over, which meanders six miles through green meadows, pouring its limpid waters into the great Lake George, where they seem to remain pure and unmixed. About twenty yards from the upper edge of the bason, and directly opposite to the mouth or outlet of the creek, is a continual and amazing ebullition, where the waters are thrown up in such abundance and amazing force, as to jet and swell up two or three feet above the common surface: white sand and small particles of shells are thrown up with the waters, near to the top, when they diverge from the centre, subside with the expanding flood, and gently sink again, forming a large rim or funnel round about the aperture or mouth of the fountain, which is a vast perforation through a bed of rocks, the ragged points of which are projected out on every side. Thus far I know to be matter of real fact, and I have related it as near as I could conceive or express myself. But there are yet remaining scenes inexpressibly admirable and pleasing.

Behold, for instance, a vast circular expanse before you, the waters of which are so extremely clear as to be absolutely diaphanous or transparent as the ether; the margin of the bason ornamented with a great variety of fruitful and floriferous trees, shrubs, and plants, the pendant golden Orange dancing on the surface of the pellucid waters, the balmy air vibrating with the melody of the merry birds, tenants of the encircling aromatic grove.

At the same instant innumerable bands of fish are seen, some clothed in the most brilliant colours; the voracious crocodile stretched along at full length, as the great trunk of a tree in size; the devouring garfish, inimical trout, and all the varieties of gilded painted bream; the barbed catfish, dreaded sting-ray, skate, and flounder, spotted bass, sheeps head and ominous drum; all in their separate bands and communities, with free and unsuspicious intercourse performing their evolutions: there are no signs of enmity, no attempt to devour each other; the different bands seem peaceably and complaisantly to move a little aside, as it were to make room for others to pass by.

But behold yet something far more admirable, see whole armies descending into an abyss, into the mouth of the bubbling fountain: they disappear! are they gone for ever? is it real? I raise my eyes with terror and astonishment; I look down again to the fountain with anxiety, when behold them as it were emerging from the blue ether of another world, apparently at a vast distance; at their first appearance, no bigger than flies or minnows; now gradually enlarging, their brilliant colours begin to paint the fluid.

Now they come forward rapidly, and instantly emerge, with the elastic expanding column of crystalline waters, into the circular bason or funnel: see now how gently they rise, some upright, others obliquely, or seem to lie as it were on their sides, suffering themselves to be gently lifted or borne up by the expanding fluid towards the surface, sailing or floating like butterflies in the cerulean ether: then again they as gently descend, diverge and move off; when they rally, form again, and rejoin their kindred tribes.

This amazing and delightful scene, though real, appears at first but as a piece of excellent painting; there seems no medium; you imagine the picture to be within a few inches of your eyes, and that you may without the least difficulty touch any one of the fish, or put your finger upon the crocodile's eye, when it really is twenty or thirty feet under water.

And although this paradise of fish may seem to exhibit a just representation of the peaceable and happy state of nature which existed before the fall, yet in reality it is a mere representation; for the nature of the fish is the same as if they were in Lake George or the river; but here the water or element in which they live and move, is so perfectly clear and transparent, it places them all on an equality with regard to their ability to injure or escape from one another; (as all river fish of prey, or such as feed upon each other, as well as the unwieldy crocodile, take their prey by surprise; secreting themselves under covert or in ambush, until an opportunity offers, when they rush suddenly upon them:) but here is no covert, no ambush;

here the trout freely passes by the very nose of the alligator, and laughs in his face, and the bream by the trout.

But what is really surprising is, that the consciousness of each others safety, or some other latent cause, should so absolutely alter their conduct, for here is not the least attempt made to injure or disturb one another.

The sun passing below the horizon, and night approaching, I arose from my seat, and proceeding on arrived at my camp, kindled my fire, supped and reposed peaceably. Rising early, I employed the fore part of the day in collecting specimens of growing roots and seeds. In the afternoon, I left these Elysian springs and the aromatic groves, and briskly descended the pellucid little river, re-entering the great lake. The wind being gentle and fair for Mount Royal, I hoisted sail, and successfully crossing the N. west bay, about nine miles, came to at Rocky Point, the west cape or promontory, as we enter the river descending towards Mount Royal: these rocks are horizontal slabs or flat masses, rising out of the lake two or three feet above its surface, and seem an aggregate composition or concrete of sand, shells, and calcareous cement, of a dark gray or dusky colour. The stones are hard and firm enough for buildings, and serve very well for light hand mill-stones; and when calcined afford a coarse lime: they lie in vast horizontal masses upon one another, from one to two or three feet in thickness, and are easily separated and broken to any size or form, for the purpose of building. Rocky Point is an airy, cool, and delightful situation, commanding a most ample and pleasing prospect of the lake and its environs; but here being no wood, I re-embarked and sailed down a little farther to the island in the bay, where I went on shore at a magnificent grove of Magnolias and Oranges, desirous of augmenting my collections. I arose early next morning, and after ranging the groves and savannas, returned, embarked again, and descending, called at Mount Royal, where I enlarged my collections; and bidding adieu to the gentleman and lady who resided there, and who treated me with great hospitality on my ascent up the river, arrived in the evening at the lower trading house.

CHAP. VI.

O N MY RETURN from my voyage to the upper store, I understood from the trading company designed for Cuscowilla, that they had been very active in their preparations, and would be ready to set off in a few days. I therefore availed myself of the little time allowed me to secure and preserve my collections, against the arrival of the trading schooner, which was hourly expected, that every thing might be in readiness to be shipped on board her, in case she should load again and return for Savanna during my absence.

Every necessary being now in readiness, early on a fine morning we proceeded, attended by four men under the conduct of an old trader, whom Mr. M'Latche had delegated to treat with the Cowkeeper and other chiefs of Cuscowilla, on the subject of re-establishing the trade, &c. agreeable to the late treaty of St. Augustine.

For the first four or five miles we travelled westward, over a perfectly level plain, which appeared before and on each side of us, as a charming green meadow, thinly planted with low spreading Pine trees (P. palustris). The upper stratum of the earth is a fine white crystalline sand, the very upper surface of which being mixed or incorporated with the ashes of burnt vegetables, renders it of sufficient strength or fertility to clothe itself perfectly with a very great variety of grasses, herbage, and remarkably low shrubs, together with a very dwarf species of Palmetto (Corypha pumila stipit. serratis). Of the low shrubs, many were new to me and of a very pleasing appearance, particularly a species of annona (annona incana, floribus grandioribus paniculatis); this grows three, four, or five feet high, the leaves somewhat cuneiform or broad lanceolate, attenuating down to the petiole, of a pale or light green colour, covered with a pubescence or short fine down; the flowers very large, perfectly white and sweet scented, many connected together on large loose panicles or spikes; the fruit of the size and form of a small cucumber, the skin or exterior surface somewhat rimose or scabrous, containing a yellow pulp of the consistence of a hard custard, and very delicious, wholesome food. This seems a variety, if not the same that I first re-marked, growing on the Alatamaha near Fort Barrington, Charlotia, and many other places in Georgia and East Florida; and I observed here in plenty, the very dwarf decumbent an-nona, with narrow leaves, and various flowers already noticed at Alatamaha (annona pigmæa). Here is also abundance of the beautiful little dwarf kalmia ciliata, already described. The white berried empetrum, a very pretty evergreen, grows here on somewhat higher and drier knolls, in large patches or clumps, associated with olea Americana, several species of dwarf querci (oaks), vaccinium, Gordonia lasianthus, An-dromeda ferruginea, and a very curious and beautiful shrub which seems allied to the rhododendron, cassine, rhamnus frangula, Andromeda nitida, &c. which being of dark green foliage, diversify and enliven the landscape: but what appears very extraordinary, is to behold here, depressed and degraded, the glorious pyramidal magnolia grandiflora, associated amongst these vile dwarfs, and even some of them rising above it, though not five feet high; yet still showing large, beautiful and expansive white fragrant blossoms, and great heavy cones, on slender procumbent branches, some even lying on the earth; the ravages of fire keep them down, as is evident from the vast excrescent tuberous roots, covering sev-eral feet of ground, from which these slender shoots spring.

In such clumps and coverts are to be seen several kinds of birds, particularly a species of jay (pica glandaria cerulea non cristata): they are generally of an azure blue colour, have no crest or tuft of feathers on the head, nor are they so large as the great crested blue jay of Virginia, but are equally clam-orous. The towee birds (fringilla erythropthalma) are very nu-merous, as are a species of bluish gray butcher bird (lanius). Here were also lizards and snakes. The lizards were of that species called in Carolina, scorpions: they are from five to six inches in length, of a slender form; the tail in particular is very long and small; they are of a yellowish clay colour, varied with longitudinal lines or stripes of a dusky brown colour, from head to tail: they are wholly covered with very small squamæ, vibrate their tail, and dart forth and brandish their forked tongue after the manner of serpents, when they are surprised or in pursuit of their prey, which are scarabei, locustæ, musci,

and other insects; but I do not learn that their bite is poisonous, yet I have observed cats to be sick soon after eating them.
After passing over this extensive, level, hard, wet savanna, we
crossed a fine brook or rivulet; the water cool and pleasant;
its banks adorned with varieties of trees and shrubs, particularly the delicate cyrilla racemiflora, chionanthus, clethra, nyssa
sylvatica, Andromeda nitida, Andromeda formosissima: and
here were great quantities of a very large and beautiful filix
osmunda, growing in great tufts or clumps. After leaving the
rivulet, we passed over a wet, hard, level glade or down, covered with a fine short grass, with abundance of low saw palmetto, and a few shrubby pine trees, quercus nigra, quercus
sinuata or scarlet oak: then the path descends to a wet bay-
gale; the ground a hard, fine, white sand, covered with black
slush, which continues above two miles, when it gently rises
the higher sand hills, and directly after passes through a fine
grove of young long-leaved pines. The soil seemed here,
loose, brown, coarse, sandy loam, though fertile. The ascent
of the hill, ornamented with a variety and profusion of herbaceous plants and grasses, particularly amaryllis atamasco, clitoria, phlox, ipomea, convolvulus, verbena corymbosa, ruellia,
viola, &c. A magnificent grove of stately pines, succeeding to
the expansive wild plains we had a long time traversed, had a
pleasing effect, rousing the faculties of the mind, awakening
the imagination by its sublimity, and arresting every active,
inquisitive idea, by the variety of the scenery, and the solemn
symphony of the steady Western breezes, playing incessantly,
rising and falling through the thick and wavy foliage.

The pine groves passed, we immediately find ourselves on
the entrance of the expansive airy pine forests, on parallel
chains of low swelling mounds, called the Sand Hills; their
ascent so easy, as to be almost imperceptible to the progressive
traveller; yet at a distant view before us in some degree exhibit
the appearance of the mountainous swell of the ocean immediately after a tempest; but yet, as we approach them, they
insensibly disappear, and seem to be lost; and we should be
ready to conclude all to be a visionary scene, were it not for
the sparkling ponds and lakes, which at the same time gleam
through the open forests, before us and on every side, retaining them in the eye, until we come up with them. And

at last the imagination remains flattered and dubious, by their uniformity, being mostly circular or elliptical, and almost surrounded with expansive green meadows; and always a picturesque dark grove of live oak, magnolia, gordonia, and the fragrant orange, encircling a rocky shaded grotto of transparent water, on some border of the pond or lake; which, without the aid of any poetic fable, one might naturally suppose to be the sacred abode or temporary residence of the guardian spirit; but is actually the possession and retreat of a thundering absolute crocodile.

Arrived early in the evening at the Halfway pond, where we encamped and stayed all night. This lake spreads itself in a spacious meadow, beneath a chain of elevated sand hills: the sheet of water at this time was about three miles in circumference; the upper end, just under the hills, surrounded by a crescent of dark groves, which shaded a rocky grotto. Near this place was a sloping green bank, terminating by a point of flat rocks, which projected into the lake, and formed one point of the crescent that partly surrounded the vast grotto or bason of transparent waters, which is called by the traders a sinkhole, a singular kind of vortex or conduit, to the subterranean receptacles of the waters; but though the waters of these ponds, in the summer and dry seasons, evidently tend towards these sinks, yet it is so slowly and gradually, as to be almost imperceptible. There is always a meandering channel winding through the savannas or meadows, which receives the waters spread over them, by several lateral smaller branches, slowly conveying them along into the lake, and finally into the bason, and with them nations of the finny tribes.

Just by the little cape of flat rocks, we fixed our encampment, where I enjoyed a comprehensive and varied scene, the verdant meadows spread abroad, charmingly decorated by green points of grassy lawns and dark promontories of woodland, projecting into the green plains.

Behold now at still evening, the sun yet streaking the embroidered savannas, armies of fish were pursuing their pilgrimage to the grand pellucid fountain; and when here arrived, all quiet and peaceable, encircling the little cerulean hemisphere, they descend into the dark caverns of the earth; where, probably, they are separated from each other, by innumerable paths, or secret rocky avenues; and after encountering various obstacles, and beholding new and unthought of scenes of pleasure and disgust, after many days absence from the surface of the world emerge again from the dreary vaults, and appear exulting in gladness, and sporting in the transparent waters of some far distant lake.

The various kinds of fish and amphibious animals, that inhabit these inland lakes and waters, may be mentioned here, as many of them here assembled, pass and repass in the lucid grotto: first the crocodile alligator: the great brown spotted garr, accoutred in an impenetrable coat of mail: this admirable animal may be termed a cannibal amongst fish, as fish are his prey; when fully grown he is from five to six feet in length, and of proportionable thickness, of a dusky brown colour, spotted with black. The Indians make use of their sharp teeth to scratch or bleed themselves with, and their pointed scales to arm their arrows. This fish is sometimes eaten, and, to prepare them for food, they cover them whole in hot embers, where they bake them; the skin with the scales easily peels off, leaving the meat white and tender.

The mud fish is large, thick or round, and two feet in length; his meat white and tender, but soft and tastes of the mud, and is not much esteemed. The great devouring trout and catfish are in abundance; the golden bream or sunfish, the red bellied bream, the silver or white bream, the great yellow and great black or blue bream, also abound here. The last of these mentioned, is a large, beautiful, and delicious fish; when full grown they are nine inches in length, and five to six inches in breadth; the whole body is of a dull blue or indigo colour, marked with transverse lists or zones of a darker colour, scatteringly powdered with sky blue, gold and red specks; fins and tail of a dark purple or livid flesh colour; the ultimate angle of the branchiostega forming a spatula, the extreme end of which is broad and circular, terminating like the feather of the peacock's train, and having a brilliant spot or eye like it, being delicately painted with a fringed border of a fire colour.

The great yellow or particoloured bream is in form and proportion much like the forementioned, but larger, from a foot to fifteen inches in length; his back from head to tail is of a dark clay and dusky colour, with transverse dashes or blotches, of reddish dull purple, or bluish, according to different exposures to light; the sides and belly of a bright pale yellow; the belly faintly stained with vermilion red, insensibly blended with the yellow on the sides, and all garnished with fiery, blue, green, gold and silver specks on the scales; the branchiostega is of a yellowish clay or straw colour; the lower edge or border next the opening of the gills, is near a quarter of an inch in breadth, of a sea green or marine blue; the ulterior angle protends backwards to a considerable length, in the form of a spatula or feather, the extreme end dilated and circular, of a deep black or crow colour, reflecting green and blue, and bordered round with fiery red, somewhat like red sealing wax, representing a brilliant ruby on the side of the fish; the fins reddish, edged with a dove colour: it is deservedly esteemed a most excellent fish.

Here are, as well as in all the rivers, lakes, and ponds of East Florida, the great soft shelled tortoises*: they are very large when full grown, from twenty to thirty and forty pounds weight, extremely fat and delicious, but if eaten to excess, are apt to purge people not accustomed to eat their meat.

They are flat and very thin; two feet and a half in length, and eighteen inches in breadth across the back; in form, appearance, and texture, very much resembling the sea turtle: the whole back shell, except the vertebra or ridge, which is not at all prominent, and ribs on each side, is soft or cartilaginous, and easily reduced to a jelly when boiled; the anterior and posterior extremities of the back shell, appear to be embossed with round, horny warts or tubercles; the belly or nether shell is but small and semicartilaginous, except a narrow cross bar connecting it at each end with the back shell, which is hard and osseous; the head is large and clubbed, of nearly an oval form; the upper mandible, however, is protended forward, and truncated, somewhat resembling a swine's snout, at the extreme end of which the nostrils are placed; on each side of the root or base of this proboscis are the eyes, which are large; the upper beak is hooked and sharp, like a hawk's bill; the lips and corners of the mouth large,

*Testudo naso cylindracea elongato, truncato.

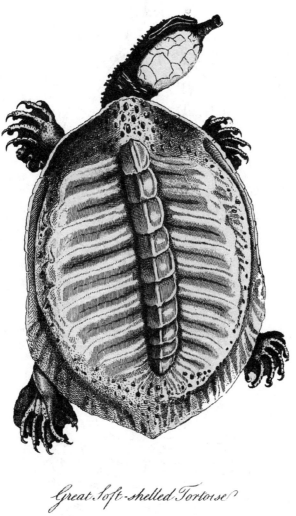

Great Soft-shelled Tortoise

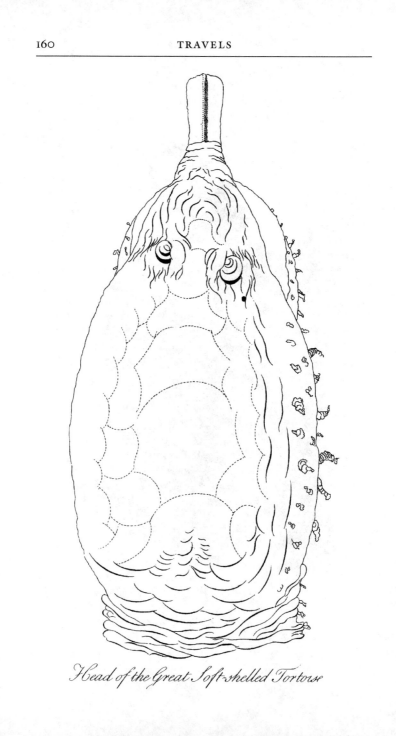

Head of the Great Soft-shelled Tortoise

tumid, wrinkled, and barbed with long, pointed warts, which he can project and contract at pleasure, which gives the creature a frightful and disagreeable countenance. They bury themselves in the slushy bottoms of rivers and ponds, under the roots of flags and other aquatic herbage, leaving a hole or aperture just sufficient for their head to play through; to such places they withdraw themselves when hungry, and there seize their prey by surprise, darting out their heads as quick as lightning, upon the unwary animal that unfortunately strolls within their reach: they can extend their neck to a surprising length, which enables them to seize young fowl swimming on the surface of the water above them, which they instantly drag down. They are seen to raise their heads above the surface of the water, in the depths of the lakes and rivers, and blow, causing a faint puffing noise, somewhat like a porpoise; probably this is for pastime, or to charge themselves with a proper supply of fresh air. They are carnivorous, feeding on any animal they can seize, particularly young ducks, frogs, and fish.

We had a large and fat one served up for our supper, which I at first apprehended we had made a very extravagant waste of, not being able to consume one half of its flesh, though excellently well cooked: my companions, however, seemed regardless, being in the midst of plenty and variety, at any time within our reach, and to be obtained with little or no trouble or fatigue on our part; when herds of deer were feeding in the green meadows before us; flocks of turkeys walking in the groves around us, and myriads of fish, of the greatest variety and delicacy, sporting in the crystalline floods before our eyes.

The vultures and ravens, crouched on the crooked limbs of the lofty pines, at a little distance from us, sharpening their beaks, in low debate, waiting to regale themselves on the offals, after our departure from camp.

At the return of the morning, by the powerful influence of light, the pulse of nature becomes more active, and the universal vibration of life insensibly and irresistibly moves the wondrous machine. How cheerful and gay all nature appears! Hark! the musical savanna cranes, ere the chirping sparrow flirts from his grassy couch, or the glorious sun gilds the tops of the pines, spread their expansive wings, leave their lofty roosts, and repair to the ample plains.

From half-way pond, we proceed Westward, through the high forests of Cuscowilla.

The appearance of the earth for five or six miles presented nearly the same scenes as heretofore.

Now the sand ridges became higher, and their bases proportionably more extensive; the savannas and ponds more expansive; the summits of the ridges more gravelly; here and there, heaps or piles of rocks, emerging out of the sand and gravel: these rocks are the same sort of concrete of sand and shells as noticed at St. Juan's and the great lake. The vegetable productions nearly the same as already mentioned.

We gently descended again over sand ridges, crossed a rapid brook, ripling over the gravelly bed, hurrying the transparent waters into a vast and beautiful lake, through a fine fruitful orange grove, which magnificently adorns the banks of the lake to a great distance on each side of the capes of the creek. This is a fine situation for a capital town. These waters are tributary to St. Juan's.

We alighted to refresh ourselves, and adjust our packs. Here are evident signs and traces of a powerful settlement of the ancients.

Sat off again, and continued travelling over a magnificent pine forest, the ridges low, but their bases extensive, with proportionable plains. The steady breezes gently and continually rising and falling, fill the high lonesome forests with an awful reverential harmony, inexpressibly sublime, and not to be enjoyed any where, but in these native wild Indian regions.

Crossing another large deep creek of St. Juan's, the country is a vast level plain, and the soil good for the distance of four or five miles, though light and sandy, producing a forest of stately pines and laurels, with some others; and a vast profusion of herbage, such as rudbeckia, helianthus, silphium, polymnia, ruellia, verbena, rhexea, convolvulus, sophora, glycine, vitia, clitorea, ipomea, urtica, salvia graveolens, viola, and many more. How cheerful and social is the rural converse of the various tribes of tree frogs, whilst they look to heaven for prolific showers! How harmonious the shrill tuneful songs of the wood thrush, and the soothing love lays of the amorous cuckoo*,

*Cuculus Caroliniensis.

seated in the cool leafy branches of the stately magnolias and shadowy elms, maples and liquidambar, together with gigantic fagus sylvatica, which shade and perfume these sequestered groves! How unexpected and enchanting the enjoyment, after traversing a burning sandy desert!

Now, again, we behold the open pine forests, and ascend the sandy hills, which continue for some miles, then gently descend again, when a level expansive savanna plain presents itself to view, which, after entering, and proceeding on, becomes wet and covered by a fine short grass, with extensive parterres of the dwarf creeping palmetto, its stipes sharply toothed or serrated, together with clumps of low shrubs, as kalmia, Andromeda, annona pygmea, myrica cerifera, empetrum, vaccinium, and others.

We now ascend a little again, and pass through a narrow pine forest; when suddenly opens to view a vastly extensive and sedgy marsh, expanding Southerly like an open fan, seemingly as boundless as the great ocean: our road crossing the head of it, about three hundred yards over; the bottom here was hard sand, a foot or more under a soft muddy surface. The traders informed me, that these vast marshes lie on the borders of a great lake, many miles in length, in magnitude exceeding Lake George, and communicating with St. Juan's by a river*; its confluence above the lower store at the Little Lake.

Observed as we passed over the sand hills, the dens of the great land tortoise, called gopher: this strange creature remains yet undescribed by historians and travellers. The first signs of this animal's existence, as we travel Southerly, are immediately after we cross the Savanna River. It is to be seen only on the high dry Sand hills. When arrived at its greatest magnitude, the upper shell is near eighteen inches in length, and ten or twelve inches in breadth; the back is very high, and the shell of a very hard bony substance, consisting of many regular compartments, united by sutures, in the manner of the other species of tortoise, and covered with thin horny plates. The nether or belly shell is large, and regularly divided transversely into five parts: these compartments are not knit

*Great Ockli-Waha.

together like the sutures of the skull, or the back shell of the tortoise, but adhere, or are connected together by a very rigid horny cartilage, which serves as hinges for him to shut up his body within his shell at pleasure. The fore part of the belly shell towards its extremity is formed somewhat like a spade, extends forward near three inches, and is about an inch and an half in breadth; its extremity is a little bifid; the posterior division of the belly shell is likewise protended backwards considerably, and is deeply bifurcated.

The legs and feet are covered with flat horny squamæ; he seems to have no clefts in them or toes, but long flattish nails or talons, somewhat in resemblance to the nails of the human fingers, five on the fore feet; the hind legs or feet appear as if truncated, or as stumps of feet, armed all round with sharp, flattish strong nails, the number undetermined or irregular; the head is of a moderate size; the upper mandible a little hooked, the edges hard and sharp; the eyes are large; the nose picked; the nostrils near together and very minute; the general colour of the animal is a light ash or clay, and at a distance, unless it is in motion, any one would disregard or overlook it as a stone or an old stump. It is astonishing what a weight one of these creatures will bear; it will easily carry any man standing on its back, on level ground. They form great and deep dens in the sand hills, casting out incredible quantities of earth. They are esteemed excellent food. The eggs are larger than a musket ball, perfectly round, and the shell hard.

After crossing over this point or branch of the marshes, we entered a noble forest, the land level, and the soil fertile, being a loose, dark brown, coarse sandy loam, on a clay or marley foundation: the forest consisted of orange groves, overtopped by grand magnolias, palms, live oaks, juglans cinerea, morus rubra, fagus sylvatica, tilia, and liquidambar; with various kinds of shrubs and herbaceous plants, particularly callicarpa, halesia, sambucus, zanthoxylon, ptelea, rhamnus frangula, rudbeckia, silphium, polymnia, indigo fera, sophora, salvia graveolens, &c. We were cheerfully received in this hospitable shade, by various tribes of birds; their sprightly songs seemed a prelude to the vicinity of human habitations. This magnificent grove was a wing of the vast forests lying upon the coast of the great and beautiful lake of Cuscowilla, at no great distance from us. Continuing eight or nine miles through this sublime forest, we entered on an open forest of lofty pines and oaks, on gently swelling sand hills, and presently saw the lake, its waters sparkling through the open groves. Near the path was a large artificial mound of earth, on a most charming, high situation, supposed to be the work of the ancient Floridans or Yamasees; with other traces of an Indian town. Here were three or four Indian habitations; the women and children saluted us with cheerfulness and complaisance. After riding near a mile farther, we arrived at Cuscowilla, near the banks: a pretty brook of water ran through the town, and entered the lake just by.

We were welcomed to the town, and conducted by the young men and maidens to the chief's house, which stood on an eminence, and was distinguished from the rest by its superior magnitude, a large flag being hoisted on a high staff at one corner. We immediately alighted: the chief, who is called the Cowkeeper, attended by several ancient men, came to us, and in a very free and sociable manner, shook our hands, or rather arms, (a form of salutation peculiar to the American Indians) saying at the same time, "You are come." We followed him to an apartment prepared for the reception of their guests.

The pipe being filled, it is handed around; after which a large bowl, with what they call "thin drink," is brought in and set down on a small low table. In this bowl is a great wooden ladle; each person takes up in it as much as he pleases, and after drinking until satisfied, returns it again into the bowl, pushing the handle towards the next person in the circle; and so it goes round.

After the usual compliments and inquiries relative to our adventures, &c. the chief trader informed the Cowkeeper, in the prefence of his council or attendants, the purport of our business, with which he expressed his satisfaction. He was then informed what the nature of my errand was, and he received me with complaisance, giving me unlimited permission to travel over the country for the purpose of collecting flowers, medicinal plants, &c. saluting me by the name of Puc Puggy, or the Flower hunter, recommending me to the friendship and protection of his people.

The next day being agreed on to hold a council and transact the business of our embassy, we acquainted the chief with our intention of making our encampment on the borders of the great ALACHUA SAVANNA, and to return at the time appointed to town, to attend the council according to agreement.

Soon after we had fixed on the time and manner of proceeding on the further settlement of the treaty, a considerable number of Indians assembled around their chief, when the conversation turned to common and familiar topics.

The chief is a tall well made man, very affable and cheerful, about sixty years of age, his eyes lively and full of fire, his countenance manly and placid, yet ferocious, or what we call savage, his nose aquiline, his dress extremely simple, but his head trimmed and ornamented in the true Creek mode. He has been a great warrior, having then attending him as slaves, many Yamasee captives, taken by himself when young. They were dressed better than he, and served and waited upon him with signs of the most abject fear. The manners and customs of the Alachuas, and most of the lower Creeks or Siminoles, appear evidently tinctured with Spanish civilization. Their religious and civil usages manifest a predilection for the Spanish customs. There are several Christians among them, many of whom wear little silver crucifixes, affixed to a wampum collar round their necks, or suspended by a small chain upon their breast. These are said to be baptized; and notwithstanding most of them speak and understand Spanish, yet they have been the most bitter and formidable Indian enemies the Spaniards ever had. The slaves, both male and female, are permitted to marry amongst them: their children are free, and considered in every respect equal to themselves; but the parents continue in a state of slavery as long as they live.

In observing these slaves, we behold at once, in their countenance and manners, the striking contrast betwixt a state of freedom and slavery. They are the tamest, the most abject creatures that we can possibly imagine: mild, peaceable, and tractable, they seem to have no will or power to act but as directed by their masters; whilst the free Indians, on the contrary, are bold, active, and clamorous. They differ as widely from each other as the bull from the ox.

The repast is now brought in, consisting of venison, stewed with bear's oil, fresh corn cakes, milk, and homony; and our drink, honey and water, very cool and agreeable. After partaking of this banquet, we took leave and departed for the great savanna.

We soon entered a level, grassy plain, interspersed with low, spreading, three-leaved Pine-trees, large patches of low shrubs, consisting of Prinos glaber, low Myrica, Kalmia glauca, Andromedas of several species, and many other shrubs, with patches of Palmetto. We continued travelling through this savanna or bay-gale, near two miles, when the land ascends a little; we then entered a hommock or dark grove, consisting of various kinds of trees, as the Magnolia grandiflora, Corypha palma, Citrus Aurantium, Quercus sempervirens, Morus rubra, Ulmus sylvatica, Tilia, Juglans cinerea, Æsculus pavia, Liquidambar, Laurus Borbonia, Hopea tinctoria, Cercis, Cornus Florida, Halesia diptera, Halesia tetraptera, Olea Americana, Callicarpa, Andromeda arborea, Sideroxylon sericium, Sid. tenax, Vitis labrusca, Hedera arborea, Hedera quinquefolia, Rhamnus volubilis, Prunus Caroliniana (pr. flor. racemosis, foliis sempervirentibus, lato-lanceolatis, acuminatis, serratis) Fagus sylvatica, Zanthoxylon clava Herculis, Acer rubrum, Acer negundo, Fraxinus excelsior, with many others already mentioned. The land still gently rising, the soil fertile, loose, loamy, and of a dark brown colour. This continues near a mile; when at once opens to view the most sudden transition from darkness to light, that can possibly be exhibited in a natural landscape.

The extensive Alachua savanna is a level green plain, above fifteen miles over, fifty miles in circumference, and scarcely a tree or bush of any kind to be seen on it. It is encircled with high, sloping hills, covered with waving forests and fragrant Orange groves, rising from an exuberantly fertile soil. The towering Magnolia grandiflora and transcendent Palm, stand conspicuous amongst them. At the same time are seen innumerable droves of cattle; the lordly bull, lowing cow, and sleek capricious heifer. The hills and groves re-echo their cheerful, social voices. Herds of sprightly deer, squadrons of the beautiful fleet Siminole horse, flocks of turkeys, civilized communities of the sonorous watchful crane, mix together, appearing

happy and contented in the enjoyment of peace, till disturbed
and affrighted by the warrior man. Behold yonder, coming
upon them through the darkened groves, sneakingly and unawares, the naked red warrior, invading the Elysian fields and
green plains of Alachua. At the terrible appearance of the
painted, fearless, uncontrouled, and free Siminole, the peaceful innocent nations are at once thrown into disorder and dis-
may. See the different tribes and bands, how they draw
towards each other! as it were deliberating upon the general
good. Suddenly they speed off with their young in the centre;
but the roebuck fears him not: here he lays himself down,
bathes and flounces in the cool flood. The red warrior, whose
plumed head flashes lightning, whoops in vain; his proud ambitious horse strains and pants; the earth glides from under
his feet, his flowing mane whistles in the wind, as he comes
up full of vain hopes. The bounding roe views his rapid approaches, rises up, lifts aloft his antlered head, erects the white
flag*, and fetching a shrill whistle, says to his fleet and free
associates, "follow;" he bounds off, and in a few minutes
distances his foe a mile; suddenly he stops, turns about, and
laughing says, "how vain! go chase meteors in the azure
plains above, or hunt butterflies in the fields about your
towns."

We approached the savanna at the south end by a narrow
isthmus of level ground, open to the light of day, and clear of
trees or bushes, and not greatly elevated above the common
level, having on our right a spacious meadow, embellished
with a little lake, one verge of which was not very distant from
us; its shore is a moderately high, circular bank, partly encircling a cove of the pond, in the form of a half moon; the
water is clear and deep, and, at the distance of some hundred
yards, was a large floating field (if I may so express myself) of
the Nymphæa nelumbo, with their golden blossoms waving
to and fro on their lofty stems. Beyond these fields of
Nymphæa were spacious plains, encompassed by dark groves,
opening to extensive Pine forests, other plains still appearing
beyond them.

This little lake and surrounding meadows would have been

*Alluding to his tail.

alone sufficient to surprise and delight the traveller; but being placed so near the great savanna, the attention is quickly drawn off, and wholly engaged in the contemplation of the unlimited, varied, and truly astonishing native wild scenes of landscape and perspective, there exhibited: how is the mind agitated and bewildered, at being thus, as it were, placed on the borders of a new world! On the first view of such an amazing display of the wisdom and power of the supreme author of nature, the mind for a moment seems suspended, and impressed with awe.

This isthmus being the common avenue or road of Indian travellers, we pitched our camp at a small distance from it, on a rising knoll near the verge of the savanna, under some spreading Live Oaks: this situation was open and airy, and gave us an unbounded prospect over the adjacent plains. Dewy evening now came on; the animating breezes, which cooled and tempered the meridian hours of this sultry season, now gently ceased; the glorious sovereign of day, calling in his bright beaming emanations, left us in his absence to the milder government and protection of the silver queen of night, attended by millions of brilliant luminaries. The thundering alligator had ended his horrifying roar; the silver plumed gannet and stork, the sage and solitary pelican of the wilderness, had already retired to their silent nocturnal habitations, in the neighbouring forests; the sonorous savanna cranes, in well disciplined squadrons, now rising from the earth, mounted aloft in spiral circles, far above the dense atmosphere of the humid plain; they again viewed the glorious sun, and the light of day still gleaming on their polished feathers, they sung their evening hymn, then in a straight line majestically descended, and alighted on the towering Palms or lofty Pines, their secure and peaceful lodging places. All around being still and silent, we repaired to rest.

Soon after sun-rise, a party of Indians on horseback appeared upon the savanna, to collect together several herds of cattle which they drove along near our camp, towards the town. One of the party came up, and informed us, the cattle belonged to the chief of Cuscowilla; that he had ordered some of the best steers of his droves to be slaughtered for a general feast for the whole town, in compliment of our arrival, and pacific negotiations.

The cattle were as large and fat as those of the rich grazing pastures of Moyomensing in Pennsylvania. The Indians drove off the lowing herds, and we soon followed them to town, in order to be at council at the appointed hour, leaving two young men of our party to protect our camp.

Upon our arrival we repaired to the public square or council-house, where the chiefs and senators were already convened; the warriors and young men assembled soon after, the business being transacted in public. As it was no more than a ratification of the late treaty of St. Augustine, with some particular commercial stipulations, with respect to the citizens of Alachua, the negotiations soon terminated to the satisfaction of both parties.

The banquet succeeded; the ribs and choicest fat pieces of the bullocks, excellently well barbecued, were brought into the apartment of the public square, constructed and appointed for feasting; bowls and kettles of stewed flesh and broth were brought in for the next course, and with it a very singular dish, the traders call it tripe soup; it is made of the belly or paunch of the beef, not overcleansed of its contents, cut and minced pretty fine, and then made into a thin soup, seasoned well with salt and aromatic herbs; but the seasoning not quite strong enough to extinguish its original savour and scent. This dish is greatly esteemed by the Indians, but is, in my judgment, the least agreeable they have amongst them.

The town of Cuscowilla, which is the capital of the Alachua tribe, contains about thirty habitations, each of which consists of two houses nearly the same size, about thirty feet in length, twelve feet wide, and about the same in height. The door is placed midway on one side or in the front. This house is divided equally, across, into two apartments, one of which is the cook room and common hall, and the other the lodging room. The other house is nearly of the same dimensions, standing about twenty yards from the dwelling house, its end fronting the door. This building is two stories high, and constructed in a different manner. It is divided transversely, as the other, but the end next the dwelling house is open on three sides, supported by posts or pillars. It has an open loft or platform, the ascent to which is by a portable stair or ladder: this is a pleasant, cool, airy situation, and here the master or chief of the family retires to repose in the hot seasons, and receives his guests or visitors. The other half of this building is closed on all sides by notched logs; the lowest or ground part is a potatoe house, and the upper story over it a granary for corn and other provisions. Their houses are constructed of a kind of frame. In the first place, strong corner pillars are fixed in the ground, with others somewhat less, ranging on a line between; these are strengthened by cross pieces of timber, and the whole with the roof is covered close with the bark of the Cypress tree. The dwelling stands near the middle of a square yard, encompassed by a low bank, formed with the earth taken out of the yard, which is always carefully swept. Their towns are clean, the inhabitants being particular in laying their filth at a proper distance from their dwellings, which undoubtedly contributes to the healthiness of their habitations.

The town stands on the most pleasant situation that could be well imagined or desired, in an inland country; upon a high swelling ridge of sand hills, within three or four hundred yards of a large and beautiful lake, the circular shore of which continually washes a sandy beach, under a moderately high sloping bank, terminated on one side by extensive forests, consisting of Orange groves, overtopped with grand Magnolias, Palms, Poplar, Tilia, Live Oaks, and others already noticed; and the opposite point of the crescent, gradually retires with hommocky projecting points, indenting the grassy marshes, and lastly terminates in infinite green plains and meadows, united with the skies and waters of the lake. Such a natural landscape, such a rural scene, is not to be imitated by the united ingenuity and labour of man. At present the ground betwixt the town and the lake is adorned by an open grove of very tall Pine trees, which standing at a considerable distance from each other, admit a delightful prospect of the sparkling waters. The lake abounds with various excellent fish and wild fowl; there are incredible numbers of the latter, especially in the winter season, when they arrive here from the north to winter.

The Indians abdicated the ancient Alachua town on the borders of the savanna, and built here, calling the new town

Cuscowilla: their reasons for removing their habitation were on account of its unhealthiness, occasioned, as they say, by the stench of the putrid fish and reptiles in the summer and autumn, driven on shore by the alligators, and the exhalations from marshes of the savanna, together with the persecution of the musquitoes.

They plant but little here about the town; only a small garden spot at each habitation, consisting of a little Corn, Beans, Tobacco, Citruls, &c. Their plantation, which supplies them with the chief of their vegetable provisions, such as Zea, Convolvulus batata, Cucurbita citrulus, Cuc. lagenaria, Cuc. pepo, Cuc. melopepo, Cuc. verrucosa, Dolichos varieties, &c. lies on the rich prolific lands bordering on the great Alachua savanna, about two miles distance. This plantation is one common enclosure, and is worked and tended by the whole community; yet every family has its particular part, according to its own appointment, marked off when planted; and this portion receives the common labour and assistance until ripe, when each family gathers and deposits in its granary its own proper share, setting apart a small gift or contribution for the public granary, which stands in the centre of the plantation.

The youth, under the supervisal of some of their ancient people, are daily stationed in their fields, and are continually whooping and hallooing, to chase away crows, jackdaws, black-birds, and such predatory animals; and the lads are armed with bows and arrows, and being trained up to it from their early youth, are sure at a mark, and in the course of the day load themselves with squirrels, birds, &c. The men in turn patrole the corn fields at night, to protect their provisions from the depredations of night rovers, as bears, raccoons, and deer; the two former being immoderately fond of young corn, when the grain is filled with a rich milk, as sweet and nourishing as cream; and the deer are as fond of the Potatoe vines.

After the feast was over, we returned to our encampment on the great savanna, towards the evening. Our companions, whom we left at the camp, were impatient for our return, having been out horse hunting in the plains and groves during our absence. They soon left us, on a visit to the town, having there some female friends, with whom they were anxious to renew their acquaintance. The Siminole girls are by no means destitute of charms to please the rougher sex: the white traders are fully sensible how greatly it is for their advantage to gain their affections and friendship in matters of trade and commerce; and if their love and esteem for each other is sincere, and upon principles of reciprocity, there are but few instances of their neglecting or betraying the interests and views of their temporary husbands; they labour and watch constantly to promote their private interests, and detect and prevent any plots or evil designs which may threaten their persons, or operate against their trade or business.

In the cool of the evening I embraced the opportunity of making a solitary excursion round the adjacent lawns. Taking my fuzee with me, I soon came up to a little clump of shrubs, upon a swelling green knoll, where I observed several large snakes entwined together. I stepped up near them; they appeared to be innocent and peaceable, having no inclination to strike at any thing, though I endeavoured to irritate them, in order to discover their disposition; nor were they anxious to escape from me. This snake is about four feet in length, and as thick as a man's wrist; the upper side of a dirty ash colour; the squamæ large, ridged, and pointed; the belly or under side of a reddish dull flesh colour; the tail part not long, but slender, like most other innocent snakes. They prey on rats, land frogs, young rabbits, birds, &c. I left them, continuing my progress and researches, delighted with the ample prospects around and over the savanna.

Stopping again at a natural shrubbery, on turning my eyes to some flowering shrubs, I observed near my feet the surprising glass snake (anguis fragilis). It seems as innocent and harmless as a worm. It is, when full grown, two feet and an half in length, and three-fourths of an inch in thickness; the abdomen or body part is remarkably short, and it seems to be all tail, which, though long, gradually attenuates to its extremity, yet not small and slender as in switch snakes. The colour and texture of the whole animal is exactly like bluish green glass, which, together with its fragility, almost persuades a stranger that it is in reality of that brittle substance: but it is only the tail part that breaks off, which it does like glass, by a very gentle stroke from a slender switch. Though it is quick and nimble in twisting about, yet it cannot run fast from one, but quickly secretes itself at the bottom of the grass or under leaves. It is a vulgar fable, that it is able to repair itself after being broken into several pieces; which pieces, common report says, by a power or faculty in the animal, voluntarily approach each other, join and heal again. The sun now low, shot the pointed shadows of the projecting promontories far on the skirts of the lucid green plain: flocks of turkeys calling upon their strolling associates, circumspectly marched onward to the groves and high forests, their nocturnal retreats. Dewy eve now arrived. I turned about and regained our encampment in good time.

The morning cool and pleasant, and the skies serene, we decamped, pursuing our progress round the Alachua savanna. Three of our companions separating from us, went a-head, and we soon lost sight of them: they again parting on different excursions, in quest of game and in search of their horses, some entered the surrounding groves and forests, others struck off into the green plains. My companion, the old trader, and myself kept together, he being the most intelligent and willing to oblige me. We coasted the green verge of the plain, under the surrounding hills, occasionally penetrating and crossing the projecting promontories, as the pathway or conveniency dictated, to avoid the waters and mud which still continued deep and boggy near the steep hills, in springy places; so that when we came to such places, we found it convenient to ascend and coast round the sides of the hills, or strike out a little into the savanna, to a moderately swelling ridge, where the ground being dry, and a delightful green turf, was pleasant travelling; but then we were under the necessity of fording creeks or rivulets, which are the conduits or drains of the shallow boggy ponds or morasses just under the hills. This range or chain of morasses continues round the south and south-west border of the savanna, and appeared to me to be fed or occasioned by the great wet bay-gale or savanna Pine lands, which lie immediately back of the high hilly forests on the great savanna, part of which we crossed in coming from Cuscowilla; which bottom is a flat, level, hard sand, lying between the sand ridge of Cuscowilla, and these eminences of the great savanna; and is a vast receptacle or reservoir of the rain waters, which being defended from the active and powerful exhalations of the meridian sun, by the shadow of the Pine trees, low shrubs, and grass, gradually filtering through the sand, drain through these hills, and present themselves in innumerable little meandering rills, at the bases of the shady heights fronting the savanna.

Our progress this day was extremely pleasant, over the green turf, having in view numerous herds of cattle and deer, and squadrons of horse, peaceably browzing on the tender, sweet grass, or strolling through the cool fragrant groves on the surrounding heights.

Beside the continued Orange groves, these heights abound with Palms, Magnolias, Red Bays, Liquidambar, and Fagus sylvatica of incredible magnitude, their trunks imitating the shafts of vast columns: we observed Cassine, Prunus, Vitis labrusca, Rhamnus volubilis, and delightful groves of Æsculus pavia, and Prunus Caroliniana, a most beautiful evergreen, decorated with its racemes of sweet, white blossoms.

Passing through a great extent of ancient Indian fields, now grown over with forests of stately trees, Orange groves, and luxuriant herbage, the old trader, my associate, informed me it was the ancient Alachua, the capital of that famous and powerful tribe, who people the hills surrounding the savanna, when, in days of old, they could assemble by thousands at ball play and other juvenile diversions and athletic exercises, over those, then happy, fields and green plains. And there is no reason to doubt of his account being true, as almost every step we take over those fertile heights, discovers remains and traces of ancient human habitations and cultivation. It is the most elevated eminence upon the savanna; and here the hills descend gradually to the savanna, by a range of gentle, grassy banks. Arriving at a swelling green knoll, at some distance in the plains, near the banks of a pond, opposite the old Alachua town, the place appointed for our meeting again together, it being near night, our associates soon after joined us, where we lodged. Early next morning we continued our tour; one division of our company directing its course across the plains to the north coast: my old companion, with myself in company, continued our former rout, coasting the savanna W. and N. W.; and by agreement we were all to meet again at night, at the E. end of the savanna.

We continued some miles crossing over, from promontory to promontory, the most enchanting green coves and vistas, scolloping and indenting the high coasts of the vast plain. Observing a company of wolves (lupus niger) under a few trees, about a quarter of a mile from shore, we rode up towards them; they observing our approach, sat on their hinder parts until we came nearly within shot of them, when they trotted off towards the forests, but stopped again and looked at us, at about two hundred yards distance: we then whooped, and made a feint to pursue them; when they separated from each other, some stretching off into the plains, and others seeking covert in the groves on shore. When we got to the trees, we observed they had been feeding on the carcase of a horse. The wolves of Florida are larger than a dog, and are perfectly black, except the females, which have a white spot on the breast; but they are not so large as the wolves of Canada and Pennsylvania, which are of a yellowish brown colour. There were a number of vultures on the trees over the carcase, who, as soon as the wolves ran off, immediately settled down upon it; they were however held in restraint and subordination by the bald eagle (falco leucocephalus).

On our route near a long projected point of the coast, we observed a large flock of turkeys: at our approach they hastened to the groves. We soon gained the promontory. On the ascending hills were vestiges of an ancient Indian town, now overshadowed with groves of the Orange, loaded with both green and ripe fruit, and embellished with their fragrant bloom, gratifying the taste, the sight, and the smell at the same instant. Leaving this delightful retreat, we soon came to the verge of the groves, when presented to view a vast verdant bay of the savanna. We discovered a herd of deer feeding at a small distance; upon the sight of us they ran off, taking shelter in the groves on the opposite point or cape of this spacious meadow. My companions being old expert hunters, quickly concerted a plan for their destruction. One of our company immediately struck off, obliquely crossing the meadow for the opposite groves, in order to intercept them, if they should continue their course up the forest, to the main; and we crossed straight over to the point, if possible to keep them in sight, and watch their motions, knowing that they would make a stand thereabouts, before they would attempt their last escape. On drawing near the point, we slackened our pace, and cautiously entered the groves; when we beheld them thoughtless and secure, flouncing in a sparkling pond, in a green meadow or cove beyond the point; some were lying down on their sides in the cool waters, whilst others were prancing like young kids; the young bucks in playsome sport, with their sharp horns hooking and spurring the others, urging them to splash the water.

I endeavoured to plead for their lives; but my old friend, though he was a sensible rational and good sort of man, would not yield to my philosophy. He requested me to mind our horses, while he made his approaches, cautiously gaining ground on them, from tree to tree, when they all suddenly sprang up and herded together: a princely buck who headed the party, whistled and bounded off; his retinue followed; but unfortunately for their chief, he led them with prodigious speed out towards the savanna very near us, and when passing by, the lucky old hunter fired and laid him prostrate upon the green turf, but a few yards from us. His affrighted followers at the instant sprang off in every direction, streaming away like meteors or phantoms, and we quickly lost sight of them. He opened his body, took out the entrails, and placed the carcase in the fork of a tree, casting his frock or hunting shirt over to protect it from the vultures and crows, who follow the hunter as regularly as his own shade.

Our companions soon arrived. We set forward again, enjoying the like scenes we had already past; observed parties of Siminole horses coursing over the plains, and frequently saw deer, turkeys, and wolves, but they knew their safety here, keeping far enough out of our reach. The wary, sharp sighted crane, circumspectly observed our progress. We saw a female of them sitting on her nest, and the male, her mate, watchfully traversing backwards and forwards, at a small distance; they suffered us to approach near them before they arose, when they spread their wings, running and tipping the ground with their feet some time, and then mounted aloft, soaring round and round over the nest. They sit upon only two eggs at a time, which are very large, long, and pointed at one end, of a pale ash colour, powdered or speckled with brown. The manner of forming their nests and sitting is very singular: choosing a tussock, and there forming a rude heap of dry grass, or such like materials, near as high as their body is from the ground, when standing upon their feet, on the summit of this they form the nest of fine soft dry grass. When they cover their eggs to hatch them, they stand over them, bearing their bodies and wings over the eggs.

We again came up to a long projecting point of the high forests, beyond which opened to view an extensive grassy cove of the savanna, several miles in circuit. We crossed straight over from this promontory to the opposite coast, and on the way were constrained to wade a mile or more through the water, though at a little distance from us it appeared as a delightful meadow, the grass growing through the water, the middle of which, however, when we came up, proved to be a large space of clear water almost deep enough to swim our horses; it being a large branch of the main creek which drains the savanna. After getting through this morass, we arrived on a delightful, level, green meadow, as usual, which continued about a mile, when we reached the firm land; and then gradually ascending, we alighted on a hard sandy beach, which exhibited evident signs of being washed by the waves of the savanna, when in the winter season it is all under water, and then presents the appearance of a large lake. The coast here is much lower than the opposite side, which we had left behind us, and rises from the meadows with a gradual sloping ascent, covered scatteringly with low spreading Live Oaks, short Palms, Zanthoxylon, Laurus Borbonia, Cassine, Sideroxylon, Quercus nigra, Q. sinuata, and others; all leaning from the bleak winds that oppress them. About one hundred yards back from this beach, the sand hills gradually rise, and the open Pine forests appear. We coasted a mile or two along the beach, then doubled a promontory of high forests, and soon after came to a swift running brook of clear water, rolling over gravel and white sand, which being brought along with it, in its descent down the steeper sandy beach, formed an easy swelling bank or bar. The waters spread greatly at this place, exhibiting a shallow glittering sheet of clear water, but just sufficient continually to cover the clear gravelly bed, and seemed to be sunk a little below the common surface of the beach. This stream, however, is soon separated into a number of rivulets, by small sandy and gravelly ridges; and the waters are finally stolen away from the sight, by a charming green meadow, but again secretly uniting under the tall grass, form a little creek, meandering through the turfy plain, marking its course by reeds and rushes, which spring up from its banks, joining the main creek that runs through the savanna, and at length delivers the water into the Great Sink. Proceeding about a mile farther, we came up to and crossed another brook larger than the former, which exhibited the like delightful appearance. We next passed over a level green lawn, a cove of the savanna, and arrived at a hilly grove. We alighted in a pleasant vista, turning our horses to graze while we amused ourselves with exploring the borders of the Great Sink. In this place a group of rocky hills almost surrounds a large bason, which is the general receptacle of the water, draining from every part of the vast savanna, by lateral conduits, winding about, and one after another joining the main creek or general conductor, which at length delivers them into this sink; where they descend by slow degrees, through rocky caverns, into the bowels of the earth, whence they are carried by secret subterraneous channels into other receptacles and basons.

We ascended a collection of eminences, covered with dark groves, which is one point of the crescent that partly encircles the sink or bason, open only on the side next the savanna, where it is joined to the great channel or general conductor of the waters. From this point over to the opposite point of the crescent (which is a similar high rocky promontory) is about one hundred yards, forming a vast semicircular cove or bason, the hills encircling it rising very steep fifty or sixty feet, high, rocky, perpendicular and bare of earth next the waters of the bason. These hills, from the top of the perpendicular, fluted, excavated walls of rock, slant off moderately up to their summits, and are covered with a very fertile, loose, black earth, which nourishes and supports a dark grove of very large trees, varieties of shrubs and herbaceous plants. These high forest trees surrounding the bason, by their great height and spread, so effectually shade the waters, that coming suddenly from the open plains, we seem at once shut up in darkness, and the waters appear black, yet are clear. When we ascend the top of the hills, we perceive the ground to be uneven, by round swelling points and corresponding hollows, overspread with gloomy shade, occasioned by the tall and spreading trees, such as live oak, morus rubra, zanthoxylon, sapindus, liquidambar, tilia, laurus borbonia, quercus dentata, juglans cinerea, and others, together with orange trees of remarkable magnitude and very fruitful. But that which is most singular and to me unaccountable, is the infundibuliform cavities, even on the top of these high hills, some twenty, thirty, and forty yards across, at their superficial rims exactly circular, as if struck with a compass, sloping gradually inwards to a point at bottom, forming an inverted cone, or like the upper wide part of a funnel: the perpendicular depth of them from the common surface is various, some descending twenty feet deep, others almost to the bed of rocks, which forms the foundation or nucleus of the hills, and indeed of the whole country of East Florida: some of them seem to be nearly filled up with earth, swept in from the common surface, but retain the same uniformity; though sometimes so close together as to be broken one into another. But as I shall have occasion to speak further of these sinks in the earth hereafter, I turn my observation to other objects in view round about me. In and about the Great Sink are to be seen incredible numbers of crocodiles, some of which are of an enormous size, and view the passenger with incredible impudence and avidity; and at this time they are so abundant, that, if permitted by them, I could walk over any part of the bason and the river upon their heads, which slowly float and turn about like knotty chuncks or logs of wood, except when they plunge or shoot forward to beat off their associates, pressing too close to each other, or taking up fish, which continually crowd in upon them from the river and creeks, draining from the savanna, especially the great trout, mudfish, catfish, and the various species of bream: the gar are rather too hard for their jaws and rough for their throats, especially here, where they have a superfluous plenty and variety of those that are every way preferable: besides, the gar being, like themselves, a warlike voracious creature, they seem to be in league or confederacy together, to enslave and devour the numerous defenceless tribes.

It is astonishing and incredible, perhaps, I may say, to relate what unspeakable numbers of fish repair to this fatal fountain or receptacle, during the latter summer season and autumn, when the powerful sun beams have evaporated the waters off the savanna; where those who are so fortunate as to effect a retreat into the conductor, and escape the devouring jaws of the fearful alligator and armed gar, descend into the earth, through the wells and cavities or vast perforations of the rocks, and from thence are conducted and carried away, by secret subterranean conduits and gloomy vaults, to other distant lakes and rivers. And it does not appear improbable, but that in some future day this vast savanna or lake of waters in the winter season will be discovered to be in a great measure filled with its finny inhabitants, who are strangers or adventurers from other lakes, ponds, and rivers, by subterraneous rivulets and communications to this rocky, dark door or outlet, whence they ascend to its surface, spread over and people the winter lake, where they breed, increase, and continue as long as it is under water, or during pleasure, for they are at all seasons to be seen ascending and descending through the rocks: but towards the autumn, when the waters have almost left the plains, they then crowd to the sink in such multitudes, as at times to be seen pressing on in great banks into the bason, being urged by pursuing bands of alligators and gar, and when entering the great bason or sink, are suddenly fallen upon by another army of the same devouring enemies, lying in wait for them. Thousands are driven on shore, where they perish and rot in banks, which was evident at the time I was there, the stench being intolerable, although then early in the summer. There are three great doors or vent holes through the rocks in the sink, two near the centre and the other one near the rim, much higher up than the other two, which was conspicuous through the clear water. The beds of rocks lay in horizontal thick strata or laminæ, one over the other, where the sink holes or outlets are. These rocks are perforated by perpendicular wells or tubes, four, five, and six feet in diameter, exactly circular as the tube of a cannon or walled well; many of these are broken into one another, forming a great ragged orifice, appearing fluted by alternate jambs and semi-circular perpendicular niches or excavations.

Having satisfied my curiosity in viewing this extraordinary place and very wonderful work of nature, we repaired to our resting place, where we found our horses and mounted again; one of the company parting from us for the buck that we had shot and left in the fork of the tree. My friend, the old trader, led the shortest way across the plain, after repassing the wet morass which had almost swum our horses in the morning. At evening we arrived at the place of our destination, where our associates soon after rejoined us with some Indians, who were merry agreeable guests as long as they staid. They were in full dress and painted; but before dark they mounted their horses, which were of the true Siminole breed, set spurs to them, uttering all at once a shrill whoop, and went off for Cuscowilla.

Though the horned cattle and horses bred in these meadows are large, sleek, sprightly, and as fat as can be in general, yet they are subject to mortal diseases. I observed several of them dreadfully mortified, their thighs and haunches ulcerated, raw, and bleeding, which, like a mortification or slow cancer, at length puts an end to their miserable existence. The traders and Indians call this disease the water-rot or scald, and say it is occasioned by the warm waters of the savanna, during the heats of summer and autumn, when these creatures wade deep to feed on the water-grass, which they are immoderately fond of; whereas the cattle which only feed and range in the high forests and pine savannas are clear of this disorder. A sacrifice to intemperance and luxury.

We had heavy rains during the night, and though very warm, yet no thunder and very little wind. It cleared away in the morning, and the day was very pleasant. Sat off for the East end of the savanna, collecting by the way and driving before us parties of horses, the property of the traders; and next morning sat off on our return to the lower store on St. John's, coasting the savanna yet a few miles, in expectation of finding the remainder of their horses, though disappointed.

We at last bid adieu to the magnificent plains of Alachua, entered the pine forests, and soon fell into the old Spanish highway, from St. Augustine across the isthmus of Florida, to St. Mark's in the bay of Apalache. Its course and distance from

E. to W. is, from St. Augustine to Fort Picolata on the river St. Juan, twenty-seven miles; thence across the river to the Poopoa Fort, three miles; thence to the Alachua Savanna, forty-five miles; thence to Talahasochte on the river Little St. Juan, seventy-five miles; thence down this river to St. Mark's, thirty miles: the whole distance from St. Augustine to St. Mark's, one hundred and eighty miles. But this road having been unfrequented for many years past, since the Creeks subdued the remnant tribes of the ancient Floridans, and drove the Spaniards from their settlements in East Florida into St. Augustine, which effectually cut off their communication between that garrison and St. Mark's; this ancient highway is grown up in many places with trees and shrubs; but yet has left so deep a track on the surface of the earth, that it may be traced for ages yet to come.

Leaving the highway on our left hand, we ascended a sandy ridge, thinly planted by nature with stately pines and oaks, of the latter genus particularly q. sinuata, f. flammula, q. nigra, q. rubra. Passed by an Indian village situated on this high airy sand ridge, consisting of four or five habitations; none of the people were at home, they were out at their hunting camps; we observed plenty of corn in their cribs. Following a hunting path eight or nine miles, through a vast pine forest and grassy savanna, well timbered, the ground covered with a charming carpet of various flowering plants, came to a large creek of excellent water, and here we found the encampment of the Indians, the inhabitants of the little town we had passed; we saw their women and children, the men being out hunting. The women presented themselves to our view as we came up, at the door of their tents, veiled in their mantle, modestly showing their faces, when we saluted them. Towards the evening we fell into the old trading path, and before night came to camp at the Halfway Pond. Next morning, after collecting together the horses, some of which had strolled away at a great distance, we pursued our journey, and in the evening arrived at the trading house on St. Juan's, from a successful and pleasant tour.

On my return to the store on St. Juan's the trading schooner was there; but as she was not to return to Georgia until the autumn, I found I had time to pursue my travels in

Florida, and might at leisure plan my excursions to collect seeds and roots in boxes, &c.

At this time the talks (or messages between the Indians and white people) were perfectly peaceable and friendly, both with the Lower Creeks and the Nation or Upper Creeks. Parties of Indians were coming in every day with their hunts; indeed the Muscogulges or Upper Creeks very seldom disturb us. Bad talks from the Nation are always very serious affairs, and to the utmost degree alarming to the white inhabitants.

The Muscogulges are under a more strict government or regular civilization than the Indians in general. They lie near their potent and declared enemy, the Chactaws. Their country having a vast frontier, naturally accessible and open to the incursions of their enemies on all sides, they find themselves under the necessity of associating in large populous towns, and these towns as near together as convenient, that they may be enabled to succour and defend one another in case of sudden invasion. This consequently occasions deer and bear to be scarce and difficult to procure, which obliges them to be vigilant and industrious; this naturally begets care and serious attention, which we may suppose in some degree forms their natural disposition and manners, and gives them that air of dignified gravity, so strikingly characteristic in their aged people, and that steadiness, just and cheerful reverence in the middle aged and youth, which sits so easy upon them, and appears so natural. For, however strange it may appear to us, the same moral duties which with us form the amiable, virtuous character, so difficult to maintain, there, without compulsion or visible restraint, operates like instinct, with a surprising harmony and natural ease, insomuch that it seems impossible for them to act out of the common high road to virtue.

We will now take a view of the Lower Creeks or Siminoles, and the natural disposition which characterises this people; when, from the striking contrast, the philosopher may approve or disapprove, as he may think proper, from the judgment and opinion given by different men.

The Siminoles are but a weak people with respect to numbers. All of them, I suppose, would not be sufficient to people one of the towns in the Muscogulge; for instance, the Uches on the main branch of the Apalachucla river, which alone contains near two thousand inhabitants. Yet this handful of people possesses a vast territory; all East Florida and the greatest part of West Florida, which being naturally cut and divided into thousands of islets, knolls, and eminences, by the innumerable rivers, lakes, swamps, vast savannas and ponds, form so many secure retreats and temporary dwelling places, that effectually guard them from any sudden invasions or attacks from their enemies; and being such a swampy, hommocky country, furnishes such a plenty and variety of supplies for the nourishment of varieties of animals, that I can venture to assert, that no part of the globe so abounds with wild game or creatures fit for the food of man.

Thus they enjoy a superabundance of the necessaries and conveniences of life, with the security of person and property, the two great concerns of mankind. The hides of deer, bears, tigers and wolves, together with honey, wax and other productions of the country, purchase their clothing, equipage, and domestic utensils from the whites. They seem to be free from want or desires. No cruel enemy to dread; nothing to give them disquietude, but the gradual encroachments of the white people. Thus contented and undisturbed, they appear as blithe and free as the birds of the air, and like them as volatile and active, tuneful and vociferous. The visage, action, and deportment of the Siminoles, form the most striking picture of happiness in this life; joy, contentment, love, and friendship, without guile or affectation, seem inherent in them, or predominant in their vital principle, for it leaves them but with the last breath of life. It even seems imposing a constraint upon their ancient chiefs and senators, to maintain a necessary decorum and solemnity, in their public councils; not even the debility and decrepitude of extreme old age, is sufficient to erase from their visages, this youthful, joyous simplicity; but like the gray eve of a serene and calm day, a gladdening, cheering blush remains on the Western horizon after the sun is set.

I doubt not but some of my countrymen who may read these accounts of the Indians, which I have endeavoured to relate according to truth, at least as they appeared to me, will charge me with partiality or prejudice in their favour.

I will, however, now endeavour to exhibit their vices, immoralities, and imperfections, from my own observations and knowledge, as well as accounts from the white traders, who reside amongst them.

The Indians make war against, kill, and destroy their own species, and their motives spring from the same erroneous source as they do in all other nations of mankind; that is, the ambition of exhibiting to their fellows a superior character of personal and national valour, and thereby immortalizing themselves, by transmitting their names with honour and lustre to posterity; or revenge of their enemy, for public or personal insults; or, lastly, to extend the borders and boundaries of their territories. But I cannot find, upon the strictest inquiry, that their bloody contests at this day are marked with deeper stains of inhumanity or savage cruelty, than what may be observed amongst the most civilized nations: they do indeed scalp their slain enemy, but they do not kill the females or children of either sex: the most ancient traders, both in the Lower and Upper Creeks, assured me they never saw an instance of either burning or tormenting their male captives; though it is said they used to do it formerly. I saw in every town in the Nation and Siminoles that I visited, more or less male captives, some extremely aged, who were free and in as good circumstances as their masters; and all slaves have their freedom when they marry, which is permitted and encouraged, when they and their offspring are every way upon an equality with their conquerors. They are given to adultery and fornication, but, I suppose, in no greater excess than other nations of men. They punish the delinquents, male and female, equally alike, by taking off their ears. This is the punishment for adultery. Infamy and disgrace is supposed to be a sufficient punishment for fornication, in either sex.

They are fond of games and gambling, and amuse themselves like children, in relating extravagant stories, to cause surprise and mirth.

They wage eternal war against deer and bear, to procure food and clothing, and other necessaries and conveniences; which is indeed carried to an unreasonable and perhaps criminal excess, since the white people have dazzled their senses with foreign superfluities.

CHAP. VII.

O N MY RETURN to the trading house, from my journey to the great savanna, I found the trading company for Little St. Juan's preparing for that post.

My mind yet elate with the various scenes of rural nature, which as a lively animated picture had been presented to my view; the deeply engraven impression, a pleasing flattering contemplation, gave strength and agility to my steps, anxiously to press forward to the delightful fields and groves of Apalatche.

The trading company for Talahasochte being now in readiness to proceed for that quarter, under the direction of our chief trader, in the cool of the morning we sat off, each of us having a good horse to ride, besides having in our caravan several pack horses laden with provisions, camp equipage, and other necessaries. A young man from St. Augustine, in the service of the governor of East Florida, accompanied us, commissioned to purchase of the Indians and traders, some Siminole horses. They are the most beautiful and sprightly species of that noble creature, perhaps any where to be seen; but are of a small breed, and as delicately formed as the American roe buck. A horse in the Creek or Muscogulge tongue is echoclucco, that is the great deer (echo is a deer, and clucco is big). The Siminole horses are said to descend originally from the Andalusian breed, brought here by the Spaniards when they first established the colony of East Florida. From the forehead to their nose is a little arched or aquiline, and so are the fine Chactaw horses among the Upper Creeks, which are said to have been brought thither from New-Mexico across Missisippi, by those nations of Indians who emigrated from the West, beyond the river. These horses are every way like the Siminole breed, only larger, and perhaps not so lively and capricious. It is a matter of conjecture and inquiry, whether or not the different soil and situation of the country may have contributed in some measure, in forming and establishing the difference in size and other qualities betwixt them. I have observed the horses and other animals in the high hilly country of Carolina, Georgia, Virginia, and all along our shores, are of a much larger and stronger make, than those which are bred in the flat country next the sea coast. A buck-skin of the Upper Creeks and Cherokees will weigh twice as heavy as those of the Siminoles or Lower Creeks, and those bred in the low flat country of Carolina.

Our first day's journey was along the Alachua roads, twenty-five miles to the Half-way Pond, where we encamped: the musquitoes were excessively troublesome the whole night:

Decamped early next morning, still pursuing the road to Alachua, until within a few miles of Cuscowilla; when the road dividing, one for the town, and the other for the great savanna, here our company separated. One party chose to pass through the town, having some concerns there. I kept with the party that went through the savanna, it being the best road, leading over a part of the savanna; when entering the groves on its borders, we travelled several miles over these fertile eminences, and delightful shady fragrant forests; then again entered upon the savanna, and crossed a charming extensive green cove or bay of it, covered with a vivid green grassy turf, when we again ascended the woodland hills, through fruitful orange groves, and under shadowy palms and magnolias. Now the pine forests opened to view. We left the magnificent savanna and its delightful groves, passing through a level, open, airy pine forest, the stately trees scatteringly planted by nature, arising straight and erect from the green carpet, embellished with various grasses and flowering plants; then gradually ascending the sand hills, we soon came into the trading path to Talahasochte; which is generally, excepting a few deviations, the old Spanish highway to St. Mark's. At about five miles distance beyond the great savanna, we came to camp late in the evening, under a little grove of live oaks, just by a group of shelly rocks, on the banks of a beautiful little lake, partly environed by meadows. The rocks, as usual in these regions, partly encircle a spacious sink or grotto, which communicates with the waters of the lake: the waters of the grotto are perfectly transparent, cool, and pleasant, and well replenished with fish. Soon after our arrival here, our companions who passed through Cuscowilla joined us. A brisk cool wind during the night kept the persecuting musquitoes at a distance.

The morning pleasant, we decamped early: proceeding on, rising gently for several miles, over sandy, gravelly ridges, we found ourselves in an elevated, high, open, airy region, somewhat rocky, on the backs of the ridges, which presented to view, on every side, the most dreary, solitary, desert waste I had ever beheld; groups of bare rocks emerging out of the naked gravel and drifts of white sand; the grass thinly scattered and but few trees; the pines, oaks, olives, and sideroxylons, poor, mishapen, and tattered; scarce an animal to be seen, or noise heard, save the symphony of the Western breeze, through the bristly pine leaves, or solitary sand-cricket's screech, or at best the more social converse of the frogs, in solemn chorus with the swift breezes, brought from distant fens and forests. Next we joyfully entered the borders of the level pine forest and savannas, which continued for many miles, never out of sight of little lakes or ponds, environed with illumined meadows, the clear waters sparkling through the tall pines.

Having a good spirited horse under me, I generally kept ahead of my companions, which I often chose to do, as circumstances offered or invited, for the sake of retirement and observation.

The high road being here open and spacious, at a good distance before me, I observed a large hawk on the ground in the middle of the road: he seemed to be in distress, endeavouring to rise; when, coming up near him, I found him closely bound up by a very long coach-whip snake, that had wreathed himself several times round the hawk's body, who had but one of his wings at liberty: beholding their struggles a while, I alighted off my horse with an intention of parting them; when, on coming up, they mutually agreed to separate themselves, each one seeking his own safety, probably considering me as their common enemy. The bird rose aloft and fled away as soon as he recovered his liberty, and the snake as eagerly made off. I soon overtook him, but could not perceive that he was wounded.

I suppose the hawk had been the aggressor, and fell upon the snake with an intention of making a prey of him; and that the snake dexterously and luckily threw himself in coils round his body, and girded him so close as to save himself from destruction.

The coach-whip snake is a beautiful creature. When full grown it is six and seven feet in length, and the largest part of its body not so thick as a cane or common walking stick; its head not larger than the end of a man's finger; its neck is very slender, and from the abdomen tapers away in the manner of a small switch or coach-whip; the top of the head and neck, for three or four inches, is as black and shining as a raven; the throat and belly as white as snow; and the upper side of the body of a chocolate colour, excepting the tail part, almost from the abdomen to the extremity, which is black. It may be proper to observe, however, that it varies in respect to the colour of the body; some I have seen almost white or cream colour, others of a pale chocolate or clay colour, but in all, the head and neck is black, and the tail dark brown or black. It is extremely swift, seeming almost to fly over the surface of the ground; and that which is very singular, it can run swiftly on its tail part only, carrying the head and body upright. One very fine one accompanied me along the road side, at a little distance, raising himself erect, now and then looking me in the face, although I proceeded on a good round trot on purpose to observe how fast they could proceed in that position. His object seemed mere curiosity or observation; with respect to venom it is as innocent as a worm, and seems to be familiar with man. It appears to be a particular inhabitant of East Florida, though I have seen some in the maritime parts of Carolina and Georgia, but in these regions it is neither so large nor beautiful.

We ascended again, passing over sand ridges of gentle elevation, savannas and open Pine forests. Masses or groups of rocks presented to view on every side, as before mentioned; and with difficulty we escaped the circular infundibuliform cavities or sinks in the surface of the earth. Generally a group of rocks, shaded by Palms, Live Oaks, and Magnolias, is situated on their limb: some are partly filled up with earth, whilst others, and the greater number of them, are partly filled with transparent cool water, which discovers the well or perforation through the rocks in the centre. This day being remarkably sultry, we came to camp early, having chosen our situation under some stately Pines, near the verge of a spacious savanna.

After some refreshment, our hunters went out into the forest, and returned towards evening. Amongst other game, they brought with them a savanna crane* which they shot in the adjoining meadows. This stately bird is about six feet in length from the toes to the extremity of the beak when extended, and the wings expand eight or nine feet; it is above five feet high when standing erect; the tail is remarkably short, but the flag or pendant feathers which fall down off the rump on each side, are very long and sharp pointed, of a delicate texture, and silky softness; the beak is very long, straight and sharp pointed; the crown of the head bare of feathers, of a reddish rose colour, thinly barbed with short, stiff, black hair; the legs and thighs are very long, and bare of feathers a great space above the knees: the plumage of this bird is generally of a pale ash colour, with shades or clouds of pale brown and sky blue, the brown prevails on the shoulders and back; the barrels of the prime quill-feathers are long and of a large diameter, leaving a large cavity when extracted from the wing: all the bones of this bird have a thin shell, and consequently a large cavity or medullary receptacle. When these birds move their wings in flight, their strokes are slow, moderate, and regular; and even, when at a considerable distance or high above us, we plainly hear the quill-feathers, their shafts and webs upon one another creak as the joints or working of a vessel in a tempestuous sea.

We had this fowl dressed for supper, and it made excellent soup; nevertheless, as long as I can get any other necessary food, I shall prefer their seraphic music in the ethereal skies, and my eyes and understanding gratified in observing their economy and social communities, in the expansive green savannas of Florida.

Next morning we arose early, and proceeding, gradually descended again, and continued many miles along a flat, level country, over delightful green savannas, decorated with hommocks or islets of dark groves, consisting of Magnolia grandiflora, Morus tilia, Zanthoxylon, Laurus Borbonia, Sideroxylon, Quercus sempervirens, Halesia diptera, Calli-

*Grus p.

carpa, Corypha palma, &c. There are always groups of whitish testaceous rocks and sinks where these hommocks are. We next crossed a wet savanna, which is the beginning of a region still lower than that we had traversed; here we crossed a rapid rivulet of exceeding cool, pleasant water, where we halted to refresh ourselves. But it must be remarked here, that this rivulet, though lively and rapid at this time, is not a permanent stream, but was formed by a heavy rain that fell the day before, as was apparent from its bed; besides it is at best but a jet of mere phantom of a brook, as the land around is rocky and hollow, abounding with wells and cavities. Soon after leaving the brook, we passed off to the left hand, along the verge of an extensive savanna, and meadows many miles in circumference, edged on one border with detached groves and pompous Palms, and embellished with a beautiful sparkling lake; its verges decorated with tall waving grass and floriferous plants; the pellucid waters gently rolling on to a dark shaded grotto, just under a semicircular swelling turfy ascent or bank, skirted by groves of Magnolias, Oaks, Laurels, and Palms. In these expansive and delightful meadows were feeding and roving troops of the fleet Siminole horse. We halted a while at this grotto; and, after refreshing ourselves, we mounted horse and proceeded across a charming lawn, part of the savanna, entering on it through a dark grove. In this extensive lawn were several troops of horse, and our company had the satisfaction of observing several belonging to themselves. One occurrence remarkable here, was a troop of horse under the controul and care of a single black dog, which seemed to differ in no respect from the wolf of Florida, except his being able to bark as the common dog. He was very careful and industrious in keeping them together; and if any one strolled from the rest at too great a distance, the dog would spring up, head the horse, and bring him back to the company. The proprietor of these horses is an Indian in Talahasochte, about ten miles distance from this place, who, out of humour and experiment, trained his dog up from a puppy to this business: he follows his master's horses only, keeping them in a separate company where they range; and when he is hungry or wants to see his master, in the evening he returns to town, but never stays at home a night.

The region we had journeyed through, since we decamped this morning, is of a far better soil and quality than we had yet seen since we left Alachua; generally a dark grayish, and sometimes brown or black loam, on a foundation of whitish marl, chalk, and testaceous limestone rocks, and ridges of a loose, coarse, reddish sand, producing stately Pines in the plains, and Live Oak, Mulberry, Magnolia, Palm, Zanthoxylon, &c. in the hommocks, and also in great plenty the perennial Indigo; it grows here five, six, and seven feet high, and as thick together as if it had been planted and cultivated. The higher ridges of hills afford great quantities of a species of iron ore, of that kind found in New-Jersey and Pennsylvania, and there called bog ore; it appears on the surface of the ground in large detached masses and smaller fragments; it is ponderous and seemed rich of that most useful metal; but one property remarkable in these ferruginious stones is, that they appear to be blistered, somewhat resembling cinders, or as if they had suffered a violent action of fire.

Leaving the charming savanna and fields of Capola, we passed several miles through delightful plains and meadows, little differing from the environs of Capola, diversified with rocky islets or hommocks of dark woodland.

We next entered a vast forest of the most stately Pine trees that can be imagined, planted by nature at a moderate distance, on a level, grassy plain, enamelled with a variety of flowering shrubs, viz. Viola, Ruella infundibuliforma, Amaryllis atamasco, Mimosa sensitiva, Mimosa intsia and many others new to me. This sublime forest continued five or six miles, when we came to dark groves of Oaks, Magnolias, Red bays, Mulberries, &c. through which proceeding near a mile, we entered open fields, and arrived at the town of Talahasochte, on the banks of Little St. Juan.

The river Little St. Juan may, with singular propriety, be termed the pellucid river. The waters are the clearest and purest of any river I ever saw, transmitting distinctly the natural form and appearance of the objects moving in the transparent floods, or reposing on the silvery bed, with the finny inhabitants sporting in its gently flowing stream.

The river at the town is about two hundred yards over, and fifteen or twenty feet in depth. The great swamp and lake

Oaquaphenogaw is said to be its source, which is about one hundred miles by land North of this place; which would give the river a course of near two hundred miles from its source to the sea, to follow its meanders; as in general our rivers, that run any considerable distance through the country to the sea, by their windings and roving about to find a passage through the ridges and heights, at least double their distance.

The Indians and traders say that this river has no branches or collateral brooks or rivers tributary to it, but that it is fed or augmented by great springs which break out through the banks. From the accounts given by them, and my own observations on the country round about, it seems a probable assertion; for there was not a creek or rivulet to be seen, running on the surface of the ground, from the great Alachua Savanna to this river, a distance of above seventy miles; yet, perhaps, no part of the earth affords a greater plenty of pure, salubrious waters. The unparalleled transparency of these waters furnishes an argument for such a conjecture, that amounts at least to a probability, were it not confirmed by ocular demonstration; for in all the flat countries of Carolina and Florida, except this isthmus, the waters of the rivers are, in some degree, turgid, and have a dark hue, owing to the annual firing of the forests and plains; and afterwards the heavy rains washing the light surface of the burnt earth into rivulets, which rivulets running rapidly over the surface of the earth, flow into the rivers, and tinge the waters the colour of lye or beer, almost down to the tide near the sea coast. But here behold how different the appearance, and how manifest the cause! for although the surface of the ground produces the same vegetable substances, the soil the same, and suffers in like manner a general conflagration, and the rains, in impetuous showers, as liberally descend upon the parched surface of the ground; yet the earth being so hollow and porous, these superabundant waters cannot constitute a rivulet or brook, to continue any distance on its surface, before they are arrested in their course and swallowed up: thence descending, they are filtered through the sands and other strata of earth, to the horizontal beds of porous rocks, which, being composed of thin separable laminæ, lying generally in obliquely horizontal directions over each other, admit these waters to pass on by gradual but constant percolation. Thus collecting and associating, they augment and form little rills, brooks, and even subterraneous rivers, which wander in darkness beneath the surface of the earth, by innumerable doublings, windings, and secret labyrinths; no doubt in some places forming vast reservoirs and subterranean lakes, inhabited by multitudes of fish and aquatic animals: and possibly, when collected into large rapid brooks, meeting irresistible obstructions in their course, they suddenly break through these perforated fluted rocks, in high perpendicular jets, nearly to their former level, flooding large districts of land. Thus by means of those subterranean courses, the waters are purified and finally carried to the banks of great rivers, where they emerge and present themselves to open daylight, with their troops of finny inhabitants, in those surprising vast fountains near the banks of this river; and likewise on and near the shores of Great St. Juan, on the east coast of the isthmus, some of which I have already given an account of.

On our arrival at Talahasochte, in the evening we repaired to the trading house formerly belonging to our chief, where were a family of Indians, who immediately and complaisantly moved out to accommodate us. The White King with most of the male inhabitants were out hunting or tending their Corn plantations.

The town is delightfully situated on the elevated east banks of the river, the ground level to near the river, when it descends suddenly to the water; I suppose the perpendicular elevation of the ground may be twenty or thirty feet. There are near thirty habitations constructed after the mode of Cuscowilla; but here is a more spacious and neat council-house.

These Indians have large handsome canoes, which they form out of the trunks of Cypress trees (Cupressus disticha), some of them commodious enough to accommodate twenty or thirty warriors. In these large canoes they descend the river on trading and hunting expeditions to the sea coast, neighbouring islands and keys, quite to the point of Florida, and some⁺imes cross the gulph, extending their navigations to the Bahama islands and even to Cuba: a crew of these adventurers had just arrived, having returned from Cuba but a few days before our arrival, with a cargo of spirituous liquors, Coffee, Sugar, and Tobacco. One of them politely presented me with a choice piece of Tobacco, which he told me he had received from the governor of Cuba.

They deal in the way of barter, carrying with them deer skins, furs, dry fish, bees-wax, honey, bear's oil, and some other articles. They say the Spaniards receive them very friend-lily, and treat them with the best spirituous liquors.

The Spaniards of Cuba likewise trade here or at St. Mark's, and other sea ports on the west coast of the isthmus, in small sloops; particularly at the bay of Calos, where are excellent fishing banks and grounds; not far from which is a consider-able town of the Siminoles, where they take great quantities of fish, which they salt and cure on shore, and barter with the Indians and traders for skins, furs, &c. and return with their cargoes to Cuba.

The trader of the town of Talahasochte informed me, that he had, when trading in that town, large supplies of goods from these Spanish trading vessels, suitable for that trade, and some very essential articles, on more advantageous terms than he could purchase at Indian stores either in Georgia or St. Augustine.

Towards the evening after the sultry heats were past, a young man of our company, having previously procured the loan of a canoe from an Indian, proposed to me a fishing excursion for trout with the bob. We set off down the river, and before we had passed two miles, caught enough for our household: he was an excellent hand at this kind of diversion: some of the fish were so large and strong in their element, as to shake his arms stoutly and drag us with the canoe over the floods before we got them in. It is in the eddy coves, under the points and turnings of the river, where the surface of the waters for some acres is covered with the leaves of the Nym-phea, Pistia, and other amphibious herbs and grass, where the haunts and retreats of this famous fish are, as well as others of various tribes.

Observing a fishing canoe of Indians turning a point below and coming towards us, who hailed us, we waited their com-ing up; they were cheerful merry fellows, and insisted on our accepting of part of their fish; they having a greater quantity and variety, especially of the bream, my favourite fish, we ex-changed some of our trout with them.

Our chief being engaged with the chiefs of the town in commercial concerns, and others of our company out in the forests with the Indians, hunting up horses belonging to the trading company; the young interpreter, my companion, who was obliging to me, and whom our chief previously recommended to me as an associate, proposed to me another little voyage down the river. This was agreeable to me, being desirous of increasing my observations during our continuance at Talahasochte; as when the White King should return to town (which was expected every hour) we intended after audience and treaty to leave them and encamp in the forests, about fifteen miles distance and nearer the range of their horses.

Having supplied ourselves with ammunition and provision, we set off in the cool of the morning, and descended pleasantly, riding on the crystal flood, which flows down with an easy, gentle, yet active current, rolling over its silvery bed. How abundantly are the waters replenished with inhabitants! the stream almost as transparent as the air we breathe; there is nothing done in secret except on its green flowery verges, where nature, at the command of the Supreme Creator, hath spread a mantle, as a covering and retreat at suitable and convenient times, but by no means a secure refuge from the voracious enemy and pursuer.

Behold the watery nations, in numerous bands roving to and fro, amidst each other; here they seem all at peace; though, incredible to relate! but a few yards off, near the verge of the green mantled shore there is eternal war, or rather slaughter. Near the banks the waters become turbid, from substances gradually diverging from each side of the swift channel, and collections of opaque particles whirled to shore by the eddies, which afford a kind of nursery for young fry, and its slimy bed is a prolific nidus for generating and rearing of infinite tribes and swarms of amphibious insects, which are the food of young fish, who in their turn become a prey to the older. Yet when those different tribes of fish are in the transparent channel, their very nature seems absolutely changed; for here is neither desire to destroy nor persecute, but all seems peace and friendship. Do they agree on a truce, a suspension of hostilities? or by some secret divine influence, is desire taken away? or they are otherwise rendered incapable of pursuing each other to destruction?

About noon we approached the admirable Manate Spring, three or four miles down the river. This charming nymphæum is the product of primitive nature, not to be imitated, much less equalled, by the united effort of human power and ingenuity! As we approach it by water, the mind of the inquiring traveller is previously entertained, and gradually led on to greater discovery; first by a view of the sublime dark grove, lifted up on shore, by a range or curved chain of hills, at a small distance from the lively green verge of the river, on the east banks; as we gently descend floating fields of the Nymphæa nelumbo, intersected with vistas of the yellow green Pistia stratiotes, which cover a bay or cove of the river opposite the circular woodland hills.

It is amazing and almost incredible, what troops and bands of fish and other watery inhabitants are now in sight, all peaceable; and in what variety of gay colours and forms, continually ascending and descending, roving and figuring amongst one another, yet every tribe associating separately. We now ascended the crystal stream; the current swift: we entered the grand fountain, the expansive circular bason, the source of which arises from under the bases of the high woodland hills, nearly half encircling it. The ebullition is astonishing, and continual, though its greatest force of fury intermits, regularly, for the space of thirty seconds of time: the waters appear of a lucid sea green colour, in some measure owing to the reflection of the leaves above: the ebullition is perpendicular upwards, from a vast ragged orifice through a bed of rocks, a great depth below the common surface of the bason, throwing up small particles or pieces of white shells, which subside with the waters at the moment of intermission, gently settling down round about the orifice, forming a vast funnel. At those moments, when the waters rush upwards, the surface of the bason immediately over the orifice is greatly swollen or raised a considerable height; and then it is impossible to keep the boat or any other floating vessel over the fountain; but the ebullition quickly subsides; yet, before the surface becomes quite even, the fountain vomits up the waters again, and so on perpetually. The bason is generally circular, about fifty yards over; and the perpetual stream from it into the river is twelve or fifteen yards wide, and ten or twelve feet in depth; the bason and stream continually peopled with prodigious numbers and variety of fish and other animals; as the alligator, and the manate* or sea cow, in the winter season. Part of a skeleton of one, which the Indians had killed last winter, lay upon the banks of the spring: the grinding teeth were about an inch in diameter; the ribs eighteen inches in length, and two inches and an half in thickness, bending with a gentle curve. This bone is esteemed equal to ivory. The flesh of this creature is counted wholesome and pleasant food; the Indians call them by a name which signifies the big beaver. My companion, who was a trader in Talahasochte last winter, saw three of them at one time in this spring: they feed chiefly on aquatic grass and weeds. The ground round about the head of the bason is generally level, for the distance of a few yards; then gradually ascends, forming moderately high hills: the soil at top is a light, grayish, sandy mould, which continues some feet in depth, lying on a stratum of yellowish clay, then clay and gravel, then sand, and so on, stratum upon stratum, down to the general foundation of testaceous rocks. In other places a deep stratum of whitish, chalky limestone. The vegetable productions which cover and ornament those eminences, are generally Live Oaks, Magnolia grandiflora, in the Creek tongue, Tolo-chlucco, which signifies the Big Bay, Laurus Borbonia or Red Bay, in the Creek tongue, Etomico, that is King's tree, Olea Americana and Liquidambar, with other trees, shrubs, and herbaceous plants common in East Florida.

The hills and groves environing this admirable fountain, affording amusing subjects of inquiry, occasioned my stay here a great part of the day; and towards evening we returned to the town.

Next day, early in the morning, we crossed the river, landing on the other shore opposite the town, swimming our horses by the side of the canoe, each of us holding his horse by the bridle whilst an Indian paddled us over. After crossing, we struck off from the river into the forests, sometimes falling into, and keeping for a time, the ancient Spanish high road

*Trichechus manatus. Sea cow.

to Pensacola, now almost obliterated: we passed four or five miles through old Spanish fields.

There are to be seen plain marks or vestiges of the old Spanish plantations and dwellings; as fence posts and wooden pillars of their houses, ditches, and even corn ridges and Batata hills. From the Indian accounts, the Spaniards had here a rich well cultivated and populous settlement, and a strong fortified post, as they likewise had at the savanna and fields of Capola; but either of them far inferior to one they had some miles farther north-west towards the Apalachuchla River, now called the Apalachean Old Fields, where yet remain vast works and buildings, as fortifications, temples, some brass cannon, mortars, heavy church bells, &c.

The same groups of whitish testaceous rocks and circular sinks, with natural wells, make their appearance in these groves and fields, as observed on the side of the river opposite to Capola; and the same trees, shrubs, and herbage without variation. Having passed five or six miles through these ancient fields and groves, the scene suddenly changes, after riding through a high forest of Oak, Magnolia, Fraxinus, Liquid-ambar, Fagus sylvatica, &c.

Now at once opens to view, perhaps, the most extensive Cane-break* that is to be seen on the face of the whole earth; right forward, about south-west, there appears no bound but the skies, the level plain, like the ocean, uniting with the firmament, and on the right and left hand, dark shaded groves, old fields, and high forests, such as we had lately passed through.

The alternate bold promontories and misty points advancing and retiring, at length, as it were, insensibly vanishing from sight, like the two points of a crescent, softly touching the horizon, represent the most magnificent amphitheatre or circus perhaps in the whole world. The ground descends gently from the groves to the edge of the Cane-break, forming a delightful green grassy lawn. The Canes are ten or twelve feet in height, and as thick as an ordinary walking staff; they grow so close together, there is no penetrating them without previously cutting a road. We came up to this vast plain where the ancient Spanish highway crosses it to Pensacola: there yet

*Cane meadows, so called by the inhabitants of Carolina, &c.

remain plain vestiges of the grand causeway, which is open like a magnificent avenue, and the Indians have a bad road or pathway on it. The ground or soil of the plain is a perfectly black, rich, soapy earth, like a stiff clay or marle, wet and boggy near the shore, but, further in, firm and hard enough in the summer season, but wet and in some places under water during the winter.

This vast plain, together with the forests contiguous to it, if permitted (by the Siminoles who are sovereigns of these realms) to be in possession and under the culture of industrious planters and mechanics, would in a little time exhibit other scenes than it does at present, delightful as it is; for by the arts of agriculture and commerce, almost every desirable thing in life might be produced and made plentiful here, and thereby establish a rich, populous, and delightful region; as this soil and climate appears to be of a nature favourable for the production of almost all the fruits of the earth, as Corn*, Rice, Indigo, Sugar-cane, Flax, Cotton, Silk, Cochineal, and all the varieties of esculent vegetables; and I suppose no part of the earth affords such endless range and exuberant pasture for cattle, deer, sheep, &c.: the waters every where, even in the holes in the earth, abound with varieties of excellent fish; and the forests and native meadows with wild game, as bear, deer, turkeys, quail, and in the winter season geese, ducks, and other fowl: and lying contiguous to one of the most beautiful navigable rivers in the world, and not more than thirty miles from St. Mark's on the great bay of Mexico, is most conveniently situated for the West India trade and the commerce of all the world.

After indulging my imagination in the contemplation of these grand diversified scenes, we turned to the right hand, riding over the charming green terrace dividing the forests from the plains, and then entering the groves again, continued eight or nine miles up the river, four or five miles distance from its banks; having continually in view, on one side or other, expansive green fields, groves, and high forests; the meadows glittering with distant lakes and ponds, alive with cattle, deer, and turkeys, and frequently presenting to view

*Zea.

remains of ancient Spanish plantations. At length, towards evening, we turned about and came within sight of the river, where falling on the Indian trading path, we continued along it to the landing-place opposite the town; when hallooing and discharging our pieces, an Indian with a canoe came presently over, and conducted us to the town before dark.

On our arrival at the trading house, our chief was visited by the head men of the town, when instantly the White King's arrival in town was announced: a messenger had before been sent in to prepare a feast, the king and his retinue having killed several bears. A fire was now kindled in the area of the public square; the royal standard was displayed, and the drum beat to give notice to the town of the royal feast.

The ribs and the choice pieces of the three great fat bears already well barbecued or broiled, were brought to the banquetting house in the square, with hot bread; and honeyed water for drink.

When the feast was over in the square (where only the chiefs and warriors were admitted, with the white people), the chief priest, attended by slaves, came with baskets and carried off the remainder of the victuals, &c. which was distributed amongst the families of the town. The king then withdrew, repairing to the council house in the square, whither the chiefs and warriors, old and young, and such of the whites as chose, repaired also; the king, war chief, and several ancient chiefs and warriors were seated on the royal cabins; the rest of the head men and warriors, old and young, sat on the cabins on the right hand of the king's: the cabins or seats on the left, and on the same elevation, are always assigned for the white people, Indians of other towns, and such of their own people as choose.

Our chief, with the rest of the white people in town, took their seats according to order: tobacco and pipes were brought; the calumet was lighted and smoaked, circulating according to the usual forms and ceremony; and afterwards black drink concluded the feast. The king conversed, drank cassine, and associated familiarly with his people and with us.

After the public entertainment was over, the young people began their music and dancing in the square, whither the young of both sexes repaired, as well as the old and middle aged: this frolick continued all night.

The White King of Talahasochte is a middle aged man, of moderate stature; and though of a lofty and majestic countenance and deportment, yet I am convinced this dignity, which really seems graceful, is not the effect of vain supercilious pride, for his smiling countenance and his cheerful familiarity bespeak magnanimity and benignity.

Next a council and treaty was held. They requested to have a trading house again established in the town, assuring us that every possible means should constantly be pursued to prevent any disturbance in future on their part; they informed us that the murderers of M'Gee * and his associates were to be put to death, that two of them were already shot, and they were in pursuit of the other.

Our chief trader in answer informed them, that the re-establishment of friendship and trade was the chief object of his visit, and that he was happy to find his old friends of Talahasochte in the same good disposition, as they ever were towards him and the white people; that it was his wish to trade with them, and that he was now come to collect his pack-horses to bring them goods. The king and the chiefs having been already acquainted with my business and pursuits amongst them, received me very kindly; the king in particular complimented me, saying that I was as one of his own children or people, and should be protected accordingly, while I remained with them, adding, "Our whole country is before you, where you may range about at pleasure, gather physic plants and flowers, and every other production:" thus the treaty terminated friendlily and peaceably.

Next day early in the morning we left the town and the river, in order to fix our encampment in the forests about

---

*M'Gee was the leader of a family of white people from Georgia destined across the isthmus, to the Mobile river: they travelled on horse-back as far as this town, where they procured canoes of the Indians, continuing their travels, descending the river and coasting the main S. W.; but at night, when on shore hunting provisions, their camp was surprised and attacked by a predatory band of Indians, who slew M'Gee and the rest of the men, and carried off the plunder and a woman to their towns.

twelve miles from the river; our companions with the pack-horses went a head to the place of rendezvous, and our chief conducted me another way to show me a very curious place, called the Alligator-Hole, which was lately formed by an ex-traordinary eruption or jet of water. It is one of those vast circular sinks, which we beheld almost every where about us as we traversed these forests, after we left the Alachua savanna. This remarkable one is on the verge of a spacious meadow, the surface of the ground round about uneven by means of gentle rising knolls: some detached groups of rocks and large spreading live oaks shade it on every side: it is about sixty yards over, and the surface of the water six or seven feet below the rim of the funnel or bason: the water is transparent, cool, and pleasant to drink, and well stored with fish; a very large alligator at present is lord or chief; many have been killed here, but the throne is never long vacant, the vast neighbouring ponds so abound with them.

The account that this gentleman, who was an eye-witness of the last eruption, gave me of its first appearance, being very wonderful, I proceed to relate what he told me whilst we were in town, which was confirmed by the Indians, and one or more of our companions, who also saw its progress, as well as by my own observations after I came to the ground.

This trader being near the place (before it had any visible existence in its present appearance), about three years ago, as he was looking for some horses which he expected to find in these parts, on a sudden was astonished by an inexpressible rushing noise, like a mighty hurricane or thunder storm; and looking round, he saw the earth overflowed by torrents of water, which came, wave after wave, rushing down a vale or plain very near him, which it filled with water, and soon began to overwhelm the higher grounds, attended with a terrific noise and tremor of the earth. Recovering from his first sur-prise, he immediately resolved to proceed for the place from whence the noise seemed to come; and soon came in sight of the incomparable fountain, and saw, with amazement, the floods rushing upwards many feet high, and the expanding waters, which prevailed every way, spreading themselves far and near. He at length concluded (he said) that the foun-tains of the deep were again broken up, and that an universal

deluge had commenced; and instantly turned about and fled
to alarm the town, about nine miles distance: but before he
could reach it, he met several of the inhabitants, who, already
alarmed by the unusual noise, were hurrying on towards the
place; upon which he returned with the Indians, taking their
stand on an eminence to watch its progress and the event. It
continued to jet and flow in this manner for several days,
forming a large, rapid creek or river, descending and following
the various courses and windings of the valley, for the distance
of seven or eight miles, emptying itself into a vast savanna,
where was a lake and sink which received and gave vent to its
waters.

The fountain, however, gradually ceased to overflow, and
finally withdrew itself beneath the common surface of the
earth, leaving this capacious bason of waters, which, though
continually near full, hath never since overflowed. There yet
remains, and will, I suppose, remain for ages, the dry bed of
the river or canal, generally four, five, and six feet below the
natural surface of the land; the perpendicular, ragged banks
of which, on each side, show the different strata of the earth;
and at places, where ridges or a swelling bank crossed and
opposed its course and fury, are vast heaps of fragments of
rocks, white chalk, stones, and pebbles, which were collected
and thrown into the lateral vallies, until the main stream prevailed over and forced them aside, overflowing the levels and
meadows, for some miles distance from the principal stream,
on either side. We continued down the great vale, along its
banks, quite to the savanna and lake where it vented itself,
while its ancient subterranean channel was gradually opening,
which, I imagine, from some hidden event or cause had been
choaked up, and which, we may suppose, was the immediate
cause of the eruption.

In the evening, having gained our encampment, on a grassy
knoll or eminence, under the cover of spreading oaks, just by
the grotto or sink of the lake, which lay as a sparkling gem
on the flowery bosom of the ample savanna; our roving associates soon came in from the ranging forests. We continued
our encampment at this place for several days, ranging around
the delightful country to a great distance, every day's excursion presenting new scenes of wonder and delight.

Early in the morning our chief invited me with him on a visit to the town, to take a final leave of the White King. We were graciously received and treated with the utmost civility and hospitality: there was a noble entertainment and repast provided against our arrival, consisting of bears ribs, venison, varieties of fish, roasted turkies (which they call the white man's dish), hot corn cakes, and a very agreeable, cooling sort of jelly, which they call conte: this is prepared from the root of the China briar (Smilax pseudo-China; Smilax aspera, fructu nigro, radice nodosa, magna, lævi, farinacea; Sloan, tom. 1. p. 31. t. 143. f. 1. habit. Jamaica, Virginia, Carolina, and Florida): they chop the roots in pieces, which are afterwards well pounded in a wooden mortar, then being mixed with clean water, in a tray or trough, they strain it through baskets; the sediment, which settles to the bottom of the second vessel, is afterwards dried in the open air, and is then a very fine reddish flour or meal: a small quantity of this mixed with warm water and sweetened with honey, when cool, becomes a beautiful, delicious jelly, very nourishing and wholesome. They also mix it with fine corn flour, which being fried in fresh bear's oil makes very good hot cakes or fritters.

On our taking leave of the king and head men, they entreated our chief to represent to the white people, their unfeigned desire to bury in oblivion the late breach of amity and intermission of commerce, which they trusted would never be reflected on the people of Talahasochte; and, lastly, that we would speedily return with merchandize as heretofore; all which was cheerfully consented to, assuring them their wishes and sentiments fully coincided with ours.

The chief trader, intending to show me some remarkable barren plains, on our return to our encampment, about noon we sat off: when we came within sight of them, I was struck with astonishment at their dreary appearance; the view Southerly seemed endless wastes, presenting rocky, gravelly and sandy barren plains, producing scarcely any vegetable substances, except a few shrubby crooked Pine trees, growing out of heaps of white rocks, which represented ruins of villages, planted over the plains; with clumps of mean shrubs, which served only to perpetuate the persecuting power and rage of fire, and to testify the aridity of the soil. The shrubs I observed were chiefly the following; Myrica cerifera, two or three varieties, one of which is very dwarfish, the leaves small, yet toothed or sinuated, of a yellowish green colour, owing to a farinaceous pubescence or vesicula which covers their surfaces; Prinos, varieties, Andromeda ferruginea, Andr. nitida, varieties, Rhamnus frangula, Sideroxylon sericium, Ilex aquifolium, Ilex myrtifolium, Empetrum, Kalmia ciliata, Cassine, and a great variety of shrub Oaks, evergreen and deciduous, some of them singularly beautiful; Corypha repens; with a great variety of herbage, particularly Cacalia, Prenanthus, Chrysocoma, Helianthus, Silphium, Lobelia, Globularia, Helenium, Polygala, varieties, Clinopodium, Cactus, various species, Euphorbia, various species, Asclepias carnosa, very beautiful and singular, Sophora, Dianthus, Cistus, Sisymbrium, Pedicularis, Gerardia, Lechea, Gnaphalium, Smilax sarsaparilla, Smilax pumila, Solidago, Aster, Lupinus filifolius, Galega, Hedysarum, &c. with various species of grasses. But there appeared vast spaces of gravel and plains of flat rocks, just even with the surface of the earth, which seemed entirely destitute of any vegetation, unless we may except some different kinds of mosses of the crustaceous sorts, as lichen, alga, &c. and coralloides. After passing several miles on the borders of these deserts, frequently alighting on them for observation and making collections, they at length gradually united or joined with infinite savannas and ponds, stretching beyond the sight southerly, parallel with the rocky barrens; being separated only by a narrow, low, rocky ridge of open groves, consisting of low, spreading Live Oaks, Zanthoxylon, Ilex, Sideroxylon, &c.; and here and there, standing either in groups or alone, the pompous Palm tree, gloriously erect or gracefully bowing towards the earth; exhibiting a most pleasing contrast and wild Indian scene of primitive unmodified nature, ample and magnificent. We at length came abreast of the expansive, glittering lake, which divided the ample meadows, one end of which stretching towards a verdant eminence, formed a little bay, which was partly encircled by groups of white chalky rocks, shaded with Live Oaks, Bays, Zanthoxylon and Palm trees. We turned our horses to graze in the green lawns, whilst we traversed the groves and meadows. Here the palmated Convolvulus trailed over the rocks, with the Hedera carnosa (fol. quinatis inciso-serratis, perennentibus), and the fantastic Clitoria, decorating the shrubs with garlands (Clit. caule volubili fol. ternatis pennatisque, flor. majore cæruleo, vexillo rotundiore, siliquis longissimis compressis).

Soon after entering the forests, we were met in the path by a small company of Indians, smiling and beckoning to us long before we joined them. This was a family of Talahasochte who had been out on a hunt, and were returning home loaded with barbecued meat, hides and honey. Their company consisted of the man, his wife and children, well mounted on fine horses, with a number of pack-horses. The man presently offered us a fawnskin of honey, which we gladly accepted, and at parting I presented him with some fish hooks, sewing needles, &c.; for in my travels amongst the Indians, I always furnished myself with such useful and acceptable little articles of light carriage, for presents. We parted, and before night rejoined our companion at the Long Pond.

On our return to camp in the evening, we were saluted by a party of young Indian warriors, who had pitched their camp on a green eminence near the lake, and at a small distance from our camp, under a little grove of Oaks and Palms. This company consisted of seven young Siminoles, under the conduct of a young prince or chief of Caloosahatche, a town southward in the isthmus. They were all dressed and painted with singular elegance, and richly ornamented with silver plates, chains, &c. after the Siminole mode, with waving plumes of feathers on their crests. On our coming up to them, they arose and shook hands; we alighted and sat a while with them by their cheerful fire.

The young prince informed our chief that he was in pursuit of a young fellow, who had fled from the town, carrying off with him one of his favourite young wives or concubines. He said merrily he would have the ears of both of them before he returned. He was rather above the middle stature, and the most perfect human figure I ever saw; of an amiable engaging countenance, air and deportment; free and familiar in conversation, yet retaining a becoming gracefulness and dignity. We arose, took leave of them, and crossed a little vale covered with a charming green turf, already illuminated by the soft light of the full moon.

Soon after joining our companions at camp, our neighbours, the prince and his associates, paid us a visit. We treated
them with the best fare we had, having till this time preserved
some of our spirituous liquors. They left us with perfect cor-
diality and cheerfulness, wishing us a good repose, and retired
to their own camp. Having a band of music with them, consisting of a drum, flutes, and a rattle gourd, they entertained
us during the night with their music, vocal and instrumental.

There is a languishing softness and melancholy air in the
Indian convivial songs, especially of the amorous class, irresistibly moving, attractive, and exquisitely pleasing, especially in
these solitary recesses, when all nature is silent.

Behold how gracious and beneficent shines the roseate
morn! Now the sun arises and fills the plains with light; his
glories appear on the forests, encompassing the meadows, and
gild the top of the terebinthine Pine and exalted Palms, now
gently rustling by the pressure of the waking breezes: the
music of the seraphic cranes resounds in the skies; in separate
squadrons they sail, encircling their precincts, slowly descend
beating the dense air, and alight on the green dewy verge of
the expansive lake; its surface yet smoking with the gray ascending mists, which, condensed aloft in clouds of vapour, are
born away by the morning breezes, and at last gradually vanish
on the distant horizon. All nature awakes to life and activity.

The ground, during our progress this morning, every where
about us presented to view those funnels, sinks and wells in
groups of rocks, amidst the groves, as already recited.

Near our next encampment, one more conspicuous than I
had elsewhere observed presenting itself, I took occasion from
this favourable circumstance of observing them in all their
variety of appearances. Its outer superficial margin was fifty or
sixty yards over, which equally and uniformly on every side
sloped downwards towards the center: on one side of it was
a considerable path-way or road leading down to the water,
worn by the frequent resort of wild creatures for drink, when
the waters were risen even or above the rocky bed, but at this
time they were sunk many yards below the surface of the
earth. We descended first to the bed of rocks, which was perforated with perpendicular tubes, exactly like a walled well,
four, five, or six feet in diameter, and may be compared to

cells in an honey-comb, through which appeared the water at bottom: many of these were broken or worn one into another, forming one vast well with uneven walls, consisting of projecting jams, pilastres, or buttresses, and excavated semicircular niches, as if a piece were taken out of a honey-comb: the bed of rocks is from fifteen to twenty feet deep or in thickness, though not of one solid mass, but of many, generally horizontal, laminæ, or strata, of various thickness, from eighteen inches to two or three feet; which admit water to weep through, trickling down, drop after drop, or chasing each other in winding little rills down to the bottom. One side of the vast cool grotto was so shattered and broken in, I thought it possible to descend down to the water at bottom; and my companion assuring me that the Indians and traders frequently go down for drink, encouraged me to make the attempt, as he agreed to accompany me.

Having provided ourselves with a long snagged sapling, called an Indian ladder, and each of us a pole, by the assistance of these we both descended safely to the bottom, which we found nearly level and not quite covered over with water; on one side was a bed of gravel and fragments of rocks or stones, and on the other a pool of water near two feet deep, which moved with a slow current under the walls on a bed of clay and gravel.

After our return to the surface of the earth, I again ranged about the groves and grottos, examining a multitude of them. Being on the margin of one in the open forest, and observing some curious vegetable productions growing on the side of the sloping funnel towards its center, the surface of the ground covered with grass and herbage; unapprehensive of danger, I descended precipitately towards the group of shrubs; when I was surprised and providentially stopped in my career, at the ground sounding hollow under my feet; and observing chasms through the ground, I quickly drew back, and returning again with a pole with which I beat in the earth, to my astonishment and dread appeared the mouth of a well through the rocks, and I observed the water glimmering at the bottom. Being wearied with excursions, we returned to our pleasant situation on the verge of the lawn.

Next day we set off on our return to the lower trading-house, proposing to encamp at a savanna, about twelve miles distance from this, where we were to halt again and stay a day or two, in order to collect together another party of horses, which had been stationed about that range. The young wild horses often breaking from the company, rendered our progress slow and troublesome; we however arrived at the appointed place long before night.

I had an opportunity this day of collecting a variety of specimens and seeds of vegetables, some of which appeared new to me, particularly Sophora, Cistus, Tradescantia, Hypoxis, Jatropa, Gerardia, Pedicularis, Mimosa sensitiva, Helonias, Melanthium, Lilium, Aletris, Agave, Cactus, Zamia, Empetrum, Erythryna, Echium, &c.

Next day, the people being again engaged in their business of ranging the forests and plains, in search of their horses, I accompanied them, and in our rambles we again visited the great savanna and lake, called the Long Pond: the lake is nearly in the middle of the spacious lawn, of an oblong form; above two miles wide and seven in length; one end approaching the high green banks adjoining the forests, where there is an enchanting grove and grotto of pellucid waters, inhabited with multitudes of fish, continually ascending and descending through the clean, white rocks, sloping from the green verged shore, by gradual steps, from smooth, flat pavements washed by the swelling undulations of the waters.

Arrived in the evening at camp, where we found the rest of our companions busily employed in securing the young freakish horses. The next day was employed in like manner, breaking and tutoring the young steeds to their duty. The day following we took a final leave of this land of meadows, lakes, groves and grottos, directing our course for the trading path. Having traversed a country, in appearance, little differing from the region lying upon Little St. Juan, we gained about twelve miles on our way; and in the evening encamped on a narrow ridge, dividing two savannas from each other, near the edge of a deep pond; here our people made a large pen or pound to secure their wild horses during the night. There was a little hommock or islet containing a few acres of high ground, at some distance from the shore, in the drowned savanna, almost every tree of which was loaded with nests of various tribes of water fowl, as ardea alba, ar. violacea, ar. cerulea, ar. stellaris cristata, ar. stellaris maxima, ar. virescens, colymbus, tantalus, mergus and others; these nests were all alive with young, generally almost full grown, not yet fledged, but covered with whitish or cream coloured soft down. We visited this bird isle, and some of our people taking sticks or poles with them, soon beat down, and loaded themselves with these squabs, and returned to camp; they were almost a lump of fat, and made us a rich supper; some we roasted, and made others into a pilloe with rice: most of them, except the bitterns and tantali, were so excessively fishy in taste and smell, I could not relish them. It is incredible what prodigious numbers there were, old and young, on this little islet, and the confused noise which they kept up continually, the young crying for food incessantly, even whilst in their throats, and the old alarmed and displeased at our near residence, and the depredations we had made upon them; their various languages, cries, and fluttering caused an inexpressible uproar, like a public fair or market in a populous trading city, when suddenly surprised by some unexpected calamitous event.

About midnight, having fallen asleep, I was awakened and greatly surprised at finding most of my companions up in arms, and furiously engaged with a large alligator but a few yards from me. One of our company, it seems, awoke in the night, and perceived the monster within a few paces of the camp, when giving the alarm to the rest, they readily came to his assistance, for it was a rare piece of sport. Some took firebrands and cast them at his head, whilst others formed javelins of saplins, pointed and hardened with fire; these they thrust down his throat into his bowels, which caused the monster to roar and bellow hideously; but his strength and fury were so great, that he easily wrenched or twisted them out of their hands, and wielding and brandishing them about, kept his enemies at a distance for a time. Some were for putting an end to his life and sufferings with a rifle ball, but the majority thought this would too soon deprive them of the diversion and pleasure of exercising their various inventions of torture: they at length however grew tired, and agreed in one opinion, that he had suffered sufficiently; and put an end to his existence. This crocodile was about twelve feet in length: we supposed that he had been allured by the fishy scent of our birds, and encouraged to undertake and pursue this hazardous adventure which cost him his life. This, with other instances already recited, may be sufficient to prove the intrepidity and subtilty of those voracious, formidable animals.

We sat off early next morning, and soon after falling into the trading path, accomplished about twenty miles of our journey; and in the evening encamped as usual, near the banks of savannas and ponds, for the benefit of water and accommodations of pasture for our creatures. Next day we passed over part of the great and beautiful Alachua Savanna, whose exuberant green meadows, with the fertile hills which immediately encircle it, would, if peopled and cultivated after the manner of the civilized countries of Europe, without crowding or incommoding families, at a moderate estimation, accommodate in the happiest manner above one hundred thousand human inhabitants, besides millions of domestic animals; and I make no doubt this place will at some future day be one of the most populous and delightful seats on earth.

We came to camp in the evening, on the banks of a creek but a few miles distance from Cuscowilla; and two days more moderate travelling brought us safe back again to the lower trading-house, on St. Juan, having been blessed with health and a prosperous journey.

On my arrival at the stores, I was happy to find all well as we had left them; and our bringing with us friendly talks from the Siminole towns, and the Nation likewise, completed the hopes and wishes of the trading company, with respect to their commercial concerns with the Indians, which, as the cheering light of the sun-beams after a dark tempestuous night, diffused joy and conviviality throughout the little community, where were a number of men with their families, who had been put out of employment and subsistence, anxiously waiting the happy event.

CHAP. VIII.

AS A LOADING could not be procured until late in the autumn, for the schooner that was to return to Georgia,
this circumstance allowed me time and opportunity to continue my excursions in this land of flowers, as well as at
the same time to augment my collections of seeds, growing
roots, &c.

I resolved upon another little voyage up the river; and after
resting a few days and refitting my bark, I got on board the
necessary stores, and furnishing myself with boxes to plant
roots in, with my fuzee, ammunition and fishing tackle, I set
sail, and in the evening arrived at Mount Royal. Next morning, being moderately calm and serene, I set sail with a gentle
leading breeze, which delightfully wafted me across the lake
to the west coast, landing on an airy, sandy beach, a pleasant,
cool situation, where I passed the night, but not without frequent attacks from the musquitoes; and next day visited the
Great Springs, where I remained until the succeeding day, increasing my collections of specimens, seeds and roots; and
then recrossed the lake to the eastern shore. This shore is
generally bolder and more rocky than the western, it being
exposed to the lash of the surf, occasioned by the W. and
N. W. winds, which are brisk and constant from nine or ten
o'clock in the morning till towards midnight, almost the year
round; though the S. winds are considerable in the spring,
and by short intervals during the summer and winter; and the
N. E. though sometimes very violent in the spring and autumn, does not continue long. The day was employed in
coasting slowly, and making collections. In the evening I made
a harbour under cover of a long point of flat rocks, which
defended the mole from the surf. Having safely moored my
bark, and chosen my camping ground just by, during the fine
evening I reconnoitred the adjacent groves and lawns. Here
is a deserted plantation, the property of Dr. Stork, where he
once resided. I observed many lovely shrubs and plants in the
old fields and Orange groves, particularly several species of
Convolvulus and Ipomea, the former having very large, white,

sweet scented flowers: they are great ramblers, climbing and strolling on the shrubs and hedges. Next morning I re-embarked, and continued traversing the bold coast north-eastward, and searching the shores at all convenient landings, where I was amply rewarded for my assiduity in the society of beauties in the blooming realms of Florida. Came to again, at an old deserted plantation, the property of a British gentleman, but some years since vacated. A very spacious frame building was settling to the ground and mouldering to earth. Here are very extensive old fields, where were growing the West-Indian or perennial Cotton and Indigo, which had been cultivated here, and some scattered remains of the ancient orange groves, which had been left standing at the clearing of the plantation.

I have often been affected with extreme regret, at beholding the destruction and devastation which has been committed or indiscreetly exercised on those extensive fruitful Orange groves, on the banks of St. Juan, by the new planters under the British government, some hundred acres of which, at a single plantation, have been entirely destroyed, to make room for the indigo, Cotton, Corn, Batatas, &c. or, as they say, to extirpate the musquitoes, alledging that groves near the dwellings are haunts and shelters for those persecuting insects. Some plantations have not a single tree standing; and where any have been left, it is only a small coppice or clump, nakedly exposed and destitute; perhaps fifty or an hundred trees standing near the dwelling-house, having no lofty cool grove of expansive Live Oaks, Laurel Magnolias, and Palms, to shade and protect them, exhibiting a mournful, sallow countenance; their native perfectly formed and glossy green foliage as if violated, defaced and torn to pieces by the bleak winds, scorched by the burning sun-beams in summer, and chilled by the winter frosts.

In the evening I took up my quarters in the beautiful isle in sight of Mount Royal. Next day, after collecting what was new and worthy of particular notice, I set sail again, and called by the way at Mount Royal. In the evening arrived safe at the stores, bringing along with me valuable collections.

CHAP. IX.

AT THE TRADING-HOUSE I found a very large party of the Lower Creeks encamped in a grove, just without the pallisadoes. This was a predatory band of the Siminoles, consisting of about forty warriors destined against the Chactaws of West Florida. They had just arrived here from St. Augustine, where they had been with a large troop of horses for sale, and furnished themselves with a very liberal supply of spirituous liquors, about twenty kegs, each containing five gallons.

These sons of Mars had the continence and fortitude to withstand the temptation of even tasting a drop of it until their arrival here, where they purposed to supply themselves with necessary articles to equip them for the expedition, and proceed on directly; but here meeting with our young traders and pack-horse men, they were soon prevailed on to broach their beloved nectar; which in the end caused some disturbance, and the consumption of most of their liquor; for after they had once got a smack of it, they never were sober for ten days, and by that time there was but little left.

In a few days this festival exhibited one of the most ludicrous bacchanalian scenes that is possible to be conceived. White and red men and women without distinction, passed the day merrily with these jovial, amorous topers, and the nights in convivial songs, dances, and sacrifices to Venus, as long as they could stand or move; for in these frolicks both sexes take such liberties with each other, and act, without constraint or shame, such scenes as they would abhor when sober or in their senses; and would endanger their ears and even their lives: but at last their liquor running low, and being most of them sick through intoxication, they became more sober; and now the dejected lifeless sots would pawn every thing they were in possession of, for a mouthful of spirits to settle their stomachs, as they termed it. This was the time for the wenches to make their market, as they had the fortitude and subtilty by dissimulation and artifice to save their share of the liquor during the frolick, and that by a very singular stratagem; for, at these riots, every fellow who joins in the club, has his own quart bottle of rum in his hand, holding it by the neck so sure, that he never looses hold of it day or night, drunk or sober, as long as the frolick continues; and with this, his beloved friend, he roves about continually, singing, roaring, and reeling to and fro, either alone, or arm in arm with a brother toper, presenting his bottle to every one, offering a drink; and is sure to meet his beloved female if he can, whom he complaisantly begs to drink with him. But the modest fair, veiling her face in a mantle, refuses, at the beginning of the frolick; but he presses and at last insists. She being furnished with an empty bottle, concealed in her mantle, at last consents, and taking a good long draught, blushes, drops her pretty face on her bosom, and artfully discharges the rum into her bottle, and by repeating this artifice soon fills it: this she privately conveys to her secret store, and then returns to the jovial game, and so on during the festival; and when the comic farce is over, the wench retails this precious cordial to them at her own price.

There were a few of the chiefs, particularly the Long Warrior their leader, who had the prudence and fortitude to resist the alluring temptation during the whole farce; but though he was a powerful chief, a king, and a very cunning man, he was not able to controul these madmen, although he was acknowledged by the Indians to have communion with powerful invisible beings or spirits, and on that account esteemed worthy of homage and great respect.

After the Indians became sober, they began to prepare for their departure. In the morning early the Long Warrior and chiefs sent a messenger to Mr. M'Latche, desiring to have a talk with him upon matters of moment: accordingly, about noon they arrived. The conference was held in the piazza of the council house: the Long Warrior and chiefs who attended him, took their seats upon a long bench adjoining the side or front of the house, reaching the whole length of it, on one hand; and the principal white traders on the other, all on the same seat. I was admitted at this conference; Mr. M'Latche and the Long Warrior sat next to each other; my late companion, the old trader, and myself sat next to him.

The Long Warrior spake, saying, that he and his companions were going to fight their enemies the Chactaws; and that some of his associates being in want of blankets, shirts, and some other articles, they declined supplying themselves with them at St. Augustine, because they had rather stick close to their old friend Mr. Spalding, and bring their buckskins, furs, and other produce of their country (which they knew were acceptable) to his trading house, to purchase what they wanted. But not having the skins, &c. with them to pay for such things as they had occasion for, they doubted not, but that on their return, they should bring with them sufficient not only to pay their debts, about to be contracted, but be able to make other considerable purchases, as the principal object of this expedition was hunting on the plentiful borders of the Chactaws. Mr. M'Latche hesitating, and expressing some dissatisfaction at his request; particularly at the length of time and great uncertainty of obtaining pay for the goods; and moreover his being only an agent for Messrs. Spalding and Co. and the magnitude and unprecedented terms of the Long Warrior's demands; required the company's assent and directions before he could comply with their request.

This answer displeased the Indian chief, and I observed great agitation and tumult in his passions, from his actions, hurry and rapidity of speech and expression. The old inter-preter who sat by asked me if I fully understood the debate; I answered that I apprehended the Long Warrior was dis-pleased; he told me he was so, and then recapitulated what had been said respecting his questions and Mr. M'Latche's answer; adding, that upon his hesitation he immediately re-plied, in seeming disgust and great expressions of anger, "Do you presume to refuse me credit; certainly you know who I am and what power I have: but perhaps you do not know, that if the matter required it, and I pleased, I could command and cause the terrible thunder* now rolling in the skies above, to descend upon your head, in rapid fiery shafts, and lay you prostrate at my feet, and consume your stores, turning them instantly into dust and ashes." Mr. M'Latche calmly replied, that he was fully sensible that the Long Warrior was a great man, a powerful chief of the bands of the respectable Simi-

*It thundered, lightened, and rained in a violent manner during these debates.

noles, that his name was terrible to his enemies, but still he doubted if any man upon earth had such power, but rather believed that thunder and lightning was under the direction of the Great Spirit; but however, since we are not disposed to deny your power, supernatural influence and intercourse with the elements and spiritual agents, or withhold the respect and homage due to so great a prince of the Siminoles, friends and allies to the white people; if you think fit now in the presence of us all here, command and cause yon terrible thunder with its rapid fiery shafts, to descend upon the top of that Live Oak* in front of us, rend it in pieces, scatter his brawny limbs on the earth and consume them to ashes before our eyes, we will then own your supernatural power and dread your displeasure.

After some silence the prince became more calm and easy, and returned for answer, that recollecting the former friendship and good understanding, which had ever subsisted betwixt the white people and red people of the Siminole bands, and in particular, the many acts of friendship and kindness received from Mr. M'Latche, he would overlook this affront; he acknowledged his reasoning and expostulations to be just and manly, that he should suppress his resentment, and withhold his power and vengeance at present. Mr. M'Latche concluded by saying, that he was not in the least intimidated by his threats of destroying him with thunder and lightning, neither was he disposed in any manner to displease the Siminoles, and should certainly comply with his requisitions, as far as he could proceed without the advice and directions of the company; and finally agreed to supply him and his followers with such things as they stood most in need of, such as shirts, blankets and some paints, one half to be paid for directly, and the remainder to stand on credit until their return from the expedition. This determination entirely satisfied the Indians. We broke up the conference in perfect amity and good humour, and they returned to their camp, and in the evening, ratified it with feasting and dancing, which continued all next day with tolerable decorum. An occurrence happened this day, by which I had an opportunity of observing their extraor-

*A large ancient Live Oak stood in the yard about fifty yards distance.

dinary veneration or dread of the rattle snake. I was in the forenoon busy in my apartment in the council-house, drawing some curious flowers; when, on a sudden, my attention was taken off by a tumult without, at the Indian camp. I stepped to the door opening to the piazza, where I met my friend the old interpreter, who informed me that there was a very large rattle snake in the Indian camp, which had taken possession of it, having driven the men, women and children out, and he heard them saying that they would send for Puc-Puggy (for that was the name which they had given me, signifying the Flower Hunter) to kill him or take him out of their camp. I answered, that I desired to have nothing to do with him, apprehending some disagreeable consequences; and desired that the Indians might be acquainted that I was engaged in business that required application and quiet, and was determined to avoid it if possible. My old friend turned about to carry my answer to the Indians. I presently heard them approaching and calling for Puc-Puggy. Starting up to escape from their sight by a back door, a party consisting of three young fellows, richly dressed and ornamented, stepped in, and with a countenance and action of noble simplicity, amity and complaisance, requested me to accompany them to their encampment. I desired them to excuse me at this time; they pleaded and entreated me to go with them, in order to free them from a great rattle snake which had entered their camp; that none of them had freedom or courage to expel him; and understanding that it was my pleasure to collect all their animals and other natural productions of their land, desired that I would come with them and take him away, that I was welcome to him. I at length consented and attended on them to their encampment, where I beheld the Indians greatly disturbed indeed. The men with sticks and tomahawks, and the women and children collected together at a distance in affright and trepidation, whilst the dreaded and revered serpent leisurely traversed their camp, visiting the fire places from one to another, picking up fragments of their provisions and licking their platters. The men gathered around me, exciting me to remove him: being armed with a lightwood knot, I approached the reptile, who instantly collected himself in a vast coil (their attitude of defence) I cast my missile weapon at him, which luckily taking his head, dispatched him instantly, and laid him trembling at my feet. I took out my knife, severed his head from his body, then turning about, the Indians complimented me with every demonstration of satisfaction and approbation for my heroism, and friendship for them. I carried off the head of the serpent bleeding in my hand as a trophy of victory; and taking out the mortal fangs, deposited them carefully amongst my collections. I had not been long retired to my apartment, before I was again roused from it by a tumult in the yard; and hearing Puc-Puggy called on, I started up, when instantly the old interpreter met me again, and told me the Indians were approaching in order to scratch me. I asked him for what? he answered for killing the rattle snake within their camp. Before I could make any reply or effect my escape, three young fellows singing, arm in arm, came up to me. I observed one of the three was a young prince who had, on my first interview with him, declared himself my friend and protector, when he told me that if ever occasion should offer in his presence, he would risk his life to defend mine or my property. This young champion stood by his two associates, one on each side of him: the two affecting a countenance and air of displeasure and importance, instantly presenting their scratching instruments, and flourishing them, spoke boldly, and said that I was too heroic and violent, that it would be good for me to lose some of my blood to make me more mild and tame, and for that purpose they were come to scratch me. They gave me no time to expostulate or reply, but attempted to lay hold on me, which I resisted; and my friend, the young prince, interposed and pushed them off, saying that I was a brave warrior and his friend; that they should not insult me; when instantly they altered their countenance and behaviour: they all whooped in chorus, took me friendly by the hand, clapped me on the shoulder, and laid their hands on their breasts in token of sincere friendship, and laughing aloud, said I was a sincere friend to the Siminoles, a worthy and brave warrior, and that no one should hereafter attempt to injure me. They then all three joined arm in arm again and went off, shouting and proclaiming

Puc-Puggy was their friend, &c. Thus it seemed that the whole was a ludicrous farce to satisfy their people and appease the manes* of the dead rattle snake.

The next day was employed by the Indians in preparations for their departure, such as taking up their goods from the trading house, collecting together their horses, making up their packs, &c. and the evening joyfully spent in songs and dances. The succeeding morning after exhibiting the war farce they decamped, proceeding on their expedition against their enemy.

*These people never kill the rattle snake or any other serpent, saying if they do so, the spirit of the killed snake will excite or influence his living kindred or relatives to revenge the injury or violence done to him when alive.

CHAP. X.

B UT LET US again resume the subject of the rattle snake; a wonderful creature, when we consider his form, nature and disposition. It is certain that he is capable by a puncture or scratch of one of his fangs, not only to kill the largest animal in America, and that in a few minutes time, but to turn the whole body into corruption; but such is the nature of this dreadful reptile, that he cannot run or creep faster than a man or child can walk, and he is never known to strike until he is first assaulted or fears himself in danger, and even then always gives the earliest warning by the rattles at the extremity of the tail. I have in the course of my travels in the Southern states (where they are the largest, most numerous and supposed to be the most venemous and vindictive) stept unknowingly so close as almost to touch one of them with my feet, and when I perceived him he was already drawn up in circular coils ready for a blow. But however incredible it may appear, the generous, I may say magnanimous creature lay as still and motionless as if inanimate, his head crouched in, his eyes almost shut. I precipitately withdrew, unless when I have been so shocked with surprise and horror as to be in a manner rivetted to the spot, for a short time not having strength to go away; when he often slowly extends himself and quietly moves off in a direct line, unless pursued, when he erects his tail as far as the rattles extend, and gives the warning alarm by intervals. But if you pursue and overtake him with a shew of enmity, he instantly throws himself into the spiral coil; his tail by the rapidity of its motion appears like a vapour, making a quick tremulous sound; his whole body swells through rage, continually rising and falling as a bellows; his beautiful particoloured skin becomes speckled and rough by dilatation; his head and neck are flattened, his cheeks swollen and his lips constricted, discovering his mortal fangs; his eyes red as burning coals, and his brandishing forked tongue of the colour of the hottest flame, continually menaces death and destruction, yet never strikes unless sure of his mark.

The rattle snake is the largest serpent yet known to exist in North America. I have heard of their having been seen formerly, at the first settling of Georgia, seven, eight and even ten feet in length, and six or eight inches diameter; but there are none of that size now to be seen; yet I have seen them about six feet in length, and above six inches in thickness, or as large as a man's leg; but their general size is four, five, and six feet in length. They are supposed to have the power of fascination in an eminent degree, so as to inthral their prey. It is generally believed that they charm birds, rabbits, squirrels and other animals, and by stedfastly looking at them possess them with infatuation: be the cause what it may, the miserable creatures undoubtedly strive by every possible means to escape, but alas! their endeavours are in vain, they at last lose the power of resistance, and flutter or move slowly, but reluctantly, towards the yawning jaws of their devourers, and creep into their mouths, or lie down and suffer themselves to be taken and swallowed.

Since, within the circle of my acquaintance, I am known to be an advocate or vindicator of the benevolent and peaceable disposition of animal creation in general, not only towards mankind, whom they seem to venerate, but also towards one another, except where hunger or the rational and necessary provocations of the sensual appetite interfere, I shall mention a few instances, amongst many, which I have had an opportunity of remarking during my travels, particularly with regard to the animal I have been treating of. I shall strictly confine myself to facts.

When on the sea coast of Georgia, I consented, with a few friends, to make a party of amusement at fishing and fowling on Sapello, one of the sea coast islands. We accordingly descended the Alatamaha, crossed the sound and landed on the North end of the island, near the inlet, fixing our encampment at a pleasant situation, under the shade of a grove of Live Oaks and Laurels*, on the high banks of a creek which we ascended, winding through a salt marsh, which had its source from a swamp and savanna in the island: our situation elevated and open, commanded a comprehensive landscape;

*Magnolia grandiflora, called by the inhabitants the Laurel.

the great ocean, the foaming surf breaking on the sandy beach, the snowy breakers on the bar, the endless chain of islands, checkered sound and high continent all appearing before us. The diverting toils of the day were not fruitless, affording us opportunities of furnishing ourselves plentifully with a variety of game, fish and oysters for our supper.

About two hundred yards from our camp was a cool spring, amidst a grove of the odoriferous Myrica: the winding path to this salubrious fountain led through a grassy savanna. I visited the spring several times in the night, but little did I know, or any of my careless drowsy companions, that every time we visited the fountain we were in imminent danger, as I am going to relate. Early in the morning, excited by unconquerable thirst, I arose and went to the spring; and having, thoughtless of harm or danger, nearly half past the dewy vale, along the serpentine foot path, my hasty steps were suddenly stopped by the sight of a hideous serpent, the formidable rattle snake, in a high spiral coil, forming a circular mound half the height of my knees, within six inches of the narrow path. As soon as I recovered my senses and strength from so sudden a surprise, I started back out of his reach, where I stood to view him: he lay quiet whilst I surveyed him, appearing no way surprised or disturbed, but kept his half-shut eyes fixed on me. My imagination and spirits were in a tumult, almost equally divided betwixt thanksgiving to the supreme Creator and preserver, and the dignified nature of the generous though terrible creature, who had suffered us all to pass many times by him during the night, without injuring us in the least, although we must have touched him, or our steps guided therefrom by a supreme guardian spirit. I hastened back to acquaint my associates, but with a determination to protect the life of the generous serpent. I presently brought my companions to the place, who were, beyond expression, surprised and terrified at the sight of the animal, and in a moment acknowledged their escape from destruction to be miraculous; and I am proud to assert, that all of us, except one person, agreed to let him lie undisturbed, and that person at length was prevailed upon to suffer him to escape.

Again, when in my youth, attending my father on a journey to the Catskill Mountains, in the government of New-york;

having nearly ascended the peak of Giliad, being youthful and vigorous in the pursuit of botanical and novel objects, I had gained the summit of a steep rocky precipice, a-head of our guide; when just entering a shady vale, I saw at the root of a small shrub, a singular and beautiful appearance, which I remember to have instantly apprehended to be a large kind of Fungus which we call Jews ears, and was just drawing back my foot to kick it over; when at the instant, my father being near, cried out, a rattle snake my son! and jerked me back, which probably saved my life. I had never before seen one. This was of the kind which our guide called a yellow one, it was very beautiful, speckled and clouded. My father pleaded for his life, but our guide was inexorable, saying he never spared the life of a rattle snake, and killed him; my father took his skin and fangs.

Some years after this, when again in company with my father on a journey into East Florida, on the banks of St. Juan, at Fort Picolata, attending the congress at a treaty between that government and the Creek Nation, for obtaining a territory from that people to annex to the new government; after the Indians and a detachment from the garrison of St. Augustine had arrived and encamped separately, near the fort, some days elapsed before the business of the treaty came on, waiting the arrival of a vessel from St. Augustine, on board of which were the presents for the Indians. My father employed this time of leisure in little excursions round about the fort; and one morning, being the day the treaty commenced, I attended him on a botanical excursion. Some time after we had been rambling in a swamp about a quarter of a mile from the camp, I being a-head a few paces, my father bid me observe the rattle snake before and just at my feet. I stopped and saw the monster formed in a high spiral coil, not half his length from my feet: another step forward would have put my life in his power, as I must have touched if not stumbled over him. The fright and perturbation of my spirits at once excited resentment; at that time I was entirely insensible to gratitude or mercy. I instantly cut off a little sapling and soon dispatched him: this serpent was about six feet in length, and as thick as an ordinary man's leg. The rencounter deterred us from proceeding on our researches for that day. So I cut off a long tough withe or vine, which fastening around the neck of the slain serpent, I dragged him after me, his scaly body sounding over the ground, and entering the camp with him in triumph, was soon surrounded by the amazed multitude, both Indians and my countrymen. The adventure soon reached the ears of the commander, who sent an officer to request that, if the snake had not bit himself, he might have him served up for his dinner. I readily delivered up the body of the snake to the cooks, and being that day invited to dine at the governor's table, saw the snake served up in several dishes; governor Grant being fond of the flesh of the rattle snake. I tasted of it but could not swallow it. I, however, was sorry after killing the serpent, when cooly recollecting every circumstance. He certainly had it in his power to kill me almost instantly, and I make no doubt but that he was conscious of it. I promised myself that I would never again be accessary to the death of a rattle snake, which promise I have invariably kept to. This dreaded animal is easily killed; a stick no thicker than a man's thumb is sufficient to kill the largest at one stroke, if well directed, either on the head or across the back; nor can they make their escape by running off, nor indeed do they attempt it when attacked.

The moccasin snake is a large and horrid serpent to all appearance, and there are very terrifying stories related of him by the inhabitants of the Southern states, where they greatly abound, particularly in East Florida: that their bite is always incurable, the flesh for a considerable space about the wound rotting to the bone, which then becomes carious, and a general mortification ensues, which infallibly destroys the patient; the members of the body rotting and dying by piecemeal: and that there is no remedy to prevent a lingering miserable death but by immediately cutting away the flesh to the bone, for some distance round about the wound. In shape and proportion of parts they much resemble the rattle snake, and are marked or clouded much after the same manner, but the colours more dull and obscure; and in their disposition seem to agree with that dreadful reptile, being slow of progression, and throwing themselves in a spiral coil ready for a blow when attacked. They have one peculiar quality, which is this, when discovered, and observing their enemy to take notice of them, after throwing themselves in a coil, they gradually raise their upper mandible or jaw until it falls back nearly touching their neck, at the same time slowly vibrating their long purple forked tongue, their crooked poisonous fangs directed right at you, which gives the creature a most terrifying appearance. They are from three to four and even five feet in length, and as thick as a man's leg; they are not numerous, yet too common, and a sufficient terror to the miserable naked slaves, who are compelled to labour in the swamps and low lands where only they abound.

I never could find any that knew an instance of any person's losing their life from the bite of them, only by hearsay. Yet I am convinced it is highly prudent for every person to be on their guard against them. They appear to be of the viper tribe, from their swelling of their body and flattening their neck when provoked, and from their large poisonous fangs: their head, mouth and eyes are remarkably large.

There is another snake in Carolina and Florida called the moccasin, very different from this; which is a very beautiful creature, and I believe not of a destructive or vindictive nature. These when grown to their greatest size are about five feet in length, and near as thick as a man's arm; their skin scaly but smooth and shining, of a pale grey and sky colour ground, uniformly marked with transverse undulatory ringlets or blotches of a deep nut brown, edged with red or bright Spanish brown. They appear innocent, very active and swift, endeavouring to escape from one; they have no poisonous fangs. These are seen in high forest lands, about rotten logs or decayed fallen limbs of trees, and they harbour about old log buildings. They seem to be a species, if not the very same snake which, in Pensylvania and Virginia, is called the wampom snake; but here in warmer Southern climes they grow to a much larger size, and from the same accident their colour may be more variable and deeper. They are by the inhabitants asserted to be dangerously venemous, their bite incurable, &c. But as I could never learn an instance of their bite being mortal or attended with any dangerous consequence, and have had frequent opportunities of observing their nature and disposition, I am inclined to pronounce them an innocent creature, with respect to mankind.

The bastard rattle snake, by some called ground rattle snake, is a dangerous little creature: their bite is certainly mortal if present medical relief is not administered: they seem to be much of the nature of the asp or adder of the old world.

This little viper is in form and colour much like the rattle snake, but not so bright and uniformly marked: their head is broader and shorter in proportion to the other parts of their body: their nose prominent and turned upwards: their tail becomes suddenly small from the vent to the extremity, which terminates with three minute articulations, resembling rattles: when irritated they turn up their tail, which vibrates so quick as to appear like a mist or vapour, but causes little or no sound or noise; yet it is the common report of the inhabitants, that they cause that remarkable vehement noise, so frequently observed in forests in the heat of summer and autumn, very terrifying to strangers, which is, probably, caused by a very sable small insect of the genus cicadae, or which are called locusts in America; yet it is possible I may be mistaken in this conjecture. This dangerous viper is from eight to ten inches in length, and of proportionable thickness. They are spiteful, snappish creatures; and throwing themselves into a little coil, they swell and flatten themselves, continually darting out their head; and they seem capable of springing beyond their length. They seem destitute of the pacific disposition and magnanimity of the rattle snake, and are unworthy of an alliance with him. No man ever saves their lives, yet they remain too numerous, even in the oldest settled parts of the country.

The green snake is a beautiful innocent creature: they are from two to three feet in length, but not so thick as a persons little finger; of the finest green colour. They are very abundant, commonly seen on the limbs of trees and shrubs: they prey upon insects and reptiles, particularly the little green chameleon: and the forked tailed hawk or kite feeds on both of them, snatching them off the boughs of the trees.

The ribband snake is another very beautiful innocent serpent: they are eighteen inches in length, and about the thickness of a man's little finger; the head is very small; the ground colour of a full, clear vermilion, variegated with transverse bars or zones of a dark brown, which people fancy represents a ribband wound round the creature's body: they are altogether inoffensive to man, and are in a manner domestic, frequenting old wooden buildings, open grounds and plantations.

The chicken snake is a large, strong and swift serpent, six or seven feet in length, but scarcely so thick as a man's wrist; they are of a cinereous, earthy colour, and striped longitudinally with broad lines or lists, of a dusky or blackish colour. They are a domestic snake, haunting about houses and plantations; and would be useful to man if tamed and properly tutored, being great devourers of rats, but they are apt to disturb hen roosts and prey upon chickens. They are as innocent as a worm with respect to venom, are easily tamed and soon become very familiar.

The pine or bull snake is very large and inoffensive with respect to mankind, but devours squirrels, birds, rabbits, and every other creature it can take as food. They are the largest snake yet known in North America, except the rattle snake, and perhaps exceed him in length: they are pied black and white: they utter a terrible loud hissing noise, sounding very hollow and like distant thunder, when irritated, or at the time of incubation, when the males contend with each other for the desired female. These serpents are also called horn snakes, from their tail terminating with a hard, horny spur, which they vibrate very quick when disturbed, but they never attempt to strike with it; they have dens in the earth, whither they retreat precipitately when apprehensive of danger.

There are many other species of snakes in the regions of Florida and Carolina; as the water snake, black snake, garter snake, copper belly, ring neck, and two or three varieties of vipers, besides those already noticed in my journal. Since I have begun to mention the animals of these regions, this may be a proper place to enumerate the other tribes which I observed during my perigrinations. I shall begin with the frogs (RANAE.)

(1) The largest frog known in Florida and on the sea coast of Carolina, is about eight or nine inches in length from the nose to the extremity of the toes: they are of a dusky brown or black colour on the upper side, and their belly or under side white, spotted and clouded with dusky spots of various size and figure; their legs and thighs also are variegated with transverse ringlets, of dark brown or black; and they are yellow

and green about their mouth and lips. They live in wet swamps and marshes, on the shores of large rivers and lakes; their voice is loud and hideous, greatly resembling the grunting of a swine; but not near as loud as the voice of the bull frog of Virginia and Pensylvania: neither do they arrive to half their size, the bull frog being frequently eighteen inches in length, and their roaring as loud as that of a bull.

(2) The bell frog, so called because their voice is fancied to be exactly like the sound of a loud cow bell. This tribe being very numerous, and uttering their voices in companies or by large districts, when one begins another answers; thus the sound is caught and repeated from one to another, to a great distance round about, causing a surprising noise for a few minutes, rising and sinking according as the wind sits, when it nearly dies away, or is softly kept up by distant districts or communities: thus the noise is repeated continually, and as one becomes familiarised to it, is not unmusical, though at first, to strangers, it seems clamorous and disgusting.

(3) A beautiful green frog inhabits the grassy, marshy shores of these large rivers. They are very numerous, and their noise exactly resembles the barking of little dogs, or the yelping of puppies: these likewise make a great clamour, but as their notes are fine, and uttered in chorus, by separate bands or communities, far and near, rising and falling with the gentle breezes, affords a pleasing kind of music.

(4) There is besides this a less green frog, which is very common about houses: their notes are remarkably like that of young chickens: these raise their chorus immediately preceding a shower of rain, with which they seem delighted.

(5) A little grey speckled frog is in prodigious numbers in and about the ponds and savannas on high land, particularly in Pine forests: their language or noise is also uttered in chorus, by large communities or separate bands; each particular note resembles the noise made by striking two pebbles together under the surface of the water, which when thousands near you utter their notes at the same time, and is wafted to your ears by a sudden flow of wind, is very surprising, and does not ill resemble the rushing noise made by a vast quantity of gravel and pebbles together, at once precipitated from a great height.

(6) There is yet an extreme diminutive species of frogs, which inhabits the grassy verges of ponds in savannas: these are called savanna crickets, are of a dark ash or dusky colour, and have a very picked nose. At the times of very great rains, in the autumn, when the savannas are in a manner inundated, they are to be seen in incredible multitudes clambering up the tall grass, weed, &c. round the verges of the savannas, bordering on the higher ground; and by an inattentive person might be taken for spiders or other insects. Their note is very feeble, not unlike the chattering of young birds or crickets.

(7) The shad frog, so called in Pensylvania from their appearing and croaking in the spring season, at the time the people fish for shad: this is a beautiful spotted frog, of a slender form, five or six inches in length from the nose to the extremities; of a dark olive green, blotched with clouds and ringlets of a dusky colour: these are remarkable jumpers and enterprising hunters, leaving their ponds to a great distance in search of prey. They abound in rivers, swamps and marshes, in the Southern regions; in the evening and sultry summer days, particularly in times of drought, are very noisy; and at some distance one would be almost persuaded that there were assemblies of men in serious debate. These have also a sucking or clucking noise, like that which is made by sucking in the tongue under the roof of the mouth. These are the kinds of water frogs that have come under my observation; yet I am persuaded that there are yet remaining several other species.

(8) The high land frogs, commonly called toads, are of two species, the red and black. The former, which is of a reddish brown or brick colour, is the largest, and may weigh upwards of one pound when full grown: they have a disagreeable look, and when irritated, they swell and raise themselves up on their four legs and croak, but are no ways venomous or hurtful to man. The other species are one third less, and of a black or dark dusky colour. The legs and thighs of both are marked with blotches and ringlets of a darker colour, which appear more conspicuous when provoked: the smaller black species are the most numerous. Early in the spring season, they assemble by numberless multitudes in the drains and ponds, when their universal croaking and shouts are great indeed, yet in some degree not unharmonious. After this breeding time

they crawl out of the water and spread themselves all over the country. Their spawn being hatched in the warm water, the larva is there nourished, passing through the like metamorphoses as the water frogs; and as soon as they obtain four feet, whilst yet no larger than crickets, they leave the fluid nursery-bed, and hop over the dry land after their parents.

The food of these amphibious creatures, when out of the water, is every kind of insect, reptile, &c. they can take, even ants and spiders; nature having furnished them with an extreme long tongue, which exudes a viscid or glutinous liquid, they being secreted under covert, spring suddenly upon their prey, or dart forth their tongue as quick as lightning, and instantly drag into their devouring jaws the unwary insect. But whether they prey upon one another, as the water frogs do, I know not.

There are several species of the lizard kind besides the alligator, which is by naturalists allowed to be a species of that genus.

The green lizard or little green chameleon is a pretty innocent creature: the largest I have seen were not more than seven inches in length: they appear commonly of a fine green colour, having a large red gill under their throat: they have the faculty of changing colour, which, notwithstanding the specious reasoning of physiologists, is a very surprising phenomenon. The striped lizard, called scorpion, and the blue bellied squamous lizards I have already mentioned. There is a large copper coloured lizard, and a very slender one of a fine blue colour, and very swift; the tail of this last, which is very long and slender, is as subject to be broken off as that of the glass snake. These two last are become very scarce, and when seen are discovered about old log buildings.

Here are several species of the tortoise, besides those already mentioned; as the small land tortoise, already described by every traveller. There is a good figure and description of him in G. Edwards's Gl. Nat. Hist. vol. II. p. 205. There are two species of fresh-water tortoises inhabiting the tide water rivers; one of which is large, weighing ten or twelve pounds, the back shell of nearly an oval form, and raised very high, the belly shell flat and entire, but deeply scolloped opposite the legs. The other species are small, comparatively, and the back shell lightly raised: both species are food for mankind and esteemed delicious.

Of beasts, the otter (lutra) is common, but more so in West-Florida, towards the mountains. The several species of mustela are common; as the mink, weasel and polecat (putorius). Racoons and opossums are in great abundance; these animals are esteemed delicious and healthy food. There are two species of wild-rats; but neither of them near as large as the European house-rat, which are common enough in the settlements of the white people. Here are very few mice; yet I have seen some, particularly in Charleston. I saw two in a little wire cage, at a gentleman's house, which were as white as snow, and their eyes red. There are yet a few beavers in East-Florida and Georgia, but they abound most in the north of Georgia, and in West-Florida, near the mountains. But the musk-rat (castor cauda lanceolata) is never seen in Carolina, Georgia or Florida, within one hundred miles of the sea coast, and very few in the most northern parts of these regions; which must be considered as a most favourable circumstance, by the people in countries where there is so much banking and draining of the land, they being the most destructive creatures to dykes.

The roe buck I have already mentioned. The bears are yet too numerous: they are a strong creature, and prey on the fruits of the country, and will likewise devour young calves, swine and sheep; but I never could learn a well attested instance of their attacking mankind. They weigh from five hundred to six hundred weight when full grown and fat: their flesh is greatly esteemed as food by the natives.

The wild cat, felis cauda truncata, (lynx) is common enough; it is a fierce and bold little animal, preying on young pigs, fawns, turkeys, &c. They are not half the size of a common cur dog, are generally of a greyish colour, and somewhat tabbied; their sides bordering on the belly are varied with yellowish brown spots, and almost black waving streaks, and brindled. I have been credibly informed that the wolves here are frequently seen pied, black and white, and of other mixed colours. They assemble in companies in the night time, howl and bark altogether, especially in cold winter nights, which is terrifying to the wandering bewildered traveller.

The foxes of Carolina and Florida are of the smaller red species; they bark in the night round about plantations, but do not bark twice in the same place; they move precipitately, and in a few minutes are heard on the opposite side of the plantation, or at a great distance: it is said that dogs are terrified at the noise, and cannot be persuaded or compelled to pursue them. They commit depredations on young pigs, lambs, poultry, &c.

The mole is not so common here as in the northern states.

The bats of Florida seem to be the same species of those in Pensylvania and Virginia, and very little different from the European.

Here are several species of squirrels, (sciurus) peculiar to the lower countries, or maritime parts of Carolina and the Floridas, and some of them are very beautiful creatures.

The great black fox squirrel is above two feet in length from the nose to the end of the tail, which for about two inches is milk white, as are the ears and nose. The red fox squirrel is of the same size and form, of a light reddish brown upper side, and white under side, the ears and tip end of the tail white.

The grey fox squirrel is rather larger than either of the foregoing; their belly white, as are the ears, nose, and tip of the tail. These three seem to be varieties of the same species.

The common grey squirrel is about half the size of the preceding.

The black squirrel is about the same size, and all over of a shining jet black.

The little grey squirrel is much less than either of the preceding species; it is of a brownish grey upper side, and white belly.

The ground squirrel, or little striped squirrel of Pensylvania and the northern regions, is never seen here, and very rarely in the mountains north-west of these territories; but the flying squirrel, (sciurus volans) is very common.

The rabbit (lepus minor, cauda abrupta, pupillis atris) is pretty common, and no ways differing from those of Pensylvania and the northern states.

Having mentioned most of the animals in these parts of America, which are most remarkable or useful, there remains, however, yet some observations on birds, which by some may be thought not impertinent.

There are but few that have fallen under my observation, but have been mentioned by the zoologists, and most of them very well figured in Catesby's, or Edwards's works.

But these authors have done very little towards elucidating the subject of the migration of birds, or accounting for the annual appearance and disappearance, and vanishing of these beautiful and entertaining beings, who visit us at certain stated seasons. Catesby has said very little on this curious subject; but Edwards more, and perhaps all, or as much as could be said in truth, by the most able and ingenious, who had not the advantage and opportunity of ocular observation; which can only be acquired by travelling, and residing a whole year at least in the various climates from north to south, to the full extent of their peregrinations; or minutely examining the tracts and observations of curious and industrious travellers who have published their memoirs on this subject. There may perhaps be some persons who consider this enquiry not to be productive of any real benefit to mankind, and pronounce such attention to natural history merely speculative, and only fit to amuse and entertain the idle virtuoso; however the ancients thought otherwise: for with them, the knowledge of the passage of birds was the study of their priests and philosophers, and was considered a matter of real and indispensable use to the state, next to astronomy; as we find their system and practice of agriculture was in a great degree regulated by the arrival and disappearance of birds of passage; and perhaps a calendar under such a regulation at this time, might be useful to the husbandman and gardener.

But however attentive and observant the ancients were on this branch of science, they seem to have been very ignorant or erroneous in their conjectures concerning what became of birds, after their disappearance, until their return again. In the southern and temperate climates some imagined they went to the moon: in the northern regions they supposed that they retired to caves and hollow trees, for shelter and security, where they remained in a dormant state during the cold seasons: and even at this day, very celebrated men have asserted that swallows (hirundo) at the approach of winter, voluntarily plunge into lakes and rivers, descend to the bottom, and there creep into the mud and slime, where they continue overwhelmed by ice in a torpid state, until the returning summer warms them again into life; when they rise, return to the surface of the water, immediately take wing, and again people the air. This notion, though the latest, seems the most difficult to reconcile to reason and common sense, respecting a bird so swift of flight that it can with ease and pleasure move through the air even swifter than the winds, and in a few hours time shift twenty degrees from north to south, even from frozen regions to climes where frost is never seen, and where the air and plains are replenished with flying insects of infinite variety, its favourite and only food.

Pensylvania and Virginia appear to me to be the climates in North-America, where the greatest variety and abundance of these winged emigrants choose to celebrate their nuptials, and rear their offspring, which they annually return with, to their winter habitations, in the southern regions of N. America; and most of those beautiful creatures, which annually people and harmonise our forests and groves, in the spring and summer seasons, are birds of passage from the southward. The eagle, i. e. falco leucocephalus, or bald eagle, falco maximus, or great grey eagle, falco major cauda ferrugineo, falco pullarius, falco columbarius, strix pythaulis, strix acclamatus, strix assio, tetrao tympanus, or pheasant of Pensylvania, tetrao urogallus, or mountain cock or grous of Pensylvania, tetrao minor sive coturnix, or partridge of Pensylvania, picus, or woodpeckers of several species, corvus carnivorus, or raven, corvus frugivora, or crow, corvus glandarius s. corvus cristatus, or blue jay, alauda maxima, regulus atrofuscus minor, or marsh wren, sitta, or nuthatch, meleagris, are perhaps nearly all the land birds which continue the year round in Pensylvania. I might add to these the blue bird, motacilla sialis, mock bird, turdus polyglottos, and sometimes the robin redbreast, turdus migratorius, in extraordinary warm winters; and although I do not pretend to assert as a known truth, yet it may be found on future observation that most of these above mentioned are strangers; or not really bred where they wintered; but are more northern families, or sojourners, bound southerly to more temperate habitations; thus pushing each other southerly, and possessing their vacated places, and then back again at the return of spring.

Very few tribes of birds build, or rear their young, in the south or maritime parts of Virginia and Carolina, Georgia and Florida; yet all these numerous tribes, particularly of the soft billed kinds, which breed in Pensylvania, pass in the spring season through these regions in a few weeks time, making but very short stages by the way: and again, but few of them winter there, on their return southerly: and as I have never travelled the continent south of New Orleans, or the point of Florida, where few or none of them are to be seen in the winter, I am entirely ignorant how far southward they continue their route, during their absence from Pensylvania; but perhaps none of them pass the tropic.

When in my residence in Carolina and Florida, I have seen vast flights of the house swallow (hirurdo pelasgia) and bank martin (hirundo riparia) passing onward north toward Pensylvania, where they breed in the spring, about the middle of March, and likewise in the autumn in September or October, and large flights on their return southward. And it is observable that they always avail themselves of the advantage of high and favourable winds, which likewise do all birds of passage. The pewit, or black cap flycatcher, of Catesby, is the first bird of passage which appears in the spring in Pensylvania, which is generally about the first, or middle of March; and then wherever they appear, we may plant peas and beans in the open grounds, (vicia sativa) French beans (phaseolus) sow raddishes, (raphanus) lettuce, (lactuca) onions, (cepa) pastinaca, daucus, and almost every kind of esculent garden seeds, without fear or danger from frosts; for although we have sometimes frosts after their first appearances for a night or two, yet not so severe as to injure the young plants.

In the spring of the year the small birds of passage appear very suddenly in Pennsylvania, which is not a little surprising, and no less pleasing: at once the woods, the groves, and meads, are filled with their melody, as if they dropped down from the skies. The reason or probable cause is their setting off with high and fair winds from the southward; for a strong south and south-west wind about the beginning of April never fails bringing millions of these welcome visitors.

Being willing to contribute my mite towards illustrating the subject of the peregrination of the tribes of birds of N. America, I shall subjoin a nomenclature of the birds of passage, agreeable to my observation, when on my travels from New England to New-Orleans, on the Mississippi, and point of Florida.

LAND birds which are seen in Pennsylvania, Maryland, Virginia, from S. Carolina, Georgia and Florida, N. and the sea coast Westward, to the Apalachian mountains, viz.

*THESE arrive in Pennsylvania in the spring season from the South, and after building nests, and rearing their young, return again Southerly in the autumn.

† THESE arrive in Pennsylvania in the autumn, from the North, where they continue during the winter, and return again the spring following, I suppose to breed and rear their young; and these kinds continue their journies as far South as Carolina and Florida.

‡ THESE arrive in the spring in Carolina and Florida from the South, breed and rear their young, and return South again at the approach of winter, but never reach Pennsylvania, or the Northern States.

‖ THESE are natives of Carolina and Florida, where they breed and continue the year round.

¶THESE breed and continue the year round in Pennsylvania.

STRIX. The Owl.

† Strix arcticus, capite levi, corpore toto niveo; the great white owl.

¶ Strix pythaules, capite aurito, corpore rufo; the great horned owl.

† Strix maximus, capite aurito, corpore niveo; the great horned white owl.

¶ Strix acclamator, capite levi, corpore griseo; the whooting owl.

† Strix peregrinator, capite aurito, corpore versicolore; the sharp winged owl.

¶ Strix assio, capite aurito, corpore ferrugineo; the little screech owl.

Vultur. The Vulture.

‖ Vultur aura; the turkey-buzzard.
‖ Vultur sacra; the white tailed vulture.
‖ Vultur atratus; black vulture, or carrion crow.

Falco. Eagle and Hawk.

¶ Falco regalis; the great grey eagle.
¶ F. leucocephalus; the bald eagle.
* F. piscatorius; the fishing eagle.
¶ F. Aquilinus; cauda ferrug. great eagle hawk.
¶ F. gallinarius; the hen hawk.
¶ F. pullarius; the chicken hawk.
* F. columbarius; the pigeon hawk.
¶ F. niger; the black hawk.
* F. ranivorus; the marsh hawk.
* F. sparverius; the least hawk or sparrow spark.

[a]Milvus. Kite Hawk.

‖ Falco furcatus; the forked tail hawk, or kite.
‖ F. glaucus; the sharp winged hawk, of a pale sky-blue colour, the tip of the wings black.
‖ F. subceruleus; the sharp winged hawk, of a dark or dusky blue colour.
‖ Psittacus Caroliniensis; the parrot of Carolina, or parrakeet.

Corvus. The Crow kind.

* Corvus carnivorus; the raven.
‖ C. maritimus; the great sea-side crow, or rook.
¶ C. frugivorus; the common crow.
¶ C. cristatus, s. pica glandaria; the blue jay.
¶ C. Floridanus, pica glandaria minor; the little jay of Florida.
¶ Gracula quiscula; the purple jackdaw of the sea coast.

---

[a]Kite hawks. These are characterised by having long sharp pointed wings, being of swift flight, sailing without flapping their wings, lean light bodies, and feeding out of their claws on the wing, as they gently sail round and round.

Pica glandaria cerulea non cristata, the little jay of East Florida.

* Gracula purpurea; the lesser purple jackdaw, or crow blackbird.
* Cuculus Caroliniensis; the cuckoo of Carolina.

PICUS. Woodpeckers.

|| Picus principalis; the greatest crested woodpecker, having a white back.
* P. pileatus; the great red crested black woodpecker.
* P. erythrocephalus; red headed woodpecker.
* P. auratus; the gold winged woodpecker.
¶ P. Carolinus; the red bellied woodpecker.
¶ P. pubescens; the least spotted woodpecker.
¶ P. villosus; the hairy, speckled and crested woodpecker.
¶ P. varius; yellow bellied woodpecker.
¶ Sitta Europea; grey black capped nuthatch.
† S. varia, ventre rubro; the black capped, red bellied nut-hatch.
† Certhia rufa; little brown variegated creeper.
* C. pinus; the pine creeper.
* C. picta; blue and white striped or pied creeper.
* Alcedo alcyon; the great crested king-fisher.
* Trochilus colubris; the humming bird.
* Lanius griseus; the little grey butcher-bird of Pensylvania.
* L. garrulus; the little black capped or butcher bird of Florida.
* L. tyrannus; the king bird.
* Muscicapa nunciola; the pewit, or black cap flycatcher.
* M. cristata; the great crested yellow bellied flycatcher.
* M. rapax; the lesser pewit, or brown and greenish fly-catcher.
* M. subviridis; the little olive col^d. flycatcher.
* M. cantatrix; the little domestic flycatcher or green wren.
* M. sylvicola; the little red eyed flycatcher.
* Columba Caroliniensis, the turtle dove.
|| C. passerina; the dove.
|| C. migratoria; the pigeon of passage or wild pigeon.
* Alauda magna; the great meadow lark.
† A. campestris; gutture flavo, the sky lark.

† A. migratoria; corpore toto ferrugineo, the little brown lark.

¶ Turdus migratorius; the fieldfare, or robin redbreast.

* T. rufus; the great, or fox coloured thrush.

* T. polyglottos; the mocking bird.

* T. melodes; the wood thrush.

* T. minimus, vertice auro; the least golden crown thrush.

* Oriolus Baltimore; Baltimore bird or hang nest.

* O. spurius; the goldfinch or icterus minor.

* Merula flammula; sand-hill redbird of Carolina.

* M. Marilandica; the summer red bird.

* Garrulis australis; the yellow breasted chat.

* Lucar lividus, apice nigra; the cat bird, or chicken bird.

¶ Ampelis garrulus; crown bird, or cedar bird.

GRANIVOROUS TRIBES.

¶ Meleagris Americanus; the wild turkey.

¶ Tetrao lagopus; the mountain cock, or grous.

¶ T. tympanus; the pheasant of Pensylvania.

¶ T. minor, s. coturnix; the quail or partridge.

¶ Loxia cardinalis; the red bird, or Virginia nightingale.

† L. rostro forficato; the cross beak.

* L. cerulea; the blue cross beak.

* Emberiza oryzivora; (1) the rice bird.*

† E. livida; the blue or slate coloured rice bird.

* E. varia; (2) the pied rice bird.

‡ Linaria ciris; the painted finch, or nonpareil.

* L. cyanea; the blue linnet.

¶ Carduelis Americanus, the goldfinch.

† C. minus; the lesser goldfinch.

† C. pusilus; the least finch.

* Fringilla erythrophthalma; the towhe bird.

† F. purpurea; the purple finch.

† F. cannabina; the hemp bird.

† F. rufa; the red, or fox-coloured ground or hedge sparrow.

† F. fusca; the large brown white throat sparrow.

---

*(1,2) Are generally supposed to be male and female of the same species (2) or the pied rice bird the male, and (1) or the yellow, the female.

* Passer domesticus; the little house sparrow or chipping bird.
* P. palustris; the reed sparrow.
* P. agrestis; the little field sparrow.
† P. nivalis; the snow bird.
* Calandra pratensis; the May bird.
* Sturnus prædatorius; the red winged starling, or corn thief.
* S. stercorarius; the cowpen bird.
* Motacilla sialis; the blue bird. (Rubicula Americana, Cat.)
* M. fluviatilis; the water wagtail.
* M. domestica (regulus rufus); the house wren.
¶ * M. palustris; (reg. minor) the marsh wren.
* M. Caroliniana; (reg. magnus) the great wren of Carolina, the body of a dark brown, the throat and breast of a pale clay colour.
* Regulus griseus; the little bluish grey wren.
† R. cristatus; the golden crown wren.
† R. cristatus alter vertice rubini coloris; the ruby crown wren. (G. Edwards.)
* R. peregrinus, gutture flavo; the olive coloured yellow throated wren.
* Ruticilla Americana; the redstart.
* Luscinia, s. philomela Americana; the yellow hooded titmouse.
* Parus cristatus; bluish grey crested titmouse.
¶ P. Europæus, the black cap titmouse.
* P. luteus; the summer yellow bird.
* P. cedrus uropygio flavo; the yellow rump.
* P. varius; various coloured little finch creeper.
* P. peregrinus; little chocolate breast titmouse.
* P. aureus vertice rubro; the yellow red pole.
* P. aureo vertice; the golden crown flycatcher.
* P. viridis gutture nigro; the green black throated fly-catcher.
* P. alis aureis; the golden winged flycatcher.
* P. aureus alis ceruleis; the blue winged yellow bird.
* P. griseus gutture luteo; the yellow throated creeper.
* Hirundo pelasgia cauda aculeata; the house swallow.
* H. purpurea; the great purple martin.

* H. riparia vertice purpurea; the bank martin.
* H. cerdo; the chimney swallow.
‡ Caprimulgus lucifugus; the great bat, or chuck wills widow.
* C. Americanus; nighthawk, or whip poor will.

AMPHIBIOUS, or AQUATIC BIRDS,

Or such as obtain their food, and reside, in and near the water.

GRUS. The Crane.

‖ Grus clamator, vertice papilloso, corpore niveo remigibus nigris; the great whooping crane.
‡ G. pratensis; corpore cinereo, vertice papilloso; the great savanna crane.

ARDEA. The Heron.

¶ Ardea Herodias; the great bluish grey crested heron.
* A. immaculata; the great white river heron.
* A. alba minor; the little white heron.
‡ A. purpurea cristata; the little crested purple or blue heron.
* A. varia cristata; the grey white crested heron.
‡ A. maculata cristata; the speckled crested heron, or crab-catcher.
* A. mugitans; the marsh bittern, or Indian hen.
* A. clamator, corpore subcæruleo; the quaw bird, or frog-catcher.
‡ A. subfusca stillata; the little brownish spotted bitern.
‡ A. violacea; the crested blue bittern, (called poor Job.)
* A. viriscens; the green bittern or poke.
* A. viriscens minor, the lesser green bittern.
* A. parva; the least brown and striped bittern.
* Platalea ajaja; the spoonbill, seen as far North as Alata-maha river in Georgia.

TANTALUS. The wood Pelican.

‡ Tantalus loculator; the wood pelican.
‡ T. albus; the white Spanish curlew.
‡ T. fuscus; the dusky and white Spanish curlew.

‖ T. pictus; (Ephouskyka Indian) the crying bird, beautifully speckled.

‖ T. Ichthyophagus; the gannet; perhaps little different from the Ibis.

‖ Numenius alba varia; the white godwit.

¶ N. pectore rufo; the great red breasted godwit.

¶ N. Americana; the greater godwit.

¶ N. fluvialis; the redshank or pool snipe.

¶ N. magnus rufus; the great sea coast curlew.

* N. minor campestris; the lesser field curlew.

¶ N. cinereus; the seaside lesser curlew.

* Scolopax Americana rufa; great red woodcock.

* S. minor arvensis; the meadow snipe.

* Tringa rufa; the red cootfooted tringa.

T. cinerea, gutture albo; the white throated cootfooted tringa.

T. vertice nigro; black cap cootfooted tringa.

¶ T. maculata; the spotted tringa.

¶ T grisea; the little pond snipe.

¶ T. fusca; the little brown or ash coloured pool snipe.

¶ T. parva; the little tringa of the sea shore, called sand bird.

* Morinella Americana; the turnstone or dotrel.

† Cygnus ferus; the wild swan.

† Anser Canadensis; the Canadian goose.

† A. alis cærulis; the blue winged goose.

† A. fuscus maculatus; the laughing goose.

† A. branta, corpore albo, remigibus nigris; the white brant goose.

† A. branta grisea maculata; the great particoloured brant, or grey goose.

† Anas fera torquata major, caput et collum viridi splendentia, dorsum griseo fuscum, pectore rufescente, speculum violaceum; the great wild duck, called duck and mallard.

† A. nigra maxima; the great black duck.

† A. bucephala; the bull-neck and buffaloe head.

† A. subcærulea; the blue bill.

† A. leucocephala; the black white faced duck.

† A. caudacuta; the sprig tail duck.

† A. rustica; the little brown and white duck.

† A. principalis, maculata; the various coloured duck, his neck and breast as though ornamented with chains of beads.

† A. minor picta; the little black and white duck called butterback.

Querquedulae. Teal.

* Anas sponsa; the summer duck.

† A. discors; the blue winged teal.

† A. migratoria; the least green winged teal.

* A. fistulosa; whistling duck.

† Mergus major pectore rufo; great fishing duck.

† M. cucullatus; the round crested duck.

* Colymbus migratorius; the eel crow.

‖ C. Floridanus; the great black cormorant of Florida, having a red beak.

¶ C. colubrinus, cauda elongata; the snake bird of Florida.

¶ C. musicus; the great black and white pied diver or loon.

† Colymbus arcticus; the great speckled diver.

¶ C. auritus et cornutus; the little eared brown dobchick.

¶ C. minor fuscus; little crested brown dobchick.

‡ Phaæthon aethereus; the tropic bird.

¶ Larus albus; the great white gull.

¶ L. griseus; the great grey gull.

‡ L. albus minor; the little white river gull.

‖ Onocrotalus Americanus; the American sea pelican.

‖ Petrella pintada; the pintada bird.

¶ Rynchops niger; the shearwater or razor bill.

‡ Pelicanus aquilus; the frigate, or man of war bird.

‡ P. sula; the booby.

† Sterna stolida; the sea swallow, or noddy.

Charadrus. The Plover kind.

* Charadrus vociferus; the kildea or chattering plover.

* C. maculatus; the great field spotted plover.

* C. minor; the little seaside ring necked plover.

* Hæmatopus ostrealegus; the will willet or oyster catcher.

‖ Fulica Floridana; the great blue or slate coloured coot of Florida.

* Rallus Virginianus; the soree bird or little brown rail, also called widgeon in Pennsyl.

‡ R. aquaticus minor; the little dark blue water rail.

* R. rufus Americanus; the greater brown rail.

‖ R. major subcæruleus; the blue or slate coloured water rail of Florida.

* Phoenicopterus ruber; the flamingo, seen about the point of Florida, rarely as far N. as St. Augustine.

I am convinced there are yet several kinds of land birds, and a great number of aquatic fowl, that have not come under my particular notice; therefore shall leave them to the investigation of future travelling naturalists of greater ability and industry.

There yet remain some observations on the passage, and breeding of birds, &c. which may be proper to notice in this place.

I shall first mention the rice bird, (emberiza oryzivora.) It is the commonly received opinion that they are male and female of the same species, i. e. the black pied rice bird the male, and a yellowish clay coloured one the female: the last mentioned appearing only in the autumn, when the oryza zizania are about ripening; yet in my opinion there are some strong circumstances which seem to operate against such a conjecture, though generally believed.

In the spring, about the middle of May, the black pied rice bird (which is called the male) appears in Pennsylvania; at that time the great yellow ephemera, called May fly, and a species of locusta appear in incredible multitudes, the favorite delicious food of these birds, when they are sprightly, vociferous, and pleasingly tuneful.

When I was at St. Augustine, in E. Florida, in the beginning of April, the same species of grasshoppers were in multitudes on the fields and commons about the town; when great flights of these male rice birds suddenly arrived from the South, which by feeding on these insects became extremely fat and delicious: they continued here two or three weeks, until their food became scarce, when they disappeared, I suppose pursuing their journey North after the locusta and ephemera; there were a few of the yellow kind, or true rice bird, to be seen amongst them. Now these pied rice birds seem to observe the same order and time in their migrations Northerly, with the other spring birds of passage, and are undoubtedly on their way to their breeding place; but then there are no females with them, at least not one to ten thousand of the male colour, which cannot be supposed to be a sufficient number to pair and breed by. Being in Charleston in the month of June, I observed at a gentleman's door, a cage full of rice birds, that is of the yellow or female colour, who were very merry and vociferous, having the same variable music with the pied or male kind, which I thought extraordinary; and observing it to the gentleman, he assured me that they were all of the male kind, taken the preceding spring, but had changed their colour, and would be next spring of the colour of the pied, thus changing colour with the seasons of the year. If this is really the case, it appears they are both of the same species intermixed, spring and fall. In the spring they are gay, vociferous and tuneful birds.

Ampelis garrulus; crown bird or cedar bird. These birds feed on various sorts of succulent fruit and berries, associating in little flocks or flights, and are to be seen in all the regions from Canada to New Orleans on the Mississippi, and how much farther South and South-West I know not. They observe no fixed time of appearance in Pennsylvania, but are to be seen in a few days every month of the year; so that it is difficult to determine at what season they breed, or where. The longest period of their appearance in Pennsylvania is in the spring and first of June, at the time the early cherries are ripe, when they are numerous; and in the autumn when the Cedar berries are ripe (Juniperus Americana;) they arrive in large flights, and, with the robins (turdus migratorius) and yellow rump (parus cedrus) soon strip those trees of their berries, after which they disappear again; but in November and December they appear in smaller flights, feeding on the fruit of the Persimon (Dyospyros Virginiana;) and some are seen till March, subsisting upon Smilax berries, Privet (Ligustrum vulgare) and other permanent fruits; after which they disappear until May and June. I have been informed by some people in Pennsylvania, that they have found their nests at these seasons in Pennsylvania.

Linaria ciris (emberiza ciris Linn.) or painted finch, or non-pareil of Catesby, is not seen North of Cape Fear, in North Carolina, and seldom ten miles from the sea coast, or perhaps twenty or thirty miles, near the banks of great rivers, in fragrant groves of the Orange (Citrus aurantium) Zanthoxylon, Laurus Borbonia, Cassine, Sideroxylon, &c.

Linaria cyanea (tanagra Linn.) the blue linnet, is supposed by some to be the nonpareil, in an early stage of life, not being yet arrived to his brilliancy and variety of colours; but this is certainly a mistake, for the blue linnet is longer and of a slenderer configuration, and their notes more variable, vehement and sonorous. And they inhabit the continent and sea coast islands from Mexico to Nova Scotia, from the sea coast, West beyond the Apalachean and Cherokee mountains. The songs of the nonpareil are remarkably low, soft and warbling, exceedingly tender and soothing.

Catesby, in his history of Carolina, speaking of the cat-bird (muscicapa vertice nigro) says, "They have but one note, which resembles the mewing of a cat;" a mistake very injurious to the fame of that bird; he, in reality, being one of our most eminent songsters, little inferior to the philomela or mock-bird; and, in some remarkable instances, perhaps, exceeds them both, in particular as a buffoon or mimick. He endeavours to imitate every bird and animal, and in many attempts does not ill succeed, even in rehearsing the songs, which he attentively listens to, from the shepherdess and rural swain; and will endeavour and succeed to admiration, in repeating the melodious and variable airs from instrumental music, and this in his wild state of nature. They are a kind of domestic bird during their spring and summer residence in Pensylvania, building their nests in gardens and sheltering themselves in groves near the houses. They cause great trouble and vexation to hens that have broods of chickens, by imitating their distressing cries, in which they seem to enjoy much delight, and cause some amusement to persons who are diverted at such incidents. They are the first bird heard singing in the morning, even before break of day.

They seem to be a tribe of birds separated by nature from the motacillæ, with which the zoologists have classed them, and appear allied to a tribe peculiar to America, to which

Edwards has given the name of manakin. In their nature they seem to take place between the thrush (turdus) and motacilla, their beak being longer, stronger, and straighter than the motacilla, and formed for eating fruit, which is their chief food; yet they will feed on reptile insects, but never attempt to take their prey on the wing.

Catesby is chargeable with the like mistake with respect to the little thrush (t. minor) and the fox coloured thrush (t. rufus) both eminent singers, and the latter little inferior to the mock-bird. The former for his shrill, sonorous and elevated strains in the high, shady forests; and the latter for variety, softness and constant responses in the hedges and groves near houses.

But yet Catesby has some right of claim to our excuse and justification, for his detraction of the same due to these eminent musicians of the groves and forests, when we consider that he resided and made his collections and observations, in the regions which are the winter retreats and residence of these birds, where they rarely sing; as it is observable and most true, that it is only at the time of incubation, that birds sing in their wild state of nature. The cat-bird, great and less thrush and fieldfare, seldom or never build in Carolina beneath the mountains, except the great or fox coloured thrush in a few instances; but all these breed in Pensylvania.

The parakeets (psitacus Caroliniensis) never reach so far North as Pennsylvania, which to me is unaccountable, considering they are a bird of such singularly rapid flight, that they could easily perform the journey in ten or twelve hours from North Carolina, where they are very numerous, and we abound with all the fruits which they delight in.

I was assured in Carolina, that these birds, for a month or two in the coldest winter weather, house themselves in hollow Cypress trees, clinging fast to each other like bees in a hive, where they continue in a torpid state until the warmth of the returning spring reanimates them, when they issue forth from their late dark, cold winter cloisters. But I lived several years in North Carolina and never was witness to an instance of it; yet I do not at all doubt but there have been instances of belated flocks thus surprised by sudden severe cold, and forced into such shelter, and the extraordinary severity and perseverance of the season might have benumbed them into a torpid, sleepy state; but that they all willingly should yield to so disagreeable and hazardous a situation does not seem reasonable or natural, when we consider that they are a bird of the swiftest flight and impatient of severe cold. They are easily tamed, when they become docile and familiar, but never learn to imitate the human language.

Both species of the Baltimore bird (oriolus, Linn. icterus, Cat.) are spring birds of passage and breed in Pennsylvania; they have loud and musical notes.

The yellow breasted chat (oenanthe, Cat. motacilla trochilus, Linn.) is in many instances a very singular bird; the variableness and mimickry of his notes or speech, imitating various creatures; and a surprising faculty of uttering a coarse, hollow sounding noise in their throats or crops, which at times seems to be at a great distance, though uttered by a bird very near, and vice versa. They arrive in Pennsylvania from the South, late in the month of May, breed and return again early in autumn.

It is a matter of enquiry, what should have induced the zoologists to class this bird with the motacillæ, when they discover no one characteristic to induce such an alliance; this bird having a remarkable thick, strong bill, more like the frugivorous tribes: and in my opinion they are guilty of the like oversight in classing the summer red-bird with the muscicapa, this bird having a thick, strong bill, approaching nearer the starling (sturnus.)

These historical observations being noted, we will again resume the subject of our journey.

CHAP. XI.

Aᴀꜰᴛᴇʀ the predatory band of Siminoles, under the conduct of the Long Warrior, had decamped, Mr. M'Latche invited me with him on a visit to an Indian town, about twelve miles distance from the trading-house, to regale ourselves at a feast of Water Melons and Oranges, the Indians having brought a canoe load of them to the trading-house the day preceding, which they disposed of to the traders. This was a circumstance pretty extraordinary to me, it being late in September, a season of the year when the Citruels are ripe and gone in Georgia and Carolina; but here the weather yet continued hot and sultry, and consequently this cool, exhilarating fruit was still in high relish and estimation.

After breakfasting, having each of us a Siminole horse completely equipped, we sat off: the ride was agreeable and variously entertaining. We kept no road or pathway constantly, but as Indian hunting tracks by chance suited our course, riding through high open, pine forests, green lawns and flowery savannas in youthful verdure and gaity, having been lately burnt, but now overrun with a green enamelled carpet, chequered with hommocks of trees of dark green foliage, intersected with serpentine rivulets, their banks adorned with shrubberies of various tribes, as Andromeda formosissima, And. nitida, And. viridis, And. calyculata, And. axillaris, Kalmia spuria, Annona alba, &c. About noon we arrived at the town, the same little village I passed by on my ascent of the river, on the banks of the little lake below Charlotia.

We were received and entertained friendlily by the Indians, the chief of the village conducting us to a grand, airy pavilion in the center of the village. It was four-square; a range of pillars or posts on each side supporting a canopy composed of Palmetto leaves, woven or thatched together, which shaded a level platform in the centre, that was ascended to from each side by two steps or flights, each about twelve inches high, and seven or eight feet in breadth, all covered with carpets or mats, curiously woven of split canes dyed of various colours. Here being seated or reclining ourselves, after smoking tobacco, baskets of the choicest fruits were brought and set before us.

The fields surrounding the towns and groves were plentifully stored with Corn, Citruels, Pumkins, Squashes, Beans, Peas, Potatoes, Peaches, Figs, Oranges, &c.

Towards evening we took our leave, and arrived at the stores before night, having in the course of the day collected a variety of curious specimens of vegetables, seeds and roots.

The company being busily employed in forming their packs of leather and loading the vessel, and I being eager to augment my collections during my stay here, I crossed the river with a gang of our people, who were transporting a party of horses to range in the meadows and plains on the side opposite to the trading-house: we carried them over in a large flat or scow. The river was here above a mile wide, but divided into a number of streams by numerous islands, which occasioned the voyage to be very troublesome, as most of the horses were lately taken wild out of their ranges, and many of them young and untutored. Being under the necessity of passing near the points of the islands, they grew restless and impatient to land, and it was with great difficulty we kept them on board; and at last, when within a quarter of a mile of the opposite shore, passing between two islands, the horses became ungovernable, and most of them plunged into the river and forced over board one of our people. I being a pretty good swimmer, in the midst of the bustle, and to avoid being beat over and perhaps wounded, leapt out and caught hold of the dock of one of the horses. We all landed safe on one of the islands, about one hundred and fifty yards distance, and the flat followed us. After a deal of trouble and loss of time, we got the horses again into the scow, where securing them by withs and vines, we again sat off, and soon landed safe on the main, at a high bluff or bank of the river, where, after turning the horses to pasture, and resting ourselves, we sat off on a visit to a plantation on the river, six or eight miles distance. On the way thither we discovered a bee tree, which we cut down, and regaled ourselves on the delicious honey; leaving one of our companions to protect the remainder until our return with a tub, to collect it and carry it with us; and in the evening we all returned safe with our sweet booty to the trading-house.

The vessel being loaded and ready to depart, I got all my collections on board. My trusty and fortunate bark I presented to the old interpreter, Job Wiggens, often my travelling companion, friend and benefactor; and taking an affectionate and final leave of the worthy C. M'Latche and the whole trading company, we set sail in a neat little schooner for Frederica in Georgia, about the last of September. We had a pleasant and prosperous voyage down the grand river St. Juan's, frequently visiting the plantations on the banks of the river, especially at such times as opposed by contrary winds; and according to promise did not neglect calling on the generous and friendly Mr. Marshall who received me so politely, and treated me with such unparalleled friendship and hospitality, when ascending the river alone last spring.

We never once went out to sea during the voyage; for when we had descended the river below the Cow-ford, we entered the sound by a channel between Fort George island and the main, through which we passed, and continued sailing between the sea coast islands and the main to Frederica on St. Simon's.

On my arrival at Frederica, I was again, as usual, friendlily received and accommodated by the excellent John Spalding, Esq; and here learning that the honourable Henry Lawrens, Esq. had a large ship loading at Sunbury for Liverpool, I determined to embrace so favourable an offer for conveying my collections to Europe; and hearing at the same time that Mr. Lawrens was daily expected in a vessel of his own, at his plantations on Broton Island and New Hope, in order to take a loading of rice for the cargo of the ship at Sunbury, I transported my collections to Broton; where meeting with Mr. Lawrens, he generously permitted me to put my things on board his vessel, and gave me room with himself in the cabin; and the merchant in Liverpool, to whom the ship was consigned, being his friend and correspondent, and a friend of Dr. Fothergill's, Mr. Lawrens proposed to recommend my collections and letters to his care.

These favourable circumstances thus co-operating, after bidding adieu to my friends and liberal patrons in these parts, I embarked on board this vessel, and after a short and pleasant passage through the sound, arrived at Sunbury, from whence, after shipping my collections, I sat sail again for Charleston, South Carolina; where being arrived, I spent the season in short excursions until next spring; and during this time of my recess I had leisure to plan my future travels, agreeably to Dr. Fothergill's instructions, and the council and advice of Dr. Chalmers of Charleston, with other gentlemen of that city, eminent for the promotion of science and encouraging merit and industry.

It was agreed that my future rout should be directed West and South-West, into the Cherokee country and the regions of the Muscogulges or Creeks.

PART III

CHAP. I.

APRIL 22d, 1776, I sat off from Charleston for the Cherokee nation, and after riding this day about twenty-five miles, arrived in the evening at Jacksonsburg, a village on Ponpon river. The next day's journey was about the same distance, to a public house or inn on the road.

The next day, early in the morning, I sat off again, and about noon stopped at a public house to dine. After the meridian heats were abated, proceeding on till evening, I obtained good quarters at a private house, having rode this day about thirty miles. At this plantation I observed a large orchard of the European Mulberry tree (Morus alba) some of which were grafted on stocks of the native Mulberry (Morus rubra); these trees were cultivated for the purpose of feeding silk-worms (phalaena bombyx). Having breakfasted, I sat forward again.

I soon entered a high forest, continuing the space of fifteen miles to the Three Sisters, a public ferry on Savanna river: the country generally very level; the soil a dark, loose, fertile mould, on a stratum of cinereous-coloured tenacious clay; the ground shaded with its native forests, consisting of the great Black Oak, Quercus tinctoria, Q. rubra, Q. phellos, Q. prinus, Q. hemispherica, Juglans nigra, J. rustica, J. exaltata, Magnolia grandiflora, Fraxinus excelsior, Acer rubrum, Liriodendron tulipifera, Populus heterophylla, Morus rubra, Nyssa sylvatica, Platanus occidentalis, Tilia, Ulmus campestris, U. subifer, Laurus sassafras, L. Borbonia, Ilex aquifolium, Fagus sylvatica, Cornus Florida, Halesia, Æsculus pavia, Sambucus, Callicarpa, and Stewartia malachodendron, with a variety of other trees and shrubs. This ancient sublime forest, frequently intersected with extensive avenues, vistas and green lawns, opening to extensive savannas and far distant Rice plantations, agreeably employs the imagination, and captivates the senses by scenes of magnificence and grandeur.

The gay mock-bird, vocal and joyous, mounts aloft on silvered wings, rolls over and over, then gently descends, and presides in the choir of the tuneful tribes.

Having dined at the ferry, I crossed the river into Georgia: on landing and ascending the bank, which has here a North prospect, I observed the Dirca palustris, growing six or seven feet high. I rode about twelve miles further through Pine Forests and savannas. In the evening I took up my quarters at a delightful habitation, though not a common tavern. Having ordered my horse a stable and provender, and refreshed my spirits with a draught of cooling liquor, I betook myself to contemplation in the groves and lawns. Directing my steps towards the river, I observed in a high Pine forest on the border of a savanna, a great number of cattle herded together, and on my nearer approach discovered it to be a cow pen; on my coming up I was kindly saluted by my host and his wife, who I found were superintending a number of slaves, women, boys and girls, that were milking the cows. Here were about forty milch cows and as many young calves; for in these Southern countries the calves run with the cows a whole year, the people milking them at the same time. The pen, including two or three acres of ground, more or less, according to the stock, adjoining a rivulet or run of water, is enclosed by a fence: in this enclosure the calves are kept while the cows are out at range: a small part of this pen is partitioned off to receive the cows, when they come up at evening: here are several stakes drove into the ground, and there is a gate in the partition fence for a communication between the two pens. When the milkmaid has taken her share of milk, she looses the calf, who strips the cow, which is next morning turned out again to range.

I found these people, contrary to what a traveller might, perhaps, reasonably expect, from their occupation and remote situation from the capital or any commercial town, to be civil and courteous; and though educated as it were in the woods, no strangers to sensibility, and those moral virtues which grace and ornament the most approved and admired characters in civil society.

After the vessels were filled with milk, the daily and liberal supply of the friendly kine; and the good wife, with her maids and servants, were returning with it to the dairy; the gentleman was at leisure to attend to my inquiries and observations, which he did with complaisance, and apparent pleasure. On my observing to him that his stock of horned cattle must be very considerable to afford so many milch cows at one time, he answered, that he had about fifteen hundred head: "my stock is but young, having lately removed from some distance to this place; I found it convenient to part with most of my old stock and begin here anew; Heaven is pleased to bless my endeavours and industry with success even beyond my own expectations." Yet continuing my interrogatories on this subject: your stock I apprehend must be very profitable, being so convenient to the capital and sea port, in affording a vast quantity of beef, butter and cheese, for the market, and must thereby contribute greatly towards your emolument: "yes, I find my stock of cattle very profitable, and I constantly contribute towards supplying the markets with beef; but as to the articles of butter and cheese, I make no more than what is expended in my own household, and I have a considerable family of black people, who, though they are slaves, must be fed, and cared for: those I have, were either chosen for their good qualities, or born in the family, and I find from long experience and observation, that the better they are fed, clothed and treated, the more service and profit we may expect to derive from their labour: in short, I find my flock produces no more milk, or any article of food or nourishment, than what is expended to the best advantage amongst my family and slaves."

He added, come along with me towards the river bank, where I have some men at work squaring Pine and Cypress timber for the West-India market; I will show you their days work, when you will readily grant that I have reason to acknowledge myself sufficiently gratified for the little attention bestowed towards them. At yonder little new habitation near the bluff on the banks of the river, I have settled my eldest son; it is but a few days since he was married to a deserving young woman.

Having at length arrived near the high banks of the majestic Savanna, we stood at the timber landing: almost every object in our progress contributed to demonstrate this good man's system of economy to be not only practicable but eligible; and the slaves appeared on all sides as a crowd of witnesses to justify his industry, humanity and liberal spirit.

The slaves comparatively of a gigantic stature, fat and muscular, were mounted on the massive timber logs; the regular heavy strokes of their gleaming axes re-echoed in the deep forests; at the same time, contented and joyful, the sooty sons of Afric forgetting their bondage, in chorus sung the virtues and beneficence of their master in songs of their own composition.

The log or timber landing is a capacious open area, the lofty pines* having been felled and cleared away for a considerable distance round about, near an almost perpendicular bluff or steep bank of the river, rising up immediately from the water to the height of sixty or seventy feet. The logs being dragged by timber wheels to this yard, and landed as near the brink of this high bank as possible with safety, and laid by the side of each other, are rolled off and precipitated down the bank into the river, where being formed into rafts, they are conducted by slaves down to Savanna, about fifty miles below this place.

Having contemplated these scenes of art and industry, my venerable host, in company with his son, conducted me to the neat habitation, which is situated in a spacious airy forest, a little distance from the river bank, commanding a comprehensive and varied project; an extensive reach of the river in front; on the right hand a spacious lawn or savanna; on the left the timber yard; the vast fertile low lands and forests on the river upwards; and the plantations adjoining. A cool evening arrived after a sultry day. As we approach the door, conducted by the young man, his lovely bride arrayed in native innocence and becoming modesty, with an air and smile of grace and benignity, meets and salutes us! what a Venus! what an Adonis! said I in silent transport; every action and feature seem to reveal the celestial endowments of the mind: though a native sprightliness and sensibility appear, yet virtue and discretion direct and rule. The dress of this beauteous sylvan queen was plain but clean, neat and elegant, all of cotton, and of her own spinning and weaving.

Next morning early I sat forward prosecuting my tour. I pursued the high road leading from Savanna to Augusta for the distance of one hundred miles or more, and then recrossed

*Pinus palustris, Linn. the long leaved Pitch Pine, or yellow Pine.

the river at Silver Bluff, a pleasant villa, the property and seat of G. Golphin, esquire, a gentleman of very distinguished talents and great liberality, who possessed the most extensive trade, connexions and influence, amongst the South and South-West Indian tribes, particularly with the Creeks and Chactaws; of whom I fortunately obtained letters of recommendation and credit to the principal traders residing in the Indian towns.

Silver Bluff is a very celebrated place. It is a considerable height upon the Carolina shore of the Savanna river, perhaps thirty feet higher than the low lands on the opposite shore, which are subject to be overflowed in the spring and fall. This steep bank rises perpendicularly out of the river, discovering various strata of earth; the surface for a considerable depth is a loose sandy loam, with a mixture of sea shells, especially ostreæ; the next stratum is clay, then sand, next marl, then clays again of various colours and qualities, which last insensibly mix or unite with a deep stratum of blackish or dark slate coloured saline and sulphureous earth, which seems to be of an aluminous or vitriolic quality, and lies in nearly horizontal lamina or strata of various thickness. We discovered bellemnites, pyrites, marcasites and sulphureous nodules, shining like brass, some single of various forms, and others conglomerated, lying in this black slaty-like micaceous earth; as also sticks, limbs and trunks of trees, leaves, acorns, and their cups, all transmuted or changed black, hard and shining as charcoal: we also see animal substances, as if petrified, or what are called sharks' teeth, (dentes carchariæ); but these heterogeneous substances or petrifactions are the most abundant and conspicuous where there is a looser kind of earth, either immediately upon this vast stratum of black earth, or in the divisions of the laminæ. The surface of the ground upon this bluff, extends a mile and a half or two miles on the river, and is from an half mile to a mile in breadth, nearly level, and a good fertile soil; as is evident from the vast Oaks, Hickory, Mulberry, Black walnut and other trees and shrubs, which are left standing in the old fields which are spread abroad to a great distance; and discovers various monuments and vestiges of the residence of the ancients; as Indian conical mounts, terraces, areas, &c. as well as remains or traces of fortresses of regular formation, as if constructed after the modes of European military architects, which are supposed to be ancient camps of the Spaniards who formerly fixed themselves at this place in hopes of finding silver.

But perhaps Mr. Golphin's buildings and improvements will prove to be the foundation of monuments of infinitely greater celebrity and permanency than either of the preceding establishments.

The place which at this day is called fort Moore, is a stupendous bluff, or high perpendicular bank of earth, rising out of the river on the Carolina shore, perhaps ninety or one hundred feet above the common surface of the water; and exhibits a singular and pleasing spectacle to a stranger, especially from the opposite shore, or as we pass up or down the river, presenting a view of prodigious walls of party-coloured earths, chiefly clays and marl of various colours, as brown, red, yellow, blue, purple, white, &c. in horizontal strata, one over the other.

Waiting for the ferry boat to carry me over, I walked almost round the under side of the bluff, betwixt its steep wall and the water of the river, which glided rapidly under my feet. I came to the carcase of a calf, which the people told me had fallen down from the edge of the precipice above, being invited too far by grass and sweet herbs, which they say frequently happens at this place. In early times, the Carolinians had a fort, and kept a good garrison here as a frontier and Indian trading post; but Augusta superseding it, this place was dismantled: and since that time, which probably cannot exceed thirty years, the river hath so much encroached upon the Carolina shore, that its bed now lies where the site of the fort then was: indeed some told me that the opposite Georgia shore, where there is now a fine house and corn field, occupies the place.

The site of Augusta is perhaps the most delightful and eligible of any in Georgia for a city. An extensive level plain on the banks of a fine navigable river, which has its numerous sources in the Cherokee mountains, a fruitful and temperate region, whence, after roving and winding about those fertile heights, they meander through a fertile hilly country, and one after another combine in forming the Tugilo and Broad rivers, and then the famous Savanna river; thence they continue near an hundred miles more, following its meanders and falls over the cataracts at Augusta, which cross the river at the upper end of the town. These falls are four or five feet perpendicular height in the summer season when the river is low. From these cataracts upwards, this river with all its tributaries, as Broad river, Little river, Tugilo, &c. is one continued rapid, with some short intervals of still water, navigable for canoes. But from Augusta downwards to the ocean, a distance of near three hundred miles by water, the Savanna uninterruptedly flows with a gentle meandring course, and is navigable for vessels of twenty or thirty tons burthen to Savanna, where ships of three hundred tons lie in a capacious and secure harbour.

Augusta thus seated at the head of navigation, and just below the conflux of several of its most considerable branches, without a competitor, commands the trade and commerce of vast fruitful regions above it, and from every side to a great distance; and I do not hesitate to pronounce as my opinion, will very soon become the metropolis of Georgia.*

I chose to take this route up Savanna river, in preference to the straight and shorter road from Charleston to the Cherokee country by fort Ninety Six, because by keeping near this great river, I had frequent opportunities of visiting its steep banks, vast swamps and low grounds; and had the advantage, without great delay, or deviating from the main high road, of observing the various soils and situations of the countries through which this famous river pursues its course, and of examining their various productions, mineral, vegetable and animal: whereas had I pursued the great trading path by Ninety six, I should have been led over a high, dry, sandy and gravelly ridge, and a great part of the distance an old settled or resorted part of the country, and consequently void of the varieties of original or novel productions of nature.

Before I leave Augusta, I shall recite a curious phenomenon, which may furnish ample matter for philosophical discussion to the curious naturalists. On the Georgia side of the river, about fifteen miles below Silver Bluff, the high road crosses a

*A few years after the above remark, the seat of government was removed from Savanna to Augusta.

ridge of high swelling hills of uncommon elevation, and perhaps seventy feet higher than the surface of the river. These
hills, from three feet below the common vegetative surface,
to the depth of twenty or thirty feet, are composed entirely
of fossil oyster shells, internally of the colour and consistency
of clear white marble: the shells are of incredible magnitude,
generally fifteen or twenty inches in length, from six to eight
wide, and two to four in thickness, and their hollows sufficient
to receive an ordinary man's foot: they appear all to have been
opened before the period of petrifaction, a transmutation they
seem evidently to have suffered; they are undoubtedly very
ancient or perhaps antideluvian. The adjacent inhabitants burn
them to lime for building, for which purpose they serve very
well; and would undoubtedly afford an excellent manure
when their lands require it, these hills being now remarkably
fertile. The heaps of shells lie upon a stratum of a yellowish
sandy mould, of several feet in depth, upon a foundation of
soft white rocks, that has the outward appearance of free-
stone, but on strict examination is really a testaceous concrete
or composition of sand and pulverised sea shells: in short, this
testaceous rock approaches near in quality and appearance to
the Bahama or Bermudian white rock.

These hills are shaded with glorious Magnolia grandiflora,
Morus rubra, Tilia, Quercus, Ulmus, Juglans, &c. with aromatic groves of fragrant Callicanthus Floridus, Rhododendron
ferrugineum, Laurus Indica, &c., Æsculus pavia, Cornus Florida, Azalea coccinea, Philadelphus inodorus and others; but
who would have expected to see the Dirca palustris and
Dodecatheon meadea grow in abundance in this hot climate!
it is true they are seen in the rich and deep shaded vales,
between the hills and North exposure; but they attain to
a degree of magnitude and splendour never seen in Pennsylvania.

CHAP. II.

AFTER conferring with gentlemen in Augusta, coversant in Indian affairs, concerning my future travels in those distant, unexplored regions, and obtaining letters to their agents in the Indian territories, I set off, proceeding for Fort James Dartmouth, at the confluence of Broad River with Savanna, the road leading me near the banks of the river for the distance of near thirty miles, crossing two or three of its considerable branches, besides rivulets and smaller brooks. The surface of the land uneven, by means of ridges or chains of swelling hills and corresponding vales, with level downs; the soil a loose, grayish-brown loamy mould on the hills, but darker and more cohesive and humid in the vales and downs; this superficial, vegetative earth, covers a deep stratum of very tenacious yellowish clay: the downs afford grass and various herbage; the vales and hills, forest trees and shrubs of various tribes, i. e. Quercus tinctoria, Q. alba, Q. rubra, Q. lobata, Acer rubrum, A. Saccharinum, A. glaucum, Morus rubra, Gleditsia triacanthus, Juglans hickory, various species, Quercus phillos, Quer. dentata, s. hemispherica, Quercus aquatica, or Maryland Water Oak, Ulmus sylvatica, Liriodendron, Liquid-amber, Diospyros, Cornus Florida, Prunus Indica, Prunus padus and Æsculus pavia; and, near water courses in the vales, Stewartia malachodendron, Halesia, Æsculus sylvatica, Styrax, Carpinus, Magnolia acuminata, Mag. tripetala, Mag. auriculata, Azalea, &c. The rich humid lands in the vales bordering on creeks and bases of the hills, likewise produce various trees, shrubs and plants, as Cercis, Corylus, Ptelea, Evonimus, Philadelphus inodorus, Staphylea trifoliata, Chionanthus, Hamamelis, Callicarpa, Sambucus, Cornus alba, Viburnum dentatum, Spirea opulifolia, Cornus sanguinea, Cephalanthus, &c. and of herbaceæ a vast variety and abundance, as Verbesina, Rudbeckia, Phaseolus, Tripsacum, Aconitum napellus, Delphinium, Angelica lucida, Tradescantia, Trillium sessile, Trillium cernuum, Actæa, Chelone, Glycine apios, Convalliaria racemosa, Mediola, Carduus, Bidens frondosa, Arum triphyllum, Coreopsis alternifolia, Circæa, Commelina, Aster, Solidago, Eupatorium,

Helianthus, and Silphium, together with a variety of other tribes and species new to me. In the evening I arrived at Little river, and took up my quarters at a public house on its banks, near its confluence with the Savanna. This is a beautiful rapid water, about fifty yards over. On a branch of this river is situated the town of Wrightsborough.

Near the ford, on the banks of this river, I first observed a very curious shrub, a beautiful evergreen, which appears to be allied to the Rhododendron, though the seed vessels seem to bear more the characteristics of the Kalmia. This shrub grows in copses or little groves, in open, high situations, where trees of large growth are but scatteringly planted; many simple stems arise together from a root or source erect, four, five and six feet high; their limbs or branches, which are produced towards the top of the stems, also stand nearly erect, lightly diverging from the main stems, which are furnished with moderately large ovate pointed intire leaves, of a pale or yellowish green colour; these leaves are of a firm, compact texture, both surfaces smooth and shining, and stand nearly erect upon short petioles; the branches terminate with long, loose panicles or spikes of white flowers, whose segments are five, long and narrow.

I arose early next morning and continued my journey for Fort James. This day's progress was agreeably entertaining, from the novelty and variety of objects and views: the wild country now almost depopulated, vast forests, expansive plains and detached groves; then chains of hills whose gravelly, dry, barren summits present detached piles of rocks, which delude and flatter the hopes and expectations of the solitary traveller, full sure of hospitable habitations; heaps of white, gnawed bones of the ancient buffaloe, elk and deer, indiscriminately mixed with those of men, half grown over with moss, altogether, exhibit scenes of uncultivated nature, on reflection, perhaps, rather disagreeable to a mind of delicate feelings and sensibility, since some of these objects recognize past transactions and events, perhaps not altogether reconcileable to justice and humanity.

How harmonious and sweetly murmur the purling rills and fleeting brooks, roving along the shadowy vales, passing through dark, subterranean caverns, or dashing over steep rocky precipices, their cold, humid banks condensing the volatile vapours, which falling coalesce in crystalline drops, on the leaves and elastic twigs of the aromatic shrubs and incarnate flowers! In these cool, sequestered, rocky vales, we behold the following celebrated beauties of the hills, fragrant Calycanthus, blushing Rhododendron ferrugineum, delicate Philadelphus inodorus, which displays the white wavy mantle, with the sky robed Delphinium, perfumed Convallaria and fiery Azalea, flaming on the ascending hills or wavy surface of the gliding brooks. The epithet fiery, I annex to this most celebrated species of Azalea, as being expressive of the appearance of its flowers, which are in general of the colour of the finest red lead, orange and bright gold, as well as yellow and cream colour; these various splendid colours are not only in separate plants, but frequently all the varieties and shades are seen in separate branches on the same plant; and the clusters of the blossoms cover the shrubs in such incredible profusion on the hill sides, that suddenly opening to view from dark shades, we are alarmed with the apprehension of the hill being set on fire. This is certainly the most gay and brilliant flowering shrub yet known: it grows in little copses or clumps, in open forests as well as dark groves, with other shrubs, and about the bases of hills, especially where brooks and rivulets wind about them: the bushes seldom rise above six or seven feet in height, and generally but three, four and five, but branch and spread their tops greatly; the young leaves are but very small whilst the shrubs are in bloom, from which circumstance the plant exhibits a greater show of splendour.

Towards evening I crossed Broad river at a good ford, just above its confluence with the Savanna, and arrived at Fort James, which is a four square stockade, with saliant bastions at each angle, mounted with a block-house, where are some swivel guns, one story higher than the curtains, which are pierced with loop-holes, breast high, and defended by small arms. The fortification encloses about an acre of ground, where is the governor's or commandant's house, a good building, which is flanked on each side by buildings for the officers and barracks for the garrison, consisting of fifty ranges, including officers, each having a good horse well equipt, a rifle, two dragoon pistols, and a hanger, besides a powder horn, shot pouch and tomahawk. The fort stands on an eminence in the forks between the Savanna and Broad rivers, about one mile above Fort Charlotta, which is situated near the banks of the Savanna, on the Carolina side. Fort James is situated nearly at an equal distance from the banks of the two rivers, and from the extreme point of the land that separates them. The point or peninsula between the two rivers, for the distance of two miles back from the fort, is laid out for a town, by the name of Dartmouth, in honour to the earl of Dartmouth, who, by his interest and influence in the British councils, obtained from the king a grant and powers in favour of the Indian trading company of Georgia, to treat with the Creeks for the cession of a quantity of land sufficient to discharge their debts to the traders, for the security and defence of which territory this fortress was established.

This territory, called the New Purchase, contains about two millions of acres, lying upon the head of Great Ogechee, between the banks of the Savanna and Alatamaha, touching on the Ocone, and taking within its precincts all the waters of Broad and Little rivers; comprehending a body of excellent and fertile land, well watered by innumerable rivers, creeks and brooks.

I made a little excursion up the Savanna river, four or five miles above the fort, with the surgeon of the garrison, who was so polite as to attend me to show me some remarkable Indian monuments, which are worthy of every travellers notice. These wonderful labours of the ancients stand in a level plain, very near the bank of the river, now twenty or thirty yards from it. They consist of conical mounts of earth and four square terraces, &c. The great mount is in the form of a cone, about forty or fifty feet high, and the circumference of its base two or three hundred yards, entirely composed of the loamy rich earth of the low grounds: the top or apex is flat: a spiral path or track leading from the ground up to the top is still visible, where now grows a large, beautiful spreading Red Cedar (Juniperus Americana): there appear four niches, excavated out of the sides of this hill, at different heights from the base, fronting the four cardinal points; these niches or sentry boxes are entered into from the winding path, and seem to have been meant for resting places or look-outs. The circumjacent level grounds are cleared and planted with Indian Corn at present; and I think the proprietor of these lands, who accompanied us to this place, said that the mount itself yielded above one hundred bushels in one season: the land hereabouts is indeed exceeding fertile and productive.

It is altogether unknown to us, what could have induced the Indians to raise such a heap of earth in this place, the ground for a great space around being subject to inundations, at least once a year, from which circumstance we may conclude they had no town or settled habitations here. Some imagine these tumuli were constructed for look-out towers. It is reasonable to suppose, however, that they were to serve some important purpose in those days, as they were public works, and would have required the united labour and attention of a whole nation, circumstanced as they were, to have constructed one of them almost in an age. There are several less ones round about the great one, with some very large tetragon terraces on each side, near one hundred yards in length, and their surface four, six, eight and ten feet above the ground on which they stand.

We may however hazard a conjecture; that as there is generally a narrow space or ridge in these low lands, immediately bordering on the river's bank, which is eight or ten feet higher than the adjoining low grounds, that lie betwixt the stream and the heights of the adjacent main land, which, when the river overflows its banks, are many feet under water, when, at the same time, this ridge on the river bank is above water and dry, and at such inundations appears as an island in the river; these people might have had a town on this ridge, and this mount raised for a retreat and refuge in case of inundations, which are unforeseen and surprize them very suddenly, spring and autumn.

Having finished my collections and observations, which were extended to a considerable distance in the environs of Dartmouth; May 10th sat off again, proceeding for Keowe; rode six or eight miles up the river above the fort; crossed over into Carolina and soon got into the high road; but had not proceeded far, when I was surprised by a sudden very heavy shower of rain, attended with terrific thunder, but luckily found present shelter at a farm house, where I continued above an hour before its fury abated; when I proceeded again, and notwithstanding this detention and obstacles in consequence of the heavy rains in raising the creeks, travelled thirty five miles, and arrived in the evening at Mr. Cameron's, deputy commissary for Indian affairs for the Cherokee nation, to whom I was recommended by letters from the honourable John Stewart, superintendant, residing at Charleston, mentioning my business in the Cherokee country.

The road this day had led me over an uneven country, its surface undulated by ridges or chains of hills, sometimes rough with rocks and stones, yet generally productive of forests, with a variety of vegetables of inferior growth, i. e. Quercus, various species, Juglans hickory, varieties, Liriodendron, Fraxinus, Fagus sylvatica, Fagus castanea, Fagus pumila, s. Chinkapin, Nyssa Sylvatica, Acer rubrum, Æsculus sylvatica, Magnolia acuminata, Magnolia tripetala, Andromeda arborea, Hopea tinctoria, Æsculus pavia, Viburnum, Azalea flammea and other species; Hydrangea, Calycanthus, &c.

The season being uncommonly wet, almost daily showers of rain, frequently attended with tremendous thunder, rendered travelling disagreeable, toilsome and hazardous, through an uninhabited wilderness, abounding with rivers and brooks. I was prevailed upon by Mr. Cameron to stay at his house a few days, until the rains ceased and the rivers could be more easily forded.

The Angelica lucida or nondo grows here in abundance: its aromatic carminative root is in taste much like that of the Ginseng (Panax) though more of the taste and scent of Anise seed: it is in high estimation with the Indians as well as white inhabitants, and sells at a great price to the Southern Indians of Florida, who dwell near the sea coast where this never grows spontaneously. I observed a charming species of Malva, having panicles of large splendid purple or deep blue flowers; and another species of Malva, very singular indeed, for it is a climber; the leaves are broad, which, with the whole plant, are hoary; the flowers are very small, and of a greenish white. Here grows also in abundance a beautiful species of Delphinium; the flowers differ in no respect from those of the common branching Larkspur of the gardens; they are of a fine deep blue colour, and disposed in long sparsed spikes; the leaves are compound, almost linear, but the segments not so fine cut as those of the garden Larkspur.

The weather now settled and fair, I prepared to proceed for Fort Prince George Keowe, having obtained of the agreeable and liberal Mr. Cameron, ample testimonials and letters of recommendation to the traders in the nation: this gentleman also very obligingly sent a young Negro slave to assist and pilot me as far as Senica.

May 15th I left Lough-abber, the seat of Mr. Cameron. In the course of this day's journey I crossed several rivers and brooks, all branches of the Savanna, now called Keowe, above its confluence with the Tugilo, the West main branch. The face of the country uneven, by means of ridges of hills and water courses; the hills somewhat rocky near their summits and at the banks of rivers and creeks, but very fertile, as there is a good depth of a loose dark and most vegetative mould, on a stratum of reddish brown tenacious clay, and sometimes a deep stratum of dusky brown marl. The vegetable productions observed during this day's progress, were generally the same as already recited since leaving Dartmouth. The flaming Azaleas abound, and illuminate the hill sides; and a new and singularly beautiful species of Æsculus pavia, situated above them, towards the summits of these low hills. This conspicuously beautiful flowering shrub, grows to the height of five or six feet; many divergent crooked stems arise together from a root or source, which dividing their branches, wreath about every way, after a very irregular and free order; the exterior subdivisions of these limbs terminate with a heavy cluster or thyrsis of rose or pink coloured flowers, speckled or variegated with crimson, larger, more expansive and regular in their formation than those of the Pavia; and these heavy spikes of flowers, charged with the morning dews, bend the slender flexile stems to the ground: the compound leaves are of the configuration of those of the Pavia, but broader and their veins more prominent. The shrubs growing about the tops of the more barren grassy hills, where large trees are few and scattered, show themselves to great advantage, and make a fine appearance.

There are abundance of Grape vines (Vitis vinifera) which ramble and spread themselves over the shrubs and low trees in these situations, and I was assured produce fruit affording an excellent juice: the grapes are of various colours when ripe, of the figure and about the size of the European wine grapes. Arrived at Sinica in the evening, after travelling forty five miles through an uninhabited wilderness.

The Cherokee town of Sinica is a very respectable settlement, situated on the East bank of the Keowe river, though the greatest number of Indian habitations are on the opposite shore, where likewise stands the council-house, in a level plain betwixt the river and the range of beautiful lofty hills, which rise magnificently, and seem to bend over the green plains and the river: but the chief's house, with those of the traders, and some Indian dwellings, are seated on the ascent of the heights on the opposite shore. This situation in point of prospect far excels the other, as it overlooks the whole settlement, the extensive fruitful plains on the river above and below, and the plantations of the inhabitants, commanding a most comprehensive diversified view of the opposite elevations.

Sinica is a new town rebuilt since the late Indian war, when the Cherokees were vanquished and compelled to sue for peace, by general Middleton, commander of the Carolinian auxiliaries acting against them, when the lower and middle settlements were broken up: the number of inhabitants are now estimated at about five hundred, and they are able to muster about one hundred warriors.

Next day I left Sinica alone, and after riding about sixteen miles, chiefly through high forests of excellent land at a little distance from the river, arrived in the evening at fort Prince George Keowe.

Keowe is a most charming situation, and the adjacent heights are naturally so formed and disposed, as with little expence of military architecture to be rendered almost impregnable. It lies in a fertile vale, at this season enamelled with the incarnate fragrant strawberries and blooming plants, through which the beautiful river meanders, sometimes gently flowing, but more frequently agitated, gliding swiftly between the fruitful strawberry banks, environed at various distances by high hills and mountains, some rising boldly almost upright upon the verge of the expansive lawn, so as to overlook and shadow it, whilst others more lofty, superb, misty and blue, majestically mount far above.

The evening still and calm, all silent and peaceable, a vivifying gentle breeze continually wafted from the fragrant strawberry fields, and aromatic Calycanthean groves on the surrounding heights; the wary moor fowl thundering in the distant echoing hills: how the groves and hills ring with the shrill perpetual voice of the whip-poor-will!

Abandoned as my situation now was, yet thank heaven many objects met together at this time, and conspired to conciliate, and in some degree compose my mind, heretofore somewhat dejected and unharmonized: all alone in a wild Indian country, a thousand miles from my native land, and a vast distance from any settlements of white people. It is true, here were some of my own colour, yet they were strangers; and though friendly and hospitable, their manners and customs of living so different from what I had been accustomed to, administered but little to my consolation: some hundred miles yet to travel; the savage vindictive inhabitants lately illtreated by the frontier Virginians; blood being spilt between them and the injury not yet wiped away by formal treaty: the Cherokees extremely jealous of white people travelling about their mountains, especially if they should be seen peeping in amongst the rocks, or digging up their earth.

The vale of Keowe is seven or eight miles in extent, that is, from the little town of Kulsage* about a mile above, thence down the river six or seven miles, where a high ridge of hills on each side of the river almost terminates the vale, but opens again below the narrow ridge, and continues ten or twelve miles down to Sinica, and in width one and two miles. This fertile vale within the remembrance of some old traders with whom I conversed, was one continued settlement; the swelling sides of the adjoining hills were then covered with habitations, and the rich level grounds beneath lying on the river, was cultivated and planted, which now exhibit a very different spectacle, humiliating indeed to the present generation, the posterity and feeble remains of the once potent and renowned Cherokees: the vestiges of the ancient Indian dwellings are yet visible on the feet of the hills bordering and fronting on the vale, such as posts or pillars of their habitations, &c.

*Sugar Town.

There are several Indian mounts or tumuli, and terraces, monuments of the ancients, at the old site of Keowe, near the fort Prince George, but no Indian habitations at present; and here are several dwellings inhabited by white people concerned in the Indian trade: Mr. D. Homes is the principal trader here.

The old fort Prince George now bears no marks of a fortress, but serves for a trading house.

CHAP. III.

I WAITED two or three days at this post expecting the return of an Indian who was out hunting. This man was recommended to me as a suitable person for a protector and guide to the Indian settlements over the hills; but upon information that he would not be in shortly, and there being no other person suitable for the purpose, rather than be detained, and perhaps thereby frustrated in my purposes, I determined to set off alone and run all risks.

I crossed the river at a good ford just below the old fort. The river here is near one hundred yards over. After an agreeable progress for about two miles over delightful strawberry plains, and gently swelling green hills, I began to ascend more steep and rocky ridges. Having gained a very considerable elevation, looking around, I enjoyed a very comprehensive and delightful view: Keowe which I had but just lost sight of, appeared again, and the serpentine river speeding through the lucid green plain apparently just under my feet. After observing this delightful landscape, I continued on again three or four miles, keeping the trading path, which led me over uneven rocky land, crossing rivulets and brooks, and rapidly descending over rocky precipices; when I came into a charming vale, embellished with a delightful glittering river, which meandered through it, and crossed my road. On my left hand, upon the grassy bases of the rising hills, appeared the remains of a town of the ancients, as the tumuli, terraces, posts or pillars, old Peach and Plumb orchards, &c. sufficiently testify. These vales and swelling bases of the surrounding hills, afford vast crops of excellent grass and herbage fit for pasturage and hay; of the latter, Plantago Virginica, Sanguisorba, Geum, Fragaria, &c. The Panax quinquefolium, or Ginseng, now appears plentifully on the North exposure of the hill, growing out of the rich mellow humid earth amongst the stones or fragments of rocks.

Having crossed the vales, I began to ascend again the more lofty ridges of hills; then continued about eight miles over more gentle pyramidal hills, narrow vales and lawns, the soil exceedingly fertile, producing lofty forests and odoriferous groves of Calycanthus, near the banks of rivers, with Halesia, Philadelphus inodorus, Rhododendron ferrugineum, Azalea, Stewartia montana*, fol. ovatis acuminatis serratis, flor. niveo, staminum corona fulgida, pericarp. pomum exsuccum, apice acuminato dehiscens, Cornus Florida, Styrax, all in full bloom, and decorated with the following sweet roving climbers, Bignonia sempervirens, Big. crucigera, Lonicera sempervirens, Rosa paniculata, &c.

Now at once the mount divide; and disclose to view the ample Occonne vale, encircled by a wreath of uniform hills; their swelling bases clad in cheerful verdure, over which, issuing from between the mountains, plays along a glittering river, meandering through the meadows. Crossing these at the upper end of the vale, I began to ascend the Occonne mountain. On the foot of the hills are ruins of the ancient Occonne town. The first step after leaving the verdant beds of the hills, was a very high rocky chain of pointed hills, extremely well timbered with the following trees: Quercus tinctoria, Querc. alba, Querc. rubra, Fraxinus excelsior, Juglans hickory various species, Ulmus, Tilia, Acer saccharinum, Morus, Juglans nigra, Juglans alba, Annona glabra, Robinia pseudacacia, Magnolia acuminata, Æsculus sylvatica, with many more, particularly a species of Robinia new to me, though perhaps the same as figured and slightly described by Catesby in his Nat. Hist. Carol. This beautiful flowering tree grows twenty and thirty feet high, with a crooked leaning trunk; the branches spread greatly, and wreath about, some almost touching the ground; however there appears a singular pleasing wildness and freedom in its manner of growth; the slender subdivisions of the branches terminate with heavy compound panicles of rose or pink coloured flowers, amidst a wreath of beautiful pinnated leaves.

My next flight was up a very high peak, to the top of the Occonne mountain, where I rested; and turning about, found that I was now in a very elevated situation, from whence I enjoyed a view inexpressibly magnificent and comprehensive.

---

*This is a new species of Stewartia, unknown to the European botanists, and not mentioned in any catalogues.

The mountainous wilderness which I had lately traversed, down to the region of Augusta, appearing regularly undulated as the great ocean after a tempest; the undulations gradually depressing, yet perfectly regular, as the squama of fish, or imbrications of tile on a roof: the nearest ground to me of a perfect full green; next more glaucous; and lastly almost blue as the ether with which the most distant curve of the horizon seemed to be blended.

My imagination thus wholly engaged in the contemplation of this magnificent landscape, infinitely varied, and without bound, I was almost insensible or regardless of the charming objects more within my reach: a new species of Rhododendron foremost in the assembly of mountain beauties; next the flaming Azalea, Kalmia latifolia, incarnate Robinia, snowy mantled Philadelphus inodorus, perfumed Calycanthus, &c.

This species of Rhododendron grows six or seven feet high; many nearly erect stems arise together from the root, forming a group or coppice. The leaves are three or four inches in length, of an oblong figure, broadest toward the extremity, and terminating with an obtuse point; their upper surface of a deep green and polished; but the nether surface of a rusty iron colour, which seems to be effected by innumerable minute reddish vesicles, beneath a fine short downy pubescence; the numerous flexile branches terminate with a loose spiked raceme, or cluster of large deep rose coloured flowers, each flower being affixed in the diffused cluster of a long peduncle, which, with the whole plant, possesses an agreeable perfume.

After being recovered of the fatigue and labour in ascending the mountain, I began again to prosecute my task, proceeding through a shady forest; and soon after gained the most elevated crest of the Occonne mountain, and then began to descend the other side; the winding rough road carrying me over rocky hills and levels, shaded by incomparable forests, the soil exceedingly rich, and of an excellent quality for the production of every vegetable suited to the climate, and seeming peculiarly adapted for the cultivation of Vines (Vitis vinifera), Olives (Olea Europea), the Almond tree (Amygdalus communis), Fig (Ficus carica), and perhaps the Pomgranate, (Punica granatum), as well as Peaches (Amyg. Persica), Prunus, Pyrus, of every variety. I passed again steep rocky ascents,

and then rich levels, where grew many trees and plants common in Pennsylvania, New-York and even Canada, as Pinus
strobus, Pin. sylvestris, Pin. abies, Acer saccharinum, Acer
striatum, s. Pensylvanicum, Populus tremula, Betula nigra,
Juglans alba, &c.; but what seems remarkable, the yellow Jessamine (Bignonia sempervirens), which is killed by a very
slight frost in the open air in Pennsylvania, here, on the summits of the Cherokee mountains associates with the Canadian
vegetables, and appears roving with them in perfect bloom
and gaiety; as likewise Halesia diptera, and Hal. tetraptera,
mountain Stewartia, Styrax, Ptelea, Æsculus pavia; but all
these bear our hardest frosts in Pennsylvania. Now I enter a
charming narrow vale, through which flows a rapid large
creek, on whose banks are happily associated the shrubs
already recited, together with the following; Staphylæa, Euonymus Americana, Hamamelis, Azalea, various species, Aristolochia frutescens, s. odoratissima, which rambles over the
trees and shrubs on the prolific banks of these mountain
brooks. Passed through magnificent high forests, and then
came upon the borders of an ample meadow on the left, embroidered by the shade of a high circular amphitheatre of hills,
the circular ridges rising magnificently one over the other. On
the green turfy bases of these ascents appear the ruins of a
town of the ancients. The upper end of this spacious green
plain is divided by a promontory or spur of the ridges before
me, which projects into it: my road led me up into an opening
of the ascents through which the glittering brook which
watered the meadows ran rapidly down, dashing and roaring
over high rocky steps. Continued yet ascending until I gained
the top of an elevated rocky ridge, when appeared before me
a gap or opening between other yet more lofty ascents,
through which continued as the rough rocky road led me,
close by the winding banks of a large rapid brook, which at
length turning to the left, pouring down rocky precipices,
glided off through dark groves and high forests, conveying
streams of fertility and pleasure to the fields below.

The surface of the land now for three or four miles is level,
yet uneven, occasioned by natural mounds or rocky knobs,
but covered with a good staple of rich earth, which affords
forests of timber trees and shrubs. After this, gently de-

scending again, I travelled some miles over a varied situation of ground, exhibiting views of grand forests, dark detached groves, vales and meadows, as heretofore, and producing the like vegetable and other works of nature; the meadows affording exuberant pasturage for cattle, and the bases of the encircling hills, flowering plants, and fruitful strawberry beds: observed frequently ruins of the habitations or villages of the ancients. Crossed a delightful river, the main branch of Tugilo, when I began to ascend again, first over swelling turfy ridges, varied with groves of stately forest trees; then ascending again more steep grassy hill sides, rested on the top of mount Magnolia, which appeared to me to be the highest ridge of the Cherokee mountains, which separate the waters of Savanna river from those of the Tanase or greater main branch of the Cherokee river. This running rapidly a North-West course through the mountains, is joined from the North-East by the Holstein; thence taking a West course yet amongst the mountains, receiving into it from either hand many large rivers, leaves the mountains immediately after being joined by a large river from the East, becomes a mighty river by the name of Hogehege, thence meanders many hundred miles through a vast country consisting of forests, meadows, groves, expansive savannas, fields and swelling hills, most fertile and delightful, flows into the beautiful Ohio, and in conjunction with its transparent waters, becomes tributary to the sovereign Mississippi.

This exalted peak I named mount Magnolia, from a new and beautiful species of that celebrated family of flowering trees, which here, at the cascades of Falling Creek, grows in a high degree of perfection: I had, indeed noticed, this curious tree several times before, particularly on the high ridges betwixt Sinica and Keowe, and on ascending the first mountain after leaving Keowe, when I observed it in flower, but here it flourishes and commands our attention.

This tree,* or perhaps rather shrub, rises eighteen to thirty feet in height; there are usually many stems from a root or source, which lean a little, or slightly diverge from each other, in this respect imitating the Magnolia tripetala; the crooked

*Magnolia auriculata.

wreathing branches arising and subdividing from the main stem without order or uniformity, their extremities turn upwards, producing a very large rosaceous, perfectly white, double or polypetalous flower, which is of a most fragrant scent; this fine flower sits in the centre of a radius of very large leaves, which are of a singular figure, somewhat lanceolate, but broad towards their extremities, terminating with an acuminated point, and backwards they attenuate and become very narrow towards their bases, terminating that way with two long, narrow ears or lappets, one on each side of the insertion of the petiole; the leaves have only short footstalks, sitting very near each other, at the extremities of the floriferous branches, from whence they spread themselves after a regular order, like the spokes of a wheel, their margins touching or lightly lapping upon each other, form an expansive umbrella superbly crowned or crested with the fragrant flower, representing a white plume; the blossom is succeeded by a very large crimson cone or strobile, containing a great number of scarlet berries, which, when ripe, spring from their cells and are for a time suspended by a white silky web or thread. The leaves of those trees which grow in a rich, light humid soil, when fully expanded and at maturity, are frequently above two feet in length and six or eight inches where broadest. I discovered in the maritime parts of Georgia, particularly on the banks of the Alatamaha, another new species of Magnolia, whose leaves were nearly of the figure of those of this tree, but they were much less in size, not more than six or seven inches in length, and the strobile very small, oblong, sharp pointed and of a fine deep crimson colour; but I never saw the flower. These trees grow straight and erect, thirty feet or more in height, and of a sharp conical form, much resembling the Cucumber tree (Mag. acuminata) in figure.

The day being remarkably warm and sultry, together with the labour and fatigue of ascending the mountains, made me very thirsty and in some degree sunk my spirits. Now past mid-day, I sought a cool shaded retreat, where was water for refreshment and grazing for my horse, my faithful slave and only companion. After proceeding a little farther, descending the other side of the mountain, I perceived at some distance before me, on my right hand, a level plain supporting a grand high forest and groves: the nearer I approached, my steps were the more accelerated from the flattering prospect opening to view. I now entered upon the verge of the dark forest, charming solitude! as I advanced through the animating shades, observed on the farther grassy verge a shady grove; thither I directed my steps. On approaching these shades, between the stately columns of the superb forest trees, presented to view, rushing from rocky precipices under the shade of the pensile hills, the unparalleled cascade of Falling Creek, rolling and leaping off the rocks: the waters uniting below, spread a broad, glittering sheet over a vast convex elevation of plain smooth rocks, and are immediately received by a spacious bason, where trembling in the centre through hurry and agitation, they gently subside, encircling the painted still verge; from whence gliding swiftly, they soon form a delightful little river, which continuing to flow more moderately, is restrained for a moment, gently undulating in a little lake: they then pass on rapidly to a high perpendicular steep of rocks, from whence these delightful waters are hurried down with irresistible rapidity. I here seated myself on the moss-clad rocks, under the shade of spreading trees and floriferous fragrant shrubs, in full view of the cascades.

At this rural retirement were assembled a charming circle of mountain vegetable beauties; Magnolia auriculata, Rhododendron ferrugineum, Kalmia latifolia, Robinia montana, Azalea flammula, Rosa paniculata, Calycanthus Floridus, Philadelphus inodorus, perfumed Convalaria majalis, Anemone thalictroides, Anemone hepatica, Erythronium maculatum, Leontice thalictroides, Trillium sessile, Trillium cern, Cypripedium, Arethusa, Ophrys, Sanguinaria, Viola uvularia, Epigea, Mitchella repens, Stewartia, Halesia, Styrax, Lonicera, &c. Some of these roving beauties stroll over the mossy, shelving, humid rocks, or from off the expansive wavy boughs of trees, bending over the floods, salute their delusive shade, playing on the surface; some plunge their perfumed heads and bathe their flexile limbs in the silver stream; whilst others by the mountain breezes are tossed about, their blooming tufts bespangled with pearly and chrystaline dew-drops collected from the falling mists, glistening in the rainbow arch. Having collected some valuable specimens at this friendly retreat, I

continued my lonesome pilgrimage. My road for a considerable time led me winding and turning about the steep rocky
hills; the descent of some of which were very rough and troublesome, by means of fragments of rocks, slippery clay and
talc: but after this I entered a spacious forest, the land having
gradually acquired a more level surface: a pretty grassy vale
appears on my right, through which my wandering path led
me, close by the banks of a delightful creek, which sometimes
falling over steps of rocks, glides gently with serpentine meanders through the meadows.

After crossing this delightful brook and mead, the land rises
again with sublime magnificence, and I am led over hills and
vales, groves and high forests, vocal with the melody of the
feathered songsters; the snow-white cascades glittering on the
sides of the distant hills.

It was now afternoon; I approached a charming vale,
amidst sublimely high forests, awful shades! Darkness gathers
around; far distant thunder rolls over the trembling hills: the
black clouds with august majesty and power, move slowly
forwards, shading regions of towering hills, and threatening
all the destruction of a thunder storm: all around is now still
as death; not a whisper is heard, but a total inactivity and
silence seem to pervade the earth; the birds afraid to utter a
chirrup, in low tremulous voices take leave of each other,
seeking covert and safety: every insect is silenced, and nothing heard but the roaring of the approaching hurricane. The
mighty cloud now expands its sable wings, extending from
North to South, and is driven irresistibly on by the tumultuous winds, spreading its livid wings around the gloomy
concave, armed with terrors of thunder and fiery shafts of
lightning. Now the lofty forests bend low beneath its fury;
their limbs and wavy boughs are tossed about and catch hold
of each other; the mountains tremble and seem to reel about,
and the ancient hills to be shaken to their foundations: the
furious storm sweeps along, smoking through the vale and
over the resounding hills: the face of the earth is obscured
by the deluge descending from the firmament, and I am
deafened by the din of the thunder. The tempestuous scene
damps my spirits, and my horse sinks under me at the tremendous peals, as I hasten on for the plain.

The storm abating, I saw an Indian hunting cabin on the side of a hill, a very agreeable prospect, especially in my present condition; I made up to it and took quiet possession, there being no one to dispute it with me except a few bats and whip-poor-wills, who had repaired thither for shelter from the violence of the hurricane.

Having turned out my horse in the sweet meadows adjoining, and found some dry wood under shelter of the old cabin, I struck up a fire, dried my clothes, and comforted myself with a frugal repast of biscuit and dried beef, which was all the food my viaticum afforded me by this time, excepting a small piece of cheese which I had furnished myself with at Charleston and kept till this time.

The night was clear, calm and cool, and I rested quietly. Next morning at day break I was awakened and summoned to resume my daily task, by the shrill cries of the social night hawk and active merry mock-bird. By the time the rising sun had gilded the tops of the towering hills, the mountains and vales rang with the harmonious shouts of the pious and cheerful tenants of the groves and meads.

I observed growing in great abundance in these mountain meadows, Sanguisorba Canadensis and Heracleum maximum; the latter exhibiting a fine show, being rendered conspicuous even at a great distance, by its great height and spread, vast pennatifid leaves and expansive umbels of snow-white flowers. The swelling bases of the surrounding hills fronting the meadows presented for my acceptance the fragrant red strawberry, in painted beds of many acres surface, indeed I may safely say, many hundreds.

After passing through this meadow, the road led me over the bases of a ridge of hills, which as a bold promontory dividing the fields I had just passed, form expansive green lawns. On these towering hills appeared the ruins of the ancient famous town of Sticoe. Here was a vast Indian mount or tumulus and great terrace, on which stood the council-house, with banks encompassing their circus; here were also old Peach and Plumb orchards; some of the trees appeared yet thriving and fruitful. Presently after leaving these ruins, the vale and fields are divided by means of a spur of the mountains pushing forward: here likewise the road forked; the left-hand path continued up the mountains to the Overhill towns: I followed the vale to the right hand, and soon began again to ascend the hills, riding several miles over very rough, stony land, yielding the like vegetable productions as heretofore; and descending again gradually, by a dubious winding path, leading into a narrow vale and lawn, through which rolled on before me a delightful brook, water of the Tanase. I crossed it and continued a mile or two down the meadows; when the high mountains on each side suddenly receding, discovered the opening of the extensive and fruitful vale of Cowe, through which meanders the head branch of the Tanase, almost from its source, sixty miles, following its course down to Cowe.

I left for a little while, the stream passing swiftly and foaming over its rocky bed, lashing the steep craggy banks, and then suddenly sunk from my sight, murmuring hollow and deep under the rocky surface of the ground. On my right hand the vale expands, receiving a pretty silvery brook of water which came hastily down from the adjacent hills, and entered the river a little distance before me. I now turn from the heights on my left, the road leading into the level lawns, to avoid the hollow rocky grounds, full of holes and cavities, arching over the river, through which the waters are seen gliding along; but the river is soon liberated from these solitary and gloomy recesses, and appears waving through the green plain before me. I continued several miles, pursuing my serpentine path, through and over the meadows and green fields, and crossing the river, which is here incredibly increased in size, by the continual accession of brooks flowing in from the hills on each side, dividing their green turfy beds, forming them into parterres, vistas and verdant swelling knolls, profusely productive of flowers and fragrant strawberries, their rich juice dying my horses feet and ancles.

These swelling hills the prolific beds on which the towering mountains repose, seem to have been the common situations of the towns of the ancients, as appears from the remaining ruins of them yet to be seen, and the level rich vale and meadows in front, their planting grounds.

Continue yet ten or twelve miles down the vale, my road leading at times close to the banks of the river, the Azalea,

Kalmia, Rhododendron, Philadelphus, &c., beautifying his now elevated shores, and painting the coves with a rich and cheerful scenery, continually unfolding new prospects as I traverse the shores: the towering mountains seem continually in motion as I pass along, pompously raising their superb crests towards the lofty skies, traversing the far distant horizon.

The Tanase is now greatly increased from the conflux of the multitude of rivulets and brooks, descending from the hills on either side, generously contributing to establish his future fame, already a spacious river.

The mountains recede, the vale expands; two beautiful rivulets stream down through lateral vales, gliding in serpentine mazes over the green turfy knolls, and enter the Tanase nearly opposite to each other. Straight forward the expansive green vale seems yet infinite: now on the right hand a lofty pyramidal hill terminates a spur of the adjacent mountain, and advances almost into the river; but immediately after doubling this promontory, an expanded wing of the vale spreads on my right, down which came precipitately a very beautiful creek, which flowed into the river just before me; but now behold, high upon the side of a distant mountain overlooking the vale, the fountain of this brisk-flowing creek; the unparalleled waterfall appears as a vast edifice with crystal front, or a field of ice lying on the bosom of the hill.

I now approach the river at the fording place, which was greatly swollen by the floods of rain that fell the day before, and ran with foaming rapidity; but observing that it had fallen several feet perpendicular, and perceiving the bottom or bed of the river to be level, and covered evenly with pebbles, I ventured to cross over; however I was obliged to swim two or three yards at the deepest chanel of it, and landed safely on the banks of a fine meadow, which lay on the opposite shore, where I immediately alighted and spread abroad on the turf my linen, books and specimens of plants, &c. to dry, turned out my steed to graze and then advanced into the strawberry plains to regale on the fragrant, delicious fruit, welcomed by communities of the splendid meleagris, the capricious roe-buck, and all the free and happy tribes which possess and inhabit those prolific fields, who appeared to invite and joined with me in the participation of the bountiful repast presented to us from the lap of nature.

I mounted again, and followed the trading path about a quarter of a mile through the fields, then gently ascended the green beds of the hills, and entered the forests, being a point of a chain of hills projecting into the green vale or low lands of the rivers. This forest continued about a mile, the surface of the land level but rough, being covered with stones or fragments of rocks, and very large, smooth pebbles of various shapes and sizes, some of ten or fifteen pounds weight: I observed on each side of the road many vast heaps of these stones, Indian graves undoubtedly*.

After I left the graves, the ample vale soon offered on my right hand, through the tall forest trees, charming views, which exhibited a pleasing contrast, immediately out of the gloomy shades and scenes of death, into expansive, lucid, green, flowery fields, expanding between retiring hills, and turfy eminences, the rapid Tanase gliding through, as a vast serpent rushing after his prey.

My winding path now leads me again over the green fields into the meadows, sometimes visiting the decorated banks of the river, as it meanders through the meadows, or boldly sweeps along the bases of the mountains, its surface receiving the images reflected from the flowery banks above.

Thus was my agreeable progress for about fifteen miles, since I came upon the sources of the Tanase, at the head of this charming vale: in the evening espying a human habitation at the foot of the sloping green hills, beneath lofty forests of the mountains on the left hand, and at the same time observing a man crossing the river from the opposite shore in a canoe and coming towards me, I waited his approach, who hailing me, I answered I was for Cowe; he intreated me very civilly to call at his house, adding that he would presently come to me.

*At this place was fought a bloody and decisive battle between these Indians and the Carolinians, under the conduct of general Middleton, when a great number of Cherokee warriors were slain, which shook their power, terrified and humbled them, insomuch that they deserted most of their settlements in the low countries, and betook themselves to the mountains as less accessible to the regular forces of the white people.

I was received and entertained here until next day with the most perfect civility. After I had dined, towards evening, a company of Indian girls, inhabitants of a village in the hills at a small distance, called, having baskets of strawberries; and this man, who kept here a trading house, being married to a Cherokee woman of family, was indulged to keep a stock of cattle, and his helpmate being an excellent house-wife and a very agreeable good woman, treated us with cream and strawberries.

Next morning after breakfasting on excellent coffee, relished with bucanned venison, hot corn cakes, excellent butter and cheese, sat forwards again for Cowe, which was about fifteen miles distance, keeping the trading path which coursed through the low lands between the hills and the river, now spacious and well beaten by travellers, but somewhat intricate to a stranger, from the frequent collateral roads falling into it from villages or towns over the hills. After riding about four miles, mostly through fields and plantations, the soil incredibly fertile, arrived at the town of Echoe, consisting of many good houses, well inhabited. I passed through, and continued three miles farther to Nucasse, and three miles more brought me to Whatoga. Riding through this large town, the road carried me winding about through their little plantations of Corn, Beans, &c. up to the council-house, which was a very large dome or rotunda, situated on the top of an ancient artificial mount, and here my road terminated. All before me and on every side, appeared little plantations of young Corn, Beans, &c. divided from each other by narrow strips or borders of grass, which marked the bounds of each one's property, their habitation standing in the midst. Finding no common high road to lead me through the town, I was now at a stand how to proceed farther; when observing an Indian man at the door of his habitation, three or four hundred yards distance from me, beckoning me to come to him, I ventured to ride through their lots, being careful to do no injury to the young plants, the rising hopes of their labour and industry; crossed a little grassy vale watered by a silver stream, which gently undulated through; then ascended a green hill to the house, where I was chearfully welcomed at the door, and led in by the chief, giving the care of my horse to two handsome youths, his sons. During my continuance here, about half an hour, I experienced the most perfect and agreeable hospitality conferred on me by these happy people; I mean happy in their dispositions, in their apprehensions of rectitude with regard to our social or moral conduct. O divine simplicity and truth, friendship without fallacy or guile, hospitality disinterested, native, undefiled, unmodifyed by artificial refinements!

My venerable host gracefully and with an air of respect, led me into an airy, cool apartment; where being seated on cabins, his women brought in a refreshing repast, consisting of sodden venison, hot corn cakes, &c. with a pleasant cooling liquor made of hommony well boiled, mixed afterwards with milk; this is served up either before or after eating in a large bowl, with a very large spoon or ladle to sup it with.

After partaking of this simple but healthy and liberal collation, and the dishes cleared off, Tobacco and pipes were brought; and the chief filling one of them, whose stem, about four feet long, was sheathed in a beautiful speckled snake skin, and adorned with feathers and strings of wampum, lights it and smoaks a few whiffs, puffing the smoak first towards the sun, then to the four cardinal points, and lastly over my breast, hands it towards me, which I cheerfully received from him and smoaked; when we fell into conversation. He first enquired if I came from Charleston? if I knew John Stewart, Esq. how long since I left Charleston? &c. Having satisfied him in my answers in the best manner I could, he was greatly pleased; which I was convinced of by his attention to me, his cheerful manners, and his ordering my horse a plentiful bait of corn, which last instance of respect is conferred on those only to whom they manifest the highest esteem, saying that corn was given by the Great Spirit only for food to man.

I acquainted this ancient prince and patriarch with the nature and design of my peregrinations, and that I was now for Cowe, but having lost my road in the town, requested that I might be informed. He cheerfully replied, that he was pleased I was come in their country, where I should meet with friendship and protection, and that he would himself lead me into the right path.

After ordering my horse to the door, we went forth together, he on foot, and I leading my horse by the bridle; thus walking together near two miles, we shook hands and parted, he returning home, and I continuing my journey for Cowe.

This prince is the chief of Whatoga, a man universally beloved, and particularly esteemed by the whites for his pacific and equitable disposition, and revered by all for his exemplary virtues, just, moderate, magnanimous and intrepid.

He was tall and perfectly formed; his countenance cheerful and lofty, and at the same time truly characteristic of the red men, that is, the brow ferocious, and the eye active, piercing or fiery, as an eagle. He appeared to be about sixty years of age, yet upright and muscular, and his limbs active as youth.

After leaving my princely friend, I travelled about five miles through old plantations, now under grass, but which appeared to have been planted the last season; the soil exceeding fertile, loose, black, deep and fat. I arrived at Cowe about noon. This settlement is esteemed the capital town: it is situated on the bases of the hills on both sides of the river, near to its bank, and here terminates the great vale of Cowe, exhibiting one of the most charming natural mountainous landscapes perhaps any where to be seen; ridges of hills rising grand and sublimely one above and beyond another, some boldly and majestically advancing into the verdant plain, their feet bathed with the silver flood of the Tanase, whilst others far distant, veiled in blue mists, sublimely mounting aloft, with yet greater majesty lift up their pompous crests, and overlook vast regions.

The vale is closed at Cowe by a ridge of mighty hills, called the Jore mountain, said to be the highest land in the Cherokee country, which crosses the Tanase here.

On my arrival at this town I waited on the gentlemen to whom I was recommended by letter, and was received with respect and every demonstration of hospitality and friendship.

I took my residence with Mr. Galahan the chief trader here, an ancient respectable man, who had been many years a trader in this country, and is esteemed and beloved by the Indians for his humanity, probity and equitable dealings with them; which, to be just and candid I am obliged to observe (and blush for my countrymen at the recital) is somewhat of a prodigy; as it is a fact, I am afraid too true, that the white traders in their commerce with the Indians, get great and

frequent occasions of complaint of their dishonesty and violence: but yet there are few exceptions, as in the conduct of
this gentleman, who furnishes a living instance of the truth of
the old proverb, that "Honesty is the best policy;" for this
old honest Hibernian has often been protected by the Indians,
when all others round about him have been ruined, their
property seized and themselves driven out of the country or
slain by the injured, provoked natives.

Next day after my arrival I crossed the river in a canoe, on
a visit to a trader who resided amongst the habitations on the
other shore.

After dinner, on his mentioning some curious scenes
amongst the hills, some miles distance from the river, we
agreed to spend the afternoon in observations on the
mountains.

After riding near two miles through Indian plantations of
Corn, which was well cultivated, kept clean of weeds, and was
well advanced, being near eighteen inches in height, and the
Beans planted at the Corn-hills were above ground; we left
the fields on our right, turning towards the mountains, and
ascending through a delightful green vale or lawn, which conducted us in amongst the pyramidal hills, and crossing a brisk
flowing creek, meandering through the meads, which continued near two miles, dividing and branching in amongst the
hills. We then mounted their steep ascents, rising gradually by
ridges or steps one above another, frequently crossing narrow
fertile dales as we ascended: the air felt cool and animating,
being charged with the fragrant breath of the mountain beauties, the blooming mountain cluster Rose, blushing Rhododendron and fair Lilly of the valley. Having now attained the
summit of this very elevated ridge, we enjoyed a fine prospect
indeed; the enchanting Vale of Cowee, perhaps as celebrated
for fertility, fruitfulness and beautiful prospects as the Fields
of Pharsalia or the Vale of Tempe; the town, the elevated peeks
of the Jore mountains, a very distant prospect of the Jore
village in a beautiful lawn, lifted up many thousand feet higher
than our present situation, besides a view of many other villages and settlements on the sides of the mountains, at various
distances and elevations; the silver rivulets gliding by them,
and snow white cataracts glimmering on the sides of the lofty

hills; the bold promontories of the Jore mountain stepping into the Tanase river, whilst his foaming waters rushed between them.

After viewing this very entertaining scene, we began to descend the mountain on the other side, which exhibited the same order of gradations of ridges and vales as on our ascent; and at length rested on a very expansive, fertile plain, amidst the towering hills, over which we rode a long time, through magnificent high forests, extensive green fields, meadows and lawns. Here had formerly been a very flourishing settlement; but the Indians deserted it in search of fresh planting land, which they soon found in a rich vale but a few miles distance over a ridge of hills. Soon after entering on these charming, sequestered, prolific fields, we came to a fine little river, which crossing, and riding over fruitful strawberry beds and green lawns, on the sides of a circular ridge of hills in front of us, and going round the bases of this promontory, came to a fine meadow on an arm of the vale, through which meandered a brook, its humid vapours bedewing the fragrant strawberries which hung in heavy red clusters over the grassy verge. We crossed the rivulet; then rising a sloping, green, turfy ascent, alighted on the borders of a grand forest of stately trees, which we penetrated on foot a little distance to a horse-stamp, where was a large squadron of those useful creatures, belonging to my friend and companion, the trader, on the sight of whom they assembled together from all quarters; some at a distance saluted him with shrill neighings of gratitude, or came prancing up to lick the salt out of his hand, whilst the younger and more timorous came galloping onward, but coyly wheeled off, and fetching a circuit stood aloof; but as soon as their lord and master strewed the crystaline salty bait on the hard beaten ground, they all, old and young, docile and timorous, soon formed themselves in ranks and fell to licking up the delicious morsel.

It was a fine sight; more beautiful creatures I never saw; there were of them of all colours, sizes and dispositions. Every year, as they become of age, he sends off a troop of them down to Charleston, where they are sold to the highest bidder.

Having paid our attention to this useful part of the creation, who, if they are under our dominion, have consequently a right to our protection and favour, we returned to our trusty servants that were regaling themselves in the exuberant sweet pastures and strawberry fields in sight, and mounted again. Proceeding on our return to town, continued through part of this high forest skirting on the meadows: began to ascend the hills of a ridge which we were under the necessity of crossing; and having gained its summit, enjoyed a most enchanting view; a vast expanse of green meadows and strawberry fields; a meandering river gliding through, saluting in its various turnings the swelling, green, turfy knolls, embellished with parterres of flowers and fruitful strawberry beds; flocks of turkies strolling about them; herds of deer prancing in the meads or bounding over the hills; companies of young, innocent Cherokee virgins, some busy gathering the rich fragrant fruit, others having already filled their baskets, lay reclined under the shade of floriferous and fragrant native bowers of Magnolia, Azalea, Philadelphus, perfumed Calycanthus, sweet Yellow Jessamine and cerulean Glycine frutescens, disclosing their beauties to the fluttering breeze, and bathing their limbs in the cool fleeting streams; whilst other parties more gay and libertine, were yet collecting strawberries, or wantonly chasing their companions, tantalising them, staining their lips and cheeks with the rich fruit.

The sylvan scene of primitive innocence was enchanting, and perhaps too enticing for hearty young men long to continue idle spectators.

In fine, nature prevailing over reason, we wished at least to have a more active part in their delicious sports. Thus precipitately resolving, we cautiously made our approaches, yet undiscovered, almost to the joyous scene of action. Now, although we meant no other than an innocent frolic with this gay assembly of hamadryades, we shall leave it to the person of feeling and sensibility to form an idea to what lengths our passions might have hurried us, thus warmed and excited, had it not been for the vigilance and care of some envious matrons who lay in ambush, and espying us, gave the alarm, time enough for the nymphs to rally and assemble together. We however pursued and gained ground on a group of them, who had incautiously strolled to a greater distance from their guardians, and finding their retreat now like to be cut off, took shelter under cover of a little grove; but on perceiving themselves to be discovered by us, kept their station, peeping through the bushes; when observing our approaches, they confidently discovered themselves, and decently advanced to meet us, half unveiling their blooming faces, incarnated with the modest maiden blush, and with native innocence and cheerfulness, presented their little baskets, merrily telling us their fruit was ripe and sound.

We accepted a basket, sat down and regaled ourselves on the delicious fruit, encircled by the whole assembly of the innocent jocose sylvan nymphs: by this time the several parties, under the conduct of the elder matrons, had disposed themselves in companies on the green, turfy banks.

My young companion, the trader, by concessions and suitable apologies for the bold intrusion, having compromised the matter with them, engaged them to bring their collections to his house at a stipulated price: we parted friendly.

And now taking leave of these Elysian fields, we again mounted the hills, which we crossed, and traversing obliquely their flowery beds, arrived in town in the cool of the evening.

CHAP. IV.

Affter waiting two days at Cowe expecting a guide and protector to the Overhill towns, and at last being disappointed, I resolved to pursue the journey alone, though against the advice of the traders; the Overhill Indians being in an ill humour with the whites, in consequence of some late skirmishes between them and the frontier Virginians, most of the Overhill traders having left the nation.

Early in the morning I sat off attended by my worthy old friend Mr. Galahan, who obligingly accompanied me near fifteen miles. We passed through the Jore village, which is pleasingly situated in a little vale on the side of the mountain; a pretty rivulet or creek winds about through the vale, just under the village: here I observed a little grove of the Casine yapon, which was the only place where I had seen it grow in the Cherokee country; the Indians call it the beloved tree, and are very careful to keep it pruned and cultivated: they drink a very strong infusion of the leaves, buds and tender branches of this plant, which is so celebrated, indeed venerated by the Creeks and all the Southern maritime nations of Indians. We then continued travelling down the vale about two miles, the road deviating, turning and winding about the hills, and through groves and lawns, watered by brooks and rivulets, rapidly rushing from the towering hill on every side, and flowing into the Jore, which is a considerable branch of the Tanase.

Began now to ascend the mountain, following a small arm or branch of the vale, which led to a gap or narrow defile, compressed by the high pending hills on each side, down which came rapidly a considerable branch of the Jore, dashing and roaring over rocky precipices.

Now leaving Roaring creek on our right, and accomplishing two or three ascents or ridges, another branch of the trading path from the Overhills to Cowe came in on our right, and here my transitory companion Mr. Galahan parted from me, taking this road back to Cowe; when I was left again wandering alone in the dreary mountains, not indeed totally pathless, nor in my present situation entirely agreeable, although such scenes of primitive unmodified nature always pleased me.

May we suppose that mankind feel in their hearts a predilection for the society of each other; or are we delighted with scenes of human arts and cultivation, where the passions are flattered and entertained with variety of objects for gratification?

I found myself unable, notwithstanding the attentive admonitions and persuasive arguments of reason, entirely to erase from my mind, those impressions which I had received from the society of the amiable and polite inhabitants of Charleston; and I could not help comparing my present situation in some degree to Nebuchadnezzar's, when expelled from the society of men, and constrained to roam in the mountains and wilderness, there to herd and feed with the wild beasts of the forests.

After parting with my late companion, I went forward with all the alacrity that prudence would admit of, that I might as soon as possible see the end of my toil and hazard, being determined at all events to cross the Jore mountain, said to be the highest land in the Cherokee country.

After a gentle descent, I entered on an extremely stony narrow vale, through which coasted swiftly a large creek, twelve or fifteen yards wide, roaring over a rocky bed, which I crossed with difficulty and danger, the ford being incommoded by shelving rocks, full of holes and cliffs. After leaving this rocky creek, my path led me upon another narrow vale or glade, down which came in great haste another noisy brook, which I repeatedly crossed and recrossed, sometimes riding on narrow level grassy verges close to its banks; still ascending, the vale gradually terminated, being shut up by stupendous rocky hills on each side, leaving a very narrow gap or defile, towards which my road led me, ascending the steep sides of the mountains; when, after rising several wearisome ascents, and finding myself over-heated and tired, I halted at a little grassy lawn through which meandered a sweet rivulet. Here I turned my horse to graze, and sat down to rest on a green bank just beneath a high frowning promontory, or obtuse point of a ridge of the mountain yet above me, the friendly rivulet making a circuit by my feet; and now a little

rested, I took out of my wallet some biscuit and cheese, and
a peace of neat's tongue, composing myself to ease and refreshment: when suddenly appeared within a few yards, advancing towards me from behind the point, a stout likely
young Indian fellow, armed with a rifle gun, and two dogs
attending. Upon sight of me he stood, and seemed a little
surprised, as I was very much; but instantly recollecting himself and assuming a countenance of benignity and cheerfulness, he came briskly to me and shook hands heartily, and
smilingly inquired from whence I came, and whither going;
but speaking only in the Cherokee tongue, our conversation
was not continued to a great length. I presented him with
some choice Tobacco, which was accepted with courtesy and
evident pleasure, and to my inquiries concerning the roads
and distance to the Overhill towns, he answered me with perfect cheerfulness and good temper. We then again shook
hands and parted in friendship; he descended the hills, singing
as he went.

Of vegetable productions observed in this region, were the
following viz. Acer striatum, Ac. rubrum, Juglans nigra, Jug.
alba, Jug. Hiccory, Magnolia acuminata, Quercus alba, Q.
tinctoria, Q. rubra, Q. prinus, with the other varieties common in Virginia: Panax ginseng, Angelica lucida, Convallaria
majalis, Halesia, Stewartia, Styrax, Staphylea, Evonimus, Viburnum, Cornus Florida, Betula nigra, Morus, Tilia, Ulmus,
Fraxinus, Hopea tinctoria, Annona, Bignonia sempervirens,
Aristolochia frutescens, Bignonia radicans, &c. Being now refreshed by a simple but healthy meal, I began again to ascend
the Jore mountains, which I at length accomplished, and
rested on the most elevated peak; from whence I beheld with
rapture and astonishment a sublimely awful scene of power
and magnificence, a world of mountains piled upon mountains. Having contemplated this amazing prospect of grandeur, I descended the pinnacles, and again falling into the
trading path, continued gently descending through a grassy
plain, scatteringly planted with large trees, and at a distance
surrounded with high forests. I was on this elevated region
sensible of an alteration in the air, from warm to cold, and
found that vegetation was here greatly behind, in plants of the
same kind of the country below; for instance, when I left

Charleston, the yellow Jasmine was rather past the blooming days, and here the buds were just beginning to swell, though some were in bloom. Continued more than a mile through this elevated plain to the pitch of the mountain, from whence presented to view an expansive prospect, exhibiting scenes of mountainous landscape, westward, vast and varied, perhaps not to be exceeded any where.

My first descent and progress down the west side of the mountain was remarkably gradual, easy and pleasant, through grassy open forests for the distance of two or three miles; when my changeable path suddenly turned round an obtuse point of a ridge, and descended precipitately down a steep rocky hill for a mile or more, which was very troublesome, being incommoded with shattered fragments of the mountains, and in other places with boggy sinks, occasioned by oozy springs and rills stagnate sinking in micaceous earth: some of these steep soft rocky banks or precipices seem to be continually crumbling to earth; and in these mouldering cliffs I discovered veins or strata of most pure and clear white earth*, having a faint bluish or pearl colour gleam, somewhat exhibiting the appearance of the little cliffs or wavy crests of new fallen snowdrifts: we likewise observe in these dissolving rocky cliffs, veins of isinglass (Mica S. vitrum Muscoviticum), some of the flakes or laminæ incredibly large, entire and transparent, and would serve the purpose of lights for windows very well, or for lanthorns; and here appeared strata of black lead (stibium).

At length, after much toil and exercise, I was a little relieved by a narrow grassy vale or lawn at the foot of this steep descent, through which coursed along a considerable rapid brook, on whose banks grew in great perfection the glorious Magnolia auriculata, together with the other conspicuous flowering and aromatic shrubs already mentioned; and I observed here in the rich bottoms near the creek, a new species of Hydrastis, having very large sinuated leaves and white flowers; after this I continued several miles over ridges and grassy vales, watered with delightful rivulets.

*Mica nitida: specimens of this earth have been exported to England, for the purpose of making Porcelain or China ware.

Next day proceeding on eight or ten miles, generally through spacious high forests and flowery lawns; the soil prolific, being of an excellent quality for agriculture; came near the banks of a large creek or river, where this high forest ended on my left hand, the trees became more scattered and insensibly united with a grassy glade or lawn bordering on the river; on the opposite bank of which appeared a very extensive forest, consisting entirely of the Hemlock spruce (P. abies), almost encircled by distant ridges of lofty hills.

Soon after crossing this large branch of the Tanase, I observed, descending the heights at some distance, a company of Indians, all well mounted on horse back; they came rapidly forward: on their nearer approach I observed a chief at the head of the carravan, and apprehending him to be the Little Carpenter, emperor or grand chief of the Cherokees, as they came up I turned off from the path to make way, in token of respect, which compliment was accepted, and gratefully and magnanimously returned; for his highness with a gracious and cheerful smile came up to me, and clapping his hand on his breast, offered it to me, saying, I am Ata-cul-culla; and heartily shook hands with me, and asked me if I knew it. I answered, that the Good Spirit who goes before me spoke to me, and said, that is the great Ata-cul-culla; and added, that I was of the tribe of white men, of Pennsylvania, who esteem themselves brothers and friends to the red men, but particularly so to the Cherokees, and that notwithstanding we dwelt at so great a distance, we were united in love and friendship, and that the name of Ata-cul-culla was dear to his white brothers of Pennsylvania.

After this compliment, which seemed to be acceptable, he inquired if I came lately from Charleston, and if John Stewart was well, saying that he was going to see him. I replied, that I came lately from Charleston on a friendly visit to the Cherokees; that I had the honour of a personal acquaintance with the superintendant, the beloved man, whom, I saw well but the day before I set off, and who, by letters to the principal white men in the nation, recommended me to the friendship and protection of the Cherokees. To which the great chief was pleased to answer very respectfully, that I was welcome in their country as a friend and brother; and then shaking hands heartily bid me farewel, and his retinue confirmed it by an united voice of assent. After giving my name to the chief, requesting my compliments to the superintendant, the emperor moved, continuing his journey for Charleston; and I, yet persisting in my intention of visiting the Overhill towns, continued on. Leaving the great forest I mounted the high hills, descending them again on the other side, and so on repeatedly for several miles, without observing any variation in the natural productions since passing the Jore: and perceiving the slow progress of vegetation in this mountainous, high country; and, upon serious consideration, it appearing very plainly that I could not, with entire safety, range the Overhill settlements until the treaty was over, which would not come on till late in June; I suddenly came to a resolution to defer these researches at this time, and leave them for the employment of another season and more favourable opportunity, and return to Dartmouth in Georgia, to be ready to join a company of adventurers who were to set off in July for Mobile in West Florida. The leader of this company had been recommended to me as a fit person to assist me on so long and hazardous a journey, through the vast territories of the Creeks.

Therefore next day I turned about on my return, proceeding moderately, being engaged in noting such objects as appeared to be of any moment, and collecting specimens; and in the evening of next day arrived again at Cowe.

Next morning Mr. Galahan conducted me to the chief of Cowe, who during my absence had returned from the chace. The remainder of this day I spent in observations in and about the town, reviewing my specimens, &c.

The town of Cowe consists of about one hundred dwellings, near the banks of the Tanase, on both sides of the river.

The Cherokees construct their habitations on a different plan from the Creeks; that is, but one oblong four square building, of one story high; the materials consisting of logs or trunks of trees, stripped of their bark, notched at their ends, fixed one upon another, and afterwards plaistered well, both inside and out, with clay well tempered with dry grass, and the whole covered or roofed with the bark of the chesnut tree or long broad shingles. This building is however partitioned transversely, forming three apartments, which communicate with each other by inside doors; each house or habitation has besides a little conical house, covered with dirt, which is called the winter or hot-house; this stands a few yards distance from the mansion-house, opposite the front door.

The council or town-house is a large rotunda, capable of accommodating several hundred people: it stands on the top of an ancient artificial mount of earth, of about twenty feet perpendicular, and the rotunda on the top of it being above thirty feet more, gives the whole fabric an elevation of about sixty feet from the common surface of the ground. But it may be proper to observe, that this mount on which the rotunda stands, is of a much ancienter date than the building, and perhaps was raised for another purpose. The Cherokees themselves are as ignorant as we are, by what people or for what purpose these artificial hills were raised; they have various stories concerning them, the best of which amount to no more than mere conjecture, and leave us entirely in the dark; but they have a tradition common with the other nations of Indians, that they found them in much the same condition as they now appear, when their forefathers arrived from the West and possessed themselves of the country, after vanquishing the nations of red men who then inhabited it, who themselves found these mounts when they took possession of the country, the former possessors delivering the same story concerning them: perhaps they were designed and apropriated by the people who constructed them, to some religious purpose, as great altars and temples similar to the high places and sacred groves anciently amongst the Canaanites and other nations of Palestine and Judea.

The rotunda is constructed after the following manner: they first fix in the ground a circular range of posts or trunks of trees, about six feet high, at equal distances, which are notched at top, to receive into them from one to another, a range of beams or wall plates; within this is another circular order of very large and strong pillars, above twelve feet high, notched in like manner at top, to receive another range of wall plates; and within this is yet another or third range of stronger and higher pillars, but fewer in number, and standing at a greater distance from each other; and lastly, in the centre stands a very strong pillar, which forms the pinnacle of the building, and to which the rafters centre at top; these rafters are strengthened and bound together by cross beams and laths, which sustain the roof or covering, which is a layer of bark neatly placed, and tight enough to exclude the rain, and sometimes they cast a thin superficies of earth over all. There is but one large door, which serves at the same time to admit light from without and the smoak to escape when a fire is kindled; but as there is but a small fire kept, sufficient to give light at night, and that fed with dry small sound wood divested of its bark, there is but little smoak. All around the inside of the building, betwixt the second range of pillars and the wall, is a range of cabins or sophas, consisting of two or three steps, one above or behind the other, in theatrical order, where the assembly sit or lean down; these sophas are covered with mats or carpets, very curiously made of thin splints of Ash or Oak, woven or platted together; near the great pillar in the centre the fire is kindled for light, near which the musicians seat themselves, and round about this the performers exhibit their dances and other shows at public festivals, which happen almost every night throughout the year.

About the close of the evening I accompanied Mr. Galahan and other white traders to the rotunda, where was a grand festival, music and dancing. This assembly was held principally to rehearse the ball-play dance, this town being challenged to play against another the next day.

The people being assembled and seated in order, and the musicians having taken their station, the ball opens, first with a long harangue or oration, spoken by an aged chief, in commendation of the manly exercise of the ball-play, recounting the many and brilliant victories which the town of Cowe had gained over the other towns in the nation, not forgetting or neglecting to recite his own exploits, together with those of other aged men now present, coadjutors in the performance of these athletic games in their youthful days.

This oration was delivered with great spirit and eloquence, and was meant to influence the passions of the young men present, excite them to emulation, and inspire them with ambition.

This prologue being at an end, the musicians began, both vocal and instrumental; when presently a company of girls, hand in hand, dressed in clean white robes and ornamented with beads, bracelets and a profusion of gay ribbands, entering the door, immediately began to sing their responses in a gentle, low, and sweet voice, and formed themselves in a semicircular file or line, in two ranks, back to back, facing the spectators and musicians, moving slowly round and round. This continued about a quarter of an hour, when we were surprised by a sudden very loud and shrill whoop, uttered at once by a company of young fellows, who came in briskly after one another, with rackets or hurls in one hand. These champions likewise were well dressed, painted, and ornamented with silver bracelets, gorgets and wampum, neatly ornamented with moccasins and high waving plumes in their diadems: they immediately formed themselves in a semicircular rank also, in front of the girls, when these changed their order, and formed a single rank parallel to the men, raising their voices in responses to the tunes of the young champions, the semicircles continually moving round. There was something singular and diverting in their step and motions, and I imagine not to be learned to exactness but with great attention and perseverance. The step, if it can be so termed, was performed after the following manner; first, the motion began at one end of the semicircle, gently rising up and down upon their toes and heels alternately, when the first was up on tip-toe, the next began to raise the heel, and by the time the first rested again on the heel, the second was on tip toe, thus from one end of the rank to the other, so that some were always up and some down, alternately and regularly, without the least baulk or confusion; and they at the same time, and in the same motion, moved on obliquely or sideways, so that the circle performed a double or complex motion in its progression, and at stated times exhibited a grand or universal movement, instantly and unexpectedly to the spectators, by each rank turning to right and left, taking each others places: the movements were managed with inconceivable alertness and address, and accompanied with an instantaneous and universal elevation of the voice, and shrill short whoop.

The Cherokees, besides the ball play dance, have a variety of others equally entertaining. The men especially exercise themselves with a variety of gesticulations and capers, some of which are ludicrous and diverting enough; and they have others which are of the martial order, and others of the chace; these seem to be somewhat of a tragical nature, wherein they exhibit astonishing feats of military prowess, masculine strength and activity. Indeed all their dances and musical entertainments seem to be theatrical exhibitions or plays, varied with comic and sometimes lascivious interludes: the women however conduct themselves with a very becoming grace and decency, insomuch that in amorous interludes, when their responses and gestures seem consenting to natural liberties, they veil themselves, just discovering a glance of their sparkling eyes and blushing faces, expressive of sensibility.

Next morning early I set off on my return, and meeting with no material occurrences on the road, in two days arrived safe at Keowe, where I tarried two or three days, employed in augmenting my collections of specimens, and waiting for Mr. Galahan, who was to call on me here, to accompany him to Sinica, where he and other traders were to meet Mr. Cameron, the deputy commissary, to hold a congress at that town, with the chiefs of the Lower Cherokees, to consult preliminaries introductory to a general congress and treaty with these Indians, which was to be convened next June, and held in the Overhill towns.

I observed in the environs of Keowe, on the bases of the rocky hills, immediately ascending from the low grounds near the river bank, a great number of very singular antiquities, the work of the ancients; they seem to me to have been altars for sacrifice or sepulchres: they were constructed of four flat stones, two set on an edge for the sides, one closed one end, and a very large flat one lay horizontally at top, so that the other end was open; this fabric was four or five feet in length, two feet high, and three in width. I inquired of the trader what they were, who could not tell me certainly, but supposed them to be ancient Indian ovens; the Indians can give no account of them: they are on the surface of the ground and are of different dimensions.

I accompanied the traders to Sinica, where we found the commissary and the Indian chiefs convened in counsel: continued at Sinica sometime, employing myself in observations, and making collections of every thing worthy of notice: and finding the Indians to be yet unsettled in their determination, and not in a good humour, I abandoned the project of visiting the regions beyond the Cherokee mountains for this season; set off for my return to fort James, Dartmouth, lodged this night in the forests near the banks of a delightful large creek, a branch of Keowe river, and next day arrived safe at Dartmouth.

List of the towns and villages in the Cherokee nation inhabited at this day, viz.

No.	1	Echoe	On the Tanase East of the Jore mountains.
	2	Nucasse	
	3	Whatoga	
	4	Cowe	4 towns.
	5	Ticoloosa	Inland on the branches of the Tanase.
	6	Jore	
	7	Conisca	
	8	Nowe	4 towns.
	9	Tomothle	On the Tanase over the Jore mountains.
	10	Noewe	
	11	Tellico	
	12	Clennuse	
	13	Ocunnolufte	
	14	Chewe	8 towns
	15	Quanuse	
	16	Tellowe	
	17	Tellico	Inland towns on the branches of the Tanase and other waters over the Jore mountains.
	18	Chatuga	
	19	Hiwasse	
	20	Chewase	
	21	Nuanha	5 towns.

22 Tallase
23 Chelowe
24 Sette   Overhill towns on the Tanase
25 Chote great   or Cherokee river.
26 Toco   6 towns.
27 Tahasse

28 Tamahle
29 Tuskege
30 —— Big Island   Overhill towns on the Tanase
31 Nilaque   or Cherokee river.
32 Niowe   5 towns.

Lower towns East of the mountains, viz.
No. 1 Sinica
       2 Keowe   On the Savanna or Keowe
       3 Kulsage   river.

       4 Tugilo
       5 Estotowe   On Tugilo river.

       6 Qualatche
       7 Chote   On Flint river.

Towns on the waters of other rivers.
Estotowe great. Allagae. Jore. Nae oche.
In all forty-three towns.

PARUS GUTTURE NIGRO.

PLATE 17

a. a contraction of these Grows Growth - perfecter

B. the Ette common one of the lateral shoots of antiquar koth are a some pale.

Sooty tinged Fly

The grant other to-fize Sugar Maple—

Our Sugar Maple as it appears when the Seeds the are fully ripe.— William Bartram September 12 1793.

PLATE 18

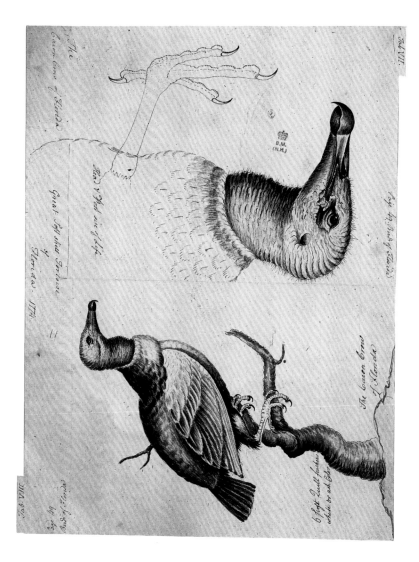

PLATE 19

Ortulan
or
Rice Bird
Pat. Nat. Carolina

Fig. 1

Fig. 2

Fig. 4

Fig. 3

Tab. V

22

PLATE 20

PLATE 21

The great Mud Tortoise from
Pennsylvania ———— Called the Snaping Turtle

WB

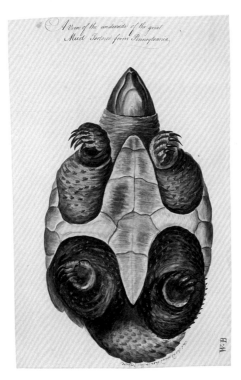

A View of the underside of the great
Mud Tortoise from Pennsylvania.

W.B

PLATE 22

The Rattle snake taken upon the banks of ye Esopeso River

PLATE 23

PLATE 24

PLATE 25

MAGNOLIA AWRICULATA. *Bart. Journ.*

a. Strobilus or Cone

W. Bartram Delin. Prouchard Sculp.

PLATE 26

ŒNOTHERA grandiflora. Bart. Journ.

PLATE 27

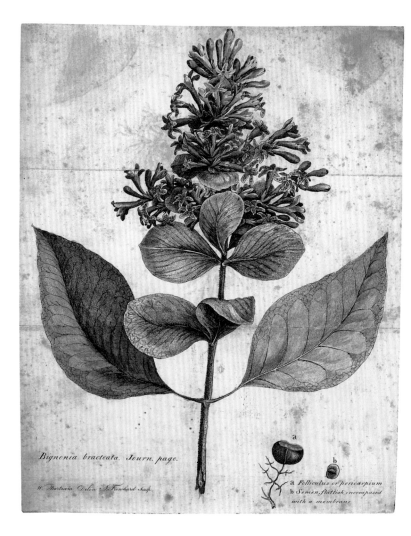

Bignonia bracteata. Journ. page.

W. Bartram Delin. & J. Rouchard Sculp.

a *Folliculus or pericarpium*
b *Semen, flatish, encompased
with a membrane*

PLATE 28

ÆSCULUS polygamia. Bart. Journ.

W. Bartram Delin. Trenchard Sculp.

PLATE 29

Franklinia alatamaha.   *A beautiful flowering tree.*

discovered growing near the banks of the R. Alatamaha in Georgia.

Willm Bartram. Delin. 1788.

PLATE 30

PLATE 31

PLATE 32

CHAP. V.

B EING returned from the Cherokee country to Dartmouth, I understood that the company of adventurers for West Florida were very forward in their preparations, and would be ready to set off in a few weeks, so that I had but a little time allowed me to make provision and equip myself for the prosecution of so long and hazardous a journey.

Our place of rendezvous was at fort Charlotte, on the opposite side of the river Savanna, and about a mile from fort James. I had a desire to make little botanical excursions towards the head of Broad river, in order to collect some curiosities which I had observed thereabouts; which being accomplished,

June 22d set out from fort Charlotte in company with Mr. Whitfield, who was chief of our caravan. We travelled about twenty miles, and lodged at the farm of Mons. St. Pierre, a French gentleman, who received and entertained us with great politeness and hospitality. The mansion-house is situated on the top of a very high hill near the banks of the river Savanna, overlooking his very extensive and well cultivated plantations of Indian Corn (Zea) Rice, Wheat, Oats, Indigo, Convolvulus Batata, &c. these are rich low lands, lying very level betwixt these natural heights and the river; his gardens occupy the gentle descent on one side of the mount, and a very thriving vineyard consisting of about five acres is on the other side.

Next morning after breakfast we set off again, continuing nine or ten miles farther down the river, when we stopped at a plantation, the property of one of our companions, where we were joined by the rest of the company. After dining here we prepared to depart; and the gentleman of the house taking an affectionate leave of his wife and children, we sat off again, and proceeding six miles farther down the river, we crossed over into Georgia, taking a road which led us into the great trading path from Augusta to the Creek nation. As the soil, situation and productions of these parts, for several days journey, differ very little from the Northern districts of Georgia, already recited, when on the survey of the New Purchase, I apprehend it needless to enter again into a detail of particulars, since it would produce but little more than a recapitulation of that journey.

Early in the evening of the 27th we arrived at the Flat-rock, where we lodged. This is a common rendezvous or camping place for traders and Indians. It is an expansive clean flat or horizontal rock, but a little above the surface of the ground, and near the banks of a delightful rivulet of excellent water, which is one of the head branches of Great Ogeche: in the loose rich soil verging round this rock, grew several very curious herbaceous plants, particularly one of singular elegance and beauty, which I take to be a species of Ipomea (Ipomea, caule erecto, ramoso, tripedali, fol. radicalibus, pinnatifidis, linearibus, humi-stratis, florib. incarnatis intus maculis coccineis adsperso). It grows erect, three feet high, with a strong stem, which is decorated with plumed or pinnatifid linear leaves, somewhat resembling those of the Delphinium or Ipomea quamoclit; from about one half its length upwards, it sends out on all sides, ascendant branches which divide again and again; these terminate with large tubular or funnel-formed flowers; their limbs equally divided into five segments; these beautiful flowers are of a perfect rose colour, elegantly besprinkled on the inside of their petals with crimson specks; the flowers are in great abundance, and together with the branches and delicately fine cut leaves, compose a conical spike or compound pannicle. I saw a species of this plant, if not the very same, growing on the sea coast islands near St. Augustine. The blue flowered Malva and Delphinium were its associates about the Flat-rock.

There are extensive cane brakes or cane meadows spread abroad round about, which afford the most acceptable and nourishing food for cattle.

This evening two companies of Indian traders from Augusta arrived and encamped near us; and as they were bound to the Nation, we concluded to unite in company with them, they generously offering us their assistance, having many spare horses and others lightly loaded, several of ours by this time being jaded: this was a favourable opportunity of relief in case of necessity.

Next morning as soon as the horses were packed and in readiness, we decamped and set forward together.

I thought it worthy of taking notice of a singular method the traders make use of to reduce the wild young horses to their hard duty. When any one persists in refusing to receive his load, if threats, the discipline of the whip and other common abuse prove insufficient, after being haltered, a pack-horse-man catches the tip end of one of his ears betwixt his teeth and pinches it, when instantly the furious strong creature, trembling, stands perfectly still until he is loaded.

Our caravan consisting of about twenty men and sixty horses, we made a formidable appearance, having now little to apprehend from predatory bands or out-laws.

This day's journey was for the most part over high gravelly ridges, and on the most elevated hills, appeared emerging out of the earth, rocky cliffs of a dark reddish brown colour; their composition seemed to be a coarse, sandy, ferruginous concrete, but so firmly cemented as to constitute a perfect hard stone or rock, and appeared to be excavated or worn into cavities and furrows by the violence of the dashing billows and rapid currents of the ocean, which heretofore probably washed them; there were however strata or veins in these rocks, of a finer composition and compact consistence, and seemed ponderous rich iron ore. A little depth below the sandy gravelly surface, lies a stratum of very compact reddish yellow clay and fragments of ochre. The trees and shrubs common on these gravelly ridges are as follows, Diospyros, Quercus rubra, Q. nigra, Q. tinctoria or great Black Oak, Q. alba, Q. lobata, post White Oak, Q. incana, foliis ovalibus integerrimis subtus incanis, Pinus lutea, Pinus tæda, foliis geminatis et trinis, strobilo ovato brevi, cortice rimoso, Pinus palustris, foliis trinis longissimis, strobilo elongata, Cornus Florida, Andromeda arborea, Nyssa sylvatica, Juglans hiccory, Prunus padus, &c. Of herbaceæ, Solidago, Eupatorium, Sylphium, Rudbeckia, Gerardia, Asclepias, Agave Virginica, Eryngium, Thapsia, Euphorbia, Polymnia, &c.

In the course of this day's journey we crossed two considerable rivulets, running swiftly over rocky beds. There is some very good land on the gradual descents of the ridges and their bottoms bordering on creeks, and very extensive grassy savannas and cane meadows always in view on one hand or the other. At evening we came to camp on the banks of a beautiful creek, a branch of Great Ogeche, called Rocky Comfort, where we found excellent accommodations, here being pleasant grassy open plains to spread our beds upon, environed with extensive cane meadows, affording the best of food for our quadrupeds.

The next day's journey led us over a level district; the land generally very fertile and of a good quality for agriculture, the vegetable surface being of a dark, loose, rich mould, on a stratum of stiff reddish brown clay. Crossing several considerable creeks, branches of the Ocone, North branch of the Alatamaha, at evening, July 1st, encamped on the banks of the Ocone, in a delightful grove of forest trees, consisting of Oak, Ash, Mulberry, Hiccory, Black Walnut, Elm, Sassafras, Gleditsia, &c. This flourishing grove was an appendage of the high forests we had passed through, and projected into an extensive, green, open, level plain, consisting of old Indian fields and plantations, being the rich low lands of the river, and stretching along its banks upwards to a very great distance, charmingly diversified and decorated with detached groves and clumps of various trees and shrubs, and indented on its verge by advancing and retreating promontories of the high land.

Our encampment was fixed on the site of the old Ocone town, which, about sixty years ago, was evacuated by the Indians, who, finding their situation disagreeable from its vicinity to the white people, left it, moving upwards into the Nation or Upper Creeks, and there built a town; but that situation not suiting their roving disposition, they grew sickly and tired of it, and resolved to seek an habitation more agreeable to their minds. They all arose, directing their migration South-Eastward towards the sea coast; and in the course of their journey, observing the delightful appearance of the extensive plains of Alachua and the fertile hills environing it, they sat down and built a town on the banks of a spacious and beautiful lake, at a small distance from the plains, naming this new town, Cuscowilla: this situation pleased them, the vast desarts, forests, lake and savannas around, affording unbounded range of the best hunting ground for bear and deer, their favourite game. But although this situation was healthy and delightful to the utmost degree, affording them variety and plenty of every desirable thing in their estimation, yet troubles and afflictions found them out. This territory, to the promontory of Florida, was then claimed by the Tomocos, Utinas, Calloosas, Yamases and other remnant tribes of the ancient Floridans and the more Northern refugees, driven away by the Carolinians, now in alliance and under the protection of the Spaniards, who assisting them, attacked the new settlement and for many years were very troublesome; but the Alachuas or Ocones being strengthened by other emigrants and fugitive bands from the Upper Creeks, with whom they were confederated, and who gradually established other towns in this low country, stretching a line of settlements across the isthmus, extending from the Alatamaha to the bay of Apalache; these uniting were at length able to face their enemies and even attack them in their own settlements; and in the end, with the assistance of the Upper Creeks, their uncles, vanquished their enemies and destroyed them, and then fell upon the Spanish settlements, which also they entirely broke up. But having treated of these matters in the journal of my travels into East Florida, I end this digression and proceed again on my journey.

After crossing the Ocone by fording it, which is about two hundred and fifty yards over, we travelled about twenty miles, and came to camp in the evening; passed over a pleasant territory, presenting varying scenes of gentle swelling hills and levels, affording sublime forests, contrasted by expansive illumined green fields, native meadows and Cane brakes; the vegetables, trees, shrubs and plants the same as already noticed without any material variation. The next day's journey was about twenty miles, having crossed the Oakmulge by fording it three or four hundred yards over. This river is the main branch of the beautiful Alatamaha: on the East bank of the river lie the famous Oakmulge fields, where are yet conspicuous very wonderful remains of the power and grandeur of the ancients of this part of America, in the ruins of a capital town and settlement, as vast artificial hills, terraces, &c. already particularly mentioned in my tour through the lower districts of Georgia. The Oakmulge here is about forty miles distance from the Ocone, the other arm of the Alatamaha. In the evening we came to camp near the banks of Stony Creek, a large rapid water about six miles beyond the river.

Next day we travelled about twenty miles farther, crossing two considerable creeks named Great and Little Tobosochte; and at evening encamped close by a beautiful large brook called Sweet Water, the glittering waving flood passing along actively over a bed of pebbles and gravel. The territory through which we passed from the banks of the Oakmulge to this place, exhibited a delightful diversified rural scene, and promises a happy, fruitful and salubrious region, when culti-vated by industrious inhabitants; generally ridges of low swelling hills and plains supporting grand forests, vast Cane meadows, savannas and verdant lawns.

I observed here a very singular and beautiful shrub, which I suppose is a species of Hydrangia (H. quercifolia). It grows in coppices or clumps near or on the banks of rivers and creeks; many stems usually arise from a root, spreading itself greatly on all sides by suckers or offsets; the stems grow five or six feet high, declining or diverging from each other, and are covered with several barks or rinds, the last of which being of a cinereous dirt colour and very thin, at a certain age of the stems or shoots, cracks through to the next bark, and is peeled off by the winds, discovering the under, smooth, dark reddish brown bark, which also cracks and peels off the next year, in like manner as the former; thus every year forming a new bark; the stems divide regularly or oppositely, though the branches are crooked or wreathe about horizontally, and these again divide, forming others which terminate with large heavy panicles or thyrsi of flowers; but these flowers are of two kinds: the numerous partial spikes which compose the panicles and consist of a multitude of very small fruitful flowers, terminate with one or more very large expansive neutral or mock flow-ers, standing on a long, slender, stiff peduncle; these flowers are composed of four broad oval petals or segments, of a dark rose or crimson colour at first, but as they become older ac-quire a deeper red or purplish hue, and lastly are of a brown or ferruginous colour; these have no perfect parts of genera-tion of either sex, but discover in their centre two, three or

Andromeda Pulverulenta.

Hydrangea Quercifolia.

four papillæ or rudiments; these neutral flowers, with the whole pannicle, are truly permanent, remaining on the plant for years, until they dry and decay: the leaves which clothe the plants are very large, pinnatifid or palmated, and serrated or toothed, very much resembling the leaves of some of our Oaks; they sit opposite, supported by slender petioles, and are of a fine, full green colour.

Next day after noon we crossed Flint river by fording it, about two hundred and fifty yards over, and at evening came to camp near the banks of a large and deep creek, a branch of the Flint. The high land excellent, affording grand forests, and the low ground vast timber and Canes of great height and thickness, Arundo gigantea. I observed growing on the steep dry banks of this creek, a species of shrub Hypericum, of extraordinary show and beauty (Hypericum aureum). It grows erect, three or four feet high, forming a globular top, representing a perfect little tree; the leaves are large, oblong, firm of texture, smooth and shining; the flowers are very large, their petals broad and conspicuous, which, with their tufts of golden filaments, give the little bushes a very splendid appearance.

The adjacent low grounds and Cane swamp afforded excellent food and range for our horses, who, by this time, through fatigue of constant travelling, heat of the climate and season, were tired and dispirited: we came to camp sooner than usual, and started later next day, that they might have time to rest and recruit themselves. The territory lying upon this creek, and the space between it and the river, present every appearance of a delightful and fruitful region in some future day, it being a rich soil, and exceedingly well situated for every branch of agriculture and grazing, diversified with hills and dales, savannas and vast Cane meadows, and watered by innumerable rivulets and brooks, all contiguous to the Flint river: an arm of the great Chata Uche or Apalachucla offers an uninterrupted navigation to the bay of Mexico and the Atlantic ocean, and thence to the West India islands and over the whole world.

Our horses being hunted up and packed, sat forward again, proceeding moderately, ascending a higher country and more uneven by means of ridges of gentle hills; the country however very pleasing, being diversified with expansive groves, savannas and Cane meadows, abounding with creeks and brooks gliding through the plains or roving about the hills, their banks bordered with forests and groves, consisting of varieties of trees, shrubs and plants; the summits of the hills frequently presenting to view piles and cliffs of the ferruginous rocks, the same species as observed on the ridges between the Flat-rock and Rocky Comfort.

Next day we travelled but a few miles; the heat and the burning flies tormenting our horses to such a degree, as to excite compassion even in the hearts of pack-horsemen. These biting flies are of several species, and their numbers incredible. We travelled almost from sun-rise to his setting, amidst a flying host of these persecuting spirits, who formed a vast cloud around our caravan so thick as to obscure every distant object; but our van always bore the brunt of the conflict; the head, neck, and shoulders of the leading horses were continually in a gore of blood: some of these flies were near as large as humble bees; this is the hippobosca. They are armed with a strong sharp beak or proboscis, shaped like a lancet, and sheathed in flexible thin valves; with this beak they instantly pierce the veins of the creatures, making a large orifice from whence the blood springs in large drops, rolling down as tears, causing a fierce pain or aching for a considerable time after the wound is made. There are three or four species of this genus of less size but equally vexatious, as they are vastly more numerous, active and sanguineous; particularly, one about half the size of the first mentioned, the next less, of a dusky colour with a green head; another yet somewhat less, of a splendid green and the head of a gold colour; the sting of this is intolerable, no less acute than a prick from a red-hot needle, or a spark of fire on the skin; these are called the burning flies. Besides the preceding tormentors, there are three or four species of the asilus or smaller biting flies; one of a grayish dusky colour; another much of the same colour, having spotted wings and a green head; and another very small and perfectly black: this last species lies in ambush in shrubby thickets and Cane brakes near water: whenever we approach the cool shades near creeks, impatient for repose and relief, almost sinking under the persecutions from the evil spirits, who continually surround and

follow us over the burning desert ridges and plains, and here
are in some hopes of momentary peace and quietness, under
cover of the cool humid groves, we are surprized and quickly
invested with dark clouds of these persecuting demons, besides musquitoes and gnats (culex et cynips).

The next day being in like manner oppressed and harrassed
by the stinging flies and heats: we halted at noon, being unable longer to support ourselves under such grievances, even
in our present situation charming to the senses; on the ac-
clivity of a high swelling ridge planted with open airy groves
of the superb terebinthine Pines, glittering rills playing beneath, and pellucid brooks meandering through an expansive
green savanna, their banks ornamented with coppices of
blooming aromatic shrubs and plants perfuming the air. The
meridian heats just allayed, the sun is veiled in a dark cloud,
rising North-Westward; the air still, gloomy and sultry; the
animal spirits sink under the conflict, and we fall into a kind
of mortal torpor rather than refreshing repose; and startled or
terrified at each others plaintive murmurs and groans. Now
the earth trembles under the peals of incessant distant thunder, the hurricane comes on roaring, and I am shocked again
to life: I raise my head and rub open my eyes, pained with
gleams and flashes of lightning; when just attempting to wake
my afflicted brethren and companions, almost overwhelmed
with floods of rain, the dark cloud opens over my head, de-
veloping a vast river of the etherial fire; I am instantly struck
dumb, inactive and benumbed; at length the pulse of life begins to vibrate, the animal spirits begin to exert their powers,
and I am by degrees revived.

In the evening this surprisingly heavy tempest passed off,
we had a serene sky and a pleasant cool night; having had
time enough to collect a great quantity of wood and Pine
knots to feed our fires and keep up a light in our camp, which
was a lucky precaution, as we found it absolutely necessary to
dry our clothes and warm ourselves, for all our skins and bedding were cast over the packs of merchandize to prevent them
and our provision from being injured by the deluge of rain.
Next day was cool and pleasant, the air having recovered its
elasticity and vivific spirit: I found myself cheerful and invig-
orated; indeed all around us appeared reanimated, and nature

presented her cheerful countenance; the vegetables smiled in their blooming decorations and sparkling crystalline dewdrops. The birds sung merrily in the groves, and the alert roe buck whistled and bounded over the ample meads and green turfy hills. After leaving our encampment, we travelled over a delightful territory, presenting to view variable sylvan scenes, consisting of chains of low hills affording high forests, with expansive savannas, Cane meadows, and lawns between, watered with rivulets and glittering brooks. Towards evening we came to camp on the banks of Pintchlucco, a large branch of the Chata Uche river.

The next day's journey was over an uneven hilly country, but the soil generally fertile and of a quality and situation favourable to agriculture and grazing, the summits of the ridges rough with ferruginous rocks, in high cliffs and fragments, scattered over the surface of the ground: observed also high cliffs of stiff reddish brown clay, with veins or strata of ferruginous stones, either in detached masses or conglomerated nodules or hematites with veins or masses of ochre.

Next day, after traversing a very delightful territory, exhibiting a charming rural scenery of primitive nature, gently descending and passing alternately easy declivities or magnificent terraces supporting sublime forests, almost endless grassy fields, detached groves and green lawns for the distance of nine or ten miles, we arrived at the banks of the Chata Uche river opposite the Uche town; where, after unloading our horses, the Indians came over to us in large canoes, by means of which, with the cheerful and liberal assistance of the Indians, ferried over the merchandize, and afterwards driving our horses altogether into the river swam them over: the river here is about three or four hundred yards wide, carries fifteen or twenty feet water, and flows down with an active current; the water is clear, cool and salubrious.

The Uche town is situated in a vast plain, on the gradual ascent as we rise from a narrow strip of low ground immediately bordering on the river: it is the largest, most compact and best situated Indian town I ever saw; the habitations are large and neatly built; the walls of the houses are constructed of a wooden frame, then lathed and plaistered inside and out with a reddish well tempered clay or mortar, which gives them the appearance of red brick walls; and these houses are neatly covered or roofed with Cypress bark or shingles of that tree. The town appeared to be populous and thriving, full of youth and young children: I suppose the number of inhabitants, men, women and children, might amount to one thousand or fifteen hundred, as it is said they are able to muster five hundred gun-men or warriors. Their own national language is altogether or radically different from the Creek or Muscogulge tongue, and is called the Savanna or Savanuca tongue; I was told by the traders it was the same with, or a dialect of, the Shawanese. They are in confederacy with the Creeks, but do not mix with them; and, on account of their numbers and strength, are of importance enough to excite and draw upon them the jealousy of the whole Muscogulge confederacy, and are usually at variance, yet are wise enough to unite against a common enemy, to support the interest and glory of the general Creek confederacy.

After a little refreshment at this beautiful town, we repacked and set off again for the Apalachucla town, where we arrived after riding over a level plain, consisting of ancient Indian plantations, a beautiful landscape diversified with groves and lawns.

This is esteemed the mother town or Capital of the Creek or Muscogulge confederacy: sacred to peace; no captives are put to death or human blood spilt here. And when a general peace is proposed, deputies from all the towns in the confederacy assemble at this capital, in order to deliberate upon a subject of so high importance for the prosperity of the commonwealth.

And on the contrary the great Coweta town, about twelve miles higher up this river, is called the bloody town, where the Micos, chiefs, and warriors assemble when a general war is proposed; and here captives and state malefactors are put to death.

The time of my continuance here, which was about a week, was employed in excursions round about this settlement. One day the chief trader of Apalachucla obliged me with his company on a walk of about a mile and an half down the river, to view the ruins and site of the ancient Apalachucla: it had been situated on a peninsula formed by a doubling of the river, and indeed appears to have been a very famous capital by the artificial mounds or terraces, and a very populous settlement, from its extent and expansive old fields, stretching beyond the scope of the sight along the low grounds of the river. We viewed the mounds or terraces, on which formerly stood their town house or rotunda and square or areopagus, and a little behind these, on a level height or natural step, above the low grounds, is a vast artificial terrace or four square mound, now seven or eight feet higher than the common surface of the ground; in front of one square or side of this mound adjoins a very extensive oblong square yard or artificial level plain, sunk a little below the common surface, and surrounded with a bank or narrow terrace, formed with the earth thrown out of this yard at the time of its formation: the Creeks or present inhabitants have a tradition that this was the work of the ancients, many ages prior to their arrival and possessing this country.

This old town was evacuated about twenty years ago by the general consent of the inhabitants, on account of its unhealthy situation, owing to the frequent inundations of the river over the low grounds; and moreover they grew timorous and dejected, apprehending themselves to be haunted and possessed with vengeful spirits, on account of human blood that had been undeservedly * spilt in this old town, having been repeatedly warned by apparitions and dreams to leave it.

At the time of their leaving this old town, like the ruin or dispersion of the ancient Babel, the inhabitants separated from each other, forming several bands under the conduct or auspices of the chief of each family or tribe. The greatest number, however, chose to sit down and build the present new Apalachucla town, upon a high bank of the river above the in-

---

*About fifty or sixty years ago almost all the white traders then in the nation were massacred in this town, whither they had repaired from the different towns, in hopes of an asylum or refuge, in consequence of the alarm, having been timely apprized of the hostile intentions of the Indians by their temporary wives. They all met together in one house, under the avowed protection of the chiefs of the town, waiting the event; but whilst the chiefs were assembled in council, deliberating on ways and means to protect them, the Indians in multitudes surrounded the house and set fire to it; they all, to the number of eighteen or twenty, perished with the house in the flames. The trader showed me the ruins of the house where they were burnt.

undations. The other bands pursued different routs, as their inclinations led them, settling villages lower down the river; some continued their migration towards the sea coast, seeking their kindred and countrymen amongst the Lower Creeks in East Florida, where they settled themselves. My intelligent friend, the trader of Apalachucla, having from a long residence amongst these Indians acquired an extensive knowledge of their customs and affairs, I inquired of him what were his sentiments with respect to their wandering, unsettled disposition; their so frequently breaking up their old towns and settling new ones, &c. His answers and opinions were the necessity they were under of having fresh or new strong land for their plantations, and new, convenient and extensive range or hunting ground, which unavoidably forces them into contentions and wars with their confederates and neighbouring tribes; to avoid which they had rather move and seek a plentiful and peaceable retreat, even at a distance, than contend with friends and relatives or embroil themselves in destructive wars with their neighbours, when either can be avoided with so little inconvenience. With regard to the Muscogulges, the first object in order to obtain these conveniencies was the destruction of the Yamases, who held the possession of Florida, and were in close alliance with the Spaniards, their declared and most inveterate enemy, which they at length fully accomplished; and by this conquest they gained a vast and invaluable territory, comprehending a delightful region, and most plentiful country for their favourite game, bear and deer. But not yet satisfied, having already so far conquered the powerful Cherokees, as, in a manner, to force them to alliance, and compelled the warlike Chicasaws to sue for peace and alliance with them; they then grew arrogant and insatiable, and turned their covetous looks towards the potent and intrepid Chactaws, the only Indian enemy they had to fear, meaning to break them up and possess themselves of that extensive, fruitful and delightful country, and make it a part of their vast empire. But the Chactaws, a powerful, hardy, subtile and intrepid race, estimated at twenty thousand warriors, are likely to afford sufficient exercise for the proud and restless spirits of the Muscogulges, at least for some years to come; and they appear to be so equally matched with the Chactaws, that it seems doubtful which of these powerful nations will rise victorious. The Creeks have sworn, it seems, that they never will make peace with this enemy as long as the rivers flow or the sun pursues his course through the skies.

Thus we see that war or the exercise of arms originates from the same motives, and operates in the spirits of the wild red men of America, as it formerly did with the renowned Greeks and Romans, or modern civilized nations, and not from a ferocious, capricious desire of shedding human blood as carnivorous savages: neither does the eager avarice of plunder stimulate them to acts of madness and cruelty, that being a trifling object in their estimation, a duffield blanket, a polished rifle gun, or embroidered mantle; no, their martial prowess and objects of desire and ambition proceed from greater principles and more magnanimous intentions, even that of reuniting all nations and languages under one universal confederacy or common wealth.

The vegetable productions in the rich low ground, near the banks of this great river, of trees and shrubs, are as follow; Platanus occidentalis, Liriodendron tulipifera, Populus heterophylla, Laurus sassafras, Laurus Barbonia, Laurus benzoin, Betula lenta, Salix fluvialis, Magnolia grandiflora, Annona glabra, Ulmus campestris, Ulmus suberifera, Carpinus, Quercus, various species, Juglans, various species, Æsculus pavia, Æsculus sylvatica, s. Virginiana, Morus, Hopea tinctoria, Fagus sylvatica, of surprising magnitude and comeliness, &c. The land rises from the river with sublime magnificence, gradually retreating by flights or steps one behind and above the other, in beautiful theatrical order, each step or terrace holding up a level plain; and as we travel back from the river, the steps are higher, and the corresponding levels are more and more expansive: the ascents produce grand high forests, and the plains present to view a delightful varied landscape, consisting of extensive grassy fields, detached groves of high forest trees, and clumps of lower trees, evergreen shrubs, and herbage; green knolls, with serpentine, wavy, glittering brooks coursing through the green plains; and dark promontories, or obtuse projections of the side-long acclivities, alternately advancing or receding on the verge of the illumined native fields, to the utmost extent of sight. The summits of the acclivities afford, besides the forest trees already recited, Halesia, Ptelea, Circis, Cornus Florida and Amorpha. The upper mound or terrace holds up a dilated level plain of excellent land, for the distance of five or six miles in width, which is a high forest of the majestic trees already mentioned, as Quercus tinctoria, Juglans nigra, Morus, Ulmus, Tilia, Gleditsia, Juglans hiccory, &c. The land after this distance, though almost flat and level, becomes leaner; the vegetative mould or surface is shallower, on a stratum of tenaceous humid clay, for the distance of fifteen or twenty miles, more or less, according to the distance of the next great river; presenting to our view a fine expanse of level grassy plains, detached forests and groves of Quercus alba, Q. lobata, Q. phillos, Q. hemispherica, Q. aquatica, with entire groves of the splendid Nyssa sylvatica and perfumed Liquidambar styraciflua, vast Cane meadows, and lastly a chain of grassy savannas. Immediately from this we began to ascend gradually the most elevated, gravelly and stony ridge, consisting of parallel chains of broken swelling hills, the very highest chain frequently presenting to view cliffs of the ferruginous rocks and red clay already noticed. This last mentioned high ridge divides the waters of the great rivers from each other, whence arise the sources of their numerous lateral branches, gradually increasing as they wind about the hills, fertilizing the vales and level plains, by their inundations, as they pour forth from the vast humid forests and shaded prolific hills, and lastly, flow down, with an easy, meandering, steady course, into the rivers to which they are tributary.

Our horses by this time having recruited themselves, by ranging at liberty and feeding in the rich young cane swamps, in the vicinity of Apalachucla, we resumed our journey for Mobile, having here repaired our equipage, and replenished ourselves with fresh supplies of provisions. Our caravan was now reduced to its original number; the companies of traders who joined us at the Flat-rock, on our arrival at this town separated from us, betaking themselves to the several towns in the Nation, where they were respectively bound. I shall just mention a very curious non-descript shrub, which I observed growing in the shady forests, beneath the ascents, next bordering on the rich low lands of the river.

This stoloniferous shrub grows five or six feet in height; many stems usually ascend from one root or the same source; these several stems diverge from each other, or incline a little towards the earth, covered with a smooth whitish bark, divided oppositely, and the branches wreath and twist about, being ornamented with compound leaves; there being five lanceolate serrated leaves, associated upon one general long slender petiole, which stand oppositely, on the branches, which terminate with a spike, or panicle of white flowers, having an agreeable scent: from the characters of the flowers, this shrub appears to be a species of Æsculus or Pavia, but as I could find none of the fruit and but a few flowers, quite out of season and imperfect, I am not certain.

CHAP. VI.

J ULY 13TH we left the Apalachucla town, and three days journey brought us to Talasse, a town on the Tallapoose river, the North East great branch of the Alabama or Mobile river; having passed over a vast level plain country of expansive savannas, groves, Cane swamps and open Pine forests, watered by innumerable rivulets and brooks, tributary to Apalachucla and Mobile. We now altered our course, turning to the left hand, Southerly, and descending near the river banks, continually in sight of the Indian plantations and commons adjacent to their towns. Passed by Otasse, an ancient famous Muscogulge town. The next settlement we came to was Coolome, where we stayed two days, and having letters for Mr. Germany, the principal trader of Coolome, I meant to consult with him in matters relative to my affairs and future proceedings.

Here are very extensive old fields, the abandoned plantations and commons of the old town, on the East side of the river; but the settlement is removed, and the new town now stands on the opposite shore, in a charming fruitful plain, under an elevated ridge of hills, the swelling beds or bases of which are covered with a pleasing verdure of grass; but the last ascent is steeper, and towards the summit discovers shelving rocky cliffs, which appear to be continually splitting and bursting to pieces, scattering their thin exfoliations over the tops of the grassy knolls beneath. The plain is narrow where the town is built: their houses are neat commodious buildings, a wooden frame with plaistered walls, and roofed with Cypress bark or shingles; every habitation consists of four oblong square houses, of one story, of the same form and dimensions, and so situated as to form an exact square, encompassing an area or court yard of about a quarter of an acre of ground, leaving an entrance into it at each corner. Here is a beautiful new square or areopagus, in the centre of the new town; but the stores of the principal trader, and two or three Indian habitations, stand near the banks of the opposite shore on the site of the old Coolome town. The Tallapoose river is here three hundred yards over, and about fifteen or twenty feet deep: the water is very clear, agreeable to the taste, esteemed salubrious, and runs with a steady, active current.

Being now recruited and refitted, having obtained a guide to set us in the great trading path for West Florida, early in the morning we sat off for Mobile: our progress for about eighteen miles was through a magnificent forest, just without or skirting on the Indian plantations, frequently having a view of their distant towns, over plains or old fields; and at evening we came to camp under shelter of a grove of Venerable spreading oaks, on the verge of the great plains; their enormous limbs loaded with Tillandsia usneadscites, waving in the winds: these Oaks were some shelter to us from the violence of an extraordinary shower of rain, which suddenly came down in such floods as to inundate the earth, and kept us standing on our feet the whole night, for the surface of the ground was under water almost till morning. Early next morning, our guide having performed his duty, took leave, returning home, and we continued on our journey, entering on the great plains. We had not proceeded far before our people roused a litter of young wolves, to which giving chase, we soon caught one of them, it being entangled in high grass; one of our people caught it by the hind legs and another beat out its brains with the but of his gun,—barbarous sport!— This creature was about half the size of a small cur-dog, and quite black.

We continued over these expansive illumined grassy plains, or native fields, above twenty miles in length, and in width eight or nine, lying parallel to the river, which was about ten miles distance; they are invested by high forests, extensive points or promontories, which project into the plains on each side, dividing them into many vast fields opening on either hand as we passed along, which presents a magnificent and pleasing sylvan landscape of primitive, uncultivated nature. Crossed several very considerable creeks, their serpentine courses being directed across the plain by gently swelling knolls perceptible at a distance, but which seem to vanish or disappear as we come upon them; the creeks were waters of the Alabama, the name of the East arm of the Mobile below the confluence of the Tallapoose. These rivulets were orna-

mented by groves of various trees and shrubs, which do not
spread far from their banks. I observed amongst them the wild
Crab (Pyrus coronaria), and Prunus Indica or wild Plumb,
Cornus Florida, and on the grassy turf adjoining grew abundance of Strawberry vines: the surface of the plains or fields
is clad with tall grass, intermixed with a variety of herbage.
The most conspicuous, both for beauty and novelty, is a tall
species of Silphium; the radical leaves are large, long and
lightly sinuated, but those which garnish the stem are few and
less sinuated; these leaves, with the whole plant, except the
flowers, appear of a whitish green colour, which is owing to
a fine soft silky down or pubescence; the flower stem, which
is eight or ten feet in length when standing erect, terminates
upwards with a long heavy spike of large golden yellow radiated flowers; the stem is usually seen bowing on one side or
other, occasioned by the weight of the flowers, and many of
them are broken, just under the panicle or spike, by their own
weight, after storms and heavy rains, which often crack or split
the stem, from whence exudes a gummy or resinous substance, which the sun and air harden into semi-pellucid drops
or tears of a pale amber colour. This resin possesses a very
agreeable fragrance and bitterish taste, somewhat like frank-
incense or turpentine; it is chewed by the Indians and traders,
to cleanse their teeth and mouth, and sweeten their breath.

The upper stratum or vegetable mould of these plains is
perfectly black, soapy and rich, especially after rains, and renders the road very slippery: it lies on a deep bed of white,
testaceous, limestone rocks, which in some places resemble
chalk, and in other places are strata or subterrene banks of
various kinds of sea shells, as ostrea, &c.: these dissolving near
the surface of the earth, and mixing with the superficial
mould, render it extremely productive.

Immediately after leaving the plains we enter the grand high
forests. There were stately trees of the Robinea pseudacacia,
Tilia, Morus, Ulmus, Juglans exaltata, Juglans nigra, Pyrus
coronaria, Cornus Florida, Cercis, &c. Our road now for several miles led us near the Alabama, within two or three miles
of its banks: the surface of the land is broken into hills and
vales, some of them of considerable elevation, covered with
forests of stately trees, such as already mentioned, but they

are of a much larger growth than those of the same kind which grow in the Southern or inhabited parts of Georgia and Carolina. We now left the river at a good distance, the Alabama bearing away Southerly, and entered a vast open forest which continued above seventy miles, East and West, without any considerable variation, generally a level plain, except near the banks of creeks that course through: the soil on the surface is a dusky brownish mould or sandy loam, on a foundation of stiff clay; and the surface, pebbles or gravel mixed with clay on the summits of the ridges: the forests consist chiefly of Oak, Hiccory, Ash, Sour Gum (Nyssa sylvatica), Sweet Gum (Liquidambar styraciflua), Beech, Mulberry, Scarlet maple, Black walnut, Dog wood, Cornus Florida, Æsculus pavia, Prunus Indica, Ptelea, and an abundance of Chesnut (Fag. castanea) on the hills, with Pinus tæda and Pinus lutea. During our progress over this vast high forest, we crossed extensive open plains, the soil gravelly, producing a few trees and shrubs or undergrowth, which were entangled with Grape vines (Vitis campestris) of a peculiar species; the bunches (racemes) of fruit were very large, as were the grapes that composed them, though yet green and not fully grown, but when ripe they are of various colours, and their juice sweet and rich. The Indians gather great quantities of them, which they prepare for keeping, by first sweating them on hurdles over a gentle fire, and afterwards drying them on their bunches in the sun and air, and store them up for provision. These Grape vines do not climb into high trees, but creep along from one low shrub to another, extending their branches to a great distance horizontally round about; and it is very pleasing to behold the clusters pendant from the vines, almost touching the earth; indeed some of them lie upon the ground.

We now entered a very remarkable grove of Dog wood trees (Cornus Florida), which continued nine or ten miles unalterable, except here and there a towering Magnolia grandiflora; the land on which they stand is an exact level; the surface a shallow, loose, black mould, on a stratum of stiff, yellowish clay. These trees were about twelve feet high, spreading horizontally; their limbs meeting and interlocking with each other, formed one vast, shady, cool grove, so dense and humid as to exclude the sun-beams, and prevent the intrusion of almost every other vegetable, affording us a most desirable shelter from the fervid sun-beams at noon-day. This admirable grove by way of eminence has acquired the name of the Dog woods.

During a progress of near seventy miles, through this high forest, there constantly presented to view on one hand or the other, spacious groves of this fine flowering tree, which must, in the spring season, when covered with blosoms, present a most pleasing scene; when at the same time a variety of other sweet shrubs display their beauty, adorned in their gay apparel, as the Halesia, Stewartia, Æsculus pavia, Æsc. alba, Æsc. Florid. ramis divaricatis, thyrsis grandis, flosculis expansis incarnatis, Azalea, &c., entangled with garlands of Bignonia crucigera, Big. radicans, Big. sempervirens, Glycine frutescens, Lonicera sempervirens, &c., and at the same time the superb Magnolia grandiflora, standing in front of the dark groves, towering far above the common level.

The evening cool, we encamped on the banks of a glittering rivulet amidst a spicy grove of the Illicium Floridanum.

Early next morning we arose, hunted up our horses and proceeded on, continuing about twenty miles, over a district which presented to view another landscape; expansive plains of Cane meadows, and detached groves, contrasted by swelling ridges, and vales supporting grand forests of the trees already noted, embellished with delightful creeks and brooks, the low grounds producing very tall canes, and the higher banks groves of the Illicium, Callicanthus, Stewartia, Halesia, Styrax and others, particulary Magnolia auriculata. In the evening we forded the river Schambe about fifty yards over, the stream active but shallow, which carries its waters into the bay of Pensacola. Came to camp, on the banks of a beautiful creek, by a charming grove of the Illicium Floridanum: from this we travelled over a level country above fifty miles, very gently but perceptibly descending South-Eastward before us: this district exhibited a landscape very different from what had presented to view since we left the nation, and not much unlike the low countries of Carolina; it is in fact one vast flat grassy savanna and Cane meadows, intersected or variously scrolled over with narrow forests and groves, on the banks of creeks and rivulets, or hommocks and swamps at their sources; with long leaved

Pines, scatteringly planted, amongst the grass; and on the high sandy knolls and swelling ridges, Quercus nigra, Quercus flammula, Quercus incana, with various other trees and shrubs as already noted, inhabiting such situations. The rivulets however exhibited a different appearance; they are shallower, course more swiftly over gravelly beds, and their banks are adorned with Illicium groves, Magnolias, Azaleas, Halesia, Andromedas, &c. The highest hills near large creeks afford high forests with abundance of Chesnut trees.

We now approached the bay Mobile, gently ascending a hilly district, being the highest forest adjoining the extensive rich low lands of the river: these heights are somewhat encumbered with pebbles, fragments and cliffs of rusty ferruginous rocks; the stones were ponderous and indicated very rich iron ore: here was a small district of good land, on the acclivities and bases of these ridges, and a level forest below, watered by a fine creek, running into the Mobile. From hence we proceeded, again descending, and travelled about nine miles generally over a level country consisting of savannas, Cane swamps, and gentle rising knolls, producing Pinus tæda, Nyssa sylvatica, Quercus rubra, Fagus castanea, Fraxinus, with other trees. Arrived at Taensa, a pretty high bluff, on the Eastern channel of the great Mobile river, about thirty miles above fort Condé, or city of Mobile, at the head of the bay.

Next day early in the morning I embarked in a boat, and proceeded for Mobile, along the banks of islands (near twenty miles) which lay in the middle of the river, between the Eastern and Western shores of the main: the banks of these low flat rich islands are well cultivated, having on them extensive farms and some good habitations, chiefly the property of French gentlemen, who reside in the city, as being more pleasant and healthy. Leaving these islands, we continued ten or twelve miles between the Eastern main and a chain of low grassy islands, too low and wet for cultivation; then crossed over the head of the bay, and arrived in town in the evening.

The city of Mobile is situated on the easy ascent of a rising bank, extending near half a mile back on the level plain above; it has been near a mile in length, though now chiefly in ruins, many houses vacant and mouldering to earth; yet there are a few good buildings inhabited by French gentlemen, English,

Scotch and Irish, and emigrants from the Northern British colonies. Messrs. Swanson and M'Gillivray who have the management of the Indian trade carried on with the Chicasaws, Chactaws, Upper and Lower Creeks, &c., have made here very extraordinary improvements in buildings.

The fort Condé, which stands very near the bay, towards the lower end of the town, is a large regular fortress of brick.

The principal French buildings are constructed of brick, and are of one story, but on an extensive scale, four square, encompassing on three sides a large area or court yard: the principal apartment is on the side fronting the street; they seem in some degree to have copied after the Creek habitation in the general plan: those of the poorer class are constructed of a strong frame of Cypress, filled in with brick, plaistered and white-washed inside and out.

July 31st, 1778, the air being very hot and sultry, thermometer up at 87, we had excessive thunder, and repeated heavy showers of rain, from morning until evening.

Not having an immediate opportunity from hence to Manchac, a British settlement on the Mississippi, I endeavoured to procure a light canoe, with which I designed to pursue my travels along shore to the settlements about Pearl river.

August 5th, set off from Mobile up the river in a trading boat, and was landed at Taensa bluff, the seat of Major Farmer, to make good my engagements, in consequence of an invitation from that worthy gentleman, to spend some days in his family: here I obtained the use of a light canoe, to continue my voyage up the river. The settlement of Taensa is on the site of an ancient town of a tribe of Indians of that name, which is apparent from many artificial mounds of earth and other ruins. Besides Mr. Farmer's dwellings, there are many others inhabited by French families; who are chiefly his tenants. It is a most delightful situation, commanding a spacious prospect up and down the river, and the low lands of his extensive plantations on the opposite shore. In my excursions about this place, I observed many curious vegetable productions, particularly a species of Myrica (Myrica inodora): this very beautiful evergreen shrub, which the French inhabitants call the Wax tree, grows in wet sandy ground about the edges of swamps; it rises erect nine or ten feet, dividing itself into a multitude of nearly erect branches, which are garnished with many shining deep green entire leaves of a lanceolate figure; the branches produce abundance of large round berries, nearly the size of bird cherries, which are covered with a scale or coat of white wax; no part of this plant possesses any degree of fragrance. It is in high estimation with the inhabitants for the production of wax for candles, for which purpose it answers equally well with bees-wax, or preferably, as it is harder and more lasting in burning.

Early on a fine morning I set sail up the river, took the East channel, and passed along by well cultivated plantations on the fertile islands, in the river on my left hand: these islands exhibit every show of fertility; the native productions exceed any thing I had ever seen, particularly the Reeds or Canes (Arundo gigantea) grow to a great height and thickness.

Early one morning, passing along by some old uncultivated fields, a few miles above Taensa, I was struck with surprize at the appearance of a blooming plant, gilded with the richest golden yellow: stepping on shore, I discovered it to be a new species of the Oenothera (Oenothera grandiflora, caule erecto, ramoso, piloso, 7, 8 pedali, foliis semi-amplexi-caulibus, lanceolatis, serratodentatis, floribus magnis, fulgidis, sessilibus, capsulis cylindricis, 4 angulis,) perhaps the most pompous and brilliant herbaceous plant yet known to exist. It is an annual or biennial, rising erect seven or eight feet, branching on all sides from near the earth upwards, the lower branches extensive, and the succeeding gradually shorter to the top of the plant, forming a pyramid in figure; the leaves are of a broad lanceolate shape, dentated or deeply serrated, terminating with a slender point, and of a deep full green colour; the large expanded flowers, that so ornament this plant, are of a splendid perfect yellow colour; but when they contract again, before they drop off, the underside of the petals next the calyx becomes of a reddish flesh colour, inclining to vermillion; the flowers begin to open in the evening, are fully expanded during the night, and are in their beauty next morning, but close and wither before noon. Their is a daily profuse succession for many weeks, and one single plant at the same instant presents to view many hundred flowers. I have measured these flowers above five inches in diameter, they have an agreeable scent.

After leaving these splendid fields of the golden Oenothera, I passed by old deserted plantations and high forests; and now having advanced above ten miles, landed at a bluff, where mooring my bark in a safe harbour, I ascended the bank of the river, and penetrating the groves, came presently to old fields, where I observed ruins of ancient habitations, there being abundance of Peach and Fig trees, loaded with fruit, which affording a very acceptable desert after the heats and toil of the day, and evening drawing on apace, I concluded to take up my quarters here for the night. The Fig trees were large as well as their fruit, which was when ripe, of the shape of pears, and as large, and of a dark bluish purple colour.

Next morning I arose early, continuing my voyage; passed by, on each hand, high forests and rich swamps, and frequently ruins of ancient French plantations; the Canes and Cypress trees of an astonishing magnitude, as were the trees of other tribes, indicating an excellent soil. Came to at noon, and advancing forward from the river, and penetrating the awful shades, passed between the stately columns of the Magnolia grandiflora, and came to the ascents supporting the high forests and expansive plains above —— What a sylvan scene is here! the pompous Magnolia reigns sovereign of the forests; how sweet the aromatic Illicium groves! how gaily flutter the radiated wings of the Magnolia auriculata, each branch supporting an expanded umbrella, superbly crested with a silver plume, fragrant blossom, or crimson studded strobile and fruits! I recline on the verdant bank, and view the beauties of the groves, Æsculus pavia, Prunus nemoralis, floribus racemosis, foliis sempervirentibus, nitidis, Æsculus alba, Hydrangia quercifolia, Cassine, Magnolia pyramidata, foliis ovatis, oblongis, acuminatis, basi auriculatis, strobilo oblongo ovato, Myrica, Rhamnus frangula, Halesea, Bignonia, Azalea, Lonicera, Sideroxylon, with many more.

Returned to the river, re-embarked, and at evening came to, in sight of the confluence or junction of the two large arms of the great Mobile river, i.e. the Tombigbe or Chicasaw with the Alabama or Coosau. About one hundred and fifty miles above this conflux, at Ft. Thoulouse, the Alabama receives into it from the East the great Talapoose river, when the former takes the name of Coosau, which it bears to its source,

which is in the So. West promontories of the Cherokee or
Apalachian Mountains in the Chicasaw territories.

Observed very large alligators, basking on the shores, as
well as swimming in the river and lagoons.

Next morning entered the Tombigbe, and ascended that
fine river. Just within its Capes, on the left hand, is a large
lagoon, or capacious bay of still water, containing many acres
in surface, which at a distant view presents a very singular and
diverting scene; a delusive green wavy plain of the Nymphæa
Nelumbo: the surface of the water is overspread with its round
floating leaves, whilst these are shadowed by a forest of umbrageous leaves with gay flowers, waving to and fro on flexible
stems, three or four feet high: these fine flowers are double
as a rose, and when expanded are seven or eight inches in
diameter, of a lively lemon yellow colour. The feed vessel
when ripe, is a large truncated, dry, porous capsule, its plane
or disk regularly perforated, each cell containing an oval osseous gland or nut, of the size of a filbert; when these are fully
grown, before they become quite hard, they are sweet and
pleasant eating, and taste like chesnuts: I fed freely on them
without any injury, but found them laxative. I have observed
this aquatic plant, in my travels along the Eastern shores of
this continent, in the large rivers and lakes, from New-Jersey
to this place, particularly in a large pond or lake near Cape
Fear river in North Carolina, which is about two miles over
and twelve feet water, notwithstanding which its surface is
almost covered with the leaves of this plant; it also abounds
in Wakamaw lake near the same river, and in Savanna river at
Augusta, and all over East Florida.

Proceeding up the river, came to at a very high steep bluff
of red and particoloured tenacious clay, under a deep stratum
of loose sandy mould: after ascending this steep bank of the
river, I found myself in an old field, and penetrating the forests
surrounding, observed them to be young growth, covering
very extensive old plantations, which was evident from the
ridges and hillocks which once raised their Corn (Zea), Batatas, &c. I suppose this to be the site of an ancient fortified
post of the French, as there appear vestiges of a rampart and
other traces of a fortress; perhaps fort Louis de la Mobile; but
in all probability it will not remain long visible, the stream of

the river making daily encroachments on it, by carrying away the land on which it stood.

Observed here amongst other vegetable productions, a new species, or at least a variety, of Halesia diptera: these trees are of the size and figure of ordinary Mulberry trees, their stems short, and tops regular and spreading, and the leaves large and broad, in size and figure resembling those of our common wild Mulberry.

Opposite this bluff, on the other side of the river, is a district of swamp or low land, the richest I ever saw, or perhaps any where to be seen: as for the trees I shall forbear to describe them, because it would appear incredible; let it suffice to mention, that the Cypress, Ash, Platanus, Populus, Liquidambar, and others, are by far the tallest, straightest and every way the most enormous that I have seen or heard of. And as a proof of the extraordinary fertility of the soil, the reeds or canes (Arundo gigantea) grow here thirty or forty feet high, and as thick as a man's arm, or three or four inches in diameter; I suppose one joint of some of them would contain above a quart of water; and these reeds serve very well for setting poles, or masts for barks and canoes. Continued yet ascending this fine river, passing by the most delightful and fertile situations: observed frequently, on bluffs of high land, deserted plantations, the houses always burnt down to the ground, and ancient Indian villages. But perceiving little variation in the natural vegetable productions, the current of the river pressing down with increased force and velocity, I turned about, descending the river, and next evening came to at a large well cultivated plantation, where I lodged all night, and the evening following returned to Taensa.

Next day I felt symptoms of a fever, which in a few days laid me up and became dangerous. But a dose of Tart. Emet. broke its violence; and care and good attendance, after a few days in some degree restored my health, at least, so far as to enable me to rove about the neighbouring forests; and here being informed of a certain plant of extraordinary medical virtues, and in high estimation with the inhabitants, which grew in the hilly land about thirty miles higher up the river, I resolved to set out in search of it, the Major being so polite and obliging as to furnish me with horses to ride, and a Negro to pilot and take care of me.

Sat off in the morning, and in the course of the day's journey crossed several creeks and brooks, one of which swam our horses. On passing by a swamp at the head of a bay or lagoon of the river, I observed a species of Cypress; it differs a little from the white Cedar of New-Jersey and Pennsylvania (Cupressus thyoides), the trunk is short and the limbs spread horizontally, the branches fuller of leaves and the cones larger and of a crimson or reddish purple colour when ripe.

After leaving the low grounds and ascending the hills, discovered the plant I went in search of, which I had before frequently observed in my descent from the Creek nation down towards Taensa. This plant appears to be a species of Collinsonia; it is diuretic and carminative, and esteemed a powerful febrifuge, an infusion of its tops is ordinarily drunk at breakfast, and is of an exceeding pleasant taste and flavour: when in flower, which is the time the inhabitants gather it for preservation and use, it possesses a lively aromatic scent, partaking of lemon and aniseed. Lodged this night at a plantation near the river, and met with civility and good entertainment. The man and his three sons are famous hunters. I was assured from good authority that the old gentleman, for his own part, kills three hundred deer annually, besides bears, tygers, and wolves.

Next morning early, sat off again, on my return, and taking a different path back, for the sake of variety, though somewhat farther about and at a greater distance from the banks of the river, observed abundance of the tall blue Sage: it grows six or seven feet high; many stems arise from one root or source; these stems are thick, woody and quadrangular, the angles obtuse: the narrow lanceolate and serrated leaves are placed opposite, and are sessile, lightly embracing the branches, which terminate with spikes of large flowers of a celestial blue colour.

These stony gravelly heights produce a variety of herbaceous plants, but one in particular I shall mention on account of its singular beauty: I believe it is a species of Gerardea (Gerardea flammea); it grows erect, a single stem from a root, three or four feet in height, branching very regularly from about one half its length upwards, forming a cone or pyramid, profusely garnished with large tubular labiated scarlet or flame coloured flowers, which give the plant a very splendid appearance, even at a great distance. Returned home in the evening fully satisfied with the day's excursion, from the discovery of many curious and beautiful vegetables.

Having advice from Mobile of an opportunity to Manchac, although my health was not established, feverish symptoms continuing to lurk about me, I resolved, notwithstanding, immediately to embrace this offer, and embarked again, descending the river to the city in company with Dr. Grant, a physician of the garrison, and late in the evening arrived in town, having suffered a smart fit of the fever by the way.

In the course of conversation with the doctor, I remarked that during my travels since leaving the Creek nation, and when there, I had not seen any honey bees. He replied, that there were few or none West of the Isthmus of Florida, and but one hive in Mobile, which was lately brought there from Europe, the English supposing that there were none in the country, not finding any when they took possession of it after the Spanish and French. I had been assured by the traders that there were none in West Florida, which to me seemed extraordinary and almost incredible, since they are so numerous all along the Eastern continent from Nova Scotia to East Florida, even in the wild forests, as to be thought, by the generality of the inhabitants, aborigines of this continent.

The boat in which I had taken a passage to Pearl river, not being in readiness to depart for several days to come, I sought opportunities to fill up this time to the best advantage possible; and hearing of a boat going to the river Perdedo, for the purpose of securing the remains of a wreck, I apprehended this a favourable time to go and search that coast, the captain civilly offering me a passage and birth with him in a handsome light sailing-boat. Set sail early on a fine morning, and having a brisk leading breeze, came to in the evening just within Mobile point; collected a quantity of drift wood to keep up a light and smoke away the musquitoes, and rested well on the clean sandy beach until the cool morning awoke us. We hoisted sail again, and soon doubled the point or East promontory of the cape of the bay, stretching out many miles and pointing towards Dauphin island, between which and this cape is the ship channel.

Coasting along the sea-shore Eastward, we soon came up to the wreck, which being already stripped of her sails, &c., our captain kept on for Pensacola, where we arrived late in the evening.

My arrival at this capital, at present the seat of government, was merely accidental and undesigned; and having left at Mobile all my papers and testimonials, I designed to conceal my avocations, but my name being made known to Dr. Lorimer, one of the honourable council, he sent me a very polite invitation, and requested that he might acquaint governor Chester of my arrival, who he knew would expect that I should wait on him, and would be pleased to see me. I begged to be excused, at this time, as the boat would sail back for Mobile in a few hours, in which I was under the necessity of returning, or must lose my passage to the Mississipi; but during this expostulation I received a letter from Mr. Livingston the secretary, whom I waited upon, and was received very respectfully and treated with the utmost politeness and affability. Soon after, the governor's chariot passed by, his excellency returning from a morning visit to his farm a few miles from Pensacola. Mr. Livingston went with me and introduced me to the governor, who commended my pursuits, and invited me to continue in West Florida in researches after subjects of natural history, &c., nobly offering to bear my expences, and a residence in his own family as long as I chose to continue in the colony; very judiciously observing, that a complete investigation of its natural history could not be accomplished in a short space of time, since it would require the revolution of the seasons to discover and view vegetable nature in all her various perfections.

The captain of our fortunate bark by this time being ready to sail, I took leave of his excellency the governor, and bid adieu to my friends Dr. Lorimer, Mr. Livingston, and others: set sail about noon on our return, and came to again within the capes of Mobile river.

Since I have hitherto given a superficial account of the towns, ports, improvements and other remarkable productions of nature, and human arts and industry, during the course of my perigrination, I shall not pass by Pensacola and its environs. This city commands some natural advantages, superior to any other port in this province, in point of naval commerce, and such as human art and strength can never supply. It is delightfully situated upon gentle rising ascents environing a spacious harbour, safe and capacious enough to shelter all the navies of Europe, and excellent ground for anchorage; the West end of St. Rose island stretches across the great bay St. Maria Galves, and its South-West projecting point forms the harbour of Pensacola, which, with the road or entrance, is defended by a block-house built on the extremity of that point, which at the same time serves the purpose of a fortress and look-out tower. There are several rivers which run into this great bay from the continent, but none of them navigable for large craft, to any considerable distance into the country: the Shambe is the largest, which admits shallops some miles up, and perriauguas upwards of fifty miles. There are some spots of good high land, and rich swamps, favourable for the production of rice on the banks of this river, which have given rise to some plantations producing Indigo, Rice, Corn, Batatas, &c. These rivers dividing and spreading abroad their numerous branches, over the expansive flat low country (between the two great rivers Apalachucla and Mobile), which consists of savannas and cane meadows, fill them with brooks and water courses, and render them exuberant pasture for cattle.

There are several hundred habitations in Pensacola: the governor's palace is a large stone building ornamented with a tower, built by the Spaniards. The town is defended by a large stockado fortress, the plan a tetragon with salient angles at each corner, where is a block-house or round tower, one story higher than the curtains, where are light cannon mounted: it is constructed of wood. Within this fortress is the council chamber; here the records are kept, houses for the officers and barracks for the accommodation of the garrison, arsenal, magazine, &c. The secretary resides in a spacious, neat building: there are several merchants and gentlemen of other professions, who have respectable and convenient buildings in the town.

There were growing on the sand hills, environing Pensacola, several curious non-described plants; particularly one of the verticillate order, about eighteen inches in height: the flowers, which formed loose spikes, were large and of a fine scarlet colour; but not having time to examine the fructification, or collect good specimens, I am ignorant of what order or genus it belongs to. And in the level wet savannas grew plentifully a new and very elegant species of Saracinia (Saracinia lacunosa); the leaves of this plant, which are twelve or fourteen inches in length, stand nearly erect, are round, tubular and ventricose—but not ridged with longitudinal angles or prominent nerves, as the leaves of the Saracinia flava are; the aperture at top may be shut up by a cap or lid, of a helmet form, which is an appendage of the leaf, turning over the orifice in that singular manner; the ventricose, or inflated part of the leaf, which is of a pale, but vivid green colour, is beautifully ornamented with rose coloured studs or blisters, and the inner surface curiously inscribed, or variegated, with crimson veins or fibres. It was past the time for flowering, but the plant in any situation is a very great curiosity.

Next morning early we arose from our hard sandy sea-beaten couch, being disturbed the whole night by the troublesome musquitoes; set sail, and before night returned safe to the city of Mobile.

CHAP. VII.

T HE NEXT DAY after my return to Mobile, I found myself
very ill, and not a little alarmed by an excessive pain in
my head, attended with a high fever; this disorder soon settled
in my eyes, nature pursuing that way to expel the malady,
causing a most painful defluxion of pellucid, corrosive water;
notwithstanding, I next day set off on board a large trading
boat, the property of a French gentleman, and commanded
by him (he being general interpreter for the Chactaw nation),
on his return to his plantations, on the banks of Pearl river:
our bark was large, well equipped for sailing, and manned with
three stout Negroes, to row in case of necessity. We embarked
in the evening, and came to about six miles below the town,
at a pleasant farm, the master of which (who was a Frenchman) entertained us in a very polite and friendly manner. The
wind favourable, next morning early we set sail again, and
having made extraordinary way, about noon came up abreast
of a high steep bluff, or perpendicular cliff of high land,
touching on the bay of the West coast, where we went on
shore, to give liberty to the slaves to rest and refresh themselves. In the mean time I accompanied the captain on an
excursion into the spacious level forests, which spread abroad
from the shore to a great distance back; observed vestiges of
an ancient fortress and settlement, and there yet remain a few
pieces of iron cannon; but what principally attracted my notice, was three vast iron pots or kettles, each of many hundred
gallons contents: upon inquiry, my associate informed me they
were for the purpose of boiling tar to pitch, there being vast
forests of Pine trees in the vicinity of this place. In Carolina
the inhabitants pursue a different method; when they design
to make pitch, they dig large holes in the ground, near the
tar kiln, which they line with a thick coat of good clay, into
which they conduct a sufficient quantity of tar, and set it on
fire, suffering it to flame and evaporate a length of time sufficient to convert it into pitch, and when cool, lade it into
barrels, and so on until they have consumed all the tar, or
made a sufficient quantity of pitch for their purpose.

After re-imbarking, and leaving this bluff a few miles, we put in to shore again, and came to a farm house, a little distance from the water, where we supplied ourselves with Corn meal, Batatas, bacon, &c. The French gentleman (proprietor of the plantation) was near eighty years old, his hair almost white with age, yet he appeared active, strong and muscular; and his mother who was present, was one hundred and five years old, active and cheerful, her eyes seemed as brisk and sparkling as youth, but she was of a diminutive size, not half the stature and weight of her son: it was now above fifty years since she came into America from old France.

I embarked again, proceeding down the bay, and in the evening doubled the west point or cape of the bay, being a promontory of the main, between which and Dauphin island, we entered the channel Oleron. From this time, until we arrived at this gentleman's habitation on Pearl river, I was incapable of making any observations, for my eyes could not bear the light, as the least ray admitted seemed as the piercing of a sword: and by the time I had arrived at Pearl river, the excruciating pain had rendered me almost frantic and stupified for want of sleep, of which I was totally deprived; and the corroding water, every few minutes, streaming from my eyes, had stripped the skin off my face, in the same manner as scalding water would have done. I continued three days with this friendly Frenchman, who tried every remedy, that he or his family could recollect, to administer relief, but to no purpose. My situation was now become dangerous, and I expected to sink under the malady, as I believe my friends here did. At last the man informed me, that on Pearl island, about twelve miles distance, resided an English gentleman, who had a variety of medicines, and if I chose to go to him he would take me there. I accordingly bid adieu to this hospitable family, and set off with him in a convenient boat; before night arrived at Mr. Rumsey's, who received me kindly, and treated me with the utmost humanity, during a stay of four or five weeks. The night however after my arrival here I sincerely thought would be my last, and my torments were so extreme as to desire it: having survived this tedious night, I in some degree recovered my senses, and asked Mr. Rumsey if he had any Cantharides; he soon prepared a blistering plaister for me, which I directed to be placed betwixt my shoulders; this produced the desired relief, and more than answered my expectation, for it had not been there a quarter of an hour before I fell asleep, and remained so a whole day, when I awoke intirely relieved from pain, my senses in perfect harmony and mind composed. I do not know how to express myself on this occasion; all was peace and tranquillity: although I had my sight imperfectly, yet my body seemed but as a light shadow, and my existence as a pleasing delirium, for I sometimes doubted of its reality. I however from that moment began to mend, until my health was perfectly restored; but it was several weeks before I could expose my eyes to open day light, and at last I found my left eye considerably injured, which suffered the greatest pain and weight of the disease.

As soon as I acquired strength to walk about, and bear the least impression of open day light on my eyes, I made frequent, indeed I may say daily excursions in and about this island, strolling through its awful shades, venerable groves and sublime forests, consisting of the Live Oaks and Magnolia grandiflora, Laurus Borbonia, Olea Americana, Fagus sylvatica, Laur. Sassafras, Quercus hemispherica, Tilia, Liquidambar styraciflua, Morus, Gleditsia, Callicarpa, Halesia, &c.

The island is six or seven miles in length, and four or five in width, including the salt marshes and plains, which invest it on every side, I believe we may only except a narrow strand at the South end of it, washed by Lake Borgone at the Regullets, which is a promontory composed of banks of sea-shells and sand cast up by the force of winds, and the surf of the Lake; these shells are chiefly a small species of white clam shells, called les coquilles. Here are a few shrubs growing on these shelly heights, viz. Rhamnus frangula, Sideroxylon, Myrica, Zanthoxylon clava Herculis, Juniperus Americana, Lysium salsum; together with several new genera and species of the herbaceous, and suffruticose tribes, Croton, Stillingia, &c., but particularly a species of Mimosa (Mimosa virgata), which in respect of the elegancy of its pinnated leaves, cannot be exceeded by any of that celebrated family. It is a perennial plant, sending up many nearly erect stems from the root or source; these divide themselves into many ascendant slender rods like branches, which are ornamented with double pinnated leaves, of a most delicate formation. The compound flowers, are of a pale, greenish yellow, collected together in a small oblong head, upon a long slender peduncle, the legumes are large, lunated and flat, placed in a spiral or contorted manner, each containing several hard compressed seeds or little beans.

The interior and by far the greater part of the island consists of high land; the soil to appearance a heap of sea sand in some places, with an admixture of sea shells; this soil, notwithstanding its sandy and steril appearance, when divested of its natural vegetative attire, has, from what cause I know not, a continual resource of fertility within itself: the surface of the earth, after being cleared of its original vegetable productions, exposed a few seasons to the sun, winds, and triturations of agriculture, appears scarcely any thing but heaps of white sand, yet it produces Corn (Zea), Indigo, Batatas, Beans, Peas, Cotton, Tobacco, and almost every sort of esculent vegetable, in a degree of luxuriancy very surprizing and unexpected, year after year, incessantly, without any addition of artificial manure or compost: there is indeed a foundation of strong adhesive clay, consisting of strata of various colours, which I discovered by examining a well, lately dug in Mr. Rumsey's yard; but lying at a great depth under the surface, the roots of small shrubs and herbage, cannot reach near to it, or receive any benefit, unless we may suppose, that ascending fumes or exhalations, from this bed of clay, may have a vivific nutritive quality, and be received by the fibres of the roots, or being condensed in the atmosphere by nocturnal chills, fall with dews upon the leaves and twigs of these plants, and there absorbed, become nutritive or exhilerating to them.

Besides the native forest trees and shrubs already noted, manured fruit trees arrive in this island to the utmost degree of perfection, as Pears, Peaches, Figs, Grape Vines, Plumbs, &c.; of the last mentioned genus, there is a native species grows in this island, which produces its large oblong crimson fruit in prodigious abundance; the fruit, though of a most enticing appearance, is rather too tart, yet agreeable eating, at sultry noon, in this burning climate; it affords a most delicious and reviving marmalade, when preserved in sugar, and makes excellent tarts; the tree grows about twelve feet high, the top spreading, the branches spiny and the leaves broad, nervous, serrated, and terminating with a subulated point.

My eyes having acquired sufficient strength to endure the open day light, I set off from Pearl island, for Manchac on the Mississipi, in a handsome large boat with three Negroes to navigate her. Leaving the friendly Mr. Rumsey's seat on Pearl Island, we descended a creek from the landing near his house; this creek led us about a mile, winding through salt sedgy marshes, into Lake Pontchartrain, along whose North shores we coasted about twenty miles, having low, reedy marshes, on our starboard: these marshes were very extensive between us and the far distant high forests on the main: at evening the shore became bolder, with sandy elevations, affording a few dwarf Oaks, Zanthoxylon, Myrica and Rham. frangula. We came to in a little bay, kindled a fire, and after supper betook ourselves to repose; our situation open, airy and cool, on clean sand banks, we rested quietly, though sometimes roused by alarms from the crocodiles, which are here in great numbers, and of an enormous bulk and strength.

Next day early we got under way, pursuing our former course, nearly Westward, keeping the North shore several leagues. Immediately back of this high sandy strand, (which is cast up by the beating surf and winds, setting from seaward, across the widest part of the lake) the ground suddenly falls, and becomes extensive flat Cypress swamps, the sources of creeks and rivers, which run into the lake, or Pearl River, or other places; the high forests of the main now gradually approaching the lake, advance up to the very shore, where we find houses, plantations and new settlements: we came to at one of them charmingly situated, set sail again, and came up to the mouth of the beautiful Taensapaoa, which takes that name from a nation of Indians, who formerly possessed the territories lying on its banks, which are fertile and delightful regions. This river is narrow at its entrance, but deep, and said to be navigable for large barks and perriauguas upwards of fifty miles: just within its capes, on the leeward shore, are heights, or a group of low hills (composed of the small clam shells, called les coquilles), which gradually depress as we retreat back from the river, and the surface of the land is more level; these shells dissolving and mixing with the surface, render the vegetative mould black, rich, and productive. Here are a few habitations, and some fields cleared and cultivated; but the inhabitants neglect agriculture, and generally employ themselves in hunting and fishing: we however furnished ourselves here with a sufficiency of excellent Batatas. I observed no new vegetable productions, except a species of Cleome (Cleome lupinifolia); this plant possesses a very strong scent, somewhat like Gum Assafetida, notwithstanding which the inhabitants give it a place in soups and sauces.

From Taensapaoa, we still coasted Westward, three or four miles, to the straits that communicate with the lake Maurepas; entering which and continuing six or eight miles, having low swampy land on each side, the channel divides, forming an island in the middle of the pass: we took the right hand channel, which continues three or four miles, when the channels reunite in full view of the charming lake. We came to at an elevated point, or promontory, on the starboard main shore, it being the North cape, from whence I enjoyed a very pleasing and complete view of the beautiful lake Maurepas; entering which next morning, a steady favourable gale soon wafted us nine or ten miles over to the mouth of the river Amite; ascended between its low banks; the land on each side a level swamp, about two feet above the surface of the water, supporting a thick forest of trees, consisting chiefly of Fraxinus, Nyssa aquatica, Nyssa multiflora, Cupressus disticha, Quercus phillos, Acer rubrum, Ac. negundo, Acer glaucum, Sambucus, Laurus Borbonia, Carpinus, Ulmus, and others. The soil or earth humid, black and rich. There is scarcely a perceptible current: the water dark, deep, turgid and stagnate, being from shore to shore covered with a scum or pellicle of a green and purplish cast, and perpetually throwing up from the muddy bottom to its surface minute air bladders or bubbles: in short, these dark loathsome waters, from every appearance, seem to be a strong extract or tincture of the leaves of the trees, herbs and reeds, arising from the shores, and which almost overspread them, and float on the surface, insomuch that a great part of these stagnate rivers, during the summer and autumnal seasons, are constrained to pass under a load of grass and weeds; which are continually vegetating and spreading over the surface from the banks, until the rising floods of winter and spring, rushing down from the main, sweep them away, and purify the waters. Late in the evening we discovered a narrow ridge of land close to the river bank, high and dry enough to suffer us to kindle a fire, and space sufficient to spread our bedding on. But here, fire and smoke were insufficient to expel the hosts of musquitoes that invested our camp, and kept us awake during the long and tedious night, so that the aligators had no chance of taking us napping. We were glad to rise early in the morning, proceeding up the Amite. The land now gradually rises, the banks become higher, the soil drier and firmer four or five feet above the surface of the river; the trees are of an incredible magnitude, particularly Platanus occidentalis, Fraxinus, ulmus, Quercus hemispherica, &c. The Canna Indica grows here in surprising luxuriance, presenting a glorious show; the stem rises six, seven and nine feet high, terminating upwards with spikes of scarlet flowers.

Now having advanced near thirty miles up the Amite, we arrived at a very large plantation, the property of a Scotch gentleman, who received me with civility, entreating me to reside with him; but being impatient to get to the river, and pleading the necessity of prosecuting my travels with alacrity, on account of the season being so far advanced, I was permitted to proceed, and set off next morning. Still ascending the Amite about twenty miles farther, arrived at the forks, where the Iberville comes in on the left hand, ascending which a little way, we soon came to the landing, where are warehouses for depositing merchandize, this being the extremity of navigation up this canal, and here small vessels load and unload. From this place to Manchac, on the banks of the Mississipi, just above the mouth of the canal, is nine miles by land; the road straight, spacious, and perfectly level, under the shadow of a grand forest; the trees of the first order in magnitude and beauty, as Magnolia grandiflora, Liriodendron tulipifera, Platanus, Juglans nigra, Fraxinus excelsior, Morus rubra, Laurus sassafras, Laurus Borbonia, Tilea, Liquidambar styraciflua, &c.

At evening arrived at Manchac, when I directed my steps
to the banks of the Mississipi, where I stood for a time as it
were fascinated by the magnificence of the great sire* of rivers.

The depth of the river here, even in this season, at its lowest
ebb, is astonishing, not less than forty fathoms; and the width
about a mile or somewhat less: but it is not expansion of surface alone that strikes us with ideas of magnificence; the altitude and theatrical ascents of its pensile banks, the steady
course of the mighty flood, the trees, high forests, even every
particular object, as well as societies, bear the stamp of superiority and excellence; all unite or combine in exhibiting a
prospect of the grand sublime. The banks of the river at Manchac, though frequently overflowed by the vernal inundations,
are about fifty feet perpendicular height above the surface of
the water (by which the channel at those times must be about
two hundred and ninety feet deep); and these precipices being
an accumulation of the sediment of muddy waters, annually
brought down with the floods, of a light loamy consistence,
continually cracking and parting, present to view deep yawning chasms, in time split off, as the active perpetual current
undermines; and the mighty masses of earth tumble headlong
into the river, whose impetuous current sweeps away and
lodges them elsewhere. There are yet visible some remains of
a high artificial bank, in front of the buildings of the town,
formerly cast up by the French, to resist the inundations, but
found to be ineffectual, and now in part tumbled down the
precipice: as the river daily encroaches on the bluff, some of
the habitations are in danger, and must be very soon removed
or swallowed up in the deep gulph of waters. A few of the
buildings that have been established by the English, since
taking possession of the colony, are large and commodious,
particularly the warehouses of Messrs. Swanson & Co. Indian
traders and merchants.

The Spaniards have a small fortress and garrison on the
point of land below the Iberville, close by the banks of the
river, which has a communication with Manchac, by a slender
narrow wooden bridge across the channel of Iberville, supported on wooden pillars, and not a bow shot from the

*Which is the meaning of the word Mississipi.

habitations of Manchac. The Iberville in the summer season
is dry, and its bed twelve or fifteen feet above the surface of
the Mississippi; but in the winter and spring has a great depth
of water, and a very rapid stream which flows into the Amite,
thence down through the lakes into the bay of Pearls to the
ocean.

Having recommendations to the inhabitants of Batonrouge,
now called New-Richmond, more than forty miles higher up
the river, one of these gentlemen being present at Manchac,
gave me a friendly and polite invitation to accompany him on
his return home. A pleasant morning; we sat off after breakfast, well accommodated in a handsome convenient boat,
rowed by three blacks. Two miles above Manchac we put in
to shore at Alabama: this Indian village is delightfully situated
on several swelling green hills, gradually ascending from the
verge of the river: the people are a remnant of the ancient
Alabama nation, who inhabited the East arm of the great Mobile river, which bears their name to this day, now possessed
by the Creeks or Muscogulges, who conquered the former.

My friend having purchased some baskets and earthen-
ware, the manufactures of the people, we left the village, and
proceeding twelve miles higher up the river, landed again at
a very large and well cultivated plantation, where we lodged
all night. Observed growing in a spacious garden adjacent to
the house, many useful as well as curious exotics, particularly
the delicate and sweet Tube-rose (Polyanthus tuberosa): it
grows here in the open garden; the flowers were very large
and abundant on the stems, which were five, six or seven feet
high, but I saw none here having double flowers. In one corner of the garden was a pond or marsh, round about which
grew luxuriantly the Scotch grass (Panicum hirtellum, gramen
panicum maximum, spica divisa, aristis armatum, Sloan, Jam.
Cat. p. 30): the people introduced this valuable grass from the
West-India islands: they mow or reap it at any time, and feed
it green to cows or horses; it is nourishing food for all cattle.
The Humble plant (Mimosa pudica) grows here five or six
feet high, rambling like Brier vines over the fences and shrubs,
all about the garden. The people here say it is an indigenous
plant, but this I doubt, as it is not seen growing wild in the
forests and fields, and it differs in no respect from that which

we protect in green houses and stoves, except in the extent and luxuriancy of its branches, which may be owing to the productive virgin mould and temperature of the climate. They however pay no attention to its culture, but rather condemn it as a noxious troublesome weed, for wherever it gets footing, it spreads itself by its seed in so great abundance as to oppress and even extirpate more useful vegetables.

Next day we likewise visited several delightful and spacious plantations on the banks of the river, during our progress upwards: in the evening arrived at my friend's habitation, a very delightful villa, with extensive plantations of Corn (Zea), Indigo, Cotton and some Rice.

A day or two after our arrival we agreed upon a visit to Point Coupè, a flourishing French settlement on the Spanish shore of the Mississipi.

Early next morning we set off in a neat Cypress boat with three oars, proceeding up the river; and by night got to a large plantation near the White cliffs, now called Brown's cliffs, in honour of the late governor of West Florida, now of the Bahama Islands, who is proprietor of a large district of country, lying on and adjacent to the Cliffs. At the time of my residence with Mr. Rumsey at Pearl island, governor Brown, then on his passage to his government of the Bahamas, paid Mr. Rumsey a visit, who politely introduced me to his excellency, acquainting him with my character and pursuits: he desired me to explore his territory, and give him my opinion of the quality of the White plains.

August 27th, 1777, having in readiness horses well equipt, early in the morning we set off for the plains. About a mile from the river we crossed a deep gully and small rivulet, then immediately entered the Cane forests, following a straight avenue cut through them, off from the river, which continued about eight miles, the ground gradually but imperceptibly rising before us: when at once opened to view expansive plains, which are a range of native grassy fields of many miles extent, lying parallel with the river, surrounded and intersected with Cane brakes and high forests of stately trees; the soil black, extremely rich and productive, but the virgin mould becomes thinner and less fertile as it verges on to the plains, which are so barren as scarcely to produce a bush or even grass, in the middle or highest parts. The upper stratum or surface of the earth is a whitish clay or chalk, with veins of sea shells, chiefly of those little clams called les coquilles, or interspersed with the white earth or clay, so tenacious and hard as to render it quite steril; scarcely any vegetable growth to be seen, except short grass, or crustaceous mosses; and some places quite bare, where it is on the surface; but where it lies from eighteen inches to two or three feet below, it has the virtue of fertilizing the virgin mould above, rendering it black, humid, soapy, and incredibly productive.

I observed two or three scrubby Pine trees or rather dwarf bushes, upon the highest ridge of these plains, which are viewed here as a curiosity, there being no Pine forests within several leagues distance from the banks of this great river, but, on the contrary, seemingly an endless wilderness of Canes, and the most magnificent forests of the trees already noted, but particularly Platanus occidentalis, Liriodendron, Magnolia grandiflora, Liquidambar styraciflua, Juglans nigra, Juglans exaltata, Tilea, Morus rubra, Gleditsia triacanthus, Laurus Borbonia, and Laurus sassafras; this last grows here to a vast tree, forty or fifty feet straight trunk; its timber is found to be useful, sawn into boards and scantling, or hewn into posts for building and fencing.

On the more fertile borders of the plains, adjoining the surrounding forests, are Sideroxylon, Pyrus coronaria, and Strawberry vines (Fragaria) but no fruit on them; the inhabitants assured me they bore fruit in their season, very large, of a fine red colour, delicious and fragrant.

Having made our tour and observations on the White plains, we returned to the river at the close of the day, and next morning sat off for Point Coupè: passed under the high painted cliffs, and then set our course across the Mississippi, which is here near two miles over: touched at a large island near the middle of the river, being led there, a little out of our way, in pursuit of a bear crossing from the main, but he out-swam us, reached the island, and made a safe retreat in the forests entangled with vines; we however pursued him on shore, but to no purpose. After resting a while, we re-embarked and continued on our voyage, coasting the East shore of the island to the upper end; here we landed again, on an extended projecting point of clean sand and pebbles, where were to be seen pieces of coal sticking in the gravel and sand, together with other fragments of the fossil kingdom, brought down by inundations and lodged there. We observed a large kind of muscle in the sand; the shell of an oval form, having horns or protuberances near half an inch in length and as thick as a crow quill, which I suppose serve the purpose of grapnels to hold their ground against the violence of the current. Here were great numbers of wild fowl wading in the shoal water that covers the sandy points, to a vast distance from the shores: they were geese, brant, gannet, and the great and beautiful whooping crane (grus alber.) Embarked again, doubled the point of the island and arrived at Point Coupè in the evening.

We made our visit to a French gentleman, an ancient man and wealthy planter, who, according to the history he favoured us with of his own life and adventures, must have been very aged; his hair was of a silky white, yet his complexion was florid and constitution athletic. He said that soon after he came to America, with many families of his countrymen, they ascended the river to the Cliffs of the Natches, where they sat down, being entertained by the natives; and under cover of a strong fortress and garrison, established a settlement, and by cultivating the land and forming plantations, in league and friendship with the Indians, in a few years they became a populous, rich and growing colony; when through the imprudent and tyrannical conduct of the commandant towards the Natches, the ancients of the country, a very powerful and civilized nation of red men, who were sovereigns of the soil, and possessed the country round about them, they became tired of these comers, and exasperated at their cruelty and licentiousness, at length determining to revenge themselves of such inhumanity and ingratitude, secretly conspired their destruction; and their measures were so well concerted with other Indian tribes, that if it had not been for the treachery of one of their princesses, with whom the commander was in favour (for by her influence her nation attempted the destruction of the settlement, before their auxiliaries joined them, which afforded an opportunity for some few of the settlers to escape), they would have fully accomplished their purpose. However

the settlement was entirely broken up, most of the inhabitants
being slaughtered in one night, and the few who escaped betook themselves to their canoes, descending the river until
they arrived at this place, where they established themselves
again; and this gentleman had only time and opportunity to
take into his boat one heifer calf, which he assured us was the
mother of the numerous herds he now possesses, consisting
of many hundred head. Here is now a very respectable village,
defended by a strong fortress and garrison of Spaniards, the
commander being governor of the district.

The French here are able, ingenious and industrious planters: they live easy and plentifully, and are far more regular
and commendable in the enjoyment of their earnings than
their neighbours the English: their dress of their own manufactures, well wrought and neatly made up, yet not extravagant or foppish; manners and conversation easy, moral and
entertaining.

Next morning we sat off again on our return home, and
called by the way at the Cliffs, which is a perpendicular bank
or bluff, rising up out of the river near one hundred feet above
the present surface of the water, whose active current sweeps
along by it. From eight or nine feet below the loamy vegetative mould at top, to within four or five feet of the water,
these cliffs present to view strata of clay, marle and chalk, of
all colours, as brown, red, yellow, white, blue and purple;
there are separate strata of these various colours, as well as
mixed or particoloured: the lowest stratum next the water is
exactly of the same black mud or rich soil as the adjacent low
Cypress swamps, above and below the bluff; and here in the
cliffs we see vast stumps of Cypress and other trees, which at
this day grow in these low, wet swamps, and which range on
a level with them. These stumps are sound, stand upright, and
seem to be rotted off about two or three feet above the spread
of their roots; their trunks, limbs, &c. lie in all directions
about them. But when these swampy forests were growing,
and by what cause they were cut off and overwhelmed by the
various strata of earth, which now rise near one hundred feet
above, at the brink of the cliffs, and two or three times that
height but a few hundred yards back, are enquiries perhaps
not easily answered. The swelling heights rising gradually over

and beyond this precipice are now adorned with high forests of stately Magnolia, Liquidambar, Fagus, Quercus, Laurus, Morus, Juglans, Tilia, Halesia, Æsculus, Callicarpa, Liriodendron, &c. Arrived in the evening at the plantation below the Cliffs, and the next day got safe back to my friend's habitation.

Observed few vegetable productions different from what grow in Carolina and Georgia; perhaps in the spring and early summer season, here may be some new plants, particularly in the high forests and ridges, at some distance from the river: there is however growing in the rich high lands, near on the banks of the river, which I observed in the settlement of Baton Rouge, an arborescent aromatic vine, which mounts to the tops of the highest trees, by twisting or writhing spirally round them; some of these vines are as thick as a man's leg, of a soft spungy texture, and flexible, covered with a Cinnamon coloured bark, which is highly aromatic or spicy. The large oblong leaves sit opposite on the branches, and are of a full deep green colour; but its season of flowering being past, and the seed scattered, I am entirely ignorant to what genus it belongs; perhaps it is a non-descript or new genus. Here is likewise a new and beautiful species of Verbena, with decumbent branches and lacerated deep green leaves; the branches terminate with corymbi of violet blue flowers: this pretty plant grows in old fields where there is a good soil.

The severe disorder in my eyes subverted the plan of my peregrinations, and contracted the span of my pilgrimage South-Westward. This disappointment affected me very sensibly, but resignation and reason resuming their empire over my mind, I submitted, and determined to return to Carolina.

Receiving information that the company's schooner was ready to sail for Mobile, I embarked on board a trading boat for Manchac, where arriving in the evening, I took leave next morning of Messrs. Swanson and Co. and set off for the forks of the Amite, and next day sat sail, descending the tardy current of the Amite. Observing two bears crossing the river a-head, though our pieces were ready charged, and the yawl along side to receive us, we pursued them in vain, they swam swiftly across and escaped in the forests on the island of Orleans. The breeze dying away at evening, we came to anchor, and had variety of amusements at fishing and fowling.

Next day, November 13th, 1777, with a steady leading breeze, entered and sailed over the lake Maurepas, and through the streights into the Pontchartrain, and continued under sail; but at midnight, by keeping too near the West shore, we ran aground on a sand-bar, where we lay beating the hard sandy bottom until morning, and our yawl parting from us in the night, which we never recovered, we were left to the mercy of the winds and floods; but before noon the wind coming briskly from North-East, driving the sea into the lake, we got off, made sail again, and before night passed through the Regullets, entering the ocean through the bay of Pearls, sailing through the sound betwixt Cat island and the strand of the continent; passing by the beautiful bay St. Louis, into which descend many delightful rivers, which flow from the lower or maritime settlements of the Chactaws or Flatheads. Continuing through the sound between the oyster banks and shoals of Ship and Horn islands, and the high and bold coast of Biloxi on the main, got through the narrow pass Aux Christians, and soon came up abreast of Isle Dauphin, betwixt whose shoals and the West Cape of Mobile Bay we got aground on some sunken oyster banks; but next day a brisk Southerly wind raised the sea on the coast, which lifted us off again, and setting sail, we shot through the Pass au Oleron, and entering the bay, by night came to anchor safe again at the city of Mobile.

After having made up my collections of growing roots, seeds and curious specimens, left them to the care of Messrs. Swanson and M'Gillavry, to be forwarded to Dr. Fothergill of London. I prepared to set off again to Augusta in Georgia, through the Creek Nation, the only practicable way of returning by land, being frustrated of pursuing my intended rout which I had meditated, through the territories of the Siminoles or Lower Creeks, they being a treacherous people, lying so far from the eye and controul of the nation with whom they are confederate, that there had lately been depredations and murders committed by them at the bay of Apalache, on some families of white people who were migrating from Georgia, with an intention of settling on the Mobile. Having to pass the distance of near two hundred miles to the first town of the nation, through a solitary, uninhabited wilderness, the bloody field of Schambe, where those contending bands of American bravos, Creeks and Chactaws, often meet in dire conflict; for the better convenience and security, I joined company with a caravan of traders, now about setting off for the nation.

Observed growing in a garden in Mobile, two large trees of the Juglans pecan, and the Dioscorea bulbifera: this last curious plant bears a large kidney shaped root, one, two or three at the bosom of the leaves, several feet from the ground, as they climb up poles or supports set by their roots; these roots when boiled or roasted are esteemed a pleasant wholesome food, and taste like the ordinary Yam.

CHAP. VIII.

NOVEMBER 27TH, 1777, sat off from Mobile, in a large boat with the principal trader of the company, and at evening arrived at Taensa, where were the pack-horsemen with the merchandize, and next morning as soon as we had our horses in readiness, I took my last leave of Major Farmer, and left Taensa. Our caravan consisted of between twenty and thirty horses, sixteen of which were loaded, two pack-horsemen, and myself, under the direction of Mr. Tap——y the chief trader. One of our young men was a Mustee Creek, his mother being a Chactaw slave, and his father a half breed, betwixt a Creek and a white man. I loaded one horse with my effects, some presents to the Indians, to enable me to purchase a fresh horse, in case of necessity; for my old trusty slave which had served me faithfully almost three years, having carried me on his back at least six thousand miles, was by this time almost worn out, and I expected every hour he would give up, especially after I found the manner of these traders' travelling. They seldom decamp until the sun is high and hot; each one having a whip made of the toughest cow-skin, they start all at once, the horses having ranged themselves in regular Indian file, the veteran in the van, and the younger in the rear; then the chief drives with the crack of his whip, and a whoop or shriek, which rings through the forests and plains, speaks in Indian, commanding them to proceed, which is repeated by all the company, when we start at once, keeping up a brisk and constant trot, which is incessantly urged and continued as long as the miserable creatures are able to move forward; and then come to camp, though frequently in the middle of the afternoon, which is the pleasantest time of the day for travelling: and every horse has a bell on, which being stopped when we start in the morning with a twist of grass or leaves, soon shakes out, and they are never stopped again during the day. The constant ringing and clattering of the bells, smacking of the whips, whooping and too frequent cursing these miserable quadrupeds, cause an incessant uproar and confusion, inexpressibly disagreeable.

After three days travelling in this mad manner, my old servant was on the point of giving out, and several of the company's horses were tired, but were relieved of their burthens by the led horses which attended for that purpose. I was now driven to disagreeable extremities, and had no other alternative, but either to leave my horse in the woods, pay a very extravagant hire for a doubtful passage to the Nation, or separate myself from my companions, and wait the recovery of my horse alone: the chief gave me no other comfortable advice in this dilemma, than that, there was a company of traders on the road a-head of us from the Nation, to Mobile, who had a large gang of led horses with them for sale, when they should arrive; and expected from the advice which he had received at Mobile before we set off from thence, that this company must be very near to us, and probably would be up to-morrow, or at least in two or three days: and this man condescended so far as to moderate a little his mode of travelling, that I might have a chance of keeping up with them until the evening of next day; besides I had the comfort of observing that the traders and pack-horsemen carried themselves towards me with evident signs of humanity and friendship, often expressing sentiments of sympathy, and saying I must not be left alone to perish in the wilderness.

Although my apprehensions on this occasion were somewhat tumultuous, since there was little hope, on the principle of reason, should I be left alone, of escaping cruel captivity, and perhaps being murdered by the Chactaws (for the company of traders was my only security, as the Indians never attack the traders on the road, though they be trading with nations at enmity with them) yet I had secret hopes of relief and deliverance, that cheered me, and inspired confidence and peace of mind.

Now I am come within the atmosphere of the Illicium groves, how reanimating is the fragrance! every part of this plant above ground possesses an aromatic scent, but the large stillated pericarpe is the most fragrant part of it, which continually perspires an oleagenous sweat, as warm and vivific as cloves or mace. I never saw it grow naturally further North than Lat. 33°, on the Mobile river and its branches, and but one place in East Florida near Lake George, Lat. 28°.

About the middle of the afternoon, we were joyfully surprised at the distant prospect of the trading company coming
up, and we soon met, saluting each other several times with
a general Indian whoop, or shout of friendship; then each
company came to camp within a few paces of each other; and
before night I struck up a bargain with them for a handsome
strong young horse, which cost me about ten pounds sterling.
I was now constrained to leave my old slave behind, to feed
in rich cane pastures, where he was to remain and recruit until
the return of his new master from Mobile; from whom I extorted a promise to use him gently, and if possible, not to
make a pack-horse of him.

Next morning we decamped, proceeding again on my travels, now alert and cheerful. Crossed a brisk rivulet ripling over
a gravelly bed, and winding through aromatic groves of the
Illicium Floridanum, then gently descended to the high forests, leaving Deadman's creek, for at this creek a white man
was found dead, supposed to have been murdered, from
which circumstance it has its name.

A few days before we arrived at the Nation, we met a company of emigrants from Georgia; a man, his wife, a young
woman, several young children, and three stout young men,
with about a dozen horses loaded with their property. They
informed us their design was to settle on the Alabama, a few
miles above the confluence of the Tombigbe.

Being now near the Nation, the chief trader with another
of our company sat off a-head for his town, to give notice to
the Nation, as he said, of his approach with the merchandize,
each of them taking the best horse they could pick out of the
gang, leaving the goods to the conduct and care of the young
Mustee and myself. Early in the evening we came to the banks
of a large deep creek, a considerable branch of the Alabama:
the waters ran furiously, being overcharged with the floods of
rain which had fallen the day before. We discovered immediately that there was no possibility of crossing it by fording; its
depth and rapidity would have swept our horses, loads and
all, instantly from our sight: my companion, after consideration, said we must make a raft to ferry over our goods, which
we immediately set about, after unloading our horses and
turning them out to range. I undertook to collect dry canes,

and my companion, dry timber or logs and vines to bind them together: having gathered the necessary materials, and laid them in order on the brinks of the river, ready to work upon, we betook ourselves to repose, and early next morning sat about building our raft. This was a novel scene to me, and I could not, until finished and put to practice, well comprehend how it could possibly answer the effect desired. In the first place we laid, parallel to each other, dry, found trunks of trees, about nine feet in length, and eight or nine inches diameter; which binding fast together with grape vines and withs, until we had formed this first floor, about twelve or fourteen feet in length, we then bound the dry canes in bundles, each near as thick as a man's body, with which we formed the upper stratum, laying them close by the side of each other and binding them fast: after this manner our raft was constructed. Then having two strong grape vines, each long enough to cross the river, we fastened one to each end of the raft; which now being completed, and loading on as much as it would safely carry, the Indian took the end of one of the vines in his mouth, plunged into the river and swam over with it, and the vine fixed to the other end was committed to my charge, to steady the raft and haul it back again after being unloaded. As soon as he had safe landed and hauled taught his vine, I pushed off the raft, which he drew over as quick as possible, I steadying it with my vine: in this manner, though with inexpressible danger of losing our effects, we ferried all safe over. The last load, with other articles, contained my property, with all my clothes, which I stripped off, except my breeches, for they contained matters of more value and consequence than all the rest of my property put together; besides I did not choose to expose myself entirely naked to the alligators and serpents in crossing the flood. Now seeing all the goods safe over, and the horses at a landing place on the banks of the river about fifty yards above, I drove them all in together, when, seeing them safe landed, I plunged in after them, and being a tolerable swimmer, soon reached the opposite shore. But my difficulties at this place were not yet at an end, for our horses all landed just below the mouth of a considerable branch of this river, of fifteen or twenty feet width, and its perpendicular banks almost as many feet in height above its

swift waters, over which we were obliged to carry every article
of our effects, and this by no other bridge than a sapling felled
across it, which is called a raccoon bridge; and over this my
Indian friend would trip as quick and light as that quadruped,
with one hundred weight of leather on his back, when I was
scarcely able to shuffle myself along over it astride. At last
having re-packed and sat off again, without any material occurrence intervening, in the evening we arrived at the banks
of the great Tallapoose river, and came to camp under shelter
of some Indian cabins, in expansive fields, close to the river
bank, opposite the town of Savannuca. Late in the evening a
young white man, in great haste and seeming confusion,
joined our camp, who immediately related, that being on his
journey from Pensacola, it happened that the very night after
we had passed the company of emigrants, he met them and
joined their camp in the evening; when, just at dark, the Chactaws surrounded them, plundered their camp, and carried all
the people off captive, except himself, he having the good
fortune to escape with his horse, though closely pursued.

Next morning very early, though very cold and the surface
of the earth as hoary as if covered with a fall of snow, the
trader standing on the opposite shore entirely naked, except
a breech-clout, and encircled by a company of red men in the
like habit, hailed us, and presently, with canoes, brought us
all over with the merchandize, and conducted us safe to the
town of Mucclasse, a mile or two distant.

The next day was a day of rest and audience: the following
was devoted to feasting, and the evening concluded in cele-
brating the nuptials of the young Mustee with a Creek girl of
Mucclasse, daughter of the chief and sister to our trader's wife.
The trader's house and stores formed a compleat square, after
the mode of the habitations of the Muscogulges, that is, four
oblong buildings of equal dimensions, two opposite to each
other, encompassing an area of about a quarter of an acre; on
one side of this a fence enclosed a yard of near an acre of
ground, at one of the farther corners of which a booth or
pavilion was formed of green boughs, having two Laurel trees
planted in front (Magnolia grandiflora). This was the secret
nuptial chamber. Dancing, music and feasting continued the
forepart of the night, and towards morning the happy couple

privately withdrew, and continued alone all the next day, no one presuming to approach the sacred, mysterious thalame.

The trader obliged me with his company on a visit to the Alabama, an Indian town at the confluence of the two fine rivers, the Tallapoose and Coosau, which here resign their names to the great Alabama, where are to be seen traces of the ancient French fortress, Thoulouse; here are yet lying, half buried in the earth, a few pieces of ordnance, four and six pounders. I observed, in a very thriving condition, two or three very large apple trees, planted here by the French. This is, perhaps, one of the most eligible situations for a city in the world; a level plain between the conflux of two majestic rivers, which are exactly of equal magnitude in appearance, each navigable for vessels and perriauguas at least five hundred miles above it, and spreading their numerous branches over the most fertile and delightful regions, many hundred miles before we reach their sources in the Apalachean mountains.

Stayed all night at Alabama, where we had a grand entertainment at the public square, with music and dancing, and returned next day to Mucclasse; where being informed of a company of traders about setting off from Tuckabatche for Augusta, I made a visit to that town to know the truth of it, but on my arrival there they were gone; but being informed of another caravan who were to start from the Ottasse town in two or three weeks time, I returned to Mucclasse in order to prepare for my departure.

On my arrival, I was not a little surprised at a tragical revolution in the family of my friend the trader, his stores shut up, and guarded by a party of Indians: in a few minutes however, the whole affair was related to me. It appeared that this son of Adonis, had been detected in an amorous intrigue, with the wife of a young chief, the day after his arrival: the chief was out on a hunt, but arrived next day; and upon information of the affair, the fact being confirmed, he with his friends and kindred resolved to exact legal satisfaction, which in this case is cutting off both ears of the delinquent, close to the head, which is called cropping. This being determined upon, he took the most secret and effectual methods to effect his purpose. About a dozen young Indian fellows, conducted by their chief (the injured husband), having provided and armed

themselves with knotty cudgels of green Hiccory, which they
concealed under their mantles, in the dusk of the evening paid
a pretended friendly visit to the trader at his own house, when
the chief feigning a private matter of business, took him aside
in the yard; then whistling through his fingers (the signal pre-
concerted) he was instantly surrounded, knocked down, and
then stripped to his skin, and beaten with their knotty blud-
geons; however he had the subtilty to feign himself speechless
before they really killed him, which he supposed was their
intention: when he had now lain for dead, the executioner
drew out his knife with an intention of taking off his ears: this
small respite gave him time to reflect a little; when he instantly
sprang up, ran off, leaped the fence, and had the good fortune
to get into a dark swamp, overgrown with vines and thickets,
where he miraculously eluded the earnest researches of his
enemies, and finally made a safe retreat to the house of his
father-in-law, the chief of the town, throwing himself under
his protection, who gave his word that he would do him all
the favour that lay in his power. This account I had from his
own mouth, for hearing of my return, the next morning after
my arrival, he sent a trusty messenger, by whom I found
means of access to him. He farther informed me, that there
had been a council of the chiefs of the town convened, to
deliberate on the affair, and their final determination was that
he must lose his ears, or forfeit all his goods, which amounted
to upwards of one thousand pounds sterling, and even that
forfeiture would not save his ears, unless Mr. Golphin interposed in his behalf; and after all, the injured Indian declares
that he will have his life. He entreated me with tears to make
what speed I could to Silver Bluff, represent his dangerous
situation to Mr. Golphin, and solicit that gentleman's most
speedy and effectual interference; which I assured him I would
undertake.

Now having all things prepared for my departure, early in
the morning, after taking leave of my distressed friend the
trader of Mucclasse, I sat off; passed through continued plantations and Indian towns on my way up the Tallapoose river,
being every where treated by the inhabitants with marks of
friendship, even as though I had been their countryman and
relation. Called by the way at the beautiful town of Coolome,

where I tarried some time with Mr. Germany the chief trader of the town, an elderly gentleman, but active, cheerful and very agreeable, who received and treated me with the utmost civility and friendship: his wife is a Creek woman, of a very amiable and worthy character and disposition, industrious, prudent and affectionate; and by her he had several children, whom he is desirous to send to Savanna or Charleston, for their education, but cannot prevail on his wife to consent to it: this affair affects him very sensibly, for he has acumulated a pretty fortune by his industry and commendable conduct.

Leaving Coolome, I re-crossed the river at Tuccabache, an ancient and large town; thence continued up the river, and at evening arrived at Attasse, where I continued near a week, waiting the preparations of the traders, with whom I was to join in company to Augusta.

The next day after my arrival, I was introduced to the ancient chiefs, at the public square or areopagus; and in the evening, in company with the traders, who are numerous in this town, repaired to the great rotunda, where were assembled the greatest number of ancient venerable chiefs and warriors that I had ever beheld: we spent the evening and greater part of the night together, in drinking Cassine and smoking Tobacco. The great council house or rotunda is appropriated to much the same purpose as the public square, but more private, and seems particularly dedicated to political affairs; women and youth are never admitted; and I suppose it is death for a female to presume to enter the door, or approach within its pale. It is a vast conical building or circular dome, capable of accommodating many hundred people; constructed and furnished within, exactly in the same manner as those of the Cherokees already described, but much larger than any I had seen of them: there are people appointed to take care of it, to have it daily swept clean, and to provide canes for fuel, or to give light.

As their vigils and manner of conducting their vespers and mystical fire in this rotunda, are extremely singular, and altogether different from the customs and usages of any other people, I shall proceed to describe them. In the first place, the governor or officer who has the management of this business, with his servants attending, orders the black drink to be brewed, which is a decoction or infusion of the leaves and tender shoots of the Cassine: this is done under an open shed or pavilion, at twenty or thirty yards distance, directly opposite the door of the council-house. Next he orders bundles of dry canes to be brought in: these are previously split and broken in pieces to about the length of two feet, and then placed obliquely crossways upon one another on the floor, forming a spiral circle round about the great centre pillar, rising to a foot or eighteen inches in height from the ground; and this circle spreading as it proceeds round and round, often repeated from right to left, every revolution encreases its diameter, and at length extends to the distance of ten or twelve feet from the centre, more or less, according to the length of time the assembly or meeting is to continue. By the time these preparations are accomplished, it is night, and the assembly have taken their seats in order. The exterior extremity or outer end of the spiral circle takes fire and immediately rises into a bright flame (but how this is effected I did not plainly apprehend; I saw no person set fire to it; there might have been fire left on the earth, however I neither saw nor smelt fire or smoke until the blaze instantly ascended upwards), which gradually and slowly creeps round the centre pillar, with the course of the sun, feeding on the dry canes, and affords a cheerful, gentle and sufficient light until the circle is consumed, when the council breaks up. Soon after this illumination takes place, the aged chiefs and warriors are seated on their cabins or sophas, on the side of the house opposite the door, in three classes or ranks, rising a little, one above or behind the other; and the white people and red people of confederate towns in the like order on the left hand; a transverse range of pillars, supporting a thin clay wall about breast high, separating them: the king's cabin or seat is in front; the next to the back of it the head warrior's; and the third or last accommodates the young warriors, &c. The great war chief's seat or place is on the same cabin with, and immediately to the left hand of the king, and next to the white people; and to the right hand of the mico or king the most venerable headmen and warriors are seated. The assembly being now seated in order, and the house illuminated, two middle aged men, who perform the office of slaves or servants, pro tempore, come in together at the door, each having very large conch shells full of black drink, and advance with slow, uniform and steady steps, their eyes or countenances lifted up, singing very low but sweetly; they come within six or eight paces of the king's and white people's cabins, when they stop together, and each rests his shell on a tripos or little table, but presently takes it up again, and, bowing very low, advances obsequiously, crossing or intersecting each other about midway: he who rested his shell before the white people now stands before the king, and the other who stopped before the king stands before the white people; when each presents his shell, one to the king and the other to the chief of the white people, and as soon as he raises it to his mouth, the slave utters or sings two notes, each of which continues as long as he has breath; and as long as these notes continue, so long must the person drink, or at least keep the shell to his mouth. These two long notes are very solemn, and at once strike the imagination with a religious awe or homage to the Supreme, sounding somewhat like a-hoo—ojah and a-lu—yah. After this manner the whole assembly are treated, as long as the drink and light continue to hold out; and as soon as the drinking begins, tobacco and pipes are brought. The skin of a wild cat or young tyger stuffed with tobacco is brought, and laid at the king's feet, with the great or royal pipe beautifully adorned; the skin is usually of the animals of the king's family or tribe, as the wild-cat, otter, bear, rattle-snake, &c. A skin of tobacco is likewise brought and cast at the feet of the white chief of the town, and from him it passes from one to another to fill their pipes from, though each person has besides his own peculiar skin of tobacco. The king or chief smokes first in the great pipe a few whiffs, blowing it off ceremoniously, first towards the sun, or as it is generally supposed to the Great Spirit, for it is puffed upwards, next towards the four cardinal points, then towards the white people in the house; then the great pipe is taken from the hand of the mico by a slave, and presented to the chief white man, and then to the great war chief, whence it circulates through the rank of head men and warriors, then returns to the king. After this each one fills his pipe from his own or his neighbour's skin.

The great or public square generally stands alone, in the centre and highest part of the town: it consists of four-square or cubical buildings, or houses of one story, uniform, and of the same dimensions, so situated as to form an exact tetragon, encompassing an area of half an acre of ground, more or less, according to the strength or largeness of the town, or will of the inhabitants: there is a passage or avenue at each corner of equal width: each building is constructed of a wooden frame fixed strongly in the earth, the walls filled in, and neatly plaistered with clay mortar; close on three sides, that is the back and two ends, except within about two feet of the wall plate or eves, which is left open for the purpose of a window and to admit a free passage of the air; the front or side next to the area is quite open like a piazza. One of these buildings is properly the council house, where the mico, chiefs, and warriors, with the citizens who have business, or choose to repair thither, assemble every day in council, to hear, decide and rectify all grievances, complaints and contentions, arising betwixt the citizens; give audience to ambassadors, and strangers; hear news and talks from confederate towns, allies or distant nations; consult about the particular affairs of the town, as erecting habitations for new citizens, or establishing young families, concerning agriculture, &c. This building is somewhat different from the other three: it is closely shut up on three sides, that is, the back and two ends, and besides, a partition wall longitudinally from end to end divides it into two apartments, the back part totally dark, only three small arched apertures or holes opening into it from the front apartment or piazza, and little larger than just to admit a man to crawl in upon his hands and knees. This secluded place appears to me to be designed as a sanctuary* dedicated to religion, or rather priest craft; for here are deposited all the sacred things, as the physic pot, rattles, chaplets of deer's hoofs and other apparatus of conjuration; and likewise the calumet or great pipe of peace, the imperial standard, or eagle's tail, which is made of the feathers

*Sanctorium or sacred temple; and it is said to be death for any person but the mico, war-chief and high priest to enter in, and none are admitted but by permission of the priests, who guard it day and night.

of the white eagle's tail* curiously formed and displayed like an open fan on a sceptre or staff, as white and clean as possible when displayed for peace, but when for war, the feathers are painted or tinged with vermillion. The piazza or front of this building, is equally divided into three apartments, by two transverse walls or partitions, about breast high, each having three orders or ranges of seats or cabins stepping one above and behind the other, which accommodate the senate and audience, in the like order as observed in the rotunda. The other three buildings which compose the square, are alike furnished with three ranges of cabins or sophas, and serve for a banqueting-house, to shelter and accommodate the audience and spectators at all times, particularly at feasts or public entertainments, where all classes of citizens resort day and night in the summer or moderate season; the children and females however are seldom or never seen in the public square.

The pillars and walls of the houses of the square are decorated with various paintings and sculptures; which I suppose to be hieroglyphic, and as an historic legendary of political and sacerdotal affairs: but they are extremely picturesque or caricature, as men in variety of attitudes, some ludicrous enough, others having the head of some kind of animal, as those of a duck, turkey, bear, fox, wolf, buck, &c. and again those kind of creatures are represented having the human head. These designs are not ill executed; the outlines bold, free and well proportioned. The pillars supporting the front or piazza of the council-house of the square, are ingeniously formed in the likeness of vast speckled serpents, ascending upwards; the Ottasses being of the snake family or tribe. At this time the town was fasting, taking medicine, and I think I may say praying, to avert a grievous calamity of sickness, which had lately afflicted them, and laid in the grave abundance of their citizens. They fast seven or eight days, during which time they eat or drink nothing but a meagre gruel, made of a little corn-flour and water; taking at the same time by way of medicine or physic, a strong decoction of the roots of the Iris versicolor, which is a powerful carthartic: they hold this root in high estimation, every town cultivates a little plan-

*Vultur sacra.

tation of it, having a large artificial pond, just without the town, planted and almost overgrown with it, where they usually dig clay for pottery, and mortar and plaster for their buildings, and I observed where they had lately been digging up this root.

In the midst of a large oblong square adjoining this town (which was surrounded with a low bank or terrace) is standing a high pillar, round like a pin or needle; it is about forty feet in height, and between two and three feet in diameter at the earth, gradually tapering upwards to a point; it is one piece of pine wood, and arises from the centre of a low, circular, artificial hill, but it leans a little to one side. I inquired of the Indians and traders what it was designed for, who answered they knew not: the Indians said that their ancestors found it in the same situation, when they first arrived and possessed the country, adding, that the red men or Indians, then the possessors, whom they vanquished, were as ignorant as themselves concerning it, saying that their ancestors likewise found it standing so. This monument, simple as it is, may be worthy the observations of a traveller, since it naturally excites at least the following queries: for what purpose was it designed? its great antiquity and incorruptibility—what method or machines they employed to bring it to the spot, and how they raised it erect? There is no tree or species of the pine, whose wood, i.e. so large a portion of the trunk, is supposed to be incorruptible, exposed in the open air to all weathers, but the long-leaved Pine (Pin. palustris), and there is none growing within twelve or fifteen miles of this place, that tree being naturally produced only on the high, dry, barren ridges, where there is a sandy soil and grassy wet savannas. A great number of men uniting their strength, probably carried it to the place on handspikes, or some such contrivance.

On the Sabbath day before I set off from this place, I could not help observing the solemnity of the town, the silence and the retiredness of the red inhabitants; but a very few of them were to be seen, the doors of their dwellings shut, and if a child chanced to stray out, it was quickly drawn in doors again. I asked the meaning of this, and was immediately answered, that it being the white people's beloved day or Sabbath, the Indians kept it religiously sacred to the Great Spirit.

Last night was clear and cold, wind North West, and this morning, January 2d, 1788, the face of the earth was perfectly white with a beautiful sparkling frost. Sat off for Augusta with a company of traders, four men with about thirty horses, twenty of which were loaded with leather and furs, each pack or load supposed to weigh one hundred and fifty pounds upon an average. In three days we arrived at the Apalachucla or Chata Uche river; crossed at the point towns Chehaw and Usseta: these towns almost join each other, yet speak two languages, as radically different perhaps as the Muscogulge's and Chinese. After leaving the river we met with nothing material, or worth particular observation, until our arrival at Oakmulge, towards evening, where we encamped in expansive ancient Indian fields, in view of the foaming flood of the river, now raging over its banks. Here were two companies of traders from Augusta, bound to the Nation, consisting of fifteen or twenty men, with seventy or eighty horses, most of which had their loads of merchandize: they crossed the river this morning and lost six horses in the attempt; they were drowned, being entangled in the vines under water at landing. But the river now falling again, we were in hopes that by next morning the waters would be again confined within the banks. We immediately sat about rigging our portable leather boat, about eight feet long, which was of thick soal leather, folded up and carried on the top of a pack of deer-skins. The people soon got her rigged, which was effected after the following manner. We, in the first place, cut down a White-Oak sapling, and by notching this at each end, bent it up, which formed the keel, stem and stern post of one piece; this was placed in the bottom of the boat, and pretty strong hoop-poles being fixed in the bottom across the keel, turning up their ends, expanded the hull of the boat, which being fastened by throngs to two other poles bent round, the outside of the rim formed the gunwhales: thus in an hour's time our bark was rigged, to which afterwards we added two little oars or sculls. Our boat being now in readiness, and our horses turned out to pasture, each one retired to repose, or to such exercise as most effectually contributed to divert the mind. I was at this time rather dejected, and sought comfort in retirement, turning my course to the expansive fields, fragrant groves and sublime forests. Returned to camp by dusk, where I found my companions cheerful and thoughtless rather to an extreme. It was a calm still evening and warm; the wood-cock (scolopax) chirruping high up in the air, gently descends by a spiral circular tract, and alights on the humid plain: this bird appears in Pennsylvania early in the spring, when the Elm and Maple begin to flower; and here the scarlet Maple, Elm and Elder began to show their flowers; the yellow Jasmin was just ready to open its fragrant golden blossoms, and the gay Azalea also preparing to expand its beauties.

The morning cool and pleasant: after reconnoitering the shores of the rivers, and consulting with our brethern in distress, who had not yet decamped, resolving to stay and lend their assistance in passing over this rapid gulph, we were encouraged to proceed; and launching our bark into the raging flood, after many successful trips ferried over all the goods, then drove in our horses altogether, and had the pleasure of seeing them all safely landed on the opposite shore; and lastly I embarked with three of our people, and several packs of leather; we then put off from shore, bidding adieu to our generous friends left behind, who re-echoed our shouts upon our safe landing. We proceeded again, crossed the Oconne in the same manner, and with the like success, and came to camp in the fertile fields, on the banks of that beautiful river; and proceeding thence next day, in the evening came to camp on the waters of great Ogeche. The following day, after crossing several of its considerable branches, came to camp; and next day crossed the main branch of that famous river, which being wide and very rapid proved difficult and dangerous fording; yet we crossed without any loss, but some of our pack-horses were badly bruised, being swept off their feet and dashed against the rocks, my horse too being carried away with the current, and plunging off sunken shelving rocks into deep holes, I got very wet, but I kept my seat and landed safe: however I suffered much, it being a cold freezing day. We came to camp early, and raising great fires with Pine knots and other wood, we dried ourselves and kept warm during the long night, and after two days more hard travelling we arrived at Augusta.

Being under a necessity of making two or three days stay here, in order to refit myself, for by this time my stock of

cloaths was entirely worn out, I took this opportunity of visiting my friend doctor Wells at his plantations near the city.
And now being again new clothed and furnished with a tolerable Indian poney, I took leave of my host and prepared to
depart for Savanna.

Soon after I left Augusta, proceeding for Savanna, the capital, a gentleman overtook me on the road, who was a native of
Ireland, and had lately arrived in this part of America with a
view of settling a plantation in Georgia, particularly for the
culture of those very useful fruits and vegetables that are cultivated up the Mediterranean, and which so largely contribute
towards supporting that lucrative branch of commerce, the
Levant trade; viz. Vitis vinifera, for wine, Vitis Corinthiaca, for
Currants, Vitis Allobrogica, for Raisins, Olives, Figs, Morus,
for feeding silkworms, Amygdalus communis, Pistachia, Capparis, Citrus aurantium, Citrus limon, Citrus verrucosa, the
great sweet scented Citron, &c. He was very ingenious, desirous of information, and as liberal and free of communicating
his own acquisitions and discoveries in useful science, and consequently a very agreeable companion. On our journey down
we stopped a while to rest and refresh ourselves at the Great
Springs, near the road, on our left hand, about midway between Augusta and Savanna. This amazing fountain of transparent cool water, breaks suddenly out of the earth, at the
basis of a moderately elevated hill or bank, forming at once a
bason near twenty yards over, ascending through a horizontal
bed of soft rocks, of a heterogeneous composition, chiefly a
testaceous concretion of broken, entire and pulverised sea
shells, sand, &c. constituting a coarse kind of lime-stone. The
ebullition is copious, active and continual, over the ragged
apertures in the rocks, which lie seven or eight feet below,
swelling the surface considerably immediately above it. The
waters descend swiftly from the fountain, forming at once a
large brook, six or eight yards over, and five or six feet deep.
There are multitudes of fish in the fountain, of various tribes,
chiefly the several species of bream, trout, cat-fish and garr: it
was amusing to behold the fish continually ascending and
descending through the rocky apertures. Observed that we
crossed no stream or brook of water within twelve or fifteen
miles of this fountain, but had in view vast savannas, swamps

and Cane meadows, at no great distance from our road, on our right hand, which we may presume were the resources or reservoirs which contributed to the supplies of this delightful grotto. Here were growing on the ascents from the fountain, Magnolia grandiflora, Laurus Borbonia, Quercus semper-virens, Callicarpa; at a little distance, a grove of the Cassine; and in an old field, just by, are to be seen some small Indian mounts. We travelled several miles over ridges of low swelling hills, whose surfaces were covered with particoloured pebbles, streaked and clouded with red, white, brown and yellow: they were mostly broken or shivered to pieces, I believe by the ancients in forming arrow-heads, darts, knives, &c., for I observed frequently some of these misshapen implements amongst them, some broken and others spoiled in the making. These stones seemed to be a species of jasper or agate.

On my way down I also called at Silver Bluff, and waited on the honourable G. Golphin, Esq. to acknowledge my obliga-tions to him, and likewise to fulfil my engagements on the part of Mr. T——y, trader of Mucclasse. Mr. Golphin assured me that he was in a disagreeable predicament, and that he feared the worst, but said he would do all in his power to save him.

After five days pleasant travelling we arrived at Savanna in good health.

List of the towns and tribes in league, and which constitute the powerful confederacy or empire of the Creeks or Mus-cogulges.

Towns on the Tallapoose or Oakfuske river, viz.

Oakfuske, upper.	
Oakfuske, lower.	
Ufale, upper.	
Ufale, lower.	
Sokaspoge.	
Tallase, great.	These speak the Muscogulge or
Coolome.	Creek tongue, called the
Chuaclahatche.	Mother tongue.
Otasse.	
Cluale.	
Fusahatche.	
Tuccabatche.	
Cunhutke.	

Towns on the Tallapoose or Oakfuske river, viz.

Mucclasse.	Speak the Stincard tongue.
Alabama.	
Savannuca.	Speak the Uche tongue.
Whittumke.	} Speak the Stincard tongue.
Coosaudda.	

Towns on the Coosau river, viz.

Abacooche.	Speaks a dialect of Chicasaw.
Pocontallahasse.	
Hiccory ground, (traders' name).	} Speak the Muscogulge tongue.
Natche.	Speaks Muscog. and Chicasaw.

Towns on the branches of the Coosau river, viz.

Wiccakaw.	
Fish pond, traders name.	} Speak the Muscogulge
Hillaba.	tongue.
Kiolege.	

Towns on the Apalachucla or Chata Uche river, viz.

Apalachucla.	
Tucpauska.	
Chockeclucca.	
Chata Uche.	
Checlucca-ninne.	} Speak the Muscogulge tongue.
Hothletega.	
Coweta.	
Usseta.	
Uche.	Speaks the Savannuca tongue.
Hooseche.	Speaks the Muscog. tongue.
Chehaw.	
Echeta.	
Occone.	} Speak the Stincard.
Swaglaw, great.	
Swaglaw, little.	

Towns on Flint river, comprehending the
Siminoles or Lower Creeks.

Suola-nocha.
Cuscowilla or Allachua.
Talahasochte.
Caloosahatche.

——Great island.	Traders name.
——Great hammock.	Traders name.
——Capon.	Traders name.
——St. Mark's.	Traders name.
——Forks.	Traders name.

With many others of less note.

The Siminoles speak both the Muscogulge and Stincard tongues.

In all fifty-five towns, besides many villages not enumerated; and reckoning two hundred inhabitants to each town on an average, which is a moderate computation, would give eleven thousand inhabitants.

It appears to me pretty clearly, from divers circumstances, that this powerful empire or confederacy of the Creeks or Muscogulges, arose from, and established itself upon, the ruins of that of the Natches, agreeably to monsieur Duprat. According to the Muscogulges account of themselves, they arrived from the South-West, beyond the Mississipi, some time before the English settled the colony of Carolina, and built Charleston; and their story concerning their country and people, from whence they sprang, the cause of leaving their native land, the progress of their migration, &c., is very similar to that celebrated historian's account of the Natches. They might have been included as allies and confederates in that vast and powerful empire of red men. The Muscogulges gradually pushing and extending their settlements on their North-East border, until the dissolution of the Natches empire; being then the most numerous, warlike and powerful tribe, they began to subjugate the various tribes or bands which formerly constituted the Natches, and uniting them with themselves, formed a new confederacy under the name of the Muscogulges.

The Muscogulge tongue is now the national or sovereign language; those of the Chicasaws, Chactaws, and even the remains of the Natches, if we are to credit the Creeks and traders, being dialects of the Muscogulge: and probably, when the Natches were sovereigns, they called their own the national tongue, and the Creeks, Chicasaws, &c., only dialects of theirs. It is uncertain which is really the mother tongue.

As for those numerous remnant bands or tribes, included at this day within the Muscogulge confederacy, who generally speak the Stincard language, (which is radically different from the Muscogulge) they are, beyond a doubt, the shattered remains of the various nations who inhabited the lower or maritime parts of Carolina and Florida, from Cape Fear, West to the Mississipi. The language of the Uches and Savannucas is a third radically different from the Muscogulge and Stincard, and seems to be a more Northern tongue; I suppose a language that prevailed amongst the numerous tribes who formerly possessed and inhabited the maritime parts of Maryland and Virginia. I was told by an old trader that the Savannucas and Shawanese speak the same language, or very near alike.

CHAP. IX.

AFTER my return from the Creek nation, I employed myself during the spring and fore part of summer, in revisiting the several districts in Georgia and the East borders of Florida, where I had noted the most curious subjects; collecting them together, and shipping them off to England. In the course of these excursions and researches, I had the opportunity of observing the new flowering shrub, resembling the Gordonia*, in perfect bloom, as well as bearing ripe fruit. It is a flowering tree, of the first order for beauty and fragrance of blossoms: the tree grows fifteen or twenty feet high, branching alternately; the leaves are oblong, broadest towards their extremities, and terminate with an acute point, which is generally a little reflexed; they are lightly serrated, attenuate downwards, and sessile, or have very short petioles; they are placed in alternate order, and towards the extremities of the twigs are crouded together, but stand more sparsedly below; the flowers are very large, expand themselves perfectly, are of a snow white colour, and ornamented with a crown or tassel of gold coloured refulgent staminæ in their centre, the inferior petal or segment of the corolla is hollow, formed like a cap or helmet, and entirely includes the other four, until the moment of expansion; its exterior surface is covered with a short silky hair; the borders of the petals are crisped or plicated: these large, white flowers stand single and sessile in the bosom of the leaves, and being near together towards the extremities of the twigs, and usually many expanded at the same time, make a gay appearance: the fruit is a large, round, dry, woody apple or pericarp, opening at each end oppositely by five alternate fissures, containing ten cells, each replete with dry woody cuneiform seed. This very curious tree was first taken notice

*On first observing the fructification and habit of this tree, I was inclined to believe it a species of Gordonia; but afterwards, upon stricter examination, and comparing its flowers and fruit with those of the Gordonia lasianthus, I presently found striking characteristics abundantly sufficient to separate it from that genus, and to establish it the head of a new tribe, which we have honoured with the name of the illustrious Dr. Benjamin Franklin. Franklinia Alatamaha.

of about ten or twelve years ago, at this place, when I attended my father (John Bartram) on a botanical excursion; but, it being then late in the autumn, we could form no opinion to what class or tribe it belonged.

We never saw it grow in any other place, nor have I ever since seen it growing wild, in all my travels, from Pennsylvania to Point Coupe, on the banks of the Mississipi, which must be allowed a very singular and unaccountable circumstance; at this place there are two or three acres of ground where it grows plentifully.

The other new, singular and beautiful shrub*, now here in full bloom, I never saw grow but at two other places in all my travels, and there very sparingly, except in East Florida, in the neighbourhood of the sea-coast.

*I gave it the name of Bignonia bracteate, extempore.

CHAP. X.

HAVING now completed my collections in Georgia, I took leave of these Southern regions, proceeding on my return to Charleston. Left Savanna in the evening, in consequence of a pressing invitation from the honourable Jonathan Bryan, Esq., who was returning from the capital, to his villa, about eight miles up Savanna river; a very delightful situation, where are spacious gardens, furnished with a variety of fruit trees and flowering shrubs. Observed in a low wet place at the corner of the garden, the Ado (Arum esculentum); this plant is much cultivated in the maritime parts of Georgia and Florida, for the sake of its large Turnip-like root, which when boiled or roasted, is excellent food, and tastes like the Yam; the leaves of this magnificent plant are very large, and of a beautiful green colour, the spatha large and circulated, the spadix terminates with a very long subulated tongue, naked and perfectly white: perhaps this may be the Arum Colocasia. They have likewise another species of the esculent Arum, called Tannier, which is a large and beautiful plant, and much cultivated and esteemed for food, particularly by the Negroes.

At night, soon after our arrival, several of his servants came home with horse loads of wild pigeons (Columba migratoria), which it seems they had collected in a short space of time at a neighbouring Bay swamp: they take them by torch light: the birds have particular roosting places, where they associate in incredible multitudes at evening, on low trees and bushes, in hommocks or higher knolls in the interior parts of vast swamps. Many people go out together on this kind of sport, when dark: some take with them little fascines of fat Pine splinters for torches; others sacks or bags; and others furnish themselves with poles or staves: thus accoutered and prepared, they approach the roosts; the sudden blaze of light confounds, blinds and affrights the birds, whereby multitudes drop off the limbs to the ground, and others are beaten off with the staves, being by the sudden consternation, entirely helpless, and easily taken and put into the sacks. It is chiefly the sweet small acorns of the Quercus phillos, Quercus aquatica, Quercus sempervirens, Quercus flammula, and others, which induce these birds to migrate in the autumn to those Southern regions; where they spend their days agreeably, and feast luxuriously, during the rigour of the colds in the North, whither they return at the approach of summer to breed.

Sat off next day, and crossed the river at Zubley's ferry, about fifty miles above Savanna, and in three days after arrived at Charleston.

Observed, by the way near Jacksonsburg, Ponpon, Aster fruticosus, growing plentifully in good moist ground, usually by the banks of canals. It is a most charming autumnal flowering shrub; it will rise to the height of eight or ten feet, when supported by neighbouring trees.

After a few days residence in Charleston, I sat off on my return to my native land; crossed Cowper river, about nine miles above the city, where the water was a mile wide, and the ferry-house being on the opposite shore, I hoisted my travelling blanket on a pole for a signal, which being white, the people soon came to me and carried me safe over. In three days more easy travelling, I crossed Winyaw bay, just below George town; and in two days more, got to the West end of Long bay, where I lodged at a large Indigo plantation. Sat off early next morning, and after crossing over the sand ridges, which afford little else but Quercus pumila, Myrica cerifera, Cassine, Sideroxylon and Andromeda entangled with various species of Smilax, got on the bay, which is a hard sand beach, exposed for the distance of fifteen miles to the continual lash of the Atlantic ocean. At about low water mark, are cliffs of rocks of the helmintholithus, being a very firm concrete or petrifaction, consisting of various kinds of seashells, fine sand and pulverized shells: there is a reef of these rocks, thirty or forty yards farther out than low water mark, which lift their rugged backs above water, and brave the continual strokes of the waves, which, however, assisted by the constant friction of the sands, make continual inroads upon them, and bore them into holes and cavities, when tempestuous seas rend them to pieces, scattering the fragments over the sandy shore. It is pleasant riding on this clean hard sand, paved with shells of various colours.

Observed a number of persons coming up a head, whom I soon perceived to be a party of Negroes. I had every reason to dread the consequence; for this being a desolate place, I was by this time several miles from any house or plantation, and had reason to apprehend this to be a predatory band of Negroes; people being frequently attacked, robbed, and sometimes murdered by them at this place. I was unarmed, alone, and my horse tired; thus situated every way in their power, I had no alternative but to be resigned and prepare to meet them. As soon as I saw them distinctly a mile or two off, I immediately alighted to rest, and give breath to my horse, intending to attempt my safety by flight, if upon near approach they should betray hostile designs. Thus prepared, when we drew near to each other, I mounted and rode briskly up; and though armed with clubs, axes and hoes, they opened to right and left, and let me pass peaceably. Their chief informed me whom they belonged to, and said they were going to man a new quarter at the West end of the bay; I however kept a sharp eye about me, apprehending that this might possibly have been an advanced division, and their intentions were to ambuscade and surround me; but they kept on quietly, and I was no more alarmed by them. After noon, I crossed the swash at the east end of the bay, and in the evening got to good quarters. Next morning early I sat off again, and soon crossed Little River at the boundary; which is on the line that separates North and South Carolina: in an old field, on the banks of this river, a little distance from the public house, stands a single tree of the Magnolia grandiflora, which is said to be the most northern settlement of that tree. Passed this day over expansive savannas, charmingly decorated with late autumnal flowers, as Helianthus, Rudbeckia, Silphium, Solidago, Helenium, Serratula, Cacalia, Aster, Lilium Martagon, Gentiana cærulea, Chironia, Gentiana saponaria, Asclepias coccinea, Hypericum, Rhexia pulcherrima, &c. &c.

Observed likewise in these Savannas abundance of the ludicrous Dionæa muscipula (Dionæa, Ellis epis. ad Linnæum, miraculum naturæ, folia biloba, radicalia, ciliata, conduplicanda, sensibilia, insecta incarcerantia. Syst. vegetab. p. 335).

This wonderful plant seems to be distinguished in the creation, by the Author of nature, with faculties eminently superior to every other vegetable production*; specimens of it were first communicated to the curious of the old world by John Bartram, the American botanist and traveller, who contributed as much, if not more, than any other man towards enriching the North American botanical nomenclature, as well as its natural history.

After traversing these ample savannas, I gradually ascended sand hills to open Pine forests; at evening got to Old town near Brunswick, where I lodged. Brunswick is a sea-port town on the Clarendon, or Cape Fear river, about thirty miles above the capes; it is about thirty years since this was the seat of government, when Arthur Dobbs, Esq. was governor and commander in chief of the province of North Carolina. Continued up the West side of North West of Cape Fear river, and rested two or three days at the seat of F. Lucas, Esq., a few miles above Livingston's creek, a considerable branch of the North West. This creek heads in vast swamps, in the vicinity of the beautiful lake Wakamaw, which is the source of a fine river of that name, and runs a South course seventy or eighty miles, delivering its waters into Winyaw bay at Georgetown. The Wakamaw lake is twenty six miles in circuit; the lands on its Eastern shores are fertile, and the situation delightful, gradually ascending from pleasing eminences; bounded on the North-West coast by vast rich swamps, fit for the production of Rice: the lake is twelve miles West from —— Moore's, Esq., whose villa is on the banks of the North West.

Proceeding again up the North West, crossed Carver's creek, and stopped at Ashwood, the ancient seat of Colonel William Bartram. The house stands on the high banks of the river, near seventy feet in height above the surface of the water; this high bluff continues two or three miles on the river, and commands a magnificent prospect of the low lands opposite, when in their native state, presenting to the view grand forests and expansive Cane meadows: the trees which compose these forests are generally of the following tribes, Quercus

---

*See some account of it in the introduction.

tinctoria, Querc. alba, Querc. phillos, Querc. aquatica, Querc. hemispherica, Fraxinus excelsior, Platanus occidentalis, Lirio-dendron tulipifera, Liquidambar styraciflua, Ulmus, Tilia, Jug-lans hiccory, Juglans cinerea, Juglans nigra, Morus rubra, Gle-ditsia triacanthus, Hopea tinctoria, Nyssa aquatica, Nyssa sylvatica, Carpinus and many more; the Cupressus disticha as stately and beautiful as I have seen any where. When these lands are cleared of their timber and cultivated, they produce abundantly, particularly, Wheat, Zea, Cotton, Hemp, Flax, with variety of excellent vegetables. This perpendicular bank of the river, by which the waters swiftly glide along, discovers at once the various strata of the earth of this low maritime country. For the most part, the upper stratum consists of a light, sandy, pale, yellowish mould or loam, for ten or twelve feet in depth (except the flat level land back from the rivers, where the clays or marle approach very near the surface, and the ridges of sand hills, where the clays lie much deeper): this sandy mould or loam lies upon a deep bed of black or dark slate coloured saline and sulphureous earth, which is com-posed of horizontal thin flakes or laminæ, separated by means of very thin, almost imperceptible veins or strata of fine mi-caceous particles, which drain or percolate a clear water, con-tinually exuding, or trickling down, and forming little rills and diminutive cataracts, being conducted by perpendicular chinks or fissures: in some places, a portion of this clear water or transparent vapour, seems to coagulate on the edges of the veins and fissures, leaving a reddish curd or jelly-like substance sticking to them, which I should suppose indicates it to spring from a ferruginous source, especially since it discovers a cha-lybeate scent and taste: in other places, these fissures show evidently a crystallization of exceeding fine white salts, which have an aluminous or vitriolic scent: they are pyrites, marca-sites, or sulphureous nodules, shining like brass, of various sizes and forms, some single and others conglomerated: other places present to view, strata of heterogeneous matter, lying between the upper loamy stratum and the bed of black saline earth, consisting of various kinds of sea shells, some whole, others broken to pieces, and even pulverized, which fill up the cavities of the entire shells, and the interstices betwixt them: at other places we observe, two or three feet below the surface or virgin mould, a stratum of four, five, or six feet in depth, of brownish marle, on a bed of testaceous rocks; a petrifaction composed apparently of various kinds of sea shells, belemnites, sand, &c., combined or united with a calcareous cement: these masses of rocks are in some places detached by veins and strata of a heterogeneous earth, consisting of sea shells and other marine productions, as well as terrestrial, which seem to be fossile, or in some degree of petrifaction, or otherwise transmuted, particularly those curious productions called birds bills, or sharks teeth (dentes carchariæ), belemnites, &c., loosely mixed with a desiccated earth composed of sand, clay, particles of marle, vegetable rubbish, &c. And again we observe shells, marcasites, belemnites, dentes carchariæ, with pieces of wood transmuted, black and hard as sea coal, singly interspersed in the black vitriolic strata of earth: when this black earth is exposed to the sun and dry air, the little thin laminæ separate, and soon discover a fine, white crystallization, or aluminous powder; but this very soon disappears, being again incorporated with the general mass, which gradually dissolves or falls like quick-lime, and appears then a grayish, extremely fine, dry micaceous powder, which smells like gunpowder.

The North West of Cape Fear, here at Ashwood, is near three hundred yards over (when the stream is low and within its banks), and is eighty or ninety miles above the capes. Observed growing hereabouts a great variety of very curious and beautiful flowering and sweet scented shrubs, particularly Callicarpa, Æsculus pavia, floribus coccineis, caule suffruticoso, Æsculus sylvatica, floribus ex albo et carneo eleganter variegatis, caule arboreo, Ptelea trifoliata, Styrax, Stewartia, Fothergilla, Amorpha, Myrica, Stillingia fruticosa, foliis lanceolatis, utrinque glabris, fructu tricocco, Olea Americana, foliis lanceolato-ellipticis, baccisatro-purpureis (Purple berried bay), Catesby, Ilex dahoon, Cassine Yapon, Azalea, varieties, Kalmea, Cyrilla, Liquidambar peregrinum, Sideroxylon, Andromeda lucida, &c.

Leaving Ashwood, and continuing up the West side of the river, about forty miles, in the banks of a creek, five or six feet below the sandy surface, are to be seen projecting out many feet in length, trunks of trees petrified to very hard stone; they lie between the upper sandy stratum and the common bed of blackish vitriolic earth; and these stone trees are to be seen in the same situation, sticking out of the perpendicular banks or bluffs of the river in this region: there are several trunks of large trees with their bark, stumps of their limbs and roots, lying petrified on the sand hills and Pine forests, near the road about this creek, not far from the saw-mills.

Crossed Rock-fish, a large branch of the North West, near its mouth or confluence, and at evening arrived at Cross-Creeks, another very considerable branch of the river, flowing in through its West banks. This creek gave name to a fine inland trading town, on some heights or swelling hills, from whence the creek descends precipitately, then gently meanders near a mile, through lower level lands, to its confluence with the river, affording most convenient mill-seats: these prospects induced active, enterprising men to avail themselves of such advantages pointed out to them by nature; they built mills, which drew people to the place, and these observing eligible situations for other profitable improvements, bought lots and erected tenements, where they exercised mechanic arts, as smiths, wheelwrights, carpenters, coopers, tanners, &c. And at length merchants were encouraged to adventure and settle: in short, within eight or ten years, from a grist-mill, saw-mill, smith-shop and a tavern, arose a flourishing commercial town, the seat of government of the county of Cumberland. The leading men of the county, seeing plainly the superior advantages of this situation, on the banks of a famous navigable river, petitioned the Assembly for a charter to empower them to purchase a district, sufficient for founding a large town; which being granted, they immediately proceeded to mark out its precincts, and named the new city Cambelton, a compliment to —— Cambel, Esq., a gentleman of merit, and a citizen of the county. When I was here about twenty years ago, this town was marking out its bounds, and there were then about twenty habitations; and now there are above a thousand houses, many wealthy merchants, and respectable public buildings, a vast resort of inhabitants and travellers, and continual brisk commerce by waggons, from the back settlements, with large trading boats, to and from Wilmington, the seaport and flourishing trading town on the Clarendon, about forty miles above the capes, which is about one hundred miles below this town. The Clarendon or Cape Fear river has its source in the Cherokee mountains, where its numerous confederate streams unite; after leaving the first ridges of the mountains, it assumes the name of Haw river, and coursing the hilly fertile country, above one hundred and fifty miles, receives through its West banks the West branch, called Deep River, and after this union, takes the name of the North-West of Cape Fear, from whence down to Cambelton, about eighty miles, it is navigable for perriauguas of considerable burthen.

Observed near Cambelton a very curious scandent Fern (Pteris scandens) rambling over low bushes, in humid situations; the lower larger fronds were digitated, or rather radiated, but towards the tops or extremities of the branches they became trifid, hastated, and lastly lanceolate: it is a delicate plant, of a yellowish lively green, and would be an ornament in a garden.

Sat off again to Cambelton, continuing yet up the North West about sixty miles; crossed over this branch, and soon after crossed the Roanoke, and then rested a few days at Mr. Lucas's a worthy old gentleman, a planter on Meherren river. Observed strolling over his fences and stables, a very singular and useful species of the Gourd (Cucurbita lagenaria); its neck or handle is above two feet in length, and not above an inch in diameter; its belly round, which would contain about a pint; it makes excellent ladles, funnels, &c. At a little distance from Mr. Lucas's, at the head of a swamp near the high road, I observed a very curious species of Prinos, which grows seven or eight feet high, the leaves broad, lanceolate, sharply serrated, nervous, and of a deep green colour; but its striking beauty consists in profuse clusters of fruit, collected about the cases or origin of the last spring's shoots; these berries are nearly round, about the size of middling grapes, of a fine clear scarlet colour, covered or invested with an incarnate mist or nebulæ.

Being now arrived on the South border of Virginia, and the hoary frigid season far advanced, I shall pass as speedily as possible from hence to Pennsylvania, my native country; since those cultivated regions of Virginia and Maryland, through which I design to travel, have been over and over explored, and described by very able men in every branch of natural history.

After leaving Meherren, I soon arrived at Alexandria in Virginia, a fine city on the West banks of the Patowmac, about the 26th of December, having had excellent roads, and pleasant, moderate weather, neither snow nor ice to be seen, except a slight fall of snow from a flying cloud, the day before I reached this place; but this evening it clouded up from the West, the wind North-east and cold. Next morning the snow was eight or ten inches deep on the ground, and the wind shifting to North-west, cleared up intensely cold: I however sat off and crossed the river just below the falls, and landed at Georgetown in Maryland. The snow was now deep every where around, the air cold to an extreme, and the roads deep under snow or slippery with ice, rendered the travelling uncomfortable.

Being now arrived at Wright's ferry, on the Susquehanna, I began anxiously to look towards home, but here I found almost insuperable embarrassments: the river being but half frozen over, there was no possibility of crossing here; but hearing that people crossed at Anderson's, about five miles above, early next morning I sat off again up the river, in company with several travellers, some for Philadelphia: arriving at the ferry, we were joined by a number of traders, with their pack-horses loaded with leather and furs, where we all agreed to venture over together; and keeping at a moderate distance from each other, examining well our icy bridge, and being careful of our steps, we landed safe on the opposite shore, got to Lancaster in the evening, and next morning sat forward again towards Philadelphia, and in two days more arrived at my father's house on the banks of the river Schuylkill, within four miles of the city, January 1778.

PART IV.

An Account of the
Persons, Manners, Customs and Government,
of the
Muscogulges, or Creeks,
Cherokees, Chactaws, &c.
Aborigines of the Continent of
North America.

CHAP. I.

DESCRIPTION OF THE CHARACTER, CUSTOMS AND
PERSONS OF THE AMERICAN ABORIGINES, FROM
MY OWN OBSERVATIONS, AS WELL AS FROM THE
GENERAL AND IMPARTIAL REPORT OF ANCIENT,
RESPECTABLE MEN, EITHER OF THEIR OWN
PEOPLE, OR WHITE TRADERS, WHO HAVE SPENT
MANY DAYS OF THEIR LIVES AMONGST THEM.

PERSONS and QUALIFICATIONS.

THE MALES of the Cherokees, Muscogulges, Siminoles, Chicasaws, Chactaws, and confederate tribes of the Creeks, are tall, erect, and moderately robust; their limbs well shaped, so as generally to form a perfect human figure; their features regular, and countenance open, dignified and placid; yet the forehead and brow so formed, as to strike you instantly with heroism and bravery; the eye though rather small, yet active and full of fire; the iris always black, and the nose commonly inclining to the aquiline.

Their countenance and actions exhibit an air of magnanimity, superiority and independence.

Their complexion, of a reddish brown or copper colour; their hair long, lank, coarse, and black as a raven, and reflecting the like lustre at different exposures to the light.

The women of the Cherokees, are tall, slender, erect and of a delicate frame; their features formed with perfect symmetry, their countenance cheerful and friendly, and they move with a becoming grace and dignity.

The Muscogulge women, though remarkably short of stature, are well formed; their visage round, features regular and beautiful; the brow high and arched; the eye large, black and languishing, expressive of modesty, diffidence, and bashfulness; these charms are their defensive and offensive weapons, and they know very well how to play them off, and under cover of these alluring graces, are concealed the most subtile artifice; they are however loving and affectionate: they are, I believe, the smallest race of women yet known, seldom above five feet high, and I believe the greater number never arrive to that stature; their hands and feet not larger than those of Europeans of nine or ten years of age: yet the men are of gigantic stature, a full size larger than Europeans; many of them above six feet, and few under that, or five feet eight or ten inches. Their complexion much darker than any of the tribes to the North of them that I have seen. This description will I believe comprehend the Muscogulges, their confederates, the Chactaws, and I believe the Chicasaws (though I have never seen their women), excepting however some bands of the Siminoles, Uches and Savannucas, who are rather taller and slenderer, and their complexion brighter.

The Cherokees are yet taller and more robust than the Muscogulges, and by far the largest race of men I have seen*; their complexions brighter and somewhat of the olive cast, especially the adults; and some of their young women are nearly as fair and blooming as European women.

The Cherokees in their dispositions and manners are grave and steady; dignified and circumspect in their deportment; rather slow and reserved in conversation; yet frank, cheerful, and humane; tenacious of the liberties and natural rights of man; secret, deliberate and determined in their councils; honest, just and liberal, and ready always to sacrifice every pleasure and gratification, even their blood, and life itself, to defend

---

*There are, however, some exceptions to this general observation, as I have myself witnessed. Their present grand chief or emperor (the Little Carpenter, Atta-kul-kulla) is a man of remarkably small stature, slender, and of a delicate frame, the only instance I saw in the nation: but he is a man of superior abilities.

their territory and maintain their rights. They do homage to the Muscogulges with reluctance, and are impatient under that galling yoke. I was witness to a most humiliating lash, which they passively received from their red masters, at the great congress and treaty of Augusta, when these people acceded with the Creeks, to the cession of the New Purchase; where were about three hundred of the Creeks, a great part of whom were warriors, and about one hundred Cherokees.

The first day of convention opened with settling the preliminaries, one article of which was a demand on the part of the Georgians, to a territory lying on the Tugilo, and claimed by them both, which it seems the Cherokees had, previous to the opening of congress, privately conveyed to the Georgians, unknown to the Creeks. The Georgians mentioning this as a matter settled, the Creeks demanded in council, on what foundation they built that claim, saying they had never ceded these lands. The Georgians answered, that they bought them of their friends and brothers the Cherokees. The Creeks nettled and incensed at this, a chief and warrior started up, and with an agitated and terrific countenance, frowning menaces and disdain, fixed his eyes on the Cherokee chiefs, and asked them what right they had to give away their lands, calling them old women, and saying they had long ago obliged them to wear the petticoat; a most humiliating and degrading stroke, in the presence of the chiefs of the whole Muscogulge confederacy, of the Chicasaws, principal men and citizens of Georgia, Carolina, Virginia, Maryland and Pennsylvania, in the face of their own chiefs and citizens, and amidst the laugh and jeers of the assembly, especially the young men of Virginia, their old enemies and dreaded neighbours: but humiliating as it really was, they were obliged to bear the stigma passively, and even without a reply.

And moreover, these arrogant bravos and usurpers carried their pride and importance to such lengths, as even to threaten to dissolve the congress and return home, unless the Georgians consented to annul the secret treaty with the Cherokees, and receive that territory immediately from them, as acknowledging their exclusive right of alienation; which was complied with, though violently extorted from the Cherokees, contrary to right and sanction of treaties; since the Savanna river and its waters were acknowledged to be the natural and just bounds of territory betwixt the Cherokees and Muscogulges.

The national character of the Muscogulges, when considered in a political view, exhibits a portraiture of a great or illustrious heroe. A proud, haughty and arrogant race of men; they are brave and valiant in war, ambitious of conquest, restless and perpetually exercising their arms, yet magnanimous and merciful to a vanquished enemy, when he submits and seeks their friendship and protection: always uniting the vanquished tribes in confederacy with them; when they immediately enjoy, unexceptionably, every right of free citizens, and are from that moment united in one common band of brotherhood. They were never known to exterminate a tribe, except the Yamasees, who would never submit on any terms, but fought it out to the last, only about forty or fifty of them escaping at the last decisive battle, who threw themselves under the protection of the Spaniards at St. Augustine.

According to their own account, which I believe to be true, after their arrival in this country, they joined in alliance and perpetual amity with the British colonists of South Carolina and Georgia, which they never openly violated; but on the contrary, pursued every step to strengthen the alliance; and their aged chiefs to this day, speak of it with tears of joy, and exult in that memorable transaction, as one of the most glorious events in the annals of their nation.

As an instance of their ideas of political impartial justice, and homage to the Supreme Being, as the high arbiter of human transactions, who alone claims the right of taking away the life of man, I beg leave to offer to the reader's consideration, the following event, as I had it from the mouth of a Spaniard, a respectable inhabitant of East Florida.

The son of the Spanish governor of St. Augustine, together with two young gentlemen, his friends and associates, conceived a design of amusing themselves in a party of sport, at hunting and fishing. Having provided themselves with a convenient bark, ammunition, fishing tackle, &c., they set sail, directing their course South, along the coast, towards the point of Florida, putting into bays and rivers, as conveniency and the prospect of game invited them. The pleasing rural and diversified scenes of the Florida coast, imperceptibly allured them far to the south, beyond the Spanish fortified post. Unfortunate youths! regardless of the advice and injunctions of their parents and friends, still pursuing the delusive objects, they entered a harbour at evening, with a view of chasing the roe-buck, and hunting up the sturdy bear, solacing themselves with delicious fruits, and reposing under aromatic shades; when, alas! cruel unexpected event! in the beatific moments of their slumbers, they were surrounded, arrested and carried off by a predatory band of Creek Indians, proud of the capture, so rich a prize; they hurry away into cruel bondage the hapless youths, conducting them by devious paths through dreary swamps and boundless savannas, to the Nation.

At that time the Indians were at furious war with the Spaniards, scarcely any bounds set to their cruelties on either side: in short, the miserable youths were condemned to be burnt.

But there were English traders in these towns, who learning the character of the captives, and expecting great rewards from the Spanish governor, if they could deliver them, petitioned the Indians on their behalf, expressing their wishes to obtain their rescue, offering a great ransom; acquainting them at the same time, that they were young men of high rank, and one of them the governor's son.

Upon this, the head men, or chiefs of the whole nation, were convened, and after solemn and mature deliberation, they returned the traders their final answer and determination, which was as follows:

"Brothers and friends. We have been considering upon this business concerning the captives—and that, under the eye and fear of the Great Spirit. You know that these people are our cruel enemies; they save no lives of us red men, who fall in their power. You say that the youth is the son of the Spanish governor; we believe it; we are sorry he has fallen into our hands, but he is our enemy: the two young men (his friends) are equally our enemies; we are sorry to see them here; but we know no difference in their flesh and blood; they are equally our enemies; if we save one we must save all three: but we cannot do it; the red men require their blood to appease the spirits of their slain relatives; they have entrusted us with the guardianship of our laws and rights, we cannot betray them.

"However, we have a sacred prescription relative to this affair, which allows us to extend mercy to a certain degree: a third is saved by lot; the Great Spirit allows us to put it to that decision; he is no respecter of persons." The lots were cast. The governor's son was taken and burnt.

If we consider them with respect to their private character or in a moral view, they must, I think, claim our approbation, if we divest ourselves of prejudice and think freely. As moral men they certainly stand in no need of European civilization.

They are just, honest, liberal and hospitable to strangers; considerate, loving and affectionate to their wives and relations; fond of their children; industrious, frugal, temperate and persevering; charitable and forbearing. I have been weeks and months amongst them and in their towns, and never observed the least sign of contention or wrangling: never saw an instance of an Indian beating his wife, or even reproving her in anger. In this case they stand as examples of reproof to the most civilized nations, as not being defective in justice, gratitude and a good understanding; for indeed their wives merit their esteem and the most gentle treatment, they being industrious, frugal, careful, loving and affectionate.

The Muscogulges are more volatile, sprightly and talkative than their Northern neighbours, the Cherokees; and, though far more distant from the white settlements than any nation East of the Mississipi or Ohio, appear evidently to have made greater advances towards the refinements of true civilization, which cannot, in the least degree, be attributed to the good examples of the white people.

Their internal police and family economy at once engage the notice of European travellers, and incontrovertibly place these people in an illustrious point of view: their liberality, intimacy and friendly intercourse one with another, without any restraint of ceremonious formality, as if they were even insensible of the use or necessity of associating the passions or affections of avarice, ambition or covetousness.

A man goes forth on his business or avocations; he calls in at another town; if he wants victuals, rest or social conversation, he confidently approaches the door of the first house he chooses, saying "I am come;" the good man or woman replies, "You are; it's well." Immediately victuals and drink are ready; he eats and drinks a little, then smokes tobacco, and converses either of private matters, public talks, or the news of the town. He rises and says, "I go!" the other answers, "You do!" He then proceeds again, and steps in at the next habitation he likes, or repairs to the public square, where are people always conversing by day, or dancing all night, or to some more private assembly, as he likes; he needs no one to introduce him, any more than the black-bird or thrush, when he repairs to the fruitful groves, to regale on their luxuries, and entertain the fond female with evening songs.

It is astonishing, though a fact, as well as a sharp reproof to the white people, if they will allow themselves liberty to reflect and form a just estimate, and I must own elevates these people to the first rank amongst mankind, that they have been able to resist the continual efforts of the complicated host of vices, that have for ages over-run the nations of the old world, and so contaminated their morals; yet more so, since such vast armies of these evil spirits have invaded this continent, and closely invested them on all sides. Astonishing indeed! when we behold the ill, immoral conduct of too many white people, who reside amongst them: notwithstanding which, it seems natural, eligible, and even easy, for these simple, illiterate people, to put in practice those beautiful lectures delivered to us by the ancient sages and philosophers, and recorded for our instruction.

I saw a young Indian in the Nation, who when present, and beholding the scenes of mad intemperance and folly acted by the white men in the town, clapped his hand to his breast, and with a smile, looked aloft as if struck with astonishment, and wrapt in love and adoration to the Deity; as who should say, "O thou Great and Good Spirit! we are indeed sensible of thy benignity and favour to us red men, in denying us the understanding of white men. We did not know before they came amongst us that mankind could become so base, and fall so below the dignity of their nature. Defend us from their manners, laws and power."

The Muscogulges, with their confederates, the Chactaws, Chicasaws, and perhaps the Cherokees, eminently deserve the encomium of all nations, for their wisdom and virtue in resisting and even repelling the greatest, and even the common enemy of mankind, at least of most of the European nations, I mean spirituous liquors.

The first and most cogent article in all their treaties with the white people, is, that there shall not be any kind of spirituous liquors sold or brought into their towns; and the traders are allowed but two kegs (five gallons each) which is supposed to be sufficient for a company, to serve them on the road; and if any of this remains on their approaching the towns, they must spill it on the ground or secrete it on the road, for it must not come into the town.

On my journey from Mobile to the Nation, just after we had passed the junction of the Pensacola road with our path, two young traders overtook us on their way to the Nation. We inquired what news? They informed us that they were running about forty kegs of Jamaica spirits (which by dashing would have made at least eighty kegs) to the Nation; and after having left the town three or four days, they were surprised on the road in the evening, just after they had come to camp, by a party of Creeks, who discovering their species of merchandize, they forthwith struck their tomahawks into every keg, giving the liquor to the thirsty sand, not tasting a drop of it themselves; and they had enough to do to keep the tomahawks from their own skulls.

How are we to account for their excellent policy in civil government; it cannot derive its influence from coercive laws, for they have no such artificial system. Divine wisdom dictates and they obey.

We see and know full well the direful effects of this torrent of evil, which has its source in hell; and we know surely, as well as these savages, how to divert its course and suppress its inundations. Do we want wisdom and virtue? let our youth then repair to the venerable councils of the Muscogulges.

CHAP. II.

ON THEIR GOVERNMENT AND CIVIL SOCIETY.

THE constitution or system of their police is simply natural, and as little complicated as that which is supposed to direct or rule the approved economy of the ant and the bee; and seems to be nothing more than the simple dictates of natural reason, plain to every one, yet recommended to them by their wise and virtuous elders as divine, because necessary for securing mutual happiness: equally binding and effectual, as being proposed and assented to in the general combination: every one's conscience being a sufficient conviction (the golden rule, do as you would be done by) instantly presents to view, and produces a society of peace and love, which in effect better maintains human happiness, than the most complicated system of modern politics, or sumptuary laws, enforced by coercive means: for here the people are all on an equality, as to the possession and enjoyments of the common necessaries and conveniences of life, for luxuries and superfluities they have none.

This natural constitution is simply subordinate; and the supreme, sovereign or executive power resides in a council of elderly chiefs, warriors and others, respectable for wisdom, valour and virtue.

At the head of this venerable senate, presides their mico or king, which signifies a magistrate or chief ruler: the governors of Carolina, Georgia, &c., are called micos; and the king of England is called Ant-apala-mico-clucco*, that is the great king, over or beyond the great water.

The king, although he is acknowledged to be the first and greatest man in the town or tribe, and honoured with every due and rational mark of love and esteem, and when presiding in council, with a humility and homage as reverent as that paid to the most despotic monarch in Europe or the East, and when absent, his seat is not filled by any other person, yet he is not dreaded; and when out of the council, he associates

*Clucco signifies great or excellent.

with the people as a common man, converses with them, and they with him, in perfect ease and familiarity.

The mico or king, though elective, yet his advancement to that supreme dignity must be understood in a very different light from the elective monarchs of the old world, where the progress to magistracy is generally effected by schism and the influence of friends gained by craft, bribery, and often by more violent efforts; and after the throne is obtained, by measures little better than usurpation, he must be protected and supported there, by the same base means that carried him thither.

But here behold the majesty of the Muscogulge mico! he does not either publicly or privately beg of the people to place him in a situation to command and rule them: no, his appearance is altogether mysterious; as a beneficent deity he rises king over them, as the sun rises to bless the earth!

No one will tell you how or when he became their king; but he is universally acknowledged to be the greatest person among them, and he is loved, esteemed and reverenced, although he associates, eats, drinks and dances with them in common as another man; his dress is the same, and a stranger could not distinguish the king's habitation, from that of any other citizen, by any sort of splendour or magnificence; yet he perceives they act as though their mico beheld them, himself invisible. In a word, their mico seems to them the representative of Providence or the Great Spirit, whom they acknowledge to preside over and influence their councils and public proceedings. He personally presides daily in their councils, either at the rotunda or public square: and even here his voice, in regard to business in hand, is regarded no more, than any other chief's or senator's, no farther than his advice, as being the best and wisest man of the tribe, and not by virtue of regal prerogative. But whether their ultimate decisions require unanimity, or only a majority of voices, I am uncertain; but probably where there is a majority, the minority voluntarily accede.

The most active part the mico takes is in the civil government of the town or tribe: here he has the power and prerogative of calling a council, to deliberate on peace and war, or all public concerns, as inquiring into, and deciding upon complaints and differences; but he has not the least shadow of exclusive executive power. He is complimented with the first visits of strangers, giving audience to ambassadors, with presents, and he has also the disposal of the public granary.

The next man in order of dignity and power, is the great war chief: he represents and exercises the dignity of the mico, in his absence, in council; his voice is of the greatest weight, in military affairs; his power and authority are entirely independent of the mico, though when a mico goes on an expedition, he heads the army, and is there the war chief. There are many of these war chiefs in a town or tribe, who are captains or leaders of military parties; they are elderly men, who in their youthful days have distinguished themselves in war by valour, subtility and intrepidity; and these veteran chiefs, in a great degree, constitute their truly dignified and venerable senates.

There is in every town or tribe a high priest, usually called by the white people jugglers, or conjurers, besides several juniors or graduates. But the ancient high priest or seer, presides in spiritual affairs, and is a person of consequence; he maintains and exercises great influence in the state, particularly in military affairs; the senate never determine on an expedition against their enemy without his counsel and assistance. These people generally believe that their seer has communion with powerful invisible spirits, who they suppose have a share in the rule and government of human affairs, as well as the elements; that he can predict the result of an expedition; and his influence is so great, that they have been known frequently to stop, and turn back an army, when within a days journey of their enemy, after a march of several hundred miles; and indeed their predictions have surprized many people. They foretel rain or drought, and pretend to bring rain at pleasure, cure diseases, and exercise witchcraft, invoke or expel evil spirits, and even assume the power of directing thunder and lightning.

These Indians are by no means idolaters, unless their puffing the tobacco smoke towards the sun, and rejoicing at the appearance of the new moon*, may be termed so. So far from

* I have observed the young fellows very merry and jocose, at the appearance of the new moon, saying, how ashamed she looks under the veil, since sleeping with the sun these two or three nights, she is ashamed to show her face, &c.

idolatry are they, that they have no images amongst them, nor any religious rite or ceremony that I could perceive; but adore the Great Spirit, the giver and taker away of the breath of life, with the most profound and respectful homage. They believe in a future state, where the spirit exists, which they call the world of spirits, where they enjoy different degrees of tranquillity or comfort, agreeably to their life spent here: a person who in his life has been an industrious hunter, provided well for his family, an intrepid and active warrior, just, upright, and done all the good he could, will, they say, in the world of spirits, live in a warm, pleasant country, where are expansive, green, flowery savannas and high forests, watered with rivers of pure waters, replenished with deer, and every species of game; a serene, unclouded and peaceful sky; in short, where there is fulness of pleasure, uninterrupted.

They have many accounts of trances and visions of their people, who have been supposed to be dead, but afterwards reviving, have related their visions, which tend to enforce the practice of virtue and the moral duties.

Before I went amongst the Indians, I had often heard it reported, that these people, when their parents, through extreme old age, become decrepid and helpless, in compassion for their miseries, send them to the other world, by a stroke of the tomahawk or bullet. Such a degree of depravity and species of impiety always appeared to me so incredibly inhuman and horrid, that it was with the utmost difficulty I assumed resolution sufficient to inquire into it.

The traders assured me that they knew no instance of such barbarism; but that there had been instances of the communities performing such a deed at the earnest request of the victim.

When I was at Mucclasse town, early one morning, at the invitation of the chief trader, we repaired to the public square, taking with us some presents for the Indian chiefs. On our arrival we took our seats in a circle of venerable men, round a fire in the centre of the area: other citizens were continually coming in, and amongst them I was struck with awe and veneration at the appearance of a very aged man; his hair, what little he had, was as white as snow; he was conducted by three young men, one having hold of each arm, and the third behind to steady him. On his approach the whole circle saluted him, "welcome," and made way for him: he looked as smiling and cheerful as youth, yet stone-blind by extreme old age: he was the most ancient chief of the town, and they all seemed to reverence him. Soon after the old man had seated himself, I distributed my presents, giving him a very fine handkerchief and a twist of choice tobacco, which passed through the hands of an elderly chief who sat next him, telling him it was a present from one of their white brothers, lately arrived in the nation from Charleston: he received the present with a smile, and thanked me, returning the favour immediately with his own stone pipe and cat skin of tobacco: and then complimented me with a long oration, the purport of which was the value he set on the friendship of the Carolinians. He said, that when he was a young man they had no iron hatchets, pots, hoes, knives, razors nor guns, that they then made use of their own stone axes, clay pots, flint knives, bows and arrows; and that he was the first man who brought the white people's goods into his town, which he did on his back from Charleston, five hundred miles on foot, for they had no horses then amongst them.

The trader then related to me an anecdote concerning this ancient patriarch, which occurred not long before.

One morning after his attendants had led him to the council fire, before seating himself, he addressed himself to the people after this manner—

"You yet love me; what can I do now to merit your regard? nothing; I am good for nothing; I cannot see to shoot the buck or hunt up the sturdy bear; I know I am but a burthen to you; I have lived long enough; now let my spirit go; I want to see the warriors of my youth in the country of spirits: (bareing his breast) here is the hatchet, take it and strike." They answered with one united voice, "We will not; we cannot; we want you here."

CHAP. III.

THE YOUTH of both sexes are fond of decorating themselves with external ornaments. The men shave their head, leaving only a narrow crest or comb, beginning at the crown of the head, where it is about two inches broad and about the same height, and stands frized upright; but this crest tending backwards, gradually widens, covering the hinder part of the head and back of the neck: the lank hair behind is ornamented with pendant silver quills, and then jointed or articulated silver plates; and usually the middle fascicle of hair, being by far the longest, is wrapped in a large quill of silver, or the joint of a small reed, curiously sculptured and painted, the hair continuing through it terminates in a tail or tassel.

Their ears are lacerated, separating the border or cartilaginous limb, which at first is bound round very close and tight with leather strings or thongs, and anointed with fresh bear's oil, until healed: a piece of lead being fastened to it, by its weight extends this cartilage an incredible length, which afterwards being craped, or bound round in brass or silver wire, extends semicircularly like a bow or crescent; and it is then very elastic, even so as to spring and bound about with the least motion or flexure of the body: this is decorated with soft white plumes of heron feathers.

A very curious diadem or band, about four inches broad, and ingeniously wrought or woven, and curiously decorated with stones, beads, wampum, porcupine quills, &c., encircles their temples; the front peak of it being embellished with a high waving plume, of crane or heron feathers.

The clothing of their body is very simple and frugal. Sometimes a ruffled shirt of fine linen, next the skin, and a flap, which covers their lower parts; this garment somewhat resembles the ancient Roman breeches, or the kilt of the Highlanders; it usually consists of a piece of blue cloth, about eighteen inches wide; this they pass between their thighs, and both ends being taken up and drawn through a belt round their waist, the ends fall down, one before, and the other behind, not quite to the knee; this flap is usually plaited and indented at the ends, and ornamented with beads, tinsel lace, &c.

The leg is furnished with cloth boots; they reach from the ancle to the calf, and are ornamented with lace, beads, silver bells, &c.

The stillepica or moccasin defends and adorns the feet; it seems to be an imitation of the ancient buskin or sandal, very ingeniously made of deer skins, dressed very soft, and curiously ornamented according to fancy.

Beside this attire, they have a large mantle of the finest cloth they are able to purchase, always either of a scarlet or blue colour; this mantle is fancifully decorated with rich lace or fringe round the border, and often with little round silver, or brass bells. Some have a short cloak, just large enough to cover the shoulders and breast; this is most ingeniously constructed, of feathers woven or placed in a natural imbricated manner, usually of the scarlet feathers of the flamingo, or others of the gayest colour.

They have large silver crescents, or gorgets, which being suspended by a ribband round the neck, lie upon the breast; and the arms are ornamented with silver bands, or bracelets, and silver and gold chains, &c. a collar invests the neck.

The head, neck and breast, are painted with vermillion, and some of the warriors have the skin of the breast, and muscular parts of the body, very curiously inscribed, or adorned, with hieroglyphick scrolls, flowers, figures of animals, stars, crescents, and the sun in the centre of the breast. This painting of the flesh, I understand, is performed in their youth, by pricking the skin with a needle, until the blood starts, and rubbing in a blueish tinct, which is as permanent as their life. The shirt hangs loose about the waist, like a frock, or split down before, resembling a gown, and is sometimes wrapped close, and the waist encircled by a curious belt or sash.

The dress of the females is somewhat different from that of the men: their flap or petticoat is made after a different manner, is larger and longer, reaching almost to the middle of the leg, and is put on differently; they have no shirt or shift, but a little short waistcoat, usually made of callico, printed linen, or fine cloth, decorated with lace, beads, &c. They never wear boots or stockings, but their buskins reach to the middle of the leg. They never cut their hair, but plait it in wreaths, which are turned up, and fastened on the crown, with a silver broach, forming a wreathed top-knot, decorated with an incredible quantity of silk ribbands, of various colours, which stream down on every side, almost, to the ground. They never paint, except those of a particular class, when disposed to grant certain favours to the other sex.

But these decorations are only to be considered as indulgencies on particular occasions, and the privilege of youth; as at weddings, festivals, dances, &c., or when the men assemble to act the war farce, on the evening immediately preceding their march on a hostile expedition: for usually they are almost naked, contenting themselves with the flap and sometimes a shirt, boots and moccasins. The mantle is seldom worn by the men, except at night, in the winter season, when extremely cold; and by the women at dances, when it serves the purpose of a veil; and the females always wear the jacket, flap, and buskin, even children as soon or before they can walk; whereas the male youth go perfectly naked until they are twelve or fifteen years of age.

The junior priests or students constantly wear the mantle or robe, which is white; and they have a great owl skin cased and stuffed very ingeniously, so well executed, as almost to represent the living bird, having large sparkling glass beads, or buttons, fixed in the head for eyes: this ensign of wisdom and divination, they wear sometimes as a crest on the top of the head, at other times the image fits on the arm, or is borne on the hand. These bachelors are also distinguishable from the other people, by their taciturnity, grave and solemn countenance, dignified step, and singing to themselves songs or hymns, in a low sweet voice, as they stroll about the towns.

These people like all other nations, are fond of music and dancing: their music is both vocal and instrumental; but of the latter they have scarcely any thing worth the name; the tambour, rattle-gourd, and a kind of flute, made of a joint of reed or the tibia of the deer's leg: on this instrument they perform badly, and at best it is rather a hideous melancholy discord, than harmony. It is only young fellows who amuse themselves on this howling instrument; but the tambour and rattle, accompanied with their sweet low voices, produce a pathetic harmony, keeping exact time together, and the countenance of the musician, at proper times, seems to express the solemn elevated state of the mind: at that time there seems not only a harmony between him and his instrument, but it instantly touches the feelings of the attentive audience, as the influence of an active and powerful spirit; there is then an united universal sensation of delight and peaceful union of souls throughout the assembly.

Their music, vocal and instrumental, united, keeps exact time with the performers or dancers.

They have an endless variety of steps, but the most common, and that which I term the most civil, and indeed the most admired and practised amongst themselves, is a slow shuffling alternate step; both feet move forward one after the other, first the right foot foremost, and next the left, moving one after the other, in opposite circles, i. e. first a circle of young men, and within, a circle of young women, moving together opposite ways, the men with the course of the sun, and the females contrary to it; the men strike their arm with the open hand, and the girls clap hands, and raise their shrill sweet voices, answering an elevated shout of the men at stated times of termination of the stanzas; and the girls perform an interlude or chorus separately.

To accompany their dances they have songs, of different classes, as martial, bacchanalian and amorous; which last, I must confess, are extravagantly libidinous; and they have moral songs, which seem to be the most esteemed and practised, and answer the purpose of religious lectures.

Some of their most favourite songs and dances, they have from their enemies, the Chactaws; for it seems these people are very eminent for poetry and music; every town amongst them strives to excel each other in composing new songs for dances; and by a custom amongst them, they must have at least one new song, for exhibition, at every annual busk.

The young mustee, who came with me to the Mucclasses from Mobile, having Chactaw blood in his veins from his mother, was a sensible young fellow, and by his father had been instructed in reading, writing and arithmetic, and could speak

English very well. He took it into his head to travel into the Chactaw country: his views were magnanimous, and his designs in the highest degree commendable, nothing less than to inform himself of every species of arts and sciences, that might be of use and advantage when introduced into his own country, but more particularly music and poetry. With these views he privately left the Nation, went to Mobile, and there entered into the service of the trading company to the Chactaws, as a white man; his easy, communicative, active and familiar disposition and manners, being agreeable to that people, procured him access every where, and favoured his subtilty and artifice: at length, however, the Chactaws hearing of his lineage and consanguinity with the Creeks, by the father's side, pronounced him a Creek, and consequently an enemy and a spy amongst them, and secretly resolved to dispatch him. The young philosopher got notice of their suspicions, and hostile intentions, in time to make his escape; though closely pursued, he kept a head of his sanguinary pursuers, arrived at Mobile, and threw himself under the protection of the English, entered the service of the trader of Mucclasse, who was then setting off for the Nation, and notwithstanding the speed with which we travelled, narrowly escaped the ardour and vigilance of his pursuing enemies, who surprised a company of emigrants, in the desarts of Schambe, the very night after we met them, expecting to intercept him thereabout.

The young traveller having learned all their most celebrated new songs and poetry, at a great dance and festival in the Mucclasse, a day or two after our arrival, the youth pressed him to give out some of his new songs; he complied with their entreaties, and the songs and dance went round with harmony and eclat. There was a young Chactaw slave girl in the circle, who soon after discovered very affecting sensations of affliction and distress of mind, and before the conclusion of the dance, many of her companions complimented her with sympathetic sighs and tears, from their own sparkling eyes. As soon as I had an opportunity, I inquired of the young Orpheus, the cause of that song being so distressing to the young slave. He replied, that when she was lately taken captive, her father and brothers were slain in the contest, and she understanding the sense of the song, called to remembrance the tragical fate of her family, and could not forbear weeping at the recital.

The meaning of the chorus was,

> All men must surely die,
> Tho' no one knows how soon,
> Yet when the time shall come,
> The event may be joyful.

These doleful moral songs or elegies, have a quick and sensible effect on their passions, and discover a lively affection and sensibility: their countenance now dejected, again, by an easy transition, becomes gently elevated, as if in solemn address or supplication, accompanied with a tremulous, sweet, lamentable voice: a stranger is for a moment lost to himself as it were, or his mind, associated with the person immediately affected, is in danger of revealing his own distress unawares.

They have a variety of games for exercise and pastime; some particular to the men, some to the female sex, and others wherein both sexes are engaged.

The ball play is esteemed the most noble and manly exercise. This game is exhibited in an extensive level plain, usually contiguous to the town: the inhabitants of one town play against another, in consequence of a challenge, when the youth of both sexes are often engaged, and sometimes stake their whole substance. Here they perform amazing feats of strength and agility. The game principally consists in taking and carrying off the ball from the opposite party, after being hurled into the air, midway between two high pillars, which are the goals, and the party who bears off the ball to their pillar wins the game; each person has a racquet or hurl, which is an implement of a very curious construction, somewhat resembling a ladle or little hoop-net, with a handle near three feet in length, the hoop and handle of wood, and the netting of thongs of raw hide, or tendons of an animal.

The foot ball is likewise a favourite, manly diversion with them. Feasting and dancing in the square at evening, ends all their games.

They have besides, feasts or festivals almost for every month in the year, which are chiefly dedicated to hunting and agriculture.

The busk, or feast of first fruits, is their principal festival; this seems to end the last, and begin the new year.

It commences in August, when their new crops of corn are arrived to perfect maturity: and every town celebrates the busk separately, when their own harvest is ready.

If they have any religious rite or ceremony, this festival is its most solemn celebration.

When a town celebrates the busk, having previously provided themselves with new cloaths, new pots, pans and other household utensils and furniture, they collect all their worn out clothes and other despicable things, sweep and cleanse their houses, squares, and the whole town, of their filth, which with all the remaining grain and other old provisions, they cast together into one common heap, and consume it with fire. After having taken medicine, and fasted for three days, all the fire in the town is extinguished. During this fast they abstain from the gratification of every appetite and passion whatever. A general amnesty is proclaimed, all malefactors may return to their town, and they are absolved from their crimes, which are now forgotten, and they restored to favour.

On the fourth morning, the high priest, by rubbing dry wood together, produces new fire in the public square, from whence every habitation in the town is supplied with the new and pure flame.

Then the women go forth to the harvest field, and bring from thence new corn and fruits, which being prepared in the best manner, in various dishes, and drink withal, is brought with solemnity to the square, where the people are assembled, apparelled in their new clothes and decorations. The men having regaled themselves, the remainder is carried off and distributed amongst the families of the town. The women and children solace themselves in their separate families, and in the evening repair to the public square, where they dance, sing, and rejoice during the whole night, observing a proper and exemplary decorum: this continues three days, and the four following days they receive visits, and rejoice with their friends from neighbouring towns, who have purified and prepared themselves.

CHAP. IV.

CONCERNING PROPERTY, AGRICULTURE, ARTS AND MANUFACTURES.

IT HAS been said by historians, who have written concerning the customs and usages of the aborigines of America, that they have every thing in common, and no private property; which are terms in my opinion too vague and general, when applied to these people. From my own frequent opportunities of observation, and the information of respectable characters, who have spent many years amongst them, I venture to set this matter in a just view before my readers.

I shall begin with the produce of their agricultural labours.

An Indian town is generally so situated, as to be convenient for procuring game, secure from sudden invasion, having a large district of excellent arable land adjoining, or in its vicinity, if possible on an isthmus betwixt two waters, or where the doubling of a river forms a peninsula. Such a situation generally comprises a sufficient body of excellent land for planting Corn, Potatoes, Beans, Squash, Pumpkins, Citruls, Melons, &c., and is taken in with a small expence and trouble of fencing, to secure the crops from the invasion of predatory animals. At other times however they choose such a convenient fertile spot at some distance from their town, when circumstances will not admit of having both together.

This is their common plantation, and the whole town plant in one vast field together; but yet the part or share of every individual family or habitation, is separated from the next adjoining, by a narrow strip, or verge of grass, or any other natural or artificial boundary.

In the spring, the ground being already prepared, on one and the same day, early in the morning, the whole town is summoned, by the sound of a conch shell, from the mouth of the overseer, to meet at the public square, whither the people repair with their hoes and axes; and from thence proceed to their plantation, where they begin to plant, not every one in his own little district, assigned and laid out, but the whole community united begins on one certain part of the field, where they plant on until finished; and when their rising crops are ready for dressing and cleansing, they proceed after the same order, and so on day after day, until the crop is laid by for ripening. After the feast of the busk is over, and all the grain is ripe, the whole town again assemble, and every man carries off the fruits of his labour, from the part first allotted to him, which he deposits in his own granary; which is individually his own. But previous to their carrying off their crops from the field, there is a large crib or granary, erected in the plantation, which is called the king's crib; and to this each family carries and deposits a certain quantity, according to his ability or inclination, or none at all if he so chooses: this in appearance seems a tribute or revenue to the mico; but in fact is designed for another purpose, i. e. that of a public treasury, supplied by a few and voluntary contributions, and to which every citizen has the right of free and equal access, when his own private stores are consumed; to serve as a surplus to fly to for succour; to assist neighbouring towns, whose crops may have failed; accommodate strangers, or travellers; afford provisions or supplies, when they go forth on hostile expeditions; and for all other exigencies of the state: and this treasure is at the disposal of the king or mico; which is surely a royal attribute, to have an exclusive right and ability in a community to distribute comfort and blessings to the necessitous.

As to mechanic arts or manufactures, at present they have scarcely any thing worth observation, since they are supplied with necessaries, conveniencies, and even superfluities by the white traders. The men perform nothing except erecting their mean habitations, forming their canoes, stone pipes, tambour, eagles tail or standard, and some other trifling matters; for war and hunting are their principal employments. The women are more vigilant, and turn their attention to various manual employments; they make all their pottery or earthen-ware, moccasins, spin and weave the curious belts and diadems for men, fabricate lace, fringe, embroider and decorate their apparel, &c. &c.

CHAP. V.

As to their marriage ceremonies, they are very simple, yet differ greatly in the various nations and tribes. Amongst some of the bands in the Muscogulge confederacy, I was informed the mystery is performed after the following manner. When a young man has fixed his affections, and is determined to marry, he takes a Cane or Reed, such as they stick down at the hills of their Bean vines for their support: with this (after having obtained her parents' or nearest relations' consent) he repairs to the habitation of his beloved, attended by his friends and associates, and in the presence of the wedding guests, he sticks his Reed down, upright in the ground; when soon after his sweet-heart comes forth with another Reed, which she sticks down by the side of his, when they are married: then they exchange Reeds, which are laid by as evidences or certificates of the marriage, which is celebrated with feasting, music and dancing: each one of their relations and friends, at the wedding, contribute something towards establishing the new family. As soon as the wedding is over, the town is convened, and the council orders or recommends a new habitation to be constructed for the accommodation of the new family; every man in the town joins in the work, which is begun and finished in a day's time.

The greatest accomplishments to recommend a young man to his favourite maid, are to prove himself a brave warrior, and a cunning, industrious hunter.

They marry only for a year's time, and, according to ancient custom, at the expiration of the year they renew the marriage: but there is seldom an instance of their separating after they have children. If it should so happen, the mother takes the children under her own protection, though the father is obliged to contribute towards their maintainance during their minority and the mother's widowhood.

The Muscogulges allow of polygamy in the utmost latitude;

every man takes as many wives as he chooses, but the first is queen, and the others her handmaids and associates.

It is common for a great man amongst them, who has already half a dozen wives, if he sees a child of eight or nine years of age, who pleases him, and he can agree with her parents or guardians, to marry her and take her into his house at that age.

Adultery is always punished with cropping, which is the only corporal punishment amongst them; and death or outlawry for murder; and infamy for less crimes, as fornication, theft, &c., which produces such repeated marks and reflections of ridicule and contempt, that it generally ends in voluntary banishment; and these renegadoes and vagabonds are generally the ruffians who commit depredations and murders on the frontiers.

The Muscogulges bury their deceased in the earth. They dig a four-square deep pit under the cabin or couch which the deceased lay on, in his house, lining the grave with Cypress bark, where they place the corpse in a sitting posture, as if it were alive; depositing with him his gun, tomahawk, pipe, and such other matters as he had the greatest value for in his life time. His eldest wife, or the queen dowager, has the second choice of his possessions, and the remaining effects are divided amongst his other wives and children.

The Chactaws pay their last duties and respect to the deceased in a very different manner. As soon as a person is dead, they erect a scaffold eighteen or twenty feet high, in a grove adjacent to the town, where they lay the corpse, lightly covered with a mantle: here it is suffered to remain, visited and protected by the friends and relations, until the flesh becomes putrid, so as easily to part from the bones; then undertakers, who make it their business, carefully strip the flesh from the bones, wash and cleanse them, and when dry and purified by the air, having provided a curiously wrought chest or coffin, fabricated of bones and splints, they place all the bones therein; it is then deposited in the bone-house, a building erected for that purpose in every town. And when this house is full, a general solemn funeral takes place; the nearest kindred or friends of the deceased, on a day appointed, repair to the bone-house, take up the respective coffins, and following one another in order of seniority, the nearest relations and connexions attending their respective corpse, and the multitude following after them, all as one family, with united voice of alternate Allelujah and lamentation, slowly proceed to the place of general interment, where they place the coffins in order, forming a pyramid*; and lastly, cover all over with earth, which raises a conical hill or mount. Then they return to town in order of solemn procession, concluding the day with a festival, which is called the feast of the dead.

The Chactaws are called by the traders flats, or flat-heads, all the males having the fore and hind part of their skulls artificially flattened, or compressed; which is effected after the following manner. As soon as the child is born, the nurse provides a cradle or wooden case, hollowed and fashioned, to receive the infant, lying prostrate on its back, that part of the case where the head reposes, being fashioned like a brick mould. In this portable machine the little boy is fixed, a bag of sand being laid on his forehead, which by continual gentle compression, gives the head somewhat the form of a brick from the temples upwards; and by these means they have high and lofty foreheads, sloping off backwards. These men are not so neat in the trim of their heads, as the Muscogulges are, and they are remarkably slovenly and negligent in every part of their dress; but otherwise they are said to be ingenious, sensible and virtuous men; bold and intrepid, yet quiet and peaceable, and are acknowledged by the Creeks to be brave.

They are supposed to be most ingenious and industrious husbandmen, having large plantations, or country farms, where they employ much of their time in agricultural improvements, after the manner of the white people; by which means their territories are more generally cultivated, and better inhabited, than any other Indian republic that we know of. The number of their inhabitants is said greatly to exceed the whole Muscogulge confederacy, although their territories are not a fourth part as extensive. It appeared to me from observation,

*Some ingenious men, whom I have conversed with, have given it as their opinion, that all those pyramidal artificial hills, usually called Indian mounts, were raised on these occasions, and are generally sepulchres. However I am of a different opinion.

and what information I could get, that the Indians entertain rational notions of the soul's immortality, and of a future state of social existence; and accordingly, in order to inculcate morality, and promote human happiness, they applaud praiseworthy actions, as commendable and necessary for the support of civil society, and maintaining the dignity and strength of their nation or tribe, as well as securing an excellent and tranquil state and degree in the world of spirits, after their decease. And they say the Great Spirit favours all good and brave men.

CHAP. VI.

LANGUAGE AND MANNERS.

THE Muscogulge language is spoken throughout the confederacy, (although consisting of many nations, who have a speech peculiar to themselves) as also by their friends and allies, the Natches. The Chicasaw and Chactaw, the Muscogulges say are dialects of theirs.

This language is very agreeable to the ear, courteous, gentle and musical: the letter R is not sounded in one word of their language: the women in particular speak so fine and musical, as to represent the singing of birds; and when heard and not seen, one might imagine it to be the prattling of young children. The men's speech is indeed more strong and sonorous, but not harsh, and in no instance guttural, and I believe the letter R is not used to express any word, in any language of the confederacy.

The Cherokee tongue, on the contrary, is very loud, somewhat rough and very sonorous, sounding the letter R frequently, yet very agreeable and pleasant to the ear. All the Indian languages are truly rhetorical, or figurative, assisting their speech by tropes; their hands, flexure of the head, the brow, in short, every member, naturally associate, and give their assistance to render their harangues eloquent, persuasive and effectual.

The pyramidal hills or artificial mounts, and high-ways, or avenues, leading from them to artificial lakes or ponds, vast tetragon terraces, chunk yards*, and obelisks or pillars of wood, are the only monuments of labour, ingenuity and magnificence, that I have seen worthy of notice, or remark. The region lying between Savanna river and Oakmulge, East and West, and from the sea coast to the Cherokee or Apalachean mountains, North and South, is the most remarkable for these

*Chunk yard, a term given by the white traders, to the oblong four square yards, adjoining the high mounts and rotundas of the modern Indians.—In the centre of these stands the obelisk, and at each corner of the farther end stands a slave post or strong stake, where the captives that are burnt alive are bound.

high conical hills, tetragon terraces and chunk yards. This region was possessed by the Cherokees, since the arrival of the Europeans, but they were afterwards dispossessed by the Muscogulges, and all that country was probably, many ages preceeding the Cherokee invasion, inhabited by one nation or confederacy, who were ruled by the same system of laws, customs and language, but so ancient, that the Cherokees, Creeks, or the nation they conquered, could render no account for what purpose these monuments were raised. The mounts and cubical yards adjoining them, seem to have been raised in part for ornament and recreation, and likewise to serve some other public purpose, since they are always so situated as to command the most extensive prospect over the town and country adjacent. The tetragon terraces seem to be the foundation of a fortress; and perhaps the great pyramidal mounts, served the purpose of look out towers, and high places for sacrifice. The sunken area, called by white traders the chunk yard, very likely served the same conveniency that it has been appropriated to by the more modern and even present nations of Indians, that is, the place where they burnt and otherwise tortured the unhappy captives that were condemned to die; as the area is surrounded by a bank, and sometimes two of them, one behind and above the other, as seats, to accommodate the spectators at such tragical scenes, as well as the exhibition of games, shows, and dances. From the river St. Juans, southerly to the point of the peninsula of Florida, are to be seen high pyramidal mounts, with spacious and extensive avenues, leading from them out of the town, to an artificial lake or pond of water; these were evidently designed in part for ornament or monuments of magnificence, to perpetuate the power and grandeur of the nation, and not inconsiderable neither, for they exhibit scenes of power and grandeur, and must have been public edifices.

The great mounts, highways, and artificial lakes up S. Juans, on the East shore, just at the entrance of the great Lake George, one on the opposite shore, on the bank of the Little Lake, another on Dunn's Island, a little below Charlotteville, one on the large beautiful island just without the Capes of Lake George, in sight of Mount Royal, and a spacious one on the West banks of the Musquitoe river near New Smyrna, are the most remarkable of this sort that occurred to me; but undoubtedly many more are yet to be discovered farther South in the peninsula; however I observed none Westward, after I left St. Juans on my journey to little St. Juan, near the bay of Apalache.

But in all the region of the Muscogulge country, South-West from the Oakmulge River quite to the Tallapoose, down to the city of Mobile, and thence along the sea coast, to the Mississipi, I saw no signs of mountains or highways, except at Taensa, where were several inconsiderable conical mountains; and but one instance of the tetragon terraces, which was at the Apalachucla old town, on the West banks of that river: here were yet remaining conspicuous monuments, as vast four square terraces, chunk yards, &c., almost equalling those eminent ones at the Oakmulge fields; but no high conical mounts. Those Indians have a tradition that these remains are the ruins of an ancient Indian town and fortress. I was not in the interior parts of the Chactaw territories, and therefore am ignorant whether there are any mounts or monuments there.

To conclude this subject concerning the monuments of the Americans, I deem it necessary to observe as my opinion, that none of them that I have seen discover the least signs of the arts, sciences, or architecture of the Europeans or other inhabitants of the old world; yet evidently betray every sign or mark of the most distant antiquity.

INDEX.

A

C

TRAVELS IN
GEORGIA AND FLORIDA,
1773–74

A REPORT TO
DR. JOHN FOTHERGILL

Travels in Georgia and Florida, 1773–74

A Report to Dr. John Fothergill

VOLUME I

Philadelphia, March 20th 1774

WENT onboard the Brig^{tn}. Charlestown Paquet Wright commander bound for South Carolina. we were favoured with a fair wind down the River to Rede Island when the Flood Tide met us. We came to Anchor in company with a Brig^{tn}. bound to the same Port we were; early in the morning we got under way & left sight of the Capes of Delawar. This night the wind coming about, in the morning we found it ahead, the gale increasing in its strength blew up a violent Storm which obliged us to lye too for two days & nights. the third day the Storm abated; the fury of the Ellements subsided, & the face of the angry Ocian remain'd calm & pleasant during the whole Voyage. Many small birds of the Finch kind were blown onboard: they were very gentle & glad to find a place of rest for their feet; after their wearied wings had gain'd new strength by this short repose, they lifted themselves aloft & were born away by favour of the fliting Winds, to their summer habitations In the North. These little Birds were of a brown colour head & Neck purple. Next day appeared a sail a Starn of us & comeing up with us we hail'd her, she proved to be the Brig^{tn}. that parted from us in the Storm. The Capt. told us, they suffered greatly in the Gale, that they could not have rode it out many hours longer. Two horses they had onboard intended for Charlestown were wash't off deck & went away. & the Packs of Hay after them which the Capt. said was to serve them on their Passage.

March 30th. At Night arived in Sight of the Light house which stands on an Island just within the Barr. In the morning we saild up to Charlestown.

Went to the house of a very Antient & honourable Family who recieved me friendly dureing my abode in this Town. waited on Do^r. Chalmers Who was pleased to confer with me on subjects relating to my persuits of natural Knowledge.

But finding my continuance in this Province would be productive of little or nothing for your advantage or amusement, I resolved to push my discoveries into Georgia, and hearing of the Congress to be held At Augusta between the Creek Indians and the White People which was to be in june, With the conscent of Doct^r. Chalmers, waited on the Honble. John Stewart Esqr. Superintendant for Indian affairs, in order to lay before that Gentleman my designs of Traveling in the Indian Countries. M^r. Stewart Rec^d. me very Pollitely & generously offered to take me in his company to Augusta when he went. & there explain to the Deputies appointed to be amongst the Indian Nations, my Business.

But knowing that many Vegitable Near the Sea coast of Georgia wuld differ in ther kinds from those growing in the upper & hilley parts about Augusta, & being much earlyer in flower I should loose the oppertunity of get^g. Specimens & seeds. So chose rather to go to Savanah in Georgia, that I might employ my time untill the meeting of the Indians, in serching the natural productions of the Maritime parts of the Province of Georgia.

The Superintendant gave me a Letter to His Excell^y. S^r. James Wright Govr. of Georgia. & told me he expected to see me at the Congress at Augusta.

The next day after staying about a Week In Charlestown, went onboard a small Schooner, bound for Georgia and in about 12 hours Sail arived safe at Savanah.

April 13th. Waited on his Excell^y. the Governer Who was Pleased to recieve me politely & offered to assist me all in his power.

April 15th. Bought a Horse & the day following set out for the Town of Sundbury. rode 15 Miles to Ferry on Gr^t. Ogeche River. crost the River. & rode 15 Miles to Midway Meeting house. Went into meeting being intraduced by some of my fellow Travilers being inhabitants of that part of the Country. heard a good Sermon by Mr. Percey, a Methodest Missioner sent by the Count^ss. of Huntington, (Rector of th Orphan house Collige). This congregation was respectable & genteel. the Religious and Pious Sperit throughout the whole Audiance reflects a shineing light on the Character of the inhabitants Midway & Newport.

After meeting rode nine Miles to Sunbury. This Pretty Town is situated on the sound apposite St. Catherin Island, & commands an agreeable prospect of the Inlet 4 or 5 Miles from the Barr. There are about one hundred houses in the Town neatly built of wood framed, having pleasant Piasas round them. the inhabitants are genteel & wealthy, either Merchants, or Planters from the Country who resort here in the Summer & Autum, to pertake of the Salubrious Sea breese, Bathing & sporting on the Sea Islands. The Barr is a good one. Vessell carying 16 feet water over it. Here is a Custom house and Naval Office for the incouragement of Commerce.

I went over to one of the Sea Islands, but discover'd nothing new, or much worth your notice. On a high bluff observed a mound or Tumulous of Oister Shells; observed a clay urn, the Shells being removed from it but found nothing in it but sand & dust. it was about 18 Inches high & one foot in diameter, it was marked or carved on the outer surface in imitation of Basket work.

The vegitable Productions were the same as on other small Islands on the coast of Carolina and Georgia; The Great Live Oak, & dwarf evergreen Oaks, Water Oaks, Red Bay, Zanthoxilon, Frangula, Red Cedar, purple Berried Bay.

Haveing recieved an invitation when in Savana from one of the most considerable Plant^{rs}: in this part of the Province. I left the pleasant Town of Sunbury & went to his house. his Plantation is very large containing great quantities of Rice Land & being advantagiously situated for the command of water over his Rice fields, he employs upwards of an hundred Negroes on this Plantation & expects to make 1600 Barrells of Rice this season, His house is situated on a Peninsula of High Land which commands a most agreeable prospect of his vast extendsive Rice fields which nearly sorounds him on all sides. he has no Orched of Fruite Trees which is a common neglect of the Planters through the Province.

Being invited by one of this Gentlemans Neighbours I waited on him, who has likewise a large and well regulated Rice Plantation. stayed a fiew days in this Settlement and was most hospitably entertain'd in the Family of the good M^{r}. B. Andrews, a member of the House of Assembly of this

Province and a worthy Elder of the Meeting in Midway Parish. during my stay here imployed my time in serching out the Natural productions of the Country, took notice of a pretty species of Asphodelus called here by the Inhabitants Fly poison, having a long loose spike of white Flowers. They gather the Roots which they bruise & steep over night, in water, in which they put honey or Treakle, which they expose in a broad Dish or Platter on a Table in the Rooms of the House unto which the Flys swarm & almost instantly after taisting the fatal Nectar turn giddy & die in incredible numbers. on this account it is a most usefull Plant in a Country so infested with these troublesom little Animals. the same root is used as effectually in destroying Crows, Rats &^{c}. Here too I observed the very singular Species of Ledum or Adromeda, whose little white campanulate Flowers, become monstrous excressences, every Part of the Flower, inlarging proportionably, & being of a deep flesh or rose colour afford a very agreeable apperance, some approaching to the size of a Teacup and is on this account extremely singular & very beautifull. It is a beautifull evergreen Shrub: the wood when dry being very sollid close & fine grained. & indures a polish resembling Box wood or Elder.

Sat out for the River Alatamaha & in 3 days arived at Darien. waited on L. M^{c}antosh Esqr. who was pleased to recieve me in the most friendly maner and on being acquainted with my Travels shewed me the greatest respect & civility. there is yet remaining some ruins of the old town of Darien, & about a mile below the Town on a Bluff of the River, remains part of one of the Angles of the Fort, the River having so far incroached on the Bluff caried it with the foundation of the Fort to the Point of an Island apposite which increases constantly & the deepest part of this entrance of the River, runs where the Fort stood.

Darien Bluff is a fine situation for a Town was the water deep enough on the Barr, for large Vessells. As this beautifull River having its source in or very near the Appalatchean Mountains, & thence taking a winding cource through the middle of this Province affords an extendsive navigation for small Craft, being interupted by no falls or Rapids of any acct:

Cross't this famous River at Barrington about 30 miles above the Inlet. & continued down the other side o' the River keeping a Path through the Pine Forests generally in sight of the low lands of the River. These Pine Forest affords large & usefull Timber Trees very tall & streight. cross some small branches of Turtle River through swamps & vast open meadoews & Savanahs, richly clad with green & flowers of various hue.

The next day got near the Sea coast, went by the vast Plantation belonging to Coll[l]. H. Lawrence and continued my route to the poiint of a neck of Land which lays between S[t]. Simons sound & the mouth of Turtle River. this neck of Land is laid out for a Town by the name of N: Brunswick. it is a fine situation, being nearly sorounded by S[t]. Simons & Turtle River Sounds, Turtle River is large Navigable River but runs but a small distance, & heads in vast Rich Swamps, the finest Rice Lands in the Province but chiefly belonging to Gentlemen of S[o]. Carolina are not cultivated; & thus one of the most valuable Parts of the Province lays as useless as any part of the Indian Country. S[t]. Simon's & Cumberland are the Inlets to this River, either of them carrying 18 or 20 feet water over their Barrs. & are about 3 miles from the Point of N. Brunswick and an excellent harbour within the Point.

As to the Vegitable productions observed here are the Live & Water Oaks, Guilandina, Black Mulberry, Xanthoxilon, Frangula, Olea Americana. Purple ber[d]. Bay Catesby.

May 1. sett off from M[r]. L. M[c]Antosh's for Augusta. 3[d] arived in Savanah. 4th. sett off in company with M[r]. J. M[c]Antosh who was going to attend at the Congress. got 15 Miles & took up quarters at a publick house. the day's journey was very agreeable, the Road being good and o'rshadowed by fragrant Forest Trees, mixt with Flowery & evergreen shrubs; Oak, Laurell, Althea, Magnolia, Catalpa, having their Tall streight Tronks, ornamented with wreaths & Garlands of various species of Bignoniæ, Hedera, Pyrola, with Floriferous Climbers, Woodbines, Jassimies, Syringa &[c]. Early in the morning proceeding on our journey rode about 3 miles, thro' a shade Forest of Oaks, Laurel, &[c]. the Soil being very Rich.

We now assend the sand hills, & here I first observed growing that very singular Ononis perfoliated, bearing a single yellow flower in the bosom of the leaves: Rode about 4 miles, arived at Ebenezar, a very beautifull Village, chiefly inhabited by the descendants of an antient colony of German Swiss's, who chiefly imploy themselves in the culture of Silk. The Town is laid out in large Squairs so that every family has ground sufficient to plant a Mulberry Orchard, a Garden, & a Cornfield, & as they have been, & are at this time, very industrious & temperate their little Plantations are well cultivated, The whole Stettlement, forms a delightfull Village incompassed with, Gardens, Orchids, Cornfields & Pasture grounds. They likewise plant wheat enough for each Family & Potatoes of all kinds grows with little or no Trouble And, the Pine forests & Savanahs, furnish plenty of food for the Support of their Stocks of Cattle &^{c}.

Here are very good Mills both for grist and for sawing Lumber fit for building &^{c}. Here is in this Village a very large brick Church, furnished with a Cupola & Bell, & some very neat private buildings.—After breakfasting and and taking a view of the place we persued on our journey through Pine groves, the Land flat, the soil sandy but the country everywhere clad with green grass in the forests & beautifull Savanahs, richly painted over with various col'd flowers. a pretty yellow Cistus, a beautifull Citisus, Penguicula's of various col'd flowers, Violets, & Phlox of various dies, Iris, Ixia, Bartsia and an endless variety of other, gay subjects of the Vegitable Kingdom. & here in the Pine Forests I first observed, that very pretty Yellow Flower, resembling a Lithospermum. The next morning being very pleasant, invited us, early, on our way; Went over the same sort of soil and situation of country, observing no new kinds of Vegitable; but the Land gradually rising higher by almost imperceptable Ridges decorated With Savanahs and Ponds, edged by delightfull green grass Plats, diversified with Pictures from the sorounding painted hills; at night arived at a very fine rapid brook of good water whereon stood a Gristmill, the Millpond was supplied with Water by a number of lively spring that broke through the Steep Banks of the sorounding Hills. The House where we lodged stood on a levell by the Pond very pleasant, This pleasant stream of water ran about ¼ Mile & fell into Savanah River. several fine odoriferous & Balmy Shrubs grew about

the Stoney brows of these Hills, the fragrant Calycanthus con-
tributeing to the balmie vivificing breath of the morning wak-
ened me to the Chierfull songs of the Inhabitants of the
Groves. The watchfull Savanah Crane's shrill Voice rang the
Alarm through the echoing Forests, & The gay lively Mock-
bird invited all to action, I obeyed the friendly Summons, &
began this day's progress.

The country now assumes a different appearance being
more Hilly, & uneven, checkered by little iminencces, & tho
these little mounts seem to stand single & parted from each
other by levell plats, Savanahs & Ponds, Yet one may percieve
they are ranged in Ridges & Chains which seemingly range
parralell with the Sea Coast, or transversewise between the
Rivers; every Ridge rises above them past, and so higher &
higher, as we approach the Hills near the Mountains, these
Pine Forests & Savanahs are all clad with grass, which having
been lately burnt, Nature unfolded her joyfull Vernal carpet
displaying a lovely scene of vegitable gayity, crouds of vegitable beauties dres't in their richest flowery Mantles. The
scene is varied and inlarged by the Herds & Flocks of Deer
& Turkey's, bound^g. & triping over the Hills and Savanahs,
renders the prospect of These vast Pine Forest extremely
noval & entertaining; the Numbers of little Lakes & ponds,
sparkling in the Morning to the rising sun. The Hills now
begin to rise somewhat higher, the soil a greyish sand mixt
with small gravel & Pibles with pieces of Flint. this sort of
soil may be about one foot or 18 Inches & next a deep Strata
of deep Yellow or redish tough Clay. this bed of Clay is so
very compact & hard occations the destruction of vast Forests of Pine Trees when a Hurricane comes, For the Roots
of the Pine Trees cannot penetrate this hard clay, there is no
descending Tronk or Tap root; no foot hold, to stand against
the storm, the Trees that are turn'd over have all their Roots
reflexed & flatted like a Tree growing on a Rock. having seen
large Forests of Miles in extent. turn'd up by Huricanes, But
have observed a very different affect, on those Trees growing
in lower Sandy countries, the Bed of clay laying much
deeper, these Trees have a Tap Root 8 or 10 feet in length
& here we very seldom see any rooted up, but broke or
twisted off a little above the surface of the earth. Observed

no change in Vegitation, except a greater luxuriantcy of grass in the Forests.

Having rode about 20 Miles we halted at the Bever-dams; these are vast Springs of very excell[t]. Cool water, this prodigious fountain essues from Clifts of white soft shelly Limestone Rocks at the foot of a Hill a fiew miles from the River, & immediately forms a bason of Water large enough for a small Vessell to Ride in & is the source of a large Creek, which runs 7 or 8 Miles & fall in the River, the water at the Springs may be 5 or 6 feet deep, extreamely transparent, & full of fish.

Of the vegitable particular to this place were the Magnolia grandiflora, or Laurel Tree, Catalpa & Bignonia's of different Species, Ilix Yapon, Prunus, Holly. After tarrying sometime, to refresh ourselves at this pleasant place, a very senseble relief, the day being excessive sultry & hot, without any good water to slake our thirst; We proceeded, passing over a pleasant country of uneven grassy Pine Forests & Savanahs, Crossing Several rapid brooks of Water. Observed growing in the Rich bottoms of these Creeks, Magnolia Umbrella Tree, Magnolea great Laurel Tree, Sasafras, Red Bay, Magnolea glauca, Vast tall streight & beautifull trees, Illex. White Oak, Chionanthos, & on the steep sides of the Hills the very fragrant Calicanthus, all these in blossom. having traviled near 40 Miles this day, come to Camp by the side of a fine Stream of Water. But the Musquetoes being very troublesom got very little rest, so that we were glad to decamp as soon as it was light enough to find our horses, we continued passing over hilly Pine forests & several, fine Streams of water, about noon, we stopt to refresh ourselves, at a publick house, pleasantly situated in the midst of a Pine forest, sorounded by extendsive Savanahs & Meadows of grass, where resorted abundance of Cattle, we got plenty of Milk butter &[c]. & Corn for our horses, this was a most acceptable refreshment to us as, the day was excessive hot. The wether dry & no good water on the Road, after leaving the pleasant brooks, so, our beasts began to pant & suffer; several fine horses in the Governer's Retinue which pass't before us, died in the Road by reason of the Heat & drouth. we continued passing through savanahs, Pine Forests, as before, came to bryer Creek a considerable branch of Savana River, the Hills & bottoms on this Creek is generally good Land, the Hills bearing large Timber of such sorts as indicate a good Soil; such as Black Walnut, Linden, Ash, Elm, Magnolia, Black Oak, Judas Tree, Halesia, Stewartia, & the Bottoms Cypres, Tupilo, Fringe Tree, Umbrella, Halesia, Elder, Carpinus, Of Plants Collinsonia, Lobelia, Urtica urens, & other Species, Serratula, Senecia, Podophyllon, Granadilla, of different Species, & a many more. Came to the Ferry where was a good little Plantation: very good Corn & Wheat, & a good Peach Orchard very fruitfull. Cross't over the Creek, the land broken & Hilly, frequant Brook & Swamps, rise a pretty high Ridge, generally Timbered, with, Scrubby White & Black Oak (call'd here Black Jacks, Species of Oaks peculear to this sort of Land. On this Ridge pass't by 4 or 5 very large shallow grassy Ponds, sorounded by Hilly Pine & Black Jack; Passt by other Ponds, saw Cattle & Horses grazing.

Went through a deep Swamp, & cross't a Creek that went through the middle, rise a small Hill, pass't by a Publick house, went 3 or 4 miles over a very oneven & hilly pine Forest, crosst a deep Boggy Cane Branch, rise a high Hill then decended to the low Lands of Savanah River, went a mile through a very good Bottom, Oak, Hicory, Carpinus, Beech Trees of an incredible magnitude, & Liquid Ambar Trees of a prodigious bulk, then come into the low lands next the River, went about 3 Miles to the River. The Timber of this land is of an emence bulk; Chiefly Hicory, Ash, White & black Oak, Silver leaf't Maple, Hornbeam, Papaw, or Wahoo, Linden & Cane thickets. came to the River aposite Silver Bluff at M^r. Golphins Trading House where we crosst the River. staid a day or two at this Place where were Numbers of People waiting the Congress to be held at Augusta.

May 14th. Set off with a number of People & a Party of Indians; The Road kept near the River generally very unevan, the Soil a light greyish sandy loam about 2 feet in depth then a bed of yellowish Clay. The Vegitable productions, such as heretofore, except the forests being a mixture of short leaved Pine; Black & red Oak; & hicory, Water Oak; very low dwarf Oaks, Chinquapins, Very low oak leaved Toxicodendron called by the inhabitants Poison Oak. About Noon having rode above 14 Miles come to a very high Bluff On Savanah River. here formerly stood Fort Moore. This is a very high perpendicular Bluff. The surface of the Earth being about 5 or 6 feet deep a whiteish sandy loam, then 7 or 8 feet depth of Yellowish Clay with a little mixture of sand, than 40 or 50 feet deep strata super strata alternately of exceeding fine greecey Marle, the upper strata being perfectly white as Chalk, the Next, white streaked or spotted with Red & Yellow than mix't with red & purple, than, with purple & blue. I observed that about 5 or 6 feet above the surface of the River, when at its common stated hight, a bed of quicksand & small gravel, the lowest bed or bottom a compact dark blue Clay or Marle. the Inhabitants Use these clays instead of Chalk & the col'd clays answers sufficiantly well for Paint. We cross't the River at this Place again & come into the Province of Georgia. rode 3 Miles to Augusta, in the even'g went a mile or two up the Banks of the River to view the Falls, an agreable prospect. They are a violent rushing of the Waters over & between the Rocks. The Bed of the River being contracted here & rockey. This being, The first Rockey Ridge we come to, it continues 2 or 3 Miles than a Vale or flat levell Land for 3 or 4 Miles, then comes another Ridge so alternately higher & higher up to the Mountains, & these Ridges continuing across the River Renders the Navigation of this large River very difficult from Augusta upwards, unless it be for Canoes & for them only in the Spring & Autumn when the River is high.—

May 15th. Waited on the Superintendant, who was pleased to renew his former generous offer, of assisting me in my Travells.

The Indians not being yet arived, I chose to imploy my time in searching the country round about this Place. I accepted of an invitation of a Gentleman of Wrightsburrough, a new Settlement about 30 Miles from Augusta Wet[d].; set off in evening chooseing to travell then, to avoid the excessive heat of the day; When the dark came on we bell'd out our horses, spread our blankets under the covert of some spreading Trees & rested well till morning. arose very early and proceeding pass't over Hills & Plains of Pine Forests; The earth cover'd with tall grass & abundance of Buffiloe grass, a species of very tall Asphodelus having very great tufts of long graminous leaves, sends up a long slender stalk 6 or 8 feet high adorned with a long Spike of little white flowers, this is call'd Buffiloe grass, from the Buffiloe's feeding principally on it when they frequented this part of the country. it grow in vast abundance, on the high lands from hence to The Mountains, & to an indifferent observer, in the Spring of the Year before it sends up it's stalk for flowering, would be taken for grass of the most luxuriant growth & displays A most gratefull Verdure under the tall Pines of these vast open extendsive Forests. I observed the leaves & tender flowers to be cropt by some Animals either Cattle or deer. Stay'd a day about this place but observed nothing new, so return'd to attend at the Congress. Night overtaking me 5 or 6 Miles before I got to Augusta, took a nother Road leading to the Town, which I did not observe untill being surprised at the appearance of a heap of white Rocks which I at first took to be Houses by the light of the Moon shineing upon them, I made up to the fancied buildings, which as I approached nearer, the delusion vanished & I found myself at the feet of a vast Pile of White Rocks; it being late & observing commodious dwelling under the shelving Clifts of the Rocks alighted, hobled out my horse & took possession of my lodgings. tho' dismal enough yet proved a very Hospitable retreat, from a very furious Storm of Thunder and rain, I rested pretty well & arose early & took a view of my very silent abode; I scrambled up the craggy sides of this Pile of Rocks, heaped and placed on one another to the hight of 50 feet & bout 200Yards in length; from their highest summets had a pleasant Prospect of the extendsive Forests, & green Savannahs below & all around me but could see no other Rocks, any where about; They were masses of that kind of shelly white soft Rocks in the Bahama Islands & Bermudas, perfectly white & easy to be cut with an axe, & makes the best Filtering Stones; observed, a beautifull, species of blue Delphinium and some other curious Vegitables. I left my solitary lodgings & arived safe in Augusta.

In a fiew days the business of the Congress was over, but not terminating intirely to the Satisfaction of the Parties, on either side the question, The Superintendant told me he thought it not alltogether safe to go then into the Indian Countries; My schemes on that Plan being thus frustrated, I was at a stand how to pr-ceed on my Botanical discoveries; However, The New purchased lands stipulated by the Indians, being now confirmed to us; a Party of surveyers & Trustees, was appointed by the Governer, to run & mark the lines round the new ceded Lands; in conjunction with Indian Deputies, appointed by them to see the Lines run agreeable to the treaty.

I therefore acquainted Coll. Barnet, (who conduct the English Party). with my desire of attending him on that expedition, who granted my request, & was pleased to tell me farther that he expected much pleasure in my company.

The Surveyers, Indian, Deputies, with their attendants, together with Packhorsmen, and hunters; The guides, and a Number of People who went to view the lands, being all ready, June 7th. we set off from Augusta to the number of 70 or 80 People; we proceeded but slow; taking into consideration, the length, & roughness of our Journey, the loaded Pack horses & some of the Indians being a foot, made this a necessary precaution; and which I had no reason to be offended at, having more time and oppertunity to make my observations, & for the better availing myself of this advantage, I chose to keep a small distance ahead of the Main body; by which I avoided the heat & dust rais'd by such a Number of People; & at the same time had leisure & oppertunaty to pick up any curiosities within view; thus having advanced about Fifteen Miles, came to a Branch of good Water, which ran through a large Cane brake. This being looked upon as a good & convenient Place both for us & our horses, pitched Camp, waiting for the Coll. to come up, and the Young Warrior Chief of the Creek Party being drunk, having taken too deep a draught at the Rum bottle, was not able to move a foot farther.

As I have hither to indeavoured to give a description of the Countries through which I pass and as I attempt only to exhibit to your Notice, the outward furniture of Nature, or the productions of the Surface of the earth; without, troubleing you with any notions, of their particular causes or design by Providence, such attempts I leave for the amusement of Men of Letters & Superior genus.

In my journey from the Sea coast to Augusta I have indeavourd to give you true & natural description of the first or lower division of the country,

From Augusta westwards to the Apalachian Mountains this country has quite another Aspect. The Ridges rise higher, the Rocks in Beds of Clay heave their Sturdy shoulders throug a rich & fertile mould, a mixture of Clay & sand, manured with the decayed substances of the former productions of the earth. In my progress from Augusta to this place, cross't several Branches of the River, the Beds of the Creeks being Rockey and gravelly, their Banks steep & stoney; The Hills rising pretty high & the soil Fertile, for a good distance on each side their banks, more or less, according to the bigness of the Stream; For I have observed where ever I have been, the larger the River or Creek, the greater quantity of fertile land. After passing these branches which unite into one Creek that falls in the River at Augusta, we traveled through a levell Forest (chiefly of Pine Timber mixt with Red Oak & Hicory, the Soil a thin surface of sandy greyish mould, on a Bed of yellowish or red Clay,) 7 or eight miles to this Cane Branch.

The next day about two hours by sun got on our way, Finding it expedant to conform to the motions of Our Indians: They never move camp till late in the morning. They never rise from Sleep till after the Sun; than Smoke the Pipe, & give out the Talk which is their Plan of pr-ceedings for the day delived by the chief: He rises, his left hand bearing on his Gun, his Right armed with his Tomahoc their ensign of Authority, with a Heroick air & action, a looud & determined Voice speaks, than marches a head with his Party.

Having traviled about ten Miles, through a Pine Forest, the timber very large & the earth cover'd with grass, some low Savanahs but not very extendsive; we came to a pretty large Creek; the land a little broken and hilly about it, the bed of the Creek stoney, the Soil good & Fertile, being a dark greyish mould on a Clay bottom, the Timber, Black, white & red Oak, Mulbery, Walnut, Hicory, Ash, Vines, Plumb, & the sides of Hill & Bottoms near Creeks, Mulberry, Ash, Fringtree, Magnolia, the sweet Calycanthus, Avilania, Æsculus, Rose flowerd Robinia, Ilex, Prinos. Opulus &ᶜ. thus we continued 8 or 10 Miles; came to Wrightsburrough; here we halted, in order to furnish ourselves with necessaries for the continuance of the expedition; & here We supplied ourselves with Corn Flower, Hamony, cured some Beef fit for carriage, Corn & some very good Cheese made here.

Wrightsburge is a late but thriving Settlement, on a branch of Little River which runs into Savana River. the inhabitents are for the most part emigrants from the North[n]. Colonies, under the conduct of ⸺ Mattox Esq. Who obtain'd a grant of these Lands, with a priviledge of settleing with such People as he should approve of. And he being a Quaker by proffession, most of his followers are of that Society. It is call'd Wrightsborough, in honour to the Governer S[r]. James wright, who granted M[r]. Mattox the priviledge of a Burrow in his little Colony; The Town is already laid out. & about 20 houses built; several Traders in it & Goods are sold as cheap here as at Augusta, Sugar, Rum, Salt. & dry Goods &[c]:

This Settlement being upon the head of Little River, a very considerable branch of Savanah River; the Soil is very fruitefull, hills & Vales, watered and beautified by numbers of salubrious waters, either, playing over gravelly Beds, through shadowy Vales; murmering in the hollow rocks, whence they glide over rockey precepices, are lost for a time, but soon appear again throug the Groves, presenting to view their prolific Boosom, beautifully decorated with the sorounding flowery hill & verdant lawns; all gay & Fragrant defuses a lovely & fruitfull Scenery all around. Mills are erected on the swift flowing Streams, the flowery Meads smile in their Vernal Robes, & the fruitefull Hills & Vales allready teams with Plenty of Corn & Grapes.

The Inhabitents of this part of the Country having formerly been inured to industry & Farming in the North[n] Colonies, & finding this a fruitefull Soil, turn their hands to the sam sort of Agriculture. They Plant Wheat, Barley, Flax, Hemp, Oates, corn, Cotton, Indigo, Breed Cattle, Sheep, & Make Very good Butter & Cheese.

Fruit Trees thrive very well here, Apples, Pears, Peaches, Plumbs, Nectrans, Cherries, Rasberries, & Several other fine Fruit; & Fruites bear surprisinly soon, I saw in M[r]. Mattox Garden, very fine large Apples 2 Years from the seed, & Grapes, 2 Year from Cutings. Having provided things convenient, in the best manner we possebly could. 21st June We set off for the great Buffulo lick, at the head of G[rt]. Ogeche River at the great Ridge which devides the waters of Savanah from the Alatamaha. or the Oconee, the N. W. branch of that River. The Lick at the foot of the Ridge is about 35 Miles from Savanah River and about 30 Miles from the Oconee.

This day's journey was agreeable, passing through a country agreeably diversified with gentle rising Hills & shady Vales; the Soil a dark loam on a red Clay founda^n. tops of Hills a little incumber'd with Rock. This country is well waterd with numerous little brook & Torrents. The Forest Trees & Shrubs are, Black, white & Red Oak, Hicory, of various Species, Black Walnut, Mulberry, Sumache &^{c}. Chionanthos, Sambucos, Halesia, Judas Tree, Calicarpa, Syringa, Evonimus, Hazel, scarlet Plums, Calycanthus, the Spicey Benjamin, & an infinite variety of other Shrubs and Plants; Collinsonia, Lobelia, with Crimson & Scarlet Flowers, Podophyllon, Granadilla, The sweet Nonda or wild Angelica. Gensang, & in & on the Verge of the Rapid rivulets a great Species of Plantago, in every respect like the common Plantain; except that it is of an incredible magnitude, the leaves with the footstalk commonly 3 feet in length, & in the Broadest part above 12 inches wide, the number of ribs of the leaf being the same with the common Plantain, & run in just the same direction, & by the smell & taist of the Plant seemes to possess the same virtues, but in a greater degree, it grows in the little coves, of the Rivulets & brooks where the eddie water hath collected & raised a Bed of slush or in the middle of the Creeks, where it forms a green Island, about some Rocks or trash. In the evening we Incamped by the banks of a beautifull rapid branch of Little River, where we found exceeding good food for our horses, on one side the Creek pretty high Hills, & on the other extendsive, levell Bottoms o'rgrown with Young Cains and young Bean Vines. After turning out our horses & Pitching Camp, the time betwixt this & dark I generally made use of in little excursions round about our Camp, and commonly by myself, there being few in Company That had any relish, or amusement, for that kind of knowledge that I was in persuit of; except when I could sometimes prevail on M^r. McAntosh to accompany me, who was my Companion in this journey, & whose company I was fond of, being of a lively & good disposition.

This evening I discovered a very curious Little Shrub, growing at the bottoms of these Hills, & on the steep banks of the
Creek, The Foliage & form of groath a little resembled the
Aralia, but what was the most remarkeble in it, the root affording a strong Yellow Tincture, near as fine as that of Gum
boge, It has long slender branching Roots which run & spread
about just under the surface of the earth, filling a large patch
of ground with a numerous offspring. the shrub rises about
2feet high sending up a slender bending knotty stalk covered
with a white smoothe bark which on being rubed off discovers
a perfectly lucid Yellow wood, which dies as well as the Root,
it is in my Opinion a very valuable Shrub, on this account,
where a fine Yellow dye is wanted. The Morning being fine
& Our horses by reason of the goodness of the food being
easily found, wee soon got on our way. traveling through a
very fertile Country, Hills and Vales, wooded with variety of
large Trees, crossing at every mile or two distance Brooks &
rivulets of exceeding good cool Water, which are fed by large
Cain Bottoms, which are springy swamps sorounded By Hills,
& the sides of these hill are covered with Cains almost to their
Tops, together with Tall grass & Pea & Bean Vines, & Grape
Vines, cross't several large Brooks, waters of great Ogechee,
& camp't this night at a fine Branch of that River. The next
day rode about 15 Miles passing through for the most part of
the way, a levell plain, Open Forest, generally Pine, mixt with
Red & Black Oak & Hicory, the earth coverd every where
with, a variety of Tall Grass, Buffiloe grass, frequantly
crossing, Rivulets of Water, Cain branches, & some baron low
ridges of Schrub Oaks, small Grape Vines, Black Jacks &ᶜ.
frequantly beds of flat Rocks rising above the Surface, where
abouts grow'd schrub Oaks, dwarf Plumbs, Mespilus, the little
sweet flowering Agave, a small leaved procumbent Euphor-
bium, Purslin, Nepellus; we came into an open Forest of
Pines, Scrub white Oaks, Black Jacks, Plumb, Hicory, Grapes
Vines, Rising a sort of Ridge, come to a flat levill Plain and
at the upper side of this, levell at the foot of the hills of the
great Ridge, is the great Buffiloe Lick which are vast Pits,
licked in the Clay, formerly by the Buffiloes, & now kept
smoothe & open by Cattle, deer & horses, that resort here
constantly to lick the clay, which is a greesey Marle of various

colours, Red, Yellow & white, & has a sweetish taste, but nothing saltish that I could percieve, Several Pits were grown over with a very tall broad bladed grass very tender & swett, which Our horses were emoderately fond of. the whole lick may take up an Acre & half of ground & some holes 5 or 6 feet deep. The land decends gradually & a little ways farther down becomes moist & springey from whence proceeds a gully, but this being a very dry Season found no water untill We had gone near a mile down it. passing by other small licking Pits, we come to a lively stream that made in from a Cane bottom. This is said to be the head of Gr^r. Ogechee River.

I Returned to camp at the great lick, where I found Our People and the Indians in a wharm contraversy concerning the direction of the Lines of the Lands to be marked out. however by the address & wise conduct of Coll^l. Barnet, the dispute was, soon decided to the seeming satisfaction of both parties, & the Corner Tree was pitch't on, from whence the Surveyers took their courses. Here our company devided. A party of Surveyers with the Creek Indians run the Line down the So: side of Ogeche a certain distance, thence another course to the River Alatamaha; The Coll^l.. his surveyers. with the party of Cherokee's, continued up the Ridge to the mark't Tree of the old Line, thence a N^o. course, to Savanah River a mile below the mouth of Tugilo, where the River devides and looses its name, the S^o. branch being call'd Tugilo River; and the N^o. branch Keowe River, both heading in the Cherokee Mountains.

The business being thus agree'd on, The Creeks Party seperated from us, & I joined with Coll. Barnet up the Ridge. We continued traveling Over an oneven country, frequently rockey, the Vegitable productions much the same as past, the hills coverd with large Oak & hicory Timber growing amongst tall grass & the Vales produceing large Oak & hicory, Ash, Mulberry, black Walnut, Plumb, Halesia, Avilania, Stewartia, Staphyllea, and a many other's amidst a vast abundance of Herbage, Such as, Sunflower, Othonna, Saratula, Persicaria, Collinsonia, Lobelea's of various Species, Sium's, Eupatorium's, Aster's, Vetches, Pea Vines, small Canes, & a vast luxuriancy of the graminious tribes, crossing many fine Rivulets in the distance of 7 or 8 Miles, come to a branch of broad River, now the country rises higher, & rockey, the Tops of the Hills producing, Chinquapin, dwarf Oaks, some chesnut Trees, scattering Pines, Plum, scrub Oaks & Hicory, The Soil a thin greyish loam, frequantly gravelly & Rockey on a Bed of Yellow or red hard Clay. We camped by this branch. A pleasant morning attended by the feather'd inhabitants of these shady retreats with joyfull song invites us forth. the elivated face of this Hilly country breathes an elastic pure air, inspireing health & activity, I arose & joyfully contributed My aid in the contemplation of the wonderfull Harmony & perfection in the lovely simplicity of Nature tho naked yet unviolated by the rude touch of the human hand. tho admiting that, human inventions, Arts and sciences to be a part in the progress of Nature, yet are perpetually productive of inovations, and events, that shew the defects of human Policy; What a beautifull scenery is Vegitable Nature!

We proceeding on our journey up the Ridge which is a pleasant varied situation of country, consisting of Hills, vales, Canebreaks & rich bottoms, producing Black Walnut, Mulberry, Accacia, Oak, Hicory, Grape Vines, Chesnut, Of vast bulk, sweet white flowerd Robinia, vast abundance of luxuriant grass, Peavines, Canebreaks or meadows which are the heads of the branches of the Waters of Savanah on one side of the Ridge & the Ocone on the other, which interlock here, making very beautifull and Rich meadows of Canes, grass &^{c}.

Thus we traveled 12 or 15 Miles, crosst a large branch of broad River, about 30 Yards over, the Water Runs very swift, & the bed of the River incumbered with rapid falls, the land rising very high, Rockey & somewhat Mountainous, very rough next the river with piles of perpendicular Rocks especially the Bluffs when the Ridges run up to the River. observed on the Steep sides of the Rockey precipices growing among the Rocks the great rose flower'd Chamerodedendron, the lesser Kelmea or Virginia Ivey Tree and in baren places amongst the Rocks the low sweet flowering Agave, a beautifull Nepellus, & a most beautifull Scarlet blossom somewhat resembling the flower of the Ipomea, spotted with Crimson. & a many other fine Vegitables. proceeding 2 or 3 Miles farther, come to camp by a fine Branch of Broad River, whose gentle flowing surface was o'rshadowed by the flowery lofty Hills on One side, whose aspireing tops spread their evening shadows along the ample verdant lawns before them; In this levell plain, by the Banks of this Rivulet we incamp't early in the evening, the Indians wanting time to hunt for fresh provisions: Thus having time before Night, I hasted on my Botanical excursions round about the Camp: Observing when decending the Hills to cross the Crick, a very agreeable fragrant smell like cloves defused about us in the air, the whole company being affected by it, I immediately concluded it must arise from some Vegitable, being bruised by the horses feet, I therefore designed to go in quest of it as soon as we came to camp; accordingly, I cross't the Creek and began to assend the Hills, having attained a considerable hight, the Hills pretty steep, my feet suddenly slid from under me; I catch't hold of the sweet Calyconthus, that stretched out a friendly bow to my relief, however in the scuffle to save myself I discovered the lovely subject of my reserches, by the figure of the leaf & Root took it to be a Species of Cariophylata, but as I could find no flower or part of fructification whereby to fix its tribe or family, I judged from the fragrance & clove like scent of the Root. Still mounting the Hill, gaind the summit, from whence I had a very agreable prospect of the Plains below, observed abundance, of the blue flowered Nepellus, and a very curious Shrub; grows about 2 feet high, olive shaped leaves growing opposite on slender branches, bearing very large oval fruite or berries, rather larger than an olive or Plumb. yellow when ripe, as I was informed by the Indians, they grew single in the bosom of the leaf having a short Pedicile. could find none Ripe neither could I see any flowers. The Indian hunters, cary the Root with them beliveving it to have a fascinating Power, to bring deer to them. this the Indian Doctors or Conjurers make their People believe; & for which end they hold it in high esteem & make them pay dear enough for it, this was the account I had by an Interpreter present. they do not eat the fruit tho' it has a great Pulp & seemed to have no disagreeable taste, but the Root very strong & disagreeable both smell and taste. It has also a large kernel & possibly very oiley when ripe; in fine It is a Pretty new shrub well worth Notice & may possess qualities (yet undiscovered to us) of great use to mankind. It grows in large patches on high dry stoney & rather barren land.

Observed growing at the feet of these Hills in the Rich bottoms & vales laying between them & the Creek, Avellania of two species, a new & very beautifull Species of Stewartia having long pointed Capsulas, the Petals very long & narrow, & the tuft of Anthera of a rich yellow color, Magnolia Umbrella, Magnolia altissima, Magnolia glauca, very tall streight and ellegant, having Pyramedal Tops, I suppose in general from 80 to 100feet in hight, the Vast Lawreil Tree Magnolia grandiflora, White sweet flowering Robinia, Catalpa, Æsculus scarlet & white, all or most of these in full blowe, intermixt with other Noble forest Trees of different Tribes, in particular, the Beech of a vast height & magnitude, Sugar Maple, Black Walnut, Plain Tree, The vast Liriodendron, Or Tulep trees, friend to the industrious Bee, whose fluttering leaves drop honey dew Sheding mana on the earth.

Continuing my ramble about these fruitefull Hills and vales I decended down again to the Creek & traceing its winding courses through these fragrant Groves which led me to the foot of a hill, here a group of fine flowering Trees & Shrubs drew my attention. approaching this joyfull retreat which decorated the banks of the Creek just by a cascade, This noble assembly of vegitable could scercely be paralell'd in America, & would have been dificult for a Botanest on which to fix the preemenence. The Majestick Laurel Tree or Magnolia grandaflora towers above the chiefs of this vegitable Court, whose proud crest adornd with waving plumes of the most exquisite white flowers, attended by other beautifull tribes of this noble Family of Vegitables. The Rose Laurell Magnolea Glauca, almost equaling the first in magnitude & exceeded by none, in tallness & gracefull body, its piramedal head adorned with leaves of a delicate asure green, thick seed with rose like blossoms of the most perfect whiteness. Magnolia Umbrella Tree whose horazontal branches, adornd with vast silkey leaves so unifornly disposd in form of an umbrella & crested by the finest flower, the whole presenting a most magnificient Canopy. Magnolia Altissima, Liriodendrum, Sugar maple, Pavia scarlet & white flowerd, Azalia, Stewartia, Calycanthus, & rose flower'd Chamerododendron & lesser Kelmia in the steep

rockey Bank, bending with their heavy clustres of flowers toward the water.

resting myself sometime in this retreat, observed some small
fish hoping out the water that seemed to shine with an uncommon lustre, I went nearer the Creek, where I beheld a
most diverting prospect; which was innumerable little fishes
in the clear water. these fish I call'd gold Fish from the richness of their colours, observed little gravelly hillocks in the
gravelly beds of the Creek just below a fall or Rapid about a
foot & half high, not quite so wide at bottom, all around these
hills numbers of these beautifull little watrey inhabitents,
which seemed by their actions to be feeding, when all of a
sudden they were squandered by the approach of speckled
Crayfish that sprang out from the bank or rocks in the Stream,
& at this instant these fishes produced a delightfull & entertaining appearance (, darting through the clear waters & some
into the air like streams of lightning or sinking in the water
like grains of gold) to a distant observer. who very soon collecting themselves in little squadrons again approach the gravelly hillocks. I put my hand in to the Water amongst them &
shuting to my finger took several, some of which I caried to
the Camp where they were much admired. The Coll. was so
taken with the event, returned with me to the Creek, who was
much diverted.

I am at a loss to account for this very new & pleasing Phenomena, there is no doubt, but these little mounds of gravell
are collected together by some animal, as their regularity of
form & position shews them not to be the effect of chance neither could they be placed in this manner by an eddy water. I
pulled several of them to pieces but could find no animal within
that could collect such a number of pebbles together. I am inclined to think they are collected by the Crayfish as a covert or
nursery for their young offspring from the attacks of these little
vigilant Gold Fish. observing multitudes of young crayfish
when I spread the pebbles about. The Gold fish is about 3
Inches in length, about ¾ of an Inch broad, the top & sides of
the head of an asure blue colour, the whole body of a bright
vermileon color, having a darker line extend along the sides
from the Gills to the Tail, Tail & Fins Yellow, the whole fish
when alive & wet reflecting a lustre like the rising sun.

The Indians and hunters having brought into Camp 3 deer & two or 3 Turkeys, We proceeded next day on our journey, still continuing up the ridge, frequantly crossing rapid branches of the waters of the Ocone & Savanah Rivers which enterlock in this Ridge, passing by numbers of Indian old fields and Artificial Mounds, which have antiently been Towns & settlements of people Which The present Nations know nothing off; neither can they give any satisfactory account whenc they come or for what they raised these vast mounds of earth. But this I have observed where ever I have been on the coast of America S°. of Chesapeak Bay, between the Sea coast & the Mountains. we observe One or more of them about their old Settlements, & always find abundance of human bones, pieces of earthen ware, flint Arrow head, Stone knive, Axes &ᶜ. I opened some of the smaller Tumula which near the Sea coast are heaps of Oister shells; Up the Rivers, On the sides of Lakes, great Savanahs, or other convenient places for their habitations they are composed of heaps of earth; & toward the mountains are made of small Rocks & Stones heaped together; I observed nothing remarkable in the vegitable creation on the Ridge yet, except greater abundance of Chesnut Trees & on the higher ridges, we passt several miles over a some what barren country very rockey, the Trees rather schrubby but prodigiously intangled with Grape Vines, so as to make our progress very slow & disagreeable, the grape vines were generally loaded with green fruite & seemed large for the season. The Trees here were commonly short white Oak, black Oak, hicory, Chinquapin, Chesnut, shrubby White flowerd Robinia, Calyeanthos, Hamamelis, judas tree, some Black Walnut, Mulberry but short & Schrubby: Rose flowered Robinia. The Soil a shallow greyish sandy loam on a hard yellow & redish Clay very much incumbered with Rocks & Stones. I observed whenever we come to any old Indian Settlements, One or more of these high Indian Mounds, made their appearance sorounded with little groves of Black Walnut, Mulberry, Wild Plumb & Chesnut Trees. whether these were antiantly cultivated by the natives for their fruit I cant say. but the present nations that inhabit these lands seeme very fond of all kinds of eatible fruits & Nuts & take great care to cultivate Peaches, grapes, Plumbs &ᶜ. the Chicasaw & Cheroke

Plumbs are a delicious & excellent fruit & some extraordinary fine Peaches they have in their Towns.

We took up camp by a large Branch of broad River. here the Coll. detach't a party of Surveyers to take the courses of broad River down to the Mouth, & I continued with the Coll. up to Tugilo. this is the N°. branch, & may be between 20 or 30 Yards wide. The land very high & Mountainous, the bed of the River very full of Rocks, occationing perpetual Rapids & falls. observed on the Baron rockey shores abundance of sweet scented little shrubs of the Verticilate tribe, seemed to be a Species of Satureja. it was an evergreen, Chamerodedendros, lesser Kelmia, Halesia, Abies. Rose Robinia, Hydrangia, Alnus, Carpinus, Andromeda, Hamamelis. This morning was taken up with contraversies between the Indians & the Whites concerning the courses of the Line, the Indians intimating that the Surveyers incroach't on their rights. however all things being at length settled we again proceeded amicabley. continuing up a valley of good Land, gradually assended the hills, which in some places were steep & rockey. we at last approach't a very high country, in quality a pretty good Soil, producing much the same appearance, as for several days heretofore, except rather larger & greater abundance of Forest Trees. perticularly Chesnut, Black & Red Oak, very streight tall Trees. At the desire of the Indians we came to Camp by a pretty branch of the Oconee River, in order to find the Mark't Tree, from whence the surveyers was to sett a course for the mouth of Tugilo. here the Coll. sent off a party of rangers with a guide to find it. I most willingly took a part in this excursion. we rode 10 or twelve Miles, most part through pleasant rich land being a forrest of hills & vales. The timber Trees, Black white red & Spanish Oak, Black Walnut, white flowerd Robinia, Mulberry, Beech of a vast size, beautifull & streight, Sugar Maple, Tulep Trees, Ash leaved Maple, Sumach. Top & sides of the Hills produced Vast Chesnut Trees, & under these fine Forest Trees Shrubs of various kinds, Judas, Grapes, Cornus Mas, Evonimus, Stapelia. the surface of the earth coverd with Canes, Pea vines, Vitches, tall Grass, Herbacious Tribes, Collinsonia, Urtica, Panax Ginsang, Sium, Seratula, Eupatoriums, Lobelia, Wolfsbane, the low vales & Bottoms, Vast Trees of Oak, Walnut, Beech, Maple,

Ash, Linden, Mulberry. of Shrubs, Hazel, Judas, Stewartia, Halesia, Staphylea, Canes, Peavine, Sunflower &^{c}. at length we found the station Tree which stands by an old field; this has been an Indian Town where are Groves of large Mulberry & Walnut Trees, Plumbs &^{c}. Here is a spacious levell Forest on the great Ridge about eight Miles from the Ocone River. The Surveyers having fixt on the course, we returnd to Camp with an account of our success. & this evening came to camp again at a fine Creek just by the mark't Tree. before dark I had time to make a little excursion round about & directed my course up the Creek where I was agreably entertained by the very desart appearance of this Indian country now intirely uninhabited. the vast plains of flat rocks spread about, some excavated & worn in holes & cavities, in other places heaped up & piled one upon another tho without an appearance of order or design, as I gradually assended, the Trees become more scattered, a vast desart rockey plain open'd before me whence I had a prospect of far distant Hills westward which were the high lands on Tugilo, having wandered some distance from Camp & night approaching, I returned following at a distance this murmering Brook, that reluctantly took its course through deep & gloomy vales & winding cavities in the Rocks, which at length displayed a gentle flowing piece of water, decorated round about with green flowery banks; where stood a variety of Gay flowering Shrubs & Plants, The fragrant Caliconthos, Rhododendron, lesser Kelmia, Andromeda evergreen, Azalea White & Rose col^d., Lobelia's, the beautifull blue Aconite, Hepatica, Fragraria, bearing very fine large Fruite and on little stoney Islets, the most sweet Pancratium and a most singular aquatic Plant bearing a large pale blue eregular Flower. N^o Book of Georgia Specimins of Plants, the great Plantain, with a variety of other Plants. had just time to observe these Vigitable, & took notice of abundance of the beautifull Gold Fish, the Pebley little mounds in the bed of the Creek, the diverting contest between them & the Crayfish, returnd to Camp by dusk.—This night threatened Rain, from NW^t., the day having been hot & Sultry but the gust blew over with very little rain, which indeed would have been very acceptable had it come, the Season being remarkebly dry, insomomuch that we crosst abundance of dry gulleys & brooks; however the Thunder gust left us a lively breese & the morning was agreeably Cool & pleasant, we traveled this day over a ruged uneven hilly country stoney & baren, yet produced Schrub Oaks, Hicory, Chesnut & abundance of Grape Vines, observed abundance of the little Shrub bearing yellow large fruite as mentioned growing about broad River, & a very beautiful Shrub, bearing long loose spikes of sweet white Flowers. the flowers were composed of four long narow reflexed Petals, the stamina four in number, extreamly short, each supporting a large round anthera, the Stile very long curling inwards at the extremity, The Capsul in all respects like that of the Chamerododendros. It is a Noble Evergreen—Come to camp by the banks of a Branch of Savanah River, small but rapid and ran through very extendsive Cane bottoms which afforded excellent food for our horses. The hunters went out & bro't in some venison, very acceptable to us. the Next day we passt over much the same sort of country as Yesterday & come to Camp by a pretty large Creek in a vale between pretty high Hills but the food not being extraordinary good, in the morning some of our best horses were missing, which gave us some uneasiness, as being near the Indian Nation we were apprehensive that some skulking parties of Indians had come in the Night & caried them off. But the Indians of our Party told us that being within within a fiew miles of Savana river at the mouth of Tugilo, where was extraordinary Cane breaks, the horses smell't the food & were gone off there, & offer'd to get & bring them to Camp, they went accordingly & returnd with them by noon, & we arived at Savanah River by the mouth of Tugila in the evening. Here we incamped under the Hills, about half a mile from Savanah River. the Indians & Surveyers marked a Line Tree, GR. on one side for our King and the Indian Mark on the other side. Curiosity led me on discoveries, I directed my course to the River through fertile low Lands, & coming near the River bank where the land was higher & the soil a rich loose mold, I observed a very pretty shrub, which grew plentifully but could not find any flower or fruit, & abundance of the beautifull large blue & purple flowerd Malva which presented a most agreeable shew of heavey Clustres of flowers, leaning their heavey branches some bent to the ground & other supported by diverse plant about them. went to the River bank which in some places was steep & rocks & here I discoverd a most ellegant shrub have[g]. large nearly cordated leaves, of a silver color under side, the numerous flexile branches tufted with heavey clustres of white flowers in form of large Umbels which at a distance looked like snow balls, it seemes to belong to the Tribe of Hydrangia, from the River had an agreeable prospect of Small Islands, in the River some of which were intirely coverd with the beautifull sweet Pancratium, and about the Rocks the fine large rose flowerd Rhododendron, with lesser Kelmia all in flower, the River here may be about ¼ Mile wide, The shore on the opposite side high & somewhat Mountainous. had a view of some Islands above and below, which seemed pretty high land, & covered with groves of Various forest Trees. observed some Indian boy's fishing in the River by the mouth of the Creek & went towards them, one of them was persueing a fish which he had just struck with a Reed harpoon, he soon came up with him & giving the Reed a trhust let it go & again persued him, when giving another push, held fast & presently drew up a large Trout near 2feet long, they took a great number of Bream, observed one species of a beautifull Silver colour, finely speckled with gold & purple, we returned to Camp with a load of very fine Fish, & in my way took a very large & beautifull Glass Snake. which however was not generally so acceptable as the fish, as none chose to have him in the Mess. Thus having performed happily this part of the business sett out upon, we returned down the River to Augusta, keeping near its bank along the Hill side between them & the River.

There is an eminence of Broken rockey hills from Tugilo down to the mouth of broad River (which is about forty Miles above Augusta) with a Verge of Rich low land below next to the River, wide or narrower according as the Hills approach or recede to & from it, some places the Hills come so near that we had great dificulty in passing a long & in such Places the bluffs are very high steep & Rockey; At other times the Ridge retires a good way off, then the assent is more easy and gradual, the prospect agreeable. very frequantly large Creeks & brooks of water break through the Ridge falling over the Rocks into the River, at these places are extendsive rich bottoms & vales & these Creeks are proper situations for water Mills. These vales, the lowlands on the River, & sides of the Hills produce, Cane pastures, pea vines, grape Vines, & very large Timber Trees of Walnut, Locust, Mulberry, Ash, Linden, Sugar Maple, Hazel, Calicanthus, Papaw Anona, & tops of the Hills Vast Tall & fruitefull Chesnut Trees, Oak, Hicory of various kinds, Grape Vines, some Pine & Chinquapin.

This new ceded country promises plenty & felicity. The Lands on the River are generally Rich, & those of its almost inumerable branches agreeable & healthy situations, especially for small Farms, every where little Mounts & Hills to build on & beneath them rich levell land fit for Corn & any grain with delightfull glittering streams of water runing through Cain bottoms, proper for Meadows, with abundance of water brooks for Mills. the Hills suit extreemly well for Vineyards & Olives as Nature points out by the abundant produce of fruitefull grape Vine, Native Mulberry Trees of an excellant quality for Silk. And any of This Land would produce Indigo, & no Country more proper for the culture of almost all kinds of Fruits.

Soon after my return from the Tugilo journey to Savanah the country was alarmed by an express from Augusta, that the Indians were for war, & had actually murdered Several Families not far from Augusta; upon this I was advised not to venture amongst them but as the lower Creeks in east Florida were not openly concerned in the mischief I imagined I might with safety turn my discoveries in that quarter. incouraged with this view I set off from Savanah by land for the Alatamaha, having put my Chest onboard a small Vessell bound for the River S[t]. John, E[t]. Florida, intending to follow soon by water; With much difficulty got to Darien; where being taken ill with a violent Fever, did not recover my health for several Weeks; when I made the 2[d] effort to procecute my journey to Florida, expresses arived from that country that the Indians were broke out there, had murdered several People & broke up the Indian Stores in that Colony. however I was determined to proceed at all events to that Province.

29th. From Broton Island, near the Mouth of the River Alatamaha, a Vast Rice Plantation belonging to Coll. Lawrence, and very well managed by M[r]. J. Bailey an intiligent Planter,

I went onboard a small boat for Fredrica on S^t. Simons Island, arived safe there & waited on J. Spalding Esqr. to whose generous assistance I am indebted for my good success on this expedition. M^r. Spalding acquainted me that his Stores in Florida were broke, except his lower Store on S^t. John, some of his Traders plundered & were all come in to the Store & that he should send a Vessell in a fiew days to bring all his effects away, so I waited a day or two for a Passage in his Vessell & this time I imployed in exploreing this Island. Fredrica was built by Genl. Oglethorp, Ann. . . . which he made the seat of Government whilst he commanded in this Province, has been a very considerable Town, the Fort has been a pretty building, but now almost in ruins since the seat of Government has been removed to Savanah. The Island is computed to be 16 Miles in length, & 3 or 4 broad; the high land generally fruitefull tho a light sandy soil suitable for Corn, Indigo and pulse, the east side of the Island is the most fertile, there being a ridge of Sea shell, hills, The Vegitable productions here, Viz^t. of Trees, Live Oak some of which are of a vast bulk, Red Bay, Elm, Ash, Maple, Hicory, Mulberry, Magnolia perticularly the great Laurel Tree, Linden, Liquid Ambar; of Shrubs, Zanthoxilon, Aralia spinosa, Elder, Frangula, Prinos. Of herbaceous Tribes, Nettles, Rhapuntia, Crotons, Eupatorium, Euphorbiums and that fairest flower of America The sweet Pancratium, a noble species. Holly, Tupilo, Sasafras, in the moister ground Cassena, Olia Americana. Grape Vines, Prinos & a many others. The Savanahs & Baygales afford a vast variety of Sun flowers, Asters, Andromedas evergreen, Hypericon.

M^r. Spalding was pleased to favour me with —— his advice & directions how to proceed in my Travell amongst the Floridians, and charged me with Letters to his agents there.

Went onboard, gat 9 or 10 miles when the Tide bro't us to anchor; near a Point of the Island; went on shore with the Capt. to pass away the time till the Tide should make in our favour, we took our guns, but met no game, except some Curlews & a Raccoon. return'd onboard, & presently got under way, & being favourd with a pleasant Night made good way, in the morning the wind increasing in our favour, had every prospect of a quick & pleasant Voyage; having got up with Cumberland Island, we observed a Sail a head, the People judged it to be a Schooner every day expected from the Indian Store, & soon coming up with her, found it to be so; we came too, & our Capt. sent his boat onboard, I chose to go, for information; where I learnt very discouraging accounts, very bad talks from the Indians. She had onboard most of the effects from the Stores, with a number of Traders, who had come in from the Indians, I learnd that my chest was hid on an Island in the River S^t. Johns a little way from the Store, with other goods; & some effects yet remaining at the Store, with the Agent, the Indians having declared they should have timely notice to remove with safety before any more mischief should be done; in consequence of these discouraging accounts our vessell turn'd back to Fredrica. However I chose to continue my journey to E^t. Florida, in expectation of a more favourable turn of affairs, & having some papers in my baggage that I did not like to loose, so I got put on shore at Fort William on S^o. Point of Cumberland, where lived the Pilot of S^t. Mary's River who sett me over on Amelia Island, were I was very hospitabley entertain'd by M^r. Egan, Agent for L^d. Egmont, here are great Plantations for the culture of Indigo. M^r. Egan shewed me Samples of his Indigo which was the best I had yet seen. I staid 2 or 3 days with this Gintleman on his promising me a passage with him to S^t. Johns. observed some large Indian Mounts, & the vestiges of great Towns & square of the antiant Indian Natives, Observed a very beautifull Species Lycium with a blue flower, & a coral red fruit, a most elligant Shrub, it's ever gay with flowers, ripe & green fruit, and a beautifull Tythemalus, with curious leaves being painted with a bright Vermilion Col^r. near The pedicile. Went with M^r. Egan in his boat roaed by Negroes, this night incamped on a Shell bluff withen a fiew miles of the River S^t. Johns, got some excellent Oisters which we roasted for Supper, rested very well under a vast spreading live Oak, making a fire to keep off the Musquitoes. arose early in the morning; took advantage of a strong Tide, & in a fiew hours got into the great River S^t. Johns, got 8 or 10 Miles farther up. stop't at Mon^r. Facio's who has a very large Indigo Plantation, on a high Hill on E^t. side of the River. This very civil gentleman shewed me his improvements. his Garden is very neat & contains a greater variety than any other in the Coliny. he has a variety of European Grapes imported from the Streight, Olives, Figs, Pomgranates, Filberts, Oranges, Lemons, a variety of garden flowers, from Europe &^{c}. we dined with him, than continued up the River 8 or 10 Miles, got to Pottburg a large Plantation belonging to a Gentleman in England. here we staid this Night & in the Morning M^r. Egan set off by land to Augustine, having business with the Governor. I found the Inhabitants greatly alarmed at the hostile disposition of the Indians & were generally on the flight or fortiffying themselves by Stockadeing in their houses, however I understood that the chiefs of the floridian's had been in to S^t. Augustine, promising satisfaction for what they had done, &^{c}.

I purchased a Canoe and alone continued my voyage up the River, having a Sail, some provisions, Gun and Amunition. My undertaking was I confess somewhat hazardous at such a time; The River being very wide, & my vessell small, was obliged to coast close along shore, this night I got about 7 Miles and campt on W^t. side of the River. Next day got about 5 Miles, the Wind rising pretty fresh against me, was obligd to look out for a harbour, and at last found a pretty good one which was very fortunate, for me, the River here being very broad near 3 Miles over; the gale taking me about the middle, having at last almost gain'd the Port, observed a prodigious large Alegator basking in the sedge on the shore, whether, he was a sleep or not I am not certain but approaching near he suddenly plunged in the water, directing his cours right at me & the water being very shole the monster went under my little vessell, had like to caried me away with him, however I got safe ashore & having moored my Vessell made an excursion in the forests, took notice of the beautiful Laurus cerasus bearing charming spike of flowers, a fine evergreen Shrub but past flowering; The Orange Trees were very fragrant In blossom, night coming on I returnd to Camp, struck up a fire and prepared, myself for this night solitary repose, hoping for favourable weather next morning. The much wish't morning appeared, but without hopes of getting away, the wind very high & against me; I arose early, & hearing some Turkeys struting, took my Gun & went towards them, I soon saw two large Turkey Cocks & a Hen, & had the luck to shoot the two Cock, which were very heavey & fat. I barbecued them, for Provisions, on my Voyage; bad weather still continuing all this day, & next, till towards the even^g., the wind seemed to lull; I repared to a sandy point a little distance from my harbour, to see how the River looket. the swell seemed to abate; a very agreeable smell come over the water from the Pine tops, these trees being now in flower, and soon observed incredible Clouds of small brown dragon flys, which come from the other side in such prodigious numbers, as for a time almost obscured the sun, the air was thick with them, as far as I could see upwards, but they quickly decended, down, & almost covered the Trees and ground about me, they however proved most Wellcome messengers, for a gentle Gale soon succeeded which was some more favourable to me; I got all thing aboard & soon reimbarked & had just time to cross the River to a Point of land, I long wanted to gain just before dark; having only time enough to prepare my lodgings before dark came on. Sonn after it began to rain, which continued all night & very windy. the rain abated in the morning, the wind yet very high & against me. I took a turn in the groves were I found abundance of Oranges and pretty evergreens, amongst the rest that very singular & beautifull evergreen commonly called wild Lime; saw an Indian who was indeavouring to get up to a flock of Turkeys, he discoverd me & I went up to him. he told me in english he lived at a plantation about a Mile off, he was a slave bro't from the Musqueto Shore; about Noon the wind being more favourable I got twelve mile farther; come too at Picolata Fort. which I observed was newly repared; got 2 Miles farther. stop't at an Orange grove. Next day got about 30 Miles, staid this Night at Villa Role. This place was settled about twelve years ago by D. Role Esqr. The situation is very high & pleasant. S^t. Johns being much narrower here than any where below, & very deep, here are only a few People that has the care of the houses & Stock belonging to M^r. Role. this place is at present in a ruinous state; tho I think a very proper & agreeable situation for a Town. It Is about Ninty miles above the mouth of the River, & 35 Miles by land to S^t. Augustine. Sett off soon in morning, passt by two Indian Settlements on the west side of the River; they

observed me as I passt along, but offered no incivilities, called
at the Camp on the Island, where the effects belonging to the
Store were deposited under the Care of siveral Traders, got
to the lower Store this even^g. where I was friendly received
by M^r. McLatchy Agent. After conferring with the Traderes
concerning the Temper & disposition of the Indians; who
seemed generally of opinion that the present confusion, was
occationed by some discontered young Warriors in the Nation
unknown to the Chiefs who wanted to go to war for plunder;
as the head men of the Floridans had lately declared to the
Governer in Augustine, that the Traders were robbed by a
Gang from the Nations & were in hopes that Trade & friendship would soon be restored again; After some days a party of
Traders, agreed to resque a journey to Cuscowela, an Indian
Town on Allatchua Savana to hunt up some horses belonging
to them; I embraced this opertunity to see that part of Florida
particularly the great Savanah.

April. Set off having a very good interpretor. rode a Mile
& half over low level land, almost intirely coverd with small
Dwarf Palmeto, under scattering Pine Trees, the soil a white
fine sand. came to a branch of water, the bottom a hard white
sand, the soil on each side for a small distance wet & owsey
producing Red Bay, Candle berry Myrtle, short Magnolia
glauca, then taller leaning Palmetos. then we come to a sandy
ridge, the sand dry, producing Palmetos, schrubby Oaks that
grow about 20feet high, large tall Pine Trees; These Sand Hills
or Ridges, are the highest Land of those flat Sandy Countries
of the Sea coast of Carolina & Florida deviding the waters of
different Rivers from each other, generally dry white sand,
they are generally, however, productive of grass and Palmetos,
various little Shrubs, Such as, various Species of Kelmia, Andromeda, Myrica cerifera. Prinos, little dwarf Oaks, & Chinquapins, as well as good large Pine Trees of the long leaved
species reconed the most valuable, both for Lumber, & its
yielding Turpentine, Tar & Pitch: we next come to Bay gales,
two miles through. As I shall have occation often to mention
these Bay Gales & Savanahs in describing, the different situations of these countries, I shall now indeavour to explain
them. These Rivers that do not reach the Hilly or Mountainous parts of these countries have their source in small Lakes

or Savanahs that have been Lakes or Ponds now fill'd up &
become grassy meadows or Savanahs which some times are
vast & extendsive, & beautifull bayand expression, or rather
they primarily derive from Gale bays, which are vast extendsive
wet & boggy schrubby plains, producing Red Bay, Horse-
Sugar Shrubs, Magnolia Glauca, Alcea Florida, all indifferently
call'd Bay's by the Inhabitants, mixt with sweet Gale, Candle
berry shrubs, evergreen Prinos, various Andromeds &^{c}. which
are perpetually kept low by the annual fireing the woods. these
Gale Bays are, on one side of the Savanahs, round about under
the Sand hill & Ridges, where the wet, owsing out, feeds the
Savanah with Moisture: or the Gale Bays are on the lower side
of the savanahs, where the brook begins a constant runing
stream. Next we come to a moist flat Pine Forest, the ground
coverd with low Palmitos, thus continued a Miles then we
come to a low wet extendsive Savanah, overgrown with very
tall streight Swamp Pine that seemed to be of a fiew years
growth, the soil a black sandy slush about a foot deep, on a
hard white sandy bottom, this place was about one Mile
through, producing very good tall Grass, intermixt with, various Species of Plants, Lobelia, Phlox, abundance of pretty
large white Lillies, on dry knowls. Very large Thistles, with
red Crimson & white Flowers, Loblolly Bay, very tall beautifull Trees, Magnolia glauca, finely in flower, Tall & beautifull
Cabbage Trees, (Palma vera). Thus having passt four or 5
Miles through a very wet & desagreeable Road, we got to dry
Pine Forests. we began gradually to rise on the Sand hills. We
rode 3 miles, come to a large rapid Stream of water, crosst &
went through a narow Swamp of midling good land, then rise
on the sandy pine Forrest, the ground coverd with low Palmetos, & pretty good Pine Timber continuing several miles,
rise higher Land, Pine & black Jacks. we continued rising sand
Hills, came to another Large Creek, some pretty good swamp
Land, high sandy pine Forest such as we had passt, the land
becomes now higher & more uneven, beggining to form
Chains or ridges of higher sand hills, the apperarance of which
tho sandy & barren, yet exhibits a pleasing Prospect, high pine
Forest, Hills & little Lakes & Savanahs, some round, & deep
between the hills, these Ponds & little lakes are of various sizes
& form, some 1 Miles over, other 5 or 6 Miles, some partly

sorounded with delightfull green levell meadows, other incompassed by high steep hills, & the large pine Trees, being
thinly planted about the green grassy Hills, we might from
the top of the high ridges see numbers of these little lakes at
a great distance Glittering through the Groves, & sorround-
ing us on every side, & their banks frequantly planted with
Orange Groves, all in flower, perfuming the Air, rendered our
journey this part of the day perfectly agreeable & made ample
amends for the dificulties I met with in the morning. this
evening came to camp by the side of a large Pond about 7 or
eight miles in length, bordered round with extendsive green
grassy lawns or meadow, sometimes partly dividing the waters
by long points or Peninsulas, every where inhabited with va-
rietes, of species of Herons, Biterns, Storks, Herds of Deer.
this is called long pond or halfway pond; The Musquetoes
were very troublesome, got very little rest. This morning
being very fine we early got on our way, but our People having
occation to hunt the woods for horses, we could not Reach
the Town this day. we camped by the side of a pleasant Pond.
the face of the country was much the same as pass't yesterday.
Alternately high sand hills and green Savanahs. observed the
sand hills to be the highest land, had yet seen in the istmous
& the surface of the earth about them to be coverd with Pib-
bles, pieces of white & yellow flint, pieces of course kind of
white lime stone, being concretions of small pieces of sea
shells cemented together with sand, & some masses of Rocks
of the same composition appear'd above the earth. Early this
morning we come to a very pleasant Creek, which emptied its
waters into a large pond or Lake. Now the land begins again
to fall lower. From this creek for the distance of 7 or eight
miles we travelled over a levell Pine forest & some savanahs,
overgrown with large timber & the ground richly coverd with
good grass intermixt with varieties of flowers of various species
& colours, we cross't part of a vast extendsive marsh, we then
entered a hamock, throug which we continued 3 or four
Miles. The Soil pretty good, producing Live Oak, Water Oak,
Hicory, Linden, Mulberry, Elm, Magnolia grandiflora; this
sort of Land is too high for the produce of Rice, but is very
proper for Cora, Indigo, Cotton. &^{c}. next we entered an open
pine forest throug which at a small distance presented

to view an exceeding beautifull Lake. our rode passing but a small distance from it and observing a large Indian Mount, which stood on the high banks of the Lake; I rode up to it from which I had an agreeable prospect over the Water, that has been formerly an Indian Town but unknown to the present Indian Nation Inhabiting this Country. here are a few Indian houses, but the People were gone out hunting except a fiew Women & Children.

We rode about a quarter of a mile farther and arived at the Town of Cuscowela. here abouts I observed The beautifull large white flower'd Anona, bearing a large fruite. and another Species, much smaller having extremely narow leaves, bearing a rose cold blossom, with crimson spots on the inside of the petals near their bases sorounding a large purple button containing the parts of fructification. The Town of Cuscowela consists of about 40 houses; placed pretty near to one another, sorounding a large open square, in the Center of which stands their Counsel house. the chiefs house was destinguished from the rest no other way than being a little larger, & by having a Flag hoisted at one Corner. Our Interpretor conducted us there. Assended an Indian Ladder, to a loft about 12 feet high where we sat down on Derr Skins; When very soon the Chief come to us & wellcomed us to his Town, with all posseble signs of joy & satisfaction, & told us of some bad talks just arived from the Nation, but he assured us of our safety & his protection; Presently Victuals was bro't to us, A Kettle of boiled Milk & another kettle of boiled Corn, with dryed Venison & Bears meet, Honey & Water, we laid our business before the Indians & having finished our repast, Set off For the great Savanah; rode about 3 miles through a low wet gale bay, coverd with little short Palmatos & very short & shrubby Pines. entered a Hamock of pretty good Oak Land, continued near a Miles through this dark thicket. Now on a sudden opens to view an inchanting scene, the great Allatchua Savanah. Behold, a vast Plain of water in the middle of a Pine forest 15 Miles in extent & near 50 Miles in circumferance, verged with green level meadows, in the summer season, beautifully adorned with jeting points & Promentorys of high land. the prospect is greatly beautified by the Prodigious Numbers of Wild fowl of various kinds,

Such as Cranes, Herons, Biterns, Pluvers, Coots. & Vast
herds of Cattle, Horses, & Deer Which, we see far distant, in
detachments over the vast Plain. The upper regions of the Air
contributes to this joyfull scene. the Silver plum'd Heron,
early in the morning hastening to their fisheries, croud to the
watery Plain, the Sonorrous Stork & Whooping Crains pro-
claim the near approaches of the Summers heats, descend
from the Skies in musical squadrons & decend; spreading
themselves over the wide green, all these gay inhabitants; at
even tide retire to the sorounding groves. This Vast Plain in
the winter Season is a beautifull Lake of Water, visited by an
incredible number of wild Fowl. The great Canada Goose,
Brant & grey Geese; with an endless variety of Ducks. In the
Month of November, when Cold N. & N E winds reach this
Country, the winged inhabitants of N^o. America begin to assemble here especially Water Fowl who make this Country of
E^t Florida their Winter retreat, & This Vast Savanah on account of its great extent affording proper food, Grass, Snales,
Periwinkles, Water Insects, fish & reptiles. It may be termed
the Elisium of Birds, & happy was he that reach't it, as the
Indians never molest them; but, lately the white People, traders, take incredible numbers of them; here they assemble in
such prodigious numbers, approaching like Clouds in the air
& spread themselves over the Waters, a Gun being fired
amongst them in the even^g or Morning, the affect is altogether asstonishing. they rise in that Quarter, like a Vast dark
thunder Storm, & shakes the air as a rushing tempest, but on
being disturbed in the Night, the multitude rises from all
quarters, the thunder of their Wings, with their united squal-
ing Tongues exhibits a scene of confusion & bableing as if
the desolution of Nature was at hand, This may appear more
delusive then real, true as it is. This night we came to camp
at S. W^t. end of the Savanah at an Orange Grove, after ride-
ing over a most pleasant green Meadow about 12 Miles, cros-
ing numbers of large coves from Point to point, which in
some places project in long Points of little scattering groves
of Oak, Magnolia & Pine Trees. numbers of herds of deer
scouring over the green plains find here a safe retreat, Observed here growing abundance of Nympha White Water lilly,
Common Nympha having large Yellow flowr. saw some leave,

& dried Capsulæ of the Colocacia Egyptian Bean Hybiscus, these grew in the water.

After we had came to camp, I as usual made an excursion in to the Groves, & thickets, but discoverd nothing new. except a very elegant Species of Abutilion having very large Velvetty hart shaped leaves, decorated with large flowers of a light Crimson. Observed growing about the roots of the Oak & Lawrel Trees in the shade Groves abundance of the little Mitchelia, this the Natives extol as an infaleable remedy in Nephritic complaints, penetrating this thicket, I found myself at a point bordered on one side by an extendsive green meadow sorounded by high Hills & forests & before me & all around on the other hand an almost endliss Plain of waters & green Meadows. I was amused at this noval Indian Scene. here we saw herds of deer bounding before the chace of the naked active Floridian mounted on his fleet Siminole horse, at the same time, other companies of Deer, of Horses & Herds of Cattle, some securely feeding almost out of view in the midst of the Plain on green grassy Islets, Other basking & sporting under the shadowy hill sporting on their way towards their Nocturnal retreats.

The sun sets behind the dark woody hills, the musical Stork, with all the featherd inhabitants of the Savanah in successive squadrons, with even'g song slowly move to their gloomy retreats. I retired to Camp & rested well this Night. but when awakened by the bellowing Allegator, & chattering Water hen.

The early watchfull Wattulas shrill voice, rings through the Forests & wakes all to action & hails the rising Sun.

Our company this morning devided to range about the Savanah in search of horses. I join'd company with a party round the Savanah to the Sink. towards the N E^t. end, we rode on the green verge from point to point of the jeting hommocks, frequently crossing fine green coves, which deeply scolloped the Shore, occationally entering the Groves. asscended a high Rocky hill, here was old Indian fields & Orange Groves, we went through this dark Grove of Live Oak, Magnolia &^{c}. but observed no new genera of Vigitables, we entered a spacious green Meadow, a cove of the Savanah, rous'd a gang of Deer which run off entering a grove, we came up to a point of scattering trees, when we observed them by a green pond in the midst of a green Meadow, they were diverting themselves, some skiping & plunging in & out the Water, others stretch't along on the green, when of a sudden being affrighted, they all started off, directing their course right towards us. a young buck come forward a head of the gang which our hunter shot at & laid him on the ground. the rest, sprang away bounding over the Plain, having placed our game in the fork of a Tree & throw'd a hunting shirt over him to preserve it from the Vultures till our return in the even^g We proceeded round the Savanah, frequantly rousing herds of Deer, Cattle & flocks of Turkeys. approaching a homock of Trees that stood out in the Meadow, observed a company of black wolves, we made up towards them who with a flock of Vulters & Eagles were tearing to pieces the Carkas of a horse. they stood their ground till we come within gun shot when the Wolves trotted off a little ways, then sat on their breeches Untill we passt them when they returnd to their repast, they were all black of the size of a large Dog, having a thick bushey Tail & sharp ears. The Wolves are become very numerous & mischiefous since this Country is become inhabited & the Indians get Stocks of Cattle, but were not so a fiew years ago insomuch it was a fiew Years ago a rare thing to see or hear of a wolfe. In E^t Florida. Having rode about twelve miles, we come to a Point of high land. I assended the rockey hill, come into an old Indian fields, here has been antiently an Indian Town. decended down the other side & entered a very deep cove of the Savanah, & directed our course a cross to a high point of Land, tho the meadow look't green with grass yet as wee approach't towards the mid way found the water deep, the grass growing through it, & soon took our horses off their legs, swam 40 or 50 Yards, when the water sholed. we got safe through, but a little wet, our horses were so fond of this grass could hardly get em along. We came very near to a gang of deer who were feeding almost up to their Backs in water, on seeing us near they plunged through the water & got away, we came near the woods, observed the great Wattula or Savana Crains setting on their Nests, they make their Nest of dry grass & sticks On high hillocks of Rushes & set with their long legs sticking out before them like a child in a high Chair, they lay three Eggs, which are longer than a Goos egg; We

soon gained the shore, thence we continued a mile or two &
come to small Clustre of Tree, Live Oak, Celtis, Elm & Magnolia which grew round about a deep sink or Bason of water
incompassed with Rocks composed of a greyish sandy lime
stone. rode about two miles over pleasant green lawns under
the Oak & Orange Grove hills, enter'd a point of woods &
came to a beautifull rapid brook of Cool water, flowing over
the silver leaf't Arum, the Banks adorned with Willows, Stew-
arts, Halesia, Evonimos, evergreen Prinos, Halesia, Cornus
Femina &^{c}. continued & soon crosst another fine branch of
good water. rode round the shore, & came to a high point of
Land, assended the steep hills, came to large Orange Groves,
which covers a large space of Ground, very uneven, sharp
pointed Hills & little rockey ridges, & deep holes or sinks.
thes holes, are numerous, some 50 or 100Yards over, at top
round, and narrowing to a point at bottom like a Funnell.
having clear water standing at the bottom & others dry, some
of a smooth surface of earth or the side overgrow with herbage & shrubs, other have steep walls of Rocks. continued a
little farther, & descended the Hills, when opened to view a
little cove of water, almost invoiron'd with steep rockey Banks.
This is the recepticale, or rather, passage of the Waters of this
vast Savanah, called the Sink, & here the waters gradually descend & sink down, & are discharged by hiden subterranian
Passages no one knows where; it is the common opinion of
Indians & Traders, they run into the little St Juane River that
flows into the Bay of Appalatche. This Sink is the most remarkeble Place for Allegatores, & to relate the Tales & accounts given by the Indians & Traders, would appear incredible & fabulous. however to my own certain knowledge,
they are prodigiously numerous & of a dredfull appearence. I
saw them 20 or more together in heaps uppon one another
basking in the sun on the shore round about, & the Surface
of the water almost cover'd with their monstrous heads, floating about like logs or chunks of wood.

Towards the fall of the Year the waters of the Savanah partly
by exhaleations from the Summer heats & draining into this
vast dark cool recepticle, the Fish assemble here. The Allegator are here in the Caverns of the Bank & Rocks round
about the sink, & in very dry & low times the Sink hole is

full of them, the enormous Allegator rushes out upon them, destroys incredible numbers & driving others ashore, where they die & rot on the land. I could observe no vortex or ruffeling on the surface of the water in this sink.

The Savanah is surrounded by pretty high hills, which looks like one continued high Ridge, the soil a greyish sandy loam, & on some high bluff a little rockey. when we are a top of the Ridge it continues back generally about a Mile & half the same sort of soil, which is fruitefull, producing Orange Groves, Great evergreen Magnolia, Sweet Gum, Live Oak, Elm, Linden, hicory, Mulberry, Papaw, Carpinus, Red bay, &ᶜ. Of Shrubs, Halesia, Stewartia, Sambucus, Staphylea, Cassina Holly, Winter berry, Æsculus, Calicarpia. Herbaceous Plants The beautifull Abutilon, Osteospermum, Helianthos, Aristalochia, Lobelias, Tetragonathekia, Eupatorium, Collinsonia. Back of this hamocky Ridge we again came to flat levell Pine Forest, Savanahs & Ponds as usual.

having compleeted my observations of this very singular place & examined its natural productions, we returned, the shortest way through the savanah, & by Night got to Camp, where we found the other Party already arived, with their horses, having found several. we were visited by several Indians who left us in the Night seemingly in a good disposition. Next morning after hunting up their horses, we returnd back to other end of the Savanah, where we came to Camp about four Miles from Cuscowela whither One of our Traders went & staid all Night intending to meet us here in morning. I spent this even'g in examining the woods & meadows about, observed here abundance of large Snakes, which were among the dry leaves & shrubs, two or 3 twisted together, they were of a harmless nature. I could scarcely provake them to open their Mouth & when pursued crept under the dry leaves & into holes in the dry sand. One kind were marked with black & white spots, made a loud hissing noise, when molested. The other kind, were of a dirty Yellow & bright red belly, both kinds very large, Six or 7 feet in length & thick. the last kind are very common about houses where they are very usefull in destroying Rats & other Vermin but are apt to destroy Chickins & suck Eggs. they Likewise climb up Matin Poles & dove cotes where they destroy the Young.

Set off off this morning on our return to the Store. rode about four miles round the Savanah then took off through the Homock, rode about two miles, & came to a pretty high sand ridge, which was a very agreeable open forest of Red oaks. pass't by an Indian settlement consisting of 3 or 4 houses near to each other; This is called the little Town. Decended a little & passt several Miles through low levell pine Forrest & savanahs. come to a fine large Brook called Fishing Creek, here was an Indian incampment, all the fellows were out hunting, but the Wenches & children at home, rode 7 or 8 Miles further through Pine Forests, came into the Road again. & shortly after came to Camp by a pleasant Creek near an Orange Grove.

The next morning pretty early got on our way, passing through Pine groves & Savanahs, finely ornamented with flowering shrubs, & Plants, particularly the glorious large white & rose col'd flowering Anona, & the Erythrina, which grows here to a fine tall Shrub, as likewise a species of Apuntia or Cactus, some white with the Cochanele Insect. passt by the delightful Lakes & Savanahs as mentioned heretofore & arived safe at the Store by Night.

Hearing at the Store of some Letters for me being sent by the care of his Honour the Lieu^t. Governor Moultry to a Plantation On the River about forty Miles down, I immediately took passage in a boat then going down the River. in two days got to the Place, calling at a Plantation On the west side of the River belonging to Governor Tonyn; here I was shewed some samples of the best flora Indigo I had yet seen, there were twenty hands employed on this plantation who made about twelve hundred w^t. of Indigo the last Year, & had now planted this year's crop. having rec^d. the letters which were from Do^r. Fothergill, London, by the way of Charlestown. These letters gave me great satisfaction, acquainting me of the safe arival of some Specimins of Plants of the natural productions of Georgia among which were near 50 new plants. Having got my letters I returnd up the River to the Store again, intending soon to make a tour up this River towards its source, intending to employ my time this way on natural discoveries untill a party of traders were ready to set off for Little St Juane River that runs into the Bay of Apalatche.

About this time a party of Indians from the lower Creek Nation come into the Store & with them a Runner dispatched from the Nation with a talk, the substance of which was that the whole Nation were greatly confused about the present differences; that the whole Creek confederacy were assembling at one of their principle towns to delebirate how to obtain peace & commerce again with the whites, that they were determined to oblige the Cowetas who were the agressors to give up the Murderers or sacrifice the whole Nation, by withdrawing their protection from & deliver them up to the resentment of the whites to take what satisfaction they should count necessary. By the same Missinger we were assured that the Simonoles on the Bay of Apalatche had taken & put to death the Murderers of Magee & his People, & in general that there were hopes of peace & trade again, the runner sat of next day for St Augustin. these accounts were agreable & enlivened my hopes of having yet an oppertunity of travelling with safety in this wild savage part of America.

The next day having repaired my little Vessell, & procured some necessaries, sat off up the river S^t. Johns, having very little wind & a pretty strong current against me, got about twelve miles, call'd at an Indigo Plantation belonging to M^r. Tucker a Gentleman in England; The house stands near the River On a high shelly bank, just by it is an Indian Mount having a broad streight High way leading from the Mountain to the Pine Forests. meeting here with a boat with two white men who were going about thirty miles up the River, I staid with them at Mo^t. Royal this Night with a view of haveing their company next day over the Lake, My Vessell being very little & the great Lake often very rough, thought it Needfull. I indeavoured here to hire a Young man to accompany me up the River, but being ingaged with the Plantation, could not insist, so was obliged to depend on my own labour.

Mo^t. Royal gives name to a large Plantation belonging to L^d. Egmont, was formerly an Indigo Plantation, but now given up & the hands removed to Emelia Island on the No. of this Province, there is about 150 Acres of Land cleared here & has been planted with Indigo, here is a very hadsom large Framed house, which stands about 100 Yards from the River, having sundry convenient out houses, placed in a regular maner. there are here about the houses left standing several very large wide spreading evergreen Oaks & Orange trees sour & sweet, very fruitfull,

About one hundred Yards from the River Bank & about three times that distance from the dwelling house, rises to View M^r. Royal. A very high Indian Mound of earth, of a conecal form, flat & nearly levell at top, about 20 Yards perpendicular height & about 150 Yards in circumferance at the base. Immediately from this mound runs a broad spacious road or high way streight out into the Pine forests, having a bank of earth thrown on each side about 2 & half feet high, all overgrown with shrubs & forest Trees, amongst which are some very large & ancient live Oaks as likewise grows over the mount. this highway is about 30 Yards wide & extends above a quarter of a Mile out to the Pine Forest, at the end of which opens to view an agreeable levell Savanah in the center of which is a little lake of water which is of a square form & seemes to have been dug out by the Indians, & perhaps the earth came a way to raise the mound with. From the summit of M^r. Royal you have an extendsive & agreeable view of the entrance of the great Lake, which appears between two pretty Islands, Viz^t. Drayton Island on the left & Bell Isle on the right hand, as like wise a view of two promontories on each side the mouth of the River as we enter the Lake where it is about 1 Mile wide.

The next day proving very Stormy & the wind ahead, could not move out of harbour so I continued my observations about this place, discoverd a very curious shrub, having nettle like leaves placed opposite, bearing tufts of beautifull Orange col'd flowers at the extremities of the branches, which are succeeded by clustres of asure col'd Berries, the plant has an agreeable scent, fragrant, resembling balm with a mixture of Musk. A very pretty little campanula with bright blue flowers.

The next day sat off in company with the other boat, which being larger & having a good sail took me intow, in this maner we set sail leaving M^r. Royal one of the finest situations on this River, went about 3 miles & entered the great lake George which is about twelve miles over either way; we set a course streight across for the mouth of the River. at other side, having passt by Draiton Isle, the wind came about a head &

blowing a fresh gale from thunder clouds rising up from the S W., we were obliged to put back for a harbour, but before we made the shore the gale carried a way our mast & Sail, which however we saved from going over board, & with great danger got into a harbour on the Island where we were detaind all night, but the storm clearing away. a calm & serene morning displayed an agreeable prospect over the wide spread waters of the lake, invironed with the high indented shores on every side as far as we could see. We took advantage of the calm repose of the morning & hurried through to the opposite shore & got in the River: The even^g being pleasant, & having about 6 miles to the upper Indian Store, we amused our selves with fishing with the bob, & took 7 or 8 large trout, & before Night got to the Store, where were a number of Indians who had taken possession after the Traders left it, they recieved us seemingly in a friendly maner, & having plenty of Bear Oil we drest our fish which made us a good supper.

Here I was again put to my shifts, being left alone, the People of the other boat going no farther up the River, however I got one of the men to accompany me on condition that I would return by a set time, so agreeing, we set off next day, & got about 8 Miles up the River, & came to camp at a high Orange Grove Bluff on the River opposite the mouth o' the branch of the River that came from the great E^t. Lake, call'd Lake Gordon; The River where we camped was narow not above 70 Yards over but Very deep & the stream very rapid. close to the right hand of our camp a pretty large lagoon, made into a vast marsh, which with a deep swamp surrounded us, communicating with a lagoon on the other side of us so that we were on a little high Islet, containing about 2 or 3 Acres of high land, the soil composed of a surface of black sandy Mold, on a vast heap of white Periwinkle or snale shells laying on a bed of soft limestone Rocks that lifts just above the surface of the waters of the River. These Limestone Rocks are a concrete of sand & shells that seem to have been reduced almost to powder, cemented together with whole shells of snails, Oister & muschel, This kind of Rock seems to be the bed or foundation of all the country of the Istmus of Florida at least as far as I have been, which we discover by observing the steep banks on the river S^t. Johns when we get above the great Lake. This River abounds with multitudes of Alegators or Crocadiles which are of vast size & extremely voracious; having pitch't our Camp; before night we went into the Lagoon to fish for Trout & having taken a sufficient number for supper, returning to camp; just in the mouth of the Lagoon, three alligators of a monstrous size rush't out of the weeds, & stop't before us who seemed inclin'd to dispute the pass, however we pusht on towards them. One rush't through the water at us, heaved his enormous body streight up out of the water near breast high, close by the side of our canoe, & open'd a dreadfull pair of jaws, & a bellowing throat; The other rose up behind us in like maner, pierceing the water with his strongplated Tail 5 or 6 feet high, flourishing it in the air. lashing the River into a foam, & roaring like furious waters breaking out of the earth, then plunging & rushing through the waters around us. Thus were we attacked by those River monsters & pursued to the shore where they lay threatning with terrible roaring. I jumped a shore clear, but was pursued up on land, within 3 Yards of our Tent; having a Fusee loaded with buck shott I immediatly armed myselfe & returned to the attack. he had withdrew himself in to the water but observing me approach nearer, pusht up towards me, & being within about 5 or 6 Yards I discharged my piece & blew the whole load into his body just behind his fore leg; he turn'd over & died immediately; the noise of the gun made them retire a little distance, in the mean time we got our fish out the canoe; & began to scale & clean them. Again the Allegators assembled in prodigious numbers, some rising their huge bodies out of the water, & roaring like terrible thunder & lashing the waters with mighty bodies, they drew near to us & one rise up & with a sweep of his Tail had like to robbed us of our fish, which we recover'd again, he come near again & having my gun loaded with a bullet, which I discharged at his head & I believe wounded him, he plunged in the water, in a dreadfull maner, & rise up a good way off. fireing at them several times caused them to keep at some distance. they however appeared so numerous & formidable round our port, that I began to consider my situation very desagreeable & under an absolute embargo. It is scarcely credible what an immence number of Fish these monsters destroy. especially at these

passes, the River being here, as I observed before, very Narow.
The Trout who pass here in their way to & from the numerous lakes & endless Lagoons & Marshes towards the head of
this Vast River, where they go to spawn. The Alegator post
themselves forming a line across, where we see them opening
their voracious Jaws into which the fish are intrap't. They
heave their heads and upper part of their body upright, opening their throats to swallow them, & I have seen them with
two or three great Trout in their mouth at a time, choping
them up, the fishes tail hanging out. the noise of their jaws
choping together, with the water & prey in their Throats;
their plunging through the water after their Prey & pusuing
one another altogether exhibits a very terrifying shew; Got no
rest this Night owing to the stinging of Musquitoes & Noise
& confusion of the Alegators & fish, As soon as day appeared
the Thunder of the Allegators, roaring all around us, & for
many Miles. Their noise is louder then the bellowing of the
most furious Bull, or a Lyon, more like the latter, the water
rattling in their throats, which they force out in froth & foam,
& makes the earth to tremble, & our little Island shook as by
an earth quake; When they roar their Body is swoln like an
empty Hogshead on the water, their head & Neck raisd out
of the water, his Tail raised 5 or 6 feet in the air, waving too
& fro, & lashing the surface of the water in a terrible maner
as they utter their terrable Voice, their body sinks gradually in
the water, then swelling again rises up, thus alternately as they
continue their bellowing. The deep swamps & banks of the
river's & Forest re-echoing the dreadfull roar, the noise is
communicated from one to another, fills the whole country
with a noise like dreadfull Thunder. But this is only in the
Spring of the year about the time of their incubation. The
Alegator when full grown are generally from 16 to 22feet in
length & the bigest part of their Body, commonly biger than
a 30Gall. Cask. They lay two or 300 Eggs in little mounts in
fens & Marshes which they form of mud & rotten weeds &
leaves, which I suppose fermenting by the heat of the sun
becomes warm enough to hatch their eggs. when the Young
first appear in shallow water not far from the old nest they are
about 12 or 13 Inches long, they are perfectly shaped, plated
all over, of a beautifull colour. pied all over bright yellow &

brown. not much unlike the colour of the Rattle Snake, they are then very active & illnatured, opening wide their mouth & snap^g, making a noise & barking like a little dogs & switch their tail to their mouth. they keep together in schooles the first year in the same place. The Old one either Male or female lies near, secreted in the sedge or Weeds to guard & protect the Young, who is very watchfull & furious. Thus I have indeavoured to give a description of the horrid & destructive Alegator. Very early this morning we got on our way (but not without being persued by our enemy the Alegator) continually passing through prodigious schools of Trout which seemed to croud & fill the river from shore to shore in such maner as to push each other out of water, & continually striking at small young fish that seemed to be going down the River. these small frys, were so amasingly numerous that the water seemed to shew nothing elce. they were about an inch long, very thin, of a bright silver colour & when the Trout came up with a schoole of them (which some times would be a quarter of a mile in length) the surface of the River was as it wer boiling, occationed by the incessant striking & jumping of the Trout at the small Fish; & now presented a very striking prospect to see the wretched condition of these unhappy little Fish for as constantly as The Trout came up with them and forced them out of their element into the Air, vast flight of a beautifull little white Bitterns flew out from the Shore amongst them & pick't em up in the Air. thus was the proveb verified with respect to thes fish jumping out of the Frying pan into the fire. The land on each side the River is either well timbered Swamps or very extendsive Marshes or fens. The Timber in the Swamp, Elm, Ash, Scarlet Maple, Water Oak, Red Bay, Palm Trees, & underneath small Palmetos, Elder, & variety of Shrubs & Plants, but I discoved nothing new; The Marshes very extendsive, generally between 2 & 3 feet higher than the surface of the water of the River at its common hight, but it is said they are All overflowed by the River rising over them in the Spring. February and March; The Soil is a black Rich mud or Clay & looks fit for Rice, Corn, Sugar Cane &^c.

After seven or eight Mile going we come to a Bluff of high shelly land where was a large fruiteful Orange Grove, about 3 Acres, rising pretty high in the Middle but sorounded by

Swamps & Marshes, The Trees here were Live Oak, Celtis, Red Bay, Orange Trees, & Palm, some curious little Shrubs & Plants Not discovered before, observed abundance of Bones, pieces of earthen ware, & other vestiges of the antient Indian Inhabitents.

Set off from this place & pass't 7 or 8 Miles farther. The Land on each side swamps & marshes very extendsive, & the prospect open & almost boundless, especially on the E[t]. side, which extends from the river bank eastward, over Lake Gordon, & into endless marshes, the view terminated only by the Horison, the vast plain agreeably decorated by Clumps or Islets of Live Oak, Laurel & the proud waving Palm Tree. arived at another high Bluff, where we found plenty of Orange Trees but this like the other Bluff containd but a small space of land sorounded by Swamps & Marshes. We incamped here this Night, being pestered by Musquetoes. Got off early next morning, pass by very rich swamp. saw Deer & Turkey. I shot a large bird seemed to be a species of Ibis, they make a loud screaming noise, in the marshes & Fens along the River Shores when they are disturbed. The Indians call them the Crying Bird (Efois-kika). they are as big bodied as a hen Turkey, & much of the same colour, long legs, Neck long & slender, the Bill about 6 Inches long, thick at the base, but small & bending downwards to the Point, the eyes large & placed high on the head. they are excellent food.

There are two other Species of this Bird on this River keep[g] in large Flights, One perfectly white except the tips of the greater quill feathers which are of a shining crow colour with red Bill & Legs. The other Black upper side, Breast & Belly white, Bill & Legs white, feed on Cray fish. Here are Two other Very large Birds that seem to be Species of the Ibis. The first a very large Stately bird, generally of a dark greyish or Dun color, head Neck & Bill brown, legs & Bill very long, they are the largest Bird in Florida, It seemes to be Catsby's Wood-Pelican. they are remarkebly scarce & a very solitary bird. I never saw but 3 or four and these in the most lonesome unfrequented places. Viz[t]. about the Lake & Savanahs, in retired wilds of Florida & high up the River S[t]. Johns. there was one shot near Charlestown S[o]. Carolina last Year while I was there. No one knew what it was & was looked on as a Prodigy.

They feed on Crayfish, Frogs & reptiles. The other is a large White Fowl, having the larger Quill feathers tip't with black, Legs & feet black. they are as big bodied as a common goose, are esteemed very good eating. they feed on, Crayfish, Frogs, Snales & Reptiles. they resort about the Banks & Marshes of great Rivers, Savanah & Lakes. After going 4 or 5 Miles, the land still swamp & Marshes, observed abundance of Alegatores almost every where bask^g in the Sun on the banks, some time 5 or 6 or more together heap't on one another like Great logs, the Water alive with trout. Came to a high Bluff; here the main Land on the west side came to the River; this Bluff is about 30 feet high above the River, went a shore & assended the Hill, on the Top is a large & beautifull Grove of Palm Trees & a large Orange Grove, I spent some time & rambling through this pleasat Grove went about a quarter & a Mile & come into the Pine Forests, which was open, & the grass having been lately burn't, afforded an agreeable verdure mixt with flowery plants, a delightfull brisk vivifying Air played through the salubrious Pine forest, mixed with the balmy breath from of the flowery savanahs, renderd this place very gratefull, having been so long confin'd to putred stagnate air between the low dark swamps & banks of the River. Returnd to the Boat & after finishing a small but savory repast on some Trout & a broiled bird with some boil'd Rice; left Palm hill & continued up the River, passing by Swamps & Marshes on each side, Observed frequantly the depreadations of the trout & the little Heron, still Swamps & Marshes, observed the Trees along the River Banks adornd with garland, of various species of Convolvulus, Ipomea, Eupatorium scandens, & a Species of Cucurbita which ran & spread over the bushes & Trees 20 or 30 Yards high, altogether affording a varied Noval scene exhibiting Natural Vistas, Labyrinth & Alcoves, varied with fine flowering plants, Asters, Hibiscus Althea &^c. all which reflect on the still surface of the River a very rich & Gay picture. Observed the low lands on the River to rise gradually higher above the water as we go up. The Soil a fertiles black mud or Clay; passt by several Islands of Swamp well timbered with Water Oak, a beautiful Tree green throughout the Year but the latter part of the Autumn & Winter the leaves begin to alter their colour, to yellow, Red & brown, when

they fall, but there remains yet before spring a sufficient number of green ones to give it the appearence of an evergreen.
the Tree grows very tall having a vast globlar Top. especially
when they grow in open places, fields & Savanahs & far exceeds even the immortal live Oak in form & grateful shadow;
Vast great Scarlet Maple, Ash, Gleditsia triaconthos & Elms.
Elder & Cephalanthos with vast leaves, wheather from the
Richness of the Soil or a variety, the flower the same as the
Common. continued passing between Swamps & Marshes as
before but they rise higher above the River, especially next the
water where grows tall beautiful Palms, Oak & Lawrel (Mag-
nolia). having gained Near 15 Miles, we come to a bluff on
the east side; found here Orange trees, Vast Lawrell Magnolia,
Red Cedar, Live Oak, water Oak, Vast great Liqudambar, Red
Bay, Celtis & back of this about a quarter of a mile we come
to the Pine Forests. This bluff continues about four or five
Miles, some places The high pine land comes close to the
River bank, then went about a Mile between Swamps, the
River is here above 200Yards over, very deep, & runs swift.
we entered a branch of the River that came in on the east side,
went about a quarter of a mile, pass't by a high Bluff on each
side, where are orange groves, Live Oak, Red Cedar, Bay &^{c}.
continued taking another left hand branch half a mile, deep
Swamp on one hand & an extendsive Marsh on other. we
entered a pretty lake, about 3 Miles in length & above a mile
wide, On high hills on the apposite side we had a view of
Berresford Plantation. crosst over the Lake, went to the
house, having a letter to his lordship's Agent, who being at
home recieved me very civilly. Next day I spent in examin'g
this place, the situation is high, 40 or 50 feet above the surface
of the lake, the soil is pretty good, a greyish sandy mold,
Yellow & Red Clay under; The high land produces the best
crops of Indigo, Corn &^{c}. of any yet on the River, & is the
upper House on the River. Here is the largest Indian Mount
I have Yet seen in Florida, having a long wide Causey leading
from it into the Pine Forest, lake as to M^t. Royal, I walked
above a mile along it where it insensibly terminated in the
open levell pine Forests. Visited a very amazeing large spring
that boils up from between high sand hills, & immediately
forms a large & very swift stream, of the clearest water, about

20 Yards wide & ten & twelve feet deep; it runs almost a direct course 400 or 500 Yards & discharges its transparent waters into the River, cariing its sea green color near 100Yards into the River, there are multitudes of beautifull fish resort into it, Such as Garr, Trout, Mullet, Catfish, 3 or 4 Species of Bream & Alegators, all which appear as plain as if we had them in hand tho' 8 & 10 feet deep in the water. The water is very warm, has a very disagreeable vitriolic taste & smells horridly of Sulphur. My companion not choosing to go any higher up the River, & I finding the Season rather too early for flowers or Seeds, & being apprehendsive of missing my oppertunaty to Appalatche, thought it best to return to the lower store, & pay this country another visit after my return from little S^t. Juane, so next day early in the morning, & having shipped a passenger, we had 3 hands, two to rowe, & I steered, this night we got to the Store near 40 Miles. stayed here all night, one of the men staid here, & the other continued with me to Mo^t. Royal, we got down to mouth of the River where it enters the great lake, but we found the Lake so rough and the wind so much against us we recon'd it dangerous to venture in it so we laid by, at a little hamock of high land, hopeing the wind to lull before night but it blew very hard all night & so continued next day but we pusht out, & indeavourd to cross. found the lake so rough were obliged to put back till towards the even'g, ventured out again tho' the wind hard a head, got a fiew Miles round east side of the lake. we were forst to put ashore in the sedge, hall'd our Vessell up as high as posseble & incamp't in the thickets about 200 Yards off. the wind increas't in the night with Rain, & rise the lake very high, found our canoe in the Morning knock't up in the grass & almost full of water. However we got off again & with great dificulty & danger coasted round the Lake, ten or 15 Miles. came to camp on a high sandy bank, the land round the east side of this lake is generally Pine land, sometimes a small stripe of Oak homock, some narow swamps, & a narow verge of grassy marsh next the Water, but the west side much better land. this Night the bad weather broke up & next morning with a gentle favourable gale we got over the lake & by night got to M^t. Royal. & the next day I got safe down to the lower store.——

VOLUME 2

S^r. being desirous of doing every thing that may tend towards the illustration of natural knowledge, I am glad of
this opportunity by your aid & incouragement, of extending
my reserches into Florida. I shall therefore with the highest
sense of pleasure, for your particular amusement proceed, &
indeavour to exhibit to your notice the natural productions
of these countries as they offer to my view in the plain simple dress of Nature; since by doing this I shall not only have
an opportunity of exercising the noble virtue of gratitude,
but shall have an opportunity of knowing the merit of my
labours.——

Being informed by M^r M'Latchy of a company of Traders
going to Little S^t. Juane River which runs into the Bay of
Apalatche on the west coast of itsmus of Florida. I most willingly agreed to join company with these people; who were
going to an Indian Town on that River in order to treat with
the Indians concerning some effects belonging to the Traders,
that the Indians had lately siezed.

We set off early in the morning, four of us in company, but
did not travel fast. the first part of the road being very bad,
our Pack horses could not travel fast, got about 30 Miles, &
came to Camp on high sand hills by long Pond. the Musquetoes were extreamely troublesome. got very little rest. set off
in the morning as early as we could get away, having the
horses to hunt up & pack, some of which were up to their
backs in the water of the lake where they were feeding on
water grass which all cattle are fond off, thrusting their heads
down under water to bite off the tender jointed stalks, tho'
the grass rises a foot or eighteen inches above the surface of
the water so that as a small distance, the lake looks like a fine
green meadow where perhaps there is four & five feet water.
We continued 3 or 4 miles through spacious Pine Forests diversified with green grassy hills, flowery Savanahs, & beautifull
ponds & little Lakes; about these Hills I first observed a very
singular & beautifull little shrub which spread its slender
branches round about flat on the ground, they being loaded
with fine purple stellated flowers which were succeeded by
seeds inclosed in prickly Capsulas or burrs. We now came into

the road to Alatchua Savanah and shortly afterwards our Company devided, one of the Traders having business with the Indians at Cuscowela. I went with the Party through the Savanah, being desireous to see this beautifull place at all seasons of the Year. late after noon we got to the Savanah, found the waters greatly deminished & a universal verdure appeard over the whole Plain. we went almost a streight course through it to the other end, a great part of the way the ground was hard & almost dry, as levell as a floor, cover'd with the richest green pasture. What an extensive prospect! what an unconfin'd display of liberty & freedom! numerous herds of fat Cattle, of deer, browsing or rolling on beds of ease and Plenty, & squadrons of fleet Seminole horse, who never yet felt the weight of the Coller or the galling Chains of servitude. if he submits to the short constraint of the bridle & bit, he exults in an oppertunity of shewing his lord the fierce floridian, his superiority of Strength & swiftness over his brother courser, & participates in the pleasure with his Master. After passing over this grand illuminated scene we entered a dark thicket of Orange Groves, Live Oak, Magnolia at the end of the Savanah; continued about a mile, then about a mile distance of open green meadows and dark woody Copses or old field; alternately we come into pine Forests. rise higher land & continued about a mile over a higher ridge of Pine, & pretty tall Red Oak mix't and abundance of low grape Vines, the Soil a pale reddish or brown coarse sand mixt with pieces of white & greyish coarse limestone with pieces & impressions of Seashells; there is a bed of this sort of Rock under all, some places 4 or 5 feet & 8 or 10 feet below the surface of the land, according to the situation, as on the tops of the hill these beds & masses of Rock are nearer the surface & frequently rise above the surface, sometimes 3 or 4 feet; in various direction sometimes they stand nearly edgeways & thrusting up their points; sometimes large round or oblong holes perforated through as if worn through, by the force of water. some places these masses of Rocks lye flat or horisontal, heap't one on another as if so placed by the hand of Man, but seems to be the effect of time & revolution, in the order of Nature. The land now decends a little, we came to camp under covert of a Grove of Oaks, on a high hill, close by the edge of an exten-

sive & beautifull Savanah, 9 or ten miles in length & 3 or 4
wide, near the middle was a beautifull piece of water which
sinks down in holes & chasms amongst Rocks in a cove of the
savanah just by our Camp sorounded by hills. here were two
or 3 large holes or sinks through Rocks, on the green levell
shore a little above the present sink, in these holes was extreamly clear water, which seemed to be levell, with the water
of the Savanah. In these holes & in the Sinks were abundance
of Fish, Trout & Bream which appeared very plain, the water
being so clear. I tryed to catch some with the Hook & line,
but they would not take the bait. Having walked over these
pleasant green hills & savanahs, returned to Camp. The evening being extreamely pleasant, a healthy breese was wafted
over the plain from Orange Groves on the other side, mixed
with a very agreable musk, played about us, & kept the Musquetoes off. I Shall here take notice that in the Pine Forests of
Carolina & Florida, in the coole of the evening just before sun
set a most agreeable musk fills the Air; but what it proceeds
from, No one could ever give me a satisfactory account, some
tell me it is the Allegator, & some again says it arises from the
hoof of the Buck but it seems to me to be more mild & agreeable then what Proceeds from either of these. I am inclined to
believe it is produced from a certain pretty little Plant which I
find growing abundantly in Savanahs amidst the Pine Forests,
whose flowers whilst fresh smell of the most agreeable musk,
so extreamely volatile & Transient that It ceases to emit the
smell quickly after it is crop't, so that This extraordinary Plant
seems rather to breathe forth a most agreeable musky vapour.
This night our two companions join'd us.

Arose early at the call of the watchfull Watula, whose musical voice rings through the forests, calling up the drousey
feather'd Inhabitents of the grove, & proclaims the Majesty
of the rising Sun. I take a view of the chearfull Savanah, &
proceed on our journey.

We now rise higher, ridges of Land all cover'd with a delightful verdure, decorated with numerous flowering Plants:
Vareties of Sunflowers, Phlox, Cistus plant, beautiful purple
Ixia & a variety of plants not yet seen, saw frequanty white
shelly Rocks rising above the surface of the earth, whereabouts

grows Anona, Erythrina, Grape Vine, Very tall Opuntia breed-ing Cochaniel. these hills and plains are thinly planted with very Tall stately long leaved Pine, admitting an extensive pros-pect over the hills; presenting to view on all sides little ponds & Lakes which are decorated round about with little groves of Oaks & Orange Trees; a very lively & healthy breese plays through these open Pine forests. Passed two or 3 miles over low levell pine land, seemed to be a shallow Pond, in wet weather, as the Pines are small schrubby & very thinly planted with frequant patches of evergreen Andromeda & Gale Bays, the grass thin & parch't, the soil a hard Sterile white sand, we now rise sand hills again, several miles gradually assending. The hills were now very Rockey, large masses of the coarse greyish & white shelly limestone, on a poor sandy barren soil, The timber very thin & schrubby, small Pine, black jacks, short anona & abundance of that little curous procumbent shrub bearing purple star flowers with burrs. this is the highest land I have seen in E^t. Florida, & here we have a view of a vast extended, levell country south ward which look far below us, extensive Pine forests, Savanahs, & Ponds. we continued a mile or two & came to a very extensive shallow pond sor-rounded by grassy plains on a hard poor white sandy bottom, the grass thin tall hard & disagreeable food but the pond an extensive piece of water & seems intirely sorounded by baren sand hills. this place is call'd the Generals Pond, from General Oglethorp, who met here all the Creek Chiefs with their Con-federates, of the lower Creek Towns, at a general Congress,

At this pond on account of the drought & excessive heat, we were obliged to stop to rest & water our horses, went to the pond to get drink but found the water so very hot & disagreeably turbid, & slimey, & almost in a state of fermen-tation, from the dead & rotting grass & Plants, owing to the excessive heat & drought of the season, & could not find trees sufficient to shade me from the burning heat of the air;

Towards the evening we again set on our journey and con-tinued, four or five miles, passing over barren sand hills and now we gradually decend for a mile or two, passt by some ponds and extensive Savanahs, very good pine forests, we came to a pretty steep decent, down the side of sandy rocky ridges. & now we left the baren high lands of the Istmouse, high I mean comparitively, with respect to the general levell low country of E^t. Florida, & from the top of this last ridge (which is lower then what we passt a few miles) we have a very agreeable & vastly extensive country beneath & we look over the Forests & meadow spreading away westward before us; When we decended the ridge & came on the levell we pass'd near two miles through low wet Gale Bays, here & there knowls or low ridges of of somewhat higher land coverd with large patches of low palmetos, schrub Oaks, little dwarf olive leaf't Oaks, & good large Tall Pine & Cypres Trees with intervales of tall grassy Meadows & Savanahs. came to a large wet Savanah covered with tall excellent sweet grass, rise higher Pine land, on our left a large deep swamp where grew abundance of very tall stately Cypres Trees, with Althea Florida, Nyssa, Red bay, Ash, Elm, Water Oak, Palm Trees; continued passing over midling high levell pine Forests, bearing very large Timber, the soil a reddish & dark brown sand, with small pieces of limestone, the surface of The earth, well coverd with a very good kind of grass, excellent food for Cattle; pass'd by numbers of deep holes in the earth of the shape of a funnel, some 30 or 40 Yards in circumferance, some less, some much larger, of various depths, some seemingly half full of water, & others dry, & overgrown with grass & weeds, which are often sorounded with homacks of Evergreen Oak, Bay, Magnolia call Laurel Tree, groves of Palm Trees, which look very agreeable at a distance, as they are placed generally round about & in the middle of vast Savanahs or meadows, & appear like little Islets sprinkled over these vast & boundless Meadows & Plains, & these holes are or have been sinks, Water passeges through the Rocky bed of this country, & strainers to Carry off the superfluous waters of the Surface of this part of the Country of Florida instead of of brooks or runing streams; it's remarkable that, there is not one brook or stream to be seen in this part of this Country from the great Allatchua Savanah to the River S^t. Juane near the Bay of Appalatchua. There is a bed of limestone rock which lays commonly 4 or 5 feet under the surface of the earth, & this bed of Rock may be about 15 or 20 feet deep. through this where we find these sinks or holes, are perpendicular tubes or wells as round and smooth inside as the neatest walled Well, which seems to have been so worn & perforated by the action of the water, which at first finding cracks or small fissures in the softer part of the rocks have in length of time formed these vast natural wells. there are often numbers of these tubes or wells in a cluster, which are worn or broke one into another, forming one vast well, excavated or fluted with simicircular niches resembleing a round hole made through a honey comb; and it is under this bed of Rocks on a bed of Clay the water, brooks & Rivers find a passage or communication, with greater Rivers, having had sundry oppertunaties of examining such of these sinks that were nearly dry, where I could see the passage under the bed of Rock. It is not uncommon in this country to see the waters breaking or gushing out of the earth in such inundations as to cover the country for many leagues, rushing through the forests, tearing up trees, earth & rocks, carying all before the mighty torrent, till finding other old Sinks in its way, plunges into the earth, forming a new temporary River untill finding a new hidden passage, disappears suddenly, what a strange delusion, how fabulous this appears, Yet it is most true, having seen some of these old dry beds of Rivers many miles in length & a great weadth & depth, and traced them from the place where they made the eruption out of the earth to the end where they plunged in again. & have seen others that have happened very lately; The innumerable funnel like holes every where seen in the forests all over this part of Florida which are dry & overgrown with grass & herbage, have been sinks and formerly waters as discribed above; & being left dry are filling up by the earth and trash washing into them by rains, winds &^{c}.

As These vast funnell shaped holes, natural Wells, or sinks as they are termed here, have a very singular apperance, & have not heard of any thing like to them in any other Country, I thought it worth your notice. & for that end have indeavourd to give a true Idea of them by a description of their natural & simple appearance; altho the cause & design of them appear evident, yet I am not capable of entering into the various dark mazes in the progress of Nature, & will detain you no longer on my notions of this subject. We pass't by a large round sink about 20 yards diameter, observed a prodigious large Alegator basking on the brink, he plunged in at my near approach, and disappeared. continued over a pleasant well timbered grassy Pine Forest. come to camp by the side of a wet Savanah near a pond; It being not yet sunset and observing a dark homock of Oaks at some distance, I went to it with one of our party in hopes of seeing some Bear & deer. This Grove was very extendsive, The Trees were Live Oak, Water Oak, chesnut leaved white Oak, Morus, Tilea, Elm, Magnolia great Lawrel Tree, Magnol, glauca, Carpinus, Anona, Halesia, Ptelea, Calicarpia, Sambucus. Herbaceous Plants, Eupatorium, Lobelia different species, Aristalocha, Urtica, Pyrola, Asters, Phasiolus, Vitia, Arum, especially the great Dragon. could discover no new genera. The Soil very fertile, a dark black mold on a Limestone rock. we went through to a pint of higher land where I observed there had been a dwelling place; observed some posts standing and old field, corn ridges & hillocks all overgrown with Saplings, The Traders informed me some years ago a spaniard dwelt here who kept a large Stock of Cattle, was kill'd by the Indians & his whole stock drove off by them, & from thence the Indians began to keep Stocks amongst them. returnd to camp, & made a repast on Cranes & Rice. These birds are midling good eating, make a Stew or soope. here we found excellent food for our horses, got a way early in the morning, passing through extensive Pine Forests, affording excellent Timber and grass range, went over green open planes, here observed a very ellegant Species of Mimosa, grows low, the leaves & stalks spreading on the ground amongst short green grass. It has no prickles. At touching the leaves they close together immediatly, & fall flat on the ground, they send up from the joints a peduncle 6 or 8 inches in length headeed by an oblong tuft of floscule having large yellow apices. they are of various colours, some heads are of a deep crimson rose colour, Yellow & white as snow, the flowers have an agreable scent of a damask rose with a little musk, these vast open grassy plains, in the morning presents a very chearfull aspect till towards mid day, when their beauty fades, they wither, & are no longer conspicuous, but then the next morning brings to view a new succession of gay Inhabitants & the plains assume a new scene of gayity & joy, about noon we came to a vast extensive Savanah having a

pond or lake in the middle reckoned Nine or 10 Miles long.
this Savanah is nearly surrounded with Homocky Land. we
went through part of it, and crosst the lower end over a vast
green meadow, finely painted with platts of the beautifull Mimosa, intermix't with other flowers of various colours, particularly a fine Plant, a tall Veronica Spicata. we now came into
a great homock of high land of some what uneven surface,
alternately little knowls, of high groves, & extensive green
plains or old fields diversified with copeses or Islets of Live
Oak, Palm trees & great Magnolia, little ponds & dry sinks.
we continued thus 6 or 7 miles, gently decending a green
levell Vale, flowered over with the Mimosa, On each side a
range of little Hills & groves of Oaks, Laurel, Palm trees &^{c}.
frequently open on on either hand views of other green Plains
& Vales, very extensive & ornamented with groves. These little hills & groves are frequently stoney, with limestone Rock
rising a little above the surface of the Ground, & generally
surround holes or sinks in some of which we find very good
clear water. in some are abundance of Fish such as Trout,
Bream &^{c} and Alegators. some are dry, & some seem almost
filld up. Now we enter a levell forest of short leaf't Pine mixt
with red & black oak, Red bay, Water Oak, pass'd by some
grassy Savanahs & shallow Cypress ponds thus 2 or 3 Miles,—
rise a little & went about a mile through levell Pine land mixt
with red Oak, the Soil a loose greyish sand 2 or 3 feet deep,
then a stiff yellow or red Clay, arrived in the evening at the
little Town Talahasochte on the banks of Little S^r. Juane River,
computed to be upwards of Sixty Miles nearly wastward of
Cuscowela. This little Town consists of about 20 houses, and
contains 70 or 80 Souls.

We went to the Traders house, which was torn almost to
pieces, soon after were visited, by an antient chief of the Town
& soon after by a number of the Inhabitence; The old Man
informed Our Trader that immediately after he left the Town,
the Young men concluding that, from so sudden & private a
flight from amongst them, & carying all most all his effects
away, The talk must in consequence be very bad, betwixt them
& the White People, they proceeded immediately to brake
open the house, & carried off all they could find but that the
old men had prevailed on them to deliver them up untill they

should be informed certainly how the Talks were, & that as soon as the White King came home (who was then out a hunting) he did not doubt, most part would be restored, & he farther said that they were greatly surprised and afflicted on account of the bad disposition of the Nation; declairing they themselves were inocent, & knew nothing of any harm against the whites, that they loved us as their Brethren, & were sensible they could not live but must perish without our friendship & assistance. bid us be easy & contented, & that they would all die to a man before any of us should be hurt. The Old Seer went home to his house & shortly after sent us some Venison broth, bears Oil & a Turkey & was soon after invited to a house where we had a repast of broiled Veneson, dry Bear meat, Honey & Thin drink, a sort of grewell made of Corn flower & hicory Nut Oil & Water boild together. returnd to our house in the evening when soon the antent Chief with sundry Other men came to us to smoke in the Pipe with us; at night they all returnd & left us alone.

Next morning we were visited by the Indians Who were very good humoured, expressing the highest satisfaction at our visit, went to several otheir houses where we were well treated. this day I spent in excursions round about the Town & the banks of y^e. River. returnd in even'g to the house, several hunting parties of Indians came in loaded with Venson, bear meat & honey. we were informed the White King chief of this Settlement was coming in. At night a large fire was kindled in the middle of the Square, which was soon surrounded by Indians dancing & singing. we soon heard the Drum beat in the Square & a messenger came to invite us to eat Bear Ribs and honey, it being the Kings treat, having killd some bear. they never eat the Ribs when out but bring them to the Town, where they make a feast in the square to the Warriors & hunters; We accordingly repared to the Square where the Men were assembling. they made way for us & placed us near, where the barbecued Ribs were served up in large Platters or wooden boles in One of the chief houses of the Square. We had Kettles of honey & water, with a great wooden family Spoon in each Kettle, every one in turn took a sup or quaff, discoursing of cheerfull subjects as he liked, as hunting adventure, jokeing, News of love, intreagues $\&^c$., The

Youth & Young fellows dancing, singing & wrestling about the Fire, When every one seemed satisfied with eating & drinkin, We repared to the Fire, where the King appeared & join'd us, in a circle seated round about the fire. the Youth ceased their jollity, & with drew at some distance, the Men pass the Pipe about the Ring, and discourse of more serious affairs with the greatest gravity & decorum. the King recieved us with great seeming satisfaction & joy & being informed of our business, by our Trader, he expressed the warmest wishes & hopes of the Store being settled again in his Town, declairing how wretched they would be if the white people withdrew their friendship & protection from their town. The King went home; we returnd to the feast, & after taking another whet at the Bear ribs & talked over the news of the times, broke up in peace & mirth, every one taking his steps as his inclination led him, the Old Chief who was their Priest or Conjurer, caried off the remains of the victuals & retired. I continued for some time in the Square, till the Youth broke up their dancing & Mirth:

The next morning having got a Canoe of one of the Indians, we went a fishing in the River for Trout, In a bout an hours time we took above twenty, we returned & overtook an Indian who with his wife & & Child had been fishing, they were deep loaded with fish. we returnd in the even'g, I walked about 2 Miles to the Indian Plantation; where the whole Town Plants in one great field, I suppose containing about 20 Acres, all Planted with Corn, Pumkins, Water Mellons, Beans, Pease, Squashes, & some Rice and Potatoes; The traders being imploy'd in hunting up their horses. I indeavoured to get an oppertunity to go down to the River to the mouth. hoping to make some discoveries there & desired our Interpretor to mention it to the Indians; he did, the Chief answered that as there had lately been murder committed thereabouts on some white People, & this matter not yet being cleared, the Nation having lately forbid the white People travelling on that coast, & that he could not answer for any mischief that might befall us from any hunting parties that frequently visit this part of Florida from the Nation.

However next morning having borrowed a canoe of some of the Indians under colour of going to fish, I made a trip of

about 6 or 7 Miles down the River, having visited a very great
and most beautifull Fountain or Spring which boils up from
between the hills about 300 yards from the River, throwing
up great quantities of white small pieces of Shells & white
shell Rock which, glittering through the limped climent as
they rise to the surface, subside & fall again round about on
every side; The bason of the fountain is nearly round and
about 100 Yards in circumferance, the banks round about of
a moderate steep assent cover'd with broken white shell, &
the water gradually deepens to the center of the fountain,
where it is many fathoms deep, the fountain is full of Fish and
Alegators & at a great depth in the water appear as plain as if
they were close at hand. The creek that runs from this immence fountain is above twenty Yards wide & runs very swift
into the River, carying its sea green transparent waters near
100 Yards a cross the River, the depth of the water of the
Creek 10 or 12 feets, where we see a continual concourse of
fish of various Kinds Such as Garr, Catfish, Mullet, Trout,
Bream of various species, Silverfish, & Pike, and the monstrous amphabious Maneta: a Skeleton of which I saw on the
bank, of the Spring, which the Indians had lately killed. The
Indians kill them for food, are esteemed good eating; the
grinding teeth were about 1½ Inch in diameter. The ribs
about 3 Inches in diameter in the thickest part & 18 Inches in
length, very solid bone & ponderous. The hills that nearly
incompassed The Spring were about 15 or 20 Yards in height
next the River but the land falls away considerably from the
top of the hills & becomes a lower flat or nearly levell forest
of Pine, Oak, Bay, Magnolia & Cabbage Trees. the Soil of the
hills a loose greyish sandy mold on shelly & limestone Rocks.
the water of the Spring cool & agreeable to drink. The Indians
and Traders say this fountain vents the waters of the great
Alatchua Savanah. Observed growing on shoal pints & shores
of the Spring large patches of very luxurient Water Cresses,
bearing beautifull clustres of sweet white flowers, but had no
more taste then the water. The vegitables I observed growing
about this place, Were The great Magnolia called by the Inhabitants of Carolina & Florida Laurel, by the Indians, Tolo
chlucco or big Bay, Red Bay, Ehto Mico or King Tree, Purple
berried Bay Catesby: Live Oak, hycory, Water Oak, Ilex,

Ptelia, Halesia, Calicarpa, Lycium, Ledum, Andromeda. Plants, Urtica, Helianthos, Eupatorium, Aristalochia, Asarebecca, Uvularia, Solidago &ᶜ. but observed no new genera. We left this beautifull Fountain, and continued a fiew miles down the River, where it began to widen. here seemed to appear vast rich Swamps adjoining this River. I could not prevail with the Man to go any further, for fear of meeting with Indians & offending the Town so we return'd to the Town, having taken in our way a great Number of fine Trout. This day the Traders had a conferrence with the Indians at the Square concerning some horses they had, amongst em the Indian, having obtain'd leave to hunt among their Stock. The next morning I went with them horsehunting. We crosst the River at the town, where it is about 300 Yards over, we continued a Mile & half up the River bank, through pretty high levell swamp land produceing Vast large tall & streight Cypress Trees, Tupilo, & that very singular Tree, that seemes to be a Species of Tupilo, bearing vast quantites of fruite nearly of the Shape & Size of the olive somewhat compress't, of a fine crimson Scarlet & Orange Colour, when ripe containing a pleasant sharp accid juice, sometimes used to make punch, & are calld wild Lemmons, and makes a very beautifull appearance. I observed in this swamp another very singular & elligant evergreen shrub. but being too early for the Flower, cant form any judgment of its tribe or family; We rise a little and enter the Pine forests. we followed the trading path about 4 Miles, came to a great Homack the Traders say 12 or 15 Miles in extent. observed in 3 or four miles going abundance of old fields, diversified with small homocks & groves of Live Oak, Laurel, Palm trees, Grape Vines &ᶜ. with Ponds & holes of water. we went by an ancient Settlement in these old fields & Meadows, I suppose Spanish as there were some Posts standing & ditches, Corn hills & ridges. we continued some miles through Cain thickets, observed limestone Rocks in the homocks and round the holes of water. we enterd an extensive green meadow, saw gangs of Cattle & horses, amongst these were the horses our Traders were in quest off, having drove up the horses, drove them towards the Town, saw abundance of Turkeys & deer in these fields & meadows, shot some Turkeys & continued along. drove through a large Savanah and pond, the water shallow, took notice of a bundance large snail shells round about on the shore, some half as big as my fist & on examination found multitudes of them in the mud & slush at the bottom of the pond, in the Savanah. they breed here in prodigious numbers, fixing their Spawn or ovulee in clusters round about bull Rushes, Reeds & Sticks in the water, two or 300 in a cluster. they are perfectly round, of the size of Pease, the shell thin hard & brittle, they look clear like pearls. These vast Periwinkles or Snail are bred in Vast numbers in the muddy shores of this River & Great St Juane, insomuch that the Rushes, Reeds, sticks & trees near the waters are white, being almost cover'd with their Eggs, a foot or 18 Inches above the water, and afford food for fish & young allegators, &^{c}. We got safe over the River with Our horses, & at Night joind the Indians in the Square where the Youth were merry, singing & dancing round the Fire. These People spending a great part of their time in feasting & Dancing. A Siminole comes in from the Chace, he lays his game down before his hywah & throws himself on his bearskin spread for him under the shade, in the evening, his friends repare to his repast, sings & dances over his War & hunting exploits till tired, falls a sleep; in the Night he awakes, stretches himself along on his back, sings himself to sleep again, thus they devide their time. I took an excursion with the Traders about 12 or 15 Miles up the River, we come to Camp by the side of a large Homock facing an extensive green meadow, at Night some Indians came to our Camp, we purchased a Deer of them, giving them some Rice for it, after some time they left us, mounted their sprightly active siminoles, started off whooping and singing through the extended savanah. we soon lost sight of them. the next day finding some horses, returnd to Town, where we continued two or 3 days waiting the arrival of some Indians who had some horses belonging to us; The Indians arrived & setling matters with them on the best terms we could, set off back again for the Store at Great St Juane. Our company went on to Camp about 15 Miles off except the chief Trader, who to oblige me we continued together. Taking another Road that passt through a vast baren Plain of many miles in extent, in the middle was a very extensive Savanah & Pond. we rode over a very baren tract, in-

cumbered with sandy limestone. came to the Sink of the Pond
which were holes & chasms in Rocks. the waters of the Ponds
on account of the excessive dry hot season had retired from
the upper holes & Sinks, the ground being almost dry round
about, these holes were full of clear & very cool water, & full
of fish & Alegators. I could plainly see other Sinks & holes
amongst Rocks at some distance from shore, out in the Pond
where resorted abundance of Alegators. we left this place, directing our course through the Savanah for our Camp, passt
over large masses of flat Rock, the earth sounding hollow under our feet as if riding over hollow Vaults. we met an Indian
and his Wife & family who were traveling towards the Towns
from a hunt. they had several horses, some packet with Skins,
Meat & honey. The Indian with the greatest complaisance &
civility bestowed on us a Bag of honey, which we caried to
Camp. We soon assended very high hilly Pine Forest, large
timber & the earth coverd with a chearfull Verdure, & from
these high hills I had a most endless open prospect of the
Plains & savanah we had left. We continued through open
pleasant Pine forrests which became very levell, passt by Savanahs, abundance of large rockey wells and Sinks with very
good cool water, sorounded & shaded with Pleasant groves
of Live Oak, Magnolia, Bay, Palm Trees, Persimmoms, Nyssa,
Halesia, Ptlea &[c]. Towards the evening came to Camp, where
our People were already arived and fixt the Camp by the side
of a large Grove, at the upper end of the Long Pond; We were
detained here some days longer in search of their horses. This
time I indeavoured to imploy to some advantage in exploreing
the country round about this lake and making my remarks.
this day all the hunters went out & left me to keep Camp;
Our place was situated very agreeably by the Grove close to
the vast extendsive Savanah: I left the dog to watch Camp,
took my Gun, & travers't round to the far Point of this high
grove, walking miles over the richest, green flowery carpet
that is posseble for fancy to concieve, intermixt & wraught by
nature with a thousand different flowers of various colours, a
vast watrey plain in the middle sparkling through the groves
& jeting points. This Savanah is computed to be about 10
Miles in length & 4 or 5 wide, scarcely a tree or bush to be
seen in it, but above twice that extent including other smaller

Savanahs & meadows dependant on it & seperated by Groves, homacks, & old fields, so that for 30 or 40 miles round we travel'd through these meadows, & Groves. Returnd to Camp in evin'g, having discovered some pretty plants. soon after some Indians came to camp, brought some Veneson, they asked me some questions, which puzzeled me a little, but I understood they wanted to know where the Trader was gone & I had Indian enough to tell them they were gone hors hunting, which seemed to satisfie them, they left the Venison & rode off. soon after our People returnd & the Indians with them.

The Next day the Traders, having some business at the Town, invited me along with them, we sat off early in the cool of the morning & in less then three hours got to Town. The Indians recieved us very affectionately, feasting us on the best they had.

Towards the cool of the evening we returnd again to Camp. on our way we saw a company of Indians at Camp over a Meadow. they were reposing themselves under the shadow of spreading Oaks and Palm trees, in a little grove which was open to an extensive green Savanah & Pond. These were Seven likely Young Siminole Fellows all elligantly dresst & painted after the Indian fashions with Plumes & Coronet on their heads, they were stretcht out on their Mantles spread on the shady green under a wide spreading live Oak & their Wenches at some distance cooking. Tho' these were all young fellows, they seemed to be under the conduct of one amongst them who was elder, & affected a somewhat more grave & serious Air & deportment. They told us they, were in pursuit of an Indian fellow, who had lately caried off this young chief's wench, from their Town, Their flight was to avoid being cropt, which is the punishment for the crime of Adultry amongst these people (A most savage custom indeed). however if the delinquents escape & keep out of the way untill the Busque, their anual grand feast of first fruits, is past, they save their Ears; & they may safely return to the Town, and no questions asked about the matter.

It is however dificult to escape this rigorous punishment for, as moral behavour seems to be a principle in their system of government & polity, and perhaps no people under the Sun have more perfect & refined notions of the nobler Virtues, than these wild Americans. The antients of the People well considering that any violation of these sacred fundamentals of their constitution not only reflects on their wisdom but weakens their power & influence; And the Relations of the delinquents, to wipe away the stain of infamy from their Families, readily join in the cause of virtue, & exert their utmost power, in discovering the Criminals that they may be punished.

They wellcomed us in their maner. That is, are you come, sit down. They soon fell into discourse with the Traders inquiring the news, & Talks, & soon joind in familiar subjects, very merry & jocose, sung war, & love songs & passing the Pipe about. Such a Company of handsome young fellow, I hardly ever saw together. The Young Chief was tall, rather above the middle size, had a lofty & fierce countenance, his eyes lively & piercing, his Nose Aquiline, his mouth large but so formed as to give an engaging smile in conformity with all his fetures, his Limbs well turnd & of exact proportion, his motions when talking easy, free & without the least constraints. His head was shaved smooth all except a crest of hair left about an Inch long, which was cut in a circular form from the Crown reaching to the back part of his head, All his head that was shaven & his neck to his shoulders painted with Vermilion, his crest black & shone like a Raven, his head was adorned with a Diadem or Coronet of Furs, which incircled his temples & went round just over the top of his fore hed, curiously wrought with Beads, & on the fore part of it waved, a high Plume of white Heron feathers, he had a large Silver gorget on his breast, & a Silver Mirror & Cross. The rest were elligantly dress & painted, with Coronets wrought ingeniously of split quills dyed of different colours & Plumes of blue Heron feathers. they had Red & blue Mantles or Match coats, fringed or laced, performed by their wives. After smokeing and conversing awhile, we left them and return'd to Camp, on our way One of the Traders said he could shew me a fine Spring of excellent water in the Rocks. presently we came to a little Grove, went into it. in the middle of this grove was a vast well, curiously fluted or hollowed round about the inside from top to bottom, it was near 20 feet perpindicular down to the water & the Rocks being broken away On one side we decended by sort of eregular steps to the water. the water was very cool & pleasant, we got up again but not without difficulty, the Rocks being rotten & mouldring away under our feet. & was glad when I was up & thought myself safe again; observed on one side of me just by my feet, dark cracks in the earth, & the dirt to fall in. I gave a kick with my foot, & drove the mould into a large deep perpindicular well. got a Pole & work't away the earth round about the mouth, this well was about 5 feet in diameter, round and smooth wrought through a rock, could see the water shining at the bottom, about 20 feet deep. got late to Camp. but had a pleasant ride, the even'g being cool & the moon shining very bright. the Vast tall Pines cast a dark shadow, and beautifully checquered & clouded over the green plains & Savanahs; The dark Groves & klumps of Trees, rising up to view, on every side, exhibited a pleasing visionary scene. Yet being inveloped in an almost endless savage Wilderness, at intervals damped my sperits, with a kind of gloomy horror. we percieved Our fire at camp.

I took a rout with The trader about fifteen miles up the River, rode 7 or 8 Miles, passing over Savanahs & open Forests. we assend'd high sand hills from whence we had a view of extendsive green plains and Savanahs. passt by a large rockey sink at one side of the Savanah, the water even with the surface of the Savanah, very Clear and cool, grown round about with Willow Trees. this large Sink was full of fish & Alegators. crosst over part of the Plain, entered a Pine forest, & presently opened a very extensive green grassy Vale about a mile wide, & in length extended beyond our view but made a bend to the right hand & partly shut up by a long point of high Pine groves that projected into it at the lower end of this Vale. where we come into it was a prodigious deep funnel shaped hole surrounded by high sand hills, except on that side next the Vale. here was large spreading live Oaks grew round about the top of hills & shaded the water in the sink, which was dark & black but very Cool & full of fish, Trout & bream &^{c}——. This Sink is called by the Indians & Traders the Alegator Hole from a Prodigious large Alegator, that has lived here from time immemorial. The high hills on each side the vale meet here & nearly surround the Sink; at a small distance on one side near the hills observed some deep wells through the Rock. I was greatly pleased to see this place. As that was the recepticle of a prodigious deluge of Waters Which about 7 or 8 Months ago, made an eruption out of the earth, at the upper end of this vale, overflowing the levell Pine forest all around for many miles, which at length found a Passage down this Vale, tareing up the earth, trees & Rocks, for 8 or 10 miles, leaving deep gullys & holes through the middle of this Vale, a track that may remain conspicuous for many Ages. being at last stopt in in its course by these hills, found a vent in these holes, and shortly afterwards disappeared. The Trader with me was an eye witness of this, being present and very near when the eruption happened: he said he was afright'd by an unusual sudden rushing noise which he compared to a violent Storm when he saw at some distance the water boiling & rising high & furiously out of the earth & was almost emediatly surrounded with the waters which he saw covering the earth around him, when he thought it high time to betake himself to flight, directing his course to their Camp which was at the Aligator hole, above described, & soon after his arival there, the waters appeard coming down the Vale, which was presently overflowed, & filled up to the sides off the hills, which too he soon left for the Town, thinking really that the dessolution of Nature was at hand. this account was confirmed to me by other Traders & the Indians at the Town, and afterward by being an eyewitness of its indeliable tracks. we returnd next day down another extensive green open Plain ornamented and diversified with Groves, extendsive Ponds and sinks, where were almost constantly in sight of Gangs of deer, Turkeys, Crains, Herons, & varieties of other fowl.

This night our Camp was alarmed by an Alegator. One of the Men getting up in the night observed him approaching. he soon alarmed us. they diverted themselves by torturing the unhappy monster. by heaving fire brands in his eyes, which inraged him & made him swell & roar terribly, they cut saplings & ramed down his throat which he easily rench't out of their hands, but they at last overcome him & killd him by such sort of torture. I am apt to believe that, he had no intention of attacking us but was passing from one pond to another, which they frequantly do, & are often kill'd in these excursions. For alltho, these monsters are so very dangerous,

& by their strength and swiftness in the Water, almost invincible. Yet when on dry land & some distance from the water, their strength & activity fails, they may be taken & destroyed.

Before I leave off in treating of this part of Florida, beg leave to observe that about this Part of the River of Little S^t. Juane appears to be a very proper & important place for a Settle ment and very necessary to strengthen a communication with the Province of West Florida; This River is large & Navigable, a great ways up, & the clearest & finest water I have seen in this Province, prodigiously replenish't with a variety of excellent River Fish. The Land on its banks fertile, & remarkebly well Timbered with Cypress & vast Pine Forest of as large a growth as any I have ever seen, & no country can well exceed it for extensive Savanahs & range for Cattle. The Indigo Plant grows so plenty & Luxurient, that the Planters have only the trouble of cutting away the Trees & stir up the soil. I have seen the greatest quantity of rich Iron Ore in these Hills near this River that I have ever seen, of the species call bog Ore. & the greatest Plenty of Stone, for building with, & there is a great likelyhood of other Valuable Minerals, in this unknown Country.

We broke up our Camp here & in 3 days traveling returnd to the Store, having collected some valuable Specimins of New Plants. by the way.

Some days after my arival at the Store, I began My second trip up S^t. Johns River, I prepared my little Vessell fit for the Voyage, & procured company to assist me over the great Lake. We set off in two Conoes, got to M^t. Royal where we stayed this night & Next morning push't out early in to the lake; The wind rising very fresh, we put into a large swift runing Creek, that come from a vast Spring five or 6 miles up to it, finding the wind to rise there was little probability of our crossing the Lake, I prevaild upon my companion to continue up the Creek, the water at the mouth of the Creek and some distance in the lake was warm & of a seagreen colour, but as we continued up; it became warmer & extreamly transperant, & difused about us a very disagreable smell. when we came towards the head The Creek widened, the water became very shallow and so full of Water grass we could hardly by any means push through it, yet at last came to the head of the

Creek, an immense fountain four or 500 Yards over where were, a great number of boiling holes throwing the water up in prodigious ebulitions, where it was a great depth & in these holes the water look't of the collour of the Skye above, & so exceedingly transparent could see the fish, Alegators & Turtle as plain as if they had been in our hands; I continued somewhat higher up to the principle Fountain which, boild up in an incredible maner out of the Chasms of deep Rock between two steep high hills.

I landed near this place, & spent some time in traversing these hills & Forests. beyond them observed some curious shrubs & plants, some of their roots & seeds I procured, & sent down to the Store by the return of the Boat that came with me. This evening we sat off & returnd down the Creek & by Sun set got to the mouth again where We found a good harbour & took up Camp, next day we got to the upper Store, where we staid all night. Next morning took leave of my companion & continued up the River alone, the wind a head & Tired, got about 8 Miles, & was obliged to take up Camp at the little Alegator Island. went into the lagoon & took some large Trout, saw abundance of Monstrous Alegators gather'd about my Camp but kept them off by fireing. Got off early in the Morn^g and went this day about 12 Miles, passing through Marshes & Swamps, the Shore on either hand close to the waters Edge most richly adorned with the gayist Vegitables. The great Rose Hibiscus, The most eligant Crimson Hybiscus, that rises tall above all Plants, spreading into inumerable branches forming a Piramedal Top larger then some Trees, bearing multitudes of Vast Crimson flowers, so resplendant when the Sun shines upon it in the morning the Eye can't behold it without injury to the sight. The smaller flower'd rose col'd Hybiscus clothed in the morning with an amazing profusion of the richest flowers, The white robed Pancratium filling the Air with the most exhilirating fragrance. behind these rise up to view on higher seats, another Order of splended Vigitable: Cephalanthos, Senesio Aboracens, Cornus, Catalpa, the Tall aspiring Amaranth, Sambucos, Palma Christa, the Indian Papaya, profusely adorn'd with garlands of the joyfull airey Climbers, As the various Bignonias. Convolvuls of various species & colours, Eupatorium scandens,

Phaseoloides, the beautifull climbing shrub Aster, unfolding her purple mantle spreading over the Shrubs & Trees all about & the Æriel Cucurbita aspiring to the tops of the highest Trees. All this reflected on the gentle flowing surface of the River in the morning exhibits an inchanting theatrical Scenery. came too at a high rockey bluff, just below was a very deep & extensive rich Swamp which lay between a lagoon of the River, & the high Pine Land on the side of hills. next the swamp, was a large Orange Grove growing over & amongst a prodigious Number of heaps of earth & shells, which had the appearnce of a buring ground, by the number of Indian Sepulchres, & I have since been informed that formerly at this place happened a great and decisive, Battle between the Creeks & Yamises, when the latter were cut to pieces, & that unhappy Nation were never after able to make any head against their conquerors but fled to Augustine & put themselves under the protection of the Spaniards. This time of the Year found the Musquetoes very troublesom, got not a wink of sleep during the Night; Set off soon in the morning, got about ten Miles, passing by vast Swamps & Marshes on each side the River Bank, passing by Islands & floating Marshes of Pistia, Persicaria, Sagitaria, Solidago, Aster, Hydracotyle, grasses, all intervoven & matted together forming, vast marshes. the current of the River & winds tearing large pieces off o' the shore fill the River with floating Islands, & in the Morning gives this vast River & Lake a very singular & entertaining appeerence. abundance of flowering Plants on them together with Various kinds of Bird, Such as Jack daws, Herons, Biterns, Coots, Black Birds & Sparows, of which there is a continual concourse flying & swiming from One Islet to another, & amongst them are abundance of Fish, Trout, Bream, Catfish, Mullet, &c. came to camp on a high bank 'twixt the Swamp & River, being a beautifull high airey bank, cover'd with green grass under vast tall spreading Palm Trees & a vast open high Levell grassy Swamp back of me, thinly Planted by Nature with Groves of tall stately Trees, Such as, Ash, Elm, Oak, Hicory, Red bay, Gleditsia, Maple, Mulberry &c. I expected from so high & airey a situation to have eluded the terrible Musquitoes but I was mistaken, for altho the Wind blew so high they were not able to keep on the wing, they swarmed close to the ground & amongst the grass so that they keep me awake all Night. it was to no purpose to make a smake to drive them off as they kept under it close to the earth amongst the grass. Next day about Noon got within a Mile of Berrisford Plantation when I was forced a shore, in an open Marsh by a most dreadfull Hurricane; & happy it was for me that I did not get up to a woody bluff which I was indeavouring for, as might have been fatal to me, for no sooner had I moored to a bush under the bank of the marsh than I beheld with astonishment and Terror the strength & fury of this Storm, the crash & wrenching of trees in the Woods a little way off of me, Trees twisted off by the top & others split to the ground, vast splinters flying like javilen in the air, the tops of the tough yielding hicory bent down into the water, but what is incredeble, I beheld the invinceble sturdy live Oak, yielding to the fury of the tempest, whose firm & almost inflexeble limbs, as thick as large Trees, twisted off, as flax or dry weeds whirl'd aloft & floating in the Air, This tempest shewed itself first in the west, by a dark bank of murmering thunder clouds, two or 3 hours before this terrible invasion, but as it rise the pointed white cap't clouds shot up swiftly through the skyes, spreading on each side. clasht by each other, casting a purple glowing flame colour over the sky, attended with continual streams of lightning & terrible Thunder. and at last these clouds from all points of the horason, met over head, & cast an universal darkness all round; it continued to rain & blow incessantly for near two hours; the rain almost fill'd my canoe & thoroughly wet all my things. after the hurricane abated I baled my Boat & got to the Plantation, where I beheld with amasement the devastation of this mighty Storm. almost every house blown away & near 20 of the largest live Oaks I had seen, which were left about the houses for shade, were torn up by the Roots, & those that stood it out had their tops almost torn to pieces & the limbs lap't to the Stump. The Indigo & corn allmost destroyed, & the People greatly terrified but by a providintial care, & which seemed really Miracalous, they escaped unhurt. I was two days here before I got my Papers dryed & lost some valuable Specimins of New Plants: But luckily had a duplicate, left behind me at the Store, In some days aft[r]: collecting some

Valuable Roots & seeds, I return'd down the River again, Not being able, for want of a hand to assist me any higher up this River. In two days, after I set off again got down to the Upper Indian Store, observing nothing new by the way, but took up some valuable Roots which I planted in a Box in my boat. I found at my arival at the Store, a party of Indians, and a trader belonging to the lower Store. I got this man to accompany me to the great East Lake, which is a part of S^t. Johns River on the east side, seven or eight miles above the upper Store. it is computed at 9 or 10 miles in length & more, by others it is said to be as long as Lake George; wet set off in the morning, & before night got to a hamock at an Orange Grove, within the Lake, made a large fire to keep off the Mus-quetoes, the while we were eating supper, two very large Bear, we heard wadeing through the water, they came within 20 Yards of us and stood, but seeing us move to get a shott at them, they, went off plunging through the water. we saw them no more, but heard them, coming to another part of the ham-ock, afterwards, but did not come near to us; Returnd next day to the Store; I made an excursion some miles round about the Store, but observed nothing curious. Set off for the lower Store, got 7 Miles On my way down the River, came to the Great Lake George. The Evening being Calm, and the face of this great Water serene & gentle, I pusht out, got safe over a large cove of it, & landed safely on a pleasan^t. [   ] sandy shore. here I injoyed a noble prospect of this grand display of waters; made me a good fire, to defend me from my enemies. The Next morning early got off, padled about 2 Miles & come to the mouth of Johnsons Springs; padled near a mile up & come to a vast Fountain, almost in every respect like the other great Spring that I visited before. I went a shore, mounted very high, hills very steep next the Creek, but fell away more gradually back, & enterd a beautifull grove of Palm Trees, large spreading live Oaks & Vast Laurel Magnolia, mounted a very high ridge, from whence had an almost endless view of a vast baren desart, altogether impenetrable so thickly over grown with short schrubby Oaoks, Bays, Yapon, Prinos & short laurel bushes (Magnolia Grandaflora) &^c. about these hills & open groves, observed abundance of the beautiful Scarlet Sage, the beautifull large yellow Malva, A noble, sweet sented Shrub bearing golden clustres of Flowers, Tall Apuntia, breeding plenty of Cochaniel. Returnd to my boat, & with a gentle favourable breese sailed over to Drayton Island; I landed here, got some Roots & seeds of some valuable Shrubs & Plants, set off and By night got over to a Promontary at the mouth of the River. the shore being very rockey & the wind blowing very high, found it very dificult & dangerous landing, it being open to the Lake but with great struggle got round a point of Marsh, into a safe harbour by dark, here I camped all Night. Next morning I traversed about this Point, came to an Orange Grove, I discovered a most singular & beautifull Species of Convolvulos. left this place & within night got safe down to the lower Store very wet & tired, having gone through a very heavey gust of Rain.

St Johns River.

Novemb^r. 6. began the first alteration of the Season, with regard to the temperature of the Air, from Summer to Autumn.

Wind S. W. attended with heavey rains & cold, night & next day wind very high & cold from N. E. evening & night high wind with cold rain. continual flights of Ducks & water foul came with the wind, about 12 OClock Night the wind shifted about S. W. then west. blew hard with much rain, in the morning shifted round N. W. this day very high wind & cold, even^g the wind fell a little but the night very cold & observed continual flights of Storks & whooping crains flying all night. The morning very cold, & observed a white frost, which killd the Goard & Potatoe Vines with abundance of other Vegitables, the wind continued very high & cold; continual flights of Storks & whooping Crains, this night very cold and flight of birds all night, next morning hard white frost; this day the Wind fell, but yet cold, & clear air. observed continual flights of Storks. they flew amazingly high & slow, observing a perticular order in their progress, their notes or voice very musical & agreeable. Altho a bird of a superior * magnitude, they move through the Skies in so

---

*The Stork is the largest bird in N^o. America. They are perfectly white, tips of the greater Quill feathers Crow black, crown of the head bare of feathers, of a flesh color. This bird is well figured by G. Edwards, I measured the Wings of one of these birds, which extended near 9 feet from tip to tip, & above 5 feet from Bill to Tail.

exalted a Sphere, that they appeared to be no biger then Pidgions, yet do they appear very conspicuous especially when in a particular position, the sun shines full upon their silver pinions, being tiped with black, their polished silver feather d[   ] flashes of light one after another, as the light is reflected from a polished [   ]. *The Whooping Crain move in the same order but not quite so high, being of a brown colour, appear high up in the air almost black. Two or 3 days continued moderately warm, the wind come round which continued 3 or 4 days very agreable, when y^c: Wind came S^o. W^t. then W^t. than N. E. clouded, blew hard with cold Rain, large flights of Wild Geese & ducks, which continued for 2 days & nights. wind came W^t. than N. W^t. very cold, abundance of ducks, biterns, Herons & other water-fowl; had 2 nights of hard white frost, than the weather moderate, now the Lakes, Ponds & Meadow, are visited & fully peopled by the feather'd tribes from the N^o. the Vast pine forest are filled with their clangor, & resound the thunder of their Wings night & Morning.

*   *   *

Panther commonly called Tyger. They are very large, strong & fierce & are too numerous, & very mischievous.

Ounce, called by the Indians Tyger cat, are nearly of the size of a small Spaniel dog, very long & slender make, have an extream long tail, Their colour is a Yellowish ground, nearly of the colour of yellow Ochre, on which are marks or spots of black, of various sizes & figures, they have very long & sharp Talons white as Ivory, the whiskers or beard about the nose & mouth very long, strong & white, the mouth large and armed with strong sharp teeth. They are swift & extreamly active, assending high Trees, & spring a great distance from the tops of Trees from one to another, & from bow to bow, They are a beautiful creature, the Florideans use their skins for Tobacoe pouches,

*The Whooping Crain is not so large as the Stork but are a large stately bird. They are of a dark ash color or brown, inhabit the Savanahs & Pine Forests. This Bird is call'd Watula by the Indians, & Whooping Crain by the white People. Figured & described by G. Edwards.—

The small Ounce or Wild Cat having a very short Tail. They are about half the sise of the Tyger cat. they are of a dark Tabbie color, This creature is too common, very fierce & bold, & do a deal of mischief about plantations in the night, carying of Geese, Poultry, lambs, Pigs &^{c}.

Wolves are here in great abundance, and of various colors, Black, Pied, Brinded & grey, the black & grey most common, they are very strong, bold & voracious, approaching Plantations in the Night, in great companies, sending out scouts or parties to look for prey.

Bos cornibus teretibus flexis Lin: syst: Nat: Buffiloe, a very large creature. This creature is become very scarce, in E^t. Florida yet there remains a fiew in the Point. The Indians bring their skins with those of Deer to Stores, the hide is covered with a short, soft curley wool or Furr, of a soft texture.

Deer. but of one Species, sometimes accidental varieties, in colour & form of horns, but not much more than half the size of those in the No^n. Colonies.

Hares, called Rabbits. these are much smaller than those in the N^o. Opossoms are very common. Pole cat not uncommon, but not so plenty as in the N^o. Mink. Wesel, not common but I have seen some. Moles are not so common. Hare are some Otters, & Beaver.

Birds of E^t. Florida.

Aquila. The greatest Grey Eagle. This is a large strong Bird. they prey upon all animals they can conquer, resort to the Sea coast & the banks of Great Waters. sitting on some eminence, they watch the flux & reflux of the Sea, observing the success of other birds of prey, which they pursue, & cause them to drop the produce of their labours, which they commonly catch ere it touches the earth. The fishing Eagle however often eludes his utmost vigilence & power, for being much lighter & active on the wing mounts aloft with greter ease, but if the eagle gets above him, the struggle is quickly over: high up in the airey regions the contest is decided, the hawk is forc't to quit his prey, When the eagle closes the points of his wings towards his body, & with collected power cleaves the elastick air & seemes to rend the skies which indeed can be only equalled by the Terror of sudden & unexpected Thunder.

early in the Spring they arive from the S°. & build their Nests on lofty Pine Trees; in the Autumn they return S°. but others arrive from the N°. & stay with us all winter so that they are to be seen all the year in this Province.

The great bald Eagle, are a strong fierce bird. they, like the grey eagle, prey upon all animals they can take, but recieve large contribution from the Fishing Eagle & other smaller birds of Prey. This likewise is a bird of passage, but breed & some continue here during the winter, coming here from the N°.

The Fishing Eagle, commonly called the Fishing Hawk, tho in the make & structure of his body is perfectly aquiline yet is more slender & delicately formed than any of the Eagles, his wings very long & sharp pointed, They keep continually about Rivers & waters & feed only on Fish, they build large Nests on the highest summits of dead Trees by the Water, are extremely fierce & watchfull about the time of incubation. they are birds of Passage, retiring S°. at the approach of winter, but early in the Spring appear in great numbers, & soon after pare together, & begin to erect their nests. This bird is the Eagle's purveyer, and is said as soon as he takes a fish he hallows out to give notice to the eagle, but this is certainly a mistaken notion, but squeels out for fear of the eagle, which he continues to do during the contest as they mount up, even to such a hight in the air as to be nearly out of sight or hearing.

There are six species of Hawks besides the little Sparow hawk: Which continue all the Year but much more numerous in the Winter season, when they arive here from the N°. Which may be distinguished thus: The great Eagle Hawk, because of his strength & fierceness, he has a red Tail, barred across with dark brown, the large Fowl hawk, having a speckled breast, he resorts about houses & preys on Poultry, the Marsh hawk a swift bird, prey on Black birds, the Ortulane & Frogs; The People of Carolina & Georgia are carefull not to destroy or molest them, as they are of the utmost service in chasing away the numerous flocks of Rice birds. they skim a long just over the top of the Rice, not suffering the rice bird to sit long in a place, & two or 3 of these hawks do more service than half a dozen Negroes constantly firing at them.

They are a slender & neat made bird, af a dark brown colour upper side; The under side of a redish yellow or brick colour, the tail long & beautiful, the Upper coverts white.

The Pidegion Hawk or long tail'd hawk, generally of a dark brown color upper side & brick color under side, the legs & Bill Yellow, the Tail very long & barred across with darker brown or dusky colour, the feathers covering the thighs very long, reaching almost to the feet. this is a smaller bird than either of the foregoing, very swift & mischievous. The Blew Hawk, this is a large beautifull bird, approaching near to the size & make of the Marsh hawk and like him flys about marshes over the tops of grass, He is of a bright bluish lead colour, the principle quill feathers almost black, the covert feathers on upper side of tail white. The Chicken hawk. Not quite so large as a small Crow, dark brown upperside, the Tail long & barred a cross, with darker colour, the upper coverts white, the breast & belly white, speckled with dusky spots. this is a neat made bird, very fierce & active & mischievous about houses amongst Poultry.

The Black Hawk is about the size of the Chicken Hawk, they are all over of a dark slate colour appearing perfectly black, they have however darker barrs across the Tail & wings. they frequent woods & shady thicket, preying on Mice, frogs & Snakes. The little Sparow Hawk is well figured & described by M. Catisby. There are besides these two beautifull species of Kite Hawks. the first is the forked tailed hawk. he is about the size of the Marsh Hawk, the Tale very long & deeply forked, his colour is principly of a light blue or lead colour, the breast & belly almost white, they are the lightest bird on the wing & scarcely ever seen setting, they feed upon the wing holding their prey in their Talons, their food is generally snakes, Lizards or the green cammelion & Tree frogs, which they snatch from the tops & bows of Trees as they fly along. the other Kite Hawk is almost in all respects like the preceeding Species but his tail is not forked, is most beautifull on the Wing & like him feed on the Wing & on the same sort of food.

There Are in this country three Species of Vultures—

The Turkey Buzard, figured as described by M. Catesby.

The Black Buzard or Caron Crow. they are a chunkyer bird

of a darker colour, have shorter wings & very short Tails, the head & Neck bare of feathers, the skin wrinkled & loose so that they may draw their head within the Skin which is of a dark purple or indigo colour, thick set with black hair. the bill is very long, streight & bent suddenly at the point, they are a heavey bird on the wing, flaping too their wings quick like a bat when flying. Tab. VII. & VIII.

The Croped Vulture. This is a very beautiful bird, not quite so large as the Turkey buzard, they are chiefly white, the back & wings of a deep nut brown, the Bill yellow, Legs white, the head & part of the neck bare of feathers, covered with a naked skin of a vermillion colour, what is remarkeble in the Bird their craw or stomack hangs like a pouch or purse bearing outside on the breast & bare of feathers. When the vast meadows & Savanahs of Florida are set on fire, they gather in flocks to the new burnt ground where they feed on the roasted snake, frogs, Lizards, Turapin's & other reptiles. where I had an oppertunity of getting one.

Here are abundance of Turkeys, two species both black, the Cock drest in the richest Garments reflecting purple Gold & [   ].

The green long tail'd Paroquett figured by Catesby. ——

Crow 2 Species, one very large keeps near the Sea coast, has a loud course voice like the Raven. the Other Species much smaller, & arive in this country in vast flights, at the approach of Winter, this is a common bird over America. Two species of Jackdaw's purple, the largest breed here & continue through the year. The smaller kind, arives here in large flights from the N°. at the approach of Winter. they breed in the northern Colonies in Pennsylvania. The Red winged Sterling. The Ortulan or Rice Bird of Catesby. the blue Ortulan or Rice bird, they are a S°. bird not ariving here till late in the summer and retire again before Frost. Several Species of the Sparows arrive here from the N°. at the approach of Winter. but the Snow bird never comes so far S°. not even to Georgia at least on the Sea coast.

Towe bird of Catesby. Winters here. The Fox col^d. Thrush, The Mevis, & small golden crown Thrush, winters here but breed in the N°. Colonies. The Mock Bird breeds here &

sings the Year through. The Catbird winters here but dont sing, they breed in the N^{on}. Colonies. Neither of the Baltimore birds breed here nor are seen in the winter but keep on farther S^o. The Robbin or fieldfare are here in the winter. The Crested Red bird here all the Year, The Summer Red bird is here in summer season. a species with black wings & Tail only pass along in the spring to the N^o. Colonies where they breed. the crested Flycatcher is here in summer, & breed here, but retire S^o. soon. The Pewit or black cap flycatcher winters here, but goes N^o. soon in the Spring. The House & Marsh Wren winters here. The Kildeer or chattering Pluver winters here. All the Woodpeckers of Catisby are here the year through except the golden winged which only winters here. The Motacilla winters here & the blue jay, of Catisby. but a smaller blue jay without a crest is here only in the Summer season, The Nonparell, & blue Linnet, is here in the Summer but go farther S^o. in the winter. the golden & ruby crown wrens winter here. The Crown bird, garulus crestata, appears here at times the whole Year. The gold Finch winters here. the Yellow rump Flycatchers are here fall & spring, but don't build here. The Cuccow is here in spring & build in the Summer, but retires So in the Autumn. the huming bird is here in the Summer. several genera of slender bill'd birds are here in the summer such as breed in the Nothern colonies that dont winter here. In The Autumn at the approach of Winter arive here three kinds of wild Geese but the Swan do not come so far S^o. The great Duck & Mallard arive here in the Winter, with a vast variety of ducks & water fowl. in the month of November pass along So vast flights of Storks & whooping Cranes. they fly very high, continuing a very agreeable musical Noise. they move very slow, & generally in a very singular order after this maner ⟨○ ○ ○⟩ great numbers however of both this species of Stork winter here & are here all the year round. Three Species of Owls, the great Horn Owls, Hen Owl & Screech Owl. Two Species of the Night hawk are here in the Summer but only the WhiperWill winters.

Of Reptiles & Amphibious Creatures of E^t. Florida:

The Green Turtle with several Species of Sea Turtle on the coast. The great soft shell Tortoise in the fresh water, the Red bellied Turapin in the fresh water Rivers, the little muskey Tortoise, The great Land Tortoise called Gopher. the Little land Turapin.

The Alegator. The Manetta, Several species of Lizards, The large Red bellied, the little squamous blue bellied, the green Lizard or Camilion.

Snakes. 1. The great Rattle Snake. 2. Little Rattle Snake call'd ground Rattle snakes because frequently howed out of the ground, they never grow above 12 or 14 inches in length, in every respect like the great Rattle Snake except, being so small & flatting their body more then him when iritated, they have only 3 Rattles, with which they make a little hissing noise but their bite not so fatal, yet dangerous, enough.

3. The Great Mockazin Snake, grows almost as large as the Rattle Snake & if posseble of a more terrible look. they are almost in every respect like the great Rattle Snake except being without Rattles, when they see their enemy approach they draw themselves up in a coil, open their frightfull jaws, throwing the upper mendable almost back to the neck, presenting two terrible fangs. their bite is said to be as fatal as that of the Rattle snake. they keep in swamp & fenns.

The high land Mocazin, these are rather longer then the Rattle Snake but not so thick, they are of very beautifull colour like the Wampom snake & I take him to be a larger species of that snake. they are much dreaded but never heard an instance of their biting any person.

The small water snake, a small species of the Mocazin, they are very numerous, & frequantly bite, but never heard of a fatal effect from it. A pretty species of yellow & brown spotted Viper, these are supposed to be dangerous. A black Viper, small about 2½ feet in length, bothe these flatten their body when iritated.

The Ribbon Snake, a beautifull, small Snake, small & round bodied, being spotted with bright Red & crow colour, grow 2½ feet in length & near an Inch thick, they are harm less.

The Glass Snake, about the size of the Ribbon snake, but not so long.

The Coach-whip Snake, they are usually about 7 feet in length & about 1½ inch in thickest part of the body, the head

& about 3 Inches of the Neck of a red brick color marked with dark brown, all the rest of the body of a pale cream color almost white & usually called the White Snake.

The Black Coach Whip Snake about the size of the foregoing, as black as a raven & extremly swift.

The Great black Snake about 6 feet long & about 2½ inches thick, a harmless Snake but of great strength & swiftness, they prey on Rabitts, Squirells, birds & other Snakes & frequantly over come the Rattle Snake, & swallow him.

The Thunderer or

No. 10. The Bull Snak, commonly called the horn Snake from his tail terminating by a hard sharp point like a young cock spurr, they are very harmless but of a monstrous size & bulk, they are frequantly above seven feet in length & 6 inches in diameter, of a pied colour black & white; when provaked they swell them selves & utter a loud thundering noise, but can t be provaked to strike but indeavour to escape in holes in dry sand hills.

11. The Great Chicken Snake, near as big as the Thunder Snake, & not so thick but rather longer, they are of an ash colour, having paralel line or stripes from head to tail. They are very swift, gliding through the forest with their head & fore part of the body lifted up two or 3 feet high. they prey on birds especially young Poultry; climbing up to the top of Marten Poles & dove cotes, destroying the young & suck the eggs.

12. The Rat catcher. This large Snake is about the Size of the chicken snake except not so long. they are, of a dirty Ash colour inclining to a straw color upper side; belly & sides bright red; They are the most inocent harmless snake, seeme dull & stupid, they resort about log house Stables & out houses; & catch Rats, moles, mice, & are very industrious & usefull, soon clearing a Plantation of such vermin, if suffer'd to stay about houses, but are seldom sufferd to be about, as they say they destroy the Chickens & Poultry.

13. The Green Snake, this is a long, extremely, small snake, of a perfectly bright Green, a little yellowish on the belly, they are allways on trees & bushes, very numerous & climb to the tops of highest Trees, in pursuite of the little green Camilion, spiders & other insects.

N° 14. Tab. V, Fig. 3. I have seen a pretty little snake about 12 inches long, small, round bodied, speckled with dark redish brown spots on a dove col'd ground, but take it to be young wampom snakes. —— These are all the different species of Snakes I have yet seen in E^t. Florida.

There are two Species of Scorpions in this Country. One small, about 2 inches in length, of a pale Olive colour, having a short articulate Tail, the sting is like that of a Wasp or bee, & not more painfull. they are frequent about old log houses amongst dirt & lumber, old cloaths, &^{c}. & commonly in the interior parts of the country—

The Other Species are much larger, of dark redish brown colour, about 4 or 5 inches long, one of the articulations of the Tail being very long & small like the small part that joins the tail to the body in a species of wasp. when they are iritated, they curle their articulate Tail up over their body & throw it out very quick, having a sting at the extremity. their sting is said to be very painfull and dangerous. I have seen them on the sea coast of istmous of Florida.

There are various Species of Spiders but never heard of any hurt from them. The most remarkeble, are the great Yellow & black streaked Spider; They spin or weave a Vast Web or Net between the Tops of very high Trees in the low Lands & Shady groves, even when the Trees are 15 or 20 feet one limb from another, the Web is very strong & knit or wove in a very beautifull & ingenious maner, they place themselves in the Center, they catch large insects Such as the Cicada, Cervus volans, small birds &^{c}. when they have sucked all the substance out of these creatures, They are carefull to bite of the webb or thred that intangled them & let the dry skeleton drop to the ground & afterwards repair their Net for fresh service. their body is about the size of a Pidgion's egg, something longer, their legs very long & armed with prickles of stiff black hair, the two fore legs are the longest, flated & broad at the middle joint; when the unhappy insect or bird is intangled in their Net & the spider finds by his struggles that he cant desingage himself, he runs speedily up & spirts out a thick white webb near as thick as a goosquill upon his prey, which spread like a cloud or white mist over him. this soon puts an end to the struggle. The other kind is much like this; full as big bodied but not so long legged and have their dwellings on lower situation amongs, tall Weed & Rushes, they weave a vast strong & ingeniously contrived web, they catch, large insects in the same manner of the other. Here is a very large Species of Spider of a particular Nature & Fearfull aspect, they are nearly as large bodied as the other kind but have very short legs, he weaves no net nor contrives any snare to take his Prey Yet is not less voracious, they take all by strength & surprise. they keep commonly about Trees & Plants: When they discover their game as The Cicada, Locust &ᶜ. they with the greatest patience, subtilety & circumspection creep up towards it by slow & wary steps, when they spring upon it seizeing it with a pare of strong sharp pincers, & at that instant with their tail fix a strong web or thread, & suffer them to be carried off their feet, & are suspended together, the unhappy captive flutters spining round backwards & forward like a nut on a small thread till his strength fails him, the voracious spider caries him off. They are covered with a soft yellowish down spotted with red & brown, the head large, having 2 firey eyes like rubies. their legs are thick & strong, each armed with a sharp crooked talon, They usually spring 2 or 3 feet on their prey. & may be called the Tyger Spider.

Here are several other kinds of spiders take their prey in the same maner, particularly three or four sorts that have their dens in large Flowers, particularly of the Synginesious Tribes as the Sunflowers, Rudbeckias & Chrysanthimums, these little subtile creatures, with their webb draw together 3 or 4 of the Radiæ of these flowers, bending the tops over together forming a little den or cave; in the farthest corner of which they secrete themselves & as these flowers are perpetually visited by swarms of flying insects, they spring out & sieze them, allways fixing a webb or thread behind least they should be caried off by the superior strength of their Prey. there are an infinite variety of kinds of Spiders, but these being the most remarkeble, I was willing to point them out.

There is no great variety of Insects different from what are native to Carolina and Virginia, & not so numerous or so great a variety as are found in the N°. Provinces; but I think are larger & of gayer colours.

The large yellow Gourd fly, Tab. X, is the most beautifull of this Genus I have ever seen, it is not of that kind which have a spiral Probosses. Here are Several beautifull Species of Phalenæ, perticularly 3 different species that spin large bags or coccoons of strong & fine Silk; After the ruffeled face of winter is calmed & Nature consents to the universal harmony of the Vernal season, these beautifull sprights begin to people the Air & haunt the fragrant Orange Groves; in the morning they break out of their dark silken tombs, hover about it for a little while untill the genial warmth of the sun animates them with vital motion. they then often flutter their wings & spread forth their silken fingers as if impatient to leave the loathsome Prison bounds, at length being arived at the period of perfection & excellence, they unfold their downey Pinions & assend to the purer regions of the skies & with inexpresseble ease & delight are wafted through the balmy air to some fragrant shady grove. The delicate structure of their wings not being formed for a long continuance in the powerful sunbeams or active waring eliments, winds & storms, they seek the peacefull retreats of flowery shady groves, where they hide themselves, untill the even^g. they fly about these groves, visit every fair flower & sip ambrosial nectar from the cup of Flora;

A very fiew days after the fly appears the fœmale deposits her Eggs in clusters on the branches or leaf of the Tree whose leaves the young worms delight to feed upon, & in a very fiew days these eggs are hatched by the warmth of the air. the little Caterpiller feeds on the young tender leaves first, till he grows & becomes stronger, when he feeds on all that's green & sappy; towards the Autumn becomes a very large green [   ] worm, & before winter wrap themselves up in silken balls, either pendant from the branches of Trees, or, wrought like sacks or baggs placed in forks of small branches, where they remain untill the (next spring the) day of resurrection.

Here are in Florida a numerous variety of Dragonflys commonly called here Musqueto hawks; The great grey dragon Fly is near 5 inches in length from head to tip of the tail. they appear pretty early in the Spring & continue till late in the Fall, they prey upon flying insects, & are destroyers of Mus-

quetoes. they are very numerous, are active soon in the morning & late in the even'g but by dark are forst to depart for
fear of the Bat [   ] take them, but the bat in turn is glad
to hide himself from the Screech Owl. The large blue bodied,
with spotted wings, they prey upon Musquetoes & Gnats.
Besides these are almost an infinite variety of smaller species
call'd Devels needles. they all feed upon smaller flying Insects.
Here is 2 species of Hornets, their Sting very painfull, especially the large pied black & white, which build large conical
Nests hanging from the bows of Trees in shady forests; the
smaller yellow, which builds their nests of the same form &
material, in the ground commonly under the roots of decayed
Trees.

Here is a large & very usefull fly much of the form of a
Hornet, but much larger & have no sting. They are called
guard flys because in some situation of this country generally
about the Sea coast & a good distance back from it they constantly swarm about cattle & horses & catch the Bot & stinging flys, which they eat & carry away to their nests in the
earth, & as soon as these very extraordinary & useful insects
arive, the tormenting biting fly immediately disappear.

Florida produces 3 or 4 species of huming Bees, the largest
nest in the ground forming a sort of comb or rather nest of
little bladders or bottles composed of a dark col'd wax, which
are full of well tasted honey.

Another Species, bore holes, in the dry logs & timber of
houses & buildings where they deposit numbers of eggs,
whereto they carry worm & caterpilers for food for the young
offspring; Either the male or fœmale, are almost constantly,
at the mouth of the nest, to prevent, the sly & roguish designs
of a Fly of quite another Tribe who if he finds an oppertunity,
slips in, and deposits eggs in the nests which prey on the
young bees & produce a swarms of a different race & family.
A smaller species, make holes in clay or mud walls of houses.

Here are great abundance of Wild honey bees, but are
certainly not native but were brought into America by the
Europeans.

Their swarms are frequently taken in the woods & caried
to the houses by the inhabitants, where they increase, are very
industrious & soon become very wealthy. The wild honey is

frequantly poisonous, especially in the spring of the Year. The People say it is occationed by the bees collecting honey from flowers of the Yellow Jessamy, a species of Bignonia, whose flowers are narcotic.

This low watry country abounds with a vast variety of Frogs, the largest Species is not so large as the great Bull Frog in Carolina & Virginia. he is about a foot long, generally of a dark green upper side, yellow about the mouth, the under side almost white clouded with darker spots or dashes. these keep in the wet, marshes of S^t. Johns River & other great waters, & make a hoarse grunting noise like hogs.

The brown & black speckled frog keeps in marshes & Savanahs.

The large dark green & speckled frog, in River swamp, Savanahs & runs.

The little luced green frogs, keeps on Rushes, Weeds & Bushes or Trees by River banks. they make a musical noise, in evening & morning all summer. when one begins to Croak, the next to him opens his pipes & so in succession, for a great distance up & down the River banks, the noise resembling the chiming of bells, these change color like the Camileon, the silver col'd treefrog. besides these, there are a great variety of little Frogs that keep only in Savanahs & ponds in the Pine forests, some about one inch in length, striped green & white, makeing a noise like chickens. others not biger then a Creeket & make a noise like them & in the savanahs as numerous as Grasshopers are in Meadows.

There is a large green & Yellow frog a long Rivers Banks, that have a loud sounding noise like large Cowbells. but these are commonly high up the Country of Carolina & Georgia.

Here are two species of Land frogs or Toads, that keep in holes in the earth or under logs & Stones in the day, but come out in the night. One species Very large & black, seems almost cover'd on upperside with a sort of protecting Plates, The other smaller & speckled, both make a horse croaking noise in even^g.

E^t. Florida abounds with a great variety of Fish both on the coast & up the numerous Rivers & fresh waters, in the salt and brackish waters are Bass, Drum, Mullit, Catfish, Whiting,

Sea trout, Sheephead, Rock, Skeats, Stingrai, Black fish, Crokers, Sun fish, Porposes, Dolphin, Shark, Jewfish & a many others in Salt waters which do not come into the Rivers. In Brackish & fresh waters are Mullet, Sheep head, Bass, Drum, Garr, Catfish. In Fresh water Rivers, Lakes & Ponds are Garr, Trout an excellent large fish, Catfish, Bream, of four different Species, Silverfish, Minies.

Here is no great variety of Shell fish either on the Sea shore or up Rivers or on the Land. The common are Oisters, Clams, Scollope, Cockles, small Limpets, Echinus, Sea Muscles,

Up the Rivers, are two species of Winkles, The great and small, some snales, Musels, On the land are 3 sorts of small Snales.

Of the Fungi there is no great variety of Genera.

Of the Musci here are a numerous variety.

Filices, a great variety and some admirably beautifull.

Algæ Several genera.

Lithophyta. Several Genera, as Sponge, Corallum, Tubipora, Millepora &c.

Of the Stone creation, Here is some variety.

Petras, Cos, Quartzum, Spatum, Schistus,

Mineræ, Pyrites, Ferrum, Hæmatites.

Fossilia, Glarea, Argilla, Arena, Marga. Concrega, Calculus gastrici Pecorum, Concha, Cancri Oculi ♋. Petrificata. Echini, Conchites, Cochlites, Cornu amomis.

Vegitable productions which the Florideans use for food:

Granadilla,

Fruit when ripe is as large as a Goose Egg, yellow, & of a very fragrant smell and an agreeable taste, the juice very sweet, inlivened with a little tartness. This fruit the Indians are very fond off, eaten singly, as other fruits or prepared in this manner; When ripe they gather great quantities & throw in heaps, to mellow. when they get yellow & begin to shrivell they spread them about to air, then beat them with parch'd corn flower, in a Mortar, which soon becomes like dough but continue beating till the whole is dry as flower, then they sift it. to clear out the seeds & skins whiche being too hard & tough to marsh up with the rest. this flower has an agreable smell & taste, & by mixing a very little of this

meal or flower with warm water make an agreeable wholesome kind of jelly. They like wise make Cakes or fritters of
it.——

Pumkins they use in the same maner, & barbecue them over
fire & smoke.

Peaches are prepared like it & barbecued. Grapes they barbecue in bunches.

Convolvulus radice tuberora esculenta. Patates.

These roots they eat boil'd & roasted, as the white People
do, these they likewise barbecue & keep all winter.——

Diospyros floribus dioicis Gron. virg:

Pursimmons the Indians delight to eat, they have a method
of preserving them by drying them; & marshing them up,
throw^g. out the stone & mix the pulp with corn flower, bake
Cakes, which will keep, a long time, & when they eat the Cake
they stew them with fat Venson & bair Oil.

Peaches, they slice, take out the stone, & marsh up with
parch't corn, beating all to dry flower, this they mix with other
corn flower & bake loaves or Cakes or barbecue the Peaches
whole on hyrdles over a gentle fire & smoke, in this maner
they do Grapes, Patates, sliced Pumkins & all other such
fruites & roots & keep in dry stores, & when they want to
cook or make use of them, they stew them in a little water,
they plump up & look & taste as when fresh. Green Corn
Pease & Beans they use this way &^{c}.——

Smilax aspera nodosa, radice rubra majora Plum.

China Root vulgo. The Indians dig up these roots, which
they chop to pieces with a hatchet, this they reduce in a
wooden mortar & Pestle as fine as posseble and mix it with
water in a large tub, stiring it about well, with a stick, & whilst
the water is thick & turgid, pour it off into another Vessell,
which when dry leaves a seddement or fine red flower or meal
at the bottom of the Vessell, This powder they keep for food,
& call it Contee, when they make use of it they mix a little
of the farena with warm water which very soon becomes a
thick redish jelly, which when sweetened with honey Or Sugar,
is very agreeable & is esteamed as nourishing & extremely
coveted by the Indians. they make very good fritters or Pan
Cakes of this flower, mixing it with corn flower & fried in
Bears Oil.

Glycine radice tuberosa Gron. virg. Apios americana.

The Indians gather the Roots of this Plant which they roast or boil. they eat like yams or Potatoes. the consistance of the Root is farinacious, white as snow, but has an earthy taste yet very wholesome and agreable enough after being used to eat them, the Plant grows in rich low vales or bottoms where the soil is loose & light. the roots grow in strings like beads, each articulation about the size of a hens egg. The Indians gather these Roots in the autumn after the Plant has flowered & the top withers. they are much used by the Floridians. The Traders call them Indian Patates.

Arum acaule, foliis hastato-cordatis acutis, angulis obtusis Hort. cliff.

Indian Turnip.

The Floridians roast or boil the root of this plant, They also cultivate Edoe's & Taniers, large species of Arum bro't here from W^t. Ind. Islands.

Citrus.

Malus Aurantia major,

Here are two sorts or varieties of Oranges, which grow wild all over the Istmos of Florida. The large sour Orange & the Bitter-swett both of which the Indians are emoderately fond of, they sometimes roast the sower oranges in the ashes, which eats something like a roasted apple.

These two species of Oranges grows, on high shell bluff on the Banks of Rivers, Lakes & Ponds, & at all inlets on the Sea coast. they grow in groves or copses together not commonly mixing with other Trees yet some other sorts of Trees will grow scatteringly amongst them, as a fiew large live Oaks, Celtis, Zanthoxilon, Palm, Ilisium. they grow only on the richest high land in the country, which occations the destruction of abundance, since this kind of soil is the most proper for the Planter to begin to clear & plant.

Whether the Orange Tree is an exotick, brot in here by the Spaniards or a Native to this country, is a question, I have inquired of some of the old spaniards at Augustine, who tell me they were first bro't in by the spaniards & spread over the Country by the Indians.

Quercus foliis lanciolatis integerrimis glabris. Gron. Virg.

Live Oak. The Acrons of this species of Oak is commonly

used as food by the Indians of the Istmous. This fruit is as sweet & as mild as a Chesnut. The Indians beat them to flower in wooden morters, & mix with corn flower which makes good bread: they also beat the acorn to pieces then heat them in water over the fire, which afford a great deal of very sweet mild oil, which they use in cookery insted of Bear Oil or Butter, they roast the acorn & eat them as we do chesnuts—

Juglaus cineria.

The Indians hold in great esteem all kinds of sweet Hicory nuts. they crack the nuts, & beat them in morters, this they boil in water & save the Oil, but the most favorite dish the Indians have amongst them is Corn thin Drink seasoned with hicory nut Oil. They pick out the kernel, beat them to a paste & boil with Indian Corn flower, which being season'd with a lixivium made of Pea straw ashes, gives it a consistance & taste someth^g. like cream or rich new milk & is called by the Traders hicory milk.

Gleditsia, spinis triplicibus axillaribus Lin. Spes. Plant. Honey Locust. The Indians use the fruit as food & make good beer of it.

Fagus

Castania Sativa. Castania pumila virginiana. Chesnut & Chinquapin. Both these fruites or Nuts are used for common food by the Floridians. they roast & boil them & make very good Bread of them.

Carica, Foliorum iobis sinuatis Hort. Cleff.

Papaya fructu oblongo, melonis effigee. Ehret.

The Floridians eat this fruite when ripe,

A Thorny evergreen shrub, calld wild limes or Tallow nuts. the fruit resembles a large yellow plumb, the pulp when ripe is of the consistance, looks & tastes like a custard having a little tartness. but very agreeable, This shrub, bears green & ripe fruit & flowers all the Year round, the Natives esteem this fruit & is the most agreable wild fruit in the Itmous.

Palma, dactylifera minor.

The low prickley Palmeto, bears vast quantities of oval yellow or brown sweet fruite, of the size of a Persimmon, which the Indians admire greatly. they are very healthy & fatning. Cattle, Horses, Hogs, Bears, dogs, Wolves, Men, birds & almost every animal in the land feed on it & get extra fat when this fruit is ripe, it makes an excellent strong sweet drink like beer. & it is emagined would yeild a good Sperit or brandy. This fruit is what fattens the bear in this country & I have seen seven or 8 bear siting on their breeches in view at the same time, feeding on this fruite, & the Bees collect abundance of honey from it.

Morus

Morus foliis subtus tomentosis, amentis longis dioicis. Gron. Virg.

The fruit of the black mulberry is a considerable part in the food of the Indians, they dry the fruite on boards in large cakes, which they keep in store, & stew it with bread, parch't corn flower & oil.

Besides these principle articles they eat almost all kinds of berries, Root & Nuts, Water Mellons, Musk Mellons, Squashes, Beans & Peas.—

I indeavoured to get a true account of the origen of the Indians of that part of Florida commonly called the Creek Nation; And being acquainted with a considerable Trader who resided for many Years amongst them, and spoke their Language perfectly well: & there being present at this time a very sensible and a very ancient Indian Chief of that People. I desired him to inquire of the old Chief, whether they who call them selves Muscogulges, were the Aborigines of Florida; He answered. That the land now inhabited by them, was, when they came to possess it, under the dominion of the Cherokees, or Mountainers, which was about the time that S°. Carolina was planted by the English, who drawing away the Savanahs or Yamases, the Indians of the lower parts of Carolina; who moved along southerly, took possession of the Sea Coast & small Islands, of Georgia & Florida, & joining with the Spaniards of Augustine drove away the Cherokes back to the Mountains. But they the Muscoges or Creeks ariving, Who they say come a long way from the Sun setting from a great River called burntstone River, They say they are decendants from two great & powerful Nations, who became so numerous their Country was not able to contain them, united in the same league to go in search of a new Country, that the lower Creeks came from the head of that great River & the Muscoges lived lower down. both People uniting in their migrations, they crosst many River & at last the great River (Messisepe), they arived in this country; But met with opposition from the Spaniards of Augustine, who not recieving them friendly, they moved along farther & setled on the Okmulge River, part of the Alatamaha, & hearing of the English or white People Northerly, some of their Chiefs went to them, at Charlestown in S°. Carolina, who took them friendly by the hand, calling them Brothers: They were glad, recieving at the same time Hatchets, knives, Kettles, Guns, & Cloathing, which was very acceptable to them; having till then very fiew Necessaries, only Bows to kill Deer & Bear with, Flint knives & hatchets, Clay potts & skins for cloathing; And that in consideration of the friendship & commerce with the whites, they made an everlasting league & allience with the English, against their enemies, the Spanierds & Yamases, who they say they have intirely conquerd and extirpated except a small remnant of Yamasees they have recieved amongst them, who dwell near the Appalatches. But inquiring farther who were the Antient Natives of E^t. Florida. He said he could not tell, but, he said that, when they the Muscogulges come there, the People were very few, wild and wandering about the country without any setled habitations, living very poor & wretched, eating Fish, Oisters or what they could pick up. That the greatest part were conquered by the Spaniards, that there was a little Town of them, near the Bay of Calos, called Calusahatche, & this nation they called Calosulges-Ulge in the Muscoge Tongue signifying People or Nation, there were some remnants of other different Nations antients of the Itmous, & of some that were very famous & powerfull: The Names & Vestigies of their Towns still remaining, particularly a very powerfull & warlike Nation, called Painted People, from their painting their Bodies all over with various colours & Figures of Animals, Birds, Beasts, Frogs, fish, Alegators, Plants & Flowers, & another Great Nation call'd Bat Necks: some of these People were alive when we came in this land, but all These Antient People are destroy'd & carried into Slavery, except a few which the Spaniards caried away with them to Cuba; when that country was deliverd up to the English. This is the substance of the accounts I got from The antient Chief concerning his Nation & Country.

MISCELLANEOUS WRITINGS

Contents

Observations on the Creek and Cherokee Indians

I. HISTORY AND TRADITIONS OF THE MUSCOGULGES.

Query.

Have those tribes of Indians which you have visited any traditions concerning their *Origin*, their *Progress*, or *Migrations*, which you consider worthy of notice? If they have, what are those *Traditions*? Which of the nations of which you have any knowledge seem to have the most accurate, and least suspicious, traditions concerning their origin, etc.? Have you any reason for believing that the Cherokees, Creeks, or any other of the Southern tribes with which you are acquainted, crossed the river Mississippi, in their progress to the country which they now inhabit? If any of these tribes crossed that *great river*, do you think it is possible to determine, with any degree of certainty, the period or periods when they did cross it? Can you form any conjecture which part or parts of the country, bordering on the Mississippi, these tribes passed through in their migrations towards the *East*?

Answer.

The *Cricks*,* or, as they call themselves, *Muscoges*, or *Muscogulges*,[†] are a very powerful confederacy, consisting of many tribes, or remnants of conquered nations, united; perhaps

---

*Cricks is a name given them by the English traders formerly, when they first began to trade amongst them, for the following reason, i. e., they observed that in their conversation, when they had occasion to mention the name of the Indian nation, if any of the Indians were present, they discovered evident signs of disgust, as supposing the traders were plotting some mischief against their nation, etc., so that they gave them this nickname, *Cricks*.

[†]*Ulge* signifies a nation, or people, in their language, as Spanish-*ulge*, English-*ulge*, etc. *Este* likewise signifies nation, or people, but whether in another tongue, or more extended sense, I know not. The *white people* they call *Este-Hulke*; the *red* men, or Indians, they call *Este-Chate*; and so of the Spaniards, whom they call *yellow men*, *Este-Cane*; and black men, or negroes, *Este-Huste*. *Este* seems a specific term for all mankind, comprehending the whole human race in four divisions, white, red, yellow, and black. *Ulge* seems an individual designation of nations and tribes.

about sixty towns, thirty of which speak the *Muscogulge tongue*, and are the progeny or descendants of a powerful band of a nation bearing that name, who, many years since (on their nation becoming very numerous, and filling their native country with inhabitants, by which the game and other necessary produce of their country became scarce and difficult to procure) were induced to separate themselves from, and go in search of, new and plentiful regions. They directed their migrations eastward, leaving with great regret and difficulty their native land, containing their relations and friends, which was on the banks of a large and beautiful river, called the Red River, from great quantities of red stone, of which they formed their tobacco-pipes. Their migrations continued a long time, and under great hardships and embarrassments, they being continually attacked by hostile Indian nations, till at length they arrived at the banks of the *Great River*, i. e., that which they crossed, when they began to think of establishing a permanent residence; but, being yet assaulted and disturbed by surrounding nations, they pushed eastward as far as the *Ockamulge*;* when, hearing of the settlements of the white people, i. e., Spaniards, at St. Augustine, they sent ambassadors to treat with them on terms of mutual favor; but not being kindly received, and hearing of other nations of white people further to the N. E., i. e., in Carolina (the English at this time were founding the colony of South Carolina at Charleston), they sent deputies or ambassadors to Charleston, offering their friendship and alliance, to continue for ever (as long as the rivers flow and the sun continues his course). A *treaty* immediately took place, and they joined their arms with the Carolinians, who assisted them against the surrounding Indian nations, which were then in the Spanish interest,

---

*This river is the South great branch of the *Altamaha*, where are to be seen, to this day, admirable remains of a vast town, extensive plantations, and monuments of the labor, and skill, and industry of the ancients, as *mounts, terraces, areas*, etc., which the present generation of the Muscogulges say are the ruins of their camps and first settlements: but this I can venture to deny, and suppose it a boast of the Creeks, to aggrandize their name and nation; for these monuments discover evident signs of being of much more ancient date. However, it is likely enough that the Muscogulges might have expelled the *then* inhabitants, taken possession of the town, and fortified and established themselves there.

whom they at length subjugated, and, in the end, proved the destruction of the Spanish colony of East Florida. The Muscogulges, by uniting the remnant tribes of their conquered foes, grew stronger, and daily extended their empire. There are now, besides the Muscogulge towns, or those towns whose inhabitants speak that tongue, almost as many languages or dialects as there are towns. It seems apparent, by this account,* that the Muscogulges crossed the Mississippi some where about the Chickasaw county, below the confluence of the Ohio, as they mention crossing but one large river, i. e., the Mississippi, or *Great River.*

They, the Natchez, Chickasaws, and Choctaws, seem to possess a common origin, as they all speak a dialect of the same country: and it is certain they all crossed the Mississippi, as they say of themselves, and long since the Spanish invasion and conquest of Mexico; for these Indians, viz., the *Choctaws*, say they brought with them across the river those fine horses called the Chickasaw and Choctaw breeds. The Seminole horses, or those beautiful creatures bred amongst the Lower Creeks, which are of the Andalusian breed, were introduced by the Spaniards at St. Augustine.

As to the Cherokees, they are altogether a separate nation from the Muscogulges, of much more ancient establishment in the regions they inhabit. I made no inquiry concerning their original descent or migrations to these parts. But I understood that they came from the West, or sun-setting. Their empire, or confederacy, was once very strong and extensive. Before the league of the Creeks† and Carolinians, their empire extended from within forty miles of the sea-coast, N. W. to the Ohio, comprehending all the region lying in the waters of the Cherokee river, quite to its confluence with the Ohio, and also of the great East branches of the Ohio, upwards beyond the Cunhawa, Sante, and Pede, north-eastward. And it is remarkable that those great *pyramidal or conical mounts of earth, tetragon terraces, and cubican yards*, are to be seen in

*This account I had from the most ancient and respectable men of the Muscogulges, through the best old traders and good interpreters, at different times and in various towns; and I believe it to be true as mere tradition can possibly be.

†When I speak of the Creeks and Muscogulges, I mean the same people.

all this vast territory.* Yet it is certain they were not the people who constructed them, as they own themselves, nor were they built by the people from whom they took possession of the country.

Their language is radically different from that of the Creeks, sounding the letter R frequently; in short, there is not one word in their respective languages alike.

II. PROBABLE ORIGIN AND RELATIONS.

Query.

Have you any reasons for believing that any of the tribes of Indians, which you have visited were derived from either the Mexicans or the Peruvians? If you have, what are those reasons?

Answer.

I have no reason, from what I have observed myself, or from information derived from others, to suppose that any of the nations or tribes came from the old Mexicans or Peruvians, unless we believe the accounts which the Natchez give of themselves, as related by M. Du Pratz; and that account should, I imagine, be understood as referring to New Mexico, because their account of their original country and migrations was from the west, or sun-setting, which would be west from their country on the Mississippi, near about the latitude of Santa Fe, N. latitude 34 or 35.

*The largest of these I ever saw stands upon the banks of the Savannah river, eight miles above Dartmouth, and about ninety miles above Augusta, which was nearly the centre of the Cherokee Empire, at the most flourishing period of its history.

There are many artificial mounts of earth along the sea-coast through Carolina and Georgia about this distance from it, and in the settlements N. W., which bear the name of Cherokee Mounts, particularly one about ten or twelve miles from Savannah, near what are now called the Cherokee Ponds. Here, on the road to Augusta, are many ponds and savannas. Indeed, there are people yet living who remember to have seen Cherokee towns inhabited, but a few miles above the city of Savannah, and afterwards possessed and inhabited by the Muscogulges.

The Spanish invasion of these regions and subsequent colonization, after the discovery of the mines and the establishment of forts, in order to possess the country, work the mines and extend their researches, would very probably cause many tribes of the natives to decamp, in search of more peaceful abodes at a distance from such troublesome neighbors, and these nations, by a N. E. course, would likely, in their opinion, get at the greatest distance from those dreaded bearded men, their common enemy (not yet having heard of other colonies or invasions of the bearded men), and thus propel one another as waves driven before the winds. The *Chickasaws, Choctaws,* and *Muscogulges,* appear to have arrived some time since the Natchez, particularly the two former tribes, and the Creeks last. The Natchez might have come from a region nearest the borders of the empire of Old Mexico; because it seems they were most polished and civilized, and were most tinctured with Mexican idolatry* and superstitions. They had a complex system of legislation, their princes were hereditary, their sovereignty absolute, and their power unlimited. The Natchez might have arrived soon after the Spaniards had conquered the Mexican Empire and began to extend their conquests towards the north (for there is no mention of their bringing horses with them, these creatures not being yet so increased as to become wild in the country, or so plentiful as to become an article of commerce between the wild Indians and Spaniards).† For, according to Du Pratz, their Empire had arrived at a prodigious latitude and strength some years before the French attempted to settle in their country, when it appeared to be greatly on the decline. It must have taken many years to have thus increased from a wretched fugitive band, supposing that they had been

---

*For although they believed in a Great Spirit, yet they adored the sun and moon. They had a temple dedicated to the sun, where they kept the eternal fire, guarded by a high priest and sacred virgins consecrated for that purpose. And though they did not offer human victims to the sun, nor eat human flesh, yet they burnt and otherwise put to death captives taken in war. And though it does not appear that they put to death slaves or other persons at the demise of their princes, sovereigns, or *Suns,* yet their slaves, concubines or relations offered themselves to death, in order to attend the souls of their sovereigns.

†*Wild Indians,* such nations as were not conquered by the Old Mexicans and made tributary, which they called *Chickimacs,* aborigines or barbarians.

frightened away from their original country by the Spanish invasions and conquests.

It seems that the arrival of the Chickasaws and Creeks, as well as Choctaws, might have been about the time that the Spaniards, French, and English began their establishments in New England, Virginia, Carolina and Florida, which I believe will appear to be about the period of the Spanish invasion, conquest, and establishment of power in New Mexico. The Choctaws, I believe, came the last, and in considerable force. According to the account of Du Pratz, derived from the Natchez, they appeared suddenly, as if they rose out of the earth. The Creeks have much the same idea of their arrival,— like the arrival and settling of a swarm of bees, as they express themselves on the subject. Yet it is certain that all these nations or bands, i. e., the Natchez, Chickasaws, Muscogulges, and Choctaws, were derived from the same region; for they all speak dialects of the same language, generally so near alike, that they are able to converse with each other without the aid of interpreters. Thus we may conclude that their arrival in the country which they now possess, was one after another, at so considerable a length of time intervening (perhaps a generation or two), each contending for empire and the honor and glory of their tribes, that they in part forgot or disregarded their ancient lineage and affinity.

III. HIEROGLYPHICAL SIGNS– PICTURE RECORDS.

Query.

Have you observed among any of the tribes of *Indians* which you have visited, any *Paintings* superior in execution to those of the Northern Indians, as we find them on trees and rocks? If you have, what did those paintings commonly represent? and among what tribes of Indians did you observe them? Are any of the Indian tribes very curious in preserving the memory of events by paintings? If such paintings are made use of by the Indians, do you know, or do you suppose, that they were acquainted with any signs or symbols to denote attributes or qualities of various kinds? Thus, how would these Indians convey an idea of *courage* or of *cowardice*, of *good* or *evil*, etc.?

Answer.

The paintings which I observed among the Creeks were commonly on the clay-plastered walls of their houses, particularly on the walls of the houses comprising the *Public Square* (see Plan on a subsequent page) or Areopagus; they were, I think, hieroglyphics, or mystical writings, for the same use and purpose as those mentioned by historians, to be found on the obelisks, pyramids, and other monuments of the ancient Egyptians, and much after the same style and taste, much caricatured and picturesque; and though I never saw an instance of the *chiaro-oscuro*, yet the outlines are bold, natural, and turned or designed to convey some meaning, passion, or admonition, and thus may be said to speak to those who can read them. The walls are plastered very smooth with red clay; then the figures or symbols are drawn with white clay, paste, or *chalk*; and if the walls are plastered with clay of a whitish or stone color, then the figures are drawn with red, brown, or bluish chalk or paste.

Almost all kinds of animals, sometimes plants, flowers, trees, etc., are the subjects; figures of mankind in various attitudes, some very ludicrous and even obscene; even the *privates* of men are sometimes represented, but never an instance of indelicacy in a female figure.

Men are often depicted having the head and other members of different kinds of animals, as a *wolf, buck, hare, horse, buffalo, snake, duck, turkey, tiger, cat, crocodile*, etc., etc. All these animals are, on the other hand, depicted having the human head, members, etc.; and animals having the head and other members of different animals, so as to appear monstrous.*

But the most beautiful painting now to be found among the Muscogulges, is on the skin and bodies of their ancient chiefs and *micos*, which is of a bluish, lead, or indigo color. It is the breast, trunk, muscular or fleshy part of the arms and thighs, and sometimes almost every part of the surface of the

---

*I am sensible that these specimens of their paintings will, to us, who have made such incomparable progress and refinement in the arts and sciences, appear trifling and ludicrous; but as you desired me to be particular and omit nothing, I hope to be excused. Yet I think they are the wretched remains of something of greater use and consequence amongst their ancestors.

body, that is thus beautifully depicted or written over with *hieroglyphics*: commonly the sun, moon, and planets occupy the breast; zones or belts, or beautiful fanciful scrolls, wind round the trunk of the body, thighs, arms, and legs, dividing the body into many fields or tablets, which are ornamented or filled up with innumerable figures, as representations of animals of the chase,—a sketch of a landscape, representing an engagement or battle with their enemy, or some creature of the chase,—and a thousand other fancies. These paintings are admirably well executed, and seem to be inimitable. They are performed by exceedingly fine punctures, and seem like *mezzo-tinto*, or very ingenious impressions from the best executed engravings. They are no doubt hieroglyphics, or mystical writings or records of their tribes or families, or of memorable events, etc., etc.

When I was at Manchack on the Mississippi, at M'Gillivray's and Swanson's trading-houses, I saw several buffalo hides with the wool on them. The flesh side of the skins was depicted and painted very beautifully; the performance was admirable —I may say inimitable by the most ingenious artists among Europeans, or people of the Old World, unless taught by the Indians. The painted hides were the work of the Illinois Indians, near Fort Chartens, where the Company had trading-houses and traders, who purchased them of the Indians, and sent them down here to go to Europe. I was asked six dollars apiece for them, which I thought cheap, considering their curiosity, but had no opportunity of conveying one home. The subjects or figures in the composition were much like those inscriptions or paintings on the bodies of the chiefs and warriors. Their borders were exceedingly pleasing: red, black, and blue were the colors, on a buff ground.

IV. COMPARATIVE RELIGIOUS ADVANCEMENT.

Query.

Which of the tribes of Indians, visited by you, are the most polished in their *Religion*, in their *Manners*, in their *Language*, in their *Government*, etc., etc.?

Answer.

If adopting or imitating the manners and customs of the white people is to be termed civilization, perhaps the Cherokees have made the greatest advance.

But I presume, if we are to form and establish our judgments from the opinions and rules laid down by the greatest doctors of morality, philosophers, and divines, either of the ancients or moderns, the Muscogulges must have our approbation, and engage our esteem.

Their religion is, perhaps, as pure as that which was in the beginning revealed to the first families of mankind. They have no notion or conception of any other God but the *Great Spirit* on high, the giver and taker away of the breath of life: which is as much as to say that eternal Supreme Being who created and governs the universe. They worship none else.

They pay a kind of homage to the *sun, moon,* and *planets,* as the mediators or ministers of the Great Spirit, in dispensing his attributes for their comfort and well-being in this life. They have some religious rites and forms, which are managed by their priests or doctors, who make the people believe, by their cunning and craft, that they have a supernatural spiritual communication with invisible spirits of good and evil, and that they have the power of invoking the elements and dispensing their attributes, good and bad. They make the people believe that, by conjuration, they can bring rain, fine weather, heat, cooling breezes, thunder and lightning, bring on or expel and cure sickness, etc., etc.

V. GOVERNMENT; CHIEFS AND PRIESTS.

Query.

What appear to be the great outlines of the *Government* of the Cherokees, Creeks, and other tribes of Indians with which you are acquainted? Are their governments in general *elective,* or are they *hereditary?* If elective, is the person elected chosen for life, or only for a certain time, or so long as he shall conduct himself to the satisfaction of the people? If hereditary, is the power of the king or sachem very considerable? Or is it chiefly a nominal power? These are questions of considerable magnitude.

Answer.

The government or system of legislation amongst all the nations of Indians I have visited, seems to be exactly similar.

It is the most simple, natural, and rational that can be imagined or desired. The same spirit that dictated to Montesquieu the idea of a rational government, seems to superintend and guide the Indians. And if I should say no more upon the subject, perhaps you would be better able to form to yourself a notion of their government.

All that I can say, from my own observation, will amount to little more than mere conjecture, and leave the subject in a doubtful situation; for, at best, it will be but the apprehensions or conjectures of a traveller from cursory and superficial views, perhaps aided and perhaps led astray by the accounts given him by the traders or other white people, who have resided among them. These, from motives of avarice or contempt of the Indians in general, through prejudice, seldom carry their observations or inquiries beyond common report, which we may be assured is against the Indians. And as they improve their commerce with them only for their immediate private interest, their stories cannot always be depended upon.

The whole region of the Muscogulge Empire or Confederacy comprehends a territory of at least 500 miles square.* It embraces the Upper and Lower Creeks or Seminoles, as also the *Uches, Alabamas, Occones,* and many more tribes, who, altogether, make between 60 and 70 towns or villages. Every town and village is to be considered as an independent nation or tribe having its *Mico* or Chief. Every individual inhabitant has an equal right to the soil and to hunt and range over this region, except within the jurisdiction of each town or village, which I believe seldom extends beyond its habitations and planting grounds. Perhaps the *Uches* are to be excepted. They claim an exclusive property, by right of a contract or treaty

---

*500 miles square; E. and W. from Savannah river to the Mobile, comprehending all its branches to their sources; and S. and N. from the extremity of the Peninsula of E. Florida to the Cherokee or Appalachian mountains.

made when they entered into alliance with the Muscogulges; but though they sometimes put the Creeks in mind of this privilege, when their hunters make too free with their hunting grounds, yet the dispute seldom goes further, as the Confederacy are cautious of offending the Uches, and yield to their common interest and safety.

The system of Government in each town or tribe may be described thus:—

1st.—The *Mico* or King.

2d.—The great War-Chief, ancient Warriors, or heads of tribes or families, that constitute the town or nation.

3d.—The younger warriors or hunters, or the commonalty.

The *Mico* is considered the first man in dignity and power in the nation or town, and is the supreme civil magistrate; yet he is, in fact, no more than president of the national council of his own tribe and town, and has no executive power independent of the council, which is convened every day in the forenoon, and held in the Public Square.

The great War-Chief heads the army of the tribe, and herein consists his dignity and power. The elder warriors, ancient heads of families, and younger warriors compose the divan or daily national council, where the *Mico* presides; the great War-Chief seated next to him, on the left hand, at the head of the ancient and celebrated warriors; and next to the *Mico*, on his right hand, is the second head-man of the tribe, at the head of chiefs of tribes and families, younger warriors, etc.

They show the king due respect and the most profound homage, especially when assembled in the Great *Rotunda* or winter council-house. To him only they bow very low, almost to his feet, when the waiters hand him the shell of *black drink*;* but when out of the council any where, they use only common civility, and converse freely with him, as with a common man. He dresses no better than an ordinary citizen, and his house is in no way distinguished from the rest, otherwise than by being larger, according as his ability

---

Black drink, a strong decoction or infusion of the leaves and tender tops of the *cassine*, or *Ilex yapon*, which is drunk constantly every evening by the chief and warriors in the Great Rotunda, with great ceremony, perhaps religious. They call this *cassine* the *beloved tree*. This infusion is perhaps one of the most active and powerful diuretics of any vegetable yet known.

or private riches may enable him, for he exacts no sort of tribute. He goes out to hunt with his family, and even goes to the field with his axe and hoe to work every day during the season of labor. But he has the disposal of the corn and fruits in the public or national granary. He is complimented with the first fruits, and gives audience to ambassadors, deputies, and strangers who come to the town or tribe, receives presents, etc.* He alone has the privilege of giving a public feast to the whole town, consisting of barbecued bear or fat bulls or steers, which he must kill himself; and this is called the king's feast, or royal feast. And when he intends to give this frolic, after a successful hunt, he sends messengers to prepare the village. They display the king's standard in front and at one corner of his house, and hoist a flag in the Public Square, beat drums about the town, and the inhabitants dress and paint themselves, for there is dancing and frolicking all that night.

They have an ancient high-priest, with juniors in every town and tribe. The high-priest is a person of great power and consequence in the state. He always sits in council, and his advice in affairs of war is of the greatest weight and importance, and he or one of his disciples always attends a war party.

It sometimes happens that the king is war-chief and high-priest, and then his power is very formidable and sometimes dangerous to the liberty of citizens, and he must be a very cunning man if the tomahawk or rifle do not cut him short.

And if I may be allowed, in this place, to venture a conjecture, the first Montezuma and the Incas, founders of the mighty empires of Mexico and Peru, were cunning usurpers of this stamp. Such were the absolute kings of the ancient Floridians; for history tells us of the king of *Calos* in the Peninsula of Florida, who assumed a communion and familiarity with powerful invisible spirits, to whom he sacrificed captives, and thus he kept his subjects in awe.

---

*The power and dignity of the king is for life, or during good behavior; he is elected, but in what manner he is chosen I could not satisfactorily ascertain. It appears to me the most mysterious part of the system. It is not in a public manner like our elections, or the traders would have been able to tell me. Perhaps it is done in secret, in the Great Rotunda, where the whites are not admitted; or in the Sanctorum, or high-priest's apartment, in the Public Square.

I myself was the other day present, when the great warrior-chief, King of the Seminoles, assumed the power and dignity of a demi-god; when, at the head of his party of warriors, with an air of surprising arrogance and pomp, he threatened Mr. McLatche that, if he did not comply with his requisitions, he would command the thunder and lightning to descend upon his head, and reduce his stores to ashes.

VI. RELIGIOUS IDEAS AND DOCTRINES.

Query.

What appear to be the great outlines of the *Religion* or *Religions* of those tribes of Indians which you have visited? Does the existence of a *God* appear to be generally received? Do you remember the *name* or *names* by which any of the tribes call or designate their God? Does the doctrine of the *Immortality of the Soul*, or a doctrine in any respect similar to it, appear to be general? Have they any idea of the doctrine of rewards and punishments in a Future State?

Answer.

After what I have hinted in my answers to your questions, in a preceding section, upon the above subject, there is little more to be said concerning their religion.

All that I observed was, that every nation I was amongst seemed individually to believe in a Supreme God or Creator, which, in their different languages, they call by a name signifying the *Great* or *Universal Spirit, the giver and taker away of the breath of life*: thus the traders all interpret the word or words which mean the *one Eternal Supreme Creator*, the *Soul and Governor of the Universe*. They have no appointed time to assemble and worship the Great Spirit, but they frequently, in word and actions, address themselves to God in thanksgiving and adoration, as when escaping from some imminent danger and calamity; they utter also ejaculations of praise and homage at beholding extraordinary instances of the works and power of God in the visible creation, or the harmony and influence of His attributes in the intellectual system.

But they worship no *idols*, either of their own formation or the production of nature.

They assemble and feast at the appearance of the new-moon, when they seem to be in great mirth and gladness, but, I believe, make no offerings to that planet.

They seem to do homage to the sun, as the *symbol* of the power and beneficence of the Great Spirit, or as his *minister*. Thus at treaties, they first puff or blow the smoke from the great pipe or calumet up towards that luminary; they look up towards it with great reverence and earnestness when they confirm their talks or speeches in council, as a witness of their contracts; as also when they make their martial harangues and speeches at the head of their armies, when setting out, or making the onset, etc.

They venerate *Fire*, and have some mysterious rites and ceremonies which I could never perfectly comprehend.

They seem to keep the *Eternal Fire* in the Great Rotunda, where it is guarded by the priests.

In their great annual festival, called the *Busque* or feast of *First Fruits*, they put out all the fires of the nation or town; and then the high-priest, by friction of dry woods and the addition of *resin*, produces new fire in the Great Temple or Rotunda, from whence the whole town is supplied. But so far are the Muscogulges from having a corps of consecrated virgins to guard and keep this fire, that the women are not allowed to step within the pale of the Rotunda, and it is death for any to enter it. None but a priest can carry the fire forth.

The *Spiral Fire*, on the hearth or floor of the Rotunda, is very curious; it seems to light up in a flame of itself at the appointed time, but how this is done I know not.

All the Indians whom I have been amongst, are so confirmed in the doctrine of the Immortality of the Soul, that they would certainly judge any man to be out of his reason that should doubt of it; they also believe that every creature has a spirit or soul that exists in a future state. Some historians have gone so far as to assert that a pattern or spiritual likeness of every thing living, as well as inanimate, exists in another world.

They believe in *rewards and punishments in a future state*, just in the same manner which we do; that virtue and merit will be rewarded with felicity; and that wickedness, on the contrary, will be attended with infamy and misery.

They believe in *visions, dreams,* and *trances*. They relate abundance of stories of men that have been dead or thought dead for many hours and days, who have revived again, giving an account of their transit to and from the world of souls, and describing the condition and situation of the place and spirits residing there. And these people have always returned to life with doctrines and admonitions tending to encourage and enforce virtue and morality.

VII. PHYSICAL CHARACTERISTICS.

Query.

Which is the fairest and most comely tribe of the Southern Indians? Are the Indian *women* generally fairer than the Indian men? Are the Indian *children* born with the copper tinge or color? Or does this color first make its appearance some days after birth? We hear much in writers of white and spotted Indians, as at the Isthmus of Darien: have you ever seen or heard of such white or spotted Indians among any of the tribes with which you are acquainted? If you have, some account of these phenomena will be very interesting to me. Do you remember the names of any of the *plants* that the Indians, which you have visited, make use of in painting or staining their skins? Is the *Succoon* (the *Sanguinaria Canadensis* of Linnaeus), one of the plants employed by the Northern Indians as a pigment, found as far south as the countries of the Cherokees, Creeks, etc.?

Answer.

The Cherokees are the largest race of men I ever saw. They are as comely as any, and their complexions are very bright, being of the olive cast of the Asiatics; this is the obvious reason which I suppose led the traders to give them the by-name of the Breeds, supposing them to be mixed with the white people. But though some of them are evidently adulterated by the traders, yet the natural complexion is tawny.

The women are tall, slim, and of a graceful figure, and have captivating features and manners, and I think their complexion is rather fairer than the men's.

The *Muscogulges* are in stature nearly equal to the Cherokees, have fine features, and are every way handsome men. Their noses are very often aquiline; they are well limbed, countenances upright, and their eyes brisk and fiery; but their complexions are of a dark copper color.

Their women are very small, in appearance not more than half the size of the men; but they have regular and beautiful features, the eyes large, with high-arched eyebrows, and their complexions little, if any, brighter than those of the men.

There are some tribes in the confederacy which much resemble the Cherokees, in stature and color, etc., viz.: the *Uches, Savannahs,* and some of the Seminoles.

I have seen Indian infants of a few weeks old; their color was like that of a healthy, male, European countryman or laborer of middle age, though inclining a little more to the red or copper tinge; but they soon become of the Indian copper. I believe this change comes naturally, as I never, from constant inquiry, could learn that the Indians had any artificial means of changing their color.

The Indians who have commerce with the whites make very little use of colors or paints of the native production of their country, since they have neglected their own manufactures for those supplied them cheaply and in abundance from Europe. I believe they are in general ignorant themselves of their own country's productions. The *poccoon* or *Sanguenaria; Galium,* bark of the *Acer rubrum, Toxicodendron radicans, Rhus triphyllon,* and some other vegetable pigments are yet in use by the women, who still amuse themselves in manufacturing some few things, as belts and coronets for their husbands, *feather cloaks,* moccasons, etc.

I have never heard of any white, speckled, or pied people among them.

It is reasonable to suppose that, anciently, when necessity obliged them, the Indians were more ingenious and industrious in manufactures than now. Therefore, we must seek for their arts and sciences among nations far distant from the settlements of the white people, or recover them by inquiry and experiments of our own.

There is one remarkable circumstance respecting the hair of the head of the Indians, which I do not know to have been observed by travellers or historians. Besides the lankness, extraordinary natural length, and perhaps coarseness of the hair of the head, it is of a shining black or brown color, showing the same splendor and changeableness at different exposures to the light. The traders informed me that they preserved its perfect blackness and splendor by the use of the red farinaceous or fursy covering of the berries of the common sumach (*Rhus glabrum*). Over night they rub this red powder in their hair, as much as it will contain, tying it up close with a handkerchief till morning, when they carefully comb it out and dress their hair with clear bears' oil.

But, notwithstanding this care and assiduity, it must at last submit to old age, and I have seen the hair of the extreme aged as white as cotton wool. I have observed quantities of this red powder in their houses.

VIII. SOCIAL RELATIONS.

Query.

What is the condition of the women among the tribes of Indians which you visited? We are told by many writers that the condition or state of the Indian women is the picture of misery and oppression; is this actually the case? Do the Indian women ever, so far as you know, preside at the councils of the Sachems, especially when war and other matters of consequence are considered in their councils? Have you ever heard or known of any instance or instances of women who have presided over any nation or nations of Indians?

Answer.

I have every reasonable argument from my own observation, as well as the accounts of the whites residing among the Indians, to be convinced that the condition of the women is as happy, compared with that of the men, as the condition of

women in any part of the world. Their business or employment is chiefly in the house, as it is with other women, except
at the season when their crops are growing, when they generally turn out with their husbands or parents, but they are
by no means compelled to such labor. There are not one-third
as many females as males seen at work in their plantations: for,
at this season of the year, by a law of the people, they do not
hunt, the game not being in season till after their crops or
harvest is gathered in, so the males have little else with which
to employ themselves; and the Indians are by no means that
lazy, slothful, sleepy people, they are commonly reported to
be. Besides, you may depend upon my assertion that there is
no people any where who love their women more than these
Indians do, or men of better understanding in distinguishing
the merits of the opposite sex, or more faithful in rendering
suitable compensation. They are courteous and polite to the
women, and gentle, tender and fondling, even to an appearance of effeminacy, to their offspring. An Indian never attempts, nay, he cannot use towards a woman amongst them
any indelicacy or indecency, either in action or language.

I never saw or heard of an instance of an Indian beating his
wife or other female, or reproving them in anger or in harsh
language. And the women make a suitable and grateful return;
for they are discreet, modest, loving, faithful, and affectionate
to their husbands.

In the hunting season, that is in autumn and winter, the
men are generally out in the forests, when the whole care of
the house falls on the women, who are then obliged to un-
dergo a good deal of labor, such as cutting and bringing home
the winter's wood, which they toat on their back or head a
great distance, especially those of the ancient large towns,
where the commons and old fields extend some miles to the
woodland. But this labor is in part alleviated by the assistance
of the old men, who are past their hunting days and no longer
participate in the wars, who remain in the towns. They have
likewise the aid of horses in this work. The women also gather
an incredible amount of nuts and acorns, which they manufacture into oil for annual consumption. They make all the
pottery or earthenware, which is very considerable, as some of
their pots hold near a barrel, and are of a tender and fragile

composition; you may see mounts of fragments of earthen-ware around their towns, for every fragment, however small, is cast into these heaps.

I neither knew nor heard of any instances of the females bearing rule, or presiding either in council or the field; but, according to report, the Cherokees and Creeks can boast of their Semiramis, Zenobia, and Cleopatra. When I was passing through the Cherokee country, we crossed a very fine stream, a branch of *Tugilo* Creek, which is called War-woman's Creek. I inquired of my companion, an ancient trader, the cause of so singular a name. He answered, that it arose from a deci-sive battle which the Cherokees formerly gained over their enemies on the banks of this creek, through the valor and stratagem of an Indian woman, who was present. She was afterwards raised to the dignity and honor of a Queen or Chief of the nation, as a reward for her superior virtues and abilities, and presided in the State during her life.

The Creeks speak to this day with the highest encomiums and pride of a widow of their grand Chief or Mico, whose superior wisdom interposed between these nations and the English, about the time of the establishment of the colony of Georgia (under the conduct of General Oglethorp), and re-stored peace between them, which grew firmer and stronger every day till the dissolution of the British government in that region. This woman married Rev. Dr. Bozemoth, of the new-founded colony, a very worthy man, who had, as a dowry with his queen, a large and fertile island on the coast of Georgia, together with a territory on the main. If I mistake not, Dr. Bozemoth afterwards returned to England with his wife, who even there was esteemed a celebrated woman for her virtues and talents.* The Seminoles, or Lower Creeks, also boast of a great queen or empress in former days, whose empire, ac-cording to their account, must have been in East Florida, be-

---

*As to this latter part of the history, I am not certain whether she remained to the end of her life in Europe, or returned again to Georgia; and also I may, perhaps, be incorrect as to the entire particulars of the story. But the main of the history is true, as every Georgian and Indian knows, and rejoices at having the names of those persons mentioned. Any gentleman of Georgia will avow to its authenticity, and, perhaps, upon inquiry, will give you a more accurate account than I can.

tween the St. Mary's and St. Juan rivers and the imperial city of *Alachua*. She was powerful and beneficent, and so celebrated a beauty that all the kings to a vast distance round about, at certain seasons, annually resorted to her court with large trains of their chiefs, etc., bearing presents for the queen, not as tributaries, but out of compliment and respect to her merit. Great numbers of the kings, chiefs, etc., continued for the stated period, representing sports, feats of arms, and other divertisements, to divert and compliment this celebrated queen. She was carried about under a rich canopy of feathers, on the shoulders of princes and nobles, etc.

Her reign was about the time the Europeans first visited these coasts. The Spanish inhabitants of East Florida have got a tradition of these matters, and relate accounts much like the above.

IX. CHUNKY-YARDS, OR EARTHWORKS.

Query.

In the letter which you wrote to me concerning the *Mounts*, etc., you make mention of the *Chunky-Yard* of the Cherokee Indians. What is the nature, use, etc., of this yard? Is this Chunky-Yard confined to the Cherokee Indians? or have you observed it among the other tribes of Indians? A sketch of the *Chunky-Yard* will be very acceptable.

Answer.

The *Chunky-Yards* of the Creeks, so called by the traders, is a cubiform area, generally in the centre of the town, because the Public Square and the Rotunda, or great winter Council-house, stand at the two opposite corners of it. It is generally very extensive, especially in the large old towns,* is exactly level, and sunk two, sometimes three, feet below the banks or terraces surrounding it, which are sometimes two, one above

---

*The Chunky-Yards are of different sizes, according to the largeness and fame of the town they belong to; some are 200 or 300 yards in length, and of proportionable breadth.

and behind the other, and are formed of earth cast out of the area at the time of its formation; these banks or terraces serve the purposes of seats for the spectators. In the centre of the yard there is a low circular mount or eminence, in the centre of which stands erect the *chunky-pole*, which is a high obelisk, or four square pillar declining upwards to an obtuse point, in shape and proportion much resembling the Egyptian obelisk. This is of wood, the heart or inward resinous part of the sound pine-tree, and is very durable; it is generally from thirty to forty feet high, and to the top of this is fastened some object to shoot at with bows and arrows, the rifle, etc., at certain times appointed. Near each corner of the lower and further end of the yard stands erect a less pillar or pole, about twelve feet high: these are called the *slave-posts*, because to them are bound the captives condemned to be burnt, and these posts are usually decorated with the scalps of their slain enemies; the scalps with the hair on them, and strained on a little hoop, usually five or six inches in width, are suspended by a string six or seven inches in length round about the top of the pole, where they remain as long as they last. I have seen some that have been there so long as to lose all the hair, and the skin remaining white as parchment or paper. The pole is usually crowned with the white dry skull of an enemy. In some of these towns I have counted six or eight scalps fluttering on one pole in these yards. Thus it appears evidently enough that this area is designed for a public place of exhibition of shows and games, and formerly some of the scenes were of the most tragical and barbarous nature, as torturing the miserable captives with fire in various ways, and causing or forcing them to run the gauntlet naked, chunked and beat almost to death with burning chunks and fire-brands, and at last burnt to ashes.

I inquired of the traders for what reason this area was called the *Chunky-Yard*; they were in general ignorant, yet they all seemed to agree in a lame story of its originating from its being the place where the Indians formerly put to death and tortured their captives—or from the Indian name for it, which bears such a signification.

The Indians do not now torture their captives after that cruel manner as formerly; but there are some old traders who have been present at the burning of captives.

I observed no Chunky-Yards, chunky-pole, or slave-posts in use in any of the Cherokee towns: and when I have mentioned in my journal, chunky-yards in the Cherokee country, it must be understood that I have seen the remains or vestiges of them in the ancient ruins of towns; for in the present Cherokee towns that I visited, though there were the ancient mounts and signs of the yard adjoining, yet the yard was either built upon or turned into a garden spot or the like.

Indeed, I am convinced that the Chunky-Yards now, or lately, in use amongst the Creeks, are of very ancient date— not the formation of the present Indians. But in most towns they are cleaned out and kept in repair, being swept very clean every day, and the poles kept up and decorated in the manner I have mentioned.

X. TENURE OF LANDS AND PROPERTY.

Query.

Does there appear to be a *community of goods* among the tribes you have visited? Or have the members of each tribe their own *exclusive property* in *Lands, Produce* of these Lands, etc.?

Answer.

As I have already observed, in answer to your fifth question, the soil, with all its appurtenances of the whole Muscogulge Confederacy or Empire, is equally the right and property of every individual inhabitant, except within the pale or precinct of each town, where *meum* and *teum*, or distinctions of property, take place. And though I believe that the whole territory comprehended within the claims of the Confederacy is divided by lines and boundaries amongst the different tribes (as, for instance, the *Uches*, as mentioned 2d, 5th, the Savannahs, Alabamas, and other tribes who speak the *Stinkard* tongue, who make, perhaps, one-third of the Confederacy; the Muscogulges, who are the head or imperial tribe and founders of the Confederacy, and speak the *Muscoge* or national tongue, and whose towns and villages perhaps claim the other two thirds of the territory); yet every individual citizen of the Confederacy has the same equal right to hunt and range, where he pleases, in the forests and unoccupied lands, and to range stocks of cattle, horses, etc.

All that a man earns by his labor or industry belongs to himself; he has the use and disposal of it according to the custom and usages of the people. He may clear, settle, and plant as much land as he pleases, and wherever he will within the boundaries of his tribe. There are, however, very few instances amongst the Creeks, of farms or private plantations out of sight of the town. I was at one belonging to a chief of the town of the Apalachuklas, about six miles from the town, on or near the banks of the river; I went to pay him a visit with an old trader, my fellow pilgrim, in consequence of an invitation to breakfast with him. He is called the *Bosten* or Boatswain by the traders. As a prince, he received us with politeness and most perfect good breeding. His villa was beautifully situated and well constructed. It was composed of three oblong uniform frame buildings, and a fourth, four-square, fronting the principal house or common hall, after this manner, encompassing one area. The hall was his lodging-house, large and commodious; the two wings were, one a cookhouse, the other a skin or ware-house; and the large square one was a vast open *pavilion*, supporting a canopy of cedar roof by two rows of columns or pillars, one within the other. Between each range of pillars was a platform, or what the traders call cabins, a sort of sofa raised about two feet above

Fig. 1.

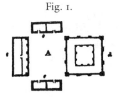

the common ground, and ascended by two steps; this was covered with checkered mats of curious manufacture, woven of splints of canes dyed of different colors; the middle was a four-square stage or platform, raised nine inches or a foot higher than the cabins or sofas, and also covered with mats.

In this delightful airy place we were received, and entertained by this prince. We had excellent coffee served up in china ware, by young negro slaves. We had plenty of excellent sugar, honey, choice warm corn cakes, venison steaks, and barbacued meat. We spent the fore part of the day with him, and returned to town at evening, well pleased with the honors and distinctions shown us by that man of excellent character. He had near one hundred acres of fertile land in good fence, most of which is usually planted, and attended to by his own family, which consists of about thirty people, among which were about fifteen negroes, several of which were married to Indians, and enjoyed equal privileges with them; but they are slaves till they marry, when they become Indians or free citizens.

This truly great and worthy man has acquired his riches by trading with the white people. He carries his merchandise on horses to the Altamaha river, where, having large and convenient boats, he descends the river to Frederica, and sometimes continues his voyage to Sunbury and Savannah, when he disposes of his goods (i. e., deerskins, furs, hides, tallow, oils, honey, wax, etc., etc.), and with the receipts thereof purchases sugar, coffee, and every other kind of goods suitable to the Indian markets. I have dwelt so long on this subject, which may be called a digression, because it may (amongst many more instances I could produce, were it required of me) serve to convince those prejudiced, ignorant, obstinate people, that assert that it is impossible for the Creeks to be brought over to our modes of civil society (though so contrary to their notions of civilization, and, perhaps, in some degree, irreconcilable to right reason). However, I am not for levelling things down to the simplicity of Indians, yet I may be allowed to conjecture that we may possibly better our condition in civil society, by paying some more respect to and impartially examining the system of legislation, religion, morality, and economy of these despised, persecuted *wild people*, or as they are learnedly called, *bipeds*—I suppose meaning a creature differing from quadrupeds.

But to return to the subject in question. Every town or community assigns a piece or parcel of land as near as may be to the town, for the sake of convenience. This is called the *town plantation*, where every family or citizen has his parcel or share, according to desire or convenience, or the largeness of his family. The shares are bounded by a strip of grass ground, poles set up, or any other natural or artificial boundary, so that the whole plantation is a collection of lots joining each other, comprised in one enclosure or general boundary.

In the spring, when the season arrives, all the citizens, as one family, prepare the ground and begin to plant, commencing at one end or the other, as convenience may direct for the general good, and so continue on until finished; and when the young plants arise and require culture, they dress and husband them until the crops are ripe. The work is directed by an overseer elected or appointed annually, I suppose in rotation throughout all the families of the town. He rises at daybreak, makes his progress through the town, and, with a singular loud cry, awakens the people to their daily labors, who by sunrise assemble at the Public Square, each one with his hoe and axe, where they form themselves into one body or band, headed by their superintendent, who leads them to the field in the same order as if they were going to battle, when they begin their work, and continue till evening. The females do not march out with the men, but follow in detached parties, bearing the provisions of the day.

When the fruits of their labors are ripe and in fit order to gather in, they all on the same day repair to the plantation: each gathers the produce of his own proper lot, brings it to town, and deposits it in his own *crib*, allotting a certain portion for the Public Granary, which is called the King's crib, because its contents are at his disposal, though not his private property, but considered as the tribute or free contribution of the citizens of the State, at the disposal of the king.

The design of the common granary is for the wisest and best of purposes, with respect to their people, i. e., a store or resource to repair to in cases of necessity. Thus when a family's private stores fall short, in cases of accident or otherwise, they are entitled to assistance and supply from the public granary, by applying to the king. It also serves to aid other towns which may be in want; and affords provisions for their armies, for travellers, sojourners, etc., etc.

Thus the Mico becomes the provider or *Father of his People*, or of *mankind*—the greatest and most godlike character upon earth.

Besides the general plantation, each inhabitant in the town incloses a garden spot adjoining his house, where he plants corn, rice, squashes, etc., which, by early planting and close attention, affords an earlier supply than the distant plantations.

Now, although it appears that these people enjoy all the advantages of freedom and private property, and have laws, usages, and customs, which secure each one his rights according to reason, justice, and equality, the whole tribe seems as one family or community, and, in fact, all their possessions are in common; for they have neither locks nor bars to their doors, and there is a common and continual intercourse between the families of a tribe; indeed, throughout the Confederacy, they seem as one great family, perfectly known and acquainted with each other whenever they meet.

If one goes to another's house and is in want of any necessary that he or she sees, and says, I have need of such a thing, it is regarded only as a polite way of asking for it, and the request is forthwith granted, without ceremony or emotion; for he knows he is welcome to the like generous and friendly return at any time. Indeed, they seem to consider all the Indians of the earth as one great family or community, who have separated themselves as convenience or necessity have directed, and formed innumerable nations,—climates, situations, revolutions, renovations, or other unknown causes, having marked the different nations and tribes by different stature, color, complexion, manners, customs, language, etc., etc.

Their philanthropy and hospitality are perhaps the most universal and liberal of any people we have any account of; they call all men, either of their own land or of the most distant nations, by the name of *brother*. The Israelites called all of their own nation and religion brothers or brethren. But the aborigines, or red men of America, offer this salutation to every individual of every nation, color, or language whatever; and this is universal throughout the nations of the continent, unless we are to except the *Esquemaux*, who appear to be another race, and with good reason are supposed to be an

European colony, much later than the colonization of the red race, supposing them to be not absolutely aborigines. Such is their hospitality to strangers, that I know a Creek Indian would not only receive into his house a traveller or sojourner, of whatever nation, color, or language (without distinction of rank or any other exception of person), and there treat him as a brother or his own child so long as he pleased to stay, and that without the least hope or thought of interest or reward, but serve him with the best of every thing his abilities could afford. He would divide with you the last grain of corn or piece of flesh, offer you the most valuable things in his possession that he imagines would be acceptable, nay, would part with every thing rather than contend for them, or let a stranger remain or go away necessitous. And this to an enemy whom they know or suspect has come through his accident or misfortune among them, or fallen into their hands: in this case they would conduct him safe beyond their frontiers, and then tell him to go and take care of himself.

Even a white man, whom they have reason to know is their most formidable, cruel, barbarous, and unrelenting foe, they would cherish as long as he might choose to stay, or else guard him to his country. If he came peaceably to his town, or even if he met him alone in the dreary forest, naked, hungry, bewildered, lost, the Indian would give him his only blanket, half his provisions, and take him to his wigwam, where he would repose securely and quietly, and in the morning conduct him safe back to his own frontier—and all this, even though he had been the day before beaten, bruised, and shot at by a white man. Thus they are hospitable, forgiving, gentle, humane, and grateful, without precept or scholastic education; and this by nature or some other unknown cause, without the least desire or expectation of applause or reward.

XI. DISEASES AND REMEDIES.

Query.

What appear to be the most common *diseases* among the tribes of Indians with which you are acquainted? What are their *remedies* for those diseases? Have you any reasons for believing that the *venereal* disease was known among the N. A. Indians *before* the discovery of the continent by the Europeans? Is it a frequent or common disease *at present* among the Indians? If so, do they appear to be acquainted with any remedy or remedies for it? If any remedies, what are they?

Answer.

The Indians seem in general healthier than the whites, have fewer diseases, and those they have not so acute or contagious as those amongst us.

The small-pox sometimes visits them, and is the most dreaded of all diseases.

Dysentery, pleurisy, intermittent fevers, epilepsy and asthma, they have at times.

The hooping-cough is fatal among their children, and worms very frequent. But (besides their well-known remedy, *spigelia anthelmintica*), to prevent the troublesome and fatal effects of this disease, they use a strong *lixivium* prepared from ashes of bean-stalks and other vegetables, in all their food prepared from corn (*zea*), which otherwise, they say, breeds worms in their stomachs.

They have the venereal disease amongst them in some of its stages; but by their continence, temperance, powerful remedies, skill in applying them, and care, it is a disease which may be said to be uncommon. In some towns it is scarcely known, and in none rises to that state of virulency which we call a *pox*, unless sometimes amongst the white traders, who themselves say, as well as the Indians, that it might be eradicated if the traders did not carry it with them to the nations when they return with their merchandise; these contract the disorder before they set off, and it generally becomes virulent by the time they arrive, when they apply to the Indian doctors to get cured.

However, I am inclined to believe that this infernal disease originated in America, from the variety of remedies found among the Indians, all of which are vegetable. I imagine that the disease is more prevalent, as well as more malignant, among the northern tribes.

The vegetables which I discovered to be used as remedies, were generally very powerful cathartics. Of this class are several species of the *Iris*, viz., *Ir. versicolor*, *Ir. verna*. And for the same purpose they have a high estimation of a species of either *Croton* or *Styllingia*, I am in doubt which; I think it is unknown to Europeans (*Cr. decumbens*): it is in great account in the medicines of Dr. Howard, of N. Carolina, in curing the *yaws*, and is called the *yaw-weed*. A great number of leaning, simple stems, arise from a large perennial root; these stalks are furnished with lanciolate, entire leaves, both surfaces smooth. The stems terminate with spikes of male and female flowers; the latter are succeeded by tricoccous seed-vessels, each cell containing a single seed; the capsule, after excluding the seed, contracts and becomes of a triangular figure, much resembling a cocked hat, which has given that name to the plant, i. e., the "cock-up-hat." In autumn, before the stems decay, the leaves change to yellow, red, and crimson colors, before they fall off.

I have been particular in the history of this plant, because it is known to possess very singular and powerful qualities. It is common on the light, dry, high lands of Carolina, Georgia, and Florida.

Several species of *Smilax*, the woody vines of *Bignonia crucigera*, some of the *bays* (*laurus*), are of great account with the Indians as remedies.

But the Indians, in the cure of all complaints, depend most upon regimen, and a rigid abstinence in respect to exciting drinks, as well as the gratification of other passions and appetites.

The Cherokees use the *Lobelia syphilitica*, and another plant of still greater power and efficacy, which the traders told me of, but would not undertake to show it to me under twenty guineas reward, for fear of the Indians, who endeavor to conceal the knowledge of it from the whites, lest its great virtues should excite their researches for it to its extirpation, etc.

The vines or climbing stems of the climber (*Bignonia crucigera*) are equally divided longitudinally into four parts by the same number of their membranes, somewhat resembling a piece of white tape, by which means, when the vine is cut through and divided transversely, it presents to view the likeness of a cross. This membrane is of a sweet, pleasant taste. The country people of Carolina chop these vines to pieces, together with *china brier* and sassafras roots, and boil them in their beer in the spring, for diet drink, in order to attenuate and purify the blood and juices. It is a principal ingredient in Howard's famous infusion for curing the *yaws*, etc., the use and virtues of which he obtained from Indian doctors.

The caustic and detergent properties of the white nettle (roots) of Carolina and Florida (*Jatropha urens*), used for cleansing old ulcers and consuming proud-flesh, and likewise the dissolvent and diuretant powers of the root of the *convolvulus panduratus*, so much esteemed as a remedy in nephritic complaints, were discovered by the Indians to the inhabitants of Carolina.*

I was informed by the people, that in order to prepare and administer both these remedies, they dig up the roots and divide and cut them into thin pieces, in order for their more speedy drying in the shade, and then reduce them to powder, the former being plentifully spread over the ulcer, and the powder of the latter swallowed with any proper liquid vehicle; they are the most efficacious if used as fresh as possible,—I suppose losing their virtues by desiccation or being exposed to the air.

Through the emollient and discutient power of the *swamp lily* (*saururus cernuus*), and the virtues of the *hypo* or *May-apple* (*podophyllum peltatum*),—the root of which is the most effectual and safe emetic, and also cathartic and equally efficacious in expelling worms from the stomach,— the lives of many thousands of the people of the Southern States are preserved, both of children and adults. In these countries it is of infinitely more value than the Spanish Ipecacuanha. I speak not only from my own experience, having been relieved by it, but likewise from numberless instances where I have seen its almost infallible good effects. The roots are dug up in the autumn and winter, and spread to dry in an airy loft, when they are occasionally reduced to powder by the usual trituration (for the roots will retain their efficacy when dried). Thirty grains of this fine sieved powder is

---

*The white nettle roots are good and wholesome food when roasted and boiled: they are about the size of a large carrot when well grown, but few of them are allowed to become large, the swine are so fond of them.

sufficient to operate on common constitutions, and half that quantity on children, but a weak dose is sufficient for a cathartic; either way it never fails to clear the stomach of worms.

In fine, I look upon this and the *saururus* to be two as valuable medicines as any we know of, at least in the Southern States. The virtues of both were communicated to the white inhabitants by the Indians.

Panax ginseng and *Nonda*, or white root (or *"belly-ache root"*),* perhaps *angelica lucida*. These roots are of the highest esteem among the Cherokees and Creeks; the virtues of the former are well known; of the latter, its friendly carminative qualities are well known for relieving all the disorders of the stomach, a dry belly-ache and disorders of the intestines, colic, hysterics, etc. The patient chews the root and swallows the juice, or smokes it when dry with tobacco. Even the smell of the root is of good effect. The Lower Creeks, in whose country it does not grow, will gladly give two or three buckskins for a single root of it.

XII. FOOD, AND MEANS OF SUBSISTENCE.

Query.

Does the food of the Indians appear to be principally animal or vegetable? What are the principal vegetables employed for food by them? What vegetables do they cultivate for food besides *maize*, different species of gourds, etc.? What are the principal vegetables of which they make their bread? Do you think the tribes you visited were acquainted with the use of salt before they became acquainted with the Europeans? If you think they were not, what substances did they employ as substitutes?

---

*The Creeks and Cherokees call it by a name signifying "white root." In Virginia it is called *Nonda*, I suppose an Indian name. It is a plant highly worthy of cultivation, grows naturally in a good, loose soil (moist), near to and all over the Cherokee and Apalachian mountains. My father (John Bartram) planted it in his garden, where it flourished equally as well as in its native soil. But the ground-mice, which are immoderately fond of its root, as well as that of the *Ginseng*, after several years destroyed it.

Answer.

Their animal food consists chiefly of venison, bears' flesh, turkeys, hares, wild fowl, and domestic poultry; and also of domestic kine, as beeves, goats, and swine—never horses' flesh, though they have horses in great plenty; neither do they eat the flesh of dogs, cats, or any such creatures as are usually rejected by white people.

Their vegetable food consists chiefly of *corn* (*zea*), rice, *convolvulus batatas*, or those nourishing roots usually called sweet or Spanish potatoes (but in the Creek Confederacy they never plant or eat the Irish potato). All the species of the *phaseolus* and *dolichos* in use among the whites, are cultivated by the Creeks, Cherokees, etc., and make up a great part of their food. All the species of *cucurbita*, as squashes, pumpkins, water-melons, etc.; but of the *cucumeres*, they cultivate none of the species as yet, neither do they cultivate our farinaceous grains, as wheat, barley, spelts, rye, buckwheat, etc. (not having got the use of the plough amongst them, though it has been introduced some years ago). The chiefs rejected it, alleging that it would starve their old people who employed themselves in planting, and selling their produce to the traders, for their support and maintenance; seeing that by permitting the traders to use the plough, one or two persons could easily raise more grain than all the old people of the town could do by using the hoe. Turnips, parsnips, salads, etc., they have no knowledge of. Rice (*oryza*) they plant in hills on high dry ground, in their gardens; by this management a few grains in a hill (the hills about four feet apart) spread every way incredibly, and seem more prolific than cultivated in water, as in the white settlements of Carolina; the heads or *panicles* are larger and heavier, and the grain is larger, firmer, or more farinaceous, much sweeter, and more nourishing.* Each family raises enough of this excellent grain for its own use.

*The rice planters of N. Carolina raise very little of their rice in flooded fields (the natural situation of their country not admitting of it), but plant in the rich low lands on the borders of streams, or swamps; and though this kind of agriculture is more troublesome and expensive, yet they find their advantage in a more farinaceous grain, more substantial and sweeter, inasmuch as their rice brings a much higher price at the foreign markets.

But, besides the cultivated fruits above recited, with peaches, oranges,* plums (Chickasaw plums), figs, and some apples, they have in use a vast variety of wild or native vegetables, both fruits and roots, viz.: *diospyros, morus rubra, gleditsia, multiloba, s. triacanthus*; all the species of juglans and acorns, from which they extract a very sweet oil, which enters into all their cookery, and several species of *palms*, which furnish them with a great variety of agreeable and nourishing food. Grapes, too, they have in great variety and abundance, which they feed on occasionally when ripe; they also prepare them for keeping, and lay up for winter and spring time.† A species of smilax (S. pseudochina) affords them a delicious and nourishing food, which is prepared from its vast, tuberous roots.

They dig up these roots, and while yet fresh and full of juice, chop them in pieces, and then macerate them well in wooden mortars; this substance they put in vessels nearly filled with clean water, when, being well mixed with paddles, whilst the finer parts are yet floating in the liquid, they decant it off into other vessels, leaving the farinaceous substance at the bottom, which, being taken out and dried, is an impalpable powder or farina, of a reddish color. This, when mixed in boiling water, becomes a beautiful jelly, which, sweetened with honey or sugar, affords a most nourishing food for children or aged people; or when mixed with fine corn flour, and fried in fresh bears' grease, makes excellent *fritters*.

I conclude these articles with mentioning a vegetable which I had but a slight opportunity of observing, just as I left the Creek country, on the waters of the Mobile river. It is a species of *palma*. It has no stalk or stem above ground; the leaves spread regularly all round, are flabelliform when fully expanded, otherwise cucullated, their stipes very short, scarcely

*Oranges and figs are not much cultivated in the *Nation* or Upper Creeks; but in the Lower Creek country, near the sea-coast, they are in greater abundance, particularly the orange. Many sorts are now become wild all over East Florida.

†Vitis Vinifera; I call them so because they approach, as respects the largeness of their fruit and their shape and flavor, much nearer to the grapes of Europe and Asia, of which wine is made, and are specifically different from our wild grape, and as different from the fox or bull grape of Pennsylvania and Carolina.

appearing at a slight view; in the centre is produced a kind of dense panicle or general receptacle of the fruit, of the form and size of a sugar-loaf. There is a vast collection of plums or drupes, of the size and figure of ordinary plums, which are covered with a fibrous, farinaceous, pulpy coating of considerable thickness; this substance, which, to the best of my remembrance, resembles manna in texture, color, and taste, is of the consistence of coarse brown sugar, mixed with particles or lumps of loaf sugar. It is a delicious and nourishing food, and diligently sought after. There were several of these clusters brought into the Ottasse town just before I left it, of which I ate freely with the Indians, and think in substance and taste it is most of any thing like manna; it is a little bitterish and stinging on the palate, at first using it, but soon becomes familiar and desirable.

I own I am not able to give an accurate botanical account of this very curious and valuable vegetable, because it was disclosed to my observation just on my departure; and although I saw several of the plants on the road, yet being obliged to follow the mad career of a man travelling with pack-horses, I had left the country of its native growth before I had an opportunity or leisure to examine it,—an omission which I have severely regretted. I am convinced it is an object of itself worth a journey to these regions to examine.

XIII. FOSSIL REMAINS.

Query.

Did you observe, in any part or parts of the countries through which you passed, any large teeth or bones, similar to those which are found near the river Ohio, etc.? Have the Indians, so far as you know, any tradition concerning these bones? If they have, what is the tradition?

Answer.

I observed not the least sign or mention of any large teeth or bones of the kind you refer to, except some tradition of the same story recited concerning the big bones on the Ohio, which stories you are well acquainted with.

I, indeed, frequently in the forests of W. Florida and N. of Georgia, observed very large bones, as those of the thigh and tibia, and some remarkably large grinders (dent. mol.); but suppose them to belong to the buffalo (*urus*). They were all unchanged bone, not petrified or fossil, which all the specimens of the great bones I have seen appear to be.

POSTSCRIPT.

I have added the following rough drawings of the *Ancient Indian Monuments*, consisting of *public buildings, areas, vestiges of towns*, etc., which I hope may serve in some degree to explain or illustrate my answers and conjectures. They are, to the best of my remembrance, as near the truth as I could express. However, if I have erred in any way, I hope they may be corrected and rectified by the observations of future and more accurate and industrious travellers. *But as Time changes the face of things, I wish they could be searched out and faithfully recorded, before the devastations of artificial refinements, ambition, and avarice, totally deface these simple and most ancient remains of the American Aborigines.*

PLAN OF THE ANCIENT CHUNKY-YARD.

The subjoined plan (fig. 2) will illustrate the form and character of these yards.

A, the great area, surrounded by terraces or banks.

B, a circular eminence, at one end of the yard, commonly nine or ten feet higher than the ground round about. Upon this mound stands the great *Rotunda, Hot House,* or *Winter Council House,* of the present Creeks. It was probably designed and used by the ancients who constructed it, for the same purpose.

C, a square terrace or eminence, about the same height with the circular one just described, occupying a position at the other end of the yard. Upon this stands the *Public Square.*

Fig. 2.

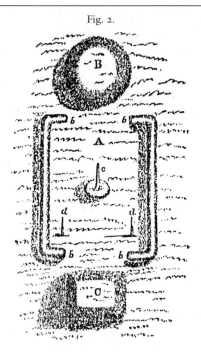

The banks inclosing the yard are indicated by the letters *b*, *b*, *b*, *b*; *c* indicates the "*Chunk-Pole*," and *d*, *d*, the "*Slave-Posts.*"

Sometimes the square, instead of being open at the ends, as shown in the plan, is closed upon all sides by the banks. In the lately built, or new Creek towns, they do not raise a mound for the foundation of their Rotundas or Public Squares. The yard, however, is retained, and the public buildings occupy nearly the same position in respect to it. They also retain the central obelisk and the slave-posts.

THE PUBLIC SQUARE.

The Public Square of the Creeks consists of four buildings of equal size, placed one upon each side of a quadrangular court. The principal or Council House is divided transversely into three equal apartments, separated from each other by a low clay wall. This building is also divided longitudinally into two nearly equal parts; the foremost or front is an open piazza, where are seats for the council. The middle apartment is for the king (*mico*), the great war chief, second head man, and other venerable and worthy chiefs and warriors. The two others are for the warriors and citizens generally. The back apartment of this house is quite close and dark, and without entrances, except three very low arched holes or doors for admitting the priests. Here are deposited all the most valuable public things, as the eagle's tail or national standard, the sacred calumet, the drums, and all the apparatus of the priests. None but the priests having the care of these articles are admitted; and it is said to be certain death for any other person to enter.

Fronting this is another building, called the "Banqueting House;" and the edifices upon either hand are halls to accommodate the people on public occasions, as feasts, festivals, etc. The three buildings last mentioned are very much alike, and differ from the Council House only in not having the close back apartment.

ARRANGEMENT OF THE PUBLIC BUILDINGS.

This is the most common plan or arrangement of the Chunky-Yard, Public Square, and Rotunda of the *modern* Creek towns.

Fig. 3.

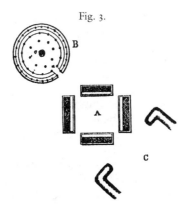

A, the Public Square or area.

B, the Rotunda; *a*, the door opening towards the square; the three circular lines show the two rows of seats, sofas, or cabins; the punctures show the pillars or columns which support the building; *c*, the great central pillar, or column, surrounded by the spiral fire, which gives light to the house.

C, part of the Chunky-Yard.

CREEK TOWNS AND DWELLINGS.

The general position of the Chunk-Yard and Public Buildings of the Creeks, in respect to the dwellings of the Indians themselves, is shown in the following engraved plan:—

Fig. 4.

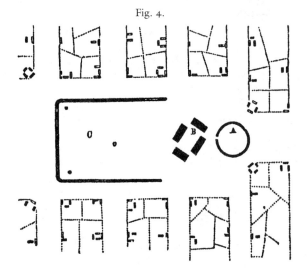

A is the Rotunda; *B*, the Public Square; *C*, the grand area or Chunky-Yard. The habitations of the people are placed with considerable regularity in streets or ranges, as indicated in the plan.

The dwellings of the Upper Creeks consist of little squares, or rather of four dwelling-houses inclosing a square area, exactly on the plan of the Public Square. (*See cut, fig.* 1, *p.* 549.)

Every family, however, has not four of these houses; some have but three, others not more than two, and some but one, according to the circumstances of the individual, or the number of his family. Those who have four buildings have a particular use for each building. One serves as a cook-room and winter lodging-house, another as a summer lodging-house and hall for receiving visitors, and a third for a granary or provision house, etc. The last is commonly two stories high, and divided into two apartments, transversely, the lower story of one end being a potato house, for keeping such other roots and fruits as require to be kept close, or defended from cold in winter. The chamber over it is the corn crib. At the other end of this building, both upper and lower stories are open on their sides: the lower story serves for a shed for their saddles, pack-saddles, and gears, and other lumber; the loft over it is a very spacious, airy, pleasant pavilion, where the chief of the family reposes in the hot seasons, and receives his guests, etc. The fourth house (which completes the square) is a skin or ware-house, if the proprietor is a wealthy man, and engaged in trade or traffic, where he keeps his deer-skins, furs, merchandise, etc., and treats his customers. Smaller or less wealthy families make one, two, or three houses serve all their purposes as well as they can.

The Lower Creeks or Seminoles are not so regular or ingenious in their building, either public or private. They have neither the Chunky-Yard nor Rotunda, and the Public Square is an imperfect one, having but two or three houses at furthest. Indeed they do not require it; as their towns are small, and consequently their councils just sufficient for the government or regulation of the town or little tribe: for in all great and public matters they are influenced by the Nation, or Upper Creeks.

Their private habitations consist generally of two buildings: one a large oblong house, which serves for a cook-room, eating-house, and lodging-rooms, in three apartments under one roof; the other not quite so large, which is situated eight or ten yards distant, one end opposite the principal house. This is two stories high, of the same construction, and serving the same purpose with the granary or provision house of the Upper Creeks.

The Cherokees, too, differ greatly from the Muscogulges, in respect to their buildings. They have neither the Square nor the Chunky-Yard. Their Summer Council House is a spacious open loft or pavilion, on the top of a very large oblong building; and the Rotunda, or great Hot or Town House, is the Council House in cold seasons.

Their private houses or habitations consist of one large oblong-square log building, divided transversely into several apartments; and a round hot-house stands a little distance off, for a winter lodging-house.

Fig. 5.

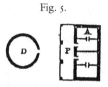

ANCIENT REMAINS.

In the Cherokee country, all over Carolina, and the Northern and Eastern parts of Georgia, wherever the ruins of ancient Indian towns appear, we see always beside these remains one vast, conical-pointed mound. To mounds of this kind I refer when I speak of *pyramidal mounds*. To the south and west of the Altamaha, I observed none of these in any part of the Muscogulge country, but always flat or square structures. The vast mounds upon the St. John's, Alachua, d Musquito rivers, differ from those amongst the Cherokee with respect to their adjuncts and appendages, particularly in respect to the great highway or avenue, sunk below the common level of the earth, extending from them, and terminating either in a vast savanna or natural plain, or an artificial pond or lake. A remarkable example occurs at Mount Royal, from whence opens a glorious view of Lake George and its environs.

Fig. 6, is a perspective plan of this great mound and its avenues, the latter leading off to an expansive savanna or natural meadow. A, the mound, about forty feet in perpendicular height; B, the highway leading from the mound in a straight line to the pond C, about half a mile distant. What may have

Fig. 6.

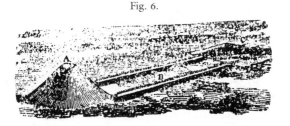

been the motive for making this pond I cannot conjecture, since they are situated close to the banks of the river San Juan. It could not, therefore, be for the conveniency of water. Perhaps they raised the mound with the earth taken out of the pond. The sketch of the mound also illustrates the character of the mounds in the Cherokee country; but the last have not the highway or avenue, and are always accompanied by vast square terraces, placed upon one side or the other. On the other hand, we never see the square terraces accompanying the high mounds of East Florida.

Account of the Species, Hybrids, and Other Varieties of the Vine of North-America

THE most obvious characters which distinguish the Grape-Vines of America from those of the old continent, are, 1. The berries of all the American species and varieties that I have seen, approach the figure of an oblate spheroid; that is, the poles are flattened, and the transverse diameter is longer than the polar: however, I have observed that Alexander's grape, and some of the bullet grapes, approach nearer to an oval or ellipsis, which is the figure of all foreign or European grapes that I have seen; viz. a prolate spheroid.—2. Most of the American species and varieties have a glaucous and yellowish pubescence on the under surface of their leaves.—3. All that I have observed in the northern and eastern districts of the United States are *polygamous*, i.e. those vines which bear fruit (female) have hermaphrodite flowers (pentandria monogynia); but the males have only five stamina, without any female organ, and are always barren. One would suppose, from WALTER so strongly marking this character as to induce him to place Vitis in the class *Dioecia*, when LINNÆUS and the other European botanists had placed it in Pentandria (he himself being an European), that all the grape-vines of the old continent are hermaphroditous and Pentandrian. I know not, from my own observation, whether the bull-grape of Carolina is hermaphroditous or dioecious, and therefore rest satisfied with Walter's assertion.

With regard to the vine of America, I find a great difficulty in discriminating the species from varieties or hybrids, which, perhaps, may be partly accounted for from some of our vines being dioecious, and there being a much greater number of male vines than of fruit-bearing ones, whose *farina fecundans*, mixing with the air and winds, is carried to a great distance to the female organs of hermaphrodite flowers. I shall now give my opinion of the distinct species or established races from which all the varieties or mules have originated.

1st. The COMMON BLUE GRAPE, or BUNCH GRAPE, *Vitis sylvestris*, or *V. occidentalis*. This is the most common grape.

The acini or berries are of the oblate figure, of various sizes on different plants, and of as various tastes. Some are sweet and pleasant enough, having a musky flavour. They are nearly as large as the Burgundy grape; are black when ripe, having a glaucous bloom, like the damson plum. The leaves of this species are large; their under surface covered with a clay-coloured down or pubescence. They are tri-lobed, each lobe subdivided or dentated. Some varieties have very deep sinuosities, almost touching the mid-rib.

2d. FOX-GRAPE, *Vitis vulpina* of Bartram. *V. foliis cordatis subtrilobis, dentatis; subtus tomentosis*, Linn. *Spec. plant. V. vulpina dicta Virginiana alba*; Pluckn. *alm.* 392. *Vitis vulpina dicta acinis peramplis purpureis in racemo paucis, sapore fœtido et ingrato præditis, cute crassa carnosa.* Clayt. n. 696. The last part of the description is decisive; every word true when applied to our fox-grape of Pennsylvania; and Dr. Clayton's authority should be relied on, as he was a native of Virginia, spent his life there, and was an excellent botanist. The leaves of the fox-grape are large and lobated, not much unlike those of the common bunch grape, but not so deeply sinuated and toothed; their under surface thickly covered with a yellow pubescence or down; the fruit bunches short, having few acini or berries on them, but these few are large, and of an oblate figure. Some are as large as a musket-ball, and are of different sizes and colours; black, red, purple, green and white, when ripe. All possess a strong rancid smell and taste, have a thick coriacious skin, and a tough jelly-like pulp or tegument which encloses the seeds. Between this nucleus and the skin is a sweet lively juice, but a little acerb or stinging to the mouth if pressed hard in eating them. There is another property of this grape which alone is sufficient to prove it to be the *Vit. vulpina*, that is, the strong rancid smell of its ripe fruit, very like the effluvia arising from the body of the fox, which gave rise to the specific name of this vine, and not, as many have imagined, from its being the favourite food of the animal; for the fox (at least the American species) seldom eats grapes or other fruit if he can get animal food.

The vines, though they make vigorous and extensive shoots, never mount high, but ramble over shrubs and low trees to a great distance from the original root. This appears to be the V. taurina of Walter, and the labrusca of Linnæus.

3d. BULL-GRAPE, *Vitis taurina* of Bartram, *Vit. vulpina* of Linnæus and Walter. This excellent grape is called by the inhabitants of Georgia, Carolina and Florida, *Bull-grape*. The preceding species is called *fox-grape* from Pennsylvania to Florida. The bull-grape has a stiff, ligneous, smooth stem, of pale ash-colour, and mounts to a great height by climbing up trees. The leaves are cordated and serrated, thin, and both surfaces naked or smooth. The racimes or fruit bunches short, containing 15 or 20 grapes at a medium. The berries or *acini* are large, near the size of a rifle-ball; of a black colour when ripe; having a bluish nebule over them, which being rubbed off, they appear of a deep blood-colour. In figure they approach to an ellipsis or prolate spheroid: however, at a little distance they appear black and round. This species is deservedly esteemed the best native grape in America, and would make a rich and delicious wine. The juice is sweet, rich and lively; and there is but little of the tough jelly-like substance enclosing the seed. The skin of the grape is rather thick, yet there is a sweet melting pulp within, which mixes with the saccharine juice when eaten. This undoubtedly is the first American grape which merits attention and cultivation for wine. It thrives in every soil and situation from the sea-coast to the mountains; it even thrives and is fruitful when growing in the barren sand-hills of Carolina and Florida.

4th. WINTER-GRAPE, *Vitis scrotina*. Cotyledon palmated. This is a vine remarkable for its sweet flowers. It mounts to the top of high trees; the stems and twigs more hard and ligneous than the bunch grape, to which I think it approaches the nearest. The leaves are small, cordated, smooth, thin and serrated. The fruit bunches branched, but the berries small and black, not so large as currants: the fruit not ripe till late in the autumn, and the juice extremely sour and ill-tasted, so that even birds will not eat them till winter frosts have meliorated them.

I shall now mention the varieties that appear to me to have arisen from a commixture of the several species or races.

Alexander's or *Tasker's grape* is a large grape, black or blue, the size of the fruit of the *Vit. vinifera* of the old continent. The grapes approach to the elliptical figure. They are, when fully ripe, perfectly black, and as sweet as any grape. Many persons think them too luscious. Before they are quite ripe some think they possess a little of the stingy taste of the fox-grape, but my taste never could discover it. It has been supposed to be a hybrid between *Vit. sylvestris* (common bunch grape) and *Vit. vinifera*, because it was found on the rocky hills near the river Schuylkill, above the upper ferry, in the neighbourhood of an old vineyard of European grapes; but I believe it to be an American.

Bland's grape. This is an excellent grape. The bunches large, branched, and well shaped, six or eight inches in length. The berries large, about the size of the common white grape of Europe, and round or oblate; when perfectly ripe, of a dark purple or red wine colour; the juice sweet and lively, having a little musky flavour, with a small portion of an agreeable astringency, somewhat like our best bunch or wild grapes, though much sweeter than any of them. If this grape is what I take it to be, a genuine American, it is a hybrid or variety. It was found in Virginia, where it is called the Virginia mus-kadell, and sent to me by the late Col. Bland. This excellent grape bids the fairest, next to the bull-grape, to afford a good wine.

There seems to be no end to the varieties of Vit. sylvestris, or *bunch grape*, in size and taste of the fruit, as also in the leaves. There is a middle-sized round grape, called *Raccoon-grape*, which appears to be much of the nature of the fox-grape: they are black when ripe; have much of the stingy taste and rancid smell of the fox-grape, and the tough jelly pulp that envelopes the seed; the skin thick; but they are not more than half the size of the fox-grape.

Thus it appears to me that we have in the United States four species of *Vitis* or grape vines, viz.

1. *Vitis sylvestris*, or *Vit. Americana*, or *occidentalis*, common bunch grape.

2. *V. vulpina*, fox-grape.

3. *V. taurina*, bullet-grape.

4. *V. serotina*, winter-grape, by some called Bermudian grape, and innumerable varieties and hybrids.

By varieties I mean different sorts of an individual species;

and by hybrids, spurious offspring by intermixture of species. Of the latter sort are,

1. Alexander's or Tasker's grape.
2. Bland's grape.
3. Raccoon-grape.

Anecdotes of an American Crow

IT IS a difficult task to give a history of our Crow. And I hesitate not to aver, that it would require the pen of a very able biographer to do justice to his talents.

Before I enter on this subject minutely, it may be necessary to remark, that we do not here speak of the crow, collectively, as giving an account of the whole race (since I am convinced, that these birds differ as widely as men do from each other, in point of talents and acquirements), but of a particular bird of that species, which I reared from the nest.

He was, for a long time, comparatively a helpless, dependent creature, having a very small degree of activity or vivacity, every sense seeming to be asleep, or in embryo, until he had nearly attained his finished dimensions, and figure, and the use of all his members. Then, we were surprised, and daily amused with the progressive developement of his senses, expanding and maturating as the wings of the youthful phalæna, when disengaged from its nympha-shell.

These senses, however, seemed, as in man, to be only the organs or instruments of his intellectual powers, and of their effects, as directed towards the accomplishment of various designs, and the gratification of the passions.

This was a bird of a happy temper, and good disposition. He was tractable and benevolent, docile and humble, whilst his genius demonstrated extraordinary acuteness, and lively sensations. All these good qualities were greatly in his favour, for they procured him friends and patrons, even among *men*, whose society and regard contributed to illustrate the powers of his understanding. But what appeared most extraordinary, he seemed to have the wit to select and treasure up in his mind, and the sagacity to practise, that kind of knowledge which procured him the most advantage and profit.

He had great talents, and a strong propensity to imitation. When I was engaged in weeding in the garden, he would often fly to me, and, after very attentively observing me in pulling up the small weeds and grass, he would fall to work, and with his strong beak, pluck up the grass; and the more so, when I complimented him with encouraging expressions. He enjoyed great pleasure and amusement in seeing me write, and would attempt to take the pen out of my hand, and my spectacles from my nose. The latter article he was so pleased with, that I found it necessary to put them out of his reach, when I had done using them. But, one time, in particular, having left them a moment, the crow being then out of my sight, recollecting the bird's mischievous tricks, I returned quickly, and found him upon the table, rifling my inkstand, books, and paper. When he saw me coming, he took up my spectacles, and flew off with them. I found it vain to pretend to overtake him; but standing to observe his operations with my spectacles, I saw him settle down at the root of an apple-tree, where, after amusing himself, for awhile, I observed, that he was hiding them in the grass, and covering them with chips and sticks, often looking round about, to see whether I was watching him. When he thought he had sufficiently secreted them, he turned about, advancing towards me, at my call. When he had come near me, I ran towards the tree, to regain my property. But he, judging of my intentions, by my actions, flew, and arriving there before me, picked them up again, and flew off with them, into another apple-tree. I now almost despaired of ever getting them again. However, I returned back to a house, a little distance off, and there secreting myself, I had a full view of him, and waited to see the event. After some time had elapsed, during which I heard a great noise and talk from him, of which I understood not a word, he left the tree, with my spectacles dangling in his mouth, and alighted, with them, on the ground. After some time, and a great deal of caution and contrivance in choosing and rejecting different places, he hid them again, as he thought very effectually, in the grass, carrying and placing over them chips, dry leaves, &c., and often pushing them down with his bill. After he had finished this work, he flew up into a tree, hard by, and there continued a long time, talking to himself, and making much noise; bragging, as I supposed, of his achievements. At last, he returned to the house, where not finding me, he betook himself to other amusements. Having noted the place, where he had hid my spectacles, I hastened thither, and after some time recovered them.

This bird had an excellent memory. He soon learned the name which we had given him, which was Tom; and would commonly come when he was called, unless engaged in some favourite amusement, or soon after correction: for when he had run to great lengths in mischief, I was under the necessity of whipping him; which I did with a little switch. He would, in general, bear correction with wonderful patience and humility, supplicating with piteous and penitent cries and actions. But sometimes, when chastisement became intolerable, he would suddenly start off, and take refuge in the next tree. Here he would console himself with chattering, and adjusting his feathers, if he was not lucky enough to carry off with him some of my property, such as a pen-knife, or a piece of paper; in this case, he would boast and brag very loudly. At other times, he would soon return, and with every token of penitence and submission, approach me for forgiveness and reconciliation. On these occasions, he would sometimes return, and settle on the ground, near my feet, and diffidently advance, with soft-soothing expressions, and a sort of circumlocution; and sit silently by me, for a considerable time. At other times, he would confidently come and settle upon my shoulder, and there solicit my favour and pardon, with soothing expressions, and caressing gesticulations; not omitting to tickle me about the neck, ears, &c.

Tom appeared to be influenced by a lively sense of domination (an attribute prevalent in the animal creation): but, nevertheless, his ambition, in this respect, seemed to be moderated by a degree of reason, or reflection. He was, certainly, by no means tyrannical, or cruel. It must be confessed, however, that he aimed to be master of every animal around him, in order to secure his independence and his self-preservation, and for the acquisition and defence of his natural rights. Yet, in general, he was peaceable and social with all the animals about him.

He was the most troublesome and teazing to a large dog, whom he could never conquer. This old dog, from natural fidelity, and a particular attachment, commonly lay down near me, when I was at rest, reading or writing under the shade of a pear-tree, in the garden, near the house. Tom (I believe from a passion of jealousy) would approach me, with his usual caresses, and flattery, and after securing my notice and re-gard, he would address the dog in some degree of complai-sance, and by words and actions; and, if he could obtain access to him, would tickle him with his bill, jump upon him, and compose himself, for a little while. It was evident, how-ever, that this seeming sociability was mere artifice to gain an opportunity to practise some mischievous trick; for no sooner did he observe the old dog to be dozing, than he would be sure to pinch his lips, and pluck his beard. At length, how-ever, these bold and hazardous achievements had nearly cost him his life: for, one time, the dog being highly provoked, he made so sudden and fierce a snap, that the crow narrowly escaped with his head. After this, Tom was wary, and used every caution and deliberation in his approaches, examining the dog's eyes and movements, to be sure that he was really asleep, and at last would not venture nearer than his tail, and then by slow, silent, and wary steps, in a sideways, or oblique manner, spreading his legs, and reaching forward. In this po-sition, he would pluck the long hairs of the dog's tail. But he would always take care to place his feet in such a manner as to be ready to start off, when the dog was roused and snapped at him.

It would be endless (observes my ingenious friend, in the conclusion of his entertaining account of the crow) to recount instances of this bird's understanding, cunning, and opera-tions, which, certainly, exhibited incontestible demonstrations of a regular combination of ideas, premeditation, reflection, and contrivance, which influenced his operations.

Some Account of the Late
Mr. John Bartram, of Pennsylvania

R ICHARD BARTRAM, the grandfather of the subject of this
sketch, came from England to America with the adherents of the famous William Penn, proprietor of Pennsylvania,
towards the close of the seventeenth century. He settled a
plantation in the township of Marpole, and county of Chester,
at the distance of twelve miles from Philadelphia.

From Richard descended two sons, John and Isaac. The
former inherited the paternal estate in Marpole, and the latter
settled upon another plantation in Darby, at a few miles distance. John, the elder, had two sons by his first marriage,
namely, James and John, early in the beginning of the eigh-
teenth century; and by his second marriage, a son and a
daughter, named William and Elizabeth. Soon after his second
marriage, he removed to North-Carolina, where he settled a
plantation at a place called Whitoc, and there, with the
greatest part of the settlement, fell a victim to the rage of the
Whitoc-Indians. The widow and her two children were carried
away captives by the Indians, but were afterwards redeemed,
and returned to Pennsylvania.

John, the celebrated botanist and naturalist, inherited the
estate in Darby, which was left to him by his uncle Isaac. Being
born in a newly-settled colony, of not more than fifty years'
establishment, in a country where the sciences of the old continent were little known, it cannot be supposed, that he could
derive great advantages or assistance from school-learning or
literature. He had, however, all or most of the education that
could, at that time, be acquired in country-schools; and whenever an opportunity offered, he studied such of the Latin and
Greek grammars and classics, as his circumstances enabled him
to purchase. And he always sought the society of the most
learned and virtuous men.

He had a very early inclination to the study of physic and
surgery. He even acquired so much knowledge in the practice
of the latter science, as to be very useful; and, in many instances, he gave great relief to his poor neighbours, who were

unable to apply for medicines and assistance to the physicians of the city (Philadelphia). It is extremely probable, that, as most of his medicines were derived from the vegetable kingdom, this circumstance might point out to him the necessity of, and excite a desire for, the study of Botany.

He seemed to have been designed for the study and contemplation of Nature, and the culture of philosophy. Although he was bred a farmer or husbandman, as a means of procuring a subsistence, he pursued his avocations as a philosopher, being ever attentive to the works and operations of Nature. While engaged in ploughing his fields, and mowing his meadows, his inquisitive eye and mind were frequently exercised in the contemplation of vegetables; the beauty and harmony displayed in their mechanism; the admirable order of system, which the great Author of the universe has established throughout their various tribes, and the equally wonderful powers of their generation, the progress of their growth, and the various stages of their maturity and perfection.

He was, perhaps, the first Anglo-American, who conceived the idea of establishing a BOTANIC GARDEN, for the reception and cultivation of the various vegetables, natives of the country, as well as of exotics, and of travelling for the discovery and acquisition of them. He purchased a convenient piece of ground, on the banks of the Schuylkill, at the distance of about three miles from Philadelphia; a happy situation, possessing every soil and exposure, adapted to the various nature of vegetables. Here he built, with his own hands, a large and comfortable house, of hewn stone, and laid out a garden containing about five acres of ground.

He began his travels at his own expence. His various excursions rewarded his labours with the possession of a great variety of new, beautiful, and useful trees, shrubs, and herbaceous plants. His garden, at length, attracting the visits and notice of many virtuous and ingenious persons, he was encouraged to persist in his labours.

Not yet content with having thus begun the establishment of this school of science and philosophy, in the blooming fields of FLORA, he sought farther means for its perfection and importance, by communicating his discoveries and collections to the curious in Europe and elsewhere, for the benefit of science, commerce, and the useful arts.

Having arranged his various collections and observations in natural history, one of his particular friends undertook to convey them to the celebrated Peter Collinson, of London. This laid the foundation of that friendship, and correspondence, which continued uninterrupted, and even increasing, for near fifty years of the lives of these two eminent men. Collinson, ever the disinterested friend, communicated, from time to time, to the learned in Europe, the discoveries and observations of Bartram. It was principally through the interest of Collinson, that he became acquainted, and entered into a correspondence, with many of the most celebrated literary characters in Europe, and was elected a member of the Royal Society of London, of that of Stockholm, &c.

He employed much of his time in travelling through the different provinces of North-America, at that time subject to England. Neither dangers nor difficulties impeded or confined his researches after objects in natural history. The summits of our highest mountains were ascended and explored by him. The lakes Ontario, Iriquois, and George; the shores and sources of the rivers Hudson, Delaware, Schuylkill, Susquehanna, Allegeny, and St. Juan were visited by him, at an early period, when it was truly a perilous undertaking to travel in the territories, or even on the frontiers, of the aborigines.

He travelled several thousand miles in Carolina and Florida. At the advanced age of near seventy years, embarking on board of a vessel at Philadelphia, he sat sail for Charleston, in South-Carolina. From thence he proceeded, by land, through part of Carolina and Georgia, to St. Augustine, in East-Florida. When arrived at the last-mentioned place, being then appointed botanist and naturalist for the King of England, for exploring the provinces, he received his orders to search for the sources of the great River St. Juan.

Leaving St. Augustine, he travelled, by land, to the banks of the river, and, embarking in a boat at Picolata, ascended that great and beautiful river (near 400 miles), to its sources, attending carefully to its various branches, and the lakes connected with it. Having ascended on one side of the river, he

descended by the other side, until the confluence of the Picolata with the sea.

In the course of this voyage or journey, he made an accurate
draught and survey of the various widths, depths, courses, and
distances, both of the main stream, and of the lakes and
branches. He also noted the situation and quality of the soil,
the vegetable and animal productions, together with other interesting observations, all of which were highly approved of
by the Governor, and sent to the Board of Trade and Plantations, in England, by whose direction they were ordered to
be published, for the benefit of the new colony.

Mr. Bartram was a man of modest and gentle manners,
frank, cheerful, and of great good-nature; a lover of justice,
truth, and charity. He was himself an example of filial, con-
jugal, and parental affection. His humanity, gentleness, and
compassion were manifested upon all occasions, and were
even extended to the animal creation. He was never known
to have been at enmity with any man. During the whole
course of his life, there was not a single instance of his engaging in a litigious contest with any of his neighbours, or
others. He zealously testified against slavery; and, that his
philanthropic precepts, on this subject, might have their due
weight and force, he gave liberty to a most valuable male slave,
then in the prime of his life, who had been bred up in the
family almost from his infancy.

He was, through life, a striking example of temperance, especially in the use of vinous and spirituous liquors: not from
a passion of parsimony, but from a principle of morality. His
common drink was pure water, small-beer, or cyder mixed
with milk. Nevertheless, he always kept a good and plentiful
table. Once a year, commonly on new year's day, he made a
liberal entertainment for his relations, and particular friends.

His stature was rather above the middle size, and upright.
His visage was long, and his countenance expressive of a
degree of dignity, with a happy mixture of animation and
sensibility.

He was naturally industrious and active, both in body and
mind; observing, that he never could find more time than he
could employ to satisfaction and advantage, either in improving
conversation, or in some healthy and useful bodily exercise: and

he was astonished to hear men complaining, that they were weary of their time, and knew not what they should do.

He was born and educated in the sect called Quakers. But his religious creed may, perhaps, be best collected from a pious distich, engraven by his own hand, in very conspicuous characters, upon a stone placed over the front window of the apartment, which was destined for study and philosophical retirement.

> 'Tis God alone, Almighty Lord,
> The Holy One by me ador'd.   J. B.
> 1770.

This may show the simplicity and sincerity of his heart, which never harboured, or gave countenance to, dissimulation. His mind was frequently employed, and he enjoyed the highest pleasure, in the contemplation of Nature, as exhibited in the great volume of Creation. He generally concluded the narratives of his journies with pious and philosophical reflections upon the Majesty and Power, the Perfection and the Beneficence, of the Creator.

He had a high veneration for the moral and religious precepts of the Scriptures, both old and new. He read them often, particularly on the sabbath-day; and recommended to his children and family the following precept, as comprehending the great principles of moral duty in man:

"Do Justice, love Mercy, and Walk Humbly before God."

He never coveted old age, and often observed to his children and friends, that he sincerely desired, that he might not live longer than he could afford assistance to himself: for he was unwilling to be a burthen to his friends, or useless in society; and that when death came to perform his office, there might not be much delay. His wishes, in these respects, were gratified in a remarkable manner: for although he lived to be about eighty years of age, yet he was cheerful and active to almost the last hours. His illness was very short. About half an hour before he expired, he seemed, though but for a few moments, to be in considerable agony, and pronounced these words, "I want to die."

Description of an
American Species of Certhia,
or Creeper

C. *rectricibus inequalibus, apice subulatis, subnudis.*

Bill long, slender, bent downwards, sharp-pointed, and somewhat flexible. The under mandible flesh-coloured next its base.

Upper side of the head, neck, and back of a dusky brown-colour; the feathers dark in their middle, and edged with light brown, or clay-colour.

Cheeks, lower part of the back, and upper coverts of the tail, of a bright-yellowish-clay colour. Throat, breast, belly, and under coverts of the tail white.

Wings of a dark-dusky or black colour, variegated with oblique bars of white on the primary and secondary quill-feathers. The tips of the feathers of the spurious wing (*ala notha*), and the first and second coverts are likewise elegantly marked with white.

Tail of a reddish-brick, or cinnamon colour: the feathers of unequal length; the middle or upper one longest, the others, on each side, gradually diminishing: each feather terminates in a slender sharp point, which (like the Woodpecker's) assists the bird in climbing and ascending trees.

Legs and feet of a dark flesh-colour, and formed as in other birds of this family, having four toes, three forward, and one backward, armed with strong talons.

Length of the bird, from the bill to the extremity of the tail, about five inches.

This species of Certhia is an autumnal bird of passage, from the north. They arrive, and appear in the environs of Philadelphia about the first of October (sooner or later, according to the severity of the season), and continue with us during the winter, if it be temperate. Or they pass on, southerly, as far as Carolina and Florida, where they winter, but return northerly in the spring, to breed, and rear their young. I have not heard of their breeding in Pennsylvania: yet they may breed in the most northern district of the state.

Their place of residence is in the woods, or high forests, where we see them climbing up, and running about, the trunks of large trees, searching the crevices of the bark for spiders and other insects, which constitute their food. And for this purpose, their slender, crooked beak is well adapted. They utter a feeble, chirping note.

This species of Certhia has the form and habits of the wood-pecker, except in the position of its toes. Neither is its bill, like that of the woodpecker, strong, and shaped for the purpose of perforating wood.

We know nothing, as yet, of the construction of its nest, or its manner of breeding.

Kingsess, December 27th, 1804.

Conjectures Relative to
the Scite of Bristol,
in Pennsylvania

IN PERUSING the First Part of your *Medical and Physical Journal*, I particularly noticed, in Dr. Gregg's *Topographical and Medical Sketch of Bristol, in Pennsylvania*, his conjecture, that the ground on which "the town stands has been *made ground*."

I suppose it was a peninsula of New-Jersey; and that the low ground back of, and N. W. of the borough, which he describes as being, at present, low marsh, meadows, and ponds, was formerly the bed or channel of the River Delaware; and that, at that time, the present bed of the river was a low isthmus, which connected it with the firm land of the Jerseys.

I will now give you the reasons which confirm me in the truth of this supposition.

First. Dr. Gregg observed, at the depth of about twenty-five feet below the surface, logs and limbs of trees, which he thought were those of Pine.

Secondly. When I was at Bristol, thirty or forty years ago, I observed the soil to be exactly the same with that of the Jersey-shore, opposite; and that both places produced the same vegetables. In particular, I observed growing in the wood-lands, close to the town, the Lupinus perennis, or Perennial Lupin.

Thirdly. Dr. Gregg observes, that the "tide regularly ebbs and flows" over great part of the morass, which insulates the borough; and that up the pond even to the Delaware, the ground is gravelly and dry, just as the bed of the river is now. The channels of rivers are continually changing place, in some part or other, owing to obstructions in their course, inundations, &c.

When the disruption to which I allude took place; whether prior to the arrival of the white people, or since that period, is a matter worthy of investigation.

Preface to
A Catalogue of Trees, Shrubs,
and Herbaceous Plants,
Indigenous to the
United States of America

Cultivated and Disposed of by
John Bartram & Son,
at their Botanical Garden, Kingsess, near Philadelphia

Aᴛ ᴛʜᴇ repeated request of our correspondents and friends, both in Europe and at home, to furnish them with a *Catalogue* of the plants of *Kingsess Botanic Gardens*, we have undertaken the task, though arduous, and now present them with the following alphabetical arrangement of them, in three orders, *viz.*

I. Tʀᴇᴇs and Sʜʀᴜʙs. II. Hᴇʀʙᴀᴄᴇᴏᴜs Pʟᴀɴᴛs and Gʀᴀssᴇs. III. Fᴇʀɴs, Mᴏssᴇs and Fᴜɴɢɪ. And for the greater conveniency of gardeners and purchasers, we have given them under two divisions or chapters, *i. e.* I. Iɴᴅɪɢᴇ-ɴᴏᴜs. II. Exᴏᴛɪᴄ.

As this *Nomenclature* is intended principally for the use of the Gardener and Agriculturalist, we have, therefore, given the generally approved names, as exhibited in Linnæus's *Systema Vegetabilium*, and *Species Plantarum*, and for such as have been discovered and named since the last edition of Linnæus, we have consulted *Willdenow*, the *Hort. Kewensis*, *Walter's Flora Caroliniensis*, and other moderns; but have rejected the innovations introduced by some late botanists of eminence and ability, as being of little or no benefit in practical garden-ing, leaving them for the amusement of systematic botanists and scientific gentlemen, who may at their pleasure recur to their works.

As several of the articles enumerated in this Catalogue have been lately discovered, and have not yet been established in foreign botanical publications; and, as there are some others of which it is difficult to determine the species, owing to vague descriptions and contradictory synonyms, we have taken the liberty to give names to these, which may be either altered or established, as further researches shall develop their true character. But as these are few, and as we have made use of terms descriptive and characteristic, we trust to the liberality and candour of our correspondents; and request as a favour, that our friends and the ingenious Botanists, who may consider our errors as not beneath their notice and criticism, will be so candid as freely to point them out for our information, that we may be enabled to give to the public a more correct and useful edition in future.

KINGSESS GARDENS were begun about 80 years since, by JOHN BARTRAM the elder, at a time when there were no establishments of this nature in Pennsylvania, if any in the colonies, unless we may except that of Doctor Clayton, in Virginia, which, though inferior in extent, was furnished with a considerable variety. They are situated on the west banks of the Schuylkill, four miles from Philadelphia, and contain about eight acres of land. The mansion and green houses stand on an eminence from which the garden descends by gentle slopes to the edge of the river; and on either side the ground rises into hills of moderate elevation, to the summits of which its borders extend. From this scite are distinctly seen the winding course of the Schuylkill, its broad-spread meadows and cultivated farms, for many miles up and down; and the river Delaware, with the variety of vessels which it is constantly bearing to and from the metropolis of America. Beyond this there is an uninterrupted view of the Jersey shore, from the eastern to the southern horizon. The whole comprehends an extensive prospect, rich in the beauty of its scenery and endless in diversity.

The worthy founder of these gardens, discovered in his early youth, a love for philosophy, and natural history in general. He was, however, particularly drawn to the study of Botany, from considering the importance of vegetables in the practice of medicine, and their indispensable use in the various departments of human economy. But at that time Botany was but little attended to in America; and in the old world the works of the great Linnæus had not appeared; he had, therefore, no other aid in studying the great book of nature than his own persevering genius. His view in the establishment was to make it a deposite of the vegetables of these United States, (then British Colonies), as well as those of Europe and other parts of the earth, that they might be the more convenient for investigation. He soon furnished his grounds with the curious and beautiful vegetables in the environs, and by degrees with those more distant, which were arranged according to their natural soil and situation, either in the garden, or on his plantation, which consisted of between 200 and 300 acres of land, the whole of which he termed his garden.

The novelty of this horticultural scene, attracted the notice of the ingenious and curious; and coming to the knowledge of Europeans, several scientific men in England, particularly of the Royal Society, united to encourage the founder to undertake journeys towards the western frontiers, in order to discover and collect curious and nondescript productions in nature, particularly vegetables, that they might be sent to Europe.

Thus these extensive gardens became the Seminary of American vegetables, from whence they were distributed to Europe, and other regions of the civilized world. They may with propriety and truth be called the *Botanical Academy of Pennsylvania*, since, being near Philadelphia, the Professors of Botany, Chemistry, and Materia Medica, attended by their youthful train of pupils, annually assemble here during the Floral season.

The revered founder lived to see his garden flourish beyond his most sanguine expectations, and extend its reputation both at home and abroad, as the Botanic Garden of America. In this condition it descended to his son, whose care it has been to preserve its well-earned fame, as well by continuing the collection already there, as by making annual excursions to increase the variety. Finding old age coming on, he has lately associated his son with him in the concern, and hopes by their united exertions, the gardens will continue to be worthy of the attention of the lovers of science and the admirers of nature.

Observations on the Pea Fly or Beetle, and Fruit Curculio

Read July 14th, 1789.

THE PEA FLY, *Bruchus pisi*, is a small beetle of that kind which we call wevel, but is more than twice their size, of an ovate form and brownish colour, particularly their upper side or elytron, which is uniformly besprinkled with specks, and strokes of a light colour, as likewise the back or upper part of the thorax, near the suture or joint. The bill is short, depressed, and armed with a hair of serrated forceps, the under side and legs are black, or of a very dark, dusky colour, the femora are armed with a sharp tooth, or acute projection at the knee joint, and the whole insect is covered with fine hair.

They feed when in the caterpillar or grub state, on the green garden or field pea, as soon as the pods (legumes) have arrived to a state of maturity, sufficient to shew the peas which are within them: in the evening, or on a cloudy day, the female deposits her eggs on the outside of the pods, these eggs or nits soon hatch, and the young larva or worm eats directly through, and enters the tender young pea, where it lodges, and remains feeding on its contents, until it changes to a chrysalis, and thence to a fly or beetle, before the succeeding spring, but do not eat their way out until the colds and frosts are past, which is about the beginning of April, when we generally begin to plant peas; and if they should open a door they do not choose to leave their old habitations until the peas are planted, unless the peas are purposely exposed to the hot sun beams, when most of them break through, creep out and fly off, and conceal themselves under proper shelter, from the arid heats of the noontide sun, and chills of the night, until the new crops of peas are ripe enough to invite them forth to the active scenes of life, as well as to fulfil the duties enjoined them by the author of creation, to increase, and multiply. After they have disseminated their eggs, they perish; scarcely a pea amongst a thousand escapes them.

But that which is surprising and difficult to account for, is, that the worm leaves the *rostellum* or sprout untouched or at least uninjured, for almost every pea vegetates and thrives vigorously, notwithstanding the corculum* and plumula seem to be consumed. Whether the sprout is of a disagreeable taste to them, or of a noxious quality, or whether they are apprised of the evil consequence of destroying the sprout, which in the end, would exterminate the race, and thus by a wonderful continence and perseverance in rectitude, set us an example of virtue, worthy of imitation, I know not. The pea fly is a troublesome, mischievous insect, for although they do not destroy the green pea, or diminish its quantity or nutritive qualities, yet it certainly contaminates and renders them disgustful to a delicate palate; for when a fine dish of them is served up, we know there is a maggot in every one, the morbid speck sufficiently betrays it, though yet so small, as scarcely discernable with the assistance of a microscope, and perhaps whilst the peas are very young, do not lessen their native peculiar delicious taste; but when they are full grown, the latent evil becomes too apparent, and when quite ripe, there is little more than the fair superficial appearance of a pea, a mere shell enveloping a fat chrysalis.

I can suggest no method of destroying this voracious insect, unless the planters who suffer by their ravages, would consent to consume in the autumn, of one and the same year, all their peas when dry ripe, by feeding them off to their cattle, and import a new stock of seed from Europe. The method would, if not exterminate them, at least diminish their numbers, for in the autumn there is not one alive but the young rising generation, in the bowels of the peas which would individually be cut off by this process.

I believe these insects, since the importation and cultivation of the green pea from Europe, have avoided every other kind of vegetable and confined themselves entirely to this, on account of its superior delicacy.—They do not meddle with any of our native pulses, that I have observed; such as the caravances, dolichos, phaseoli, lupini, vicia, &c. yet there is in

*Corculum is the rudiment of the young plant. Plumula is the first apparent expansion, of the infant plant upwards, which appears above ground, after the seed or pea has sprouted.

Carolina, a smaller yellowish species of this insect, which is, if possible, more numerous and voracious; they are destructive to all kinds of esculent legumes, particularly so to all species of caravances, and these, in the manner of the common little black wevel, lay their knits on the dry peas, which hatch and propagate continually, the year round, and devour perpetually while there is a pea remaining for them. The common black wevel (curculio piceus) in Carolina and Florida, are particularly destructive to the mayz, (indian corn) and oryza (rice) after it is divested of its husk, and prepared for exportation; then there is no way of saving it, not even in casks, for any length of time, but is entirely safe in the husk, or in the rough, as the planters term it.

Curculio oblongus rufo-testacius, Coleopteris angulato tuberculatis notatis, proboscide longa, deorsum arcuata.

This insect is of the genus we call wevel, but is much larger than the common black one which infests grain in our granaries. They are of an oblong form, and of a brown testaceous colour, yet varied with spots or clouds of yellow or white, and the elytron or shell which covers the wings, is studded with pointed tubercles, as are the thighs, legs and thorax. The proboscis is truncated, and terminates with a serrated or toothed forceps, with which they gnaw the green fruit: near the extremity of the proboscis, are two articulated antennæ, the eyes are placed near the base or origin of the proboscis; the legs are six in number, two of which are placed on the thorax, near the joint, and the other four are on the sides of the body near the abdomen; the whole insect is covered with hair.

This is the mischievous insect which destroys all our stone fruit, plumbs, pears, nectarins, cherries &c. and I believe apples, the European walnut, and other fruits. But it is not in the fly or beetle state that they do this mischief, but in that of the caterpillar or worm. In the spring when the young fruit is about half grown or younger, the female is furnished with a sharp spatula or gauge at the extremity of her abdomen, somewhat like the point of a lancet, with which she pierces the rind of the tender green fruit, at the same instant depositing an egg or knit just under the raised cuticle of the wound, which is like to that made by the nib of a pen. This egg soon hatches, and the little larva immediately eats inward, descending to the stone or kernel of the fruit, round about which it feeds, between it and the pulpy rind, or enters the kernel, which is yet very tender and delicate; but in this last circumstance, the destroyer generally falls a victim to his own intemperance and gluttony, for such fruit generally drop before they are half ripe, and consequently before the metamorphosis of the grub, but such as feed only on the interior pulp round about the stone, continue on the tree until the ripening of the fruit, and thus live out their time. When the fruit drops off, the worm creeps out, enters the earth, and the following spring becomes a beetle or curculio. About the time of the setting of the young fruit, they creep out of the earth, ascend or fly into the trees, copulate, and are then attentive only to the work of generation.

Such is the prolific nature of this insect, that each female lays many hundred eggs, and a few flies are abundantly sufficient to destroy the fruit of a large tree.

Many methods have been thought of and practised to remedy the evil, but none have as yet been attended with success, perhaps through want of perseverance.

During my travels southward, (from Pennsylvania to Florida,) I had sufficient opportunities to observe that the fruit trees on the sea coast and brackish water, were free from the ravages of this destructive insect; this suggested to me an idea, that the saline vapours were pernicious to them, and hence I imagined, that if we were to go to the trifling expence of showering our choicest fruit trees with a weak solution of common sea salt, once or twice a week, it might answer the same end of preserving the fruit, and by persevering farther in a little more expence, in extending the same care to our orchards, we might in a few years expel them. But this is only a conjecture, having never made the experiment.

[January 1808. The foregoing paper being found among the papers of the society, was sent to Mr. Bartram for the purpose of revision, and to enable him to add such additional facts, as might have occurred to him. He returned it with the following note.]

"I have nothing more to add, but that the spring following, I put the experiment of showering a plum tree on tryal, with a weak solution of sea salt dissolved in water, but being too strong of salt, most of the leaves and fruit fell off in consequence of it, otherwise the experiment might have produced the desired effect, as what fruit remained were not touched by the insect, though small and disfigured by the strength of the brine; yet a few arrived to their natural size and ripened, so that I am induced to believe, that with care in tempering the solution, it will be found to be the best and cheapest remedy against the ravages and encrease of those pernicious insects yet discovered. It should be so weak as just to taste of salt.

I have lately reason to recommend fresh oyster shells, pulverized in the manner that plaister of Paris is prepared for manure, put about the roots of peach and plum trees &c. as effectual in keeping off the peach *Zygæna*, and also *Cerambix* which destroys apple trees.

Quere, whether oyster shells powdered, would not be found to be as good a manure, as plaister or lime? perhaps more lasting, and less expensive as they could be prepared with less labour and expence."

W. B.

PLATE 33

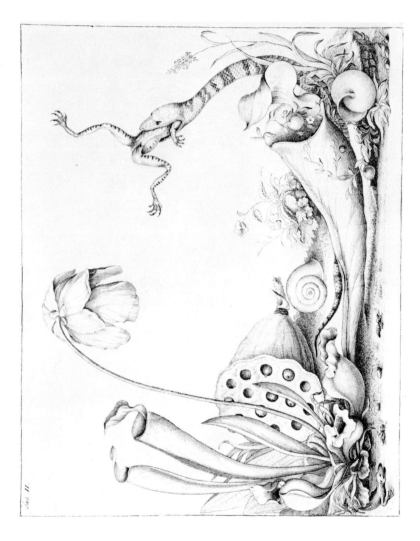

Tab. II.

PLATE 34

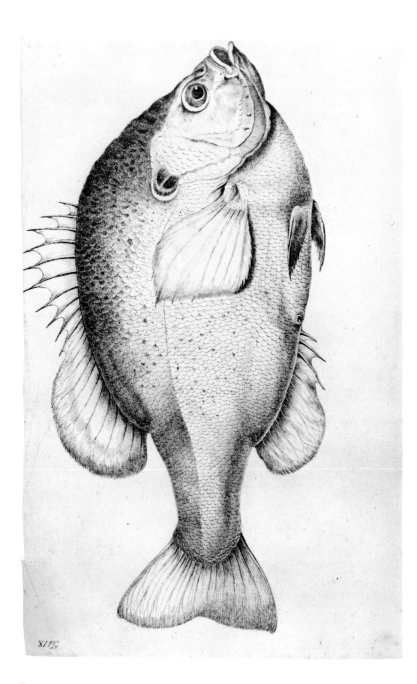

XI 92.

PLATE 35

PLATE 36

Tab. XIX.

PLATE 37

PLATE 38

PLATE 39

PLATE 40

Magnolia acuminata. / *Cucumber Tree.*
Linn.
America

PLATE 41

Lanius Cerviscii

PLATE 42

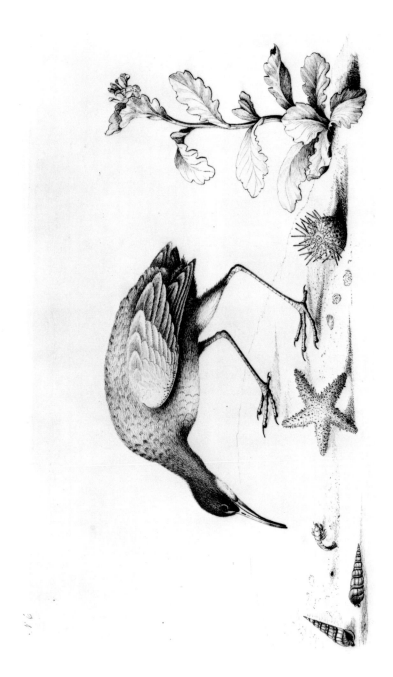

PLATE 43

Silphium terebinthenum   *Syng. polyg. necessaria.*

PLATE 44

PLATE 45

N.º 7.

PLATE 46

N.2

N.1.
Wild Lemmon's
grows in the Province of Georgia
The Flowers are green the Fruits the size of a Damson Plumb
N.2 A very early Flowering Hawthorn
grows in same Province

PLATE 47

PLATE 48

CHRONOLOGY

NOTE ON THE TEXTS

NOTES

GLOSSARY

INDEX

Chronology

1739   Born William Bartram on April 20 (April 9, Old Style), along with twin sister Elizabeth, in Kingsessing, Pennsylvania, son of Quakers Ann Mendenhall and John Bartram, a farmer, botanist, naturalist, and writer. Siblings are half brother Isaac, b. 1725, son from father's first marriage, brothers James, b. 1730, and Moses, b. 1732, and sister Mary, b. 1736. (Great-grandparents John and Elizabeth Bartram emigrated from Derbyshire, England, in 1683 as part of the first wave of Quaker immigration to the new colony of Pennsylvania, and settled in Darby, west of Philadelphia. Grandparents William Bartram and Elizah Hunt married in 1696; they had two sons, John, b. 1699, and James, b. 1701, before Elizah's death in 1701. Grandfather married Elizabeth Smith in 1707 and was declared "out of unity" with the Darby Monthly Meeting of the Religious Society of Friends in 1708 for reasons that are unclear. He then bought land in North Carolina east of present-day Swansboro and moved there in 1711 with Elizabeth and their infant daughter, Elizabeth, leaving John and James behind with his family in Chester County, Pennsylvania. Grandfather was killed on September 22, 1711, in a raid by Tuscarora Indians; Elizabeth, her daughter, and her three-month-old son William were taken prisoner, but were released in 1712 and returned to Pennsylvania. Father John Bartram married Mary Maris in 1723; she died in 1727. Father purchased a stone house and 112 acres of land in Kingsessing, on the west bank of the Schuylkill River across from Philadelphia, in 1728. On October 10, 1729, he married Ann Mendenhall, the daughter of Benjamin Mendenhall, an English Quaker wheelwright who immigrated to Pennsylvania around 1686. Father raised wheat, oats, flax, and corn on Kingsessing farm, and began one of the first botanical gardens in English North America on the land around the house. In 1733 he began sending seeds, plant and animal specimens, and observations on natural history to Peter Collinson, an English Quaker merchant, botanist, and member of the Royal Society. In the years following, father's botanical work became increasingly known among horticulturists and naturalists in North America, Britain, and Europe, including Mark Catesby, Sir Hans Sloane, and Carolus Linnaeus.)

1741   Sister Ann born.

1743   Brother John born. Father joins Benjamin Franklin in founding American Philosophical Society.

1748   Brother Benjamin born. Swedish botanist and author Peter Kalm, a former student of Carolus Linnaeus, makes first of several visits to the Bartram house.

1752   Begins attending the Academy of Philadelphia (precursor to the College of Philadelphia), where he is tutored by Charles Thomson, later secretary of the Continental Congress; curriculum includes Greek, Latin, English, rhetoric, history, geography, mathematics, astronomy, and natural philosophy.

1753   Draws birds and plants (some of his drawings are sent to Collinson by his father). Accompanies father on plant and seed collecting expedition to the Catskill Mountains of New York in September. Meets botanist and nature artist Jane Colden, daughter of Cadwallader Colden, scientist and surveyor general of New York, at the Colden home near Newburgh.

1754   Returns to Catskills with father in late summer and meets Cadwallader Colden. Alexander Garden, a Scottish naturalist and physician who had recently immigrated to Charleston, South Carolina, visits the Bartram home in the fall.

1755   Accompanies father on botanical expedition to Connecticut and New York.

1756   Bartram declines offer from Alexander Garden to become an apprentice physician. Father declines offer of printing apprenticeship for Bartram from Benjamin Franklin on the grounds that the printing trade is too difficult to succeed in financially. Bartram becomes apprentice to Philadelphia merchant James Child, who owns store on Water Street. Sends preserved and dried small birds to George Edwards, English author and illustrator of *A Natural History of Un-*

common Birds (Edwards will describe the specimens in his *Gleanings of Natural History*, published 1758–64).

1758   Drawings by Bartram of a "Horn tailed Turtle" and a "Small mud-turtle" appear in the *Gentleman's Magazine* in London. Father is disowned by Darby Monthly Meeting for denying the divinity of Jesus, but continues to attend Meeting with his family.

1760   Begins keeping a commonplace book around this time (will make periodic entries in it for over 50 years).

1761   Ends mercantile apprenticeship. With financial support from father, sets up as a merchant on the Cape Fear River in present-day Bladen County, North Carolina. Lives at "Ashwood," the home of his uncle, Colonel William Bartram, on the Wilmington–Fayetteville Road.

1762   Visits Philadelphia in June to attend to business affairs, then returns to the South in September with his father and brother Moses. Travels with them through Virginia to the Yadkin River in western North Carolina, then goes with brother to Ashwood while father continues on botanical trip through the Carolinas and Virginia.

1765   Father is appointed botanist for the North American colonies by George III. At his father's request, Bartram sells his trading stock and closes his business to accompany father on a botanical expedition to Florida. Father arrives at Ashwood in July and explores nearby countryside with Bartram. Travels with father to Charleston, South Carolina, in August, where they stay with planter Thomas Lamboll and see Alexander Garden and merchant Henry Laurens (who later serves as president of the Continental Congress, 1777–78). In September the Bartrams go to Savannah, Georgia, then go up the Savannah River and visit Augusta before returning to Savannah. After exploring the coastal region of Georgia, they reach St. Augustine, Florida, on October 11. Bartram visits nearby Anastasia Island to gather specimens, and in November attends meeting at Picolata between Governor James Grant and Indian agent John Stuart and leaders of the Creek Indians. Leaves St. Augustine with father on December 19 on expedition to find source of the St. Johns River.

1766   Travels by boat up the St. Johns until January 12, when dense reeds and plants south of Lake Harney block further progress upriver. Makes drawings and paintings during his travels, some of which father sends to Collinson. Returns to St. Augustine on February 13; when his father sails for Charleston in March, Bartram remains in Florida, intending to start a rice and indigo plantation on the St. Johns six miles from Picolata despite father's opposition. While in Charleston father buys three men, two women, and a boy as slaves for the plantation and sends them to Florida in April, along with tools, provisions, and seeds. (Importation of a minimum number of slaves into Florida was required in order to receive a land patent.) During the summer Bartram is ill with fever, and little progress is made in clearing and planting the land. Visited twice by Henry Laurens, who writes to Bartram's father describing "the forlorn state of poor Billy Bartram." After hearing from Laurens, father advises Bartram to dispose of the plantation and return home. Abandons plantation in autumn (fate of plantation slaves is unknown). Begins working on surveying projects along the Mosquito River with cartographer Gerald De Brahm. Sails from St. Augustine in November and is shipwrecked off the Florida coast near present-day New Smyrna.

1767   Returns to St. Augustine. Writes to Collinson asking if work as an illustrator is available in London. Goes back to Philadelphia in the fall. Works as an agricultural laborer (later returns to working as a merchant).

1768   Elected in February as a corresponding member of the American Society Held in Philadelphia for Promoting Useful Knowledge (in 1769 the Society merges with the American Philosophical Society and becomes the American Philosophical Society for Promoting Useful Knowledge; there is no record that Bartram ever attended any of its meetings). Reads widely about beliefs of the Greeks, Romans, and American Indians. Copies quotations from William Shenstone on gardens and moral behavior into his commonplace book. In July Collinson writes that Margaret Cavendish Bentinck, Duchess of Portland, a leading English collector of marine shells, has commissioned Bartram to draw all land, river, and sea shells *"from the very least to the greatest"* for a fee of £21 (Bartram will send a number of drawings to her in following years). Collinson dies in England on August 11. In autumn, Dr. John Fothergill, an English Quaker physician and owner of one of the largest botanical gardens in England, commissions Bartram to draw mollusks and turtles for an initial fee of £21.

1770   Flees Philadelphia to escape creditors and returns to Cape Fear region of North Carolina, hoping to collect debts owed to him. (Father writes to Fothergill on September 30, before he receives letter from Bartram: "Poor Billy hath had ye greatest misfortunes in trade that could be & gone thro ye most grievous disapointments & is now absconded I know not whither.") Uncle William Bartram dies on October 24.

1771   Father writes to Bartram on April 25 that his brother-in-law, George Bartram, has settled with Bartram's creditors for £100 and "allso paid that troublesome man who threatened thee on his own account I think ye day before thee went away."

1772   Bartram considers abandoning mercantile career and returning to St. Augustine to draw and study nature. Writes to parents that he must "retreat within myself to the only business I was born for, and which I am only good for (If I am intitled to use that phrase for any thing)." Father reponds in July, opposing his return to Florida: "I don't intend to have any more of my estate spent there or to ye southward upon any pretense whatever." Sends drawings to Fothergill and proposes in accompanying letter that he return to Florida to collect plants. In October Fothergill responds, agreeing to the Florida expedition and sending detailed instructions for collecting seeds, shipping live specimens, and making drawings. Fothergill also writes to Dr. Lionel Chalmers of Charleston and arranges for Bartram to be paid £50 per year, with an additional allowance for expenses. Bartram returns to Philadelphia in the late fall.

1773   Sails from Philadelphia on March 20 and arrives on March 31 in Charleston, where he stays with Thomas Lamboll. Receives money from Chalmers before sailing to Savannah in mid-April. Travels south to site of present-day Brunswick, Georgia, then returns to Savannah. Becomes friends with Lachlan McIntosh, a Scottish immigrant living in Darien, Georgia, and his son, John. Witnesses treaty negotiations with Creek Indians at Augusta in mid-May, then travels with John McIntosh and a large surveying party through northeastern Georgia. Visits the Oconee River near present-day Athens and the mouth of the Tugaloo River before returning to Savannah in July. Falls ill for weeks with fever while at Darien. Spends winter in Savannah.

1774   Travels to Florida in March and goes up St. Johns River to Spalding's Lower Store, a trading post six miles southwest of present-day Palatka. Becomes friends with Charles McLatchie, the agent who runs the store. Visits the Alachua Savanna near present-day Gainesville in April, probably traveling with trader and interpreter Job Wiggens. Given name "Puc Puggy" ("Flower Hunter") by Seminole Indians. Goes up the St. Johns in May as far as Blue Springs, near present-day Orange City, then returns to Spalding's Lower Store in June. Travels in western Florida as far as the Suwannee River, June–July. Makes second trip up the St. Johns to Lake George, August–September. Sends specimens to Fothergill in England (will send 209 dried plant specimens and 59 zoological and botanical drawings to Fothergill between 1774 and 1776, as well as a two-part report on his travels; the first part may have been sent from Spalding's Lower Store in the autumn of 1774). Spends autumn in Florida and Georgia.

1775   Arrives on March 25 in Charleston, where he stays with Mary Thomas, daughter of Thomas Lamboll. During this time Bartram may have prepared and sent the second part of his report to Fothergill (edited by Francis Harper, the report is published for the first time in the *Transactions of the American Philosophical Society* in 1943). Revolutionary War begins on April 19 with battles of Lexington and Concord in Massachusetts (news does not reach Charleston until early May). Leaves Charleston on April 22 and goes to Augusta, Georgia, then travels through northeastern Georgia and northwestern South Carolina into the mountains of western North Carolina, arriving around May 22 in Cowee, a settlement near present-day West's Mills in Macon County, North Carolina. While traveling alone in the vicinity of present-day Andrews, Cherokee County, on May 27, Bartram decides not to proceed further into Cherokee territory and instead returns to Georgia by way of northwestern South Carolina. Travels westward across central Georgia with large party of traders, reaching the Oconee River at Rock Landing, four miles below present-day Milledgeville, on July 1. Crosses the Chattahoochee River into Alabama in mid-July and reaches Mobile around July 26. Travels up the Tombigbee River during August, then returns to Mobile. Sails to Pensacola, Florida, where on September 5 he obtains permission from the British governor to travel and collect botanical specimens in West Florida. Returns to Mobile and then sails westward through Mississippi Sound. Suffers increasing pain in his eyes, possibly from poison-ivy infection or from scarlet fever. Recovers while staying for several weeks at "Pearl Island" in Louisiana, near the mouth of the Pearl River. Crosses Lake Pontchartrain and Lake Maurepas and reaches the eastern bank of the Mississippi around October 21. Visits Baton Rouge, then crosses the Mississippi and goes to Point Coupee, about 35 miles upriver from Baton Rouge, in late October. Leaves Baton Rouge on November 10 and returns to Mobile around November 16. Remains in Mobile until late November, then travels to the Creek Indian settlements along the Tallapoosa River in Alabama.

1776   Crosses Chattahoochee River in January and travels through central Georgia to Augusta. Spends spring and summer in Georgia. May have volunteered to assist Georgia troops, led by Lachlan McIntosh, preparing to repel a rumored British invasion from Florida (attack does not take place). Ships last plant specimens to Fothergill. Leaves Savannah and travels overland to Pennsylvania.

1777   Arrives in Philadelphia in January. Father dies on September 22. Bartram inherits £200, and his brother John inherits the house and gardens in Kingsessing, where Bartram will live and work for the rest of his life. British army occupies Philadelphia on September 25. Garden is neglected during occupation and becomes overgrown.

1778   British evacuate Philadelphia on June 18. Bartram signs affirmation of "Allegiance and Fidelity" to the General Assembly of Pennsylvania on August 26.

1780   John Fothergill dies in England on December 26.

1782   Elected professor of botany by the trustees of the Univer-
            sity of the State of Pennsylvania (successor to the College
            of Philadelphia and predecessor to the University of Penn-
            sylvania). Although there is no record that Bartram for-
            mally declined the post, he apparently never lectured at the
            university.

1784   Mother dies.

1785   Brothers Isaac and Moses announce in an advertisement in
            the April 22 *Pennsylvania Packet* that Bartram will settle
            any long-standing debts with the "legacy left him by his
            father, John Bartram." Botanist Humphry Marshall, a
            cousin of Bartram's father, publishes *Arbustum Ameri-
            canum*, containing many botanical descriptions contrib-
            uted by Bartram.

1786   Philadelphia publisher Enoch Story Jr. issues broadside so-
            liciting subscriptions for the printing of Bartram's *Travels.*
            Receives a trunk from Mary Lamboll Thomas containing
            specimens, papers, and books that he had left in Charleston
            in 1776. French botanist André Michaux visits Bartram's
            garden in September. Bartram falls nearly 20 feet out of a
            cypress tree while gathering seeds in his garden and suffers
            a compound fracture of his right leg (injury apparently in-
            hibits physical activity for the remainder of his life). Cor-
            responds with Benjamin Smith Barton, a young Pennsyl-
            vania naturalist studying medicine in Great Britain.

1787   George Washington, who is attending the Constitutional
            Convention in Philadelphia, visits Bartram's garden on
            June 10. Several convention delegates, including Alexander
            Hamilton, James Madison, Alexander Martin, George
            Mason, John Rutledge, Caleb Strong, and Hugh William-
            son, visit the garden on July 14, accompanied by botanist
            Manasseh Cutler.

1788   Bartram sends 38 plant specimens and four drawings from
            his travels in the South to Robert Barclay, a wealthy Eng-
            lish amateur botanist. In an accompanying letter to Barclay,
            Bartram writes that he is sending the specimens "expecting
            or desiring no other gratuity than the bare mention of my
            being the discoverer . . ."

1789 With André Michaux, travels south from Philadelphia for a day, then returns home while Michaux continues on to Wilmington. Benjamin Smith Barton, who has returned to Philadelphia and been appointed professor of natural history and botany at the University, begins bringing his classes to Bartram's garden. Encouraged by Barton, Bartram writes "Observations on the Creek and Cherokee Indians" (manuscript is published for the first time in the *Transactions of the American Ethnological Society* in 1853). Reads "Observations on the Pea Fly or Beetle, and Fruit Curculio" at a meeting of the Philadelphia Society for Promoting Agriculture. *Hortus Kewensis* by William Aiton, which lists at least 21 plant species discovered by Bartram, is published in London.

1790 Begins keeping a meteorological diary on January 1 (makes daily entries in it through September 12, 1791). Philadelphia publishers James and Johnson issue new proposal for printing the *Travels* and receive subscriptions from President Washington, Vice-President John Adams, and Secretary of State Thomas Jefferson.

1791 *Travels through North & South Carolina, Georgia, East & West Florida, the Cherokee country, the extensive territories of the Muscogulges, or Creek Confederacy, and the country of the Chactaws; containing an account of the Soil and Natural Productions of those regions, together with observations on the Manners of the Indians* is deposited for copyright by Bartram on August 26 and published in Philadelphia by James and Johnson.

1792 British edition of the *Travels* published in London by Joseph Johnson.

1793 Irish edition of the *Travels* is published in Dublin in April, and a German translation is published in Berlin later in the year.

1794 Henry Wansey, an English Quaker who visits the garden in June, records in his diary that when one of his companions made joking reference to the encounters with alligators described in the *Travels*, Bartram "became so reserved, that we could get but little conversation with him."

Second edition of the *Travels* is published in England (Coleridge and Wordsworth will own copies of this edition, and Coleridge will copy passages into his journal).

1797 Bartram begins keeping a second commonplace book in which he makes periodic entries about weather, philosophy, bird migrations, animal habits, plant and flower cycles, and his reading (keeps book through 1802). Playwright William Dunlap and novelist Charles Brockden Brown visit Bartram's garden on May 9. Dunlap records in his diary: "Arrived at the Botanist's Garden, we approached an old man who, with a rake in his hand, was breaking the clods of earth in a tulip bed. His hat was old and flapped over his face, his coarse shirt was seen near his neck, as he wore no cravat or kerchief; his waistcoat and breeches were both of leather, and his shoes were tied with leather strings. We approached and accosted him. He ceased his work, and entered into conversation with the ease and politeness of nature's noblemen. His countenance was expressive of benignity and happiness. This was the botanist, traveller, and philosopher we had come to see."

1798 Benjamin Smith Barton publishes Part I of his treatise on medicinal plants, *Collections for an Essay towards a Materia Medica of the United States* in Philadelphia, based on Bartram's 89-page manuscript "Pharmacopoeia."

1799 French translation of the *Travels* published in Paris by Libraires Carteret et Brosson. Dr. Benjamin Rush visits the garden in August.

1801 Second French edition of the *Travels* is published in Paris by Libraire Maradau.

1802 Bartram begins a new "weather diary" on January 1, in which he makes daily observations of temperature, wind, precipitation, bird migration, animal habits, plants cycles, and an occasional comment on human events (continues this diary through the end of 1822, with one major gap from September 20, 1808, to April 18, 1818). Becomes friends with Alexander Wilson, a Scottish immigrant who is teaching school at nearby Gray's Ferry on the Schuylkill River. Naturalist

Constantin Rafinesque makes the first of many visits to Bartram's garden.

1803   Bartram provides most of the illustrations and a large, though unacknowledged, amount of the information contained in *Elements of Botany*, published by Benjamin Smith Barton. Contributes a drawing and notes, attributed to "a very intelligent gentleman," to *An Investigation of the Properties of the Sanguinaria canadensis or Puccoon*, botanical study by William Downey.

1804   William Darlington visits the garden with Barton's botany class (Darlington later becomes a leading American botanist, and in 1849 publishes an edition of the correspondence of John Bartram and Humphry Marshall). Alexander Wilson begins sending color drawings of birds to Bartram for his criticism (in 1805 Wilson writes to Bartram that his ornithological drawings "owe their existence" to "your inspiration"). Wilson's poem "The Rural Walk," which is set in Bartram's garden, appears in August in *The Literary Magazine, and American Register*. Around this time Bartram meets Wilson's close friend George Ord, who later becomes a prominent American naturalist. In September Bartram drafts a letter to his nephew Dr. James Howell Bartram, a ship's surgeon who is about to sail to India and Java, advising him on questions of moral conduct, eating and personal health while traveling, and personal improvement, and asking him to give his regards to naturalist Thomas Horsfield, a former student of Barton's now serving as a surgeon with the Dutch army on Java. Bartram publishes "Anecdotes of an American Crow" and "Some account of the late Mr. John Bartram, of Pennsylvania" in the *Philadelphia Medical and Physical Journal*, edited by Benjamin Smith Barton.

1805   Publishes "Description of an American Species of Certhia, or Creeper" in the *Philadelphia Medical and Physical Journal*. Bartram sends the horns from a "Stone Buck" (pronghorn) to President Jefferson after Jefferson expresses an interest in them (horns had been given to Bartram's father). Jefferson invites Bartram to serve as natural history adviser to an expedition up the Red River led by Thomas Freeman.

1806   In February Bartram declines Jefferson's invitation, citing
        his age and infirmities. He recommends Alexander Wilson
        in his place, but Jefferson does not respond to this advice,
        or to Wilson's offer to join the Red River expedition.

1807   Bartram writes preface to *A Catalogue of Trees, Shrubs, and
        Herbaceous Plants*, which is offered for sale at the garden.
        Advises visitors on herbal medicine.

1808   Charles Willson Peale paints a portrait of Bartram for his
        gallery of noted Americans. English naturalist Thomas
        Nuttall visits the garden. Bartram writes letter on October
        29 introducing Benjamin Say, husband of his niece Ann
        Bonsall, to President Jefferson (Say had recently been
        elected to Congress). Bartram's paper from 1789, "Obser-
        vations on the Pea Fly or Beetle, and Fruit Curculio," is
        published in the first volume of the *Memoirs* of the Phila-
        delphia Society for Promoting Agriculture. Alexander
        Wilson publishes the first volume of his series *American
        Ornithology* (seven more volumes appear by 1813).

1809   In November Wilson proposes that Bartram join him in a
        collecting and exploring trip to St. Louis, but Bartram de-
        clines, citing his age and poor health.

1810   Encourages great-nephew Thomas Say to begin collecting
        beetles and butterflies (Say later becomes an entomologist
        and conchologist and publishes *American Entomology; or
        Descriptions of the Insects of North America* in three vol-
        umes, 1824–28).

1811   Wilson stays at the Kingsessing house during the summer
        (he will also live there for several months in 1812).

1812   The Academy of Natural Sciences is founded in Philadel-
        phia and Bartram is elected a member. Brother John Bar-
        tram dies, leaving the family house and gardens to his
        daughter Ann, a botanist and artist, and her husband, Rob-
        ert Carr. Bartram continues to live in the Kingsessing
        house with the Carrs.

1813   Alexander Wilson dies on August 23.

1815   A paper on the "Cryingbird" (limpkin) by Benjamin Smith
        Barton appears in the *Transactions* of the Linnaean Society
        in London along with an engraving of a drawing attributed
        to Bartram. Barton dies on December 19.

1818   Bartram's drawing of *Pyrola umbellata*, originally engraved
        for the second edition of Barton's *Elements of Botany*, ap-
        pears without acknowledgment as a frontispiece to the
        "third American edition" of *An Introduction to Botany* by
        Priscilla Bell Wakefield.

1823   Dies on July 22 at his Kingsessing house from a ruptured
        lung artery. After funeral on July 23 Bartram is buried at
        an unrecorded location.

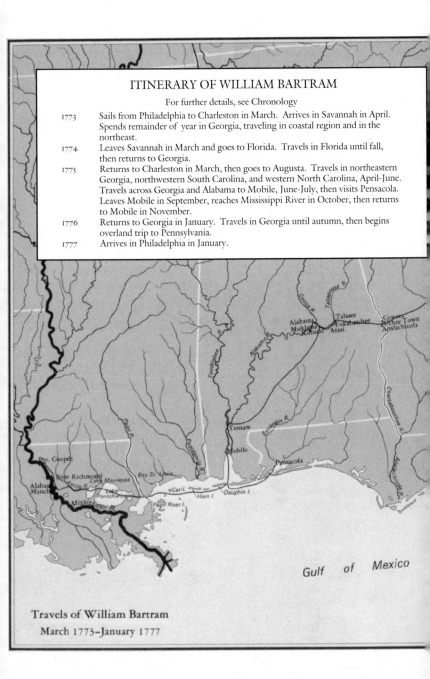

ITINERARY OF WILLIAM BARTRAM

For further details, see Chronology

1773   Sails from Philadelphia to Charleston in March. Arrives in Savannah in April. Spends remainder of year in Georgia, traveling in coastal region and in the northeast.

1774   Leaves Savannah in March and goes to Florida. Travels in Florida until fall, then returns to Georgia.

1775   Returns to Charleston in March, then goes to Augusta. Travels in northeastern Georgia, northwestern South Carolina, and western North Carolina, April-June. Travels across Georgia and Alabama to Mobile, June-July, then visits Pensacola. Leaves Mobile in September, reaches Mississippi River in October, then returns to Mobile in November.

1776   Returns to Georgia in January. Travels in Georgia until autumn, then begins overland trip to Pennsylvania.

1777   Arrives in Philadelphia in January.

Travels of William Bartram
March 1773–January 1777

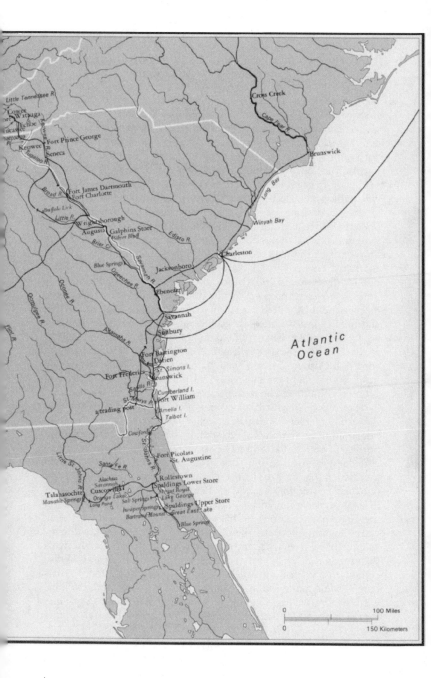

Little Tennessee R.
Cowee
Wataga
Echoe
Tucasee
Chattooga
Keowee
Fort Prince George
Seneca

Broad R.
Fort James Dartmouth
Fort Charlotte
Buffalo Lick
Little R.
Wrightsborough
Augusta
Galphins Store
Silver Bluff
Briar Cr.
Blue Springs
Savannah R.
Jacksonboro
Greene R.
Ebenezer
Savannah
Oconee R.
Ogeechee R.
Altamaha R.
Sunbury
Ocmulgee R.
Fort Barrington
Darien
Fort Frederica
St. Simons I.
Brunswick
Cumberland I.
Satilla R.
St. Marys R.
Fort William
a trading post
Amelia I.
Talbot I.
Cowford
St. Johns R.
Flint R.
Fort Picolata
St. Augustine
Santa Fe R.
Alachua
Rollestown
Savannah
Cuscowilla
Spalding Lower Store
Mount Royal
Talahasochte
Long Pond
Orange Lake
Salt Springs
Lake George
Manatee Springs
Juniper springs
Spaldings Upper Store
Bartrams Mount
Great East Lake
Blue Spring

Cross Creek
Cape Fear R.
Brunswick

Long Bay

Winyah Bay
Charleston

Atlantic
Ocean

0   100 Miles
0   150 Kilometers

Note on the Texts

This volume presents the texts of two travel narratives by William Bartram, *Travels Through North and South Carolina, Georgia, East and West Florida, the Cherokee Country, the Extensive Territories of the Muscogulges or Creek Confederacy, and the Country of the Chactaws; containing an account of the Soil and Natural Productions of those regions, together with observations on the Manners of the Indians* and *Travels in Georgia and Florida, 1773–74: A Report to Dr. John Fothergill*, as well as eight essays that include observations on American Indians, botany, ornithology, geology, and entomology.

William Bartram traveled extensively in the American South from 1773 until 1777, collecting plant specimens and making botanical and zoological drawings for his English patron, Dr. John Fothergill. Sometime after his return to Philadelphia in 1777, Bartram began to write a narrative of his travels. The Philadelphia publisher Enoch Story Jr. issued a broadside in 1786 soliciting subscriptions for printing Bartram's *Travels*; but for reasons that are not clear, Story did not publish the book. In 1790 James and Johnson, another Philadelphia firm, issued a new proposal for the printing of the *Travels* and asked for subscriptions. The book was published in Philadelphia by James and Johnson, with a title page dated 1791, sometime between August 26, 1791, when Bartram deposited the title for copyright, and January 27, 1792, when the Pennsylvania botanist Henry Muhlenberg recorded in his journal that he had "perused William Bartram's Florida travel book." Bartram apparently did not proofread the James and Johnson edition, and he is known to have been very dissatisfied with it. The edition contained numerous typographical errors, especially in the setting of scientific names, as well as heavy punctuation that does not conform to Bartram's usage in other manuscripts (the manuscript of the *Travels* is not known to be extant). Bartram included an errata correcting 28 errors in the James and Johnson edition in a copy of the *Travels* that he gave to his neighbor William Hamilton in 1799; but there was no opportunity for Bartram to make these corrections in a future American edition, since the *Travels* was not reprinted in the United States during his lifetime.

An English edition of the *Travels* was published in London by Joseph Johnson in 1792, and it contained significantly fewer errors than the Philadelphia setting. Collation of the American and English editions shows that the English edition more closely follows Bartram's style of punctuation. Therefore the text printed in this volume is taken from the first English edition of *Travels Through North and South Carolina, Georgia, East and West Florida, the Cherokee Country, the Extensive Territories of the Muscogulges or Creek Confederacy, and the Country of the Chactaws; containing an account of the Soil and Natural Productions of those regions, together with observations on the Manners of the Indians,* published by Joseph Johnson in 1792. Thirteen corrections from Bartram's list of errata are incorporated in the text printed here: at page 17, line 5, "Drosera" replaces "Drossea"; at 32.16, "Ciris" replaces "Ceris"; at 39.29, "linear" replaces "lineal"; at 39.35, "Annona triloba" replaces "Antrilobe"; at 55.6, "cercis" replaces "cercea"; at 106.10–11, "standard" replaces "starol"; at 164.2, "rigid" replaces "ridgy"; at 193.16, "ferruginious" replaces "terrigenous"; at 208.23, "Caloosahatche" replaces "Talahasochte"; at 211.11–12, "Jatropha" replaces "Iatropa"; at 256.22, "prinus" replaces "prinos"; at 277.15–16, "Euonymus" replaces "Euonimus"; and at 280.29, "Trillium cern" replaces "Trillium cesnum". (The remaining 15 errors noted by Bartram in the 1791 American edition were corrected in the 1792 English edition.)

While in the South, Bartram wrote a report to Dr. Fothergill covering his travels in 1773 and 1774. The untitled report was sent to him in two separate volumes: the first was probably sent from Florida in autumn 1774, the second probably from Charleston, South Carolina, in spring 1775. Following Fothergill's death, Bartram's report eventually became the property of the British Museum (Natural History). In 1943 the manuscript, edited and annotated by Francis Harper, was published for the first time in the *Transactions of the American Philosophical Society* under the title *Travels in Georgia and Florida, 1773–74: A Report to Dr. John Fothergill.* Working from a photostatic copy of the report, Harper presented the manuscript in a text in which punctuation and letters inadvertently omitted by Bartram were presented in roman type and enclosed in brackets; in this volume, these editorial emendations are accepted and printed without brackets. In cases where Harper was unable to determine Bartram's intentions from the photostatic copy, he sometimes presented conjectural readings set in italic type and enclosed in brackets and sometimes offered no conjectural readings. In the present volume, the conjectural readings are accepted and printed in roman type without brackets; the places where no conjectures were made are indicated by bracketed spaces, e.g., [   ]. The text of *Travels in Georgia and Florida, 1773–74: A Report to Dr. John Fothergill* printed here is taken from *Transactions of the American Philosophical Society,* New Series—Volume XXXIII, Part II (Philadelphia: American Philosophical Society, 1943), pp. 121–242.

The eight essays included in this volume are arranged in the approximate order of their composition, and each text is taken from its first publication. The following is a list of the sources of the texts printed here:

"Observations on the Creek and Cherokee Indians" was written in 1789, probably in response to inquiries from naturalist Benjamin Smith Barton, but did not appear during Bartram's lifetime. His manuscript, edited by E. G. Squier, was first published in *Transactions of the American Ethnological Society*, Volume III, Part I (New York: 1853), pp. 1–81.

"Account of the Species, Hybrids, and Other Varieties of the Vine of North-America" was written in 1802 and published in *The Medical Repository*, Series 2, Volume I (New York: 1803), pp. 19–24.

"Anecdotes of an American Crow" and "Some Account of the Late Mr. John Bartram, of Pennsylvania" were published in the *Philadelphia Medical and Physical Journal*, Volume I, Part I (Philadelphia: 1804), at pp. 89–95 and pp. 115–24 respectively.

"Description of an American species of Certhia, or Creeper" and "Conjectures relative to the Scite of Bristol, in Pennsylvania" were published in the *Philadelphia Medical and Physical Journal*, Volume II, Part I (Philadelphia: 1805) at pp. 103–6 and pp. 131–33 respectively.

The "Preface to *A Catalogue of Trees, Shrubs, and Herbaceous Plants, Indigenous to the United States of America; cultivated and disposed of by John Bartram & Son, At their Botanical Garden, Kingsess, near Philadelphia: to which is added a Catalogue of Foreign Plants, collected from various parts of the globe*" appeared in the catalogue, which was printed in Philadelphia by Bartram and Reynolds in 1807 for sale at the Bartram family garden.

"Observations on the Pea Fly or Beetle, and Fruit Curculio" was read by Bartram at a meeting of the Philadelphia Society for Promoting Agriculture in 1789 and then published with a newly written addendum in the *Memoirs of the Philadelphia Society for Promoting Agriculture* (Philadelphia: 1808), pp. 317–23.

This volume presents the texts of the original printings chosen for inclusion here; it does not attempt to reproduce features of 18th-century typography, such as the long "s". The texts, including the original index to the *Travels*, are printed without change, except for the correction of typographical errors and the change of page numbers to conform to the pagination of the present volume. Spelling, punctuation, and capitalization are often expressive features, and they are not altered, even when inconsistent or irregular. The following is a list of typographical errors corrected, cited by page and line number: 7.9, India; 10.25, lanks; 14.25, tœda; 30.35, squamosa; 30.38, humila; 31.10, parva; 31.35, opossums; 40.39, breunis; 49.35, Della; 50.8, Sambricus; 59.2, malva; 105.31, stratoites; 133.22, Creeks; 153.28, incarna; 199.39, Trichecus; 200.10, South-west; 202.36, conclude; 235.9, estates; 238.18, midde; 240.36, glundaria; 241.7, peilatus; 248.30, Americana; they; 256.1, PART II; 258.13, constanly; 265.40, throgh; 279.1, subdiving; 288.19, mountaneous; 289.23–24, contiued; 289.32, Keowe; 293.10, Gallahan; 293.23, in laws; 304.5, Joco; 305.23, These; 315.12, aud; 344.9, iuhabitants; 362.35, virgils; 369.22, lanidng; 371.35, Ghuaclahatche; 373.1, conprehending; 375.1, CHAP. XI; 384.40, wich; 388.20, frowing; 413.19, to it by; 441.4, nould; 474.12, their;; 534.16, M'Gillvany's; 542.29, Sanguenaria; 542.29, Gallium; 542.30, Toxcodendron; 542.30–31, Rhustruphydon; 545.22 of of; 547.6, pillars; 549.12, Apalachians; 556.15, three pieces; 557.9, *Norida*; 557.31, *Norida*; 559.32, slips; 565.12, council; 569.10, Bartram,; 569.12, *Pluckn.*

Notes

In the notes below, the reference numbers denote page and line of this volume (the line count includes titles and headings). No note is made for material included in standard desk-reference books such as Webster's *Collegiate*, *Biographical*, and *Geographical* dictionaries. Footnotes in the text are the author's own. The map on pages 608–9 is from *Atlas of Early American History*, ed. by Lester J. Cappon, Barbara Bartz Petchenik, and John Hamilton Long (Princeton: Princeton University Press, 1976). For identifications of plants and animals, see the Glossary. For present-day names of some of the sites Bartram visited, see the Index. For further background than is provided in the notes, see: *The Travels of William Bartram: Naturalist's Edition*, ed. by Francis Harper (New Haven: Yale University Press, 1958); *Travels in Georgia and Florida. 1773–74: A Report to Dr. John Fothergill*, ed. by Harper, in *Transactions of the American Philosophical Society 33* (1943); Edmund Berkeley and Dorothy Smith Berkeley, *The Life and Travels of John Bartram: From Lake Ontario to the River St. John* (Gainesville: University Press of Florida, 1982); *The Correspondence of John Bartram, 1734–1777*, ed. by Berkeley and Berkeley (Gainesville: University Press of Florida, 1992); John R. Swanton, *The Indians of the Southeastern United States* (Washington, D.C.: Smithsonian Institution Press, 1979; first published by the U.S. Government Printing Office as no. 197 of Bureau of American Ethnology bulletin, 1946); Charles Hudson, *The Southeastern Indians* (Knoxville: University of Tennessee Press, 1976); and *William Bartram on the Southeastern Indians*, ed. by Gregory A. Waselkov and Kathryn E. Holland Braund (Lincoln: University of Nebraska Press, 1995). The scholarship of Francis Harper has been an essential aid in the preparation of this volume. The paintings and drawings on the plates were selected with the assistance of Amy Meyers of the Huntington Library, San Marino, California.

TRAVELS THROUGH NORTH AND SOUTH CAROLINA, GEORGIA, EAST AND WEST FLORIDA

3.1–15   TRAVELS . . . INDIANS.] Bartram's report to Dr. Fothergill (pages 427–522 in this volume) provides a more accurate account of the order in which he visited areas of the South in 1773–74; for a more detailed account of the sequence of his travels, see the Chronology in this volume. The 1791 American edition of the *Travels* included the following dedication: "To His Excellency Thomas Mifflin, Esq., President of the State of Pennsylvania, This

Volume of Travels is Gratefully Inscribed, By his respectful friend and servant William Bartram."

13.15–16   Royal Society] Eight of John Bartram's papers were published in the Royal Society of London's *Philosophical Transactions.* He was a member of the Royal Academy of Sciences of Stockholm.

16.21–24   stiff hairs . . . perish] Bartram is credited with being the first to distinctly describe how insects are trapped in the Sarracenia.

22.12   papiles] Bartram's anglicized plural of the genus *Papilio* (butterfly).

24.29–25.17   In the consideration . . . aware.] A manuscript document, bearing the initials W B but not written in Bartram's hand, is in the Henry Knox Papers at the Pierpont Morgan Library in New York. It was printed for the first time in *William Bartram on the Southeastern Indians,* edited and annotated by Gregory A. Waselkov and Kathryn E. Holland Braund (Lincoln: University of Nebraska Press, 1995), under the title "Some Hints & Observations, concerning the civilization, of the Indians, or Aborigines of America." Though the manuscript in the Knox papers may be a revision of the original document (which is not known to be extant), there is good reason to believe that it is based on something Bartram wrote. At the beginning of his first administration, President Washington asked Secretary of War Henry Knox to study relations between the United States and the Indians and to make recommendations for future frontier policy. Knox solicited information from many sources while conducting his study in 1789, and it seems likely that he received the Bartram document at this time. Bartram may have written the passage on Indian policy in the "Introduction" to the *Travels* at about the same time as he composed the observations on the Indians contained in the document in the Knox papers. The text of "Some Hints & Observations, concerning the civilization, of the Indians, or Aborigines of America" is printed below:

The Spanish settlements, in Florida, extend but a small distance from the Sea Coast: For they are very careful, not to disturb, or offend the Indians, by dispossessing them, or even hunting on their Lands.

They consider them as Brethren & fellow Citizens, and use all rational means to engage their friendship, to make them good Christians & consequently good Men.

I could wish the Citizens of these States, would shew their approbation of so worthy an example, by endeavouring to conciliate the affections of the Indians, especially of those Nations within the limits of the United States. Particular notice should be taken of the tribes to the S.W. the Cherokes, Muscogulges,* Chicasa's and Chactaws. The Siminoles, although confederates to the Muscoges, are at present within the limits of the Spanish claims of Florida, and consequently, in a political view, they do not immediately concern us.

*Creeks

The Tribes above mentioned, lay contiguous to one another, and taken collectively, comprehend a vast territory, and a very respectable number of Inhabitants, who are intrepid, and warlike. Although they are not, strictly consider'd, Aborigines of these Countries; yet they have possess'd the Soil, for some Ages past, and the Bones, and other sacred reliques of their Ancestors lie buried in the dust about their Towns.

Our Ancestors who first landed on these Coasts, were received by the Fathers, and Grandfathers of those Tribes, in the most friendly, and hospitable manner. They humanely & cheerfully treated them as wellcome Guests: But to give a stronger proof of their affection, they call'd them *"Beloved Brethren"* and voluntarily evacuated their Towns to accommodate them. Every necessary & conveniency, which the country afforded was brought as an inducement for our Ancestors to remain amongst them, or to repeat their Visits. The Indians regarded them with love, and reverence. Benevolence taught those natives to act in the excellent characters of Friends & Guardians, & to establish their White Brothers family, on their Border. The white family increased & flourished. The Spanish another more powerful family of White People, who had before settled a Plantation a little to the S^d, with envy, saw the progress of the English family. Stimulated by Rage, they determined against right, and justice, to commence hostilities & destroy them: But the natives with one hand, with one Spirit, engaged in defence of the English, and in the end expeld their envious neighbour.

These instances of magnanimity & friendship, in the Natives, in my opinion, should not only recall, that gratitude which seems to have been expeld from our Breasts, but excite in us, sentiments of generosity & compassion, toward their unfortunate offspring.

Man, after he has subjugated his powerful opponent, is too apt to conclude rashly, & act tyrannically.

We unreasonably ask, to what purpose do we observe any terms, with cruel, barbarous Savages, who are continually seeking opportunities to massacre our Brethren & Relatives on the Frontiers?

Wretches, who in the late glorious contest, joined our Enemy to cut our Throats!

Let us join as one Man, to cut them off & disposses them of those Lands, which are *ours by right of conquest.*

Our injustice & avarice, in pressing upon their Borders & dispossessing them of their Lands, together with the outrage committed against their Persons & encroachments made on their hunting Grounds by the Frontiers, provoke them to retaliation.

Their joining, or taking part with our Enemy, during the late Contest, is I believe, understood in a too general sense. We ought at least to discriminate. I pass'd through the Muscogulge confederacy at the most critical period of the contest; that was, when a declaration of Independence was made.

I endeavour'd to discover the sentiments of the Indians, with regard to it, and I found that they were nearly unanimous in reprobating the hostile proceedings, of the English, against their white Children. Mr Golphin was of the opinion, that at least two thirds of the Confederacy, were decidedly in favor of Congress; That Gentleman, had so powerful an Interest, that he displaced every British Commissary, who was amongst them, & gave those offices to the Friends of Liberty. He himself was unanimously chosen by them, as their *Beloved Man*, or *Superintendant.*

I question wether there was one of the Towns, who joined their Forces with the British; if it has been the case; they were some Bands of the Lower Creeks, or Siminoles, who were far distant from the Nation, & immediately under the influence & controul, of the British, of East, and West Florida.

Now let us consider what a sacrifice, these virtuous Men, made to humanity, & honor. For fifty Years, they had constantly enjoy'd superfluous supplies of Merchandize, which were convey'd to them, from Charlston, Savana, Pensocola, and Movile. They were now entirely ignorant of any of the arts, whereby, to supply themselves with necessary clothing; they had almost forgotten how to make earthen Potts, & not one amongst them knew how to form a Stone axe, or wooden Hough. All their dependance had rested upon the Traders, who supplied them with European Manufactures; but from these, they were now entirely precluded. Yet amidst all their difficulties, they stood firm to our advocate, Mr Golphin, even to the termination of the Contest. There was not a hostile Indian, who cross'd the Altamaha, nor even St Mary's, during the whole time I remained at Georgia: not one Family disturb'd altho' they were under the most alarming apprehensions. When I was at Genl McAntoshes, on the Altamaha, the English attempted to invade Georgia. They advanced to the Banks of St Mary's, possess'd themselves of it, & took Shelter in the Old Indian trading House. A few Indians were in company. A Small party of the Georgians marched from the Altamaha, to oppose them & they gain'd the banks before the Enemy had pass'd the Flood. Hostilities commenced by the Parties firing at each other across the River. The British were under cover of the evacuated trading Houses, & the Georgians sheilded themselves behind the Trees, on the Rivers Banks. The conflict had continued for some time, when the Chief of the Indians threw down his Gun & boldly stepping out from the corner of a House, he took off his Hat, & whirling it up in the Air, as he advanced to the River Side, amidst showers of Bullets, he spoke aloud to the Georgians, declaring that they were Brother's & friends & that he knew not any cause why they should spill each others Blood. Neither I (said he) nor my Companions the Red-Men, will fire another Gun. He turned about, shouted & immediately led off the Indians. This put an end to the contest at that time.

In order to recover the friendship & union of our neighbouring, uncivilized nations, perhaps no more eligeble, or laudable step can be pursued, than the introduction of our Language, System of Legislation, Religion, Manners Arts & Sciences; & by the reestablishment of Trade & Commerce, in a peaceable & friendly manner, amongst them. These beget an intercourse by insensible gradations, act like facination, & while they charm & please them, we effect a revolution, & secure a permanently peaceable dominion without violence or injustice.

This way of sharing a possession in those vacant & desirable Regions, is certainly, of all others, the most consistent with those divine precepts, of our holy *Religion*, which should guide all our actions. Those sacred Tutors, teach us that all the nations & Tribes of Men, are Brethren & the offspring of one Family: They instruct us that every nation is equally entitled to those bountiful blessings of Providence, the furniture and produce of the Earth, & the benign influence of the Planets.

By them we are also commanded to banish violence & war, & sit down together in peace & goodwill toward each other; conversing & praising God.

Would we pursue those Rules, then indeed, might we sit down, in peace & full security, under the shade of the fruitful Trees. Then without the dread of resentment, from some violated & incensed foe, might the contented & cheerful Patriarchs behold their innocent Youths, sporting on the verdant Lawns, or on the verges of glittering Lakes. Happy should we be in our possessions, & at the return of Silent Eve, we could listen to the musick of the Lute, or behold our bleating flocks, bounding over the distant Hills.

Our Minds would then be at rest, or in rapture with the inexpressible consolation, that we had not oppos'd the will of God, nor conteracted the dictates of the moral Law, inscribed on every human Heart.

We seem not to be apprehensive of our dangerous situation, from the wisdom & superior policy, of our rival Neighbours, who surround us by Land. They practice every art & policy, to gain & secure the friendship of the Indians, and to avail themselves of the advantages arising from their intimacy: as from their Trade or Commerce, & aid in War, from their Arms.

They obtain their ends, by the most rational methods; those are the introduction of their Systems of civilisation. Were we to act right, we should do the same, & dissipate the dark Clouds of Prejudice, which have been hovering about our Heads from our Infancy. We ought to consider them, as they are in reality, as our Brethren & fellow Citizens, & treat them as such; notwithstanding, their manners & modes of Government are somewhat different from ours.

The People of Georgia, Virginia, Pensylvania &ᶜ, are distinct, independent States, or Tribes, with respect to their internal Legislation, & each govern'd by its own Laws, & manners; nor in these affairs will they submit to the controul of any other Sovereign Power.

But in external matters, which regard the general good of the confederacy, they acknowledge & do homage to the supreme Sovereign of the U. States, in the Federal compact.

Just in this view do the American Aborigines, comprehend the rights of homage or Sovereignty.

Every Tribe which constitutes the Muscogulge Confederacy has seperate customs & many of them different Systems of Legislation. Yet they do homage to a Sovereign Power, which is represented in their grand National Council, when very important Affairs require it; & indeed they have an Emperor, or *Great Mico* acknowledged amongst them.

If we examine all the Treaties, betwixt the Indians & Europeans, from the earliest invasions of the latter, down to our own times, we shall find that the Indians, consider'd the Europeans in no other view, than as powerful, enterprising Visitants. As a mark of perfectly good breeding, they hailed them, Brothers & friends, & gave them Lands to settle on equal terms with themselves. They always consider'd the Europeans as worthy of being elected their Guardians, & Protectors & as a compliment, they call'd them Brothers, & their Kings & Governors, Fathers, elder Brothers.

Surely it is very absurd to suppose they would give all their Country away, abandon their aged Parents, & consign themselves & Posterity to slavery, for the purpose of gratifying the evil & caprice of avaricious Strangers. We might almost as easily imagine that these innocent People, would tamely suffer those Strangers to cut off their Arms & Legs, or deprive them of their Members, which are necessary for procreation. We find, as they ever have been, that they now are most tenacious of their freedom, independence & other unalienable rights of Men.

Their Systems of Government, civil & Religious Customs, are in general similar to those of other Nations. Their Form, Intelects & powers of Speech the same. Their Religion or homage to the *Great, or Sovereign Spirit*, is the same intelectual System, as acknowledged by the wisest & most virtuous nations in the old World.

Their Ideas, with respect to the duties, & conduct of Individuals, to their Superiors, coincide with those of the most perfect Government on Earth.

Are these People not worthy of our Friendship? Are they not worthy of our care? These are the abandoned Posterity, of the friends of our Progenitors; whom, some of us say, those Progenitors cut off; or drove over the *Mississippi.*

We now want Citizens to people hundreds of thousands of acres of Land already within our precincts.

Who has a stronger claim to this Country than the Indians? If priority of possession gives the best Right, surely they have it? But were we to think & act as just & grateful Men, & to suffer ourselves to consider that their Ancestors were the friends and Protectors of the infant states of Carolina & Georgia, we should soon find that they have a right, infinitely superior to any other claims.

We exclaim, "*they are Savages & will be wild Savages:* They live by hunting & War; they are idle, obstreperous, and predatory Vagabonds; & will never be subject to a civilized Government. They claim & hold more Land than would conveniently maintain a thousand times as many white People, as Indians; & *our Children will soon want room.*"

With respect to the universal objection that they will never become civilized; I must acknowledge that I am of a different opinion from my Countrymen.

I have been among them particularly the Muscoges or Cricks, & resided some time in their Towns. I then embraced every opportunity of discovering the disposition of their Minds. I found they strongly inclined to our modes of civilization.

They admire our Religion & would be pleased to have Missionaries sent, to introduce & teach it to them. They appear more sincerely religious than we ourselves, they keep strictly & I may say holy the Sabbath Day,* in all their Towns.

They wish to learn our arts of spinning, weaving, Smithing, painting, & Sculpture &c: & would like to have work houses established for teaching their Youth the useful ones. It is also my opinion that nothing would please them more, than having Schools settled in their Towns, to instruct their Children in reading, writing and arithmetick.

They want Sheep & horned Cattle & would be happy with our arts, and improvements in Agriculture. On their vast natural Plains, their Hills & Commons encircling their Towns, they could raise Sheep enough to supply Wool for the Manufactories of the United States, without clearing one acre of Woodland. Besides they have a natural Range for inumerable Stocks of horned Cattle & Horses; which would become articles of Commerce with us. Their climate is suitable to the culture of chochineal, & it is a business which would be agreeable to their dispositions.

They might & would raise Cotton enough to clothe themselves, to satisfy the demands of the United States, & to supply foreign Markets.

Their Language is beautiful, copious & easily learned. It is adapted to our Idioms, & it would be an easy matter to translate the Bible & other useful Books, & have them printed & distributed amongst them, in their own tongue.

If such a Scheme as their civilization was seriously consider'd, & attempted with sincerity & Spirit, I believe the Patrons would gain their full reward by seeing the good fruits of their labor arrive to a State of maturity.

The most considerable obstacle would probably be their civil, & political concerns in taxes & other publick requisitions necessary for the support of Government. These things, if conducted with moderation & prudence, might by mutual concessions become conciliated. But if attempted they will require perseverance & they must be a work of time.

Let us my Brethren convince the World, that the Citizens of the United States are Men in every Sense. Let us support our dignity in all things. Let our actions, in this memorable *age of our establishment, as a Nation or People*, be as a Mirror to succeeding Generations. Let us leave to our Children, a monument inscribed with Lessons of Virtue, which may remain from age to age, as approved examples for their Posterity: that they, in similar cases may say to one another; see how benevolently, how gratefully, how nobly, our forefathers acted!

WB

*Sunday they devote to the worship of the Grt Spirit, calling it the White Man's Beloved day.

27.10   Charleston . . . ——]   The *Charles-Town Packet* and the *Prince of Wales.*

28.27   Chalmer]   Lionel Chalmers (1715?–77), a physician born and educated in Scotland and a Bartram family friend, acted as John Fothergill's agent in superintending William Bartram's travels in the South, 1773–77. Chalmers was a patron of naturalists and the author of a treatise on the weather and diseases of South Carolina and numerous papers on pathology.

29.7–8   Sir J. Wright]   Sir James Wright (1716–85) became attorney general of South Carolina around 1739 and then served as agent for the colony in England; in 1760 he became lieutenant governor of Georgia and in 1761, captain-general and governor-in-chief. He fled to England in 1776 but was sent back to reorganize the Loyalist government in 1779, when Georgia was occupied by the British during the American Revolution, and remained until he was ordered to abandon the province in 1782.

29.17   B. Andrews]   Benjamin Andrew, a planter and member of the Georgia Assembly, supported the American cause during the Revolution; in 1777 he became president of the Georgia Executive Council and in 1780 was elected to the Continental Congress, but never attended. After the war he served as a judge for Liberty County, Georgia.

29.33   St. Helena]   Actually Ossabaw Island; St. Helena is further north, just southeast of Port Royal.

31.33   large ground rat]   Probably a now extinct form of pocket gopher.

32.15–16   Catesby . . . Carolina]   Mark Catesby, *The Natural History of Carolina, Florida, and the Bahama Islands* (1730?–48).

32.37   J. Stewart]   John Stuart, of Scottish birth, settled in Charleston in 1748 and was British superintendent of Indian affairs in the Southern Department of North America, 1762–79. Chalmers wrote John Bartram in early April 1773 that Stuart had agreed to take his son "in his Retinue, & recommend him to the Protection of the Several Indian Tribes," and had offered to do so at his own expense. In the letter, Chalmers described Stuart as "an Excellent Painter & Draughtsman, and in many Respects a Virtuoso—". Around June 1, 1775, Stuart fled to Florida to avoid being arrested on the false charge of inciting Indians against the colonists. Later, from his headquarters in Pensacola, he obeyed orders to enlist Indians in aiding the British cause. Stuart died in Pensacola in 1779.

33.10   Medway meeting]   The village of Midway, Georgia, was settled by Independents in 1752 and was named for England's Medway River; the church, burned by the British in 1778, rebuilt in 1792, and slightly damaged in the Civil War, is now a landmark building.

35.34–35   name was M'Intosh . . . colony]   Donald McIntosh; the Mc-
Intoshes were among the Scottish Highlanders who, at the invitation of Gov-
ernor James Oglethorpe (1696–1785), founder of Georgia, settled in 1736 at
New Inverness (later renamed Darien).

37.3   L. M'Intosh's]   Lachlan McIntosh (1727–1806) settled with his family at New Inverness in 1736; after his father's death he was assisted in his study
of mathematics and surveying by James Oglethorpe and worked for a time in
a counting house in Charleston, where he became a friend of Henry Laurens
(1724–92). After his return home he became a land surveyor and eventually
acquired large landholdings. McIntosh was made a brigadier general in 1776,
held a command in the Continental Army under General George Washington,
and later commanded Georgia and South Carolina regiments. Brevetted major
general in 1783, he was elected to the Continental Congress in 1784 but never
attended, served as a Congressional commissioner to deal with the southern
Indians, 1785–86, and was appointed Naval Officer of the Port of Savannah in
1789. His wife was Sarah Threadcraft McIntosh.

37.20   John M'Intosh]   McIntosh (1755–1826) rose to the rank of lieutenant colonel in the Revolutionary War and commanded troops under Andrew
Jackson at Mobile in the War of 1812.

47.30   Amelia and Talbert]   Actually Amelia and Cumberland islands; Talbot Island is just south of Amelia.

53.7–8   the treaty concluded]   Probably on June 3, 1773; on June 11 Governor Wright issued a proclamation inviting settlers into the new purchase and
announcing that its boundaries were being surveyed.

63.2   Hortus Siccus]   An arranged collection of dried plants (literally, "dry
garden").

67.15–16   Creek nation]   The Creek, or Muskogee, nation is believed to
have begun with confederations of the Coosa, Coweta, Kasihta, and Tukabahchee; European records of their towns in present South Carolina, Georgia,
and Alabama date from the 16th century. Groups that gradually gathered
around or under the dominant Muskogee included the Apalachicola, Chiaha,
Hitchiti, Okmulge, Osochi, Sawokli, and Yuchi, who mostly joined the Lower
Creeks (a name for the Creeks who settled on the lower Chattahoochee and
Ocmulge rivers), and the Alabama, Koasati, Muklasa, Pawokti, Tawasa, Tus-
kege, some Shawnee and, for a time, the Yamasee, who joined the Upper
Creeks (those on the Coosa and Tallapoosa rivers). Under Chief Alexander
McGillivray, the Upper Creeks were allied with the British during the Revo-
lutionary War. The nation was removed to Indian country in present
Oklahoma beginning in 1832.

67.19   Oakmulge fields]   Now Ocmulgee National Monument, opposite
Macon, Georgia.

68.4–6   establishing . . . Charleston]   Charleston was settled in 1670 on the west bank of the Ashley River as the capital of the new English colony of Carolina; the colony moved across the river to the present location of Charleston in 1680.

68.11–13   Savannas . . . Paticas]   Savannah was a name for the Shawnee who settled on the Savannah River around 1680; many moved to the Chattahoochee at the beginning of the 1715–17 Yamasee War, and later to the Tallapoosa River. By 1731, all the Shawnee had left the Carolinas. Ogeeche, or Hughchee, was a synonym for Yuchi; they moved to the Carolinas after 1661 and most moved to Georgia territory in 1716 and between 1729 and 1751. Wapoo may refer to people who lived by a creek of that name on Edisto Island. The first European record of the Santee is in the 17th century, when they were encountered living on the Santee River. They fought against the colonists in the Yamasee War of 1715–17, and most of the group were sent to the West Indies as slaves after being defeated in 1716 by Cusabos allied with the Carolina colonists; the remainder probably joined the Catawba, a Siouan group. The Yamasee groups in present South Carolina, due to exploitation by traders and fears that a census introduced in 1715 foreshadowed their enslavement, led the insurrection known as the Yamasee War. They and many who had sided with them fled to St. Augustine after the Creeks signed a peace treaty with the Carolinians in 1717, but their numbers were further reduced in raids by the Creeks and the British; the survivors were probably absorbed by the Seminoles and the Creeks. The Utina or Timucua (the name that extended to their related tribes in Florida and a part of southern Georgia) had ranged from the Savannah to the St. Johns rivers. They eventually were decimated in attacks by the Creeks, Yuchi, and British, and the survivors were probably absorbed by the Seminoles. The Icosans may be the South Carolina Coosa. The Coosa, a division of the Cusabo, were probably absorbed by the Creeks and the Catawba. Patica was the name of two Timucuan towns on the St. Johns River.

69.25–26   James Spalding]   Spalding (1734–94) emigrated from Scotland to Charleston, South Carolina, in 1760. After Florida was ceded to Britain in 1763 he began establishing trading posts there and became a member of its Colonial Council. He moved to Florida at the outbreak of the Revolutionary War but returned to St. Simon's around 1787 and helped to establish Georgia's sea-island cotton industry. He was married to Margery McIntosh.

74.13   pillo]   Pilau, a dish of rice and meat or fowl cooked together.

75.8–9   on Little St. Simon's]   Actually, Cumberland Island; Little St. Simon's is farther north.

76.10   Ogeeche mounts]   The shell mounds, much of which later were removed for road material, may have been of a Guale group; most of the Guale moved from Georgia to Florida around 1680 and apparently lost their identity as the Guale after joining the Yamasee in South Carolina in the early 18th century.

78.6   pettiaugers]   A popular corruption of piraguas, or periaguas, open, flat-bottomed, two-masted barges that were used in America and the West Indies, and also of pirogues, dugouts and open boats, sometimes with sails.

81.40   fusee]   Or fusil, a flintlock musket capable of firing either a bullet or buckshot.

85.14–15   council . . . governor of East Florida]   The council probably took place shortly after Patrick Tonyn (1725–1804; governor 1774–83) took office in March 1774. Several councils concerning the threat of war had also been held in the month before his inauguration.

85.32   Siminole nation]   Seminole is a Creek word meaning "one who has camped out from the regular towns," sometimes rendered "runaway." The nation grew up around the Oconee after they moved in 1750 from Lower Creek country in Georgia to Florida's Alachua Savanna. The first to confederate with them were mostly Hitchiti speaking groups, but by the later 18th to early 19th centuries the Seminole had become a primarily Muskogean people. The Oconee, an Atcik-Hata group who spoke a Muskogean language, lost their identity as a separate group before most of the nation was removed to present Oklahoma after the Second Seminole War, fought between 1835 and 1842.

95.33–35   Charlotia . . . Rolle]   Denys, or Dennis, or Denis, Rolle (1725–97) brought indentured settlers from London's slums to the place he named Charlotia (it was also known as Rollestown) around 1765. He later attempted to form another settlement there, but that enterprise also failed. He became a member of the House of Commons.

102.28–35   islands . . . third]   The first is Hog, the second, on the east, is Drayton Island; the third, which may have been Rope's Island, is referred to as Isle of Palms on page 142.33 in this volume.

112.37   little promontory]   A shell mound on "East Lake" (later called Lake Dexter), referred to as Bartram's Mound on the map, pages 608–9 in this volume. Most of it was removed for road material, as were many other mounds of this type noted by Bartram.

124.9–10   the long s]   A form of the letter s, now archaic, that was used in early editions of the *Travels*. It appeared so: $\int$.

127.26–35   It is . . . Ipomea.]   One of the many sections drawn on by François René de Chateaubriand in his American writings.

129.6–17   bluff . . . burying ground]   At what became St. Francis, midway between Lake Dexter and Beresford; the Yamasee burial places evidently were later obliterated by cultivation of the area, and the mound was used for road-building material around 1940.

133.22–23   colony . . . Turnbull]   Andrew Turnbull (1718?–92), a Scottish physician, in 1768 settled about 1,200 indentured persons from Minorca and about 300 from Italy and Greece at the site he named New Smyrna. The settlers raised and processed indigo for export and built canals and roads. Most of the surviving colonists moved to St. Augustine after Governor Tonyn in 1776 granted them the right to leave the settlement.

133.32   the surveyor]   Royal surveyor and cartographer William Gerard De Brahm.

133.39–40   spacious Indian mount]   Now known as Turtle Mound, it rises about 50 feet above Coronado Beach; the mound appeared on European maps as early as 1564.

136.38–39   *Tantalus albus . . . Tantalus versicolor]   Catesby, *Natural History of Carolina, Florida, and the Bahamas* (1732), I, 82, pl. 82, and 83, pl. 83.

137.8–10   Catesby . . . wood pelican*]   Catesby, *Natural History of Carolina . . . ,* I, 81, pl. 81.

150.3–4   inchanting . . . crystal fountain]   The description of presently-named Salt Springs, as well as other passages in the *Travels,* were an influence on Samuel Coleridge's "Kubla Khan: Or, a Vision in a Dream" (1816; written 1795). Coleridge copied parts of the *Travels* in his notebook and drew on the work for other poems, including *The Rime of the Ancient Mariner* (1798) and "Christabel" (1816).

153.13   old trader]   Probably Job Wiggens.

175.22   powerful tribe]   Probably the Potano, one of the most powerful Timucuan groups, who were encountered by DeSoto in 1539. They were driven from their town by the Spanish in 1584, allowed to return around 1601, and apparently participated in an uprising in 1656; the last record of the group is sometime after 1680.

185.23–36   as blithe . . . set.]   Chateaubriand used this description of the Seminole in the chapter "The Hunters" in *Atala* (1801).

204.4–5   Alligator-Hole . . . water]   Alligator-Hole is the present Blue Sink; Coleridge drew on this description for "Kubla Khan."

206.10–11   Sloan . . . tom. I]   Sir Hans Sloane, *Voyage to the Islands Barbados, Madeira, Nieves, St. Christophers and Jamaica, with the natural history of the herbs and trees, four-footed beasts, fishes, birds, insects, reptiles &c.,* (2 volumes, 1707, 1725), vol. 1. Sloane (1660–1753) was a British naturalist and physician, a president of the Royal Society, and correspondent of John Bartram.

214.34   Dr. Stork]   English physician William Stork, a member of the Royal Society, promoter of British immigration to Florida, and author of *An account of East-Florida, with a journal kept by John Bartram . . . upon a journey from St. Augustine up the river St. John's as far as the lakes* (3 editions,

1766–74; the later editions are titled *A description of East Florida . . .*). He had been in Florida as an agent for land grantees.

227.10–11   governor Grant] James Grant (1720–1806), born in Scotland, a career soldier and governor of Florida, 1760–71, promoted John Bartram's exploration of the St. Johns River. During the Revolutionary War he commanded British troops at Long Island, Brandywine, and Germantown; he gained the rank of major general in 1777 and general in 1796.

229.1–25   ground rattle snake . . . snake] The description of the upturned nose and swelling and flattening fit the young hognose snake; cf. the descriptions of the ground rattlesnake, page 510.7–13, and of hognose snakes ("Viper"), page 510.29–32, in this volume.

230.34–233.14   The largest . . . water frogs do] This is the most detailed account of frogs and toads in America published before 1800.

233.35   G. Edwards's . . . Hist.] British naturalist George Edwards (1693–1773), to whom Bartram had sent drawings and preserved and dried small birds, *Gleanings of Natural History* (3 vols., 1758–64), Vol. II (1760).

236.7–251.27   migration of birds . . . (sturnus).] The observations on bird migration are the first extensive American explanation of the phenomenon; these and the listings and observations of birds, here and elsewhere in the *Travels*, were the most detailed by an American ornithologist up to that time. Although Bartram was the first to provide binomial names for many bird species, his names were not accepted in ornithological nomenclature.

256.3   1776] Actually in 1775.

260.1–261.4   Silver Bluff . . . silver.] George Galphin (c. 1709–80), a native of Ireland, established his trading post in 1734 on a tract of land still called Silver Bluff, about 13 miles south of Augusta, Georgia. Based on Indian lore related by Galphin and on the chronicles of Juan Pardo, the bluff is the traditional site of Cofitachequi, capital of the province once known as Yupaha or Ybaha (a Timucuan name for the Muskogee), famous from the early chronicles of Hernando DeSoto and later romances and histories (the actual site has not been verified). The chronicles relate that in May 1540 DeSoto's army was welcomed in the town and left with more than 200 pounds of pearls from a temple, purportedly granted them by one who became known as "the Lady of Cofitachequi," either the chieftainess or her niece; they also took the woman herself (she soon escaped, taking with her a basket of the pearls). The Cofitachequi are believed to have been the Kasihta or the Coweta. Galphin, an American patriot during the Revolution, was instrumental in persuading Lower Creeks not to fight against the Americans and is believed to have donated a large amount of money to equip a fleet under John Paul Jones. He became assistant superintendent of Indian affairs.

261.9   fort Moore] The area of Fort Moore, which was three miles southeast of Augusta, was visited by Catesby in the 1720s and in 1763 by John Bartram, who was the first to scientifically describe the oyster fossils there.

262.39–40   seat of government . . . Augusta]   Savannah was the capital of Georgia 1754–86, and Augusta, 1786–95; after that the capital was Louisville, 1796–1805, Milledgeville, 1805–68, and then Atlanta, which became the temporary capital in 1868 and the permanent capital in 1877.

263.22   Bahama . . . white rock]   Limestone.

265.31   bones . . . buffaloe, elk]   This account established the record for these species in Lincoln County, Georgia, which was apparently the southernmost range of the elk in the eastern United States.

266.9–20   fiery . . . fire.]   Wordsworth used this passage in his poem "Ruth."

267.8–10   town . . . earl of Dartmouth]   William Legge (1731–1801), 2d earl of Dartmouth, for whom Dartmouth College (incorporated 1769) was named, was president of the British board of trade and foreign plantations, 1765–66, and colonial secretary, 1772–75. In 1776, as lord privy seal (1775–82), he advocated using force against the American colonies; the town that was supposed to be named for him was instead called Petersburg. Its site is now under the reservoir created by the construction of the Clark Hill Dam on the Savannah River between 1946 and 1954.

267.26–30   Indian monuments . . . great mount]   The mounds have been dated to circa 1300–1450. The smaller mounds, at what became known as the Rembert archeological site in Elbert County, Georgia, were excavated in the mid-19th century, and the great mound was destroyed by a flood in 1908. A reservoir now covers the site.

269.4   Mr. Cameron's]   Alexander Cameron in 1764 was appointed by John Stuart commissary, and soon after deputy superintendent, of Indian affairs for the Cherokee. A Loyalist, Cameron unsuccessfully attempted to dissuade the Cherokee from attacking American frontier settlements in the spring of 1776, but later fought with them against the Americans. In October 1776, after their demand to turn over Cameron and the warrior Dragging Canoe was refused, and again in December 1780, revolutionary Virginia forces burned Cherokee Overhill towns. After Stuart's death Cameron was placed in control of Indian affairs for the western area of the Southern Department of North America, 1779–81.

271.18–20   late Indian war . . . Middleton]   The Cherokee were at war with the British from November 1759 to September 1761. The South Carolina provincial regiment commanded by Colonel Thomas Middleton (1719–66) included among its numbers Isaac Huger, Francis Marion, and William Moultrie, all of whom became American officers in the Revolutionary War. Colonel James Grant commanded the British regulars. The battle of the Vale of Cowee occurred in June 1761.

271.27–28   fort . . . Keowe]   The former fort on the Keowee River was used in campaigns against the Cherokee, whose town of Keowee was destroyed in 1760.

274.11   one hundred yards]   Bartram frequently wrote "yards" when actually referring to the number of feet.

275.24–26   Robinia . . . Carol.]   Mark Catesby, *The Natural History of Carolina, Florida, and the Bahama Islands* (1748), II, appendix: 20, pl. 20.

277.31   a gap . . . lofty ascents]   Rocky Gap in the Chattooga Ridge, northwest South Carolina.

283.1   Overhill towns]   Cherokee settlements in parts of Tennessee, Georgia, and extreme southwestern North Carolina; see also page 304 in this volume.

289.33–34   Fields . . . Tempe]   Sites famous in ancient histories and stories of Thessaly in ancient Greece. Pharasalia was a district around the city of Pharsalus near the Enipeus river; the Vale of Tempe, between mounts Olympus and Ossa, is traversed by the river Pinios (anciently, Peneus).

291.14–24   companies . . . fruit.]   William Wordsworth used this passage in his poem "Ruth."

294.13–16   to Nebuchadnezzar's . . . forests.]   Cf. Daniel 4:33.

297.14–15   Little Carpenter]   Attakullakulla (c. 1700–c. 1780), who lived in the Overhill town Chote, had been among a delegation of Cherokee leaders whom Sir Alexander Cuming took to England in 1730. As a sub-chief he had rescued John Stuart when Fort Loudon was taken by forces under Chief Oconostota in the Cherokee War of 1760–61, he helped to negotiate peace with the British, and he was instrumental in Cherokee acceptance of Stuart as superintendent of Indian affairs. In May 1776 Attakullakulla was one of the older Cherokee leaders who opposed a plan by a delegation of Shawnee, Mohawks, and Delawares to attack frontier settlements, but by July 1776 most of the Cherokee nation was at war with the Americans; one of the leading warriors was Attakullakulla's son Dragging Canoe. For Stuart's flight from Charleston, see note 32.37.

298.24   I turned . . . return]   Bartram had apparently reached the valley of Junaluska Creek near present Andrews in Cherokee County, North Carolina.

303.12   towns . . . Cherokee nation]   After suffering a series of defeats during and after the American Revolution, the Cherokee were forced to cede large portions of their country. In the 19th century they developed a settled agricultural economy, adopted a written language and, in 1827, framed a written constitution and declared themselves a sovereign nation. Cherokee sovereignty was opposed by President Andrew Jackson, and in 1835, as part of a general policy of removing Indians from the southeast, the U.S. government coerced representatives of a minority of the Cherokee nation into signing the treaty of New Echota. Under the treaty, the Cherokee ceded their land east of the Mississippi in return for $5 million and seven million acres of wilderness land west of the Mississippi. In 1838–39 the U.S. army forcibly removed 18,000 Cherokee from the eastern United States; more than 4,000 men, women, and children died in army stockades or along the westward "Trail of Tears" during the removal.

308.26–309.21   Ocone . . . broke up.]   This paragraph outlines almost all the known Oconee history from about 1695; see also note 85.32.

309.6–7   Tomocos . . . Yamases]   The Tomoco were probably the Timucua. The Calusa was a large tribe or confederation on the west coast of Florida south of Tampa Bay and in the Florida Keys, whose numbers were much reduced by the mid-18th century; some are believed to have migrated to Cuba and the rest were absorbed by the Seminoles. For the Yamasee and the Utina see note 68.11–13.

313.34   Chata Uche]   Or Chattahoochee, Muskogee for "marked (or sculptured) rocks."

317.7   Their . . . language]   The Uchian language is distinctive (Yuchi, or Uchi, may be drawn from the Hitchiti word "ochesee," meaning "people of another language"); the Savannah, or Shawnee, spoke an Algonquian language. The Yuchi who eventually moved to present Oklahoma to live among the Creeks retained their own language.

317.32   Micos]   See pages 537.9–538.17 and footnote in this volume.

328.24   fort Condé]   Built by the French when they settled Mobile in 1711 and named Fort Charlotte when the area was ceded to Britain in 1763.

329.2   McGillivray]   Lachlan McGillivray (1719–1809?), was born in Scotland and immigrated in 1735 to America, where he quickly founded a successful trading company. A Loyalist during the American Revolution, he returned to Scotland when the British army evacuated Savannah in 1782, leaving his Creek wife, two daughters, and his son, Alexander McGillivray, behind. His son later became a prominent Creek leader.

329.16   1778]   Actually 1775.

329.24–25   Major Farmer]   Robert Farmar, with two British regiments, had captured Mobile in 1763, then was placed in charge of the city for several years.

329.28–29   Taensa . . . ancient town]   The Taensa moved from present Louisiana to present Alabama in 1715 and lived first in the area of Mobile on land that was given them by the French (the Tawasa had lived there from 1707 until early in 1715), then in a new town, called Tensaw, across the river; they returned to Louisiana around 1763. They no longer exist as a group.

331.38   Ft. Thoulouse]   The French established Fort Toulouse, which they referred to as Aux Alibamons, around 1717 when the British had lost influence in the area following the Yamasee War; the fort was taken by the British in 1763.

332.39   perhaps . . . Mobile]   Fort Louis de la Mobile (named for Louis XIV and the Mobile Indians) was 27 miles up the Mobile River at present Twenty-Seven-Mile Bluff. It was built when the French settled there in 1702 and abandoned when they moved downriver to establish Mobile in 1711.

333.33   Tart. Emet.]   Tartar-emetic was the common name in pharmacology for potassio-antimonious tartrate, a poisonous substance that was used medicinally to induce vomiting.

335.16–26   honey bees . . . continent.]   Honey bees are not native to America.

336.5–7   Pensacola . . . government]   Florida became a British colony, and Pensacola the capital of West Florida, in 1763; the city surrendered to the Spanish in 1781 and Florida was ceded back to Spain in 1783.

336.10   Dr. Lorimer]   John Lorimer, an early member of the American Philosophical Society, became a member of the Florida Assembly in 1766 and in 1770, deputy auditor general.

336.12–13   governor Chester]   Peter Chester, governor of West Florida 1770–81.

336.18   Mr. Livingston]   Philip Livingston Jr., provincial secretary of West Florida in Chester's administration.

343.31–32   Taensapaoa . . . Indians]   The Tangipahoa probably left the area on the Tangipahoa River around the end of the 17th century. They were related to the Acolapissa (later known as the Houma) and eventually may have merged with them while living near the Mississippi River.

347.9   one of these gentlemen]   William Dunbar (1749–1810) emigrated from Scotland in 1771 and established his plantation in West Florida near present Baton Rouge in 1773; it was plundered by a small group of Continental soldiers in 1778, and in 1792 he established another plantation in Natchez, Mississippi. After Dunbar made the first meteorological study of Mississippi in 1799, Thomas Jefferson initiated a correspondence with him and later appointed him to explore the region of the Ouachita River and to direct an expedition to the Red River country. Dunbar was elected to the American Philosophical Society and was known for his writings on plants, animals, astronomy, and other scientific subjects.

347.17   Alabama nation]   A portion of the Alabama, legendarily one of the original Southeastern tribes, moved to the banks of the Mississippi River in present Louisiana after French-held territory was ceded to Britain in 1763; most later moved to Texas, while other Alabamas joined the Seminole in

Florida. Those who remained in their own country were removed to present Oklahoma in 1836.

347.32 Sloan, Jam.] See note 206.10–11.

348.18–20 Brown's . . . Bahama Islands] Montfort Browne was governor of West Florida, 1767–69, and of the Bahamas 1774–76 and 1778–79.

348.28 August 27, 1777] Actually October 27, 1775.

350.21–23 Cliffs . . . fortress] The French post and settlement at Fort Rosalie was established in 1716 on the bluffs of present Natchez, Mississippi. The Natchez first rebelled in 1720 and were defeated in 1723. They rose again in what became known as "the great Natchez conspiracy" and on November 28, 1729, destroyed the post and settlement, killing about 200 people and taking about as many hostage. The following January French troops, aided by the Choctaw, attacked the Natchez and rescued many of the prisoners. The surviving Natchez escaped across the Mississippi to present Sicily Island, where they again were besieged by the French. About 400 were captured and sold into slavery in the West Indies; those who escaped eventually joined the Chickasaw, who had been aiding them, and later some joined the Cherokee and the Creek.

353.1 1777] Here, as at 355.2, actually 1775.

355.9 Mr. Tap——y] John Adam Tapley.

359.26 Mucclasse] Or Muklasa, a town believed to have been of a group affiliated with either the Alabama or the Koasati. The Muklasa (an Alabama and Choctaw word for "friends" or "people of one nation") were first recorded on the Tallapoosa in 1675 and last recorded as being in the area in 1799; they are said to have moved from the region to Florida around 1814.

360.21 Tuckabatche] Or Tukabahchee, the chief war town of the Upper Creeks; the Tukabahchee were one of the leading tribes of the Creek Nation.

366.29 Ottasses] The Atasi, one of the leading tribes of the Creek nation. Bartram's descriptions here are often referred to in discussions of the Creek.

368.2 January 2d, 1788] Actually in 1776.

370.2 doctor Wells] Humphrey Wells, a surgeon, probably moved to Georgia from Maryland in 1775.

373.22–24 Duprat . . . South-West] Antoine Le Page du Pratz, *Histoire de la Louisiane* (1758; translated in 1763 as *History of Louisiana, or of the Western Parts of Virginia and Carolina*).

374.3 Natches] The Natchez were distantly related to the Muskogee and spoke a distinctive language.

377.5–6 Jonathan Bryan] Bryan (1708–88) moved to Georgia from South Carolina in 1752 and served as a judge of the General Court and a royal counselor of the colony. A patriot during the Revolution, he was a member of the Committee of Safety, the Georgia state constitutional convention, 1776–77, and state congress. He was taken prisoner by the British and sent to New York, but continued to work for the American cause after his release in a prisoner exchange.

377.22   wild pigeons]   This account is one of the chief records of the now-extinct passenger pigeon (*Ectopistes migratorius*) in Georgia.

380.1   This . . . plant]   John Bartram sent a dried specimen of the Venus's-flytrap to England and John Ellis, an amateur English botanist, brought it to the attention of Linnaeus; both recognized the sensitivity of its leaves but Linnaeus did not hold that it trapped insects. See also the following note.

380.14   Arthur Dobbs]   Dobbs (1689–1765), of Irish birth, was colonial governor of North Carolina from 1754 until his death. In 1741 he persuaded the British admiralty to send an expedition in search of the Northwest Passage and was the author of *An Account of the Countries adjoining Hudson's Bay* (1744). He was a correspondent of John Bartram's concerning horticulture and other subjects. Dobbs is believed to have been the first to note the Venus's-flytrap, in a letter to Peter Collinson dated April 2, 1759, where he called it "a kind of Catch *Fly sensitive which closes upon anything that touches it*," and in another account of it in 1760, where he called it "Fly Trap Sensitive," but his reporting of the plant was not discovered until around 1835.

380.31–32   Colonel William Bartram.]   Bartram (1704–70), the half brother of John Bartram, had lived in Ashwood from about 1726 and was a militia colonel and representative in the North Carolina Assembly. His wife, Sarah, had died in 1772, and his son, William, a physician, died in 1771, but his daughter Sarah Brown (d. 1779) was living in the area, as probably was another daughter, Mary Robeson.

382.32–34   Olea Americana . . . Catesby]   Mark Catesby, *The Natural History of Carolina, Florida, and the Bahama Islands* (1731), I, 61, pl. 61.

385.32   January 1778]   Actually in 1777.

397.38   very aged man]   Perhaps the man known as the "Wolf King" who in a letter from Mucclasse dated April 29, 1766, that was written and signed by interpreter James Germany, proposed to Governor James Wright and John Stuart a cessation of trade to bring under control Indians who had opposed the treaty of Augusta.

TRAVELS IN GEORGIA AND FLORIDA, 1773–74:
A REPORT TO DR. JOHN FOTHERGILL

429.4   March 20th 1774]   Actually in 1773.

429.31   an Island]   Probably Morris Island in Charleston Harbor.

429.33   Family]   Probably the family of Thomas Lamboll (1694–1774), friends of Bartram and his father; Thomas Lamboll had been a long-time correspondent of English naturalist and merchant Peter Collinson (1694–1768).

429.35   Do^r. Chalmers]   See note 28.27.

430.6–7   John Stewart]   See note 32.37.

430.22   James Wright]   See note 29.7–8.

430.32–33   Midway Meeting house]   See note 33.10.

430.36   Count^{ss}. of Huntington]   Selina Shirley Hastings (1701–79), the countess of Huntingdon, was a philanthropist of religious and charitable organizations and a friend of the Wesleys and of George Whitefield; she donated funds to help Whitefield found his Bethesda orphanage, near Savannah.

431.40   B. Andrews]   See note 29.17.

432.24   L. M^{c}antosh]   See note 37.3.

433.10   H. Lawrence]   Henry Laurens (1724–92) had met Bartram and his father in 1765. He was a merchant trading primarily in rice and slaves until becoming a planter in 1764. He was a member of the South Carolina Assembly, 1757–63 and 1766–74, and its Council of Safety in 1775, a member of the Continental Congress, 1777–79, and its president November 1777 to December 1778. In 1780 he was captured by the British while sailing to Europe to negotiate a treaty with the Dutch and was held on suspicion of treason for about 14 months in the Tower of London, then exchanged for General Cornwallis. With Benjamin Franklin and John Jay he signed the preliminary Treaty of Paris in November 1782.

433.26   Purple . . . Catesby]   See note 382.32–34.

433.28   J. McAntosh]   See note 37.20.

434.2–17   Ebenezar . . . Church]   The former colony was settled by Lutheran Salzburgers in 1734 and its Jerusalem Church was rebuilt 1767–69.

437.27–28   Silver Bluff . . . Golphins]   See note 260.1–261.4.

438.25   Superintendant]   John Stuart (see note 32.37).

452.31   N^o]   Probably refers to a plant shipped to Fothergill.

456.2   J. Spalding]   See note 69.26.

456.9–10   Fredrica . . . Ann. . . .]   Fort Frederica was built when the colony was settled in "anno Domini" 1736. Bartram probably intended to enter the date later.

459.27   Musqueto Shore]   Mosquito, or Miskito, Coast, a region along the coast of East Nicaragua that was named for the Miskito Indians; from 1655–1850 it was a protectorate of the British.

459.31–32   Villa Role . . . D. Role]   See note 95.33–35.

460.11   Governer in Augustine]   Patrick Tonyn; see note 85.14–15.

460.18   interpretor]   Probably the trader Job Wiggens.

463.35   Allatchua Savanah.]   In the report a marginal note here, "Tab. IX," refers to a drawing of the Alachua Savanna; the drawing is reproduced on plate 2 in this volume.

469.23   Moultry]   John Moultrie, a physician, became lieutenant governor of Florida in 1763 and moved to the Bahamas after England ceded Florida back to Spain in 1783.

469.27   Governor Tonyn]   See note 85.14–15.

470.8   Cowetas]   A Muskogee group, one of the early members of the Creek nation.

470.14   Magee & his People]   See Bartram's footnote on page 203 in this volume.

472.13   bob . . . large trout]   See page 107.1–8 in this volume; for smaller trout, the bait was a bunch of worms, fowl gut, or colored rags.

473.19   Fusee]   See note 81.40.

476.34–35   Catsby's Wood-Pelican]   See note 137.6–8.

478.38   amazeing large spring]   Blue Spring, the southernmost point reached by Bartram on this journey; he had traveled farther south with his father in 1766.

480.13   M'Latchy]   Charles McLatchie, agent of Spalding's Lower Trading Store.

487.27   Talahasochte]   Muskogee for "White King's Town."

490.2   Fountain or Spring]   Manatee Spring, about seven miles west of present Chiefland, Florida.

492.19   hywah]   Wife.

496.36–37   Alegator Hole]   Present Blue Sink; see also page 204.4–5 and note.

498.31   Creek . . . Spring]   Present Salt Springs Run and Salt Springs; see also page 150.3–4 and note.

500.6–11   bluff . . . buring ground]   See note 129.6–17.

500.14   Yamises]   For the Yamasee, see note 68.11–13.

504.20   * * *]   Asterisks indicate a missing page in the manuscript of the report.

504.35–38   Whooping Crain . . . Edwards.]   George Edwards, *A Natural History of Birds* (1750), III, plates 38—"Hooping-Crane" (Bartram's "Stork") and 39—"Brown and Ash-colour'd Crane."

508.7   Tab. VII. & VIII.]   See plate 19 this volume.

512.1   N° 14. Tab. V, Fig. 3.]   See plate 20 in this volume.

514.3   Tab. X]   See plate 31 in this volume.

516.16   green frogs]   In the report, a marginal note here refers to the drawing that is reproduced on plate 20 in this volume.

517.21–25   *Petras . . .* Cornu amomis.]   Most of the Latinate names of the stones, minerals, and fossils are from Linnaeus' *Systema naturae*, vols. 2 (1767) and 3 (1768).

521.26   Cherokees]   The name is probably from the Muskogee "chilo-kee," meaning "people of another speech."

521.28–29   Savanahs or Yamasees]   See note 68.11–13.

522.26   Calosulges]   The Calusa; see note 309.6–7.

MISCELLANEOUS WRITINGS

527.1–2   *Observations . . . Indians*]   Bartram wrote this piece in response to the queries of Philadelphia physician and naturalist Benjamin Smith Barton (1766–1815). With the manuscript was the following letter:

> Thus you have,
>   Sir,
>   My observations and conjectures on these matters, with all the truth and accuracy that my slender abilities will admit of, and without reserve. If they should not answer your wishes and expectations, I desire you will ascribe it to my misapprehension of the queries, or lack of knowledge, etc., etc.
> I doubt not but you will readily excuse bad writing, composition and spelling. My weakness of sight, I hope, will plead for me, when I assure you I have been obliged to write the greater part of this with my eyes shut, and that with pain.
> I do not mention this to claim any sort of obligation from you, Sir, for all that I knew concerning these matters are due to you and to science.
>   I remain, Sir,
> With every sentiment of respect
>   and esteem, your
>   obliged friend,
>   WM. BARTRAM.
> PHILADELPHIA, Dec. 15, 1789.

528.21   Spaniards, at St. Augustine]   St. Augustine was settled by the Spanish in 1565 and burned by the English in 1586. Construction of its immense fort, San Marcos, was begun in 1672, following the founding of Charleston (see note 68.4–6). St. Augustine was ceded to the English in 1763 and retroceded to Spain in 1783.

528.25–26   founding . . . Charleston]   See note 68.4–6.

530.18   as related . . . Du Pratz]   See note 373.22–24.

530.24–25   largest of these . . . Dartmouth]   See page 267.8–30 and notes.

534.16   M'Gillivray's]   See note 329.2.

534.23   Fort Chartens]   Fort Chartres was established by the French in 1718–20 on the east bank of the Mississippi, about 12 miles north of present Kaskaskia, Illinois. It was called Fort Cavendish, 1765–72, when the territory was controlled by the British.

536.7   spirit . . . Montesquieu]   In the preface to *Spirit of the Laws* (1748), Montesquieu wrote: "I have not drawn my principles from my prejudices, but from the nature of things."

536.26–27   Seminoles . . . *Occones*]   For the Seminoles and the Oconee, see note 85.32, for the Yuchi, 68.11–13, and for the Alabama, 347.17.

538.31   king of *Calos*]   The head chief of the main Calusa town, located on Mound Key in Estero Bay, controlled more than 50 villages from Lake Okeechobee southward; the town was first visited by Spaniards in the mid-16th century.

539.5   McLatche]   See note 480.13.

542.16   *Savannahs*]   See note 68.11–13.

545.22   Georgia . . . Oglethorpe)]   Georgia, the last of the 13 colonies to be founded, was chartered by James Oglethorpe (1696–1785) in 1732; Savannah, its first settlement, was founded in 1733. The colony was intended to help defend the Carolinas against Spanish Florida and to serve as a refuge for impoverished persons who had been released from debtors' prison in England. Under the terms of the original charter, control of the colony reverted to the British crown in 1753. During the Revolutionary War the British held Savannah, 1778–82.

545.25   Rev. Dr. Bozemoth]   The Reverend Thomas Bosomworth. Mary Bosomworth (earlier Mary Musgrove and Mary Mathews) was the niece of Emperor Brims, an important chief of the Lower Creeks. She acted as an interpreter to James Oglethorpe.

548.29–30   *Uches* . . . Alabamas]   The Savannah and Alabama spoke Algonquian dialects; for the Yuchi, see note 317.7.

554.17   *lixivium*]   Water impregnated with a substance such as alkaline salts which have been extracted by lixivation (i.e., the process of separating soluble from insoluble substances by percolation).

560.11   Ottasse]   See note 366.29.

568.19   WALTER] Thomas Walter (1740–88), *Flora Caroliniana, Secundum Systema Vegetabilium Perillustris Linnae: Digesta* (1788).

569.11   Linn. *Spec. plant.*] Carolus Linnaeus, *Species Plantarum* (1753–62; supplement, 1780).

569.12   Pluckn. *alm.*] Leonard Plukenet (1642–1706), *Almagestum Botanicum sive. Phytographiae Plukenetianae Onomnasticon Methodo Synthetica digestum . . .* (1696).

569.14   Clayt.] John Clayton (c. 1685–1773), of English birth, was a Virginia physician, author of histories of Virginia, and botanist who collected plants and seeds and created a botanical garden; the results of his work are compiled in Johann Frederick Gronovius' *Flora Virginica* (1739–43; revised edition, 1762).

570.3   BULL-GRAPE] In the published article, a note by James Mease reads: "Bartram lately informed me that the word bull is an abbreviation of bullet; the grapes being so called from their approaching nearly the size of a bullet. . . ."

571.21   Col. Bland] Theodorick Bland (1742–90), a Virginia physician until he retired to become a planter in 1771, was a Revolutionary soldier, delegate to the Continental Congress, 1780–83, and a member of Congress, 1789–90; he voted against the federal Constitution in the Virginia ratifying convention of 1788.

577.3   RICHARD . . . subject] Actually, John Bartram's paternal grandfather was also named John (Richard Bartram was his paternal great-grandfather).

577.9, 12   John] Actually, William.

579.4–5   friends . . . Collinson] Joseph Breintnall (d. 1746), a Quaker, Philadelphia merchant, friend of John Bartram, and correspondent of Peter Collinson; his avocation was making leaf impressions and John Bartram helped him collect and identify specimens. Peter Collinson (1694–1768), a London merchant, avid gardener, and patron of botony who studied plants and insects and contributed to scientific journals, had been seeking someone in North America who would send him plant specimens on a regular basis; he began corresponding with Bartram in 1733.

579.13–14   celebrated literary characters] Among John Bartram's British and European correspondents were naturalists Carl von Linné, Mark Catesby, Johann F. Grenovius, Sir Hans Sloane, Thomas François Dalibard, Johann Jakob Dillenius, George Edwards, and John Fothergill.

579.14–15   Royal . . . Stockholm] See note 13.15–16.

581.25   "Do Justice . . . God."] Cf. Micah 6:8.

584.4   your] Bartram had addressed his remarks to the editor of the journal, Benjamin Smith Barton (see note 527.1–2).

584.5–6   Dr. Gregg's . . . *Pennsylvania*] Amos Gregg (d. 1808), *Philadelphia Medical and Physical Journal* (1805, I:15–22).

585.25–26   *Willdenow . . . Caroliniensis*] Carolus Ludovicus Willdenow,
Carolia Linné, Species Plantarum (1798–1812), a new edition of *Species Plantarum* with listings, according to the Linnaean system, of species discovered
after the original publication, and William Aiton, *Hortus Kewensis; or a catalogue of plants cultivated in the Royal Botanic Garden at Kew* (1789). For
Walter, see note 568.19.

586.16   Doctor Clayton]   See note 569.14.

591.36–37   paper . . . society]   Bartram had read the paper to a meeting
of the Philadelphia Society for Promoting Agriculture on July 14, 1789.

Glossary

An asterisk indicates a botanical or zoological name originated by Bartram. The appearance of Bartram's name after a scientific binomial indicates that he is credited with providing the first taxonomic description of a species.

Abies] *Tsuga Canadensis*, Canada hemlock.

Acer glaucum] Probably *Acer rubrum*, red maple.

Acer negundo] Ash-leaved maple.

Acer rubrum] Red maple.

Acer saccharinum] *Acer saccharum*, sugar maple.

Acer striatum] Probably *Acer spicatum*, mountain maple.

Aconitum napellus] Probably *Aconitum uncinatum*, clambering monkshood.

Actaea] Probably *Actaea pachypoda*, white baneberry.

Adansonia digitata] Baobab tree.

Ado] *Colocasia antiquorum*, taro, or a related species.

Aesculus] Buckeye.

Aesculus *alba] *Aesculus parviflora*, white buckeye.

Aesculus *arborea] Perhaps *Aesculus sylvatica* Bartram, Carolina buckeye.

Aesculus *Florida] Perhaps *Aesculus sylvatica* Bartram, Carolina buckeye.

Aesculus pavia] Red buckeye; in some cases, possibly *Aesculus sylvatica* Bartram, Carolina buckeye.

Aesculus *sylvatica] Carolina buckeye.

Aesculus *Virginica] Probably *Aesculus pavia*, red buckeye.

Agave virginica] Rattlesnake-master.

Agave vivipara] *Agave neglecta*, wild century-plant.

Alauda campestris] *Eremophila alpestris*, Northern Horned Lark.

Alauda magna] *Sturnella magna*, Eastern Meadowlark.

Alauda maxima] *Sturnella magna*, Eastern Meadowlark.

Alauda migratoria] *Anthus spinoletta*, Water Pipit.

Alcea florida] *Gordonia lasianthus*, loblolly-bay.

639

Alcedo alcyon]　*Megaceryle alcyon*, Eastern Belted Kingfisher.

Aletris]　Star-grass.

Alligator]　*Alligator mississipiensis*, American alligator.

Almond tree]　*Prunus communis*.

Alnus]　*Alnus rugosa*, green alder.

Amaryllis atamasco]　*Zephyranthes atamasco*, atamasco lily.

Amorpha]　Lead plant.

Ampelis garrulus]　*Bombycilla cedrorum*, Cedar Waxwing.

Amygdalus communis]　*Prunus communis*, almond tree.

Amygdalus Persica]　*Prunus persica*, peach tree.

Anas bucephala]　Probably *Bucephala albeola*, Bufflehead.

Anas caudata]　*Anas acuta*, Pintail Duck.

Anas discors]　Blue-winged Teal.

Anas fera torquata major]　*Anas platyrhynchos*, Common Mallard.

Anas leucocephala]　Perhaps the female *Aythya marila*, Greater Scaup, or the female *Aythya affinis*, Lesser Scaup.

Anas *migratoria]　*Anas crecca*, Green-winged Teal.

Anas minor picta]　Male *Bucephala albeola*, Bufflehead.

Anas nigra maxima]　Probably *Melanitta perspicillata*, Surf Scoter.

Anas *principalis]　Male *Histrionicus histrionicus*, Harlequin Duck.

Anas rustica]　Female *Bucephala albeola*, Bufflehead.

Anas sponsa]　*Aix sponsa*, Wood Duck.

Anas *subcerulea]　Composite of *Aythya marila*, Greater Scaup, and *Aythya affinis*, Lesser Scaup.

Andromeda arborea]　*Oxydendrum arboreum*, sour-wood.

Andromeda axillaris]　Presumably *Leucothoe axillaris*, fetter-bush.

Andromeda calyculata]　Undetermined.

Andromeda ferruginea]　*Lyonia ferruginea* or *Lyonia fruticosa*, stagger-bush.

Andromeda *formosissima]　*Leucothoe acuminata*, pipewood.

Andromeda lucida]　Possibly *Lyonia lucida*, hoorah bush.

Andromeda nitida]　*Lyonia lucida*, hoorah bush.

Andromeda *pulverulenta] *Zenobia pulverulenta.*

Andromeda *viridis] Undetermined.

Anemone hepatica] *Hepatica americana,* hepatica.

Anemone thalictroides] *Anemonella thalictroides,* rue anemone.

Angelica lucida] *Lingusticum canadense.*

Annona *alba] Undetermined species of genus *Asimina,* pawpaw.

Annona glabra] Probably *Asimina triloba,* Northern pawpaw.

Annona *grandiflora] *Asimina incana* Bartram, showy pawpaw.

Annona *incana] *Asimina incana* Bartram, showy pawpaw.

Annona *pigmea] *Asimina pigmea* Bartram, dwarf pawpaw.

Annona pygmea] Presumably *Asimina pigmea* Bartram, dwarf pawpaw.

Annona triloba] *Asimina triloba,* northern pawpaw.

Anser aliis ceruliis] *Chen caerulescens,* Snow Goose.

Anser branta] *Chen caerulescens,* Snow Goose.

Anser branta grisea maculata] Probably *Chen caerulescens,* Snow Goose.

Anser Canadensis] *Branta canadensis,* Canada Goose.

Anser fuscus maculatus] *Anser albifrons,* White-fronted Goose.

Anthemis nobilis] Chamomile.

Apios americana] Groundnut.

Apple tree] *Pyrus malus.*

Apricot] *Prunus armeniaca.*

Aralia spinosa] Prickly ash.

Araneus *saliens] A species of jumping spider, family *Salticidae.*

Ardea alba] *Casmerodius albus,* Great Egret.

Ardea alba minor] Either an immature *Egretta caerulea,* Little Blue Heron, or *Egretta thula,* Snowy Egret.

Ardea caerulea] *Egretta caerulea,* Little Blue Heron.

Ardea *clamator] *Nycticorax nycticorax,* Black-crowned Night Heron.

Ardea herodias] Great Blue Heron.

Ardea *immaculata] *Casmerodius albus,* Great Egret.

Ardea maculata cristata] Probably *Nyctanassa violacea,* Yellow-crowned Night Heron.

*Ardea *mugitans*] *Botaurus lentiginosus*, American Bittern.

*Ardea *parva*] *Ixobrychus exilis*, Eastern Least Bittern.

Ardea purpurea cristata] *Egretta caerulea*, Little Blue Heron.

Ardea stellaris cristata] Probably *Nyctanassa violacea*, Yellow-crowned Night Heron.

Ardea stellaris maxima] Probably *Ardea herodias wardi*, Ward's Heron.

Ardea subfusca stellata] Probably an immature *Nycticorax nycticorax*, Black-crowned Night Heron, or an immature *Nyctanassa violacea*, Yellow-crowned Night Heron.

Ardea varia cristata] Possibly *Egretta tricolor*, Louisiana Heron.

Ardea violacea] *Nyctanassa violacea*, Yellow-crowned Night Heron.

Ardea virescens] *Butorides striatus*, Green Heron.

Arethusa] Probably *Cleistes divaricata*, spreading pogonia.

*Arethusa *pulcherrima*] Possibly *Arethusa bulbosa*, swamp pink, or *Pogonia* species.

Aristolochia frutescens] Possibly *Aristolochia durior*, Dutchman's pipe.

Arum aeaule] *Peltandra virginica*, arrow arum.

Arum Colocasia] *Colocasia antiquorum*, taro.

Arum esculentum] *Colocasia antiquorum*, taro, or a related species.

Arum triphyllum] *Arisaema triphyllum*, Jack-in-the-pulpit.

Arundo gigantea] Giant cane.

Asafoetida] Gum.

Asarabacca] *Hexastylis arifolia* or *Hexastylis callifolia*, heart-leaf.

*Asclepias *carnosa*] *Asclepias humistrata*, a milkweed.

*Asclepias *coccinea*] Perhaps *Asclepsias lanceolata*, a milkweed.

*Asclepias *fragrans*] Perhaps *Podostigma pedicellata*, a milkweed.

Asilus] Deer flies, genus *Chrysops.*

Asphodelus, called "Fly poison"] *Chrosperma muscaetoxicum.*

*Aster *fructicosus*] *Aster carolinianus*, climbing aster.

Auris marina] An undetermined limpetlike gastropod mollusk.

Avellania] *Corylus* species, hazelnut.

*Azalea *coccinea*] Probably *Rhododendron speciosum*, showy azalea.

*Azalea *flammea*] Probably either *Rhododendron calendulaceum*, flame azalea, or *Rhododendron speciosum*, showy azalea.

*Azalea *flammula*] Probably *Rhododendron calendulaceum*, flame azalea.

*Azalea *nuda*] Probably *Rhododendron nidiflorum*, pink azalea.

*Azalea *rosea*] Undetermined species of *Rhododendron*.

Azalea viscosa] *Rhododendron viscosum*, swamp azalea.

Baltimore bird, both species] *Icterus galbula*, Northern Oriole (Baltimore Oriole), and *Icterus spurius*, Orchard Oriole.

Barilla] Probably *Salsola kali*, saltwort.

Barley] *Hordeum sativum.*

*Bartramia *bracteata*] *Pinckneya pubens*, Pinckneya (Georgia bark).

Bartsia] *Castilleja coccinea*, Indian paint-brush.

Basil] *Clinopodium* species.

Bat, great] *Caprimulgus carolinensis*, Chuck-will's-widow.

Batata] *Ipomoea batatas*, sweet potato.

Bay, loblolly] *Gordonia lasianthus*, loblolly-bay.

Bay, Purple berried] *Osmanthus americana*, devil wood.

Bay, Red] *Persea borbonia.*

Bay (or bay tree), Sweet] *Persea borbonia.*

Bay, dwarf Sweet] *Persea humilis.*

Bear] *Ursus americanus*, Black Bear.

Beaver] *Castor canadensis.*

Bee] *Apis mellifera*, honey bee.

Bees, humble] *Bombus* species, bumblebees.

Bees, humming] *Bombus* species, bumblebees.

Beech] *Fagus grandifolia.*

Belemnites] Possibly *Belemnitella americana*, a fossil cephalopod mollusk.

Betula lenta] Probably *Betula nigra*, river birch.

Betula nigra] Probably *Betula lenta*, black birch.

Bidens frondosa] Beggar-ticks.

*Bignonia *bracteata*] *Pinckneya pubens*, Pinckneya (Georgia bark).

Bignonia crucigera] *Bignonia capreolata*, trumpet flower.

Bignonia radicans] *Campsis radicans*, trumpet creeper.

Bignonia sempervirens] *Gelsemium sempervirens*, yellow jessamine.

Bittern, crested blue] *Nyctanassa violacea*, Yellow-crowned Night-Heron.

Bittern, green] *Butorides virescens*, Green Heron.

Bittern, least brown and striped] *Ixobrychus exilis*, Least Bittern.

Bittern, lesser green] *Butorides virescens*, Green Heron.

Bittern, little white] *Egretta thula*, Snowy Egret.

Bittern, marsh] *Botaurus lentiginosus*, American Bittern.

Black Jacks] Either *Quercis laevis* or *Quercis marilandica*, black-jack oaks.

Blossom, Scarlet, resembling Ipomea] *Gilia rubra*, standing cypress.

Blue bill] *Aythya marila*, Greater Scaup, and *Aythys affinis*, Lesser Scaup.

Blue bird] *Sialia sialis*, Eastern Bluebird.

Bomble bee] *Bombus* species.

Booby] *Sula* species.

Bos cornibus teretibus flexis] *Bison bison*, American Bison.

Brant] Probably *Chen caerulescens*, Snow Goose.

Bream, golden, or sunfish] *Chaenobryttus coronarius* Bartram.

Bream, great black or blue] *Lepomis macrochirus*, Copper-nosed Bream.

Bream, great yellow or particoloured] *Lepomis microlophus*, Shell-cracker Bream.

Bream, red bellied] *Lepomis auritus*, Red-breasted Bream.

Bream, yellow, or sun fish] *Chaenobryttus coronarius* Bartram.

Bromelia Ananas] *Ananas sativus*, pineapple.

Broom-Pine] *Pinus palustris*, longleaf pine.

Buckeye] *Aesculus* species.

Buffalo] *Bison bison*, American Bison.

Buffalo head] *Bucephala albeola*, Bufflehead.

Bufflehead] *Bucephala albeola*.

Bull frog] *Rana catesbeiana*.

Bull-neck] *Bucephala albeola*, Bufflehead.

Bull Snake] *Pituophis melanoleucus,* Pine-gopher Snake.

Bumblebee] *Bombus* species.

Butcher bird, bluish grey] *Lanius ludovicianus,* Loggerhead Shrike.

Butcher-bird, little black capped] *Lanius ludovicianus,* Loggerhead Shrike.

Butterback] Male *Bucephala albeola,* Bufflehead.

Butterfly, black, with yellow stripes and crimson spots] *Heliconius charithonius,* Zebra butterfly.

Butterfly pea] *Clitoria mariana.*

Buzzard, Black or Carrion Crow] *Coragyps atratus,* Black Vulture.

Buzzard, turkey] *Cathartes aura,* Turkey Vulture.

Cabbage tree] *Sabal palmetto,* cabbage palmetto.

Cacalia, another species than *Cacalia heterophylla*] Undetermined.

Cacalia *heterophylla] *Garberia heterophylla* Bartram, garberia.

Cacalia suffruticosa] *Garberia heterophylla* Bartram, garberia.

Cactus cochenellifer] *Nopalea cochenillifera,* cochineal plant of Mexico.

Cactus grandiflora] *Selenicereus grandiflorus,* night-blooming cereus.

Cactus melo-cactus] *Cactus melocactus,* Turk's head.

Cactus opuntia] Possibly *Opuntia ammophila.*

Calandra *pratensis] *Spiza americana,* Dickcissel.

Callicarpa] *Callicarpa americana,* French mulberry.

Calycanthus] Primarily *Calycanthus floridus,* sweet shrub.

Calycanthus floridus] Sweet shrub.

Camellia] Probably *Camellia japonica,* common camellia.

Cancer *macrourus] *Cambarus* species, crayfish.

Cancer Squilla] Stomatopod crustacean, undetermined.

Cane or reed] *Arundinaria tecta,* small cane; *Arundinaria gigantea,* giant cane.

Cane (*Arundo gigantea*)] *Arundaria gigantea,* giant cane.

Canna Indica] Possibly *Canna indica,* red canna.

Canna lutea] *Canna flaccida,* golden canna.

Cannabis] *Cannabis sativa,* hemp.

Cantharides]   A preparation of *Cantharis vesicatoria*, blister beetles.

Capparis]   *Capparis spinosa*, caper bush.

Caprimulgus Americanus]   *Chordeiles minor*, Nighthawk, and *Caprimulgus vociferus*, Whip-poor-will.

Caprimulgus *lucifugus]   *Caprimulgus carolinensis*, Chuck-will's-widow.

Capsicum]   *Capsicum frutescens*, bird pepper.

Carduelis Americanus]   *Carduelis tristis*, American Goldfinch.

Carduelis pinus]   *Carduelis pinus*, Pine Siskin.

Carduelis *pusillus]   Possibly *Carduelis flammea*, Common Redpoll.

Carduus]   *Cirsium* species, thistle.

Carica papaya]   Papaya or custard-apple.

Carnation]   *Dianthus armeria*.

Carpinus]   Probably *Carpinus caroliniana*, blue beech.

Carpinus betula]   *Carpinus caroliniana*, blue beech.

Carpinus ostrya]   *Ostrya virginiana*, hop hornbeam.

Caryophyllata]   Probably *Geum* species, avens.

Caryophyllus aromaticus]   *Eugenia aromatica*, clove tree.

Cassine]   *Ilex vomitoria*, yaupon.

Cassine *yapon]   *Ilex vomitoria*, yaupon.

Castania pumila virginiana]   *Castanea* species, chinquapin.

Castor cauda lanciolata]   *Ondatra zibethicus*, Common Muskrat.

Catalpa]   *Catalpa bignonioides*, catalpa.

Cat-bird]   *Dumetella carolinensis*, Gray Catbird.

Cattle]   *Bos taurus*.

Cedar, red]   *Juniperus virginiana* or *Juniperus* species.

Cedar, white]   *Chamaecyparis thyoides*.

Cedar bird]   *Bombycilla cedrorum*, Cedar Waxwing.

Celtis]   *Celtis* species, hackberry.

Cepa]   *Allium cepa*, onion.

Cephalanthus]   *Cephalanthus occidentalis*, button-bush.

Cercis] *Cercis canadensis*, redbud.

*Certhia *picta*] *Mniotilta varia*, Black and White Warbler.

Certhia pinus] *Dendroica pinus*, Pine Warbler.

*Certhia *rufa*] *Certhia familiaris*, Brown Creeper.

*Cervus *sylvaticus*] *Odocoileus virginianus*, White-tailed Deer.

Chamaerhododendros, rose flower'd] *Rhododendron minus*, lesser rose-bay.

Chameleon, green] *Anolis carolinensis*, Green Anole.

*Charadrius *maculatus*] Probably *Pluvialis dominica*, American Golden Plover.

*Charadrius *minor*] Probably including *Charadrius semipalmatus*, Semi-palmated Plover, *Charadrius wilsonia*, Wilson's Plover, and *Charadrius melodus*, Piping Plover.

Charadrius vociferus] Killdeer.

Chat, yellow breasted] *Icteria virens*.

Cherries] *Prunus* species.

Chestnut] *Castanea dentata*.

Chicken bird] *Dumetella carolinensis*, Gray Catbird.

China brier] *Smilax pseudo-china* or *Smilax bona-nox*.

China Root] *Smilax* species, catbrier.

Chinquapin] *Castanea* species.

Chionanthus] *Chionanthus virginica*, old man's beard.

Chipping bird] *Spizella passerina*, Chipping Sparrow.

Chironia] *Sabatia* species, marsh pink.

*Chironia *pulcherrima*] *Sabatia* species, marsh pink.

Chrysocoma] Possibly *Elephantopus* species or *Vernonia* species.

Chuck-will's-widow] *Caprimulgus carolinensis*.

Cicadae, or locusts] Cicadas.

Circaea] Probably *Circaea quadrisulcata*, enchanter's nightshade.

Cistus] Probably *Helianthemum* species, rock-rose.

Citra, ambrosial] Probably *Citrus* species, orange.

Citron, great sweet scented] *Citrus medica*.

Cituels or Citruls] *Citrullus vulgaris*, watermelon.

Citrus aurantium]   Bitter-sweet orange.

Citrus limon]   *Citrus limonia*, lemon.

Citrus *verrucosa]   Undetermined.

Cleome *lupinifolia]   *Cleome* species or *Neocleome* species, spider-flower.

Clethra]   Probably *Clethra alnifolia*, latherbush.

Clethra alnifolia]   Latherbush.

Clinopodium]   Basil.

Clitoria]   *Clitoria mariana*, butterfly pea.

Cloves]   Dried buds of *Eugenia aromatica*.

Cochineal insect]   *Coccus cacti*.

Cochleae]   Various species of gastropod mollusks.

Cochlites]   Small fossil mollusk or brachiopod.

Cocos nucifera]   Cocoa palm.

Coffee]   *Coffea* species.

Colchicum]   *Colchicum* species, autumn crocus.

Collinsonia, a species of]   *Micheliella anisata*, stone-root.

Columba Caroliniensis]   *Zenaida macroura*, Mourning Dove.

Columba migratoria]   *Ectopistes migratorius*, Passenger Pigeon (now extinct).

Columba passerina]   *Columbina passerina*, Ground Dove.

Colymbus arcticus]   Probably *Gavia pacifica*, Pacific Loon.

Colymbus auritus et cornutus]   *Podiceps auritus*, Horned Grebe.

Colymbus cauda elongata]   *Anhinga anhinga*, American Anhinga (Water Turkey).

Colymbus *colubrinus, cauda elongata]   *Anhinga anhinga*, American Anhinga (Water Turkey).

Colymbus *Floridanus]   Probably *Phalacrocorax auritus*, Double-crested Cormorant.

Colymbus *migratorius]   Probably *Phalacrocorax auritius*, Double-crested Cormorant.

Colymbus minor fuscus]   *Podilymbus podiceps*, Pied-billed Grebe.

Colymbus *musicus]   *Gavia immer*, Common Loon.

Commelina]   *Commelina* species, day-flower.

Concha mytilus]   Possibly *Mytilus* species.

Concha ostrea]   Probably *Ostrea virginica*, oyster.

Concha pecten]   Probably *Pecten* species, scallop.

Concha *venerea]   Possibly *Venus* species, Hard Clam.

Conchites]   Small fossil mollusk.

Convallaria, perfumed]   Possibly *Convallaria montana*, Alleghanian lily-of-the-valley.

Convallaria majalis]   *Convallaria montana*, Alleghanian lily-of-the-valley.

Convallaria racemosa]   *Smilacina racemosa*, false Solomon's seal.

Convolvulus, with large, white, sweet-scented flowers]   Probably *Calonyction aculeatum*, moon flower.

Convolvulus, palmated]   Possibly *Operculina dissecta*, a morning glory.

Convolvulus batata]   *Ipomoea batatas*, sweet potato.

Convolvulus dissectus]   Possibly *Operculina dissecta*, a morning glory.

Convulvulus radice tuberosa esculenta]   *Ipomea batatas*, sweet potatoes

Coot, great blue or slate colored, of Florida]   *Fulica americana*, American Coot.

Coquilles]   Probably *Rangia* species.

Corallinus]   Possibly coral.

Coralloides]   Undetermined lichen.

Coreopsis alternifolia]   Possibly *Phalacrocorax auritus*, Double-crested Cormorant.

Coreopsis bidens]   *Bidens* species, beggar-ticks.

Cormorant, great black, of Florida]   *Phalacrocorax floridanus* Bartram, Florida Cormorant.

Corn]   *Zea mays*, maize.

Corn, Indian]   *Zea mays*, maize.

Corn thief]   *Agelaius phoenicius*, Red-winged Blackbird.

Cornu ammonis]   An ammonite.

Cornus alba]   Probably *Cornus amomum*, silky dogwood.

Cornus Femina]   Probably *Cornus stricta*, swamp dogwood.

Cornus Florida] Flowering dogwood.

Cornus Mas] *Cornus florida*, flowering dogwood.

Cornus sanguinea] Probably *Cornus amomum*, silky dogwood, or *Cornus foemina*, stiff dogwood.

Corvus *carnivorus] *Corvus corax*, Northern Raven.

Corvus cristatus, seu pica glandaria] *Cyanocitta cristata*, Blue Jay.

Corvus *Floridanus, pica glandaria minor] Probably *Aphelocoma coerulescens*, Scrub Jay.

Corvus *frugivora] Probably *Corvus brachyrhynchos*, American Crow, and *Corvus ossifragus*, Fish Crow.

Corvus glandarius seu corvus cristatus] *Cyanocitta cristata*, Blue Jay.

Corvus *maritimus] Possibly *Corvus corax*, Northern Raven.

Corylus] *Corylus* species, hazelnut.

Corypha *obliqua] *Serenoa repens* Bartram, saw palmetto.

Corypha *palma] *Sabal palmetto*, cabbage palmetto.

Corypha pumila] *Sabal minor*, dwarf or blue-stem palmetto.

Corypha *repens] *Serenoa repens* Bartram, saw palmetto.

Cotton, annual] *Gossypium hirsutum*, upland cotton.

Cotton, West-Indian (or perennial)] Probably *Gossypium barbadense*, sea-island cotton.

Coturnix] *Colinus virginianus*, Bobwhite.

Cowpeas] *Vigna sinensis.*

Cowpen bird] *Molothrus ater*, Brown-headed Cowbird.

Crabcatcher] Probably *Nyctanassa violacea*, Yellow-crowned Night Heron.

Crane] Primarily *Grus canadensis* Bartram, Sandhill Crane.

Crane, savanna] *Grus canadensis* Bartram, Sandhill Crane.

Crane, whooping] *Grus americana.*

Cray-fish] *Cambarus* species.

Creeper, blue and white striped] *Mniotilta varia*, Black and White Warbler.

Creeper, little brown variegated] *Certhia americana*, Brown Creeper.

Creeper, pine] *Dendroica dominica*, Yellow-throated Warbler.

Crickets, savanna] *Hyla ocularis*, Little Grassfrog.

Crinum] Swamp lilies.

Crinum, perfumed] Probably *Crinum americanum*, a swamp lily.

*Crinum *floridanum*] Probably *Crinum americanum*, a swamp lily.

Croakers] *Micropogon undulatus*, a fish of the family Sciaenidae.

Crocodile] *Alligator mississipiensis*, American Alligator.

Cross beak] *Loxia curvirostra*, Red Crossbill.

Cross beak, blue] *Guiraca caerulea*, Blue Grosbeak.

Crow] *Corvus brachyrhynchos*, American Crow, and *Corvus ossifragus*, Fish Crow.

Crow, carrion] *Coragyps atratus*, Black Vulture.

Crow, eel] Possibly *Phalacrocorax auritus*, Double-crested Cormorant.

Crown, great sea-side] Possibly *Corvus corax*, Northern Raven.

Crown bird] *Bombycilla cedrorum*, Cedar Waxwing.

Crying bird] *Aramus guanauna*, Limpkin.

Cuckoo of Carolina] *Coccyzus americanus*, Yellow-billed Cuckoo.

Cuckoo] *Coccyzus americanus*, Yellow-billed Cuckoo.

*Cuculus *Caroliniensis*] *Coccyzus americanus*, Yellow-billed Cuckoo.

Cucumber] *Cucumis sativus.*

Cucumber tree] *Magnolia acuminata.*

Cucurbita citrullus] *Citrullus vulgaris*, watermelon.

Cucurbita lagenaria] Gourd or calabash.

Cucurbita melopepo] *Cucurbita pepo*, bush pumpkin or squash.

Cucurbita pepo] Field pumpkin.

*Cucurbita *peregrina*] Possibly *Cucurbita okeechobeensis*, Okeechobee gourd.

Cucurbita verrucosa] Cymling, a scalloped summer squash.

Culex] *Aedes, Culex, Anopheles* species, mosquito.

Cupressus disticha] *Taxodium distichum*, river cypress, and *Taxodium ascendens*, pond cypress.

Cupressus thyoides] *Chamaecyparis thyoides*, white cedar.

Curlew] *Numenius phaeopus*, Whimbrel, or *Eudocimus albus*, White Ibis.

Curlew, dusky and white Spanish] Immature *Eudocimus albus*, White Ibis.

Curlew, lesser field]   Possibly *Numenius borealis*, Eskimo Curlew.

Curlew, great sea coast]   Probably *Numenius americanus*, Long-billed Curlew.

Curlew, sea side lesser]   Probably *Numenius phaeopus*, Whimbrel.

Curlew, Spanish]   *Eudocimus albus*, White Ibis.

Curlew, White Spanish]   *Eudocimus albus*, White Ibis.

Cydonia]   *Cydonia* species, including quince, *Cydonia oblonga*.

Cygnus ferus]   *Cygnus columbianus*, Whistling Swan.

Cynips]   Gnats, order Diptera.

Cypress, a species of, resembling white cedar]   Probably *Chamaecyparis thyoides*, white cedar.

Cyprinus coronarius]   *Chaenobryttus coronarius* Bartram, yellow bream.

Cypripedium]   *Cypripedium* species, Lady's slipper.

Cypripedium calceolus]   A European species of Lady's slipper.

Cyrilla racemiflora]   Tyty.

Daphne]   Genus of ornamental shrubs.

Dates]   *Phoenix dactylifera.*

Daucus]   *Daucus carota*, carrot.

Deer]   *Odocoileus virginianus*, White-tailed Deer.

Delphinium]   *Delphinium* species, larkspur.

Delphinium peregrinum]   *Delphinium* species, larkspur.

Dianthus]   Probably *Silene baldwinii*, one of the catchflys.

Dionaea muscipula]   Venus' fly-trap, *Dionaea muscipula.*

Dioscorea bulbifera]   *Dioscorea* species, wild yam-root.

Diospyros]   *Diospyros virginiana*, common persimmon.

Diospyros Virginiana]   Persimmon.

*Diospyros *Virginica*]   *Diospyros virginiana*, persimmon.

Dirca palustris]   Leatherwood.

Diver, great black and white pied]   *Gavia immer*, Common Loon.

Diver, great speckled]   *Gavia pacifica*, Pacific Loon.

Dobchick, little crested brown]   *Podilymbus podiceps*, Pied-billed Grebe.

Dobchick, little eared brown] *Podiceps auritus*, Horned Grebe.

Dodecatheon meadia] Shooting star.

Dog] *Canis familiaris.*

Dog-wood] *Cornus florida*, flowering dogwood.

Dolichos] Probably *Vigna sinensis*, cowpea.

Dotterel] *Arenaria interpres*, Ruddy Turnstone.

Dove, Catesby's Ground] *Columbina passerina*, Ground-Dove.

Dove, turtle] *Zenaida macroura*, Mourning Dove.

Drosera rotundifolia] Round-leaved sundew.

Duck, great fishing] *Mergus serrator*, Red-breasted Merganser.

Duck, little black and white] Male *Bucephala albeola*, Bufflehead.

Duck, little brown and white] Female *Bucephala albeola*, Bufflehead.

Duck, round crested] *Lophodytes cucullatus*, Hooded Merganser.

Duck, sprig tail] *Anas acuta*, Northern Pintail.

Duck, summer] *Aix sponsa*, Wood Duck.

Duck, various coloured] Male *Histrionicus histrionicus*, Harlequin Duck.

Duck, great wild] *Anas platyrhynchos*, Common Mallard.

Eagle, bald] *Haliaeetus leucocephalus.*

Eagle, fishing] *Pandion haliaetus*, Osprey.

Eagle, great grey] Immature *Haliaeetus leucocephalus*, Bald Eagle.

Eagle, white] Probably *Sarcoramphus papa*, King Vulture. Bartram is the only person known to have recorded a sighting of this bird in territory that is now part of the United States.

Echinitis] Undetermined marine invertebrate.

Echinus] Undetermined sea urchin.

Echium] Possibly *Onosmodium virgianum*, false growell.

Eddo] *Colocasia antiquorum*, taro, or a related species.

Efois-kika] *Aramus guarauna*, Limpkin.

Ehto Mico or King Tree] *Persea borbonia*, red bay.

Elder] *Sambucus canadensis*, common elder, or *Sambucus simpsonii*, southern elder.

Elk]   *Cervus elaphus*, Elk (Wapiti).

Elm]   *Ulmus* species.

Emberiza *ciris]   *Passerina ciris*, Painted Bunting.

Emberiza *livida]   Probably *Euphagus carolinus*, Rusty Blackbird, or male *Molothrus ater*, Cowbird.

Emberiza oryzivora]   *Dolichonyx oryzivorus*, Bobolink.

Emberiza *varia]   Breeding male *Dolichonyx oryzivorus*, Bobolink.

Empetrum]   *Ceratiola ericoides*, rosemary.

Empetrum album]   *Ceratiola ericoides*, rosemary.

Ephemera]   Probably Mayflies, family Ephemeridae.

Ephouskyca]   *Aramus guarauna*, Limpkin.

Eryngium]   *Eryngium* species, button snakeroot.

Erythrina]   *Erythrina herbacea*, cardinal spear.

Erythrina corallodendrum]   *Erythrina herbacea*, cardinal spear.

Erythronium *maculatum]   *Erythronium americanum*, adder's tongue.

Euonymus Americana]   *Euonymus americanus*, strawberry bush.

Eupatorium]   *Eupatorium* species.

Eupatorium scandens]   *Mikania scandens*, climbing hemp-vine.

Euphorbia]   Probably *Euphorbia* species, spurge.

Euphorbia picta]   *Euphorbia heterophylla*, painted leaf.

Fagus]   *Fagus grandifolia*, American beech.

Fagus castanea]   *Castanea dentata*, chestnut.

Fagus pumila, seu *Chinkapin]   *Castanea pumilia*, Piedmont chinquapin.

Fagus sylvatica]   *Fagus grandifolia*, American beech.

Falco Aquilinus]   *Buteo jamaicensis*, Red-tailed Hawk.

Falco columbarius]   Merlin (Pigeon Hawk).

Falco furcatus]   *Elanoides forficatus*, Swallow-tailed Kite.

Falco gallinarius]   Probably *Accipiter cooperii*, Cooper's Hawk, or *Buteo* species.

Falco *glaucus]   *Elanus leucurus*, White-tailed Kite.

Falco leucocephalus]   Adult *Haliaeetus leucocephalus*, Bald Eagle.

Falco *major cauda ferruginea] *Buteo jamaicensis*, Red-tailed Hawk.

Falco *maximus] Immature *Haliaeetus leucocephalus*, Bald Eagle.

Falco niger] Possibly *Falco peregrinus*, Peregrine Falcon.

Falco *piscatorius] *Pandion haliaetus*, Osprey.

Falco *pullarius] Undetermined hawk, *Accipiter* or *Buteo* species.

Falco *ranivorus] *Circus cyaneus*, Northern Harrier (Marsh Hawk).

Falco *regalis] Immature *Haliaeetus leucocephalus*, Bald Eagle.

Falco sparverius] American Kestrel or Sparrow Hawk.

Falco *subcerulius] *Ictinia mississippiensis*, Mississippi Kite.

Felis cauda truncata] *Felis rufus*, Bobcat.

Fern, scandent] *Lygodium palmatum*, climbing fern.

Ficus carica] Fig trees.

Field fare] *Turdus migratorius*, American Robin.

Fig] *Ficus carica.*

Fig, common dwarf Indian] *Opuntia* species, prickly pear.

Filbert] *Corylus* species.

Filices] Ferns and fern allies.

Filix *osmunda] *Osmunda cinnamomea*, cinnamon fern, or *Osmunda regalis*, royal fern.

Filix *scandens] *Lygodium palmatum*, climbing fern.

Finch, creeper] *Parula americana*, Northern Parula.

Finch, painted] *Passerina ciris*, Painted Bunting.

Finch, purple] *Carpodacus purpureus*, Purple Finch.

Finch, small brown, with purple head and neck] *Carpodacus purpureus*, Purple Finch.

Fishing-hawk] *Pandion haliaetus*, Osprey.

Flags] *Iris* species.

Flamingo] *Phoenicopterus ruber*, Greater Flamingo.

Flax] *Linum* species.

Flounder] *Paralichthys* species (around Georgia coastal islands); *Trinectes maculatus*, Southern Hog-choker (off Florida).

Fly, yellow Gourd] *Eacles imperialis*, Imperial Moth.

Flycatcher, black cap]   *Sayornis phoebe*, Eastern Phoebe.

Flycatcher, brown and greenish]   *Contopus virens*, Eastern Wood Pewee.

Flycatcher, crested, great crested yellow bellied]   *Myiarchus crinitus*, Great Crested Flycatcher.

Flycatcher, golden crown]   Adult male *Dendroica coronata*, Yellow-rumped Warbler, in spring plumage.

Flycatcher, golden winged]   *Vermivora chrysoptera*, Golden-winged Warbler.

Flycatcher, green black throated]   *Dendroica virens*, Black-throated Green Warbler.

Flycatcher, little domestic]   *Vireo griseus*, White-eyed Vireo.

Flycatcher, little olive]   *Empidonax virescens*, Acadian Flycatcher.

Flycatcher, little red eye'd]   *Vireo olivaceus*, Red-eyed Vireo.

Flycatcher, yellow rump]   *Dendroica coronata*, Yellow-rumped Warbler (Myrtle Warbler), or *Dendroica magnolia*, Magnolia Warbler.

Fly poison]   *Chrosperma muscaetoxicum.*

Fothergilla]   *Fothergilla* species, witch alders.

Fothergilla gardeni]   Dwarf witch-alder.

Fox]   *Urocyon cinereoargenteus*, Gray Fox.

Fragaria]   *Fragaria* species, strawberry.

Frangula]   Probably *Rhamnus caroliniana*, buckthorn or Indian cherry.

*Franklinia *Alatamaha*]   *Franklinia alatamaha* Bartram, Franklin tree. The tree was last recorded growing wild in 1803; it is still cultivated.

Fraxinus]   *Fraxinus* species, ash.

*Fraxinus *aquatica*]   Perhaps *Fraxinus caroliniana*, water ash.

Fraxinus excelsior]   *Fraxinus americana*, white ash.

Frigate bird]   *Fregata magnificens*, Magnificent Frigatebird (Man-o'-war-bird).

Fringe-tree]   *Chionanthus virginica*, old man's beard.

Fringilla canabina]   Probably female and immature male *Carpodacus purpureus*, Purple Finch.

Fringilla erythrophthalma]   *Pipilo erythrophthalmus*, Rufus-sided Towhee.

Fringilla fusca]   *Zonotrichia albicollis*, White-throated Sparrow.

Fringilla purpurea]   *Carpodacus purpureus*, Purple Finch.

*Fringilla *rufa*]   *Passerella iliaca*, Fox Sparrow.

Fritillaria]   A genus of *Liliaceae*.

Frog, a beautiful green]   *Hyla cinerea*, Green Treefrog.

Frog, bell]   *Hyla cinerea*, Green Treefrog, or *Hyla gratiosa*, Barking Treefrog.

Frog, diminutive species of, called savanna crickets]   *Hyla ocularis*, Little Grassfrog.

Frog, a little grey speckled]   *Acris gryllus*, Southern Cricket Frog.

Frog, shad]   *Rana sphenocephala*, Southern Leopard Frog.

Frogs, high land, called toads]   *Bufo terrestris*, Southern Toad.

Frogs, land]   *Bufo terrestris*, Southern Toad.

Frogs, little, about one inch in length, striped green and white]   *Acris gryllus*, Southern Cricket Frog.

Frogs, little "luced" green]   *Hyla cinerea*, Green Treefrog.

Frogs, little, not bigger than a cricket]   *Hyla ocularis*, Little Grassfrog.

Frogcatcher]   *Nycticorax nycticorax*, Black-crowned Night Heron.

*Fulica *Floridana*]   *Fulica americana*, American Coot.

Fungus called Jew's ears]   *Auricularia auricula-judae.*

Galega]   Probably *Tephrosia* species, devil's shoestring.

Gannet]   *Mycteria americana*, Wood Stork.

Gar]   *Lepisosteus osseus*, Long-nosed Gar; *Cylindrosteus platostomus*, Short-nosed Gar.

Gar, great brown spotted]   *Lepisosteus osseus*, Long-nosed Gar.

Garcinia mangostana]   *Garcinia mangostand*, mangosteen (a Malayan fruit).

*Garrulus *australis*]   *Icteria virens*, Yellow-breasted Chat.

*Gentiana *caerulea*]   *Gentiana* species, gentian.

Gentiana saponaria]   Soapwort gentian.

Gerardia]   *Gerardia* species, false foxglove.

*Gerardia *flammea*]   Probably *Macranthera flammea* Bartram, a scrophulariaceous plant.

Geum]   *Geum* species, avens.

*Geum *odoratissimum*, a new species of Caryophyllata]   Undetermined.

Ginseng (*Panax*)] *Panax quinquefolius.*

Gleditsia] *Gleditsia triacanthos*, honey locust, or *Gleditsia aquatica*, water locust.

Gleditsia monosperma] *Gleditsia aquatica*, water locust.

Gleditsia triacanthos] Honey locust.

Globularia] Probably *Petalostemum* species, prairie clover.

Gloriosa superba] Climbing lily.

Glycine] Possibly *Apios americana*, ground nut.

Glycine apios] *Apios americana*, ground nut.

Glycine frutescens] *Wisteria frutescens*, American wisteria.

Glycine radice tuberosa] *Apios americana*, groundnut.

Gnaphalium] *Gnaphalium* species, everlasting.

Godwit, great red breasted] *Limosa haemastica*, Hudsonian Godwit.

Godwit, greater] Adult *Limosa fedoa*, Marbled Godwit.

Godwit, white] Juvenile *Limosa fedoa*, Marbled Godwit.

Goldfinch] *Carduelis tristis*, American Goldfinch.

Goldfinch, lesser] *Carduelis pinus*, Pine Siskin.

Gold-fish] *Notropis lutipinnis*, Bartram's Minnow.

Goose, blue winged] *Chen caerulescens*, Snow Goose.

Goose, Canadian] *Branta canadensis*, Canada Goose.

Goose, laughing] *Anser albifrons*, Greater White-fronted Goose.

Gopher] *Gopherus polyphaemus* Bartram, Gopher Tortoise.

Gordonia lasianthus] Loblolly-bay.

Gossypium] A genus including the cottons.

Gourd] *Lagenaria vulgaris.*

Gourd fly, yellow] *Eacles imperialis*, Imperial Moth.

*Gracula *purpurea*] Possibly *Quiscalus quiscula*, Common Grackle.

Gracula quiscula] *Quiscalus major*, Boat-tailed Grackle.

Granadilla] May-pop.

Grapes, European wine] *Vitis vinifera.*

*Grus *alba*] *Grus americana*, Whooping Crane.

Grus *clamator, vertice papilloso, corpore niveo remigibus nigris]   *Grus americana*, Whooping Crane.

Grus *pratensis, corpore cinereo, vertice papilloso]   *Grus canadensis* Bartram, Sandhill Crane.

Guilandina dioica]   *Gymnocladus dioica*, Kentucky coffee-tree.

Gull, great grey]   Immature individuals of both *Larus argentatus*, Herring Gull, and *Larus delawarensis*, Ring-billed Gull.

Gull, great white]   Adult individuals of both *Larus argentatus*, Herring Gull, and *Larus delawarensis*, Ring-billed Gull.

Halesia]   *Halesia* species, silverbell trees.

Halesia diptera]   Two-winged silverbell.

Halesia tetraptera]   *Halesia carolina*, four-winged silverbell.

Haliotis auris marina]   Undetermined marine mollusk.

Haliotis patella]   Undetermined marine mollusk.

Hamamelis]   *Hamamelis virginiana*, witch hazel.

Hawk, blue]   Adult male *Circus cyaneus*, Northern Harrier (Marsh Hawk).

Hawk, great eagle]   *Buteo jamaicencis*, Red-tailed Hawk.

Hawk or kite, forked tailed]   *Elanoides forficatus*, Swallow-tailed Kite.

Hawk, least]   *Falco sparverius*, American Kestrel (Sparrow Hawk).

Hawk, marsh]   *Circus cyaneus*, Northern Harrier (Marsh Hawk).

Hawk, pidgeon]   *Falco columbarius*, Merlin (Pigeon Hawk).

Hawk, sparrow]   *Falco sparverius*, American Kestrel (Sparrow Hawk).

Hedera arborea]   *Ampelopsis arborea*, pepper vine.

Hedera *carnosa]   Probably *Parthenocissus quinquefolia*, Virginia creeper.

Hedera quinquefolia]   *Parthenocissus quinquefolia*, Virginia creeper.

Hedysarum]   Probably *Lespedeza* species, bush clover, or *Desmodium* species, beggar's-ticks.

Helenium]   *Helenium* species, sneezeweed.

Helianthus]   *Helianthus* species, sunflower, or related plant.

Helonias]   Possibly *Zigadenus densus*, crow poison.

Hematopus ostrealegus]   *Hematopus palliatus*, American Oystercatcher.

Hemlock spruce]   *Tsuga canadensis*, Canada hemlock, or *Tsuga caroliniana*, Carolina hemlock.

Hemp]   *Cannabis sativa.*

Hepatica]   Hepatica americana.

Heracleum *maximum]   Heracleum lanatum, cow parsnip.

Herbaceae]   Herbaceous plants.

Heron, great bluish grey crested]   *Ardea herodias,* Great Blue Heron.

Heron, great white river]   *Casmerodius albus,* Great Egret.

Heron, little crested purple or blue]   *Egretta caerulea,* Little Blue Heron.

Heron, little white]   Immature *Egretta caerulea,* Little Blue Heron, or *Egretta thula,* Snowy Egret.

Heron, white]   Either *Egretta thula,* Snowy Egret, or *Casmerodius albus,* Great Egret.

Hibiscus althea]   Hibiscus species, rose mallow.

Hibiscus coccineus]   Blazing star.

Hibiscus, Crimson]   *Hibiscus coccineus,* blazing star.

Hibiscus, Rose]   *Hibiscus* species, rose mallow.

Hibiscus spinifex]   Pavonia spinifex, a mallow.

Hickory]   *Carya* species.

Hickory, shell-barked]   *Carya ovata.*

Hippobosca]   Tabanus species, horsefly.

Hirundo *cerdo]   Chaetura pelagica, Chimney Swift.

Hirundo pelasgia, cauda aculeata]   Hirundo rustica, Barn Swallow.

Hirundo purpurae]   Progne subis, Purple Martin.

Hirundo riparia vertice purpurea]   Riparia riparia, Bank Swallow, and *Tachycineta bicolor,* Tree Swallow.

Holly]   *Ilex opaca.*

Honey Locust]   *Gleditsia triacanthos.*

Hopea tinctoria]   Symplocos tinctoria, horse sugar.

Horse]   *Equus caballus.*

Horse-sugar Shrubs]   *Symplocos tinctoria.*

Hummingbird]   *Archilochus colubris,* Ruby-throated Hummingbird.

Hyacinthus]   A genus of Liliaceae, comprising the hyacinths.

Hydrangea, new species of]   *Hydrangea quercifolia* Bartram, oak-leaved hydrangea.

*Hydrangea *quercifolia*] *Hydrangea quercifolia* Bartram, oak-leaved hydrangea.

Hydrastis, new species of] *Trautvetteria carolinensis*, false bugbane.

*Hydrocotyle *fluitans*] *Hydrocotyle* species, water pennywort.

Hypericum] *Hypericum* species, St. John's-wort.

*Hypericum *aureum*] *Hypericum frondosum*, golden St. John's-wort.

Hypoxis] *Hypoxis* species, star-grass.

Hyssopus] *Hypericum officinalis*, hyssop.

Ibis (or Egyptian Ibis)] *Threskiornis aethiopicus.*

Ibis, black above, white below, with white bill and legs] Immature *Eudocimus albus*, White Ibis.

Ibis, white, with black-tipped wings and red bill and legs] Adult *Eudocimus albus*, White Ibis.

Icterus, golden] *Icterus galbula*, Northern Oriole (Baltimore Oriole).

Icterus minor] *Icterus spurius*, Orchard Oriole.

Ilex] Possibly *Ilex opaca*, American holly.

Ilex angustifolium] Possibly *Ilex cassine*, dahoon holly.

Ilex aquifolium] *Ilex opaca*, American holly.

Ilex dahoon] *Ilex cassine*, dahoon or cassena.

Ilex myrtifolium] *Ilex myrtifolia*, myrtle-leaved holly.

Illicium] Anise trees.

Illicium] In Alabama and probably in Georgia, *Illicium floridanum*, purple anise; elsewhere, *Illicium parviflorum*, yellow anise.

Indigo] *Indigofera tinctoria* and probably *Indigofera suffruticosa.*

Indigofera] Probably *Indigofera caroliniana*, wild indigo.

Ipomoea] Morning-glories.

Ipomoea, a scarlet blossom resembling] *Gilia rubra*, standing cypress.

Ipomoea, with erect stem, pinnatifid leaves, and red flowers] *Gilia rubra*, standing cypress.

*Ipomoea *erecta*] Probably *Gilia rubra*, standing cypress.

Ipomoea quamoclit] Cypress vine.

Iris versicolor] Blue flag.

Itea]   *Itea virginica*, Indian reed.

Iva]   Probably *Iva frutescens*, marsh elder.

Ivy Tree, Virginia]   *Kalmia latifolia*, mountain laurel.

Ixia, cerulean]   *Salpingostylis caelestina* Bartram, Bartram's celestial lily.

*Ixia *caelestina*]   *Salpingostylis caelestina* Bartram, Bartram's celestial lily.

Ixia, purple]   *Salpingostylis caelestina*, Bartram's celestial lily.

Jackdaw]   *Quiscalus major*, Boat-tailed Grackle, or *Quiscalus quiscula*, Common Grackle.

Jackdaw, lesser purple]   *Quiscalus quiscula*, Common Grackle.

Jackdaw, purple, of the sea coast]   *Quiscalus major*, Boat-tailed Grackle.

Jackdaw, purple, the largest]   *Quiscalus major*, Boat-tailed Grackle.

Jackdaw, the smaller kind]   *Quiscalus quiscula*, Common Grackle.

Jacobea, Corymbous (Senecio Jacobea)]   Probably *Senecio glabellus*, ragwort.

Jasmine, yellow]   *Gelsemium sempervirens*.

Jatropha]   *Jatropha stimulosa*, spurge nettle.

Jay, blue]   *Cyanocitta cristata*, Blue Jay.

Jay, crested blue, of Virginia]   *Cyanocitta cristata*, Blue Jay.

Jay without a crest]   *Aphelocoma coerulescens*, Scrub Jay.

Jay, little, of Florida]   *Aphelocoma coerulescens*, Scrub Jay.

Jessamine, yellow]   *Gelseminum sempervirens*.

Jew's ears]   *Auricularia auricula-judae*, a fungus.

Johnsonia]   *Callicarpa*, a genus including the French mulberry.

Judas or Judas Tree]   *Cercis canadensis*, redbud.

*Juglans *acuminata*]   Possibly *Carya glabra*, pignut hickory.

Juglans alba]   Probably *Carya tomentosa*, white heart hickory.

Juglans cinerea]   Possibly *Carya cordiformis*, bitternut hickory.

*Juglans *exaltata*]   *Carya ovata*, shell-barked hickory.

Juglans nigra]   Black walnut.

Juglans pecan]   *Carya illinoensis*, pecan.

*Juglans *rustica*]   *Carya* species, undetermined nut.

*Juniperus *Americana*]   *Juniperus virginiana*, red cedar, or *Juniperus silicicola*, southern red cedar.

Kalmia] A genus of Ericaceae, comprising the American laurels.

Kalmia, a new] *Kalmia hirsuta*, calico bush.

Kalmia angustifolia] Undetermined.

Kalmia *ciliata] *Kalmia hirsuta*, calico-bush.

Kalmia glauca] Undetermined.

Kalmia latifolia] Mountain laurel.

Kalmia, lesser] *Kalmia latifolia*, mountain laurel.

Kalmia *spuria] *Befaria racemosa*, tar flower.

Kildea] *Charadrius vociferus*, Killdeer.

King bird] *Tyrannus tyrannus*, Eastern Kingbird.

King-fisher, great crested] *Ceryle alcyon*, Eastern Belted Kingfisher.

King's tree] *Persea borbonia*, red bay.

Kite, forked tailed] *Elanoides forficatus*, Swallow-tailed Kite.

Lacerta] *Cnemidophorus sexlineatus*, Racerunner.

Lanius garrulus] *Lanius ludovicianus*, Loggerhead Shrike.

Lanius *griseus] *Lanius ludovicianus*, Migrant Shrike.

Lanius tyrannus] *Tyrannus tyrannus*, Eastern Kingbird.

Lantana (possibly *Lant. camerara*)] Shrub verbena.

Lantana, balmy] Probably *Lantana camara*, shrub verbena.

Lark, great meadow] *Sturnella magna*, Eastern Meadowlark.

Lark, little brown] *Anthus rubescens*, American Pipit.

Lark, sky] *Eremophila alpestris*, Horned Lark.

Larkspur, garden] *Delphinium* species.

Larus alba] Probably adults of *Larus argentatus*, Herring Gull, and *Larus delawarensis*, Ring-billed Gull.

Larus alba minor] Probably *Sterna hirundo*, Common Tern.

Larus *griseus] Probably immature *Larus argentatus*, Herring Gull, and *Larus delawarensis*, Ring-billed Gull.

Laura-cerasa] *Prunus caroliniana*, laurel cherry.

Laurel] *Magnolia grandiflora*, southern magnolia.

Laurel Magnolia] *Magnolia grandiflora*, southern magnolia.

Laurel Rose] *Magnolia virginiana*, sweetbay.

Laurus benzoin] Probably *Lindera benzoin*, spice-bush.

Laurus Borbonia] *Persea borbonia*, red bay.

Laurus camphora] *Cinnamomum camphora*, camphor tree.

Laurus cerasus] *Prunus caroliniana*, laurel cherry.

Laurus cinnamomum] *Cinnamomum zeylanicum*, cinnamon tree.

Laurus Indica] Undetermined.

Laurus Persica] *Persea gratissima*, avocado.

Laurus sassafras] *Sassafras albidum*, sassafras.

Lechea] *Lechea* species, pinweed.

Lemon] *Citrus limonia*.

Leontice thalictroides] *Caulophyllum thalictroides*, blue cohosh.

Lepus minor] *Sylvilagus floridanus*, Eastern Cottontail.

Lettuce, garden] *Lactuca sativa*.

Lettuce (*lactuca*)] *Lactuca sativa*.

Lettuce, Indian] *Swertia caroliniensis*.

Ligustrum vulgare] *Ligustrum vulgare*, privet.

Lilium] Probably *Lilium catesbaei*, leopard lily.

Lilium martagon] *Lilium* species, lily.

Lilium superbum] Turk's-cap lily.

Lily of the valley] *Convallaria montana*.

Lily, White] *Crinum americanum*, swamp lily.

Limes] *Citrus aurantifolia*.

Lime, Wild] *Ximenia americana*.

Limodorum] *Calopogon*, a genus including the grass-pinks.

*Linaria ciris] *Passerina ciris*, Eastern Painted Bunting.

Linaria cyanea] *Passerina cyanea*, Indigo Bunting.

Linden] *Tilia* species, basswood.

Linnet, blue] *Passerina cyanea*, Indigo Bunting.

Linum] A genus of Linaceae, including the flaxes.

Liquidambar] *Liquidambar styraciflua*, sweet gum.

Liquidambar peregrinum] *Comptonia peregrina*, sweet fern.

Liquidambar styraciflua] *Liquidambar styraciflua*, sweet gum.

Liriodendron (*Liriodendron tulipifera*)] Tulip tree.

Live oak] *Quercus virginiana.*

Lizards, blue bellied squamous] *Sceloporus undulatus*, Eastern Fence Lizard.

Lizard, green, or little green chameleon] *Anolis carolinensis*, Green Anole.

Lizard, large copper coloured] *Eumeces laticeps*, Broad-headed Skink.

Lizard, slender, of a fine blue colour] *Eumeces* species, or *Cnemidophorus sexlineatus*, Racerunner.

Lizards, slender, long-tailed, called scorpions] *Cnemidophorus sexlineatus*, Racerunner.

Lizard, striped, called scorpion] *Cnemidophorus sexlineatus*, Racerunner.

Lobelia cardinalis] Cardinal flower.

Loblolly Bay] *Gordonia lasianthus.*

Locusta, a species of] Probably *Chortophaga viridifasciata*, Green-striped locust.

Lonicera] Probably *Lonicera sempervirens*, coral honeysuckle.

Lonicera sempervirens] Coral honeysuckle.

Loxia cardinalis] *Cardinalis cardinalis*, Northern Cardinal.

Loxia cerulea] *Guiraca caerulea*, Blue Grosbeak.

Loxia rostro forficato] *Loxia curvirostra*, Red Crossbill.

**Lucar *lividus, apice nigra*] *Dumetella carolinensis*, Gray Catbird.

Lupines] *Lupinus* species.

Lupine, a beautiful species of] *Lupinus villosus*, lady lupine.

*Lupinus *biennis*] *Lupinus villosus*, lady lupine.

*Lupinus *filifolius*] Possibly *Lupinus nuttallii*, sandhill lupine.

Lupus niger] *Canis rufus*, Red Wolf.

*Luscinia, seu *philomela *Americana*] Probably *Wilsonia citrina*, Hooded Warbler.

Lutra] *Lutra canadensis*, River Otter.

*Lycium *salsum*] *Lycium carolinianum*, Christmas berry.

Lynx] *Felis rufus*, Bobcat.

Magnolia, a species differing little from *Magnolia glauca*] *Magnolia virginiana*, sweetbay.

Magnolia, towering] *Magnolia grandiflora*, southern magnolia.

Magnolia acuminata] Cucumber tree.

Magnolia altissima] *Magnolia grandiflora*, southern magnolia.

Magnolia *auriculata] *Magnolia fraseri*, mountain magnolia, or possibly *Magnolia macrophylla*, bigleaf magnolia.

Magnolia glauca] *Magnolia virginiana*, sweetbay.

Magnolia, glorious] *Magnolia grandiflora*, southern magnolia.

Magnolia, grand] *Magnolia grandiflora*, southern magnolia.

Magnolia grandiflora] Southern magnolia.

Magnolia, great evergreen] *Magnolia grandiflora*, southern magnolia.

Magnolia, great laurel tree] *Magnolia grandiflora*, southern magnolia.

Magnolia *pyramidata] Pyramid magnolia.

Magnolia tripetala] Umbrella magnolia.

Magnolia, umbrella tree] *Magnolia tripetata*, umbrella magnolia.

Mallard] *Anas platyrhynchos*, Common Mallard.

Malva] Undetermined species of mallow.

Man of war bird] *Fregata magnificens*, Magnificent Frigatebird (Man-o'-war-bird).

Manatee or sea cow] *Trichechus manatus*, Manatee.

Maple, ash leaved] *Acer negundo*.

Martin, bank] *Riparia riparia*, Bank Swallow.

Martin, great purple] *Progne subis*, Purple Martin.

May-Apple] *Passiflora incarnata*, may-pop.

May bird] *Spiza americana*, Dickcissel.

Medeola] *Medeola virginiana*, Indian cucumber-root.

Medusa] A jellyfish.

Melanthium] Possibly *Amianthium muscaetoxicum*, fly poison.

Meleagris *Americanus] *Meleagris gallopavo*, Wild Turkey.

Meleagris occidentalis] *Meleagris gallopavo*, Wild Turkey.

Melons (*Cucurbita citrullus*)] *Citrullus vulgaris*, watermelon.

Mergus] Possibly *Lophodytes cucullatus*, Hooded Merganser.

Mergus cucullatus, the round crested duck] *Lophodytes cucullatus*, Hooded Merganser.

Mergus major pectore rufo] *Mergus serrator*, Red-breasted Merganser.

*Merula *flammula*] *Piranga olivacea*, Scarlet Tanager.

*Merula *Marilandica*] *Piranga rubra*, Summer Tanager.

Mespilus] Crataegus species, hawthorn; Aronia species, chokeberry; or Amelanchier, shadbush.

Mimosa intsia] *Schrankia* species, sensitive briar.

Mimosa sensitiva] Probably *Schrankia* species, sensitive briar.

Mimosa virgata] Probably *Desmanthus illinoensis*.

Mink] *Mustela vison*.

Mitchella repens] Partridge berry.

Moccasin snake, poisonous] *Agkistrodon piscivorus*, Cottonmouth.

Mock-bird] *Mimus polyglottos*, Mockingbird.

Mole] *Scalopus aquaticus*, Eastern Mole.

Momordica] A genus of Cucurbitaceae, including the balsam-apples.

Moor fowl] *Bonasa umbellus*, Ruffed Grouse.

*Morinella *Americana*] *Arenaria interpres*, Ruddy Turnstone.

Morus] *Morus rubra*, red mulberry, and *Morus alba*, white mulberry.

Morus foliis subtus tomentosis] Probably *Morus rubrus*, red mulberry.

Mosses, crustaceous] Lichens.

Moss, long] *Tillandsia usneoides*, long or Spanish moss.

Mosquito Hawks] Odonata species, dragonflies.

*Motacilla *Caroliniana*] *Thryothorus ludovicianus*, Carolina Wren.

*Motacilla *domestica* (*regulus *rufus*)] *Troglodytes aedon*, House Wren.

*Motacilla *fluviatilis*] *Seiurus motacilla*, Louisiana Waterthrush.

*Motacilla *palustris* (*regulus *minor*)] *Cistothorus palustris*, Marsh Wren.

Motacilla sialis] *Sialia sialis*, Eastern Bluebird.

Motacilla trochilus] *Icteria virens*, Yellow-breasted Chat.

Mud fish] *Amia calva*, Bowfin.

Mulberry] *Morus rubra*, red mulberry.

Mulberry trees, European] *Morus alba*, white mulberry.

Mullet] *Mugil cephalus*, Common Mullet, or *Mugil curema*, Silver Mullet.

Musa paradisiaca] *Musa paradisiaca*, banana.

Musa sapientum] *Musa paradisiaca*, banana.

Musci] Flies.

Muscicapa *cantatrix] *Vireo griseus*, White-eyed Vireo.

Muscicapa cristata] *Myiarchus crinitus*, Great Crested Flycatcher.

Muscicapa *nunciola] *Sayornis phoebe*, Eastern Phoebe.

Muscicapa *rapax] *Contopus virens*, Eastern Wood Pewee.

Muscicapa *subviridis] Probably *Empidonax virescens*, Acadian Flycatcher.

Muscicapa *sylvicola] *Vireo olivaceus*, Red-eyed Vireo.

Muscicapa vertice nigro] *Dumetella carolinensis*, Gray Catbird.

Muskmelons] *Cucumis melo*.

Muskrats (*castor cauda lanceolata*)] *Ondatra zibethicus*, Common Muskrat.

Myrica cerifera] Wax myrtle.

Myrica *inodora] *Myrica inodora* Bartram, odorless wax myrtle.

Myrtus, broad leaved sweet] *Persea littoralis*, dune red bay.

Myrtus caryophyllata] *Eugenia aromatica*, clove tree.

Myrtus communis] Classic myrtle.

Myrtus pimenta] *Pimenta officinalis* Berg, allspice.

Mytili, fresh-water] Pelecypod mollusks, probably *Elliptio* species.

Narcissus] *Narcissus* species, including narcissi, daffodils, jonquils.

Nectarine] *Amygdalus persica*.

Nepenthes distillatoria] A Sri Lankan pitcher plant.

Nicotiana] *Nicotiana tabacum*, tobacco.

Night hawk] *Chordeiles minor*, Common Nighthawk, or *Caprimulgus vociferus*, Whip-poor-will.

Nightingale] *Cardinalis cardinalis*, Northern Cardinal.

Noddy] *Anous stolidus*, Brown Noddy.

Nondo] *Ligusticum canadense*.

Nonpareil] *Passerina ciris*, Painted Bunting.

Numenius, alba varia] Juvenile *Limosa fedoa*, Marbled Godwit.

Numenius albus] *Eudocimus albus*, White Ibis.

Numenius *Americana] Adult *Limosa fedoa*, Marbled Godwit.

Numenius *cinereus] Probably *Numenius phaeopus*, Whimbrel.

Numenius *fluvialis] Perhaps both *Tringa melanoleuca* and *Tringa flavipes*, Greater and Lesser Yellowlegs.

Numenius fuseus] *Eudocimus albus*, White Ibis.

Numenius magnus rufus] Probably *Numenius americanus*, Long-billed Curlew.

Numenius minor campestris] Possibly *Numenius borealis*, Eskimo Curlew.

Numenius pectore rufo] *Limosa haemastica*, Hudsonian Godwit.

Nuthatch] *Sitta carolinensis*, White-breasted Nuthatch.

Nuthatch, black capped, red bellied] *Sitta canadensis*, Red-breasted Nuthatch.

Nuthatch, grey black capped] *Sitta carolinensis*, White-breasted Nuthatch.

Nux moschata] Nutmeg.

Nyctanthes] A genus of Old World shrubs, jasmines.

Nymphaea nelumbo] *Nelumbo lutea*, water chinquapin.

Nyssa] *Nyssa* species, gum.

Nyssa aquatica] Probably *Nyssa sylvatica*, black gum or black tupelo.

Nyssa *coccinea, sive *Ogeeche] *Nyssa ogeche* Bartram, Ogeechee tupelo.

Nyssa multiflora] Probably *Nyssa sylvatica*.

Nyssa *Ogeeche, sive *coccinea] *Nyssa ogeche* Bartram, Ogeechee tupelo.

Nyssa sylvatica] Black gum or black tupelo.

Nyssa *tupilo] *Nyssa* species, gum.

Oak, Black] *Quercus velutina*, black oak.

Oak, chestnut leaved white] *Quercus pinus*, swamp chestnut oak.

Oak, dwarf] *Quercus* species.

Oak, evergreen] *Quercus virginiana*, live oak.

Oak, Live] Chiefly *Quercus virginiana*, live oak.

Oak, Maryland Water] *Quercus nigra*, water oak.

Oak, Narrow-leaved Wintergreen] *Quercus laurifolia*, laurel oak (Darlington oak).

Oak, Red] *Quercus rubra*, northern red oak.

Oak, Scrubby Black, or Black Jack] *Quercus marilandica* or *Quercus laevis*.

Oak, Water] *Quercus laurifolia*, laurel oak (Darlington oak), or *Quercus nigra*, water oak.

Oak, White] *Quercus alba*, white oak.

Oak, Willow-leaved] *Quercus phellos*, willow oak.

Oats] *Avena sativa*.

Oenanthe] *Icteria virens*, Yellow-breasted Chat.

Oenothera *grandiflora] Bartram's evening primrose.

Ogeechee limes] *Nyssa ogeche* Bartram.

Olea Americana] *Osmanthus americana*, devil-wood.

Olea europaea] Olives.

Olinopodium] *Clinopodium* species, basil.

Olive, Indian] *Nestronia umbellula*, oil-nut.

Olives] *Olea europaea*.

Onions (*cepa*)] *Allium cepa*.

Onocrotalus *Americanus] *Pelecanus occidentalis*, Brown Pelican.

Ononis perfoliated] *Baptisia perfoliata*, gopher-weed.

Ophrys] Probably *Listera smallii*, Small's twayblade, or *Spiranthes* species, ladies'-tresses.

Ophreys *insectoria] *Ophreys insectifera*, a European orchid.

Ophrys, spiral] Probably *Spiranthes* species, ladies'-tresses.

Opossums] *Didelphis marsupialis*.

Opuntia] *Opuntia* species, prickly pear.

Orange] *Citrus aurantium*, bitter-sweet orange, *Citrus sinensis*, sweet orange.

Orchis] A genus of orchids.

Oriolus Baltimore] *Icterus galbula*, Northern Oriole (Baltimore Oriole).

Oriolus (icterus minor)] *Icterus spurius*, Orchard Oriole.

Oriolus spurius] *Icterus spurius*, Orchard Oriole.

Ortulan or Rice Bird of Catesby] *Doliconyx oryzivorus*, Bobolink.

Oryza] *Oryza sativa*, rice.

Oryza zizania] *Zizania aquatica*, wild rice.

Osteospermum] Probably *Polymnia uvedalia*, bear-foot.

Ostrea] *Ostrea* species, oyster (fossil).

Otter] *Lutra canadensis*, River Otter.

Ounce] Either *Felis rufus*, Bobcat, or *Felis pardalis*, Ocelot.

Ounce, small] *Felis rufus*, Bobcat.

Owl, great (or great horned)] *Bubo virginianus*, Great Horned Owl.

Owl, great white] *Nyctea scandiaca*, Snowy Owl.

Owl, screech, little screech] *Otus asio*, Eastern Screech Owl.

Owl, sharp winged] Probably *Asio flammeus*, Short-eared Owl.

Owl, whooting] *Strix varia*, Barred Owl.

Oyster catcher] *Haematopus palliatus*, American Oystercatcher.

Oyster shells, fossil] *Ostrea georgiana*.

Painted finch] *Passerina ciris*, Painted Bunting.

Palm, exalted] *Roystonea elata* Bartram, royal palm, or *Sabal palmetto*, cabbage palmetto.

Palm, shadowy] *Sabal palmetto*, cabbage palmetto.

Palm trees, of a different species from the cabbage tree] *Roystonea elata* Bartram, royal palm.

Palma Christi] *Ricinus communis*, castor-oil plant.

Palma, dactylifera minor] *Serenoa repens*, saw palmetto.

Palma *elata] *Roystonea elata* Bartram, royal palm.

Palma vera] *Sabal palmetto*, cabbage palmetto.

Palmetto, dwarf prickly fan-leaved] *Serenoa repens* Bartram, saw palmetto.

Palmetto, a very dwarf species of] *Serenoa repens* Bartram, saw palmetto.

Palmetto, dwarf creeping, with stipes serrated] *Serenoa repens* Bartram, saw palmetto.

Palmetto, Dwarf Saw] *Serenoa repens* Bartram, saw palmetto.

Palmetto, saw] *Serenoa repens* Bartram.

Panax ginseng] *Panax quinquefolius*, ginseng.

Panax quinquefolium] *Panax quinquefolius*, ginseng.

Pancratium *fluitans] Probably *Hymenocallis coronaria*, spider lily.

Pancratium, odorous, sweet] *Hymenocallis* species, spider lily.

Pancratium, white robed] *Hymenocallis* species, spider lily.

Panicum *hirtellum] *Echinocloa* species, scotch grass.

Panther] *Felis concolor*, Cougar.

Papaver somniferum] Opium poppy.

Papaw] *Asimina* species, pawpaw.

Papaya, Indian] Carica papaya.

Papilio] A Linnaean genus, originally including all the butterflies.

Paroquets, Parrakeet, Parrot of Carolina] *Conuropsis carolinensis*, Carolina Parakeet (now extinct).

Partridge (of Pennsylvania)] *Colinus virginianus*, Northern Bobwhite.

Parus alis aureis] *Vermivora chrysoptera*, Golden-winged Warbler.

Parus aureus alis ceruleis] *Vermivora pinus*, Blue-winged Warbler.

Parus aureus vertice rubro] *Dendroica palmarum*, Palm Warbler.

Parus aurio vertice] Adult male *Dendroica coronata* in spring plumage, Yellow-rumped Warbler (Myrtle Warbler).

Parus *cedrus, uropygio flavo] *Dendroica coronata* in winter plumage, Yellow-rumped Warbler (Myrtle Warbler).

Parus cristatus] *Parus bicolor*, Tufted Titmouse.

Parus *Europeus] *Parus atricapillus*, Black-capped Chickadee; *Parus carolinensis*, Carolina Chickadee.

Parus griseus gutture luteo] *Dendroica dominica*, Yellow-throated Warbler.

Parus *luteus] *Dendroica petechia*, Yellow Warbler.

Parus peregrinus] *Dendroica castanea*, Bay-breasted Warbler.

Parus *varius] *Parula americana*, Northern Parula.

Parus *viridis gutture nigro] *Dendroica virens*, Black-throated Green Warbler.

Passer *agrestis] *Spizella pusilla*, Field Sparrow.

Passer *domesticus] *Spizella passerina*, Chipping Sparrow.

Passer *nivalis] *Junco hyemalis*, Dark-eyed Junco (Slate-colored Junco).

Passer *palustris] *Melospiza georgiana*, Swamp Sparrow.

Passiflora incarnata] May-pop.

Pastinaca] *Pastinaca sativa*, parsnip.

Patates, Indian] *Apios americana*, groundnut.

Patella] An undetermined mollusk.

Pavia *sylvatica] *Aesculus sylvatica* Bartram, Carolina buckeye.

Peach, or Peach trees] *Prunus persica*.

Peacock] *Pavo cristatus*.

Pear] *Pyrus communis*.

Pedicularis] Probably *Pedicularis canadensis*, wood betony.

Pelican, American sea] *Pelecanus occidentalis*, Brown Pelican.

Pelican, solitary, of the wilderness] *Mycteria americana*, Wood Stork.

Pelican, wood] *Mycteria americana*, Wood Stork.

Pelecanus aquilus] *Fregata magnificens*, Magnificent Frigatebird (Man-o'-war-bird).

Pelecanus sula] *Sula* species, Booby.

Perdicium, silvery] *Chaptalia tomentosa*, pineland daisy.

Persicaria *amphibia] *Polygonum* species, smartweed.

Persimmon] *Diospyros virginiana*.

Petrella *pintada] Perhaps *Daption capense*, Cape Petrel.

Pewit, or black cap flycatcher] *Sayornis phoebe*, Eastern Phoebe.

Pewit, lesser] *Contopus virens*, Eastern Wood Peewee.

Phaethon aethereus] Red-billed Tropic-bird.

Phalaena] A Linnaean genus originally comprising all the moths (except *Sphinx*).

Phalaena *bombyca] *Bombyx mori*, Silk-worms.

Phalaena *periodica] Probably *Malacosoma americana* Fabricius, Tent Caterpillar.

Phaseoloides] *Wisteria frutescens*, American wisteria.

Phaseolus] Either *Phaseolus polystachios*, wild bean, or *Phaseolus* species, French beans.

Pheasant of Pennsylvania] *Bonasa umbellus*, Ruffed Grouse.

Philadelphus] *Philadelphus* species, syringa.

Philadelphus inodorus] Syringa.

Philomela] Possibly *Luscinia megarhynchos*, European Nightingale.

Philomela Americana] Probably *Wilsonia citrina*, Hooded Warbler.

Phoenicopterus ruber] Greater Flamingo.

Physic-nut, or Indian Olive] *Nestronia umbellula*, oil-nut.

Pica glandaria] *Cyanocitta cristata*, Blue Jay.

Pica glandaria cerulea non cristata] *Aphelocoma coerulescens*, Scrub Jay.

Pica glandaria minor] *Aphelocoma coerulescens*, Scrub Jay.

Picus auratus] *Colaptes auratus*, Northern Flicker.

Picus erythrocephalus] *Melanerpes erythrocephalus*, Red-headed Woodpecker.

Picus Carolinus] *Melanerpes carolinus*, Red-bellied Woodpecker.

Picus pileatus] *Dryocopus pileatus*, Pileated Woodpecker.

Picus principalis] *Campephilus principalis*, Ivory-billed Woodpecker.

Picus pubescens] *Picoides pubescens*, Downy Woodpecker.

Picus varius] *Sphyrapicus varius*, Yellow-bellied Sapsucker.

Picus villosus] *Picoides villosus*, Hairy Woodpecker.

Pigs] *Sus scrofa*.

Pigeons, wild] *Ectopistes migratorius*, Passenger Pigeon (now extinct).

Pines] *Pinus* species.

Pine, Broom] *Pinus palustris*, longleaf pine.

Pine, long-leaved] *Pinus palustris*, longleaf pine.

Pine, Wild] *Tillandsia utriculata*.

Pine, yellow] *Pinus palustris*, longleaf pine.

Pinguiculas] *Pinguicula* species, butterworts.

Pinus abies] *Tsuga canadensis*, Canada hemlock.

Pinus balsamea] *Abies balsamea*, balsam fir.

Pinus Canadensis] *Tsuga canadensis*, Canada hemlock.

Pinus echinata] Shortleaf pine.

Pinus larix] *Larix laricina*, tamarack.

Pinus lutea] Possibly *Pinus elliottii*, slash pine.

Pinus palustris] Longleaf pine.

*Pinus *phoenix*] *Pinus* species, undetermined.

Pinus squarrosa] *Pinus echinata*, shortleaf pine.

Pinus strobus] White pine.

Pinus sylvestris] Undetermined *Pinus* species.

Pinus taeda] Loblolly pine.

Pipe-stem wood] *Leucothoe acuminata*, pipewood.

Pistacia] *Pistacia vera*, pistachio.

Pistia] *Pistacia stratiotes*, water lettuce.

Pisum] A genus of Leguminosae, comprising the garden or English peas.

Plantago Virginica] Hoary plantain.

Plantain, common] Plantago major.

Platalea ajaja] *Ajaia ajaja*, Roseate Spoonbill.

Platanus] *Platanus occidentalis*, sycamore.

Plover, chattering] *Charadrius vociferus*, Killdeer.

Plum] *Prunus angustifolia*, Chickasaw Plum.

Plum, ordinary] *Prunus domestica*.

Podophyllum] *Podophyllum peltatum*, mandrake.

Poinciana pulcherrima] *Caesalpinia pulcherrima*, dwarf poinciana.

Poison oak] *Rhus toxicodendron*.

Poke] *Butorides virescens*, Green Heron.

Polecat] *Mephitis mephitis*, Striped Skunk.

Polyanthus tuberosa] *Polianthes tuberosa*, tuberose.

Polygala, varieties] *Polygala* species.

Polymnia] *Polymnia uvedalia*, bear-foot.

Pomegranate] *Punica granatum*.

Pompions] *Cucurbita moschata*, Seminole pumpkins or crookneck squashes.

Poor Jobe] *Nyctanassa violacea*, Yellow-crowned Night Heron.

Poppy flower, fringed] *Papaver somniferum*.

Populus Heterophylla] Swamp cottonwood.

Populus tremula]   Possibly *Populus deltoides* Bartram, Eastern cottonwood.

Porcupine]   *Erethizon dorsatum.*

Potato]   *Ipomoea batatas*, sweet potato.

Prenanthes]   *Prenanthes* species, gall-of-the-earth.

Primula]   A genus of Primulaceae, comprising the primroses.

Prinos, curious species of]   *Ilex amelanchier*, Bartram's holly.

Prinos glaber]   *Ilex glabra*, gallberry.

Privet]   *Ligustrum vulgare.*

Prunus Caroliniana]   Laurel cherry.

Prunus cerasus]   Sour cherry.

*Prunus *Chickasaw*]   *Prunus angustifolia*, Chickasaw plum.

*Prunus *Indica*]   Possibly *Prunus angustifolia*, Chickasaw plum.

Prunus laurocerasus]   *Prunus caroliniana*, laurel cherry.

*Prunus *nemoralis*]   *Prunus caroliniana*, laurel cherry.

Prunus padus]   Probably *Prunus serotina*, wild black cherry.

Psidium]   A genus of Myrtaceae, including the guavas.

Psittacus Caroliniensis]   *Conuropsis carolinensis*, Carolina Parakeet (now extinct).

Ptelea]   *Ptelea trifoliata*, wafer ash.

*Pteris *scandens*]   *Lygodium palmatum*, climbing fern.

Punica granatum]   Pomegranate.

Purple berried bay]   *Osmanthus americana*, devil-wood.

Putorius]   *Mephitis mephitis*, Striped Skunk.

Pyrus]   A genus of Rosaceae, comprising the pears, apples, chokeberries, and mountain ashes.

Pyrus coronaria]   Possibly *Pyrus angustifolia*, narrow-leaved crab apple.

Pyrus malus]   Apple.

Quail]   *Colinus virginianus*, Northern Bobwhite.

Quaw bird]   *Nycticorax nycticorax*, Black-crowned Night Heron.

Quercus alba]   White oak.

Quercus aquatica]   *Quercus nigra*, water oak.

Quercus foliis lanciolatis integerrimis glabris] *Quercus virginiana*, live oak.

Quercus *hemispherica] *Quercus laurifolia*, laurel oak (Darlington oak).

Quercus *incana] *Quercus cinerea*, upland willow oak.

Quercus nigra] Mainly *Quercus marilandica*, black jack oak.

Quercus phellos] *Quercus phellos*, willow oak.

Quercus pumila] Oak runner.

Quercus rubra] Northern red oak.

Quercus sempervirens] *Quercus virginiana*, live oak.

Quercus *tinctoria] *Quercus velutina*, black oak.

Quinquina] *Cinchona officinalis*, quinine.

Rabbits] *Sylvilagus floridanus*, Eastern Cottontail.

Raccoons (*Ursus cauda elongata*)] *Procyon lotor*.

Radishes] *Raphanus sativus*.

Rail, blue or slate coloured water, of Florida] *Gallinula chloropus*, Common Moorhen (Florida Gallinule).

Rail, little brown] Immature *Porzana carolina*, Sora.

Rail, little dark blue water] Adult *Porzana carolina*, Sora.

Rajana] Possibly *Brunnichia cirrhosa*, eardrops.

Rallus aquaticus minor] Adult *Porzana carolina*, Sora.

Rallus major subceruleus] *Gallinula chloropus*, Common Moorhen (Florida Gallinule).

Rallus rufus Americanus] Probably *Rallus limicola*, Virginia Rail.

Rallus Virginianus] Immature *Porzana carolina*, Sora.

Rapa] *Brassica*, a genus of Cruciferae, including the mustards, cabbages, and turnips.

Raphanus] *Raphanus sativus*, radish.

Rat, common Norway] *Rattus norvegicus*, Norway Rat (Brown Rat).

Rat, house, European] *Rattus norvegicus*, Norway Rat (Brown Rat), or *Rattus rattus*, Black Rat.

Rat, ground, large] *Geomys* species, Pocket Gopher.

Rats, wild, two species of] *Sigmodon hispidus*, Cotton Rat; possibly *Peromyscus gossypinus*, Cotton Mouse.

Rattle snake, ground]   *Sistrurus miliarius*, Pigmy Rattler.

Rattle-snake, dreaded]   *Crotalus horridus*, Timber Rattlesnake.

Raven]   *Corvus corax*, Common Raven.

Razor bill]   *Rynchops niger*, Black Skimmer.

Rebicula]   *Sialia sialis*, Eastern Bluebird.

Red-belly]   *Lepomis auritus*, Red-breasted Bream.

Red bird]   *Cardinalis cardinalis*, Northern Cardinal.

Red bird, Crested]   *Cardinalis cardinalis*, Northern Cardinal.

Redbird, sand-hill, of Carolina]   *Piranga olivacea*, Scarlet Tanager.

Red-bird, summer]   *Piranga rubra*, Summer Tanager.

Red bird, with black wings and Tail]   *Piranga olivacea*, Scarlet Tanager.

Red Cedar]   *Juniperus* species.

Red pole, yellow]   *Dendroica palmarum*, Palm Warbler.

Redstart]   *Setophaga ruticilla*, American Redstart.

Reeds or Canes (*Arundo gigantea*)]   *Arundinaria gigantea*, Giant Canes.

Regulus atrofuscus minor]   *Cistothorus palustris*, Marsh Wren.

Regulus cristatus]   *Regulus satrapa*, Golden-crowned Kinglet.

Regulus cristatus alter vertice rubini coloris]   *Regulus calendula*, Ruby-crowned Kinglet.

*Regulus *griseus*]   *Polioptila caerulea*, Blue-gray Gnatcatcher.

*Regulus *magnus*]   *Thryothorus ludovicianus*, Carolina Wren.

*Regulus *minor*]   *Cistothorus palustris*, Marsh Wren.

*Regulus *peregrinus, gutture flavo*]   *Geothlypis trichas*, Common Yellowthroat.

*Regulus *rufus*]   *Troglodytes aedon*, House Wren.

Rhamnus frangula]   *Rhamnus caroliniana*, buckthorn.

Rhamnus volubilis]   *Berchemia scandens*, Rattan Vine.

Rheum rhabarbarum]   *Rheum rhaponticum*, rhubarb.

Rhexia]   Deer-grasses.

*Rhexia *pulcherrima*]   *Rhexia* species, deer-grass.

Rhizophora conjugata]   *Avicennia nitida*, black mangrove.

Rhododendron ferrugineum]   *Rhododendron minus*, lesser rose-bay.

Rhododendron, large rose flowered]   *Rhododendron minus*, lesser rose-bay.

Rhododendron, a new species of]   *Rhododendrun carolinianum*, Carolina rose-bay.

*Rhododendron *spurium*]   *Befaria racemosa*, tarflower.

Rhus vernix]   Poison sumac.

Rice]   *Oryza sativa.*

Rice bird]   *Dolichonyx oryzivorus*, Bobolink.

Rice bird, pied]   Male Bobolink, *Dolichonyx oryzivorus*, while breeding.

Robins]   *Turdus migratorius*, American Robin.

Robin redbreast]   *Turdus migratorius*, American Robin.

Robinia hispida]   Rose acacia.

Robinia, incarnate]   Probably *Robinia viscosa*, clammy locust.

*Robinia *montana*]   *Robinia* species, locust.

Robinia pseudoacacia]   Black locust.

Robinia, rose flowered]   *Robinia hispida*, rose acacia.

Robinia, white flowerd]   *Robinia pseudoacacia*, black locust.

Rockfish]   *Roccus saxatilis.*

Roebuck]   *Odocoileus virginianus*, White-tailed Deer.

*Rosa *paniculata*]   *Rosa* species, a wild rose.

Rose, mountain cluster]   *Rosa* species, a wild rose.

Rubicula Americana]   *Sialia sialis*, Eastern Bluebird.

Rudbeckia]   A genus of Compositae, cone-flowers.

Ruellia]   A genus of Acanthaceae, ruellias.

*Ruellia *infundibuliformea*]   *Ruellia* species, undetermined.

**Ruticilla Americana*]   *Setophaga ruticilla*, American Redstart.

Rynchops niger]   Black Skimmer.

Sage, Scarlet]   *Erythrina herbacea*, cardinal spear.

Sage, tall blue]   *Salvia azurea.*

Sagittaria]   *Sagittaria* species, arrowhead.

*Salix *fluvialis*]   Probably *Salix nigra*, black willow.

Salvia coccinea]   Scarlet sage.

Salvia *graveolens]   *Salvia* species, sage.

Sambucus]   *Sambucus canadensis*, common elder, or *Sambucus simpsonii*, southern elder.

Sanguinaria]   *Sanguinaria canadensis*, bloodroot.

Sanguisorba]   *Sanguisorba canadensis*, burnet.

Sanguisorba Canadensis]   *Sanguisorba canadensis*, burnet.

Sapindus]   *Sapindus marginatus*, Florida soapberry.

Sarracenia, a new species of]   *Sarracenia drummondi*, Drummond's pitcher plant.

Sarracenia flava]   Yellow trumpet.

Sarracenia *galeata]   *Sarracenia* species, a pitcher-plant.

Sarracenia *lacunosa]   *Sarracenia drummondi*, Drummond's pitcher plant.

Sarracenia purpurea]   Purple pitcher-plant.

Sarracenia, yellow]   *Sarracenia flava*, yellow trumpet.

Sassafras]   *Sassafras albidum*, sassafras.

Savanna Crane]   *Grus canadensis* Bartram, Sandhill Crane.

Scarabei]   Probably lamellicorn beetles.

Sciurus]   *Sciurus* species, tree squirrels.

Scolopax Americana rufa]   *Scolopax minor*, American Woodcock.

Scolopax minor arvensis]   *Gallinago gallinago*, Common Snipe.

Scorpions]   *Cnemidophorus sexlineatus*, Racerunner.

Scotch grass]   *Echinochloa* species.

Sea cow]   *Trichechus manatus*, Manatee.

Senecio arborescens]   *Baccharis halimifolia*, sea myrtle or groundsel tree.

Senecio Jacobea]   Probably *Senecio glabellus*, ragwort.

Serratula]   Probably *Liatris* species, button snakeroot.

Shad]   *Alosa sapidissima*.

Shearwater]   *Rynchops niger*, Black Skimmer.

Sheep]   *Ovis aries*.

Sheepshead]   *Archosargus probatocephalus*.

Shrub, beautiful, allied to *Rhododendron*] *Befaria racemosa*, tar-flower.

Shrub, a very beautiful, with long loose spikes of sweet white flowers] *Elliottia racemosa*.

Shrub, a very curious, with nettlelike leaves, orange flowers, and azure berries] *Lantana camara*, lantana.

Shrub, a very curious Little] *Xanthorrhiza simplicissima*, yellowroot.

Shrub of great singularity and beauty] *Cliftonia monophylla*, tyty.

Shrub, a little (or procumbent), with purple stellated fowers and prickly capsules] *Krameria spathulata*, sandbur.

Shrub, a noble sweet-scented, bearing golden clusters of flowers] *Illicium parviflorum*, yellow anise.

Sideroxylon] *Bumelia* species, buckthorn.

Sideroxylon Sericeum] *Bumelia* species, buckthorn.

Sideroxylon tenax] Probably *Bumelia tenax*, buckthorn.

Silk-worms] *Bombyx mori*.

Silphium] *Silphium* species, rosin-weeds.

Sisymbrium] A genus of Brassicaceae.

Sitta Europea] *Sitta carolinensis*, White-breasted Nuthatch.

*Sitta *varia, ventre rubro*] *Sitta canadensis*, Red-breasted Nuthatch.

Sium] Probably *Sium suave*, water parsley.

Skate] *Raja* species.

Smilax] *Smilax* species, catbriers.

Smilax aspera] Probably *Smilax pseudo-china*, China brier.

Smilax, pseudo China] Probably *Smilax pseudo-china*, China brier, or *Smilax bona-nox*, bamboo.

Smilax pumila] *Smilax pumila*, sarsaparilla vine.

Smilax sarsaparilla] *Smilax* species, catbrier.

Snake, black] *Coluber constrictor*, Black Snake (Racer).

Snake, Black Coach Whip] Color phase of *Masticophis flagellum*, Coachwhip.

Snake, Bull] *Pituophis melanoleucus*, Pine-gopher Snake.

Snake, chicken] *Elaphe obsoleta*, Rat Snake.

Snake, coach-whip] *Masticophis flagellum*.

Snake, glass]   *Ophisaurus* species, a limbless lizard.

Snake, glass (*anguis fragilis*)]   *Ophisaurus* species, a limbless lizard.

Snake, Great Black]   *Coluber constrictor*, Black Snake (Racer).

Snake, Great Chicken]   *Elaphe obsoleta*, Rat Snake.

Snake, green]   *Opheodrys aestivus*, Rough Green Snake.

Snake, horn]   *Pituophis melanoleucus*, Pine-gopher Snake.

Snakes, large, with black and white spots, and making a loud hissing noise]   *Pituophis melanoleucus*, Pine-gopher Snake.

Snakes, large, yellow, with red belly, and destroying vermin]   *Elaphe obsoleta*, Rat Snake.

Snake, pine or bull]   *Pituophis melanoleucus*, Pine-gopher Snake.

Snake, ring neck]   *Diadophis punctatus*, Ring-neck Snake.

Snake, rattle, great]   *Crotalus adamanteus*, Eastern Diamondback Rattlesnake, and *Crotalus horridus*, Timber Rattlesnake.

Snake, Thunder]   *Pituophis melanoleucus*, Pine-gopher Snake.

Snake, White]   *Masticophis flagellum*, Coachwhip.

Snake Birds, a species of cormorant or loon]   *Anhinga anhinga*, American Anhinga (Water Turkey).

Snipe, meadow]   *Gallinago gallinago*, Common Snipe.

Snow bird]   *Junco hyemalis*, Dark-eyed Junco (Slate-colored Junco).

Solanum tuberosum]   White potato.

Solidago]   *Solidago* species, goldenrod.

Sophora]   *Baptisia* species, wild indigo.

Soree bird]   Immature *Porzana carolina*, Sora.

Sour Gum]   *Nyssa sylvatica*, black tupelo or blackgum.

Spanish Curlews]   *Eudocimus albus*, White Ibis.

Sparrow, large brown white throat]   *Zonotrichia albicollis*, White-throated Sparrow.

Sparrow, little field]   *Spizella pusilla*, Field Sparrow.

Sparrow, little house]   *Spizella passerina*, Chipping Sparrow.

Sparrow, red, or fox-coloured ground or hedge]   *Passerella iliaca*, Fox Sparrow.

Sparrow, reed]   *Melospiza georgiana*, Swamp Sparrow.

Spider, Tiger] Large jumping spider, family Salticidae.

Spiraea opulifolia] *Physocarpus opulifolius*, ninebark.

Spoonbill] *Ajaia ajaja*, Roseate Spoonbill.

Squash] *Cucurbita* species.

Squashes (*Cucurbita verrucosa*)] Cymlings, scalloped summer squashes

Squilla] Undetermined stomatopod crustacean.

Squirrel, black] *Sciurus carolinensis*, Grey Squirrel, black phase.

Squirrel, common grey] *Sciurus carolinensis*, Grey Squirrel.

Squirrel, flying] *Glaucomys volans*, Southern Flying Squirrel.

Squirrel, great black fox] *Sciurus niger*, Fox Squirrel, black phase.

Squirrel, grey fox] *Sciurus niger*, Fox Squirrel, grey phase.

Squirrel, ground, or little striped squirrel] *Tamias striatus*, Eastern Chipmunk.

Staphylaea] *Staphylaea trifolia*, bladdernut.

Staphylaea trifoliata] *Staphylaea trifolia*, bladdernut.

Starling] *Agelaius phoeniceus*, Red-winged Blackbird.

Sterling, red winged] *Agelaius phoeniceus*, Red-winged Blackbird.

Sterna stolida] *Anous stolidus*, Brown Noddy.

Stewartia] *Stewartia malachodendron*, silky camellia, or *Stewartia ovata*, mountain camellia.

Stewartia, mountain] *Stewartia ovata*, mountain camellia.

Stewartia malachodendron] Silky camellia.

Stewartia *montana] *Stewartia ovata*, mountain camellia.

Stewartia, a new species of] *Stewartia pentagyna* or *Malachodendron pentagynum*, mountain camellia.

Stillingia] Probably *Stillingia sylvatica*, queen's delight.

Stillingia *fructicosa] *Sebastiana fructicosa* Bartram, sebastian bush.

Strawberry] *Fragaria* species.

Strix *acclamator, capite levi, corpore griseo] *Strix varia*, Barred Owl.

Strix *acclamatus] *Strix varia*, Barred Owl.

Strix *arcticus, capite levi, corpore toto niveo] *Nyctea scandiaca*, Snowy Owl.

Strix assio] *Otus asio*, Eastern Screech Owl.

Strix assio, capite aurito, corpore ferrugineo]   *Otus asio*, Eastern Screech Owl.

Strix *maximus, capite aurito, corpore niveo]   Possibly *Bubo virginianus*, Great Horned Owl.

Strix *peregrinator, capite aurito, corpore versicolor]   Probably *Asio flammeus*, Short-eared Owl.

Strix *pythaules, capite aurito, corpore rufo]   *Bubo virginianus*, Great Horned Owl.

Strix *pythaulis]   *Bubo virginianus*, Great Horned Owl.

Sturnus *predatorius]   *Agelaius phoeniceus*, Red-winged Blackbird.

Sturnus *stercorarius]   *Molothrus ater*, Eastern Cowbird.

Styrax]   *Styrax* species, storaxes.

Styrax *latifolia]   *Styrax grandifolia*, large-leaved storax.

Sugar-cane]   *Saccharum officinarum*.

Sumach]   *Rhus* species.

Summer yellow bird]   *Dendroica petechia*, Yellow Warbler.

Sunfish (sun fish)]   *Chaenobryttus coronarius* Bartram.

Swallow, chimney]   *Chaetura pelagica*, Chimney Swift.

Swallow, house]   *Hirundo rustica*, Barn Swallow.

Swallow, sea]   *Anous stolidus*, Brown Noddy.

Swan, wild]   *Cygnus columbianus*, Whistling or Tundra Swan.

Sweet Gum]   *Liquidambar styraciflua*.

Syringa]   *Syringa* species, lilacs.

Tallow-nut, or Wild Lime]   *Ximenia americana*.

Tanagra cyanea]   *Passerina cyanea*, Indigo Bunting.

Tannier]   Root or stem of various aroids including *Colocasia antiquorum*, taro.

Tantalus, or *tantali*]   *Mycteria americana*, Wood Stork, or *Eudocimus albus*, White Ibis.

Tantalus. The Wood Pelicane]   *Mycteria americana*, Wood Stork.

Tantalus alber]   *Eudocimus albus*, White Ibis.

Tantalus albus]   *Eudocimus albus*, White Ibis.

Tantalus fuscus]   *Eudocimus albus*, White Ibis, immature.

*Tantalus *Ichthyophagus*] *Mycteria americana*, Wood Stork.

Tantalus loculator] *Mycteria americana*, Wood Stork.

*Tantalus *pictus, (Ephouskyka Indian)*] *Aramus guarauna*, Limpkin.

*Tantalus *versicolor*] *Eudocimus albus*, White Ibis.

Teal, blue winged] *Anas discors*, Blue-winged Teal.

Teal, least green winged] *Anas crecca*, Green-winged Teal.

Teal, painted summer] *Aix sponsa*, Wood Duck.

Telea] *Tilia* species, basswood, or *Ptelea trifoliata*, wafer ash.

Terrapin, Little land] *Terrapene carolina*, Eastern Box Turtle.

Terrapin, Red-bellied] *Chrysemys nelsoni*, Florida Red-bellied Turtle.

Testudo naso cylindracea elongato, truncato] *Trionyx ferox*, Florida Soft-shelled Turtle.

*Testudo *Polyphaemus*] *Gopherus polyphaemus* Bartram, Gopher Turtle.

Tetragonotheca] *Tetragonotheca helianthoides*, pineland ginseng.

Tetrao lagopus] Probably *Tympanuchus cupido*, Greater Prairie Chicken.

*Tetrao *minor sive coturnix*] *Colinus virginianus*, Northern Bobwhite.

*Tetrao *minor, seu coturnix*] *Colinus virginianus*, Northern Bobwhite.

*Tetrao *tympanus*] Probably *Bonasa umbellus*, Ruffed Grouse.

Tetrao urogallus] Probably *Tympanuchus cupido*, Greater Prairie Chicken.

Thapsia] *Thaspium* species or *Zizia* species, meadow parsnip.

Theobroma] *Theobroma* species, cacao trees.

Thrush, fox coloured] *Toxostoma rufum*, Brown Thrasher.

Thrush, great or fox coloured] *Toxostoma rufum*, Brown Thrasher.

Thrush, least golden crown] *Seiurus aurocapillus*, Oven-bird.

Thrush, red] *Toxostoma rufum*, Brown Thrasher.

Thrush, wood] *Hylocichla mustelina*.

Thymus] *Thymus* species, thymes.

Tilia] *Tilia* species, basswood.

*Tillandsia *lingulata*] *Tillandsia utriculata*, a wild pine.

*Tillandsia *monostachya*] Probably *Tillandsia tenuifolia*, a wild pine.

*Tillandsia *usneascites*] *Tillandsia usneoides*, Spanish Moss.

Tithymalus] *Poinsettia heterophylla*, painted leaf.

Titmouse, bluish grey crested] *Parus bicolor*, Tufted Titmouse.

Titmouse, little chocolate breast] *Dendroica castanea*, Bay-breasted Warbler.

Titmouse, yellow hooded] *Wilsonia citrina*, Hooded Warbler.

Tobacco] *Nicotiana tabacum.*

Tolo-chlucco] *Magnolia grandiflora*, southern magnolia.

Tortoise, fresh-water, large, with high shell] *Chrysemys floridana*, Cooter.

Tortoise, great land, called Gopher] *Gopherus polyphaemus* Bartram, Gopher Turtle.

Tortoise, great soft shelled] *Trionyx ferox*, Florida Soft-shelled Turtle.

Tortoise, little muskey] *Sternotherus* species.

Tortoise, small land] *Terrapene carolina*, Eastern Box Turtle.

Towhee bird] *Pipilo erythrophthalmus*, Rufous-sided Towhee.

Toxicodendron, very low oak leaved] *Rhus toxicodendron*, poison oak.

Tradescantia] *Tradescantia* species, spiderwort.

Trichechus manatus] *Trichechus manatus*, Manatee.

Trichomanes] *Lygodium palmatum*, climbing fern.

Trillium cernuum] *Trillium cernuum*, nodding wake-robin.

Trillium sessile] Sessile-flowered wake-robin.

Tring, red cootfooted] *Phalaropus fulicarius*, Red Phalarope.

Tringa, black cap cootfooted] *Phalaropus lobatus*, Red-necked Phalarope.

Tringa cinerea, gutture albo] *Phalaropus lobatus*, Red-necked Phalarope, breeding female.

Tringa fusca] Undetermined.

Tringa griseus] Possibly *Actitis macularia*, Spotted Sandpiper, in immature or winter plumage.

Tringa maculata] *Actitis macularia*, Spotted Sandpiper, in adult summer plumage.

Tringa *parva] Various species including *Calidris pusilla*, Semipalmated Sandpiper; *Calidris minutilla*, Least Sandpiper; *Calidris alba*, Sanderling.

Tringa *rufa] *Phalaropus fulicarius*, Red Phalarope.

Tringa, spotted] *Actitis macularia*, Spotted Sandpiper, in adult summer plumage.

Tringa vertice nigro] *Phalaropus lobatus*, Red-necked Phalrope, in winter plumage.

Tringa, white throated cootfooted] *Phalaropus lobatus*, Red-necked Phalarope, breeding female.

Tripsacum] *Tripsacum dactyloides*, gama grass.

Triticum] *Triticum* species, wheats.

Triticum Cereale] Wheat (most commonly *Triticum aestivum*).

Trochilus colubris] *Archilochus colubris*, Ruby-throated Hummingbird.

Tropic bird] *Phaethon aethereus*, Red-billed Tropicbird.

Trout] *Micropterus salmonides*, Large-mouthed Bass.

Trout, salmon] *Micropterus salmonides*, Large-mouthed Bass.

Tube-rose] *Polianthes tuberosa*, tuberose.

Tulip tree] *Liriodendron tulipifera.*

Tulipa] *Tulipa* species, tulips.

Tupelo] *Nyssa* species.

Tupelo, with olive shaped crimson fruit] *Nyssa ogeche*, tupelo gum.

Turdus *melodes] *Hylocichla mustelina*, Wood Thrush.

Turdus migratorius] *Turdus migratorius*, American Robin.

Turdus *minimus, vertice aurio] *Seiurus aurocapillus*, Oven-bird.

Turdus minor] Probably *Hylocichla mustelina*, Wood Thrush.

Turdus polyglottos] *Mimus polyglottos*, Northern Mockingbird.

Turdus rufus] *Toxostoma rufum*, Brown Thrasher.

Turkeys] *Meleagris gallopavo*, Wild Turkey.

Turnip, Indian] *Peltandra virginica*, arrow arum.

Turnstone] *Arenaria interpres*, Ruddy Turnstone.

Turtle dove] *Zenaida macroura*, Mourning Dove.

Ulmus] *Ulmus* species, elm.

Ulmus campestris] Probably *Ulmus americana*, white elm.

Ulmus *suberifera] *Ulmus alata*, winged elm.

Ulmus *sylvatica] Possibly *Ulmus americana*, white elm, or *Ulmus floridana*, Florida elm.

Umbrella, or Umbrella Tree] *Magnolia tripetata*, umbrella magnolia.

Urtica] Probably *Urtica* species nettle.

Uvularia] *Uvularia* species, bellwort.

Vaccinium (Vaccinium varietas)] Probably *Vaccinium* or *Gaylussacia* species, blueberry.

Verbena] *Verbena* species, vervains.

Verbena *corymbosa] *Verbena* species, a vervain.

Verbesina] *Verbesina* species, crown-beards.

Viburnum] *Viburnum* species, arrow-woods.

Viburnum *Canadense] *Viburnum* species, arrow-wood.

Viburnum dentatum] Southern arrow-wood.

Viburnum prunifolium] Probably *Viburnum rufidulum*, Rusty Blackhaw.

Vicia] *Vicia* species, vetches.

Vicia sativa] *Pisum sativum*, English peas.

Vines (*Vitis vinifera*)] European wine grape.

Viola] *Viola* species, violets.

Violets] *Viola* species.

Viper, black] *Heterodon platyrhinos*, Eastern Hognosed Snake.

Viper, yellow and brown spotted] *Heterodon platyrhinos*, Eastern Hognosed Snake.

Vitis] *Vitis* species, grapes.

Vitis *Allobrogica] *Vitis* species, a grape.

Vitis *campestris] Possibly *Vitis labrusca*, fox grape.

Vitis *Corinthiaca] *Vitis* species, a grape.

Vitis labrusca] Possibly *Vitis rufotomentosa*, redshank grape.

Vitis vinifera] European wine grape.

Vitis vulpina] Possibly *Vitis munsoniana*, bullace.

Vultur *atratus] *Coragyps atratus*, Black Vulture.

Vultur aura] *Cathartes aura*, Turkey Vulture.

Vultur *sacra] *Sarcoramphus papa*, King Vulture. See Eagle, white.

Vulture, black] *Coragyps atratus*, Black Vulture.

Vulture, coped, or carrion crow] *Coragyps atratus*, Black Vulture.

Vulture, painted] *Sarcoramphus papa*, King Vulture. See Eagle, white.

Vulture, white tailed] *Sarcoramphus papa*, King Vulture. See Eagle, white.

Wagtail, water] *Seiurus motacilla*, Louisiana Water Thrush.

Walnut, Black] *Juglans nigra*.

Water oak] *Quercus nigra*.

Watermelons] *Citrullus vulgaris*.

Watula] *Grus canadensis* Bartram, Sandhill Crane.

Wax tree] *Myrica inodora* Bartram, odorless bayberry.

Weasel] *Mustela frenata*.

Whip-poor-will] *Caprimulgus carolinensis*, Chuck-will's-widow; *Caprimulgus vociferus*, Whip-poor-will; *Chordeiles minor*, Nighthawk.

White Root] *Ligusticum canadense*.

Whiting] *Menticirrhus* or *Umbrula* species.

Widgeon] Immature *Porzana carolina*, Sora.

Wild-cat] *Felis rufus*, Bobcat.

Wild lime or Tallow nut] *Ximenia americana*.

Will willet] *Haematopus palliatus*, American Oystercatcher.

Willets] *Catoptrophorus semipalmatus*, Willet.

Wolf] *Canis rufus*, Red Wolf, or *Canis lupus*, Gray Wolf.

Woodcock] *Philohela minor*, American Woodcock.

Woodcock, great red] *Philohela minor*, American Woodcock.

Woodpecker, gold winged] *Colaptes auratus*, Northern Flicker.

Woodpecker, greatest crested, having a white back] *Campephilus principalis*, Ivory-billed Woodpecker.

Woodpecker, great red crested black] *Dryocopus pileatus*, Pileated Woodpecker.

Woodpecker, hairy, speckled and crested] *Picoides villosus*, Hairy Woodpecker.

Woodpecker, least spotted] *Picoides pubescens*, Downy Woodpecker.

Woodpecker, red bellied] *Melanerpes carolinus*, Red-bellied Woodpecker.

Woodpecker, red headed] *Melanerpes erythrocephalus*, Red-headed Woodpecker.

Woodpecker, yellow bellied]   *Sphyrapicus varius*, Yellow-bellied Sapsucker.

Wood-pelican]   *Mycteria americana*, Wood Stork.

Wren, golden crown]   *Regulus satrapa*, Golden-crowned Kinglet.

Wren, great, of Carolina]   *Thryothorus ludovicianus*, Carolina Wren.

Wren, green]   *Vireo griseus*, White-Eyed Vireo.

Wren, house]   *Troglodytes aedon*, House Wren.

Wren, little bluish grey]   *Polioptila caerulea*, Blue-grey Gnatcatcher.

Wren, marsh]   *Cistothorus palustris*, Marsh Wren.

Wren, olive coloured yellow throated]   *Geothylpis trichas*, Common Yellowthroat.

Wren, ruby crown]   *Regulus calendula*, Ruby-crowned Kinglet.

Yam]   *Dioscorea* species.

Yaupon]   *Ilex vomitoria*, yaupon.

Yellow bird, blue winged]   *Vermivora pinus*, Blue-winged Warbler.

Yellow rump]   *Dendroica coronata* in winter plumage, Yellow-rumped Warbler (Myrtle Warbler).

Yucca gloriosa]   Spanish bayonet.

Zamia]   *Zamia integrifolia*, coontie.

Zamia pumila]   *Zamia integrifolia*, coontie.

Zanthoxylum]   Probably *Zanthoxylum clava-herculis*, Hercules' club, or toothache tree.

Zanthoxylum clava Herculis]   *Zanthoxylum clava-herculis*, Hercules' club, or toothache tree.

Zea]   *Zea mays*, maize or Indian corn.

*Zizyphus *scandens*]   Probably *Berchemia scandens*, rattan vine.

Index

CATALOGING INFORMATION

Bartram, William 1739–1823.
    [Travels through North & South Carolina, Georgia, east
& west Florida, the Cherokee country . .]
    Travels, and other writings / William Bartram.
       p. cm. — (The Library of America ; 84)
    Includes index.
    1. Southern States—Description and travel—Early works
to 1800. 2. Indians of North America—Southern States—
Early works to 1800. 3. Natural history—Southern States
—Early works to 1800. 4. Bartram, William, 1739–1823—
Journeys—Southern States.
    I. Title. II. Series.
F213.B2893 1996   95–23727
917.5—dc20
ISBN 1–883011–11–6

THE LIBRARY OF AMERICA SERIES

This book is set in 10 point Linotron Galliard,
a face designed for photocomposition by Matthew Carter
and based on the sixteenth-century face Granjon. The paper is
acid-free Ecusta Nyalite and meets the requirements for permanence
of the American National Standards Institute. The binding
material is Brillianta, a woven rayon cloth made by
Van Heek-Scholco Textielfabrieken, Holland.
The composition is by The Clarinda
Company. Printing and binding by
R.R.Donnelley & Sons Company.
Plates printed by Hull Printing.
Designed by Bruce Campbell.

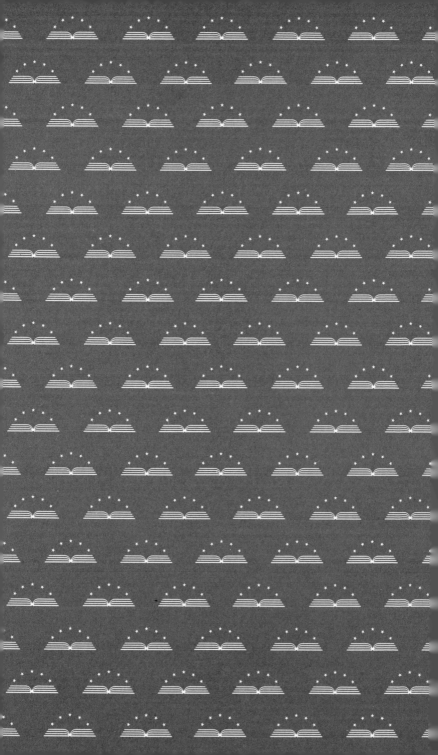